The Chinese Air Force

Evolving Concepts, Roles, and Capabilities

Center for the Study of Chinese Military Affairs (CSCMA)

The Center for the Study of Chinese Military Affairs (China Center) was established as an integral part of the National Defense University's Institute for National Strategic Studies on March 1, 2000, pursuant to Section 914 of the 2000 National Defense Authorization Act. The China Center's mission is to serve as a national focal point and resource center for multidisciplinary research and analytic exchanges on the national goals and strategic posture of the People's Republic of China and to focus on China's ability to develop, field, and deploy an effective military instrument in support of its national strategic objectives.

The Chinese Air Force

Evolving Concepts, Roles, and Capabilities

EDITED BY
RICHARD P. HALLION,
ROGER CLIFF, and
PHILLIP C. SAUNDERS

PUBLISHED BY NATIONAL DEFENSE UNIVERSITY PRESS FOR THE
CENTER FOR THE STUDY OF CHINESE MILITARY AFFAIRS
INSTITUTE FOR NATIONAL STRATEGIC STUDIES
WASHINGTON, D.C.
2012

To the Memory of

Major General John R. "Johnny" Alison, USAFR (Ret.)
1912–2011

An American patriot whose love for his country and affection for its people were matched by his affection for the Chinese people, for whom he fought strenuously and well during the Second World War

Contents

Foreword xi
David A. Deptula

Acknowledgments xiii

Introduction xvii
Richard P. Hallion

I: CONCEPTS

Chapter 1
The Concept of Airpower: Its Emergence, Evolution,
and Future 1
Forrest E. Morgan

Chapter 2
China's Quest for Joint Aerospace Power:
Concepts and Future Aspirations. 33
Mark A. Stokes

Chapter 3
The PLAAF's Evolving Influence within the PLA and
upon National Policy 71
Xiaoming Zhang

II: ORGANIZATION, LEADERSHIP, AND DOCTRINE

Chapter 4
The Organizational Structure of the PLAAF 95
Kenneth W. Allen

Chapter 5
The Missions of the People's Liberation Army Air Force . . . 133
Murray Scot Tanner

Chapter 6
The Development of the PLAAF's Doctrine. 149
Roger Cliff

Chapter 7
The PLAAF and the Integration of Air and Space Power. . . 165
Kevin Pollpeter

III: EQUIPMENT, PERSONNEL, AND EDUCATION / TRAINING

Chapter 8
Equipping the PLAAF: The Long March to Modernity 191
David Shlapak

Chapter 9
Meeting the Challenge of the Upcoming PLAAF
Leadership Reshuffle 213
You Ji

Chapter 10
Education and Training in the PLAAF 235
Kevin Lanzit

IV: INDUSTRIES AND MILITARY IMPLICATIONS

Chapter 11
China's Aviation Industry: Past, Present, and Future 257
Shen Pin-Luen

Chapter 12
China's Quest for Advanced Aviation Technologies 271
Phillip C. Saunders and Joshua K. Wiseman

Chapter 13
The Employment of Airpower in the Taiwan Strait........ 325
Hsi-hua Cheng

Chapter 14
The U.S.-China Military Balance Seen in
a Three-Game Framework 347
David Frelinger and Jessica Hart

About the Contributors............................. 371

Index 377

Foreword

In my assignment as Air Force Deputy Chief of Staff for Intelligence, I had the responsibility of monitoring air forces around the world. There is no question which country has made the greatest strides in developing its airpower capability. Over the last two decades, China's air force, the People's Liberation Army Air Force (PLAAF), has transformed itself from a large, poorly-trained force operating aircraft based on 1950s Soviet designs to a leaner and meaner force flying advanced Russian and indigenously produced fourth-generation fighters. This remarkable transformation is still a work in progress, but China has made up a lot of ground in a short time.

China's civilian and military leaders grasped the centrality of airpower in modern warfare as early as the mid 1970s, a lesson reinforced by the stunning success of the U.S.-led coalition during the first Gulf War. They set the goal of building the PLAAF into a world class, high-technology air force capable of prevailing against sophisticated adversaries in regional conflicts. China's expanding airpower capability has had a profound impact on the Asia-Pacific region (and beyond), causing countries to reassess their own air force modernization needs.

China's successful 2011 test flight of a stealth fighter prototype, the J–20, demonstrates just how ambitious its airpower goals have become. The United States and Russia are the only other countries deploying or developing true fifth-generation fighter aircraft; Beijing is now seeking to match the capabilities of the two most established aerospace powers. In addition to stealth fighter development, the Chinese aviation industry already produces two fourth-generation fighters (the indigenous J–10 and China's Su–27 copy, the J–11) which are roughly equivalent to the aircraft that make up the bulk of the existing U.S., Russian, and Western air force fleets. China has also successfully test flown a fourth-generation fighter (J–15) that can be launched from an aircraft carrier.

More sophisticated combat aircraft are just one component of the expansion of Chinese airpower. Chinese military planners are focused on development of antiaccess/area denial capabilities with an eye toward negating any potential threat to their dominance in the Western Pacific. Chinese efforts to develop an "informatized" military include a focus on integrating and networking aerospace systems, using airborne early warning and control aircraft together with space-based assets. China plans to field a large fleet of remotely piloted aircraft

(RPAs) with both combat and surveillance missions. The deployment of RPAs will enhance and extend the range of China's area denial capabilities, challenging the ability of other nations' forces to operate in the Western Pacific.

China's Second Artillery Corps now possesses a large arsenal of increasingly accurate cruise and ballistic missiles that could strike air bases in Japan and islands throughout the Pacific, and target U.S. aircraft carriers. Nonstealthy aircraft attempting to operate near China will be confronted with an increasingly capable land-based air defense network. PLAAF training has advanced in parallel with technological improvements, resulting in a better-educated and more professional cadre of officers and enlisted personnel. Even in an era of constrained resources, China's comprehensive expansion of its airpower capability should be a matter of great concern to U.S. civilian and military leaders and to U.S. friends and allies in Asia, particularly Japan, South Korea, and Taiwan.

I was honored and privileged to take part in the October 2010 conference in Taipei on the Chinese Air Force, which was jointly organized by Taiwan's Council for Advanced Policy Studies, the Carnegie Endowment for International Peace, the U.S. National Defense University, and the RAND Corporation. The organizers did a superb job in assembling a first-rate group of international experts on airpower and the Chinese military. The conference papers were discussed and debated at length as experts sought to assess Chinese air force current and future capabilities and the trajectory of the air balance across the Taiwan Strait and in the Western Pacific. The current volume contains substantially revised versions of the papers presented at the conference, benefiting greatly from conference discussions and careful editing by Richard Hallion, Roger Cliff, and Phillip Saunders. Together, the chapters offer a complete picture of where the Chinese air force is today, where it has come from, and most importantly, where it is headed.

This book should be of keen interest to policymakers, senior military leaders, the intelligence community, academics, and China watchers of every stripe. However, it is of particular relevance to senior U.S. civilian and military leaders as they make difficult decisions about funding U.S. air and naval capabilities in an environment of constrained defense resources. It is also important reading for U.S. Air Force and Navy officers, who need to understand the progress China has made in modernizing its air force, and to consider the ways Chinese leaders might employ air power in the future.

David A. Deptula, Lt General, USAF (Ret.)

Senior Military Scholar
Center for Character and Leadership Development
United States Air Force Academy

Acknowledgments

Many individuals deserve credit for ensuring the success of the 2010 International Conference on People's Liberation Army (PLA) Affairs, particularly conference organizers Arthur Ding, Secretary General, Chinese Council of Advanced Policy Studies; Roger Cliff, Senior Political Scientist of the RAND Corporation; Phillip Saunders, Director of the Center for the Study of Chinese Military Affairs at the U.S. National Defense University (NDU) Institute for National Strategic Studies; and Michael Swaine, Senior Associate, Carnegie Endowment for International Peace (CEIP). The conference could not have succeeded without the hard work of Yi-su Yang of the Chinese Council of Advanced Policy Studies (CAPS), who superbly managed the travel and logistics arrangements and coordinated meetings with Taiwan and U.S. military and government officials. The editors would also like to thank Teresa Yen and the staff at the Far Eastern Plaza hotel in Taipei.

The presenters and panelists deserve great credit for taking time from very busy schedules to prepare provocative and thoughtful papers rooted in Chinese sources and rigorous analysis, illuminating the current state and likely future of the PLA Air Force (PLAAF). The editors would like to thank discussants Xiaoming Zhang of the U.S. Air War College, Air University; Richard P. Hallion; Paul Godwin, Foreign Policy Research Institute; Benjamin Lambeth, RAND Corporation; Alexander Huang, Tamkang University; and Andrew Erickson, U.S. Naval War College for their comments on individual papers. We are also grateful to panelists Michael Swaine, Sze-Wei Chang, Taiwan University of Science and Technology, and David Deptula, RAND Corporation, for their observations on the PLAAF.

This volume also benefited greatly from the questions, comments, and discussions of conference participants, who represented nearly fifty official and unofficial think-tank, academic, political, business, and military organizations and associations. In addition to CAPS, CEIP, NDU, and RAND, these included the following:

    Academia Sinica
    Aerospace Industrial Development Corporation
    Alion Science and Technology
    American Chamber of Commerce

American Institute in Taiwan
Ancer Technology
Asia Centre
Australian Commerce and Industry Office
Center for Naval Analyses
Defense Group Incorporated
European Union Centre in Taiwan
Foreign Policy Research Institute
Foundation on Asia-Pacific Peace Studies
French Institute in Taipei
Genco International, Inc.
German Institute in Taiwan
India-Taipei Association
Institute of Chinese Communist Studies
Israel Economic and Cultural Office in Taipei
Moscow-Taipei Coordination Commission
Nanyang Technological University
National Policy Foundation
National Chengchi University
National Taiwan University
Phoenix Satellite Television Ltd.
Project 1049 Institute
Prospect Foundation
Singapore Trade Office in Taipei
Taipei Medical University
Taiwan Brain Trust
Taiwan Legislative Yuan
Taiwan Ministry of Foreign Affairs
Taiwan National Defense University
Taiwan Society for Strategic Studies
Taiwan University of Science and Technology
Tamkang University
U.S. Air Force Air War College
U.S. Air Force Pacific Air Forces
U.S. National War College
U.S. Naval War College
U.S. Pacific Command
University of New South Wales
Yuan-Ze University.

Richard Hallion would also like to thank Andrew Erickson, Associate Professor, U.S. Naval War College; Xiaoming Zhang, Associate Professor, U.S. Air Force Air War College; Polly Shen, Research Associate, Taiwan Council of Advanced Policy Studies; Maj. Gen. Tsai-mai "Mike" Tien, Superintendent, Taiwan Air Force Academy, Gangshan; Edward Chuang, Chairman, Genco International, Inc.; and Sun Tai Hsiang, Director, Aviation Museum of the Civil Aeronautics Administration, Taoyuan International Airport. Each contributed to the understanding of China's aerospace heritage, and to the issues and concerns that are examined in this work.

The editors would like to thank George Maerz (copy-editing), Frank Hoffman, and Jeff Smotherman at NDU Press and Guy Tom (cover design) and Jessica Reynolds (layout) at the Government Printing Office for their hard work in turning the draft manuscript into a finished book. National Defense University Research Analysts Isaac Kardon and Joshua Wiseman and Budget Analyst Debbie Jefferson provided administrative and other support for the conference and subsequent efforts to publish and distribute this book.

Introduction

Richard P. Hallion

The ever-accelerating transformation of the People's Republic of China (PRC) in the years since the era of Mao Zedong, particularly in its economic and military growth, has been nothing short of remarkable. Developments over the last quarter-century—effectively since the tragedy of Tiananmen Square and the collapse of the Soviet Union and Warsaw Pact alliance—have been more so still. The relationship of this increasingly robust and growing power to the established global community is a complex one, and no thornier aspect of that relationship can be found than the uneasy interplay among the PRC, Taiwan, and the countries that deal with both.

For years, professional "China watchers" scoured publications, broadcasts, and other bits of evidence for clues to what was happening within the PRC, its leadership ranks, its stance toward neighbors and the world around it, and its intentions, particularly toward Taiwan. The opening of China to the outside world—with the easing of travel and access restrictions, rapid proliferation of communications and transportations links, and consequently increasing interchanges of official and unofficial visitors, business people, academics, students, and tourists—has vastly increased awareness, appreciation, and understanding of the many interrelated challenges surrounding China's rise from a regional to a global power and its relationship to the global community.

The nature of the PRC-Taiwan relationship is one of the greatest of these challenges. For decades, both sides operated on a hair-trigger state of alert, ever ready to go to war over seemingly the slightest provocation. Numerous clashes illuminated the underlying antagonism and fulfilled the bellicose exchanges between leaders of the two countries, most notably the Yijiangshan Island campaign of 1954–1955 (the first Taiwan Strait crisis), and then the battles over the islands of Quemoy and Matsu (now Jinmen and Maˇzuˇ, the second Taiwan Strait crisis), which ushered in the era of air-to-air missiles. In the years since, there have been encouraging signs that the violence seen in years past is receding. Cross-strait dialogue is replacing bellicosity, and exchanges are replacing saber-rattling. Today, the contrails criss-crossing the Taiwan Strait are not combat aircraft climbing to battle, but civil air transports linking the two separated communities, totaling over 500 cross-strait flights per week, something inconceivable just a generation ago. When a devastating earthquake struck Sichuan province in the PRC in 2008, Taiwan's relief assistance, including direct flights by China Airlines to Chengdu, exceeded that of all other nations, reaffirming the depth of affection and shared heritage of the peoples bordering the Taiwan Strait. Nevertheless, the prospect of violence, however increasingly distant, remains, in this era of ballistic and cruise missiles, precision weapons, and cyber warfare, a daunting one.

One of the crucial areas of concern is the force disparity between the PRC and Taiwan. Even as political rhetoric softens, bringing the two sides closer, the force disparity grows ever wider, particularly in their respective airpower capabilities. Today, the traditional technological edge that Taiwan's military airpower forces enjoyed over the mainland is a thing of the past. Where a decade ago, Taiwan's airmen flew aircraft that were at least one, and in some cases two, technological generations superior to those of the PRC, today they are already in a position of inferiority, with their aging F–16A/B, AIDC F–CK–1 Ching-Kuo, and Mirage 2000 fighters increasingly outclassed and outnumbered by newer PRC aircraft such as the Su–27, J–10, J–11, and Su–30 aircraft. Where a decade ago, Taiwan's airmen could operate with relative impunity over the Taiwan Strait, facing a limited-range surface-to-air missile threat built around derivatives of the then 40-year-old Khrushchev-era SA–2, today they face far more dangerous S–300 (SA–10/20) systems that deny access over the strait, and the prospect of the S–400 which, installed along the coast of the PRC, will reach across the strait and beyond Taiwan itself.

Coupled with the PRC's introduction of precision air-to-surface munitions, air refueling, airborne early warning, large numbers of short- and medium-range ballistic missiles, land attack cruise missiles, and an increased emphasis on electronic and cyber warfare, the challenges facing Taiwan's air defenders have never been graver than at the present time. Significantly, because of the longstanding ties between the United States and Taiwan, any prospect of cross-strait conflict carries with it the implicit risk of igniting a broader and even more devastating conflict. Clearly, it is in the interest of all parties to ensure that the PRC-Taiwan relationship evolves in a peaceful, mutually beneficial fashion.

To that end, in late October 2010, a distinguished international group of experts on airpower, military affairs, and the PRC-Taiwan relationship gathered in Taipei to examine the present state and future prospects of the People's Liberation Army Air Force (PLAAF). The conference was the latest in a series of international conferences on the affairs of the People's Liberation Army (PLA) cosponsored by the Chinese Council of Advanced Policy Studies (CAPS), the Carnegie Endowment for International Peace (CEIP), the U.S. National Defense University (NDU), and the RAND Corporation. Over 3 days, speakers presented 14 papers on aspects of airpower, the PLAAF, and the implications for Taiwan, and panels discussed and debated the presentations, taking questions and comments from an audience of 115 registered attendees, with many others dropping by. The conference organizers and presenters met with President Ma Ying-jeou and other Taiwan officials, as well as civil and military representatives of the American Institute in Taiwan; they also visited Ching Chuan Kang (CCK) Air Base, home of Taiwan's 527th Tactical Fighter Wing, operating the aging indigenous AIDC F-CK–1 Ching-Kuo lightweight fighter, for a study tour and briefing on the state of Taiwan Strait air defenses.

This book is a compilation of the edited papers, reflecting comments and additions stimulated by the dialogue and discussion at the conference. As lead editor, I wish to thank the various authors for their patience and willingness in preparing their papers for this publication. For the record, there has been no attempt to "homogenize" the papers, or to seek a uniform outlook. The authors have been free to address their topics to whatever depth they chose, and to present their views without censorship or attempts to find a common view. Nevertheless, as the reader will quickly perceive, there is a remarkable congruency of thought and outlook. The conference presentations were arranged in four broad themes: concepts; PLAAF organization, leadership, and doctrine; PLAAF equipment, personnel, education, and training; and industry and military implications. That same arrangement has been followed in the four-Part structure of this book.

Forrest E. Morgan, a senior political scientist at the RAND Corporation, opens Part I with a wide-ranging survey of airpower doctrine from the time of the "Great War" to contemporary operations in Iraq and Afghanistan; he presents a classic tour through airpower theory and practice, stressing its enduring value, and making reference to the great theorists of airpower, particularly Britain's Hugh "Boom" Trenchard, Italy's Giulio Douhet, and America's William "Billy" Mitchell. He concludes that "As airpower enters its second century, it will remain the most important instrument of international security," noting that

> most analysts now agree that airpower is the quintessential strike element in a force-projection network able to conduct parallel attacks to create effects that are simultaneously tactical, operational, and strategic. . . . Propositions about airpower have generated more study and debate than have propositions about most other instruments of military force. They will continue to do so in the future, keeping the field vibrant and innovative. Clearly, the concept of airpower will remain not only relevant, but central to international security and stability as nations advance in the 21st century.

Next, Mark A. Stokes, executive director of the Project 2049 Institute, presents an intriguing survey of the PLAAF's quest for joint-service aerospace power, examining the strategic drivers underpinning its quest, evolving Chinese concepts of joint aerospace power, the challenges of force modernization, the range of technological and acquisition choices facing the PLAAF, and PLAAF interest in advanced weapons concepts such as hypersonic missiles and spaceplanes, space-based systems, and cyber warfare. He concludes:

> The gradual expansion of China's long-range precision strike capabilities is altering the regional strategic landscape. The PLA Air Force and Second Artillery are making modest progress in developing advanced capabilities with an eye toward expanding their operational range into space and into the Asia-Pacific region. For the PLA Air Force, the ability to carry out strategic strike missions at ranges of 3,000 kilometers (1,860 miles) or more is viewed as the key to becoming a truly independent service, rather than one dependent on the Second Artillery or a supporting player to the ground forces. Despite the PLAAF's aspirations to develop a force capable of an independent air campaign around China's periphery and speculation of subordination of Second Artillery conventional ballistic missile units to the PLAAF, senior PRC political and military authorities will likely continue to rely on the established capabilities of the Second Artillery for coercion, strategic strike missions, and suppression of enemy air defenses for some time to come.
>
> ... Beijing's missile-centric strategy presents a number of challenges for regional stability. Barring the fielding of effective countermeasures, Chinese conventional aerospace power, specifically short- and medium-range ballistic and extended-range land attack cruise missiles, may over time give the PLA a decisive advantage in future conflicts around China's periphery.

Xiaoming Zhang, associate professor in the Department of Leadership and Strategy at the U.S. Air Force's Air War College, furnishes a valuable historical introduction to the PLAAF, from its roots in fighter-centric defensive air warfare before and after the Korean War era, and its evolution since that time as an army air service dominated by the PLA's surface-centric thought and leadership. He traces how, over its history, the PLAAF's ability to undertake deep strike and even cross-border air support operations has been heavily constrained by the PRC's political decisionmakers. While its modern capabilities—exemplified by aircraft such as the J–10 and Su–27—have left the legacy MiG–17 (J–5), MiG–19 (J–6), and MiG–21 (J–7) era far behind, he stresses "What has not changed is the PLA's political culture, service tradition, older ways of doing things, and outdated organizational system," concluding:

> The PLA is a titanic bureaucratic amalgamation with a leaden hand of tradition that can often block innovation. Changes in doctrine, training practices, force structure, and equipment are underway, yet many traditions and cultural characteristics of the 83-year-old PLA are rigorously maintained. On top of that, there is the Party-controlled political culture and the ground force–centric predominant organizational tradition of the PLA. Both serve as constraining mechanisms that not only restrict the PLA's drive to autonomy, but also ensure its loyalty to the Party and obedience to the Party's policy."

In Part II of this volume, Kenneth W. Allen, a senior research analyst at Defense Group Incorporated, offers an in-depth examination of the PLAAF's organizational structure, noting how it has adjusted to accommodate changes in equipment, force structure, and the transformation of modern military power. Increasingly, the PLAAF has emphasized the planning and execution of joint operations. The shift toward joint operations accelerated in the early 2000s, when, as Allen notes, "PLAAF officers began to assume key joint billets, including membership on the Chinese Communist Party's (CCP's) Central Military Commission (CMC), commandant of the Academy of Military Science, commandant and political commissar of the National Defense University, and deputy director billets in the General Staff Department (GSD), General Political Department (GPD), and General Logistics Department (GLD)."

But, if much of this organizational transformation is, on the surface, quite impressive, Allen, like Xiaoming Zhang before him, highlights the traditionalist aspects of the PLA that continue to dominate the perspective of the PLAAF. He notes that "the army still dominates the majority of the leadership and working billets in all of these organizations, along with the General Armament Department (GAD), which has yet to have a PLAAF (or PLA Navy) deputy, and all seven of the Military Region (MR) Headquarters. There are no indications this pattern of army domination will change in the next decade."

Murray Scot Tanner, a China security analyst with the Center for Naval Analyses, offers a detailed examination of three of the PLAAF's mission areas: deterring infringement of China's critical national security interests, carrying out offensive operations, and maintaining China's air and space defenses. Tanner traces the PLAAF's evolution from a pre-1990s emphasis upon largely tactical air defense to a gradually evolving appreciation after Operation *Desert Storm* of airpower's suitability for executing a broader range of strategic defensive and offensive missions. In 2004, the Party's Central Military Commission approved

PLAAF plans to "integrate air and space; [and] be simultaneously prepared for offensive and defensive operations." Three years later, Zhang Yuliang pronounced that "the Air Force should give full play to its powerful aerial mobility, rapid speed, and long-distance strike capabilities, as well as its advantages in conducting multiple types of aerial missions." Tanner concludes:

> Chinese air and space analysts have devoted increasing attention to promoting China's preparation for offensive missions and its efforts to seize and maintain the initiative in combat [including] efforts to develop a ladder of signals of increasing intensity to ward off potential adversaries [stressing] the increased importance of offense in PLAAF missions . . . targeting what they see as the fragile "systems of systems" that constitute enemy combat information systems [and placing] a growing emphasis on counterattacks as a means of seizing and holding the initiative in the face of near certain large-scale air attacks.

Roger Cliff, a nonresident Senior Fellow at the Center for Strategic and Budgetary Assessments, presents a thorough review of the doctrinal development of the PLAAF, relating it to historic milestones in its development, and in the political history of the PRC. Cliff notes that the PLAAF's future success, like that of other air forces, will depend upon how well it has mastered modern airpower doctrine and thought, not simply advanced weapons technology. He notes the importance of Deng Xiaoping who, after becoming China's leader in 1978, mandated rapid military modernization, particularly of the PLAAF (though Deng, as Cliff emphasizes, was motivated as much by a desire to place the airmen under strict Party control—they had proven "politically dangerous" in the days of Lin Biao—as by a desire to improve its combat capabilities). While noting PLAAF weaknesses and deficiencies, Cliff concludes:

> The United States and Taiwan would likely find the PLAAF to be an aggressive opponent in the event of a conflict. . . . Especially at the beginning of a war, the PLA will endeavor to attack enemy air bases, ballistic-missile bases, aircraft carriers, and warships equipped with land-attack cruise missiles before enemy aircraft can take off or missile attacks can be launched . . . . By 2015 or so, the weapons systems and platforms that China . . . is likely to have [would] make a Chinese air defense campaign . . . highly challenging for U.S. air forces [and] enable China to conduct offensive operations far into the western Pacific.

In the next chapter, Kevin Pollpeter, China program manager at Defense Group Incorporated, assesses the PLAAF's growing interest in space operations. He notes that in 2009, Xu Qiliang, commander of the PLAAF, stated the following:

> The air and space era and information era have arrived at the same time and the domain of information and domain of space and air have become the new commanding height for international strategic competition.... competition among armed forces is moving toward the air and space domain and is extending from the aviation domain to near space and even deep space.

Pollpeter finds that Xu's quest for "air and space security" is intrinsically bound with the PLAAF's concept of integrated air and space operations, which envisions the air and space battlespace as a "seamless whole." The "ultimate goal" he believes the PLAAF is seeking is a "network-centric force in which disparate forces, divided by function and distance, will be fused into an organic whole through the use of information technologies" to achieve air and space superiority, precision strike, rapid maneuver, and multidimensional support to PLA forces. The PLAAF's interest in assuming command over the PLA's space presence has not met with universal support, and its notions of space presence (including a somewhat surprising level of interest in manned spacecraft) are not universally accepted either. However space doctrine and application evolve within the PLA and PLAAF, enunciating and fulfilling a national space security policy will remain a crucial goal for both, particularly as China increasingly asserts its place among the world's spacefaring peoples.

Part III begins with David Shlapak, a senior international policy analyst at the RAND Corporation, who offers a cogent survey of the PLAAF's drive to modernize and reequip its combat forces, evocatively terming it "a Long March to modernity." Shlapak traces the transformation of the PLAAF's order of battle across two crucial decades, from 1990 to 2010. Over that time, its force structure of fighters, fighter-bombers, ground attack, and bomber aircraft has steadily declined, from approximately 5,000 aircraft in 1990 to approximately 1,500 in 2010. But while overall numbers have dropped, today the PLAAF possesses the world's third-highest number of advanced fourth-generation (third-generation, by PLAAF's categorization of fighter aircraft technology) fighters, behind the United States and Russia. Matching this has been an equivalent upgrading in air-to-air and air-to-surface weapons, surface-to-air missiles, sensors, avionics, air refueling, and airborne early warning and control. Shlapak concludes:

> The progress made in recent years by the PLAAF is impressive.... As late as the early 1990s, it was likely too weak to have even defended China's home airspace against a serious, modern adversary.... [Now] the revolution in the PLAAF's order of battle is over. It has made up the four decades separating the MiG–17/MiG–19 generations from the Su–27SK

Su–30MKK generation in just 15 remarkable years. Whether or not the PLAAF can close the remaining gaps between its capabilities and those of the most advanced air forces remains to be seen. But given how it has transformed itself over the last 15 years, one would be foolish to bet heavily against it.

You Ji, an associate professor at the School of Social Science and International Studies, University of New South Wales, Australia, presents a detailed examination of the individuals comprising the PLAAF's senior leadership—those approximately three-dozen officers at or above full corps rank—tracing how, over time, the PLAAF's senior leaders have increasingly come from the ranks of airmen, particularly fighter pilots from the most prestigious and accomplished fighter regiments and air divisions. As his chapter shows, the leadership of the PLAAF is surprisingly "elderly," with a coming massive reshuffle in favor of slightly younger commanders coincident with the coming 18th Party Congress in 2012. The transformation of the PLAAF from the era of the J–5 (MiG–17) and J–6/Q–5 (MiG–19) to the era of the J–10, Su–27, and J–11 "has placed," he believes, "huge pressure for the air force to groom, select, and place talented commanders at various levels." The author concludes that the PLAAF leadership selection process

> is increasingly based upon meritocracy and even "expertocracy," . . . [reflecting] a sophisticated, institutionalized, and comprehensive personnel selection and promotion system. . . . The candidates for top leadership are inevitably well-trained, learned, and internationally exposed. The level of professionalism is very high, both in terms of their careers as airmen, and their experience as commanders. Mediocre officers simply do not make it to the top, given the extremely tough competition among peers.

Kevin Lanzit, a senior analyst with Alion Science and Technology, Incorporated, reviews the PLAAF's professional military education and training. As the PLAAF modernizes force structure and operational doctrine, it continues to modernize its education and training as well, seeking, as Lanzit states, "to transform its legacy mechanized force into a force that will be capable of fighting and winning in modern, informatized conditions." Lanzit begins with an overview of training in the Chinese air service in the pre-Communist era. Training deficiencies in the early days of the PLAAF resulted in ill-trained aircrew compared to their Soviet advisors and Western opponents, and, later, to the Taiwan airmen facing them across the Taiwan Strait. The societal disruptions accompanying the infamous "Cultural Revolution" of the late Mao era took their own toll on PLAAF competency as well. Thanks first to the reforms of Deng Xiaoping, followed by those of Jiang Zemin, Hu Jintao, and continuing to the present, the PLAAF is today more rigorously (if imperfectly) trained than at any previous time. Even so, Lanzit concludes that although progress has been "substantial," the PLAAF still "has not yet achieved the development goals it seeks for officers and NCOs [noncommissioned officers]."

Beginning Part IV, Shen Pin-Luen of the Prospect Foundation delineates the past, present, and likely future of the Chinese aircraft industry, discussing how the PRC's drive to modernize led not only to strenuous transformative efforts within the PLAAF, but also to a transformation of the Chinese aircraft industry. Its transformation resulted in a more globally inquisitive industry, one looking for inspiration in foreign design practice, but also, over time, more confident of its own abilities to pursue advanced technology programs, even complex fighter development efforts such as the J–8, J–10, J–11, and JH–7. This confidence became evident in mid-2008 with the establishment of the Commercial Aircraft Corporation of China Ltd. (COMAC), and, slightly later, with the merger of China Aviation Industry Corporation I (AVIC I) and China Aviation Industry Corporation II (AVIC II) into the China Aviation Industry Corporation (AVIC), and was reaffirmed by the first flights of the Chengdu J–20, a prototype stealth fighter roughly equivalent to the American YF–22/YF–23 of 1990, in January 2011. "The overhaul of the aviation sector is an indication that the pace of development and reform in China's aviation industry is picking up," Shen concludes, warning that "China's determination and injection of resources into the industry should not be underestimated by the outside world."

Next, Phillip C. Saunders, director of the Center for the Study of Chinese Military Affairs at National Defense University's Institute for National Strategic Studies, and Joshua K. Wiseman, a research analyst at the center, probe into the Chinese aviation industry and the PLAAF's acquisition efforts to reveal a pattern of technology acquisition they summarize as "buy, build, or steal." "Chinese leaders aspire to build a defense industry capable of producing advanced military weapons systems without dependence on foreign suppliers," they note, "but the limited capacity of China's overall economy and technological limitations on its military aviation sector have made access to foreign aircraft and technology necessary." They trace the "ongoing tension between the desire for self-reliance in defense and the need for access to advanced foreign technologies," across five periods in the evolution of China's military aerospace industry.

The first period was that of Soviet assistance from 1950 to 1960, which gave the PRC its initial experience in license-producing Soviet fighters, bombers, and transports. The second, from 1960 to 1977, was that of the Sino-Soviet split, during which China made do with incremental product refinement and development of derivatives (such as the Q–5) from existing designs. The third, from 1977 to 1989, marked China's turning to the West, during which it gained some access to Western technologies. But the Tiananmen Square repression bought this period to a close. China initiated the fourth period when it turned back to a cash-strapped Russia—and even Israel—to secure advanced fighter and missile technology exemplified in the Su-27 and J-10. The fifth (and current) period began in 2004. Since then, Western nations and Russia have become increasingly reluctant to share technology with the PRC. As a consequence, the authors conclude:

> The likelihood that China will have no foreign source of advanced military aviation technology supports two important conclusions. First, the Chinese military aviation industry will have to rely primarily on indigenous development of advanced "single-use" military aviation technologies in the future [and] China will likely rely more heavily on espionage to acquire those critical military aviation technologies it cannot acquire legitimately from foreign suppliers or develop on its own.

Next, Hsi-hua Cheng, an instructor at the Taiwan National Defense University, addresses the grim prospect of military encounters over the Taiwan Strait, including the possibility, however remote, of a forceful seizure of the island of Taiwan by an all-out PLA amphibious assault. He undertakes his analysis by studying PLA, PLAN, and PLAAF doctrinal pronouncements, the pattern of military activity, and the respective force structures on either side of the strait. While noting that since May 20, 2008, when Taiwan President Ma Ying-jeou took office, the cross-strait policies of both sides have become more peaceful and friendly, he nevertheless pointedly notes that "the PRC has never renounced the use of military force against Taiwan, and, indeed, as it has steadily modernized its forces, the PRC has continued to maintain an aggressive posture toward Taiwan."

Examining various uses of coercion and escalatory force, the author stresses the PLAAF and Second Artillery's belief in the use of joint, overwhelming power. For its part, he argues that Taiwan must employ its airpower only for self-defense. "As long as they don't step on our territory and impede our lifelines," he asserts, "they don't win and we don't lose, and our national security is secured." Under no circumstances, he believes, should Taiwan engage in a preventive strike, as "Taiwan can't afford the international liability of initiating the war." It is essential, then, that Taiwan shape its defensive forces so that they can survive a first strike, enabling defenders to "concentrate Taiwan's limited airpower to a critical time and place." Taiwan, he believes, "must construct a mobile, diffuse, and widespread air defense umbrella covering point, area, and then theater air defense," exploiting as well the synergy of advanced aircraft, helicopters, unmanned aerial systems, V/STOL (vertical and/or short takeoff and landing) technologies, hardening airfields and command facilities, and developing "a decentralized network-centric command and communication structure."

Finally, the author recommends that Taiwan "adopt a 'Starfish' strategy to enhance its survivability," noting that starfish can regenerate lost arms and that Taiwan's defense leaders "should try to apply this strategy to decentralize the commanding activity to the very basic units of its organizations, equipment, facilities, or personnel, to ensure that sustainability and survivability will expand." Above all, he notes, Taiwan must work to ensure "that the PRC has no excuses to justify an invasion of Taiwan."

In the final chapter, David Frelinger, a senior political scientist at the RAND Corporation, and Jessica Hart, an analyst at a defense contractor, offer a provocative assessment of the PLAAF's modernization and its influence upon the U.S.-China military balance. They posit an "alternative framework" looking beyond the "ossified" bipolar nature of the Cold War, noting the U.S.-China relationship "is not yet mature, and there are multiple, competing narratives about interests and goals on both sides." They employ three analytical games: the "Game of Influence" (Chinese and American military power advancing their respective national interests); the "Battle over a Third Party" (Chinese and American military power employed in a two-party conflict over Taiwan); and the "Great Power Game" (unlike the others, a zero-sum game in which military power is "the central aspect" of the U.S.-China relationship), noting that both America and China have "largely confined" themselves to the second game, the Battle over a Third Party. They conclude:

> The United States has a wide range of options that do not necessarily require a new force structure or more defense expenditures, but instead may call for an altered military and political emphasis. . . . If the United States chooses to continue to play the same game in the same way it has since the end of the Cold War, the results may be to China's advantage. But if the United States chooses to play another game where its significant military and political assets can be more fully utilized, PLAAF modernization may lead to a Pyrrhic victory for the Chinese.

Taken as a whole, the chapters of this volume provide a comprehensive picture of China's progress in building a modern air force. This effort is most visible in PLAAF investments in aircraft and in China's efforts to develop a capable military aviation industry. However, as several chapters demonstrate, improvements in organization, personnel, training, and doctrine have been equally important in terms of PLAAF development and expanding operational and combat capabilities. The overall impression is that the Chinese air force has made great progress on its "Long March to modernity."

Finally, on a personal note, this book is dedicated to a remarkable airman, Major General John R. Alison, USAFR (Ret.), who died on June 6, 2011, at the age of 98. Aside from being an extraordinary pilot and military leader (and co-founder of America's first Air Commandos), "Johnny" Alison was a fiercely dedicated patriot, whose love of country and affection and admiration for its people were matched by his affection and admiration for the people of China. As a fighter pilot in China during World War II, Alison was moved by the suffering, courage, and daily sacrifice of the Chinese people, whose optimism, passionate dedication to their homeland, and faith in its future he greatly admired. After the war, as a postwar U.S. Air Force officer, international businessman, and aviation executive, he maintained his interest in China and its citizens. All who knew him—and this editor was privileged to know him well—will recall how often he spoke of the necessity of finding a means to ensure lasting peace for the Taiwan Strait, a peace characterized by mutual respect and dignity. In a conversation less than 3 months before his death, he stressed the critical importance of promoting a stronger and beneficial unity between Taiwan and the mainland, and between the American and Chinese people, believing both would work to further the stability of East Asia. May his life serve as both example and encouragement to all those who, whatever their nationality and background, seek today to blaze a path to permanent peace so that the Taiwan Strait never again experiences the dismal and bitter horrors of civil war.

PART I
CONCEPTS

Chapter 1

The Concept of Airpower: Its Emergence, Evolution, and Future

Forrest E. Morgan

It should come as no surprise that the concept of *airpower* has changed a great deal since H.G. Wells first used the term in his 1908 science fiction novel, *The War in the Air*. Given the passage of more than a century, the world has seen dramatic advances in technology as well as changes in the geopolitical conditions in which war is fought. Yet within the ever-evolving fabric of airpower history, one can find remarkable threads of continuity. Early aircraft, though but fragile contraptions of wood and canvas, exploited the same advantages enjoyed by the sophisticated weapons systems that operate in today's 21st-century skies: the ability to cover great distances in any direction quickly, free of obstruction by surface terrain; the ability to overfly enemy armies and navies and attack them from above, across the breadth and depth of the battlespace; and the ability to take war to the heart of an enemy's society, striking vulnerable targets previously unreachable before defeating surface defenses. So there should be little wonder that the concept of airpower, while ever evolving, has also exhibited elements of continuity, as have the doctrines and strategies that conceptual thinking about airpower has inspired. In many ways and for reasons that are clearly evident, today's airmen have inherited the strategic mindset of their forebears.

This paper examines that mindset in historical context as it traces the evolution of airpower thought and considers what theoretical, technological, and political trends suggest for strategies that air forces will likely employ in the future. It explains how airpower thought, though buffeted by changes in technology and geopolitics, has been anchored on an evolving body of theory conceived to exploit the unique warfighting advantages afforded by the ability of aircraft to operate in the vertical dimension. Yet within this unifying framework, strategic thinkers have, from the earliest days of military air operations, debated whether airpower is employed most effectively as an independent instrument against targets chosen to create direct, war-winning effects at the strategic level of war, or whether it is better used in combination with surface forces at the operational level of war. I argue that these competing ideas appear to be converging in the current era, but the debate is unlikely to ever be fully resolved. That is a good thing because strategy has always benefited from rigorous examination and spirited intellectual debate. Creative thought and innovation have always been the touchstones of airpower. That heritage will continue into the future.

The Dawn of Airpower Thought

When military authorities hesitantly began acquiring "aeroplanes" in the years immediately following Orville and Wilbur Wright's first flight of a heavier-than-air craft, the missions they had in mind for these new machines flowed from the novel but limited capabilities they offered. Considering them too fragile for combat and unable to carry ordnance heavy enough to contribute anything meaningful to artillery bombardment, the U.S. Army, along with the armies of several European countries, nevertheless saw potential applications in communications and reconnaissance in the airplane's speed and the visual perspective afforded by altitude. Such were the missions in which aircraft were first employed in combat, over Libya in 1911, the Balkans the next year, and, more significantly still, in Europe when war broke out in 1914. But it did not take long for the airmen flying these machines to begin finding combat applications for the unique capabilities that the new technology provided. Almost immediately, enemy reconnaissance aircrews began harassing each other, first throwing bricks and hand grenades, later shooting at each other with handguns, rifles, and ultimately mounted machineguns. Before long, air services on both sides organized "pursuit" squadrons with aircraft and crews dedicated to the air-to-air combat mission. By mid 1916, both the Germans and the Franco-British allies had developed machinegun synchronizers, allowing them to fire ahead along the axis of flight by shooting between the propellers, thus creating the first true fighter planes.[1]

Meanwhile, aviators developed techniques to strafe and bomb enemy trenches, and they began attacking lines of communication in efforts to interdict the movement of men and materiel to the front. The Germans even pioneered the use of strategic bombing, striking London and other urban targets from lighter-than-air dirigibles, beginning in 1915. Later, in 1917, when the unwieldy Zeppelins began taking too many losses, German leaders transferred the mission to faster, more maneuverable Gotha and Giant bomber aircraft. Indeed, by the time U.S. aviators officially entered the war that same year—American volunteers had participated unofficially in the French Air Service's *Lafayette Escadrille* (originally *Escadrille Américaine*) since April 1916—all of the principal missions flown by today's air forces had already emerged in some form. Nevertheless, air operations ultimately had a negligible effect on the course of the war, due to the limitations in payload weight and bombing accuracy that constrained aircraft capabilities in that era.[2]

Despite these limitations, several visionaries saw beyond the constraints of contemporary technology to grasp the potential of how aircraft might affect the outcomes of future wars, triggering the emergence of formal airpower theory. One of these individuals was Giulio Douhet, an artillery officer in the Italian army. Douhet had watched the rapid development of combat aviation during the war and saw in the emerging capability of bomber aircraft a potential for striking enemy countries where he thought they were most vulnerable, their cities. In his 1921 book, *Command of the Air*, and several subsequent publications, he theorized that airpower could be used to end wars quickly by bombing urban areas to break the enemy's material and moral resistance.[3] Countries with the foresight to embrace the potential of airpower could thereby avoid repeating the bloody stalemate of the last war, where more than 8 million men had given their lives, many in frontal assaults against machineguns, artillery, and barbed wire, while stalled at the trenches in France.

Aircraft had the advantageous ability to strike the heart of an enemy's country without having to defeat its armies first. Though World War I had demonstrated that disciplined soldiers could withstand considerable bombardment without breaking, Douhet believed that civilians would not be so resilient. Bombers could overfly enemy armies, thus avoiding the adversary's hardened crust, and bomb major cities, causing panic and generating popular pressure to end the war. Douhet argued, however, that Italy could not afford to build the bomber force needed to carry out such a plan if it continued squandering its scarce defense resources on less effective military capabilities, such as ground and naval forces. Nor could the air service achieve its full potential if it continued to be administered by the army, because army generals would insist that aircraft be used to attack enemy forces and perform other battlefield missions in support of ground operations.

Douhet proposed that Italy, instead, build an independent air force comprised primarily of heavily armed "battle planes." In the event of war, these planes would not waste time attacking the enemy army. Rather, they would first dispose of the greatest threat that a savvy adversary could muster—the enemy air force. Douhet's first objective would be to bomb the adversary's airfields, destroying enemy planes on the ground and any that rose to challenge his battle planes, until Italy achieved command of the air. Then the air force would turn its attention to the enemy's capital and major cities, bombing the civilian population into submission and enemy leaders into surrender.[4]

Another airpower visionary during the interwar years was Britain's Air Marshal Sir Hugh Trenchard. Having commanded the Royal Flying Corps during World War I, he was an ardent believer in the war-winning potential of airpower and the chief interwar champion and architect of Britain's independent

Royal Air Force (RAF). According to historian Phillip Meilinger, "Trenchard carried three main beliefs with him from the war: air superiority was an essential prerequisite to military success; airpower was an inherently offensive weapon; and although its material effects were great, airpower's psychological effects were far greater."[5]

In the years leading to World War II, under Trenchard's guidance, the RAF developed a doctrine for strategic bombing which maintained that victory in war resulted from the collapse of civilian morale. Like Douhet, Trenchard disparaged dissipating airpower's unique capabilities in attacks on armies in the field. Rather, the RAF's principal doctrine publication, AP 1300, *Royal Air Force War Manual*, advocated bombing industrial centers to drive workers from the factories and destroy economic infrastructure—including public utilities, food and fuel supplies, transportation networks, and communications—to cause "a general undermining of the whole populace, even to the extent of destroying the nation's will to continue the struggle."[6] And like Douhet, Trenchard insisted that the RAF retain its institutional separation from the army in order to husband the resources and maintain the freedom of action needed to carry out its independent mission.[7]

While U.S. aviators were influenced by Douhet and Trenchard, they were most inspired by the very public and often caustic arguments proffered by their own airpower champion, Brigadier General William "Billy" Mitchell. As a senior U.S. air officer in France during World War I, Mitchell was well acquainted with Trenchard, and after the war he also consulted with Douhet and Italian bomber designer and manufacturer Gianni Caproni.[8] Like his European counterparts, Mitchell was an ardent believer in airpower as an independent, war-winning weapon, and he argued vociferously that the air services should be granted separation from all Army and Navy control. In Mitchell's view, air warfare was unique, and only airmen, whom he saw as a "distinctive class of ... aerial knights engaged in chivalrous combat," had the proper mindset to lead it.[9] It was a romantic image, one that he painted for public consumption at every opportunity in books, speeches, magazine articles, and newspaper editorials, often criticizing Navy leaders and even his own superiors in the Army for their hidebound attitudes and for mismanaging the air assets under their control. Ultimately, his public defiance of military authority resulted in his court martial and resignation from the Army, but he continued to extol the virtues of independent airpower in publications and speeches until his death in 1936.[10]

Officers on the faculty of the U.S. Army's Air Corps Tactical School (ACTS) at Maxwell Field, Alabama, followed the international airpower debate with interest.[11] They too believed aerial bombardment was a weapon with war-winning potential, one best employed as an independent instrument against a country's vulnerable interior, but they were less than sanguine about Douhet's and Trenchard's conviction that the key to victory lay in directly targeting the enemy's moral resistance.[12] Rather, having observed that warfare between industrial states had become very resource consumptive, they theorized that bombing an enemy's armaments industry could deny him the *capability* to wage war as well as the will to do so. Relying on deductive reasoning and circumstantial evidence—such as when a temporary closing at the only plant in the United States that manufactured a spring essential to the assembly of variable-pitch propellers brought aircraft production to a nationwide halt—ACTS theorists surmised that every industrialized nation-state had become a network of interconnected economic systems, an "industrial web," with critical points, the destruction of which would lead to its collapse.[13]

Of course, striking such critical points from the air with sufficient force and accuracy to destroy them would be challenging—it could only be done with mass raids in daylight. And the enemy would resist mass bomber raids with all the fighters and antiaircraft artillery it could muster—the bombers would have to fly high and be fast and heavily armed. But comparing the capabilities of fighters and bombers of that era, and examining the development of such new technologies as the Norden bombsight, they concluded that "high-altitude, daylight precision bombing" was not only possible, it would be key to winning a war with an industrialized state. Therefore, "an inviolable principle of ACTS was that airmen use the bomber only against vital material targets located deep within hostile territory and that it never serve in harassing operations of the Army."[14]

Although theories for employing airpower as an independent, war-winning weapon were in vogue in several of the world's leading air services, they were by no means universally accepted, and so an opposing line of thought—airpower at the *operational* level of war—arose. In Germany, for instance, desires to develop and employ strategic bombing were tempered by the need to use airpower in support of ground operations. As Germany was a continental power with contiguous borders with its traditional enemies, *Luftwaffe* planners recognized that they would likely be called upon to support the army at the onset of any future war. Nevertheless, Germany had its own interwar strategic bombing theorist in the person of Dr. Robert Knauss, a World War I combat veteran who afterwards helped shape Lufthansa, and whose ideas largely mirrored those of Douhet.[15]

The Chief of the *Luftwaffe* General Staff, Walther Wever, who advocated a balanced development of airpower capabilities, also believed strategic bombing would be an important arrow in Germany's quiver. In 1934 he ordered work to begin on a long-range "Ural Bomber" that would enable the *Luftwaffe* to bomb military and industrial targets deep in the Soviet Union.[16] However, several factors constrained the *Luftwaffe*'s development of capabilities for conducting strategic air warfare. First, the General Staff worried that the "terror bombing" that Douhet and Knauss advocated would provoke Germany's enemies to reciprocate with revenge attacks on German cities, so they blocked all attempts to have such tactics written into *Luftwaffe* doctrine.[17] Second, although there was considerable interest in the early 1930s in developing long-range bombers for use against industrial targets, the Germans failed to clear the technological hurdles that would have allowed them to develop aircraft engines powerful enough to carry heavy payloads at the altitudes and distances needed to accomplish that mission. Finally, and perhaps most importantly, the *Luftwaffe*'s most influential strategic bombing advocate, Walther Wever, met an untimely death in an air accident in 1936. With his demise, the Ural Bomber project was canceled and Reich Air Minister Hermann Goring put the *Luftwaffe* in the hands of generals more interested in developing capabilities for supporting ground operations.

Consequently, from that point onward German airpower development focused on capabilities for supporting actions at the operational level of war. The *Luftwaffe* began procuring fighters and fast medium bombers for destroying enemy airpower in the battle zone rather than by bombing aircraft production. General Ernst Udet, whom Goring appointed to direct the Office of Technical Development in 1936, insisted that all future bombers be designed as dive-bombers.[18] General Hans Jeschonnek, appointed chief of the *Luftwaffe* General Staff in 1939, was similarly enamored with dive-bombing. As a result, dive-bombing was emphasized over level bombing and aircraft such as the Junkers Ju–87 *Stuka* (for *Sturzkampfflugzeug*: "dive bomber") became exemplars of German airpower thought. Ultimately, the *Luftwaffe*'s doctrinal thrust shifted to providing interdiction bombing and close-air support (CAS) for armor and infantry actions in Germany's emerging high-speed maneuver warfare doctrine, which, soon after its first employment in Poland, was dubbed *Blitzkrieg* (Lightning War).[19]

Similar, though not identical, experiences can be seen in other countries during the interwar period. The Soviet Union had its own strategic bombing advocate in the personage of Air Force General A.N. Lapchinsky, who in the early 1920s wrote a book and several articles arguing that strategic bombing would be a major weapon in future wars. Alternatively, Army Chief of Staff Marshal Mikhail Tukhachevskii, while acknowledging a future role for strategic bombardment, maintained that airpower should be used mostly in joint operations, with light bombers, fighters, and ground-attack aviation integrated with armor and artillery employment in the execution of "deep battle" doctrine.[20] Early on, Lapchinsky's ideas found favor among Soviet aviators, ironically, not so much from a rational analysis of airpower capabilities as from a belief that strategic bombing was a "modern" form of warfare and therefore more appropriate for a military system built on Marxist-Leninist principles.[21]

However, as Soviet airpower thought matured, the orientation shifted. During Germany's 1925–1933 air mission to the Soviet Union, German instructors emphasized the importance of air-ground cooperation at the operational level of war. Later, during the Spanish Civil War (1936–1939), in which Germany and Italy deployed forces in support of the Nationalist cause and the Soviet Union supported the Republican side, air forces on both sides briefly resorted to population bombing, but ultimately enjoyed much greater success when they used their airpower in support of ground operations. By the end of the 1930s, the Soviets, like the Germans, concluded that, given limitations imposed by the technology at their disposal, airpower concepts developed around short-range ground-attack aircraft would suit their needs better than those requiring aircraft that they lacked the capability to produce.[22]

Japan and even Italy, the home of Giulio Douhet, exhibited similar patterns in thinking. Japan attempted to develop long-range bombers and the Japanese army and navy air services resorted to population bombing in Shanghai, Guangzhou, Nanjing, and Chongqing starting in 1937 in the war against China. But the Japanese experienced the same technological limitations and disappointing outcomes as did the continental powers of Europe, and they subsequently focused their greatest efforts on using airpower in support of surface forces. Italy, alternatively, never made a serious effort to develop strategic bombers. Although Italian air force leaders paid lip-service to Douhet—likely prudent, as he was a prominent Fascist—in practice they dismissed his ideas as immoral and inappropriate for Italy's geostrategic challenges, following instead the more operationally-focused ideas of Amedeo Mecozzi. As the Spanish Civil War confirmed their thinking, the Italians increasingly focused their attention on developing doctrine for using airpower in support of ground and naval operations.[23]

Applying Airpower Thought to Shape Air Strategy in World War II

The beginning of World War II saw German airpower applied at the operational level of war with stunning results. On September 1, 1939, Germany unleashed *Blitzkrieg* on Poland. The *Luftwaffe* began the operation with massive air attacks on airfields and other military targets across the country. Although the Polish air force fought with skill and bravery, it was quickly overwhelmed by superior numbers. Soon afterwards the Polish army buckled under the coordinated onslaught of hundreds of *Panzer* tanks and *Stuka* dive-bombers.[24]

This campaign first showed the world what synergies were possible in coordinated air and ground operations. Interdiction bombing made it impossible for the Poles to move troops in the open, and German armored forces quickly advanced, enveloping the Polish formations. At that point, close air support (CAS) was instrumental in crushing Polish efforts to break out of the encirclements. By the end of September, the Polish army and air force had been destroyed and Warsaw bombed into capitulation. But the small, ill-equipped Polish air force was no real challenge to the *Luftwaffe*—the real test came the following spring in the Battle of France.[25]

In May 1940 the German Army overran Luxembourg and drove multiple spearheads into the Netherlands, Belgium, and Northern France. As in the Polish campaign, the *Luftwaffe* struck airfields hard and fast, destroying a large percentage of French and Belgian aircraft on the ground. The Germans used the vertical dimension in novel ways, dropping airborne forces to seize key bridges on the Meuse and behind Dutch defenses in the canal country, and carrying out a bold glider assault, landing on the roof of the Belgian fort of Eben Emael to unhinge defenses there. Meanwhile, *Stuka* dive-bombers pounded French, British, and Belgian forces ahead of German armor divisions as the *Panzers* plunged into Belgium and France. The results in this campaign resembled those in Poland the previous September. In the face of a rapid, coordinated assault, the defenders buckled physically and morally. The campaign was over in 6 weeks. Although Germany employed airpower similarly in subsequent campaigns, often achieving tactical success, its ability to translate those achievements into strategic effects diminished as the war progressed.[26]

In the summer of 1940, with the continental Allies in Western Europe defeated, German leaders began planning operation "Sea Lion," the invasion and conquest of Great Britain. Such an effort would have presented a unique challenge for German campaign planners in terms of their ability to integrate *Luftwaffe* operations with those of two other services, but their ability to meet that challenge was never tested. Before the German army and navy could launch a cross-channel operation with any chance of success, the *Luftwaffe* would have to neutralize Britain's RAF and win command of the air. It failed to do so.

The *Luftwaffe* launched the main air assault on August 13. Although it gave the outnumbered RAF a considerable pounding for several weeks, the British held on tenaciously, rationing Fighter Command's limited resources in a sector defense scheme made possible by the use of radar to detect incoming attackers and direct fighter interceptions.[27] Even so, the *Luftwaffe* still might have exhausted RAF resistance had not Adolf Hitler, in a fit of pique in early September, redirected the German air effort away from the RAF bases and against London instead, in an effort to break British resolve with terror bombing. That effort failed as well. By September 17, it was clear that the *Luftwaffe* would be unable to secure the skies over Britain and the English Channel and Hitler "postponed" plans for Sea Lion.[28]

Blunted in the west, Germany turned east once more in 1941, unleashing *Blitzkrieg* on the Soviet Union. As in previous campaigns on the continent, the *Luftwaffe* quickly decimated Soviet airpower, destroying 1,200 aircraft the first day alone. Moreover, the Red Army, immense but stripped of competent leadership in Stalin's recent purge, lost more than 50 divisions in the first three weeks of battle.[29] Yet despite the fact that the Germans drove the Red Army from Poland to the outskirts of Moscow over the course of a few short months, the Soviet will to resist never wavered. The Russians held out, rebuilt their army and air force (with considerable U.S. material support), and turned the tide, eventually driving the *Wehrmacht* to Berlin and destroying it with the Soviet Union's own doctrine for integrating airpower with ground forces at the operational level of war—deep battle.[30]

A more balanced mix of strategic and tactical airpower application characterized the Anglo-American airpower experience in World War II, though American and British thinking sharply differed over the fundamental nature of strategic air operations. Soon after the United States entered the war in December 1941, the U.S. Army Air Forces (the USAAF, established in 1941 from the prewar U.S. Army Air Corps) had its opportunity to put its strategic bombing doctrine in action. With France fallen, Britain driven off the continent, and the Soviet Union refusing to allow Allied personnel on Soviet territory, the U.S. Army had no immediate foothold from which it could launch an operation against German ground forces, and the only way the United States could strike at its principal European enemy was to join the RAF in the strategic bombing of German industry.

As a result, prewar Air Corps doctrine was the guiding principle when four former ACTS faculty members drafted Air War Planning Document 1 (AWPD-1), the blueprint for U.S. participation in the bombing campaign—the USAAF would use high-altitude, daylight precision bombing to attack Germany's industrial web. Such an approach was inconsistent with that used by the RAF, which had already tried daylight bombing and switched to nighttime area bombing after suffering unbearable losses. However, the two doctrines were not incompatible, and the Anglo-American Allies eventually agreed to a Combined Bomber Offensive (CBO) in which the USAAF would bomb by day and the RAF by night, thereby putting the maximum pressure possible on Germany's industrial infrastructure and the forces defending it.[31]

Thus began the first sustained test of the strategic bombing theories developed between the wars.[32] Over the next 3 years, the Allies dropped over 2.7 million tons of bombs on industrial targets, first in German-occupied Western Europe and later in Germany itself. While the British effort was devoted to crippling German industry by area-bombing urban areas and industrial centers, the USAAF, guided by ACTS industrial web theory, sought to bring German war production to a halt by using precision bombing to destroy key nodes in the system. While they were confident in their ability to do this, the question that arose repeatedly throughout the war was, just what were the key nodes on which German industry most depended? Opinions differed over the course of the struggle, and though target lists never focused on one category exclusively, the weight of effort shifted from the aircraft industry in early 1943 to ball bearing plants later that year. In early 1944 the bombing came to focus more heavily on transportation and other targets in preparation for the Normandy invasion. Mid-1944 saw a shift once again to steel and, most significantly, synthetic oil production. While the destruction of none of these targets succeeded in bringing Germany's industrial production to a halt early enough to end the war before its armies were defeated on the ground, the United States Strategic Bombing Survey (USSBS) later concluded—both from physical and documentary evidence, and from the interrogations of key German military, civilian, and industrial leaders—that the attacks on fuel production had the most dramatic impact. Indeed, some analysts have since argued that strategic bombing might have had war-winning effect if synthetic fuel production had received a far greater weight of effort earlier.[33]

Strategic bombing was by no means the only way airpower was employed in the western theater in World War II. Beginning with the 1943 North Africa campaign and continuing with the invasions and reconquest of the European continent, airpower provided essential support to ground operations in all the basic missions pioneered in World War I: reconnaissance, air superiority, close air support, and interdiction. Along the way—and often through costly errors, such as the debacle at Kasserine Pass in North Africa, which resulted in airmen being given greater responsibility and authority in the conduct of air-ground operations, based largely on earlier RAF experience in the Western Desert— the Allies learned important lessons that became central tenets of U.S. Air Force and RAF doctrine in future years.[34] Chief among them was that airpower must never be divided into "penny packets" and dispersed to the control and support of individual ground commanders. Rather, its control must be centralized under the command of an airman, the only military professional who could be entrusted to sufficiently understand its unique properties and employ it effectively, to allow for the most flexible employment and the most effective massing of force against key targets. Most importantly, command of the air is essential: air superiority is a prerequisite for effective surface operations. Though controversial at the time, both of these tenets have endured and are accepted as core prerequisites even today, in the era of hyper-jointness characteristic of contemporary American and coalition military operations.[35]

The air war in the Pacific theater yielded similar lessons, though it unfolded in an order opposite that in Europe. With Japan having captured a broad defensive perimeter of islands in the first months of the war, its home islands were protected by an expanse of ocean that exceeded the range of U.S. bombers. Consequently, the USAAF was first tasked with providing support to Chinese forces in their struggle against the Japanese army on the Asian mainland and to U.S. Army and Marine ground operations in the systematic reconquest of islands in the southwest Pacific. By late 1944, however, the Marianna Islands had been recaptured and bases built on Guam, Saipan, and Tinian, putting Japan in striking range of B–29 heavy bombers.

Once again, ACTS industrial web theory–based Air Corps doctrine guided the effort, at least initially. For the first several months, the USAAF's XXI Bomber Command attempted high-altitude daylight precision bombing with high explosives, but the characteristically strong winds found at altitudes above 30,000 feet (the so-called "jetstream" blowing west-to-east over Japan and the Pacific) and Japan's dispersal of industry rendered that approach ineffective. Therefore, in March 1945 the XXI Bomber Command changed tactics, resorting to nighttime raids at low altitude using incendiaries on urban centers.[36] The results were devastating. Over the next 5 months, B–29s dropped 104,000 tons of bombs, destroying an average of 40 percent of the built-up areas in Japan's 66 largest cities.[37] Yet despite this horrific pounding, Japanese leaders were unwilling to accept Allied demands for unconditional surrender until after the USAAF dropped atomic bombs on Hiroshima on August 6 and Nagasaki on August 9. The surrender finally came on August 14, 1945. In the eyes of U.S. airmen, theories espousing the employment of airpower as an independent war-winning weapon had finally been validated.

Airpower Thought in the Early Cold War Era

By the end of World War II, the concept of airpower as an independent strategic weapon was firmly established. Although the CBO's ultimate effect on the outcome of the war in Europe was indeterminate and military analysts and scholars have since debated what factors were most instrumental in forcing Japan's capitulation, conventional wisdom immediately presumed that strategic bombing had won the war—the atomic bombs had forced Japanese leaders to accept unconditional surrender.[38] This appeared to be a harbinger of how future wars would unfold. Atomic weapons could only be delivered from the air, and only heavy bombers were large enough to carry them. Consequently, the emerging concept of atomic warfare seemed indistinguishable from strategic bombing, and airpower became widely accepted as the independent war-winning weapon that theorists had long claimed it to be.

It is ironic that at a time when the concept of strategic airpower seemed most transcendent, further development of airpower thought would grind to a halt. But that is what happened, largely as a result of the impact on thinking caused by the dramatic advance in destructiveness made possible by atomic and later nuclear weapons. Military and political leaders first saw atomic bombs simply as more powerful ordnance, weapons to be used in future wars to achieve military and political objectives more efficiently. But as USSBS investigators learned more about the extent of destruction wrought on the cities of Hiroshima and Nagasaki, it became increasingly apparent that atomic bombs were weapons in a totally different class from anything used before. The following year, RAND analyst Bernard Brodie published his now classic book, *The Absolute Weapon: Atomic Power and World Order*, in which he argued that atomic weapons were so potentially devastating that they would change the very nature of war.[39] Thirteen years later, with the United States and Soviet Union both possessing growing stockpiles of nuclear arms, Brodie would write:

> Perhaps the most elementary, the most truistic, and yet the most important point one can make is that the kind of sudden and overwhelming calamity that one is talking about today in any reference to all-out or total war would be an utterly different and immeasurably worse phenomenon from war as we have known it in the past.[40]

Much had changed by the time Brodie wrote those words. Soon after the end of World War II, America's erstwhile ally, the Soviet Union, had emerged as its rival in the long-term ideological struggle for geopolitical dominance that came to be known as the Cold War. The United States' monopoly on atomic weapons was curtailed sooner than expected when the Soviets exploded their own atom bomb in 1949, and U.S. leaders were further distressed when the Soviets tested their first thermonuclear device in August 1953, less than a year after the United States had crossed that threshold. Even so, U.S. nuclear capabilities, both in terms of numbers of bombs and of long-range bombers needed to deliver them, sufficiently outstripped those of the Soviet Union that the Eisenhower administration opted for a "New Look" policy in which the United States would save money by reducing expenditures on conventional armaments, relying instead on the threat of massive nuclear retaliation to deter Soviet aggression in Western Europe. That meant that defense budgets would be slashed, and most of the remaining money would go into nuclear weapons, heavy bombers, and defenses against Soviet bombers, versus Army and Navy personnel and equipment.

As a result, between 1954 and 1961 almost half of the entire defense budget was allocated to the Air Force, with the remaining half divided among the other three services.[41] Roughly half of the Air Force budget was, in turn, allocated to the Strategic Air Command (SAC), the early Cold War proprietor of the nuclear bombardment mission. Army and Navy leaders protested vehemently, of course, but to no avail. Despite the Korean War experience—one in which U.S.-led United Nations (UN) forces helped defend the Republic of Korea in a major conventional war against North Korean and Chinese efforts to unite the peninsula under communist rule—U.S. and British defense planners argued that all future wars would likely swiftly "go nuclear," and planned their force-structure and defense investment accordingly.

These decisions had dramatic effects on force structure and strategic thinking. The service made heavy investments in long-range strategic bombers and tankers, and crew training and exercises for the units receiving them focused almost exclusively on skills needed to scramble the strategic force, get the bombers across the Arctic, penetrate Soviet airspace, and deliver nuclear ordnance. Conversely, as Air Force planners believed the threat of nuclear retaliation would deter Soviet aggression in Europe, the greatest threat to U.S. national security was a nuclear attack on the homeland by Soviet bombers. Consequently, the U.S. Air Force procured a series of fighter interceptors designed to maximize speed for bomber interception in lieu of designs that would have balanced speed, maneuverability, and armament—capabilities needed to make them effective weapons for winning air superiority against other fighters.[42] Not even Tactical Air Command (TAC), the organization responsible for providing air support to ground operations, was immune to the prevailing nuclear dogma. Starved of funding and support by an Air Force dominated by SAC bomber generals, TAC procured the F-105 Thunderchief, an extremely fast (Mach 2 capable) fighter-bomber designed to deliver a single tactical nuclear weapon on the battlefield.[43]

More serious, though, was the effect that this thinking had on Air Force doctrine and strategy. Secure in the conviction that strategic bombing had won World War II and the belief that the next great war, if it occurred, would be won by nuclear bombardment, Air Force strategic thought and doctrine stagnated to the point of virtual paralysis. Air Force education focused on the history of strategic bombardment and largely neglected the other vital lessons learned regarding the use of airpower for CAS and interdiction. At the same time, due to the potential for catastrophic destruction entailed in nuclear war, political leaders concluded that strategy had now become too important an issue to be left in the hands of military professionals. Consequently, the next generation of relevant theories, those addressing such topics as nuclear warfighting, deterrence, escalation management, and crisis stability, came not from the intellectual center at Maxwell Field or anywhere else within the Air Force, but from a group of civilian "strategy intellectuals" at the RAND Corporation and in academia.[44] Meanwhile, as political scientist Karl Mueller has noted, SAC planners occupied themselves compiling notional target lists and "continued in general to approach strategic airpower much as their wartime predecessors had during the Combined Bomber Offensive," largely oblivious to the theories and strategies debated by prominent intellectuals and political leaders.[45]

The impacts of these decisions manifested themselves when the United States found itself at war with both conventional and unconventional adversaries in Vietnam, forcing hard-learned lessons on the national military establishment in general and the Air Force in particular. Although not designed for conventional warfare, the F–105 Thunderchief became the workhorse of the Air Force conventional deep-strike and interdiction missions during the first several years of the war, completing over 20,000 sorties. From a combination of restrictive rules of engagement, poor operational concepts, and inadequate protection of its vulnerable flight control system, almost half of the 833 F–105s produced were lost in the skies over North Vietnam, mostly due to surface-to-air missiles (SAMs) and conventional antiaircraft fire. Air-to-air combat also brought some rude surprises. The North Vietnamese air force sought-out U.S. bombers and strike aircraft, but generally avoided combat whenever confronted by Air Force and Navy fighters. When they did confront their American counterparts, however, they often proved more of a challenge than anticipated, particularly early in the war. With U.S. aircrews inadequately trained for air combat, constrained by unrealistic rules of engagement and doctrine, and flying aircraft designed principally for intercepting bombers or conducting nuclear strike missions, they often found themselves at a disadvantage against more maneuverable Soviet-built fighters.

Over time the Air Force reacquired the skills needed for air superiority and developed tactics for drawing the North Vietnamese out to fight, ultimately achieving a kill ratio of 2-to-1 over their adversaries. That was certainly better than the negative ratio suffered in the first months of the war, but unimpressive when compared to the 10-to-1 kill ratio achieved in the Korean War. Complicating matters, U.S. air commanders were unable to achieve unity of command, having divided the airspace over Vietnam into six separate "route packages" and parceled out control over them to the Army, Navy, and Air Force, respectively.[46]

The most serious problems, however, stemmed from the overall concept in which airpower was employed to obtain U.S. political objectives in the war. Seeing the conflict as a war of aggression by communist North Vietnam against a democratic South Vietnam and the southern insurgency purely as a product of northern subversion, U.S. political leaders believed the solution to the challenge lay in compelling Hanoi to cease its aggression against South Vietnam. Air Force leaders, in turn, steeped in a heritage of strategic bombing against industrialized countries, concluded that the most reasonable course of action would be to execute an intense bombing campaign to destroy 94 industrial and transportation targets that they believed would break Hanoi's will and capability to continue the war. They argued for such a campaign throughout the summer and fall of 1964 and again in February 1965 following a Viet Cong attack on the U.S. air base at Pleiku. But President Johnson was concerned about the political risks of too forceful an approach and opted, instead, for a more measured strategy.[47]

In March 1965, under President Johnson's orders and direct supervision, Air Force and Navy aircraft began Operation *Rolling Thunder*, a bombing campaign designed to gradually escalate in intensity and move progressively northward in an effort to interdict supplies headed southward and compel Hanoi to agree to peace. It was an abject failure. By the spring of 1968, U.S. aircraft had flown over 300,000 sorties and dropped over 860,000 tons of bombs, but had failed to interdict enough supplies to prevent communist forces from launching a major offensive during the Tet holiday.[48] More importantly, after 3 years of bombing, communist leaders in Hanoi remained as intractable as ever, vowing to continue the war until the United States left and Vietnam was reunified. Before the end of the year, Johnson announced that *Rolling Thunder* would soon end and he would not seek reelection as president.

Despite the discouragements encountered in Vietnam, the Air Force learned a great deal there that would make it much more effective in future conflicts. Old lessons were relearned, such as the need for skills and tactics for winning air superiority and the vital importance of unity of command. And while the Air Force continued to believe that the key to victory in war against an industrialized state would be the independent application of airpower, Air Force doctrine came to acknowledge that close air support and interdiction would also be important missions in future wars.

All of these insights had implications for force structure. Painfully aware of its technical inadequacies at the beginning of the war, the Air Force learned lessons in combat that informed designs for new, much more capable fighters, such as the F–15 Eagle, F–16 Fighting Falcon, and a plane specifically developed for supporting ground operations, the A–10 Thunderbolt II (nicknamed the "Warthog"). By the end of the Vietnam War, the Air Force was fielding its first laser-guided munitions, making interdiction strikes against bridges and railroads much more effective and far less costly in planes lost and aircrew killed or captured. And as North Vietnam, with the Soviet Union's material and technical support, developed what was then the world's most sophisticated air defense system integrating fighter defenses with radar-cued, antiaircraft artillery and SAMs, the U.S. Air Force developed suppression of enemy air defense (SEAD) systems and tactics to defeat the new threat.

Many of these emerging concepts and capabilities came to bear when the North Vietnamese army launched a major conventional invasion of South Vietnam in the spring of 1972. By then the bulk of U.S. ground forces had been withdrawn from the conflict under President Richard Nixon's "Vietnamization" program, but U.S. airpower was still available, and the President ordered it to support the badly battered Army of the Republic of Vietnam (ARVN). Operation *Linebacker*, an interdiction campaign put together to carry out that order, imposed a terrible toll on the communist invasion force.

Over the next several months, with U.S. and South Vietnamese air support, the ARVN withstood the initial onslaught, fought the communists to a standstill, and began pushing the invaders back until Hanoi finally called for a halt and agreed to negotiate an end to the war. When those negotiations broke down, President Nixon ordered the Air Force to conduct Operation *Linebacker II*, the heavy bombing of Hanoi and Haiphong using B–52 Stratofortresses. The Air Force did so from December 18 to December 29, with a 36-hour break for Christmas, flying 741 B–52 sorties, along with 769 sorties flown by other Air Force and Navy aircraft, dropping a total of more than 20,000 tons of bombs.[49] The cost was high, with 15 B–52s and 12 other planes lost, but the operation was successful. When the integrated air defense system (IADS) protecting Hanoi lost the ability to coordinate its operations and then exhausted its supply of SAMS, North Vietnamese leaders agreed to return to the bargaining table and a final agreement was struck a few weeks later. Analysts debate whether that agreement resulted more from the coercive leverage of airpower or the concessions that U.S. leaders made during negotiations, but either way, the United States was out of the Vietnam War.[50]

The Late Cold War Renaissance in Airpower Thought

As is so often the case following an unsuccessful war, U.S. military leaders entered the post-Vietnam era with a strong conviction that they needed to reform their institutions. Morale in the U.S. Army, in particular, was seriously damaged, having fought "a series of battles that were, at best, tactical stalemates," and having sunk into "a deep malaise brought about by an unpopular war, an inequitable draft system, a progressive unraveling of small-unit discipline, and a severe questioning of the competence and integrity of its senior leaders."[51] Air Force leaders were also deeply disturbed by the Vietnam experience. While many of them clung to the belief that *Linebacker II* demonstrated that the United States could have won the war had President Johnson allowed the Air Force to conduct an intense bombardment of the 94 targets it proposed in the very beginning, others, particularly those in TAC where most of the war's operational lessons had been learned, were less sanguine that strategic bombing would be the principal war-winning element of all future conflicts.[52] But SAC and the bomber pilots still dominated the Air Force. As a result, Air Force doctrine throughout the remainder of the 1970s blandly sought to relate the role of airpower "more directly to national policy and national security strategy," suggesting that the independent, strategic application of airpower remained the paramount conceptual model in official U.S. Air Force thinking.[53]

It should not surprise that, as the U.S. Army turned its attention from the jungles of Southeast Asia to the central challenge of defending Western Europe from attack by a large, mechanized, and heavily-armored Soviet Army, it would find U.S. Air Force TAC to be a willing and necessary partner in its doctrinal reforms. Still the bastard son of a SAC-dominated Air Force, TAC had also refocused on the challenges of fighting a war in Europe. During the Vietnam War the Army and TAC had relearned the World War II lesson that they needed to cooperate with each other to be effective. So, following a series of exploratory meetings in late 1973, TAC and the Army's Training and Doctrine Command (TRADOC) opened a joint office to study integration issues—the Directorate of Air-Land Force Application (ALFA)—at Langley Air Force Base, Virginia, in July 1975.[54] It marked the beginning of a resurgence of thought about the use of airpower at the operational level of war.

During the next 15 years, the TAC-TRADOC relationship produced doctrinal innovations in three phases. In the first, running until 1979, the partners worked out ways in which airpower would integrate with ground forces in support of the Army's newly developed doctrine of Active Defense. However, as Army officers studied the new concept, they began to worry that it was too defensively oriented. Given the successive waves of Soviet formations that could be thrown at North Atlantic Treaty Organization (NATO) forces, it would only be a matter of time before the defenders were overrun.[55] Therefore, in the second phase of doctrine development starting about 1980, Army planners began considering ways to extend the battlefield to engage second- and third-echelon Soviet forces before they could be brought to bear. As the primary means available for delivering firepower in the deep battle area would be airpower, this required developing procedures to closely coordinate air interdiction strikes with those from Army deep fire assets, such as Army Tactical Missile Systems (ATACMS), and with closer fires from artillery and Multiple Launch Rocket Systems (MLRS), while also providing CAS to U.S. and Allied troops in contact with Soviet forces. The Army called the new concept "AirLand Battle Doctrine." Further development over the next several years led to the third phase of innovation emerging in the mid-1980s: the evolution of AirLand Battle Doctrine into an offensive, deep-battle concept emphasizing close integration of airpower with high-speed ground maneuver operations.[56]

While all of this was happening, the U.S. Air Force was undergoing a transition in leadership—fighter pilots were beginning to outnumber bomber pilots in the highest ranks of the service. Due to the fact that more fighter pilots had seen combat in Korea and Vietnam than had bomber pilots, the majority of rated officers favored by promotion boards in succeeding years hailed from the tactical air forces. By the 1960s the effects of these pressures were beginning to be felt in the lower general officer ranks, and by the 1970s a growing number of three- and four-star generals had come from fighter cockpits. Yet even as late as when the ALFA stood up in 1975, "bomber generals still outnumbered fighter generals on the Air Staff by two to one, and the major (four-star) command positions by four to three."[57] But that ratio was finally about to change. By 1982, fighter generals outnumbered bomber generals in the major commands and no bomber generals remained in Air Staff positions. The transition culminated that year when a fighter pilot, General Charles A. Gabriel, was appointed Air Force Chief of Staff.[58]

Resurgence of Thought About Conventional Airpower at the Strategic Level of War

One might have expected the ascendance of fighter generals to result in the U.S. Air Force abandoning the concept of airpower as an independent war-winning instrument, but that was not the case. In 1988, Colonel John Warden, an F–15 pilot, published a book entitled, *The Air Campaign: Planning for Combat*, based on a thesis he wrote as a student at National Defense University.[59] Warden's argument in that treatise was reasonably evenhanded, balancing the need for offensive and defensive operations and conceding that in some conflicts the chief use of airpower might be "the destruction—or neutralization through maneuver—of some or all of the enemy's forces."[60] Nevertheless, the very title of the book ruffled Army feathers in the suggestion that an air campaign might be fought separate from an Army-led joint campaign. To the Army's growing irritation, Warden's ideas would soon become much more provocative.

By 1990, Warden had become chief of Checkmate, the Headquarters Air Force strategy analysis center. There, he developed the idea that an enemy state is a system, somewhat akin to a human body, with eyes, nerve centers, a brain, and other subsystems to provide infrastructure, organic essentials, and defense mechanisms. Warden proposed that one need not destroy an enemy's infrastructure, organic essentials, or even his defenses to defeat him. The most efficient way to victory would be to attack selected "centers of gravity" (COGs), key nodes in essential subsystems, particularly the enemy's brain and nervous system.[61] If the correct COGs were struck simultaneously, the enemy system would be unable to adjust to compensate for the failure of multiple functions. It would go into "strategic paralysis" or collapse. Warden asserted that precision weapons had provided airpower the ability to carry out such "parallel attacks" and thereby defeat enemy systems quickly, with less blood and treasure expended on both sides.[62]

Another prominent airpower thinker who emerged in the same era was David Deptula. As a lieutenant colonel, he was Warden's deputy in Checkmate and, after the latter's retirement, continued in the Air Force, reaching general officer rank.[63] Deptula, who served in Secretary of the Air Force Donald Rice's Secretarial staff group, had been principal author of the service's *Global Reach–Global Power* strategic planning framework, issued in June 1990 and subsequently forming the conceptual framework for the restructuring of the Air Force over the next 3 years. Deptula championed Warden's ideas and carried them a step forward, emphasizing the need to conduct "effects-based operations"—that is, identifying the correct COGs and striking them to create the system effects Warden advocated, versus striking targets simply to destroy the enemy's materiel.[64]

Warden and Deptula got the first test of their ideas in the 1991 Gulf War against Iraq, which hinted strongly at the conceptual convergence of operational and strategic airpower. At the request of Air Force Vice Chief of Staff General John M. Loh, the Checkmate team developed an air-targeting concept called "Instant Thunder" which they believed would be sufficient to force the Iraqi army out of Kuwait. The Instant Thunder plan entailed rapid, intense attacks on command, control, and communications systems to paralyze Saddam's ability to coordinate his forces and additional attacks on industry and infrastructure targets to compel him to withdraw from Kuwait. Warden briefed the plan to Loh, then to Chairman of the Joint Chiefs General Colin Powell, and then, at Powell's request, to U.S. Central Command (USCENTCOM) commander General Norman Schwarzkopf, who requested that Warden fly to Saudi Arabia and brief the U.S. Central Air Force (USCENTAF) Commander, Lieutenant General Charles Horner.[65] Horner accepted elements of the plan as a starting point, but considered it inadequate as it stood, putting its emphasis on the putative coercive effects of strategic attack without considering whether the Iraqi army, if unmolested from the air, might go on the offensive. Therefore, he sent Warden back to Washington, though retaining Deptula in theater to work with USCENTAF planners under the direction of Brigadier General Buster Glosson to flesh out a broader air strategy in support of the USCENTCOM plan for Operation *Desert Storm*.[66]

On January 17, 1991, USCENTCOM launched *Desert Storm*, and for the next 38 days, coalition airpower subjected Iraq to one of the most concentrated aerial bombardments seen in history. Over the first week, air strikes focused largely on strategic targets in the original Instant Thunder plan, dismembering the air defense system and hitting electrical power and command, control, and communications nodes in and around Baghdad. Then the emphasis shifted to interdiction targets and, increasingly, to Iraq's Republican Guard and regular army forces in southern Iraq and Kuwait.[67]

On February 24, USCENTCOM launched its ground offensive, following 38 days of air attack. With AirLand Battle Doctrine guiding U.S. Army operations, airpower was employed in support of coalition ground forces while continuing strategic attacks against Iraqi command, control, and infrastructure targets. The application of combined arms was devastatingly effective. One hundred hours into the ground operation, with Kuwait liberated and Iraqi forces in a desperate rout to escape envelopment in the now famous "Hail Mary" maneuver, all political objectives were accomplished and President George H.W. Bush called the offensive to a halt.

Airpower Thought and Employment Since *Desert Storm*

The dramatic effectiveness of coalition operations in *Desert Storm* set off a heated debate between U.S. military professionals as to which element of the plan was most responsible for the triumph. The Air Force was ebullient, its sentiment captured by the U.S. Air Force Historian Richard P. Hallion who wrote "Simply (if boldly) stated, airpower won the Gulf war."[68] Army leaders, on the other hand, argued that airpower alone had failed to achieve coalition objectives—after 38 days of concentrated bombing, Iraqi forces remained in Kuwait until rooted out by ground forces. Even within the Air Force, officers debated whether the war's successful outcome resulted more from the application of airpower against strategic targets or in support of coalition ground forces before and after the ground offensive began.[69] Some maintained that *Desert Storm* signaled the onset of a "military-technical revolution" or "revolution in military affairs" (later simply called, "transformation"), while others argued it was just another benchmark in the evolutionary advance of U.S. military technological capabilities. But wherever individual airmen stood in the debate, the one thing on which nearly all of them agreed was that airpower had been instrumental in winning the Gulf War and was destined to be the decisive force in all future conflicts. Afterward, two coercive air operations in the troubled Balkans not only reinforced airmen's conviction that airpower had become the premier expression of American military might, but also convinced some U.S. political leaders, for the first time since the Vietnam War, that airpower could be wielded as a potent and convenient instrument of political coercion.

From August 30 to September 14, 1994, NATO carried out Operation *Deliberate Force*, the air campaign against Serbian forces in the Bosnian civil war. This operation was NATO's response to a series of Serbian atrocities over the preceding months, which included attacks on UN peacekeepers and the sacking of Srebrenica, and culminated with the August 28 shelling of a Sarajevo marketplace, killing 37 civilians and wounding 85 others.[70] Over the next two weeks U.S. and allied aircraft struck Serbian military positions, allowing a combined ground force of Croatians, Bosnian Croats, and Bosnian Muslims to make territorial advances against the Serbs and ultimately compelling Serbian leaders to accept a NATO-brokered partition plan and enter formal peace negotiations in Dayton, Ohio.[71] In this case, airpower was applied against operational military forces in a way that created strategic effects.

Four and a half years later, NATO carried out another coercive air campaign, Operation *Allied Force*, in response to Serbia's refusal to accept UN accords regarding the treatment of Albanian Muslim citizens in Kosovo. In this operation, running from March 24 to June 10, 1999, NATO air forces began by bombing Serbian army units in the province of Kosovo and then, as more strike aircraft arrived in theater, escalated the campaign in intensity and target selection, moving to industrial and infrastructure targets in Serbia proper. After 78 days of bombing, Serbian President Slobodan Milosevic withdrew his army and paramilitary forces from Kosovo and agreed to NATO terms. Although Milosevic's capitulation was undoubtedly influenced by factors in addition to the bombing, airmen were quick to point out that, unlike prior cases, in this episode, conventional airpower had brought an adversary to terms before ground forces were engaged in the fight.[72] Here, airpower was applied as an independent instrument, and it only achieved its effect after being redirected from tactical military targets to those historically categorized as "strategic."

The consistency with which U.S. airpower was successfully employed in the 1990s only added to a growing confidence fostered by advances in technology during that period, resulting in acceleration in the development of warfighting theory. The dramatic outcome of the Gulf War had already convinced many analysts that the combined effects of stealth technology and precision weapons had placed the United States on the cusp of a military transformation. In the several years following the Gulf War, the United States crossed additional technological thresholds, adding even more to its military capabilities. The global positioning system (GPS) satellite constellation achieved full operational capability in 1995, providing precise position, navigation, and timing data everywhere in the world and empowering a new generation of all-weather precision-guided munitions. Conventional forces were granted much more access to near real-time intelligence, surveillance, and reconnaissance (ISR) data, providing them greater situational awareness than most adversaries they expected to encounter in future wars. And advances in computer networking, supported by a worldwide, omni-present backbone of satellite communications, enabled an ever-increasing ability to network operational forces together to share situational awareness and coordinate their actions in high-speed maneuver warfare. All of this fed a new generation of transformation theory based on concepts of network-centric warfare (later called net-centric warfare or NCW) in which every platform would be a sensor and all operators would share information in near real-time.

Network-centric warfare marked a further convergence of airpower thought. It was theorized that command-and-control hierarchies would flatten to accelerate decisionmaking and flexibility, thereby maximizing the ability to respond to rapid changes in the operational environment.[73] Whether this is so, advocates and critics alike have since argued that such flattening would also effectively erase the lines between the operational and strategic levels of war. Strike aircraft directly supporting surface forces would create strategic effects. Aircraft striking strategic targets, such as command-and-control nodes, would often do so to inhibit the enemy's ability to coordinate its military forces, thereby creating operational effects. All the while, networked sensors and communications would empower command authorities to monitor tactical operations in real-time and govern them directly whenever they chose to do so.[74]

These ideas had profound implications for the concept of airpower. As airpower is the most flexible, responsive, and far-ranging means of applying kinetic force, it would constitute the primary strike element of NCW in all applications across the breadth and depth of the battlespace. Airpower is fungible in target selection—strike assets tasked to service operational targets can be re-tasked against high-priority strategic targets en route when network sensors detect perishable intelligence on their whereabouts. In fact, strikers can be tasked against operational and strategic targets in the same sortie and can even launch before tasking and take target direction en route or while loitering in the battlespace. In the NCW concept, operational and strategic applications of airpower converge as one. Airpower as a concept was finally approaching unity … at least in theory.

Airpower in Overseas Contingency Operations: Theory Meets Reality

The terrorist attacks of September 11, 2001, put the United States in a quandary. An elusive nonstate actor based in Afghanistan, a country very difficult for the United States to reach with conventional military power, had confronted the Nation with deadly force. When Taliban authorities in Kabul refused to arrest and extradite Osama bin Laden and other al Qaeda leaders, the Bush administration decided that the United States would use military force to impose regime change on Afghanistan and bring the terrorists to justice. But that raised the question of how it could do that in a timely manner in a region of the world that was so inaccessible. After considering the options, U.S. leaders decided to conduct an air campaign against the Taliban and send paramilitary and special operations forces to fund and advise the Northern Alliance—a collection of militant factions that had for several years waged an unsuccessful civil war—and provide them air support in an effort to change the balance of power in Afghanistan.[75]

The campaign was a rapid success. On October 7, 2001, Operation *Enduring Force* began with airstrikes against air defense, command-and-control, and other military targets in and around Kabul. Over the next 2 weeks the target list expanded, and on October 28, with heavy U.S. air support, the Northern Alliance launched a major offensive, which culminated on November 13 when the Taliban was driven out of Kabul. U.S.-led military operations continued the rest of that year and into the next to mop up fleeing enemy forces and pockets of resistance, but unfortunately, bin Laden and other key al Qaeda and Taliban leaders evaded capture.[76]

Airpower continued its triumphal performance in conventional operations. When the Bush administration later decided to impose regime change on Iraq, the successful use of airpower in support of indigenous forces in Afghanistan prompted a debate about whether to use a similar approach against the Baathist regime. Kurdish factions in northern Iraq had challenged Baghdad authority for years, and some analysts argued that, empowered by U.S. military advisors and airpower, the Kurds could defeat Saddam's forces just as the Northern Alliance had defeated the Taliban.[77] Further study, however, convinced U.S. Secretary of Defense Donald Rumsfeld that the Iraqi army was too large and heavily armed for the Kurds to defeat by themselves, even with U.S. air support. Therefore, while he did agree to provide Kurdish forces U.S. advisors and air support to engage the Iraqi forces in the northern sector of the country, Rumsfeld ordered USCENTCOM commander General Tommy Franks to plan a conventional invasion of southern Iraq to defeat the main force of the Iraqi army and capture Baghdad.

Once again, U.S. leaders wanted to move more quickly than a typical deployment would allow. Even before September 11, Rumsfeld had reviewed Operation Plan (OPLAN) 1003–98, the standing war plan for Iraq, and found it unsatisfactory. Largely a replay of the first Gulf War, it called for a time-consuming deployment of about half a million troops. The Secretary worried that such an approach would allow Saddam time to manipulate world opinion against the United States and also threaten U.S. forces and regional friends with weapons of mass destruction. Therefore, his instructions to Franks called for an innovative plan employing a much smaller force focusing on speed, surprise, and shock. The objective would be to quickly decapitate Iraq—that is, either kill Saddam and other key Baathist leaders, or sever their ability to command and control their forces—and so shock the regime that it would collapse, capitulate, or fall to a popular uprising.[78]

Sixteen months after planning began, time consumed largely in efforts to raise a coalition and get UN approval for the use of force, U.S. and coalition forces executed Operation *Iraqi Freedom*. On March 18, 2003, a day after President Bush issued a 48-hour ultimatum, U.S. leaders received intelligence that Saddam was staying at Dora Farm, one of his properties outside Baghdad. The President authorized a strike on that location, which was carried out with Tomahawk cruise missiles and precision-guided munitions dropped from F–117 fighters, on March 19, immediately after the ultimatum expired. Saddam was not at Dora Farm when the strike occurred. The ground invasion began on March 20, and the full-fledged air attack kicked off about 12 hours after that.[79]

The air strategy for Operation *Iraqi Freedom* supported the Army's AirLand Battle Doctrine–based ground scheme of maneuver and also strongly reflected Warden's theory that parallel attacks would cause strategic paralysis, the general principle of which, by then, had been accepted as U.S. Air Force doctrine. According to Bob Woodward, who interviewed White House and Pentagon officials after the war, planners organized the targets for kinetic, electronic, and information attacks into nine prioritized groups according to what they believed to be Iraq's centers of gravity. Strikingly similar to the five-ring diagram that Warden used to prioritize the COGs in his theory, the nine COG categories identified for *Iraqi Freedom* were:[80]

- The leadership, the real inner circle of Saddam and his sons, Uday and Qusay
- Internal security and the regime intelligence, including the close-in ring of bodyguards in the Special Security Organization (SSO); the command, control, and communications network
- Weapons of mass destruction infrastructure

- Missile production, maintenance, and delivery capability
- The Republican Guard divisions and the Special Republican Guard that protected Baghdad
- Land territory inside Iraq where pressure could be exerted such as the northern Kurdish area that was effectively autonomous
- The regular Iraqi army
- Iraqi commercial and economic infrastructure; and the diplomatic infrastructure abroad that included Iraqi agents working out of their embassies
- The civilian population.

As was the case in Afghanistan, the major combat operation against Iraq in March and April 2003 was a rapid success. Although the parallel attacks neither caused Iraqi leaders to capitulate in shock nor paralyzed their ability to command and control their forces, the heavy aerial bombardment in coordination with the rapid mechanized advance of coalition ground forces had devastating effects on Iraqi regular and paramilitary forces. With Iraqi forces destroyed from the air whenever they attempted to mass and decimated by ground attack whenever they dispersed, coalition ground forces easily overcame all resistance in their drive to Baghdad. The operations plan had projected up to 125 days of "decisive combat operations" to defeat Iraq, but U.S. Marines were helping Iraqi citizens pull down a statue of Saddam in downtown Baghdad on April 9, only 20 days after the invasion began.[81] Three weeks after that, on May 1, 2003, President Bush declared Operation *Iraqi Freedom* successfully accomplished.

Fighting amorphous groups of unconventional adversaries poses its own frustrations. One could argue that stability operations in Afghanistan and Iraq have gone almost as poorly as the major combat operations of 2001 and 2003 went well. While analyzing the many problems encountered in those efforts is a challenge beyond the reach of this paper, it is worth considering the frustrations that they have presented to the U.S. and allied air forces involved. Counterinsurgency, stability, and nation-building operations are intrinsically ground-intensive efforts, with Army and Marine forces taking the lead. But military leaders have occasionally resorted to using air strikes with precision munitions against known or suspected terrorist safe houses, sometimes in urban areas, in efforts to kill key enemy leaders. Unfortunately, such actions have often proven counterproductive, with civilian casualties publicized on CNN and al Jazeera, radicalizing sympathetic Muslims locally and abroad, thereby fueling further unrest and violence.[82]

Starting about 2004, as sectarian violence and insurgencies began to gain momentum in Iraq and Afghanistan, U.S. Air Force leaders became increasingly interested in finding ways that airpower could be used more effectively in support of efforts to stabilize those countries. After tasking the RAND Corporation to study the issue, they were informed that history has shown that insurgencies are rarely won by outside powers; therefore, the best roles the U.S. Air Force could play in counterinsurgency operations, in addition to providing airlift and ISR support to coalition ground forces, would be in advising, training, and equipping partner air forces.[83] Such advice is a hard pill to swallow for a military institution whose doctrine has historically emphasized winning the Nation's wars through the lethal application of airpower.

Airpower as a Concept, and Its Continuing Relevance

As airpower enters its second century, it will remain the most important instrument of international security. Although operations against unconventional adversaries have put strains, both budgetary and conceptual, on the U.S. Air Force and its allies, the current situation does not typify the most serious threats that the great democracies will likely face in the 21st century. Pundits and prophets may argue that major war between powerful developed nations is a thing of the past and that the only threats to international security now emanate from nonstate actors, but they are, quite simply, wrong. Powerful states still exist and new ones are rising. Those states have interests and military forces to pursue them. While few if any national leaders in today's world overtly seek armed conflict, the interests of some states invariably infringe on those of others. When confrontations occur, tensions rise and cascading events can lead nations to war even when neither party sees it as a desirable course of action.

The early airpower visionaries understood that airpower is uniquely suited to deter interstate war and win such wars when deterrence fails. They appreciated the inherent value of being able to operate in the vertical dimension, with the speed, range, and flexibility to hold an enemy at risk across the breadth and depth of the battlespace and, if needed, take war to the very heart of his society. Early theorists may have debated whether airpower was most effectively employed against the enemy's surface forces or against nonmilitary targets in the rear, but the one issue on which virtually all of them agreed was that no army, navy, or government could survive for long if it ceded command of the air above it to an enemy.

Finally, airpower thinking is approaching harmony, if not unanimity. Today's transformational theories are bringing the opposing lines of thought about airpower together toward conceptual harmony, if not complete unification. Most analysts now agree that airpower is the quintessential strike element in a force-projection network able to conduct parallel attacks to create effects that are simultaneously tactical, operational, and strategic. Yet those same analysts continue to debate what target sets are most efficacious in creating desired effects, what effects are most desired, and by what mechanisms they will be created. Such questions may never be fully resolved, and that is probably for the better. Strategy has always benefited from rigorous examination and spirited intellectual debate. Propositions about airpower have generated more study and debate than have propositions about most other instruments of military force. They will continue to do so in the future, keeping the field vibrant and innovative. Clearly, the concept of airpower will remain not only relevant, but central to international security and stability as nations advance in the 21st century.

Notes

[1] Lee Kennett, *The First Air War: 1914-1918* (New York: The Free Press, 1991), 63-82.

[2] Ibid., 41-62.

[3] Giulio Douhet, *Command of the Air*, originally published in 1921, revised in 1927. Translated into English by Dino Ferrari and published in New York by Coward-McCann in 1942, and reprinted (Washington DC: Office of Air Force History, 1983), along with *The Probable Aspects of The War of The Future* (1928), *Recapitulation* (1929), and *The War of 19—* (1930).

[4] Douhet's ideas became increasingly radical over the course of his publishing career, culminating in a 1930 novel, *The War of 19—*, in which he depicted Germany employing an independent air force to bomb French and Belgian population centers, pounding both countries into submission in 48 hours. For a thoughtful discussion on the evolution of Douhet's ideas, see I.B. Holley, Jr., *Technology and Military Doctrine: Essays on a Challenging Relationship* (Maxwell Air Force Base, AL: Air University Press, 2004), 38-42.

[5] Phillip S. Meilinger, "Trenchard, Slessor, and Royal Air Force Doctrine before World War II" in *The Paths of Heaven: The Evolution of Airpower Theory*, ed. Phillip S. Meilinger, School of Advanced Airpower Studies (Maxwell Air Force Base, AL: Air University Press, 1997), 51.

[6] Ibid., 55, 66-67.

[7] Ibid., 48-49.

[8] Mark A. Clodfelter, "Molding Airpower Convictions: Development and Legacy of William Mitchell's Strategic Thought," in Meilinger (ed.), *The Paths of Heaven*, 98.

[9] Ibid., 90. Also see Barry D. Watts, *The Foundations of the U.S. Air Doctrine: The Problem of Friction in War* (Maxwell Air Force Base, AL: Air University Press, 1984), 7-11.

[10] Mitchell's most lasting contributions are his books: *Our Air Force: The Key to National Defense* (New York: Dutton, 1921); *Winged Defense* (New York: P.G. Putnam's Sons, 1925); and *Skyways* (Philadelphia: J.B. Lippincott Company, 1930).

[11] The ACTS was created at Langley Field, Virginia, in 1920, but it had its greatest influence on airpower theory and Army Air Corps doctrine after moving to Maxwell Field, Alabama, in August 1931.

[12] Although *Command of the Air* was not published in English until 1942, lecture notes from the Air Corps Tactical School reveal that the faculty was aware of Douhet's theories and addressed them in the curriculum. See Thomas H. Greer, *The Development of Air Doctrine in the Army Air Arm: 1917-1941* (Washington, DC: Office of Air Force History, 1985), 48-52.

[13] Howard D. Belote, "Warden and the Air Corps Tactical School: What Goes Around Comes Around," *Airpower Journal* 13, no. 3 (Fall 1999), 39-47.

[14] Peter Faber, "Interwar US Army Aviation and the Air Corps Tactical School: Incubators of American Airpower," in Meilinger (ed.), *The Paths of Heaven*, 219.

[15] James S. Corum, *The Luftwaffe: Creating the Operational Air War, 1918-1940* (Lawrence, KS: University of Kansas Press, 1997), 130-133.

[16] Ibid., 134-140.

[17] The *Luftwaffe*'s 1935 doctrine manual also argued that population bombing was immoral and that it would likely increase the enemy's will to resist, versus weaken it. See James S. Corum, "Airpower Thought in Continental Europe Between the Wars," in Meilinger (ed.), *The Paths of Heaven*, 173.

[18] Corum, *The Luftwaffe*, 266-268.

[19] Ibid., 243-249.

[20] Justin D. Murphy and Matthew Alan MacNeice, *Military Aircraft, 1919-1945: An Illustrated History of Their Impact* (Santa Barbara, CA: ABC-CLIO, Inc., 2008), 28.

[21] Corum, "Airpower Thought in Continental Europe Between the Wars," 165.

[22] Ibid., 164-167.

[23] Ibid., 159-162.

[24] John Keegan, *The Second World War* (New York: Penguin Books, 1989), 44-47.

[25] Williamson Murray, *Strategy for Defeat: The Luftwaffe 1933-1945* (Maxwell AFB, AL: Air University Press, 1983), 30-31.

[26] Keegan, *The Second World War*, 54-70. Also see Drew Middleton, *Crossroads of Modern Warfare: Sixteen Twentieth-Century Battles that Shaped Modern History* (Garden City, NY: Doubleday & Co., 1983), 62-69.

[27] Middleton, *Crossroads of Modern Warfare*, 86-90; Murray, *Strategy for Defeat*, 48-50.

[28] Middleton, *Crossroads of Modern Warfare*, 99.

[29] Keegan, *The Second World War*, 184-187.

[30] Ibid., 197.

[31] Haywood S. Hansell, Jr., *The Air Plan That Defeated Hitler* (Atlanta, GA.: Higgins-McArthur/Longino and Porter, 1972), 157-169.

[32] As previously mentioned, while the CBO was the first sustained test of strategic bombing, there are several prior examples in which combatants resorted to city bombing. These efforts were done with less persistence and on a much smaller scale.

[33] The United States Strategic Bombing Survey (USSBS), *Summary Report (European War)*, September 30, 1945, reprinted (Maxwell Air Force Base, AL: Air University Press, 1987), 5, 10-22.

[34] In the February 1943 battle at Kasserine Pass in North Africa, divided command arrangements and a poorly coordinated close air support system hamstrung Allied efforts to repulse a surprise attack from Rommel's Afrika Korps.

[35] Robert Frank Futrell, *Ideas, Concepts, Doctrine: Basic Thinking in the United States Air Force, Volume I, 1907-1960* (Maxwell Air Force Base, AL: Air University Press, 1989), 171-178.

[36] Ronald H. Spector, *Eagle Against the Sun: The American War with Japan* (New York: Vintage Books, 1985), 505.

[37] USSBS, *Summary Report (Pacific War)*, July 1, 1946, reprinted (Maxwell Air Force Base, AL.: Air University Press, 1987), 86, 92-94.

[38] American popular opinion holds that the atomic bombs so shocked and intimidated Japanese leaders that they felt compelled to throw in the towel for fear of further destruction. This argument has been expressed in books, such as Herbert Feis's *Japan Subdued* and numerous articles. Conversely, the USSBS concluded that Japan would probably have surrendered before November 1, 1945, the date set for the U.S. invasion of the home islands, even without the atomic bomb, due to the effects of conventional strategic bombing. Naval historians such as Kenneth J. Hagan contend that the interdiction campaign, waged primarily by submarines and secondarily by land- and carrier-based aviation, was America's most compelling weapon in the Pacific war. More recently, Robert A. Pape has asserted that Japanese leaders were persuaded to surrender only after the Soviet plunge into Manchuria, launched on August 9, only hours before the second atomic bombing, convinced them that they would be unable to inflict serious damage on an American invasion force. See Herbert Feis, *Japan Subdued: The Atomic Bomb and the End of the War in the Pacific* (Princeton, NJ: Princeton University Press, 1961); Kenneth J. Hagan, *This People's Navy: The Making of American Sea Power* (New York: The Free

Press, 1991); Robert A. Pape, *Bombing to Win: Airpower and Coercion in War* (Ithaca, NY: Cornell University Press, 1996); and USSBS, *Japan's Struggle to End the War*, (Washington, DC: Government Printing Office, 1946).

[39] Bernard Brodie, *The Absolute Weapon: Atomic Power and World Order* (New York: Harcourt Brace, 1946).

[40] Bernard Brodie, *Strategy in the Missile Age* (Princeton, NJ: Princeton University Press, 1959), 391.

[41] The average budget allocation over those years was 47 percent to the Air Force, 29 percent to the Navy and Marines combined, and 24 percent to the Army. See Alain C. Enthoven and K. Wayne Smith, *How Much is Enough? Shaping the Defense Program, 1961–1969*, RAND Document CB-403 (Santa Monica, CA.: RAND Corporation, 1971), 13–14.

[42] Examples include the F-101 Voodoo, F-102 Delta Dagger, F-104 Starfighter, and F-106 Delta Dart.

[43] Earl H. Tilford, Jr., *Setup: What the Air Force Did in Vietnam and Why* (Maxwell Air Force Base, AL: Air University Press, 1991), 33–34.

[44] Ibid., 284–287. For a detailed history of the development and influence of the U.S. strategy intellectual community, see Fred Kaplan, *The Wizards of Armageddon* (New York: Simon & Schuster, 1983).

[45] Karl P. Mueller, "Strategic Airpower and Nuclear Strategy: New Theory for a Not-So-New Apocalypse," in Meilinger (ed.), *The Paths of Heaven*, 292.

[46] William W. Momyer, *Airpower in Three Wars (WWII, Korea, Vietnam)* (Maxwell Air Force Base, AL: Air University Press, 2003), 104–112.

[47] Tilford, 93.

[48] Wayne Thompson, *To Hanoi and Back* (Washington, DC: Smithsonian Institution Press, 2002), 80; Carl Berger, ed., *The United States Air Force in Southeast Asia* (Washington, DC: Office of Air Force History, 1977), 366. Compare this to the 653,000 tons dropped in Korea and the 503,000 tons dropped in the Pacific theater in World War II.

[49] Tilford, 263.

[50] For U.S. policy and air strategy during the Vietnam War, see Mark Clodfelter, *The Limits of Airpower: The American Bombing of North Vietnam* (New York: The Free Press, 1989).

[51] Harold R. Winton, "An Ambivalent Partnership: US Army and Air Force Perspectives on Air-Ground Operations, 1973–90," in Meilinger (ed.), *The Paths of Heaven*, 402.

[52] Air Force leaders who believed they could have quickly won the war with heavy bombing included Curtis LeMay and William Momyer. Their arguments found endorsement outside the Air Force in the writings of Admiral U.S.G. Sharp, commander of U.S. Pacific Command during the war, and Army Colonel Harry G. Summers, whose books were assigned readings at the Air Force Air Command and Staff College and the Air War College in the 1980s. Clodfelter, *The Limits of Airpower*, 206–207. See U.S.G. Sharp, *Strategy for Defeat: Vietnam in Retrospect* (Novato, CA: Presidio, 1978) and Harry G. Summers, Jr., *On Strategy: A Critical Analysis of the Vietnam War* (Novato, CA: Presidio, 1982).

[53] Winton, "An Ambivalent Partnership," 407.

[54] Ibid., 411.

[55] John L. Romjue, "The Evolution of the AirLand Battle Concept," *Air University Review* 35, no. 4 (May-June 1984): 4–15.

[56] Winton, "An Ambivalent Partnership," 407.

[57] Mike Worden, *Rise of the Fighter Generals: The Problem of Air Force Leadership, 1945–1982* (Maxwell Air Force Base, AL: Air University Press, 1998), 226.

[58] Ibid.

[59] See John A. Warden III, *The Air Campaign: Planning for Combat* (Washington, DC: NDU Press, 1988).

[60] Ibid., 112.

[61] The term "center of gravity" was introduced in Western military theory by Prussian army officer Carl von Clausewitz (1780-1831), who described it as the "hub of all power and movement, on which everything depends." Warden used the term in the *The Air Campaign*, but redefined it as "that point where the enemy is most vulnerable and the point where an attack will have the best chance of being decisive." By 1990 Warden's thinking had progressed from conceiving a single center of gravity to addressing multiple centers of

gravity as described above. See Carl von Clausewitz, *On War*, translated and edited by Michael Howard and Peter Paret (Princeton, NJ: Princeton University Press, 1976), 595–596, and Warden, *The Air Campaign*, 7.

[62] See John A. Warden III, "Employing Airpower in the Twenty-first Century," in *The Future of Airpower in the Aftermath of the Gulf War*, eds. Richard H. Shultz, Jr., and Robert L. Pfaltzgraff, Jr. (Maxwell Air Force Base, AL: Air University Press, 1992), 57–82, and "The Enemy as a System" in *Airpower Journal* 9, no. 1 (Spring, 1995), 41–50.

[63] Lieutenant General Deptula was most recently Deputy Chief of Staff for Intelligence, Surveillance and Reconnaissance, Headquarters U.S. Air Force. He retired on October 1, 2010.

[64] David A. Deptula, *Effects Based Operations: Change in the Nature of Warfare* (Arlington, VA: Aerospace Education Foundation, 2001).

[65] The Instant Thunder plan focused on a list of 84 targets, which included command, control, communications and intelligence nodes; electrical power and oil refining facilities; bridges, railroads, and ports; and air defense systems. For specifics, see James A. Winnefeld, Preston Niblack, and Dana J. Johnson, *A League of Airmen: U.S. Airpower in the Gulf War*, RAND Document MR-343 (Santa Monica, CA: RAND Corporation, 1994), 68.

[66] Ibid., 65–70.

[67] Ibid., 129–32, 148–60.

[68] Richard P. Hallion, *Storm over Iraq: Airpower and the Gulf War* (Washington, DC: Smithsonian Institution Press, 1992), 1.

[69] Edward C. Mann, *Thunder and Lightning: Desert Storm and the Airpower Debates* (Maxwell AFB, AL: Air University Press, 1995), 1–5.

[70] For a detailed account of political and military events leading to Operation *Deliberate Force*, see Karl Mueller, "The Demise of Yugoslavia and the Destruction of Bosnia: Strategic Causes, Effects, and Responses," in *Deliberate Force: A Case Study in Effective Air Campaigning, Final Report of the Air University Balkans Air Campaign Study*, ed. Robert C. Owen (Maxwell Air Force Base, AL: Air University Press, 2000), 1–36.

[71] Mark C. McLaughlin, "Assessing the Effectiveness of *Deliberate Force*: Harnessing the Political-Military Connection," in Owen (ed.), *Deliberate Force*, 189–197.

[72] For an analysis of the factors that led to Milosevic's capitulation, see Stephen T. Hosmer, *The Conflict Over Kosovo: Why Milosevic Decided to Settle When He Did*, RAND Document MR-1351-AF (Santa Monica, CA: RAND Corporation, 2001).

[73] Arthur K. Cebrowski and John J. Garstka, "Network-Centric Warfare: Its Origin and Future," *Proceedings* 124, no. 1 (January 1998): 28–35. For an early exploration of the theoretical implications of warfare waged in an information-networked environment, see John Arquilla and David Ronfeldt, eds., *In Athena's Camp: Preparing for Conflict in the Information Age*, RAND Document MR-880-OSD/RC (Santa Monica, CA: RAND Corporation, 1997).

[74] See John J. Cummings, "Does Network Centric Warfare Equal Micromanagerial Warfare? Minimizing Micromanagement at the Operational Level of War," paper submitted to the Naval War College, Newport, RI, February 3, 2003; Tim L. Day, "Network Centric Warfare—Death or Renaissance of the Operational Arts and the Operational Level of War," paper submitted to the Faculty of the Naval War College, May 17, 2005; Arthur L. Money, "Network-Centric Warfare: Sense of the Report," Submitted to the Congress in partial fulfillment of Section 934 of the Defense Authorization Act for FY01 (Public Law 106-398), March 2001; Paul Murdock, "Principles of War on the Network-Centric Battlefield: Mass and Economy of Force," *Parameters* 32, no. 1 (Spring 2002), 86–95.

[75] Bob Woodward, *Bush at War* (New York: Simon & Schuster, 2002), 42–53.

[76] For a careful examination and analysis of these events, see Benjamin S. Lambeth, *Airpower Against Terror: America's Conduct of Operation Enduring Freedom*, RAND Document MG-166-CENTAF (Santa Monica, CA: RAND Corporation, 2005).

[77] For an argument in support of a broad application of the approach used in Afghanistan, see Richard Andres, Craig Willis, and Thomas Griffith, "Winning with Allies: The Strategic Value of the Afghan Model," *International Security* 30, no. 3 (Winter 2005–2006), 124–160.

[78] Bob Woodward, *Plan of Attack* (New York: Simon & Schuster, 2004), 34–44.

[79] Joseph L. Galloway, "General Tommy Franks Discusses Conducting the War in Iraq," *Knight Ridder Newspapers*, June 19, 2003; Woodward, *Plan of Attack,* 380–389 and 402.

[80] Woodward, *Plan of Attack*, 56. For Warden's five-ring diagram, see John A. Warden III, "Air Theory for the Twenty-First Century," in *Challenge and Response: Anticipating U.S. Military Security Concerns*, ed. Karl P. Magyar (Maxwell Air Force Base, AL: Air University Press, August 1994), 318.

[81] Woodward, *Plan of Attack*, 146, 408.

[82] For more on the escalatory risks of such attacks, see Forrest E. Morgan, Karl P. Mueller, Evan S. Medeiros, Kevin L. Pollpeter, and Roger Cliff, *Dangerous Thresholds: Managing Escalation in the 21st Century*, RAND Document MG-614-AF (Santa Monica, CA: RAND Corporation, 2008), 141–158.

[83] Alan J. Vick, Adam Grissom, William Rosenau, Beth Grill, and Karl P. Mueller, *Airpower in the New Counterinsurgency Era: The Strategic Importance of USAF Advisory and Assistance Missions*, RAND Document MG-509-AF (Santa Monica, CA: RAND Corporation, 2008), 109–114.

Chapter 2

China's Quest for Joint Aerospace Power: Concepts and Future Aspirations

Mark A. Stokes

The desire to fly higher, faster, and farther is shared by airmen around the world, and unimpeded access to the skies over a region convincingly demonstrates national power. Spurred by a global diffusion of technology and a desire to develop a military commensurate with its growing economic might, the People's Republic of China (PRC) is developing capabilities that could alter the strategic landscape in the Asia-Pacific region and beyond. Shaping the future strategic environment in the Asia-Pacific region, aerospace power traverses vast distances and places a premium on speed and agility that defy the laws of gravity.

Aerospace power—the strategic and operational application of military force via platforms operating in or passing through air and space—is emerging as a key instrument of Chinese statecraft. Control of the skies is a critical enabler for dominance on the Earth's surface. Gaining and maintaining air superiority and space control could provide a political and military leadership with the operational freedom needed to coerce an opponent to make concessions in political disputes. Freedom of action in the skies can offer a decisive edge on the surface. Chinese observers view air and space as a single operational medium of the future, with the English term *aerospace* best describing the merging of the twin domains.

The People's Liberation Army (PLA) is rapidly advancing its capacity to apply aerospace power in order to defend against perceived threats to national sovereignty and territorial integrity. Constrained by a relatively underdeveloped aviation establishment, the PLA is investing in aerospace capabilities that may offset shortcomings in the face of a more technologically advanced adversary.

Refining its concepts of airpower and integrated aerospace operations along with rapidly advancing technology, the PLA is embarked upon a quest to extend its operational military power vertically into space and horizontally beyond its immediate periphery. The PLA's concept of airpower is broader than its air force. Conventional manned fixed-wing air assets are only one possible means of delivering firepower at extended ranges. To date, PLA conventional air platforms have been insufficient by themselves to suppress air defenses, conduct strategic strike missions, or gain air superiority around the Chinese periphery.

Today, the PLA's growing arsenal of increasingly accurate and lethal ballistic and land attack cruise missiles serves as its primary instrument of aerospace power projection and strategic attack. Theater missiles, defined as conventional ballistic and land attack cruise missiles with ranges between 500 and 5,500 kilometers (310–3,410 miles), also enable the PLA Air Force (PLAAF) to compensate for its shortcomings in suppression of enemy air defenses needed to attain limited air superiority, conduct strategic strike, and perform other roles and missions. Over the longer term, the PLAAF aspires to gain the ability to conduct independent strategic attack missions as well as integrated air and space—that is, aerospace—operations. Whether independent or joint, a persistent surveillance network is a critical enabler for PLAAF and Second Artillery delivery of firepower against selected strategic and operational targets with precision and at increasingly extended ranges. Looking toward 2025, Chinese technical writings outline a vision for a conventional global precision strike capability.

Key drivers shaping PLA concepts of aerospace power as an instrument of national power include gaining an ability to enforce territorial claims and resolve sovereignty disputes on terms favorable to Beijing. Threat perceptions are also influencing PLA operational concepts and force modernization. A more efficient and effective system for leveraging military-related technologies is also shaping new operational and organizational concepts that best accommodate new capabilities, such as long-range precision strike and counterspace systems. Over the longer term, successful development and deployment of intermediate- and intercontinental-range conventional ballistic missiles and other precision strike assets would offer the PRC political leadership a flexible deterrent that could achieve strategic and operational effects against an enemy in a crisis.

The emergence of China as a major economic, technological, military, and political player is changing the dynamics within the Asia-Pacific region and the world at large. Various drivers energize China's evolving aerospace power theories, and can be examined through the prism of four central concepts associated with joint aerospace operations: integrated offense-defense; integrated information-firepower; strategic strike; and integrated air and space (aerospace). Various aspects of technological development and force modernization are narrowing the gap between aspiration and future capabilities.

Strategic Drivers

Four key drivers shape PRC concepts of aerospace power:

- territorial integrity
- asserting sovereignty

- threat perception
- technology diffusion.

In great measure, the PLA's rapid advance in its capacity to apply aerospace power is driven by the requirement to defend against perceived threats to national sovereignty and territorial integrity. In enforcing sovereignty claims over the last 20 years, conventional ballistic missiles have been one of the most effective tools of PRC political and military coercion. As a symbolic metric of intent, the PRC's expanding arsenal of conventional ballistic missiles across the Taiwan Strait is intended to deter political support in Taiwan for *de jure* independence and coerce the island's population to support unification with China on Beijing's terms. Whoever dominates the skies over a given geographic space, such as Taiwan, disputed territories in northern India or Japan, and the South China Sea, has a decisive advantage on the surface. Over the last 15 years, conventional ballistic and land attack cruise missiles have been perhaps the most visible and central element of PRC's coercive strategy against Taiwan. Over the next 10–15 years, more advanced conventional air assets, integrated with persistent surveillance, a single integrated air and space picture, and survivable communications architecture, could enable greater confidence in enforcing a broader range of territorial claims around China's periphery.

Traditional concepts of air defense have evolved into a broader concept for a "national aerospace security system" as a means to defend against perceived threats. At least one key driver of aerospace power development is a requirement to be familiar with and have countermeasures against advanced U.S. long-range precision strike capabilities expected to be in place by 2025.[1] To quote one long-time China watcher, "the Chinese armed forces are obsessed with defending China from long-range precision air strikes."[2] Applicable American technology efforts that fuel Chinese concern over long-range precision strike include the joint program of the Air Force, Defense Advanced Research Projects Agency (DARPA), and Lockheed-Martin called the Force Application and Launch from the Continental U.S. (FALCON) Hypersonic Technology Vehicle-2 (HTV-2) program. Under this concept, the Minotaur solid-fueled launch vehicle boosts an unmanned, maneuverable, hypersonic flight vehicle into near-space, which glides back through the atmosphere at speeds exceeding Mach 20. The launch vehicle also could be capable of launching microsatellites into space on short notice. Another program of interest is the U.S. Air Force (USAF)-Boeing X-37B Orbital Test Vehicle first boosted into space in April 2010.[3] Yet another is the USAF-Boeing-Pratt & Whitney-Rocketdyne X-51A WaveRider supersonic combustion ramjet (scramjet) demonstrator, which is dropped from a B-52 and boosted to high supersonic speeds by a rocket before its scramjet engine is initiated. The

X–51A completed its first flight in May 2010, the first successful demonstration of a hydrocarbon-fueled scramjet engine in aviation history.

A more immediate goal appears to be developing the means to deny or complicate the ability of the United States to intervene in a regional contingency around its periphery. Chinese analysts may view an expansion of the battlespace and disruption of U.S. ability to project conventional power in response to Chinese use of force to resolve territorial or sovereignty claims as a legitimate force modernization requirement. Authoritative Chinese writings indicate research into, and development of, increasingly accurate and longer range conventional strategic strike systems that could be launched from Chinese territory against land- and sea-based targets throughout the Asia-Pacific region in a crisis situation. Observers appear concerned over vulnerability to first strike against China's nuclear deterrent. As a corollary, Chinese force planners may be emulating or mirroring United States aerospace power concepts and programs, based on a perceived requirement to narrow the technological gap and attain a global status commensurate with the country's rising economic power.[4]

Technological diffusion constitutes an important driver for Chinese aerospace power. The more efficient and effective means for leveraging military-related technologies shape new operational and organizational concepts that best accommodate new capabilities, such as long-range precision strike and counterspace systems. If the technological capacity exists, the incentives to develop systems to expand the country's aerospace power may prove irresistible.[5] As a result, unforeseen breakthroughs in disruptive technologies and so-called trump card capabilities indeed could change strategic calculations in the Asia-Pacific region and beyond.[6]

Means of diffusing aerospace technology include formal and informal organizations intended to facilitate collaboration between the PLA, industry, and academia; enabling technological breakthroughs via innovative organizational changes within the PLA's acquisition and equipment system and aerospace industry; and decisive steps taken to develop new internationally competitive industries involving large, complex systems such as commercial aviation.[7] Indeed, China's defense research and development (R&D) establishment is breaking down barriers that previously hampered ability to field the complex "system of systems" characteristic of contemporary advanced aerospace power.

Evolving Chinese Concepts of Joint Aerospace Power

The PLA and supporting defense industry are in the midst of a potentially dramatic transformation in aerospace concepts and capabilities. While still in a state of flux, basic aerospace concepts appear to be guiding an ambitious force modernization program. Heavily influenced by American and other foreign strategists, basic Chinese aerospace theory is founded upon the notion that unimpeded access to skies over a region not only enables operational success on the surface, but also has intrinsic value as an instrument of national power.

Aerospace power is among the most flexible and effective of coercive tools available to political decisionmakers. At the strategic level, airpower, and more broadly aerospace power, have the potential to influence the cost-benefit calculus of an opposing political leadership. Aerospace power seeks to achieve effects at the strategic, theater, or tactical level. Unlike surface warfare, airpower is usually concentrated to directly achieve objectives with theater-wide significance, bypassing tactical objectives. Airpower, if used properly, can serve political as well as military objectives. A single airstrike may have strategic significance, in that it can produce a political outcome. In measuring the effectiveness of a coercive air campaign, one relies more on judgments of strategic, rather than tactical, effectiveness, e.g., how well bombs, missiles, and electronic attack affect targets. Strategic effectiveness describes how the destruction of target sets attains political goals.

At the operational level, air superiority determines success in a campaign for sea control, an amphibious invasion, or physical occupation of territory. As time goes on, the same may be said for space control. In a conflict, the side that enjoys unimpeded access to the skies over a region gains an overwhelming advantage on the surface.[8] Colonel John A. Warden III, a key architect of modern U.S. airpower thought and doctrine, once observed, "no country has won a war in the face of enemy air superiority, no major offensive has succeeded against an opponent who controlled the air, and no defense has sustained itself against an enemy who had air superiority." As Warden noted, "to be superior in the air, to have air superiority, means having sufficient control of the air to make air attacks on the enemy without serious opposition and, on the other hand, to be free from the danger of serious enemy air incursions."[9]

The PLA, led by the Second Artillery and increasingly the PLAAF, understands the potential role aerospace power plays in strategy and modern warfare. For a PLAAF seeking to integrate more offensive roles and missions, the goal in a conflict is to gain local or limited air superiority, which permits freedom of flight over a limited area for a finite period of time. Limited air superiority is differentiated from theater air superiority, or supremacy, in which air assets can operate anywhere within the entire combat theater with impunity.[10] Attainment of air superiority requires neutralizing or suppressing assets that can interfere with air operations, including fighters, ground-based air defenses, sensors such as radar systems, jammers, and various supporting infrastructure. Like all other systems, air defense has points of failure that could have system-wide effects if neutralized. For countering fighters and other long-range precision strike assets, history has shown that targeting runways, logistical support, aircrews, and aircraft on the ground is more cost-effective than fighting air battles, if operational surprise can be achieved.[11]

The PLA strategic studies community notes that the predominant trend transforming traditional notions of airpower (空中力量) is the seamless integration of the air and space domains, expansion of the strategic battlespace, as well as nonmilitary uses of airpower such as disaster relief.[12] A key focus is development of long-range precision strike capabilities in order to gain strategic leverage in future crises, complicate the ability of the United States to intervene (e.g., "counterintervention" (反干涉) operations), and ensure air superiority in territorial disputes around its periphery. Developmental efforts include extended range aerodynamic platforms and follow-on variants of conventional ballistic missiles, including those able to engage moving targets at sea. Over time, as its persistent sensor, data fusion, and command and control architecture increases in sophistication and range, the PLA's ability to hold at risk an expanding number of targets throughout the western Pacific Ocean, South China Sea, and elsewhere around its periphery is expected to grow.[13]

Over the years, the PLA has made significant advances in developing a force capable of applying aerospace power in a joint environment.[14] Expansion of Second Artillery conventional missile infrastructure, PLAAF long-term force modernization, and a conceptual body of literature suggest that the PLA is in the midst of a fundamental shift in joint aerospace power doctrine. PLA analysts have traditionally viewed application of aerospace power as a form of "firepower warfare," which involves the coordinated use of PLAAF strike aviation assets, Second Artillery conventional theater missiles, and information warfare.

The PRC's ballistic missile forces could operate independently in support of a deterrent or coercive campaign or in support of air, maritime, or information operations. The Second Artillery's most important mission likely would be suppression of enemy air defenses in order to facilitate air superiority and follow-on air strikes. Centrally commanded and controlled at the theater level, the Second Artillery's basic principles stress surprise and preemption, concentration of resources, and rapid reaction. The Second Artillery's force modernization program requires a significant increase in accuracy and increased numbers of ballistic missiles. At the same time, it is developing sophisticated warheads that could increase the destructiveness of the ballistic missile force.

Four evolving theoretical concepts of aerospace power shape the operational requirements needed to support national security needs:

- integrated attack-defense operations
- integrated information-firepower

- strategic strike

- integrated air and space (aerospace) operations.

While degree of emphasis varies between services, all reflect a belief in the expanding nature of the battlespace that drives long-range operational requirements, and possibly a future realignment of roles and missions.[15]

Integrated Attack-Defense Operations

Like most defense establishments, the PLA characterizes its modernization efforts as defensive in nature. To this end, aerospace power is viewed as a vital element of territorial air defense with offensive air operations as a means to suppress adversary strike capabilities at their source. As the PRC's 2008 Defense White Paper explains:

> China pursues a national defense policy which is purely defensive in nature. China places the protection of national sovereignty, security, territorial integrity, safeguarding of the interests of national development, and the interests of the Chinese people above all else.[16]

The concept of integrated defense and offense is primarily in the context of the joint air defense. Indeed, most aerospace industry studies address an antiship ballistic missile (ASBM) capability in the context of defending against sea-based assets, such as Tomahawk cruise missiles and other strike systems. Integrated attack and defense (攻防兼备) is intimately related to the concept of a joint counterair strike campaign (联合反空袭战役). In doctrinal writings, counterair strike operations theory is divided into passive defense (防护), territorial air defense (抗击), and offensive counterair operations (反击). The PLAAF and Second Artillery envision holding at risk facilities and assets around China's periphery, including air bases, aircraft carriers and other surface assets, and missile-related facilities.[17]

A general concept appears to be to develop the ability to conduct offensive counterair strikes out to a range covered by persistent surveillance assets as far as Guam, at a distance of 3,000 kilometers (1,860 miles) from the east coast of China. Second Artillery and PLAAF force modernization appears to be focused on systems able to suppress air operations on Guam, throughout the South China Sea, and other locations by the middle of this decade. Systems are under development which may place U.S. military facilities on Guam at risk by 2015.[18] To test theories, in the summer of 2009, the PLAAF and Second Artillery conducted one of the first large-scale joint live-fire exercises involving elements from four missile brigades and two PLAAF air divisions.[19]

In the traditional PLA operational lexicon, air and/or conventional missile operations are viewed within the context of an integrated joint firepower campaign that consists of strike aviation, theater missiles, and/or long-range artillery. PLA analysts view an air campaign as an integral component of "joint firepower warfare" operations (联合火力战) involving the coordinated use of PLA Air Force strike aviation assets and Second Artillery conventional theater missiles.

Integrated Information-Firepower

As early as 2004, a guiding PLA objective for developing its armed forces has been "informatization." This principle stresses the centrality of information technology in weapons systems and their application.[20] The PLA still considers itself in the early stages of integrated information-firepower (信息火力一体) with a goal of achieving its fullest capabilities by 2050.[21] The application of Chinese aerospace power against operational targets is likely to be linked with (and thus limited by) the scope and sophistication of its persistent surveillance network and related command, control, and communications system. PLA joint firepower operations theory thus envisions the seamless connection between sensors and shooters of the PLA Air Force, Second Artillery, and other firepower custodians echoing Western F2T2EA ("Find, Fix, Track, Target, Engage, Assess") theory and evolving practice undertaken over the past two decades.

The mission of firepower warfare is three-fold. First and most important, air strikes and theater missile operations, supported by information operations, are intended to create the conditions necessary for a decisive attainment of strategic and theater objectives. These conditions include the achievement of the "Three Superiorities" (三权): information dominance, air superiority, and sea superiority. Achievement of the three superiorities could, in and of itself, create the necessary conditions for termination of conflict on the PRC's terms. The second mission of firepower warfare is to support large-scale ground force operations through annihilation of or paralyzing the enemy's effective strength. The final function involves independent firepower operations in direct support of strategic and theater objectives. Independent missions involve demonstrations of force or resolve, "strategic deterrence" missions, punishment through long-range air strikes, or a series of Second Artillery strikes that are intended to achieve limited strategic or operational objectives. Firepower warfare would dominate the preliminary phase of a campaign and, under certain conditions, could *independently* achieve strategic objectives of the PRC.[22]

Limited firepower assets would be intended for use against targets whose destruction or suppression can achieve the greatest effects. Primary targets for the application of firepower include the command and control system and associated communications; strategic infrastructure; the most advanced capabilities of the opponent, including the air defense system; defense industries; and airbases and ports. From the PLA's perspective, air and conventional theater missile strikes are the most important means of firepower against deep targets.

The PRC views information operations as integral to a successful joint aerospace or firepower campaign. Coercive military operations ultimately are intended to affect the decision calculus and morale of opposing civilian and military leaders. Perceptions and decisions of an opposing leadership are shaped by the quality and amount of information which they possess. Effective military operations rely upon the ability to defend one's sources of information while exploiting and assaulting an opponent's information structure. The focus of information operations is the enemy's command system. The command system serves as the strategic and operational "vital point" (要穴), and consists of policymakers at the strategic level, the operational military command, and supporting command, control, and communications systems.

In addition to increasingly accurate and lethal theater ballistic and land attack cruise missiles and increasingly sophisticated multirole fighter aircraft, the PLA is prioritizing development of stand-off and escort jammers as well as other electronic warfare assets. At the same time, Beijing is investing in advanced command, control, communications, and intelligence systems while placing greater emphasis on training, particularly through the use of simulators.

Intelligence warfare, electronic warfare, and psychological operations are force multipliers that can enhance the effectiveness of air and missile operations in the successful attainment of limited political objectives. These capabilities are intended to confuse an adversary and increase the chances of strategic or operational surprise. From a psychological perspective, information operations can magnify the effects of air strikes with detrimental effects on an enemy leadership's morale and national will. Electronic attack and electronic defense are integral aspects of a PLA joint air campaign.

Electronic warfare is another key aspect of integrated information-firepower warfare. PLA strategists believe electronic warfare can powerfully affect the results of a military campaign and theater offensives, and perhaps help determine the outcome of a war. The PLA also has been developing a computer network attack capability. The most likely target would be automation systems, often referred to as process control systems (PCS) or supervisory control and data acquisition (SCADA) systems, which are critical to the safe, reliable, and efficient operations of critical infrastructure. PCS is used extensively in managing electric power, water, petroleum, natural gas, as well as communications systems. If a PCS system could be affected, there may be no need for physical destruction.

Counterstealth is another aspect of integrated information-firepower warfare. The PLA is seeking to reduce the advantages that low observable air assets enjoy. Most important is the ability to detect, track, and engage aircraft and land attack cruise missiles with low radar cross sections. Also focused on reducing the signature of its own assets, greater knowledge of stealth systems will increase their capabilities against U.S. low observable systems.[23]

PLA programs to counter potential adversary space capabilities also are an aspect of integrating information with firepower, and essential for denying or degrading adversary C4ISR (command, control, communications, computers, intelligence, surveillance, and reconnaissance) capabilities. For electronic defense, the PRC is investing heavily in command automation, tactical data links, electronic attack, and space-based reconnaissance and communications systems. The PLA appears to be applying principles of network-centric warfare to correlate data from increasingly sophisticated sensor architectures. Network-centric warfare equips soldiers, airmen, and soldiers with a common operational picture that significantly increases situational awareness. As a result, individuals and units equipped to participate in the network are able to synchronize action, without necessarily having to wait for orders, which in turn reduces their reaction time. In addition, the network allows for dispersed and flexible operations at lower cost. Therefore, the introduction of a networked common tactical picture based on an advanced tactical data link program is a paradigm shift that could gradually break down the PLA's traditionally stovepiped, service-oriented approach to defense.[24]

The PLA's Joint Theater Command structure would direct integrated information-firepower warfare. The Firepower Coordination Center would coordinate an air and theater missile campaign against key targets in order to achieve strategic and theater objectives. Cells would contain PLA Air Force, Second Artillery, special operations, and ground force elements that would carry out necessary liaison with their respective corps-level service headquarters. Other supporting facilities would include centers for communications, firepower coordination, intelligence information, electronic countermeasures command, and weather.

Strategic Strike

The concept of strategic strike serves as the principal rationale for creation and sustainment of a military service organization independent and distinct from ground or naval forces. For example, strategic strike serves as the raison d'être for an independent U.S. Air Force. The strategic strike mission is the principal driver for the Second Artillery's existence as an independent force, and a vision for the PLAAF.[25] From a U.S. perspective, strategic strike seeks to "weaken the adversary's ability or will to engage in conflict, and may achieve strategic objectives without necessarily having to achieve operational objectives as a precondition."[26]

The Second Artillery's conventional ballistic and ground-launched cruise missile force has been at the forefront of the PLA's strategic strike capability for almost 20 years. As the 2008 Defense White Paper notes, the "Second Artillery Force is a strategic force under the direct command and control of the

CMC [Central Military Commission], and the core force of China for strategic deterrence." In addition, "the conventional missile force of the Second Artillery Force is charged mainly with the task of conducting medium- and long-range precision strikes against key strategic and operational targets of the enemy."[27]

The PLA leadership depends upon its ballistic and land attack cruise missile force—the Second Artillery—to deter potential adversaries and defend against perceived threats to national sovereignty and territorial integrity. Increasingly accurate conventional ballistic and ground-launched cruise missiles (GLCMs) are the optimal means for suppressing enemy air defense and creating a more permissive environment for subsequent conventional air operations due to their relative immunity to defense systems. Along these lines, ballistic missiles function similarly to U.S. stealth assets. In a conflict, they can be supported by electronic attack assets which reduce early warning and confuse enemy commanders. In addition, space-based, airborne, and ground-based sensors can facilitate command and control and provide crucial strategic intelligence, theater awareness, targeting, and battle damage assessment information.

For integrated attack-defense operations and coercive air campaigns today, the PLAAF depends upon the Second Artillery for suppression of enemy air defenses and missions that would enable a more permissive operating environment. As time goes on, however, the PLAAF may become less reliant on Second Artillery support as it evolves "relatively independent" capabilities through economical "leapfrogs" (跨越式) in technology development.[28] The PLAAF has been diversifying its roles and missions, moving away from a force that once was almost exclusively responsible for air defense, interdiction, and close air support toward a service whose primary mission is deterrence and strategic attack. The PLAAF's diversification is grounded in a body of theory stipulating that an independent air strike campaign could support national objectives.[29]

According to China's 2008 Defense White Paper,

> the Air Force is working to accelerate its transition from territorial air defense to both offensive and defensive operations, and increase its capabilities for carrying out reconnaissance and early warning, air strikes, air and missile defense, and strategic projection, in an effort to build itself into a modernized strategic air force.

The PLAAF is characterized as "a strategic service of the PLA, and the main force for carrying out air operations. It is responsible for such tasks as safeguarding the country's territorial air space and territorial sovereignty, and maintaining a stable air defense posture nationwide."

With the White Paper stopping short of enshrining the strategic strike mission, PLAAF representatives have made no secret that the service's long-term vision is to be able to conduct an independent air campaign to achieve decisive strategic effects.[30] Such a goal should not be surprising. Since the publication of Giulio Douhet's *Command of the Air* in 1921, airpower proponents have envisioned the transformation of warfare through long-range strategic strikes. PLAAF representatives have argued in favor of a gradual transition from supporting roles and predominantly defensive counterair missions and close air support, to joint operations, and finally to a fully independent service able to conduct strategic strike missions at extended ranges.[31] According to one detailed Taiwan assessment, the PLAAF had set a goal to be able to conduct an air campaign within a 1,000-kilometer (620-mile) radius of China's periphery by 2010—one that has not been successful to date—and extend the range to 3,000 kilometers (1,860 miles) by 2030.[32]

The PLAAF has long struggled to assert its relevance within the PLA. In January 1979, paramount leader Deng Xiaoping enshrined airpower as a key component of overall force modernization by stating that "without air superiority, success in future war is not possible … give priority to the development of the air force … invest in the aviation industry and air force to ensure air superiority." However, as John Lewis and Xue Litai have noted, Deng's advocacy had a secondary motive, which was to assert his authority over a service that had been perceived to be politically questionable.[33]

Strategic strike is intimately related to a coercive aerospace campaign. The strategic center of gravity in a coercive aerospace campaign is the opposing leadership. Coercive force seeks to affect the amorphous and unquantifiable variable of national will, morale, and resolve, or to manipulate a leader's decision calculus by ensuring he understands that the costs of continuing a particular course of action outweigh the benefits. The challenge is to shatter the will and morale of an opponent or affect his decision calculus. In theory, an effective aerospace campaign would degrade an adversary's capabilities to such an extent that success looks impossible, defeat looks inevitable, further resistance appears futile, and the costs of continuing to resist outweigh the costs of surrendering.[34]

In a coercive aerospace campaign, PLA observers highlight the utility of well-planned preemptive strikes as a means to shock an opponent, paralyze his ability to conduct operations, and force a political solution soon after initiation of hostilities. PLAAF doctrine stresses rapid mobility, "paralysis warfare" (瘫痪战), concentration of its best assets, surprise, and pre-emption. A fundamental PLA guiding concept is to compel a political concession swiftly, using only the minimal force necessary.[35]

A more ambitious offensive air campaign is conceived as having two general phases: first strikes and follow-on strikes. PLA first-strike operations would involve Second Artillery conventional missiles, the concentrated application of the PLAAF's best assets, as well as aviation assets from other services. In theoretical operational analysis, first strikes would consist of multiple waves in order to suppress enemy air defenses. This includes preventing key enemy aviation assets from taking off, effectively preventing ground-based air defenses from organizing resistance along specific corridors, and eliminating enemy early warning assets. Achieving air superiority will facilitate follow-on air activity or landing operations.[36]

Force should be concentrated against those targets whose destruction or suppression would have the greatest strategic and operational effects. However, planning should take into consideration neutralization of targets that would permit a more permissive environment for follow-on strikes. Flexibility is important, requiring a capable and timely reconnaissance network that can evaluate results of the first strike. In general, given fundamental economy-of-force considerations, fewer aircraft are needed for follow-on strike operations. One assessment concludes that for deep-strike operations, ballistic and extended-range cruise missiles may be preferable to aircraft in order to avoid the complexity of first attaining air superiority and to take advantage of the inherent surprise aspects of missile operations.[37]

In some circumstances, an offensive air campaign would be the precursor to establishment of a coercive "air blockade."[38] As a relatively new mission, an air blockade is viewed by authoritative PRC sources as an effective means to compel an adversary to accede to Beijing's demands. A blockade could "create internal struggles and societal collapse." Air blockades involve strikes against ports and navigation routes to shut down air and maritime traffic and cut off contact with the international community as a means to achieve specific political or military objectives. Operations also include efforts to counter an enemy's attempt to break the blockade. An air blockade can weaken an enemy's capacity for operations, or compel him to accede to Beijing's demands short of war. An air blockade can take many forms, including suppressing air and naval bases, halting land transportation, or, in the case of Taiwan, cutting off traffic in the Strait. An air blockade can be carried out in conjunction with a maritime blockade or quarantine.[39]

In seeking an independent strategic strike capability, the PLAAF appears to be encroaching upon a conventional mission that the Second Artillery has monopolized for almost two decades. However, the Second Artillery serves in a supporting role in the PLA's strategy for suppressing adversary air assets on the ground or at sea. Augmenting traditional airpower, Second Artillery assets facilitate the occupation of the air domain and offset weaknesses of the PLAAF. To be sure, ballistic and land attack cruise missiles offer advantages over traditional airpower due to an assured ability to penetrate defenses, ability to prepare and launch with little warning, short time of flight, and lower mission support costs. However, ballistic and land attack cruise missiles are unable to sustain flight, are not reusable after launch, and therefore are relatively inflexible.[40]

Integrated Air and Space (Aerospace) Operations

A more ambitious and long-term force development airpower concept is "integrated air and space (aerospace) operations" (空天一体). As a preface, definitional and translation issues are important. Air and space have traditionally been viewed as separate domains, with "near-space" occupying the realm between the two. Traditional airbreathing platforms operate in accordance with the laws of aerodynamics, and are flexible and responsive. Space systems are governed by orbital mechanics, cover a broader expanse of Earth, and in the case of satellites, offer a more continuous presence. However, with air and space being defined as a single operational medium, and with an emphasis on capabilities that blur the distinction between traditional boundaries, the term *aerospace* may be more appropriate than "air and space" in describing PLA future ambitions.

China's traditional concept of airpower is centered upon air superiority (制空权) in support of ground and naval forces. However, due to what is viewed as the near inevitable militarization of space, observers stress the need to view the air and space domains as a single realm.[41] *Aerospace* implies that air and space function as a single, integrated medium. From a Chinese R&D perspective, integrated air and space operations conceptually link two defense industrial organizations: aviation (航空) and space and missiles (航天).

At least as early as 2002, opinion leaders called for establishment of a "national aerospace security system" (空天安全体系). The PLAAF appears poised to become the country's principal custodian of an evolving aerospace defense system.[42] As PLAAF Commander Xu Qiliang argued in a recent media interview, an integrated approach to aerospace operations is needed to ensure strategic dominance on the sea and ground.[43] PLAAF-affiliated analysts outline intent to leapfrog in the service's ability to conduct integrated aerospace operations.[44] With the concept of aerospace operations still in its infancy, observers note that technological and legal issues constrain the pace of development.[45] Nevertheless, as one senior PLAAF official noted, "space control is a reasonable extension of air control."[46]

The PLA's concept of integrated aerospace operations includes the zone between the atmosphere and outer space, known as "near-space." Chinese analysts view the near-space realm (often termed the "transatmosphere" in Western aerospace thought) as an area of future strategic competition. Near-space is generally characterized as the region between 20 and 100 kilometers (12.4

to 62 miles) above the earth's surface. The 100-kilometer altitude point, sometimes called the Kármán Line, is a rough border dividing the earth's atmosphere and outer space. The near-space realm is too high for fighter jets and too low for orbiting satellites, though winged boost-glide craft and high-supersonic and hypersonic transatmospheric craft such as North American's X–15 research airplane and Scaled Composites' *SpaceshipOne* have transited it.[47]

Both the PLAAF and Second Artillery indicate their intent to establish space operations as a core competency. While writings assume space assets would naturally support air operations, uncertainty surrounds the role of the PLAAF, Second Artillery, or other entities in managing space operations, including planning, programming, and budgeting functions; satellite launch, tracking, and control; ground processing; and counterspace operations. Another possible contentious issue could be future flight vehicles that operate in or transit all domains of space, near-space, and the atmosphere.[48]

Both the PLAAF and Second Artillery appear to make arguments in favor of organizational control over space-related policy, budget, and peacetime operational control. Today, China's space assets appear to be controlled by the headquarters-level General Staff and General Armaments Departments. Requirements development and ground processing and analysis of satellite imagery for military consumers appear to be the responsibility of the General Staff Department Second Department Technology Bureau.[49]

The PLAAF's argument is premised upon the concept of integrated aerospace operations, that air and space are a single integrated medium, and that space is a natural extension of air. However, its vision appears set upon control of the entire aerospace domain (制空天权). Senior prominent space and missile industry authorities associated with the China Aerospace Science and Industry Corporation (CASIC) Second Academy appear to advocate on behalf of the PLAAF, arguing that aerospace assets should be concentrated under a single military service, and that a space force should be built upon the foundation of an air force, similar to the United States, Russia, and others.[50] In addition, the battlespace for air defense operations should be extended beyond the atmosphere and into space and over sea, yet integrated under a single air defense command organization.[51] In addition to the air force, an internal Second Artillery text references a potential "Second Artillery space operations unit" (二炮太空作战部队) with an operational support function.[52]

Ownership of satellites now and in the future remains unclear. Products and services, including imagery and communications, are national assets and thus made available for military purposes. Space launch and satellite tracking and control services in peacetime appear to be under the control of the General Armaments Department (GAD). However, the PLA likely assumes that satellite assets and perhaps even static space launch facilities could be vulnerable during a conflict. Therefore, prudence dictates that satellite reserves are in place, as well as mobile launchers, most likely derivatives of the DF–21 medium-range ballistic missile (MRBM). For logistical reasons, Second Artillery could be a service provider in contingency situations due to its inherent operational responsiveness.

Integrated aerospace defense also includes an ability to counter foreign space-based surveillance, ballistic and land attack cruise missiles, and hypersonic aerospace strike vehicles in the future.[53] After outlining a 15-year, three-phased missile defense development plan in 1996, China's space and missile industry conducted successful tests in January 2007 and January 2010, thus demonstrating an ability to intercept satellites in low Earth orbit and rudimentary medium-range ballistic missiles during the mid-course portion of flight.[54]

Insufficient information is available to assess which service would be equipped with aerospace intercept systems once a viable capability is fully operational. Presumably, however, the Equipment Department of either the PLAAF or Second Artillery is overseeing R&D. One analysis explains that the aerospace defense domain would be divided along the Kármán Line—the PLAAF would assume the air defense mission for threats below 100 kilometers (62 miles) while the Second Artillery would be responsible for threats above 100 kilometers.[55]

Force Modernization and Chinese Aerospace Power

Research and development–related writings may also provide insight into evolving joint aerospace power concepts. To close the gap between aspirational theory and capabilities, the PLA has made significant investments in force modernization over the last 20 years. Looking beyond traditional fixed-wing aircraft and ballistic and land attack cruise missiles, Chinese analysts view the realm between the atmosphere and space as a new area of global competition. An integrated sensor-to-shooter architecture would serve as a foundation for aerospace operations.

Over the next 10–15 years, visionaries hope to successfully leapfrog development and leverage the merging of aviation and space and missile technologies.[56] The PLA General Armaments Department provides overall force modernization policy guidance and likely serves as approval authority for service-level R&D and acquisition contracting.[57] The GAD's Science and Technology Committee has formed at least 20 national-level technology working groups and defense R&D laboratories around the country. Presumably, the purpose is to leverage and pool resources to review progress, advise GAD on resource allocation, and learn how to overcome technological bottlenecks. Individual GAD-led technology working groups include the following:

- General Missile Technology[58]
- Precision Guidance Technology[59]
- Computer and Software Technology
- Satellite Technology
- Radar Sensor Technology
- Micro-Electromechanical Systems (MEMS) Technology[60]
- Communications, Navigation, and Tracking Technology[61]
- Integrated Military Electronics and Information Systems Technology[62]
- Simulation Technology
- Stealth Technology[63]
- Opto-Electronics Technology
- Aircraft Technology
- Target Characteristics and Signal Control
- Inertial Technology.

A shift in acquisition responsibilities may facilitate in leveraging advances in many of these basic technologies. Since at least 2003, service-level acquisition authorities have assumed many of the responsibilities that previously resided within GAD. While GAD likely retains policy and approval authority, the formation of the Second Artillery Equipment Research Academy (二炮装备研究院) and PLAAF Equipment Research Academy (空军装备研究院) is intended to integrate the various research institutes within the services and empower Equipment Departments to better translate conceptual aerospace campaign theory into operational requirements, oversee industrial research and development, and supervise operational test and evaluation.[64]

A senior PLAAF Equipment Research Academy representative responsible for requirements development outlined the integrated aerospace priorities as follows:[65]

- air-launched precision strike munitions incorporating new forms of propulsion for hypersonic long-range strike
- advanced guidance systems furnishing increased precision

- advanced hard-and-soft-kill munitions capable of neutralizing deep, buried targets and paralyzing electronics via high-power microwave (HPM) projection
- extended range air-to-air missiles capable of countering airborne surveillance aircraft and stand-off jammer platforms
- new generation, long-range air defense assets, including endo- and exoatmospheric missile defenses able to engage tactical ballistic missiles.

Along similar lines, senior PLAAF leaders have outlined force development priorities, including the capacity to carry out long-range precision strike, an ability to attain local or limited air superiority, stealth, "full spectrum" air and missile defense, new "trump card" (撒手锏) weapons systems, long-range airlift (远程投送), and unmanned aerial vehicles.[66] Over time, PLAAF capabilities are likely to expand more rapidly than in the past. For example, PLAAF Deputy Commander He Weirong outlined the PLAAF's intent to procure a next-generation fighter over the next 8 to 10 years.[67] Research, development, test, and evaluation investment is underway on developing and fielding advanced active electronically scanned array (AESA) radar, and the GAD has a dedicated expert working group with the purpose of achieving breakthroughs in stealth technology.[68]

Key R&D, systems integration, and manufacturers for aerospace systems include three space and missile groups: the China Aerospace Corporation (CASC), China Aerospace Science and Industry Corporation (CASIC), and the Aviation Industry Corporation of China (AVIC). Since the 1950s, priority has been granted to the space and missile industry (e.g., CASC and CASIC), with the aviation industry viewed as relatively backward. The aviation industry's R&D and manufacturing management practices are at least in part to blame for its relative backwardness.[69] The assignment of space and missile industry leaders to key national defense and aviation industry positions, specifically the country's large passenger aircraft program, reflects the confidence senior political leaders have in the PRC space industry and shortcomings in the aviation establishment.[70]

Merging Air and Space with Traditional Roles and Missions: Aerospace Strike Systems

Based on a broad survey of authoritative technical literature, the PLA's long-term vision for joint aerospace power appears to include an ability to deliver conventional firepower with precision to any point on Earth. In line with the PRC's traditional approach to research and development, strategic strike programs could entail four phases:[71]

- The first phase would involve fielding of an initial maritime variant of the DF–21C medium-range ballistic missile (MRBM)—an antiship ballistic missile (ASBM)—by the end of the 11th Five Year Plan (2006–2010).
- A second phase would seek to extend precision strike out to a range of 3,000 kilometers by the conclusion of the 12th Five Year Plan (2011–2015).[72]
- A third phase would result in fielding a boosted hypersonic glide missile capable of intercontinental strike by 2020.
- A final capability, deployed before 2025, would be a hypersonic scramjet-propelled cruise vehicle for global operations.

In the near term, the chances of success for fielding conventional ballistic and cruise missiles able to strike fixed and moving targets in the western Pacific Ocean and South China Sea out to a range of 2,000 kilometers are high. Consistent with the reports of ongoing testing, at least one authoritative source indicates that preparations for ASBM manufacturing were completed in 2009.[73]

The most recent additions to the PLA's extended-range conventional strike capability include ground- and air-launched land attack cruise missiles. Since successful completion of operational testing in October 2003, the PLA inventory of ground-launched cruise missiles has expanded significantly. The addition of air-launched land attack cruise missiles will further expand the PLA's extended-range strike capability.[74] The air-launched variant of the DH–10 land attack cruise missile, referred to in Taiwan sources as the YJ–100 (鹰击100), ostensibly has a 1,500-kilometer (930-mile) range.[75] When launched from a B–6 bomber in the Bohai Gulf or coastal areas over China, the missiles could reach targets throughout Japan and the South China Sea. However, if the bomber carries out missions overwater in the western Pacific, it could theoretically cover Guam. In one interview, cruise missile designer Yang Baokui highlighted six focus areas for next-generation weapons systems, including:[76]

1. increased range
2. increased precision
3. higher reliability
4. increased weapons system effects
5. easier maintenance
6. improved electronic counter-countermeasures (ECCM).

Research and development investment into next-generation extended-range precision strike systems exemplifies the PLA's evolving concept of aerospace power. With ballistic and cruise missile technology serving as the basis, investment into aerospace strike also may illustrate how service-related competition could evolve. Aerospace flight vehicles blur the distinction between the air and space domains. In discussing new generation ballistic and extended-range air- and ground-launched cruise missiles, aerospace engineers have advocated modification of existing ballistic missile designs toward ones that adopt characteristics of both ballistic and cruise missiles. As two aerospace engineers put it, "The traditional ballistic reentry mode of reentry vehicle cannot meet the demand of the new battle environment. A new-style lift reentry weapon platform is an optimal key to solve this problem."[77]

Hypersonic aerospace flight vehicles exemplify the merging of the air and space domains from both operational and industrial perspectives.[78] Aerospace strike systems under development in China could be divided into two categories: a boost-glide vehicle that is launched into a suborbital trajectory in near-space by a ballistic missile; and/or a horizontal take-off and landing strike system that utilizes an air-breathing supersonic combustion ramjet (scramjet) engine to propel a vehicle to hypersonic speeds.[79] Key areas of R&D include high lift-to-drag ratio delivery vehicles, high-temperature materials for thermal protection, precision navigation, guidance and control, and ability to maintain external radio frequency links through plasma in near-space.

Initial aerospace vehicle R&D is believed to rely on conventional ballistic missile technology for ascent into a suborbital trajectory in near-space.[80] The missile would then release a post-boost vehicle to glide and maneuver toward the intended target. Chinese engineers appear to be conducting preliminary research into a conceptual design for a suborbital flight vehicle (亚轨道飞行器) or strike system that adopts a boost-glide (助推滑翔) trajectory, or, as some engineers call it, a "Qian Xuesen trajectory" (钱学森弹道).[81] Instead of flying on a normal ballistic path that takes the missile into space before returning to Earth, the boost-glide missile skips in and out of near-space, those altitudes between 20 and 100 kilometers.[82]

Aerodynamically configured to glide toward its target, the flight vehicle adopts hybrid characteristics of both ballistic and cruise missiles. In its initial stage of flight, sources indicate the flight vehicle would reach hypersonic speeds of between Mach 8 and Mach 12.[83] Another study references an upper altitude of 60 kilometers and lower of 30 kilometers (37.2 and 18.6 miles).[84] In addition to complicating mid-course missile defenses, boost-glide flight vehicles are said to extend the range of existing ballistic missiles. One study, for example, asserts that a basic boost-glide capability could extend the range of a missile by 31.2 percent.[85]

Signifying the importance that China places on development of aerospace flight vehicles, senior political and military authorities established a steering group in 2006 and a dedicated research institute for leveraging the unique characteristics of near-space under the CASC First Academy in 2008. The CASC First Academy is China's principal organization for R&D and production of strategic ballistic missiles and space launch vehicles. Senior designers for boost-glide strike systems likely reside within the CASC First Academy 10th Research Institute (Near-space Flight Vehicle Research Institute, (临近空间飞行器研究所), which formed in October 2008 after 2 years of closed door meetings, conferences, and feasibility studies.[86] Most recently in June 2009, a CASC manufacturing facility in Chengdu (7304 Factory) initiated testing on an engine designed to support a near-space flight vehicle program.[87]

In line with the PLA's "informatization" of weapons systems, precision guidance enjoys a high R&D priority. For high-altitude target acquisition of moving targets at sea, such as aircraft carriers, China's defense R&D community appears to be investing significant resources into fielding a missile-borne synthetic aperture radar (SAR) capability that would be integrated with satellite positioning and inertial navigation systems.[88] Chinese aerospace engineers have been refining technologies for advanced flight vehicle terminal guidance, including millimeter wave, infrared, and laser detection and ranging (ladar) seekers.[89] A former high-ranking aerospace industry official opined that precision strike systems, such as an ASBM, would share many of the same guidance technologies as the antisatellite (ASAT) system that was tested in January 2007.[90]

Chinese industry publications appear to view boost-glide flight vehicles in a similar context as the U.S. Air Force FALCON program, one of a number of Prompt Global Strike–related research, development, test, and evaluation (RDT&E) programs underway in the United States. CASC First Academy, CASIC Third Academy, and PLA designers have conducted feasibility studies of common aero vehicles (CAVs), and appear to believe China could overcome technical obstacles to fielding such as system.[91] In one study, CASC First Academy engineers noted use of a ramjet engine for the post-boost vehicle and cited issues associated with heating and use of infrared terminal sensors when going after sea-based and land-based targets. After detailed analysis, First Academy designers identified 10 key technologies needed for global precision strikes. Engineers believe that a ballistic missile equipped with a post-boost-glide vehicle could enter the R&D phase in the 12th Five Year Plan.[92]

Other concepts under development also include air-launched conventional ballistic missiles and space launch vehicles. Preliminary research by the space and missile industry into air-launched solid-fueled vehicles is said to have begun in 2000.[93] Airborne platforms are viewed as fuel efficient since launch would be at a high altitude, and the missile could enjoy velocity benefits. Aerospace industry executives have outlined a conceptual design for a 1-meter diameter solid motor that could lift a 50-kilogram (110-pound) microsatellite into a 500-kilometer (310-mile) orbit from a converted B–6 bomber.[94] While not confirmed, some indications exist that some testing has taken place. Another variant, similar to a winged cruise ballistic missile, is for near-space flight.[95]

Authoritative sources indicate that preliminary R&D funds are being invested into a more advanced hypersonic aerospace flight vehicle program.[96] Next-generation flight vehicles may adopt airbreathing supersonic combustion ramjet (scramjet) engine (超燃冲压发动机) technology, enabling acceleration to hypersonic speeds in excess of Mach 5. In addition to scramjet engine technology, R&D is focused on advanced heat-resistant materials, radar and infrared signature reduction (e.g., "stealth"), micro-electromechanical systems (MEMS), smart structures, and autonomous control.[97] One Chinese study outlined results of modeling and simulating a scramjet-powered vehicle with a range between 1,000 and 2,000 kilometers (620–1,240 miles), flying toward its target at an altitude of between 25 and 30 kilometers (15.5–18.6 miles) and a speed of Mach 6.[98]

Chinese engineers have been investigating turbine-based combined cycle (TBCC) propulsion systems. More specifically, Chinese aerospace engineers have been carrying out basic research into an air-turbo rocket (ATR) propulsion system, an airbreathing system that combines elements from both turbojets and rocket engines. Simulations validated one ATR design that operates at speeds up to Mach 4 and altitudes of up to 11 kilometers (6.82 miles).[99] In a *Xinhua* interview, a founding father of China's space and missile program, Zhuang Feng'gan (庄逢甘), argued that that aerospace flight vehicle testing could begin as early as the end of the 11th Five Year Plan.[100] Hong Kong's *Wen Wei Po* reported in 2006 that R&D could be completed by 2020.[101]

As a final note, China's R&D community also has been investing resources in more exotic forms of electronic attack. In particular, efforts have been directed toward an energy weapon that produces a strong electromagnetic pulse (EMP) to neutralize electronic systems within its effective radius. Known as a high-powered microwave (高功率微波武器) device, it has been championed by many of China's most respected advocates of information warfare. PLA-affiliated research institutes have already mastered certain power sources commonly associated with microwave weapons.[102] Chinese writings indicate various applications for high-powered microwave (HPM) devices to shut down adversarial radars and C4ISR systems in an opening salvo, including directional systems for jamming the electronic systems of attacking aircraft and antiradiation missiles, and as an antisatellite weapon to degrade sensitive satellite electronic systems.[103]

Sensor Architecture for Surveillance and Integrated Aerospace Defense

Over the short term, the PLA's ability to conduct strategic and operational strike missions is likely to be restricted by the limited range of its persistent surveillance assets. Thus, to expand its battlespace awareness, the PLA is investing in four key capabilities enabling it to monitor activities in the western Pacific, the South China Sea, and the Indian Ocean:

- near-space flight vehicles
- space-based orbital platforms
- airborne platforms
- land-based over-the-horizon (OTH) and other radar systems.

The PRC has placed a relatively high priority on developing sensors for persistent surveillance from near-space. However, coverage from platforms similar to satellites in low Earth orbit could offer significant improvements in resolution. Duration of flight for near-space vehicles far exceeds that of unmanned aerial vehicles (UAVs), and their small radar and thermal cross-sections make them difficult to track and target. Powered in part by high-efficiency solar cells, near-space vehicles are viewed by PLA advocates as a relatively inexpensive means of furnishing persistent broad-area surveillance.[104] Thus, over the next decade, near-space flight vehicles (近空间飞行器) may emerge as a dominant PLA platform for a persistent region-wide surveillance capability during crisis situations.[105] In sum, despite the significant technical challenges that exist, the PLA and China's defense R&D community have become increasingly interested in near-space flight vehicles for reconnaissance, communications relay, and electronic countermeasures.[106] For reconnaissance missions, synthetic aperture radar surveillance and electronic intelligence appear to be priorities.[107]

In order to overcome technical challenges, CASIC established a new research institute in 2005 dedicated to the design, development, and manufacturing of near-space, lighter-than-air flight vehicles for surveillance purposes. Known as the the "068 Base Near-space Flight Vehicle R&D Center" and located in Hunan Province, its initial projects include the JK–5, JK–12, and JKZ–20 airships. The 068 Base has a cooperative R&D program with Russian counterparts for upper atmospheric airship control systems.[108]

Increasingly sophisticated, space-based surveillance systems would expand PLA battlespace awareness and support strike operations farther from

Chinese shores.[109] Space assets enable the monitoring of naval activities in surrounding waters and the tracking of potentially hostile air force deployments into the region. Space-based reconnaissance systems also provide imagery necessary for mission planning functions, such as navigation and terminal targeting and guidance for land attack cruise missiles (LACMs). Satellite communications also offer a survivable means of communication that will become particularly important as the PLA operates farther from its territory.

The PRC has embarked on a major dual-use, civil-military space program that is predominantly driven by the desire to stand among equals in the international community.[110] However, as in most space programs, there is a military stake. A number of authoritative journals have advocated accelerating and expanding China's space-based surveillance system, including the need for a "space-based theater electronic information system" covering an area of 3,000 square kilometers.[111] Unverified sources indicate that a strategic cueing network for long-range precision-strike missions relies on a dual-use satellite architecture that is being implemented ahead of schedule.[112]

Integrated aerospace operations assume fusion of multiple sensors, including high resolution, dual-use space-based SAR, electro-optical (EO), and possibly electronic intelligence (ELINT) satellites for surveillance and targeting. China's space industry is reportedly nearing completion of its second-generation SAR satellite, and its EO capabilities have been steadily progressing. As Chinese engineers have noted, SAR imagery is key for automated target recognition of ships at sea.[113]

While information is sparse, indications exist pointing to at least some PLA investment into developing a space-based ELINT capability.[114] Prudence would suggest at least a rudimentary space-based electronic intelligence capability already exists, perhaps as a package onboard a communications satellite or other space system. At least one design under evaluation is a constellation of small electronic reconnaissance satellites which can ensure precise location data and survivability. In a crisis situation, China may have the option of augmenting existing space-based assets with microsatellites launched on solid-fueled launch vehicles. A new CASIC business division dedicated to microsatellites—the CASIC First Academy—was established in 2002. Existing and future data relay satellites and other beyond-line-of-sight communications systems could transmit targeting data to and from the theater command elements.[115]

Not surprisingly, radar systems constitute the foundational underpinning of China's early warning network.[116] The general trend is for PLA radar coverage to expand upward into space and outward not just in the region but to global coverage. Chinese R&D is particularly focused on countering stealthy flight vehicles. Senior Colonel Liu Yongjian, a key air force acquisition authority responsible for technical radar requirements development, noted five priorities for radar development:

- expansion of the radar frequency range from "microwave" frequencies toward a broader portion of the frequency spectrum
- integration of space-based, airborne, ground-based, and maritime sensors
- integration of infrared and laser-related sensors with passive and active radars
- integration of radar functions, such as linking early warning and surveillance with seekers on strike assets
- fusion of sensor data into an integrated network.[117]

The PLAAF appears to operate high-frequency (HF) skywave-exploiting OTH radar systems as a central element of an extended-range air defense and maritime surveillance architecture.[118] Skywave OTH radar systems emit a pulse in the lower range of the frequency spectrum (3–30 MHz), which bounces off the ionosphere to illuminate a target—either air or surface—from the top down.[119] As a result, detection ranges for wide area surveillance can extend out to 1,000 to 4,000 kilometers (620–2,480 miles).[120] Able to detect stealthy aircraft, cruise missiles, and maritime surface targets, a skywave-exploiting OTH radar system could define the effective range of China's strategic strike capabilities. A PLAAF unit known as the "skywave brigade" mans a watch center south of Hubei city in Xiangfan. The brigade operates transmitter and receiver sites and ionosphere measuring stations along China's southeast coast.[121]

In addition to OTH systems, the PLA acquisition and technology and defense industry authorities have been examining other means to reduce the effectiveness of stealthy, low observable aircraft and other flight vehicles for at least 20 years. Technologies being developed include ultrawideband and bi- and multistatic radar systems, as well as synthetic aperture ladar systems.[122]

While GAD has a well-established space-tracking and control network, the PLA appears to still be working on radar systems capable of providing target queuing quality data for ballistic missile and satellite intercepts. However, a prototype long-range, large, phased-array radar has been used to support missile defense and ASAT testing over the last several years. One space surveillance radar R&D study indicated a requirement for detecting and tracking targets as small as 10 centimeters (3.93 inches) at an altitude of 500 kilometers (310 miles).[123]

In sum, the PLAAF, while technologically behind the U.S. Air Force and others, is nevertheless evolving into a force capable of dominating the skies around its periphery with support from the Second Artillery and information warfare assets. An aerospace campaign intended to coerce an adversary would emphasize preemption, surprise, and concentration of its most advanced assets to achieve a measure of shock. In order to effectively guide such a campaign, command and control would be centrally planned and executed by the Joint Theater Command, and supported by other joint command systems, including a joint Firepower Command Center, as well as command centers that would oversee component operations of the PLAAF and the Second Artillery.

In Conclusion

The Asia-Pacific region is in the midst of fundamental change, with significant implications for long-term strategic stability. The gradual expansion of China's long-range precision-strike capabilities is altering the regional strategic landscape. The PLA Air Force and Second Artillery are making modest progress in developing advanced capabilities with an eye toward expanding their operational range into space and into the Asia-Pacific region. For the PLA Air Force, the ability to carry out strategic strike missions at ranges of 3,000 kilometers (1,860 miles) or more is viewed as the key to becoming a truly independent service, rather than one dependent on the Second Artillery or a supporting player to the ground forces. Despite the PLAAF's aspirations to develop a force capable of an independent air campaign around China's periphery and speculation of subordination of Second Artillery conventional ballistic missile units to the PLAAF, senior PRC political and military authorities will likely continue to rely on the established capabilities of the Second Artillery for coercion, strategic strike missions, and suppression of enemy air defenses for some time to come.[124]

Due their speed, precision, and difficulties in fielding viable defenses, these systems—if deployed in sufficient numbers—have the potential to provide the PRC with a decisive military edge in the event of conflict over territorial or sovereignty claims. Reliance on ballistic missiles and extended-range LACMs incentivizes other militaries to develop similar capabilities.

The rapid deployment of ballistic missiles and GLCMs has dampened the requirement for an offensive-oriented air force. Another possible constraint has been the limitations of China's aviation industry and its corresponding reliance on foreign procurement of key systems. Nevertheless, over the coming decade, a more capable, technologically advancing domestic aviation industry may be better positioned to support the PLAAF's vision of becoming a world-class service capable of conducting air campaigns independent of the Second Artillery.

Beyond force modernization programs in India and Taiwan, PRC expansion of its aerospace capabilities is at least a partial driver for a modest shift in U.S. defense policies.[125] Intended to counter lower end threats, such as those of North Korea and Iran, U.S. missile defenses are likely unable to counter more sophisticated and larger Chinese ballistic missile raids, much less new generation, hypersonic, extended-range flight vehicles.[126] As a result, the United States and allies and partners in the Asia-Pacific region would need to rely on hardening and counterstrikes for defense.

Beijing's missile-centric strategy presents a number of challenges for regional stability. Barring the fielding of effective countermeasures, Chinese conventional aerospace power, specifically short- and medium-range ballistic and extended-range land attack cruise missiles, may over time give the PLA a decisive advantage in future conflicts around China's periphery. Barring a visible and decisive American response, the PRC's successful deployment of an antiship ballistic missile capability could diminish confidence in U.S. security guarantees not only in Taiwan but throughout the region as a whole.

Beijing's continued theater missile-centric strategy presents challenges that transcend the operational realm. Beijing's large infrastructure of short-range ballistic missiles opposite Taiwan fosters mistrust and discourages meaningful political dialogue that could lead toward a resolution of differences in a manner acceptable to the people of Taiwan and the international community. Beyond Taiwan, Beijing's continued reliance on and expansion of conventional theater missiles as the centerpiece of its aerospace power have the potential to create strategic competitions that increase the risks of conflict in the future. Looking out toward the future, PRC success in linking aspirations for integrated aerospace power with operational capabilities over the next 10 to 15 years is far from certain, yet clearly bears watching.

Notes

[1] For a detailed assessment of U.S. programs, see Xie Wu, "Four Major Challenges Facing an Accelerated U.S. 'Prompt Global Strike Program'" [美"快速全球打击"难获快速发展 面临四大难题], *China Daily*, June 11, 2010, at <www.chinadaily.com.cn/hqjs/jsyw/2010-06-11/content_446614_2.html>.

[2] See Dennis J. Blasko, "The Pentagon-PLA Disconnect: China's Self Assessments of Its Military Capabilities," *China Brief* 8, no. 14 (July 3, 2009).

[3] Xin Dingding, "US Spacecraft Sparks Arms Race Concerns," *China Daily*, April 24, 2010, at <www2.chinadaily.com.cn/world/2010-04/24/content_9770149.html>.

[4] The mirroring of programs may also work in reverse. DOD's answer to China's ASBM R&D appears to be DARPA's Long Range Anti-Ship Missile (LRASM) program. See program overview on DARPA's Web site at <www.darpa.mil/tto/programs/lrasm/index.html>.

[5] For an overview of the technological imperative theory, see Barry Buzan and Eric Herring, *The Arms Dynamic in World Politics* (Boulder, CO: Lynne Rienner, 1998). Also see Hasan Ozbekhan, "The Triumph of Technology: Can Implies Ought" in *An Introduction to Technological Forecasting*, ed. Joseph P. Martino (New York: Gordon and Breach, 1972), 83–92.

⁶ A disruptive technology or disruptive innovation is a term describing a technological innovation, product, or service that uses a "disruptive" strategy, rather than an "evolutionary" or "sustaining" strategy, to overturn the existing dominant technologies or status quo products in a market. See Joseph L. Bower and Clayton M. Christensen, "Disruptive Technologies: Catching the Wave," *Harvard Business Review* 73, no. 1 (January-February 1995), 43–53; and Clayton M. Christensen, *The Innovator's Dilemma* (Cambridge: Harvard Business School Press, 1997).

⁷ See Mark Stokes, "China's Commercial Aviation Sector Looks to the Future," *Project 2049 Futuregram* (March 2009).

⁸ The Joint Chiefs of Staff (JCS) defines *air superiority* as "that degree of dominance of one force over another which permits the conduct of operations by the former and its related land, sea, and air forces at a given time and place without prohibitive interference by the opposing force." See U.S. Department of Defense (DOD), Joint Publication 1–02, *Department of Defense Dictionary of Military and Associated Terms* (Washington, DC: DOD, June 13, 2007), 27. Also see Clayton Chun, *Aerospace Power in the 21ˢᵗ Century: A Primer* (Colorado Springs, CO, 2001), 1–39.

⁹ John A. Warden, *The Air Campaign: Planning for Combat* (Washington, DC: National Defense University Press, 1988), 13–24.

¹⁰ See Liu Yalou, "New Historical Starting Point in the Modernizing the Air Force" [在新的历史起点上推进空军现代化建设], *Qiushi*, January 17, 2008, at <www.chinavalue.net/Article/Archive/2008/9/18/135542.html>.

¹¹ See, for example, John A. Warden, "The Enemy as a System," *Airpower Journal* 14, no. 1 (Spring 1995), 40–45.

¹² See Chen Jie, Liu Guanying, and Long Hui [军种战略教学与科研学术研讨会观点综述], *Journal of National Defense University* 3 (2007) at <http://www.lw23.com/pdf/_02e45fdf-b6ae-4ad7-950f-11b49b0f4cf7/lunwen.pdf>.

¹³ Wayne A. Ulman, "China's Emergent Military Aerospace and Commercial Aviation Capabilities," Testimony before the U.S.-China Economic and Security Review Commission, May 20, 2010, at <www.uscc.gov/hearings/2010hearings/written_testimonies/10_05_20_wrt/10_05_20_ulman_statement.php>.

¹⁴ For a detailed account of China's aerospace campaign doctrine, see Mark Stokes, "The Chinese Joint Aerospace Campaign: Strategy, Doctrine, and Force Modernization," in *China's Revolution in Doctrinal Affairs: Emerging Trends in the Operational Art of the Chinese People's Liberation Army*, eds. James Mulvenon and David Finklestein (Arlington, VA: CNA Corporation, 2005) at <www.cna.org/documents/DoctrineBook.pdf>.

¹⁵ Chen, Liu, and Long.

¹⁶ *China's National Defense in 2008* (Beijing: Information Office of the State Council of the People's Republic of China, January 2009) at <http://www.gov.cn/english/official/2009-01/20/content_1210227_4.htm>.

¹⁷ For an overview, see Wang Houqing and Zhang Xingye et al., *Campaign Science* [战役学] (Beijing: National Defense University Press, 2000), 441–458. Also see Wang Wenrong, ed., *Strategic Science* [战略学] (Beijing: National Defense University Press, 2000), 333–334; and *Regional Counter-Air Strike Operational Research* [区域性反空袭作战研究], Huzhou City Air Defense Office, undated, at <www.hurf.gov.cn/rftd/191.html>.

¹⁸ Ulman.

¹⁹ "Second Artillery and Air Force Conduct Joint Live Fire Exercise for First Time" [二炮与空军首次进行实兵实弹导空联合演习], *Xinhua*, July 19, 2009, at <http://war.news.163.com/09/0719/13/5EJBGC2P00011MTO.html>.

²⁰ See, for example, Wang Baocun, "Information-Firepower Analysis" [信息火力战解析], *PLA Daily* (reported in Xinhua), April 22, 2004, at <http://news.xinhuanet.com/mil/2004-04/22/content_1434792.htm>. Also see "Stress Study of Information-Firepower Warfare as an Independent Form of Operation" [重视研究信息火力战 应成独立作战样式], *PLA Daily*, March 4, 2008, at <www.china.com.cn/military/txt/2008-03/04/content_11509946.htm>.

²¹ Ibid.

²² Among various sources, see Yu Guohua, *Study on Issues in Modern Offensive Campaigns* (Beijing: National Defense University Press, 1998) at <www.51ar.net/book/bookroom/ebooks/lm2_military/book003.htm>.

²³ Ulman.

²⁴ Among various sources, see David S. Alberts, John J. Garstka, and Frederick P. Stein, *Network Centric Warfare* (Washington, DC: DOD C4ISR Cooperative Research Program, September 1999). For another outstanding overview of network centric warfare, see Clay Wilson, *Network Centric Operations: Background and Oversight Issues for Congress*, Congressional Research Service Report to Congress (March 15, 2007). In accordance with Metcalf's Law, the value or power of a network increases in proportion to the square of the number of nodes on the network. Technology is advancing to the point where a common operational picture could be used on a personal display assistant (PDA). At least one key organization involved in data link development is the PLA's University of Science and Technology's Command Automation Academy [解放军理工大学,指挥自动化学院], which is associated with the General Staff Department 63ᵈ Research Institute.

²⁵ For a discussion of PLAAF views on strategic strike operations, see Zhu Hui, ed., *Strategic Air Force* [战略空军论] (Beijing: Lantian Publishing, 2009), 119–126.

²⁶ See Air Force Doctrine Document 2-1.2, *Strategic Attack* (Washington, DC: Headquarters Air Force, June 12, 2007) at <www.dtic.mil/doctrine/jel/service_pubs/afdd2_1_2.pdf>.

²⁷ *China's National Defense in 2008*, at <www.gov.cn/english/official/2009-01/20/content_1210227_9.htm>.

²⁸ "The Chinese Air Force's Economical Path to Realizing Strategic Leapfrogging" [中国空军实现战略性跨越的经济路径], *Xinhua* (August 10, 2010), at <http://news.xinhuanet.com/mil/2010-08/04/content_13964189.htm>.

²⁹ "Liu Yazhou: The Chinese Air Force Must Prepare for Integrated Offense-Defense" [刘亚洲： 中国空军必须具备攻防兼备], *Chinaweek* [中国报道周刊], May 28, 2005, at <http://www.china-week.com/html/2501.htm>. Also see Zheng Dongxiao, "From History to the Future: Chinese Air Force Development from a Macro Perspective" [从历史到未来:中国空军建军思想的宏观演进], *New West* 3 (2010).

³⁰ Concept first raised by Liu Huaqing in 1993 in "Unswervingly Follow the Path of Modern Military Construction with Chinese Characteristics" [坚定不移地沿着建设有中国特色现代化军队的道路前进], presentation before Central Party School, May 20, 1993, at <www.cass.cn/zhuanti/2008ggkf/show_News.asp?id=228926>.

³¹ See Liu, "New Historical Starting Point in the Modernizing [of] the Air Force"; Zhuang Jingqian, "Beijing Observation: Chinese Air Force Quickens Pace of Strategic Transition, Possibly by Taking Two Steps," *Zhongguo Tongxun She* (November 10, 2009) at <www.haixiainfo.com.tw/print78917.html>, accessed May 17, 2010; "From Defense to Attack: Sixty Years of PLA Air Force Development" [从防御到进攻：中国空军的60年建设], *Air Force World*, October 29, 2009, at <http://news.ifeng.com/mil/special/kongjun60/lishi/200910/1029_8387_1410457.shtml>.

³² Wang Changhe, "PLA Air Force 20 Year Review and Outlook" [中共空军20 年的回顧與展望], in *The Philosophy of War and the Study on PRC's Strategy* [戰爭哲學與中共戰略研究], Li Chentong et al. (Taipei: National Defense University War Academy, 2008), 96–97.

³³ John Wilson Lewis and Xue Litai, "China's Search for a Modern Air Force," *International Security* 24, no. 1 (Summer 1999), 64–94, at <http://iis-db.stanford.edu/pubs/20614/China's_search_for_a_modern_air_force.pdf>.

³⁴ Among various discussions, see Thomas J. Christensen, "Coercive Contradictions: *Zhanyixue*, PLA Doctrine, and Taiwan Scenarios," in *China's Revolution in Doctrinal Affairs: Emerging Trends in the Operational Art of the Chinese People's Liberation Army*, eds. James Mulvenon and David Finklestein (Alexandria, VA: CNA Corporation, December 2005) at <www.defensegroupinc.com/cira/pdf/doctrinebook_ch9.pdf>. For a relatively early PLAAF assessment of the value of coercive air operations, see Xie Fengliang [谢凤良], "Offensive Air Operations: Issues for Developing the Air Force in a New Era" [空中进攻作战： 新世纪空军发展的主题], *Sanhang Zhiguang* (July 28, 2004) at <www.univs.cn/newweb/univs/nwpu/2004-07-28/254378.html>.

³⁵ Among various sources, see Chung Chien, "High Tech War Preparation of the PLA: Taking Taiwan without Bloodshed," *Taiwan Defense Affairs* 1 (October 2000), 141–162. The guiding principle is contained in the eight-character slogan of "victory with the first fight, rapid war rapid resolution" [初战决胜, 速战速决].

³⁶ Cao Kuofa, "Issues concerning the application of airpower in landing operations" [登陆战役中空军作战运用的几个问题], *Research on Campaign Theory*, 115–120.

³⁷ Christensen, 356.

[38] Among various sources, see Hu Wenlong, ed., *Research on Joint Blockade Operations* [联合封锁作战研究], (Beijing: National Defense University Press, 1999), 3.

[39] Wang, *Strategic Science* [战略学], 334–335.

[40] Chai Deshou, "Revolution in Military Affairs Gives Birth to New Form of Warfare—Discussion of Rise and Trends in Missile Warfare" [军事变革催生新作战样式 -兼论导弹战的崛起及趋势], *PLA Daily*, July 27, 2004, at <www.chinamil.com.cn/item/newar/zzxl/28.htm>.

[41] For an illustrative overview of this argument, see Yang Mingqing, "New PLAAF Strategy and Security Concept—Integrated Aerospace Is the Strategic Choice" [我空军新战略与新安全观 空天一体是战略选择], *Liaowang*, November 10, 2009, republished and posted at <http://news.qq.com/a/20091110/000809.htm>. Also see Li Qing, "Aviation Industry Development and Research Center Deputy Senior Engineer Explains 'Integrated Aerospace'" [航工业发展研究中心副总师阐释"空天一体"], *Liaowang*, November 10, 2009, at <www.chinanews.com.cn/gn/news/2009/11-10/1956166.shtml>.

[42] "Establishing a National Aerospace Security System" [建立我国的空天安全体系], *Science News* [科学时报], February 24, 2002, at <www.cas.cn/xw/zjsd/200202/t20020224_1683499.shtml>; "Xu Qiliang: The Chinese Air Force Must Have an Aerospace Security Perspective" [许其亮：中国空军必须树立空天安全观], *Xinhua*, November 1, 2009, at <http://mil.news.sina.com.cn/2009-11-01/1424572155.html>; Zhu Hui [朱晖], "China's Aerospace Security Facing Threat of Full Range of Stealthy Unmanned Vehicles and Other Weapon Systems" [我国空天安全面临隐形战机无人机等武器威胁], *PLA Daily*, December 3, 2009, at <http://mil.eastday.com/m/20091203/u1a4853820.html>; "PLAAF Deputy Commander Chen Xiaogong Calls for Attention to Aerospace Security" [解放军空军副司令员陈小工呼吁关注空天安全], *China News Service*, March 9, 2010, at <http://military.people.com.cn/GB/1076/52984/11107476.html>; and Zhong Shan, "Discussion of Information Age of the Aerospace Century" [论信息时代的空天世纪], *China Space News*, February 4, 2010, at <www.china-spacenews.com/n435777/n435778/n674308/65983.html>.

[43] "General Xu Qiliang: The PLA Air Force Will Develop an Integrated Air and Space Operational Capability" [许其亮上将：中国空军将发展空天一体作战能力], *Xinhua*, November 11, 2009, at <http://mil.news.sina.com.cn/2009-11-05/1743572706.html>.

[44] See Shan Xu, "The Chinese Air Force's "Path of Leapfrogging" [中国空军的"跨越之路"], *Oriental Outlook* [瞭望东方周刊], August 5, 2010, at <www.lwdf.cn/oriental/cover_story/20100805141022999.htm>.

[45] <http://news.ifeng.com/mainland/detail_2010_09/14/2512164_0.shtml>.

[46] See Liu Yazhou Wenzhai at <http://wenku.baidu.com/view/ce7fa62458fb770bf78a5534.html>, 8.

[47] See Li Yiyong and Shen Huairong, "Key Technologies for Developing Near-space Flight Vehicles" [发展近空间飞行器系统的关键技术], *Journal of the Academy of Equipment Command & Technology* (October 2006), 52–55. For a U.S. perspective on near-space, see Ed "Mel" Tomme and Sigfred J. "Ziggy" Dahl, "Balloons in Today's Military? An Introduction to the Near-Space Concept," *Air & Space Power Journal* 19, no. 4 (Winter 2005). Also see Edward B. Tomme, "The Paradigm Shift to Effects-Based Space: Near-Space as a Combat Space Effects Enabler," Airpower Research Institute Research Paper 2005–01 (Maxwell Air Force Base, AL: Air University, 2005).

[48] See Roger Cliff, "The Development of China's Air Force Capabilities," Testimony presented before the U.S.-China Economic and Security Review Commission, May 20, 2010; and Ulman.

[49] Directed by Luo Wei [罗为], the bureau appears to be known by a number of names, including the 61646 Unit, Beijing Institute of Remote Sensing Information [北京遥感信息研究所], GSD Space Reconnaissance Bureau [总参航天侦察局], and GSD Space Technology Reconnaissance Bureau [总参航天技术侦察局]. Among sources, see "China's largest aerospace science and technology research institute established at Harbin Institute of Technology" [中国最大空天科学技术创新研究院在哈工大成立] at <www.gaokaoinfo.cn/gaokao.asp?id=14737>. According to one source, the institute provided imagery for earthquake support in Qinghai. See <www.cea.gov.cn/manage/html>/8a8587881632fa5c0116674a018300cf/_content/10_05/11/1273544138348.html>.

[50] Zhong Shan, "Discussion of Information Age of the Aerospace Century" [论信息时代的空天世纪], *China Space News*, February 4, 2010, at <www.china-spacenews.com/n435777/n435778/n674308/65983.html>.

[51] "Establishing a New Concept for Air Defense Operations under Informationization Conditions" [确立信息化条件下防空作战新观念], *PLA Daily*, June 21, 2005, at <www.china.com.cn/military/txt/2005-06/21/content_5894857.htm>.

⁵² Yu Jixun (ed.), Second Artillery Campaign Science [第二炮兵战役学] (Beijing: National Defense University Press, 2004), 70, 75, and 142.

⁵³ For an excellent and reasonable analysis of the January 2010 missile defense interceptor test by a well regarded independent Chinese military-technical analyst, see KKTT, "A Preliminary Analysis of China's Ground-Based Mid-Course Missile Defense Interceptor Technology Test" [我国"陆基中段反导拦截技术试验"初步分析], KKTT blog (January 12, 2010) at <http://liuqiankktt.blog.163.com/blog/static/12126421120100129195498/>. Also see Mark A. Stokes, *China's Strategic Modernization: Implications for U.S. National Security* (Carlisle, PA: U.S. Army War College, 1999), 115; and Ian Easton, "The Great Game in Space: China's Evolving ASAT Weapons Programs and Their Implications for Future U.S. Strategy," *The Project 2049 Institute Occasional Paper* (June 24, 2009).

⁵⁴ Chen Dingchang [陈定昌] is said to have served as the chief designer of the ASAT missile defense interceptor KKV, with Zhang Yiqun [张奕群] as the deputy chief designer for the KKV subsystem. Zhang is from the Second Academy's Second Design Department. A senior designer from the CASIC Fourth Academy's Fourth Design Department, Zheng Chenghuo [郑盛火], is said to be leading the development of the solid launch vehicle subsystem.

⁵⁵ Li Guoqiang [李國強], "New Strategy of the PLA Air Force" [中国空军新战略], *Wenhuipo* (Hong Kong), November 26, 2009, at <http://paper.wenweipo.com/2009/11/26/PL0911260003.htm>, accessed on May 3, 2010.

⁵⁶ Geng Yandong and Xiao Jianjun, "Preliminary Study on Aerospace Integration" [关于空天一体化的初步研究], *Journal of the Academy of Equipment Command & Technology* (December 2004), 49–52.

⁵⁷ More specifically, the GAD Comprehensive Planning Department [综合计划部] probably is responsible for overall force modernization planning and policy. Service Department's Second Artillery and Nuclear Technology Bureau [总装军兵种部二炮装备与核技术局] and Aviation Bureau [总装军兵种部航空局] probably are the coordinating bodies. For a good GAD overview, see Harlan Jencks, "The General Armaments Department," in James Mulvenon and Andrew N.D. Yang eds., *The PLA As Organization* (Washington, DC: RAND, 2002) at <www.rand.org/pubs/conf_proceedings/CF182/CF182.ch7.pdf>.

⁵⁸ Bao Weimin (包为民), director of the CASC First Academy's new 10th Research Institute (Near-Space Flight Vehicle Institute), is dual-hatted as CASC First Academy S&T Committee Director, as well as deputy director of the GAD Precision Guidance Experts Group.

⁵⁹ The Precision Guidance Expert Group has been headed by Chen Dingchang, former CASIC Second Academy Director. See "Introduction to Comrade Chen Dingchang," China Aerospace Science and Industry Corporation (September 20, 2008) at <www.casic.com.cn/n16/n1250/n10984/n17506/17672.html>. Bao Weimin serves as deputy. The 863–801 program appears to be aligned with the GAD Precision Guidance Experts Group.

⁶⁰ Qinghua University professor You Zheng [尤 政] leads the GAD MEMS technology expert group. He also served as chief designer for China's Naxing–1 [NS–1] and other microsatellite programs, a cooperative effort between Qinghua University and CASIC First Academy. Weighing 2 kilograms, the NS–1 microsatellite was launched in April 2004 and was believed a major platform for testing of defense-related MEMS systems. See "You Zheng presentation," Qinghua University (June 21, 2010) at <http://join-tsinghua.edu.cn/bkzsw/detail.jsp?seq=4003&boardid=35>.

⁶¹ Among its prominent members is Xidian University's Li Jiandong [李建东].

⁶² China Electronics Technology Corporation (CETC) Director Wang Zhigang [王志刚] directs this GAD Experts Group.

⁶³ Director of the GAD Stealth Technology Steering Group is Wu Zhe [武哲]. Born in 1957, Wu is from the Beijing University of Aeronautics and Astronautics (BUAA).

⁶⁴ "PLAAF Equipment Research Academy Responsible for More than 3000 Programs Over Last Three Years" [空军装备研究院3年来承担科研任务3000多项], *Xinhua*, February 2, 2007, at <http://news.xinhuanet.com/politics/2007-02/02/content_5688500.htm>; and "How Did the Second Artillery Corps Create More than 6,000 S&T Results?" [二炮 6000余项科研成果是如何创造的?], *PLA Daily*, February 11, 2009, at <http://news.xinhuanet.com/mil/2009-02/11/content_10798697.htm>. The PLAAF Equipment Research Academy includes a missile defense simulation laboratory. For insights into PLAAF Equipment Research Academy role in matching operational concepts, requirements, R&D, and production, see commentary by Lu Gang [吕刚], Academy Director, at <http://str.chinaiiss.com/html/>/200910/26/wa2761_1.html>. Not all seem to have agreed with the strengthening of service level responsibilities. See Zhao Xiaozhuo [赵小卓], "Renew Concepts

for Weapon and Equipment System Construction" [更新武器装备体系建设观念], *PLA Daily*, June 24, 2004, at <www.pladaily.com.cn/item/newar/zw/43.htm>.

[65] Zhang Wei, "Discussion of Accelerating Air and Space Integration Equipment Development" [试论加快空天一体战备发展], *Ground Based Air Defense Weapon Systems* [地面防空武器] (January 2003), 2–6. Zhang Wei [张伟] served as Director, PLAAF Equipment Department R&D Department. The Academy's Director is Lu Gang [吕刚]; its Senior Engineer is Gan Xiaohua [甘晓华], an engine R&D specialist.

[66] See Liu Yalou, "New Historical Starting Point in the Modernizing [of] the Air Force" [在新的历史起点上推进空军现代化建设], *Qiushi*, January 17, 2008, at <www.chinavalue.net/Article/Archive/2008/9/18/135542.html>. Also see *China's National Defense in 2008* (Beijing: State Council Information Office) at <www.china.org.cn/government/whitepaper/node_7060059.htm>, accessed on January 2, 2010.

[67] "Discussion with He Weirong: China Conducting R&D on Fourth Generation Aircraft" [对话何为荣：中国正在研制第四代战机], *Xinhua Network*, November 9, 2009, at <http://news.xinhuanet.com/mil/2009-11/09/content_12416003.htm>, accessed on March 2, 2010.

[68] China's leading figure in applied research in stealth is Dr. Wu Zhe [武哲]. An aircraft design specialist at Beijing University of Aeronautics and Astronautics (NUAA), Dr. Wu also serves as the director of PLA General Armaments Department S&T Committee's Stealth Technology Working Group [隐身技术专业组组长]. See, for example, "Changjiang University Alumni and Scholar Wu Zhe" [长江学者特聘教授武哲校友], Harbin Institute of Technology announcement (May 7, 2010) at <http://90.hit.edu.cn/news/Showfc.asp?id=1827>, accessed on May 10, 2010.

[69] See "Reforming the Aviation Industrial System from the Perspective of the Space Industrial Management System" [从航天工业管理体制特点看航空工业体制改革], China National Space Administration Web site (January 20, 2009) at <www.cnsa.gov.cn/n615708/n2259527/167282.html>. For an outstanding perspective on shifts in the aviation industry, see Tai Ming Cheung, "Remaking Cinderella: The Nature and Development of China's Aviation Industry," Testimony Before the U.S.-China Economic and Security Review Commission, Hearing on China's Emergent Military Aerospace and Commercial Aviation Capabilities, May 20, 2010, at <www.uscc.gov/hearings/2010hearings/written_testimonies/10_05_20_wrt/10_05_20_cheung_statement.php>.

[70] See Kevin Pollpeter, "The Stars of China's Space Program: The Rise of a 'Space Gang?'" *China Brief* 7, no. 17, (September 19, 2007); and Mark Stokes, "China's Commercial Aviation Sector Looks to the Future," *Project 2049 Futuregram* (March 13, 2009).

[71] This analysis is credited to a military analyst with a record of seemingly credible reporting. See KKTT, "China's Development Concept for Theater Missile Strike Power" [我国区域常规打击力量建设设想], April 2009, at <http://blog.sina.com.cn/s/blog_465311c10100gh5q.html>.

[72] Options include a more advanced solid-fuel motor, sophisticated aerodynamic maneuvering capability, and a "boost-glide" trajectory that would complicate mid-course missile defenses.

[73] For reference to ASBM testing, see Statement of Admiral Robert F. Willard, U.S. Navy, Commander U.S. Pacific Command, before the House Armed Services Committee on the U.S. Pacific Command Posture, March 23, 2010, at <http://armedservices.house.gov/pdf/s/FC032510/Willard_Testimony032510.pdf>, accessed April 14, 2010.

[74] While unclear at the present time, it appears that R&D on ground- and air-launched variants of the DH–10 were conducted in parallel. Both variants appear to have been tested in summer and fall 2003. The CASIC Third Academy design team appears to have included Liu Yongcai [刘永才] as chief designer, Zheng Riheng [郑日恒] as engine subsystem designer, Feng Dawei [冯大伟] as control subsystem designer, and Zou Zhiqin [邹志勤] as INS subsystem designer.

[75] The CASIC Third Academy classifies cruise missiles as short range (50 kilometers or less), medium range (50 to 120 kms), medium-long range (120–500 kms), long range (500–5,000 kms), very long range (5,000–8,000 kms), and intercontinental (above 8,000 kms).

[76] "Yang Baokui: Leapfrogging of China's Precision Weapons R&D" [杨宝奎：中国精确制导武器研制实现技术跨越], China Academy of Sciences Web site (April 19, 2004) at <www.cas.cn/xw/zjsd/200906/t20090608_644604.shtml>.

[77] Zhai Hua and Zhou Bozhao, "Adjustable Range Trajectory Design with Multiple Constraints for Precision Guided Vehicles"; Zhou Wenya, Chen Hongbo, and Yang Di, "Entry Guidance for Common Aero Vehicle"; and Chen Hongbo and Yang Di, "Reentry Maneuver Control Strategy Study of Common Aero Vehicle," all in *Systems and Control in Aerospace and Astronautics* (Shenzhen: International Symposium on Sys-

tems and Control in Aerospace and Astronautics, 2006), 1–4, 4–6, 638–642. The authors are from the Harbin Institute of Technology and the National University of Defense Technology, and Chen Hongbo is from CASC First Academy; see also Wang Yunliang, Tang Wei, Zhang Yong, and Li Weiji, "Aerodynamic Configuration Optimization of a Common Aero Vehicle," *Journal of Astronautics*, July 2006, funded by a Chinese Natural Sciences grant; and Zhao Ruian, "Concept of Orbital Ballistic Missiles," *Aerospace China* 1, no. 1 (2004).

[78] This observation is credited to Richard P. Hallion, "The X-Vehicles: Advancing the Limits of Technology," presentation to the Joint NASA-USAF-AIAA X-Vehicle Symposium (May 21, 2002), at <www.aiaa.org/documents/conferences/Presentations/Hallion.pdf>. See also his *Hypersonic Power Projection,* Number 6 in the *Mitchell Paper* series (Arlington: Air Force Association-Mitchell Institute for Airpower Studies, 2010).

[79] For a good overview of the Prompt Global Strike program and more specifically the deployment of conventional ballistic missiles, see Bruce M. Sugden, "*Speed Kills*: Analyzing the Deployment of Conventional Ballistic Missiles," *International Security* 34, no. 1 (2009), 113–146.

[80] Key players involved in technology policy oversight include Cui Erjie [崔尔杰] from the 701st Research Institute; Zhang Litong [张立同], a senior composite materials expert with NUAA; Wu Hongxin [吴宏鑫] from the CASC Fifth Academy's 502ᵈ Research Institute; Nie Haitao [聂海涛] from AVIC's 611 Research Institute; reentry vehicle specialist An Fuxing [安复兴] from the CASC First Academy's 14th Research Institute; scramjet engine specialist Wang Zhenguo [王振国] from the PLA National University of Defense Technology; and senior force development planner Zhu Rongchang [朱荣昌] associated with the PLAAF Headquarters Department Military Theory Department [空军司令部军事理论研究部]. See "Conference Opens on Near-space Flight Vehicle Development Trends and Issues in Major Basic Technology Program" [临近空间飞行器的发展趋势和重大基础科学问题研讨会在京召开], National Natural Science Foundation, May 12, 2006, at <www.nsfc.gov.cn/Portal0/InfoModule_375/1111.htm>.

[81] U.S. media reported the ASBM as having characteristics of a cruise missile. See Christopher P. Cavas, "Missile Threat Helped Drive DDG Cut," *Defense News*, August 4, 2008. For references to the Qian Xuesen trajectory, see Gu Wenjin, Yu Jinyong, and Zhao Hongchao, "New Concept of M-Type Missile Trajectory," *Journal of Naval Aviation Academy* 19, no. 2 (2004). Also see Hu Zhengdong et al., "Trajectory Performance Analysis and Optimization Design for Hypersonic Skip Vehicle," *Journal of Astronautics* 29, no. 1 (2008), 66–71. Also see Xu Wei, Shen Pizhong, and Xia Zhixun, "Integrated Design and Optimization for Boost-Glide Missiles," *Journal of Solid Rocket Technology* 31, no. 4 (2008), 317–320; Yang En'mi, Tang Guojin, and Chen Lei, "Schematic Study for Mid-Course Trajectories for Boost-Glide Missiles," *Journal of National University of Defense Technology* 28, no. 6 (2006); Li Yu, Cui Naigang, and Guo Jifeng, "Development and Key Technology Analysis of Boost-Glide Missile," *Tactical Missile Technology*, no. 5 (2008); and Guo Xingling and Zhang Heng, "An Analysis of the Maximum Time Rates of Heat of Long-Range Boost Glide Flight," *Journal of Astronautics* 29, no. 3 (2008), 783–788. Also see Li Yu, Yang Zhihong, and Cui Naigang, "Study on Optimal Trajectory for Boost-Glide Ballistic Missiles," *Journal of Astronautics* 29, no. 1 (January 2008), 66–71; and Li Yu, Cui Naigang, and Guo Jifeng, "Development and Key Technology Analysis of Boost-Glide Missile," *Tactical Missile Technology*, no. 5 (2008).

[82] The boost-glide concept was first developed by Eugene Sanger and other German aerospace engineers in the 1930s and refined by various researchers in America, including Hsue-shen Tsien (Dr. Qian Xuesen, the father of China's space and missile program), who worked firstly at GALCIT with Theodore von Kármán and then at the Jet Propulsion Laboratory (JPL) before returning to the PRC. In Sanger's concept, a launch vehicle would propel itself to the upper atmosphere then glide with no power until it hit denser air. It then would use kinetic energy to skip off the atmosphere back up to higher altitudes, similar to a stone skipping along water. Each skip reduces the available energy until it glides toward its target. Sanger calculated that a missile launched from Nazi Germany would require three skips to strike a target in the eastern United States. The Russians reportedly flight-tested a similar boost-glide vehicle in 2005. The "skipping" also could involve energy management or "phugoid" porpoise-like measures in which the missile pitches up and climbs, then pitches down and descends. Tsien thought more simply for his concept, first unveiled in an essay for the American Rocket Society, a forerunner of the American Institute of Aeronautics and Astronautics, and based on the aerodynamics of the Wasserfall surface-to-air missile.

[83] Guan Shiyi, "Regarding Qian Xuesen's New Concept for Ballistic Trajectory," *Winged Missiles Journal* [feihang daodan] no. 1 (2003), 1–4. For an alternative concept, see Gu Liangxian, Gong Chunlin, and Wu Wuhua, "Design and Optimization of Wavy Trajectory for Ballistic Missiles," *Acta Armamentarii* 26, no. 3 (May 2005), 353–355.

[84] Zhan Hao, Sun Dechuan, and Xia Lu, "Preliminary Design for Soaring Hypersonic Cruise Vehicle," *Journal of Solid Rocket Technology* 30, no. 1 (2007). The authors are also from the Northwest Polytechnical University's College of Astronautics.

[85] Xu Wei, Sun Pizhong, and Xia Zhixun, "Integration Design and Optimization for Boost Glide Missile" [助推-滑翔导弹总体一体化优化设计], *Journal of Solid Rocket Technology* 31, no. 4 (2008), 319.

[86] The establishment of a research institute and its place in the number scheme ("10th Research Institute") within the CASC First Academy connotes the priority being placed on near-space platforms. See Yang Jian, "CASC First Academy 10th Research Institute Established" [航天一院10所揭牌成立], *China Space News*, October 24, 2008, available in Chinese at <www.china-spacenews.com/n435777/n435778/n435783/49822.html>; Zhan Shige and Meng Qingguo, "Conference Held in Beijing on Developmental Prospects for Near-space Flight Vehicles," *Bulletin of National Natural Science Foundation* (May 12, 2006) at <www.nsfc.gov.cn/Portal0/InfoModule_375/1111.htm>.

[87] "A Certain CASC 7304 Factory Engine Moves into the High Altitude, Long Endurance Domain" [航天7304厂某发动机迈向无人机中高空长航时领域], *China Space News*, June 22, 2009.

[88] For general overviews, see Chen Haidong and Yu Menglun, "Concept for Maneuvering Re-Entry Vehicle Integrated Guidance" [机动再入飞行器的复合制导方案研究], *Journal of Astronautics* [*Yuhang xuebao*] 22, no. 5 (September 2001), 72–76; and Wang Qiang, Huang Jianchong, and Jiang Qiuxi, "The Chief Development Trends of Synthetic Aperture Radar" [合成孔径雷达的主要发展方向], *Modern Defense Technology* (April 2007), 81–88. The authors are from the PLA's Institute of Electronic Engineering in Hefei, Anhui province. Also see Gao Feng, "The Application of Radar Homing Technology in Long Range Guided Missiles," *Aerospace Shanghai*, 2004 (5), 25–29; and Qin Yuliang, Wang Jiantao, Wang Hongqiang, and Li Xiang, "Overview of Missile-Borne Synthetic Aperture Radar" [弹载合成孔径雷达技术研究综述], *Signal Processing* [*xinhao chuli*] (April 2009), 630–635. The authors are from the National University of Defense Technology (NUDT), which hosts a National Laboratory for Precision Guidance and Automated Target Recognition [精确制导自动目标识别国家重点实验室].

[89] Millimeter wave (MMW) technology is a key research area under the 863 Program. The Center for Space Science and Applied Research within the China Academy of Sciences and Dongnan University host a key national laboratory for testing of MMW systems. For an example of one authoritative discussion of adapting air defense interceptor MMW terminal guidance to antiship missiles, see Xia Guifen, Su Hongyan, Ge Zhiqiang, and Huang Peikang, "Study on the High Frequency Resolution Technology on the MMW Radar Seeker," *Journal of Projectiles, Rockets, Missiles, and Guidance* 29, no. 2 (2009), 58–60. The authors are from the Beijing Institute of Remote Sensing Equipment (CASIC 25th Research Institute). For a general survey comparing MMW to other types of terminal guidance, see Yang Shuqian, "Development and Prospects of Precision Guidance Munitions," *Aerospace Control* [*Hangtian kongzhi*] (August 2004), 17–20. Also see Xia Guifen, Zhu Huaicheng, et al., "Study on the Frequency Profile Modeling Technology of the MMW Radar Seeker," *Systems Engineering and Electronics* [*Xitong gongcheng yu dianzi jishu*] 30, no. 9 (2008). The authors are from the CASIC Second Academy's 25th Research Institute.

[90] See "Qi Faren: Anti-Satellite Technology Can Be Used to Attack Aircraft Carrier," *Ming Pao*, March 5, 2007, A4. CASIC—most likely the Second Academy—contracted with the GAD for the ASAT test. The missile was launched from Xichang Space Center and targeted an aging Feng Yun 1C (FY–1C) polar orbit satellite launched in 1999. The successful test supposedly came after three misses on November 30, 2006, April 20, 2006, and October 26, 2005. See Jeffrey Lewis, "When Did China Start ASAT Testing," January 22, 2007, *Arms Control Wonk* blog at <http://lewis.armscontrolwonk.com/archive/1369/when-did-china-start-asat-testing>.

[91] For a CASC First Academy assessment of the U.S. program, see Tong Xionghui, "Forecast and Analysis of USA's Future Conventional Prompt Global Strike System" [美国未来全球快速精确打击体系预测分析], *Missiles and Space Vehicles* (May 2008). Also see Wang Yunliang, Tang Wei, Zhang Yong, and Li Weiji, "Aerodynamic Configuration Optimization of a Common Aero Vehicle" [通用航空飞行器气动布局设计优化], *Journal of Astronautics* [*Yuhang xuebao*] 27, no. 4 (2006). The authors are from the Northwest Polytechnology University and China Aerodynamics Research and Development Center (CARDC).

[92] Chen Xinmin and Yu Menglun, "Design Method of Missile Baseline Concept Based on Function Analysis" [基于功能分析法的导弹基准方案设计方法], *Missiles and Space Vehicles* (April 2008); and Chen Hongbo and Yang Di, "Reentry Maneuver Control Strategy Study of Common Aero Vehicle," in the previously cited *Systems and Control in Aerospace and Astronautics*, 638–642. See Yong En'mi, Tang Guojin, and Chen Lei,

"Three-Dimensional Optimal Trajectory for Global Range of CAV," in *Systems and Control in Aerospace and Astronautics*, (Shenzhen: ISSCAA, 2006), 1396–1400.

[93] Shi Fashu, Yuan Bin, and Chen Shi'nian, "Developmental Prospects for China's Air-Launched Solid-Fuelled Launch Vehicles," *China Aerospace* no. 2 (2003). As a reference, Orbital Sciences offers small satellite air-launch with its Pegasus booster, launched from a converted Lockheed L–1011 Tristar airliner. See also "Jane's Defense Reveals China's Most Recent Aircraft Carrier Surgical Killer" [*jiandi fangfu bao zhongguo zuixin hangmu dashaqi waike shuli*] (August 26, 2008) at <www.chnqiang.com/article/2008/0826/article_34759.shtml>.

[94] See Gan Shaosong, Huang Zuyin, Ye Dingyou, and Gao Bo, "Concepts for Development of Our Country's Solid Launch Vehicles," undated and unsourced (likely 2005). The authors are from the CASC Fourth Academy, the primary competitors to the CASIC Sixth Academy.

[95] The three-stage launch vehicle has a weight of 13,000 kilograms (28,660 pounds). The launch vehicle separates from the aircraft at the altitude of 11,000 meters (36,089 feet) and the airspeed of 206.93 meters per second (687.76 feet per second). Entering its "winged" flight mode, it accelerates to 2,250 meters per second (7,382 feet per second) and reaches the altitude of 39,751 meters (130,417 feet). For Russian reporting, see "International Air and Space Demonstration," *Aviatsiya I Kosmonavtika*, February 28, 2007.

[96] "Key Fundamental Issues in the Major Research Plan for Aerospace Flight Vehicles" [空天飞行器的若干重大基础问题重大研究计划], undated, National Natural Science Foundation Web site, at <www.nsfc.gov.cn/nsfc/cen/00/kxb/sw/introduction/2004introdu-6.htm>.

[97] *Basic Issues in the 2005 Aerospace Flight Vehicle Program* [空天飞行器的若干重大基础问题], at <www.nsfc.gov.cn/nsfc/cen/02/html>created/2004jh/2005_06_28.htm>.

[98] See Che Jing and Tang Shuo, "Research on Integrated Optimization Design of Hypersonic Cruise Vehicle," National Natural Science Foundation study, August 21, 2006. The authors are from the Northwest Polytechnical University College of Astronautics, which hosts a GAD-funded flight vehicle laboratory. One leading figure overseeing scramjet engine R&D is Liu Xingzhou [刘兴洲] from the CASIC Third Academy. See "CASIC's Liu Xingzhou Reviews and Assesses Domestic Scramjet Engine Research" [中国航天科工集团刘兴洲院士为我校师生做国内超燃冲压发动机研究的回顾与分析], BUAA News, November 8, 2007, at <http://news.buaa.edu.cn/dispnews.php?type=1&nid=15667&s_table=news_txt> and "The Eternal Pursuit" [永恒的追求], *Scientific Chinese*, September 30, 2007, at <www.scichi.com/new/Article/1486.html>.

[99] Chen Xiang, Chen Yuchun, Tu Qiuye, Zhang Hong, and Cai Yuanhu, "Research on Performance of Air-Turbo Rocket," *Journal of Projectiles, Rockets, Missiles, and Guidance* 29, no. 2 (2009), 162–165. The authors are from the Northwest Polytechnology University's School of Power and Energy. Li Huifeng, Chen Jindong, and Li Naying, "Research on Midcourse Navigation of Hypersonic Cruise Air Vehicles," *Modern Defense Technology* 34, no. 6. The authors are from the Beijing University of Aeronautics and Astronautics (BUAA) Space College.

[100] "Expert: China's Scramjet Engine Achieves Breakthrough: Aerospace Plane Enters a New Phase" [独家：中国超燃冲压发动机取得突破 空天飞行器 进入试验阶段] (December 11, 2007) at <www.zaobao.com/special/newspapers/2007/12/hongkong071211o.html>.

[101] Peng Kailei, "Chinese 'Lifting Body' Outline Revealed for First Time" [中國「穿梭機」外形首度曝光], *Wenweipo*, December 1, 2006, at <http://paper.wenweipo.com/2006/12/01/YO0612010003.htm>.

[102] Since the mid-1990s, the PRC is said to have received assistance from Russian scientists who are considered to be the leading experts in the world on nuclear and nonnuclear radio frequency weapons.

[103] For detailed discussion of HPM systems, see Mark A. Stokes, *China's Strategic Modernization: Implications for the United States* (Carlisle, PA: Strategic Studies Institute, 1999). Also see Lin Zheng, "New Advances in Electronic Warfare," in *Proceedings of '96 Conference Sponsored by Journal "Huoli Yu Zhihui Congzhi"* (October 1996), 16–21, in *FBIS-CST*-97-012; Zhang Zhenzhou, "Longitudinal Tranmission of Exploding Electromagnetic Waves," in *Xiandai Fangyu Jishu* (April 1995), 47–58, in *CAMA* 2, no. 5. Also see Qin Zhiyuan, "HPM Weapons in Tomorrow's War," paper presented at 1997 COSTIND-sponsored international conference on RMA. For reference to use of HPM devices to counter JTIDS, see Wen Guangjun, Li Shigun, Guo Weili, Li Jiayin, and Li Lemin, "Study on the Possibility of Jamming JTIDS Signal with High Power Microwave Source." [高功率微波源干扰JTIDS信号的可能性分析], *Journal of Sichuan Institute of Light Industry And Chemical Technology* 19, no. 3 (1999). For use of HPM to neutralize SATCOM, see Zhou Jiabo, "Exploration of Space Communications Countermeasures" [空间信息对抗初探], *Radar and Electronic Warfare* [雷达与电子战], (January 2007), 7–14.

[104] For a general Chinese analysis, see Wang Shengkai, Quan Shouwen, Li Binhua, and Ma Qin, "Near-space and Near-space Flight Vehicles" [临近空间和临近空间飞行器], *CONMILIT* [*Xiandai junshi*] no. 7 (2007), 36–39.

[105] Guo Weimin, Si Wanbing, Gui Qishan, and He Jiafan, "Coordination and Applicability of Near-space Flight Vehicles in Missile Warfare" [导弹作战中临近空间飞行器与航天器的协同应用], *Winged Missiles* [飞航导弹], (May 2008).

[106] For a representative Second Artillery overview, see Li Chao, Luo Chuanyong, and Wang Hongli, "Research into Near-space Flight Vehicle Applications for the Second Artillery" [近空间飞行器在第二炮兵部队的应用研究], *Journal of Projectiles and Guidance* (January 2009); Tang Jiapeng, Guan Shixi, Ling Guilong, and Duan Na, "Study on Propulsion System of Near-space Vehicles," *Journal of Projectiles, Rockets, Missiles, and Guidance* (June 2009), 145–148. Also see Li Zhen, Li Haiyang, and Yong En'mi, "Analysis of Trajectory Characteristics of Near-space Kinetic Weapons," *Journal of Projectiles, Rockets, Missiles, and Guidance* (June 2009), 183–185.

[107] Wang Wenqin, Cai Jingye Cai, and Peng Qicong, "Conceptual Design of Near-Space Synthetic Aperture Radar for High-Resolution and Wide-Swath Imaging," *Aerospace Science and Technology* (2009), 1–8. Wang is from the University of Electronic Science and Technology of China (UESTC) and claims to be a leading advocate within China for near-space SAR remote sensing.

[108] See Duan Dongbei, "Airship's R&D and Application to Aeronautics and Astronautics in China," briefing, CASIC Hunan Astronautic Industry Corporation, April 2008, at <www.veatal.com/iso_album/duandongbei.pdf>. AVIC's 605 Research Institute also is involved in airship R&D.

[109] For examples of U.S. overviews of China's space modernization, see Andrew S. Erickson, "Eyes in the Sky," *U.S. Naval Institute Proceedings* 136, no. 4 (April 2010), 36–41; Gregory Kulacki and Jeffrey G. Lewis, *A Place for One's Mat: China's Space Program, 1956–2003* (Cambridge, MA: American Academy of Arts and Sciences, 2009) at <www.amacad.org/publications/spaceChina.pdf>, accessed April 16, 2010; Kevin Pollpeter, "The Chinese Vision of Space Military Operations," in *China's Revolution in Doctrinal Affairs: Emerging Trends in the Operational Art of the Chinese People's Liberation Army*, eds. James Mulvenon and David Finklestein (Virginia: CNA Corporation, December 2005), 329–369, at <www.defensegroupinc.com/cira/pdf/doctrinebook_ch9.pdf>; Larry M. Wortzel, *The Chinese People's Liberation Army and Space Warfare: Emerging United States-China Military Competition* (Washington, DC: American Enterprise Institute, 2007) at <www.aei.org/paper/26977>; Dean Cheng "China's Space Program: Civilian, Commercial, and Military Aspects," CNA Corporation Conference Report, May 2006; Phillip C. Saunders, "China's Future in Space: Implications for U.S. Security," *AdAstra* (Spring 2005), 21–23, at <www.space.com/adastra/china_implications_0505.html>; Eric Hagt and Matthew Durnin, "China's Antiship Ballistic Missile: Developments and Missing Links," *Naval War College Review* 62, no. 4 (Autumn 2009), 87–115; and Joan Johnson-Freese, "China's Space Ambitions," *IFRI Proliferation Paper*, Summer 2007, at <www.ifri.org/downloads/China_Space_Johnson_Freese.pdf>.

[110] For a good overview of this thesis, see Kulacki and Lewis.

[111] For one widely cited article published 10 years ago, see Ma Genhai, "Considerations Regarding China's Military Use Satellite System Entering the Next Century," *Journal of the Institute of Command and Control Technology* [Zhihui jishu xueyuan xuebao] 10, no. 6 (1999). Also see Zhu Bin and Chen Xuan, "A Space-Based Electronic Information System for Long Range Precision Strike," *Aerospace China*, no. 3 (2007).

[112] Qiu and Long assert that a program to deploy a space-based reconnaissance architecture, programmed under the 863 program for 2015–2020, was advanced in 2004. The total scope of the space architecture is unknown at the current time. However, in their 2006/7 *Modern Ships* article, Qiu and Long assess that during a crisis, 24 satellites could be available, including 6 EO satellites, 10 radar reconnaissance satellites, 2 maritime satellites, and 6 electronic reconnaissance satellites with a visit rate of 40 minutes. For emergencies, microsatellites, with a life of 1–2 weeks, can augment large ones and be launched from mobile platforms within 12 hours of an order.

[113] Chen Deyuan and Tu Guofang, "SAR Image Enhancement Using Multi-scale Products for Targets Detection," *Remote Sensing Journal* [Yaogan xuebao] *(March 2007),* 185–192. Authors are from the Institute of Electronics, Chinese Academy of Sciences.

[114] See Yuan Xiaokang [袁孝康], "Satellite Electronic Reconnaissance, Antijamming," *Shanghai Hangtian*, October 9, 1996, 32–37, in FBIS–CST–97–011; and Yuan Xiaokang, "Some Problems of Space Electronic Reconnaissance," *Hangtian Dianzi Duikang* (March 1996), 1–5, in CAMA 3, no. 4. Yuan is a key engineer involved in space-based antenna systems design, including both ELINT and SAR, from the SAST 509th Research Institute (Shanghai Institute of Satellite Engineering). Also see Jiang Zisen, Li Wei, and Wang Hongbin, "Electronic Reconnaissance Satellites" [电子侦察卫星], *Satellite and Network* (April 2007).

[115] "China Blasts Off First Data Relay Satellite," *Xinhua News Agency*, April 26, 2008. For an example of the data relay satellite being used for missile guidance, see Chen Lihu, Wang Shilian, and Zhang Eryang,

"Modeling and Simulation of Missile Satellite-Missile Link Channel in Flying-Control Data-Link" [基于卫星中继的导弹飞控数据链链路分析], *Systems Engineering And Electronics* 29, no. 6 (2007). The chief designer of the satellite was Ye Peijian [叶培建]. Also see Wu Ting-yong, Wu Shiqi, and Ling Xiang, "A MEO Tracking and Data Relay Satellite System Constellation Scheme for China," *Journal of Electronic Science and Technology of China* (December 2005).

[116] The Nanjing Research of Electronic Technology (NRIET, 14th Research Institute; 南京电子技术研究所) is China's primary entity responsible for developing air and space surveillance radar systems. Range for detection of airbreathing or ballistic missile targets depends upon aperture of the radar, frequency, power, elevation of the radar, and altitude/radar cross-section of the target. UHF radar systems operate at 300 MHz to 1 GHz and are primarily used for long-range early warning and space tracking. Legacy PAVE PAWS, UEWR, MEADS, and Taiwan's Surveillance Radar Program (SRP) are examples of long-range early warning UHF radar systems. The SRP is perhaps the most robust UHF radar design in the world today. L-Band (1–2GHz) and S-Band (2–4 GHz) are primarily for air surveillance systems. X-Band (8–12 GHz) radar systems, such as the Ground-Based Radar (GBR), are for search and fire control.

[117] "Radar Patrolling as the Thousand Mile Sky 'Eye'" [雷达巡视万里蓝天的"眼睛"], *PLA Daily*, April 26, 2010, at <www.mod.gov.cn/wqzb/2010-04/26/content_4150035.htm>. Senior Colonel Liu Yongjian [刘永坚] directs the PLAAF Equipment Research Academy's Radar Institute.

[118] For an excellent Western analysis of Chinese OTH-B radar development, see Sean O'Connor, "OTH Radar and ASBM Threat, *IMINT and Analysis*, November 11, 2008 at <http://geimint.blogspot.com/2008/11/oth-radar-and-asbm-threat.html>. Skywave involves ionospheric refraction of propagated electromagnetic waves at great distance from their point of origin.

[119] Xin Guo, Ni Jin-Lin, and Liu Guo-Sui, "Ship Detection with Short Coherent Integration Time in Over-the-Horizon Radar," Conference Paper, International Conference on Radar (RADAR 2003), Adelaide, Australia on September 3–5, 2003. The three authors are from the 14th Research Institute and the Research Center of Electronic Engineering Technology, Nanjing University of Science and Technology. Also see Tang Xiaodong, Han Yunjie, and Zhou Wenyu, "Skywave Over the Horizon Backscatter Radar," 2001 CIE International Radar Conference Proceedings, January 2, 2001. Authors are from the Nanjing Research Institute of Electronic Technology.

[120] Another type of OTH radar—a surface wave system—also operates in the HF band, and relies on "electromagnetic coupling" of the HF waves to the sea surface. This coupling provides a means to detect targets over the horizon beyond the line-of-sight limit experienced by conventional microwave radar systems. Surface wave systems usually have a surveillance range no more than 400 kilometers. Therefore, they are mostly used for local area defense against low-flying missiles and also for some monitoring of ship traffic. Surface wave radars are large and require sophisticated frequency management systems in order to operate via the ever-changing ionosphere.

[121] See "Introduction to Yingpan Village" [营盘村简介], Xiangfan City Web site, at <www.xftxbsc.gov.cn/newview.asp?id=408&menutype=4>; and "Second CPPCC Session of Xiangfan City Opens" [襄樊市政协十二届二次会议隆重开幕], *Hubei News*, February 3, 2009, at <http://news.cnhubei.com/xwhbyw/xwwc/200902/t566879.shtml>, accessed February 9, 2010.

[122] Zhao Shanghong, Yang Xiaotie, and Xie Xiaoping, "Ultra-Wideband Impulse Radar and Counter-Stealth Technology" [超宽带冲击雷达与反隐形技术], *Journal of Air Force Engineering University*, January 2000, 82–85. China Academy of Engineering Physics (CAEP) appears to be a key organization involved in conducting preliminary R&D into ultra wideband (UWB) radar. For background on ladar, see R.L. Lucke, L.J. Rickard, M. Bashkansky, J.F. Reintjes, and E.E. Funk, "Synthetic Aperture Ladar," U.S. Naval Research Laboratory, at <www.nrl.navy.mil/research/nrl-review/2003/remote-sensing/lucke/>.

[123] See Chao Shaoying and Yang Wenjun, "Requirement Analysis of Phased Array Radar for Space-Object Surveillance" [用于空间目标监视的相控阵雷达需求分析], *Modern Radar* 28, no. 1 (2006) at <http://d.wanfangdata.com.cn/Periodical_xdld200601005.aspx>. The Nanjing Research Institute of Electronic Technology (NRIET, or the CETC 14th Research Institute).

[124] For an example of an interesting speculative assessment, see "Model for Integrated Aerospace Development" [空天一体化建设模式], *Dragon Rising*, March 28, 2010, at <http://riyueliuguang.blog.163.com/blog/static/12207485020102281039190 3/>. Also see Huang Zijuan, "Expert: China's Air Force Moving toward Integrated Aerospace and Long Range Air Strike Capabilities" [专家: 我空军须向空天一体转型 具远程空中打击力量], *People's Daily* (September 24, 2009) at <http://military.people.com.cn/GB/8221/74407/169171/169174/10111982.html>.

[125] Andrew Erickson and David Yang, "On the Verge of a Game-Changer: A Chinese Antiship Ballistic Missile Could Alter the Rules in the Pacific and Place U.S. Navy Carrier Strike Groups in Jeopardy," *U.S. Naval Institute Proceedings* 135, no. 3 (May 2009), 26–32; Paul S. Giarra, "A Chinese Anti-Ship Ballistic Missile: Implications for the USN," testimony before the U.S.-China Economic and Security Commission (June 11, 2009) at <www.uscc.gov/hearings/2009hearings/written_testimonies/09_06_11_wrts/09_06_11_giarra_statement.pdf>; Andrew F. Krepinevich, *Why AirSea Battle?* (Washington DC: Center for Strategic and Budgetary Assessments, 2010) at <www.csbaonline.org/4Publications/PubLibrary/R.20100219.Why_AirSea_Battle/R.20100219.Why_AirSea_Battle.pdf>; and Roger Cliff, Mark Burles, Michael S. Chase, Derek Eaton, and Kevin L. Pollpeter, *Entering The Dragon's Lair: Chinese Anti-Access Strategies and Their Implications for the United States* (Arlington, VA: RAND Corporation, 2007) at <www.rand.org/pubs/monographs/2007/RAND_MG524.pdf>.

[126] *Ballistic Missile Defense Review Report*, Department of Defense, February 2010, at <http://www.defense.gov/bmdr/docs/BMDR%20as%20of%2026JAN10%200630_for%20web.pdf>.

Chapter 3

The PLAAF's Evolving Influence within the PLA and upon National Policy

Xiaoming Zhang

The rise of China as a global economic and political power in recent years raises concerns for many policymakers, strategists, and scholars about Chinese military modernization—concerns that might provide a new perspective on global security for years to come.[1] At the center of this concern is the fact that the People's Liberation Army (PLA) Air Force (PLAAF) has gained offensive capability by equipping itself with an increasing number of third- and fourth-generation fighters, airborne early warning aircraft, aerial refueling tankers, intelligence collection and jamming aircraft, and long-range antiaircraft missile systems. But what matters most is not so much the growth of Chinese airpower capability per se; rather, it is how China might use its new military strength, especially its air and naval power. One area of particular interest to defense analysts is the evolving influence of the PLAAF within the PLA and in China's own national policymaking.

Airpower and its influence have primarily dominated in Western political thought. Given China's growing economic and military power as well as changes in its bureaucratic politics, security interests, and technology, it is logical to examine the following concerns as they relate to the PLAAF:

- concepts for airpower as an instrument of statecraft
- influence within the PLA and in national policymaking
- vision of future roles and missions
- organization, leadership, personnel, and doctrine
- capabilities
- political and military implications of all of the above for Taiwan and the United States.

In 2007, a U.S. Army War College and National Bureau of Asian Research project, *Right Sizing the People's Liberation Army: Exploring the Contours of China's Military*, produced two separate studies of the latest development of the PLAAF and its growing capability.[2] Using different methodologies, these two studies—one a scenario-based approach to articulate impending developments of the Chinese air force, and the other focused on institutional and doctrinal developments since the 1990s—addressed concerns such as the PLAAF's current status and influence within the PLA and what role the PLAAF currently plays in national policymaking. The studies contend that perceptions of the international threat environment, technological limitations, lack of advanced aircraft, and budget concerns would act as constraints on the PLAAF's modernization efforts, and any significant progress in force modernization would take at least 10–15 years to reach.[3]

This chapter is inclined to argue that while the PLAAF is transforming, the PLA's political culture and organizational system pose a serious challenge to China's current effort to embrace an air force that is capable of both offensive and defensive operations, and especially to the PLAAF's own ambition to "bear the brunt of the operations, and play a sustained, independent role" in modern warfare. These challenges include the PLA's and PLAAF's tradition, perception of itself and each other, older way of doing things, outdated organizational structure, and limited funding under the current system. The PLAAF's current development is about more than changing doctrine and buying advanced systems. An appropriate organizational change is necessary. It will take far longer to nourish an institutional culture that enables the PLAAF to embrace both offensive and defensive capability as an independent strategic force.

Analyzing the current and future state of PLAAF modernization necessitates examining the historical development of the Chinese air force and its experiences (during the Korean War, the 1950s Taiwan Strait crises, and the air defense engagements against Nationalist and American intrusions); it also requires an examination of the historical evolution of the political culture of the PLAAF over the years, including utilization of the senior leadership's military thought as guidance to keep the development of the air force politically correct and thus reliable. It is against this historical background that the author has made his assessment of the current development of the PLAAF. The conclusion following from this is that the army-dominated organizational system and the emergence of different services' cultures continue to limit the PLAAF's influence within the PLA, its relationship with other services, and the role it currently plays in national policymaking. This situation exists despite China's experiencing profound changes in bureaucratic politics, in its security interests, and in its technology and military capabilities.

The PLAAF's Early Experiences

The present understanding of the PLAAF's development cannot be disassociated from an overview of its early experiences. The doctrinal guidance for PLAAF development was Chinese defensive thinking. From the outset, the PLAAF leadership preferred to build an air force that possessed more fighters than bombers. Its theory was that the role of fighters dovetailed well with the defensive cast of Chinese military thought. Bombers attacked enemy countries and territories—an aggressive act—but fighters were defensive in nature and, if successful in fending off attacks, would ensure air superiority.[4] The PLAAF's immediate mission, therefore, was to attain air superiority over the Nationalist Chinese on Taiwan, provide support to the planned amphibious assault on Taiwan, and then develop itself into a force capable of defending China's airspace and waters.

The Korean War provided the impetus for the rapid expansion of the air force in both aviation personnel and equipment. A large number of officers and troops were transferred from ground forces to form 26 aviation divisions, four independent regiments, and eight aviation and three mechanical schools operating throughout the conflict on the Korean Peninsula.[5] The existing ground force structure was simply grafted onto the air force, and army officers were chosen to command the air force. The PLAAF leadership was accustomed to believe that the building of an air force on the foundation of the ground forces was a necessary principle for its future success. Thus, its primary mission was to provide support for ground troops, and the air force would take the victories of ground operations as its own.[6] The air force was created as an independent service of the PLA under the direct control of the Central Military Commission (CMC), the highest military authority of the People's Republic of China (PRC).[7] This ground-centric army bias accounts for the PLAAF leadership's inclination at the time to perceive the air force as a support unit of the PLA. They did not consider airpower essential in a strategic sense, valuing it only for the tactical support it could provide to the ground forces during operations.[8] Such thinking, moreover, justified an army-centric and -dominated PLA system that subsequently prevented the air force from operating as an independent service.

The Korean War experience was a driving force for the PLAAF to further emphasize air defense and procurement of fighters to constitute the largest and most important element of the Chinese air force. The Chinese leaders gleaned a mixed understanding of airpower from the Korean conflict. While recognizing America's air superiority, Chinese leaders discounted the role airpower had played. They found it particularly interesting that air bombardment inflicted fewer casualties upon Communist forces than ground fire. Given their confidence in the human factor—that men could overcome weapons—and their own guerrilla war experience, they remained convinced that PLA ground forces could overwhelm stronger opponents and win any future war.[9] It is thus not surprising that Chinese political leaders and generals maintained their view that future wars would be conducted in the context of ground operations, with airpower used to supplement the power of the army. This air defense experience thus resulted in the PLAAF's continuing to emphasize an air defense strategy and the development of fighter planes, radar, and ground antiaircraft systems, while devoting only a small portion of the overall force structure to delivering limited air-to-surface ordnance.

Throughout the 1950s, the PLAAF constantly engaged in air combat against the Nationalist Chinese air force for the control of airspace over the coastal areas of Zhejiang and Fujian provinces (right across the strait from Taiwan). Air battles over the Taiwan Strait intensified in the summer of 1958.[10] As during the Korean War, the PLAAF took a passive stance and waited to respond to intrusions by the Nationalist air force, which was much smaller, but was thus free to choose the time and method of aerial combat. The PLAAF, by contrast, had to depend on ground control intercept (GCI) to scramble its fighters. Furthermore, the capability of the air force was restricted by political considerations and the limited range of the MiG–17 fighter. Nevertheless, operations against the Nationalists over the southeast coastal areas in the 1950s gave the Chinese valuable experience in employing airpower in air defense.

This trend continued into the late 1950s and then the 1960s as one major focus of the PLAAF's day-to-day activity was constantly scrambling its fighters to intercept intruding Nationalist and American aircraft, many of them spy planes (in sequence, the McDonnell F2H–2P, Lockheed RF–80C, Lockheed P2V–5, Martin P4M, North American RF–86A/F, Republic RF–84F, North American RF–100A, Martin RB–57A/D, McDonnell RF–101A, various Lockheed U–2s, Lockheed RF–104G, and unmanned Ryan Firebee drones that routinely flew over Chinese airspace), but also engaging and shooting down aircraft that accidently approached or overflew its borders, including, shortly after the Korean War, a Cathay Pacific DC–4 airliner, and several American aircraft shot down during the Vietnam War.[11]

The incidents of intruding overflights took place in the midst of an upsurge in political radicalism within the PRC that emphasized political factors and the promotion of Mao's cult of personality. The downing of every intruder was described more like a political victory than a military one. Celebrations were held and awards were given to those involved in combat actions. Senior party and state leaders, including Chairman Mao and Premier Zhou Enlai, always received the men responsible for the shoot-downs, making headline news across the country. Senior military leaders also used these events to promote the air force, proclaiming that "all military services must learn from the air force."[12] Chinese accounts of the PLAAF's role in these conflicts, including a claim that the PLAAF is the only air force in the world to have ever defeated the U.S. Air Force (USAF), have become important components of the service tradition, continuing to influence the Chinese air force to think of itself in a continuum linking the past to the present, and thence to the future.[13]

The PLAAF's Unique Political Culture

Over the years, the PLAAF developed a unique political culture that has not only influenced its development, but is crucial to understanding the Chinese air force. The PLAAF is accustomed to use the Chinese leadership's instructions and speeches as guidance to define its doctrine, mission, and force structure in order to maintain political support. This PLAAF tradition continues to influence thinking and efforts to pursue development of a modern air force. Despite their long revolutionary experience, Chinese leaders, particularly Mao Zedong, the founder and strategist of the PLA, had no knowledge of air and naval warfare. Even so, the PLAAF codifies their sporadic instructions as profound military thought guiding the development of Chinese airpower.[14] This approach is attributed partly to traditional Chinese filial piety and partly to the Chinese Communist Party's highly doctrinaire and centralized institutional system.

At the onset of its establishment, the PLAAF used the chairman's message of encouragement to the air force, "creating a powerful air force to eliminate the remnant enemy [the KMT legacy forces that had evacuated the mainland for Taiwan] and consolidate national defense," to characterize the air force's contemporary and future task.[15] While recognizing the importance of airpower in national consolidation and development, none of the Chinese leaders offered any systematic thinking on the air force and airpower employment. One common view shared by these political and military leaders was the use of air force to ensure command of China's airspace through air defense. Although a few of them occasionally talked about the use of bombers to strike deeply into the enemy's rear positions, they never seemed to imply any offensive action beyond China's own territory.[16]

Studies of the military thoughts of Chinese leaders on the air force and its employment dominated the PLAAF's theoretical inquiry. As a result, for most of its existence until recently, no serious efforts were made to explore the differing means of employing airpower within the framework of China's defense strategy. Even now, PLAAF studies still incorporate the military thoughts of these past political leaders in their current pursuit of modern airpower theory. Thus, PLAAF thinking and doctrine are still imbued with the PLA's traditional political jargon. This at-best pseudoscientific approach accounts for the PLAAF's failure to ascribe the military thoughts of the earlier leaders to the PLAAF's longtime perception of itself as a homeland defense force, whose task was, first and foremost, to defend China's airspace and thus maintain only a limited role and modest capability to support the army and navy.[17] The legacy of the Chinese leadership's minimalist understanding of the actual role that airpower can play is evident in the PLAAF's self-perpetuating view of itself in an unbroken string of memories about victories and heroism in the past, including a claim that it is the only air force in the world to have ever defeated the USAF. The PLAAF's self-aggrandizing depiction, however intellectually dishonest it may be, has nevertheless become an important component of its service tradition.[18]

More Political Than Military in Its Decisionmaking

The West tends to see the PLA as having too much autonomy in China's civil-military relations. In fact, as commanders of a Party-controlled armed service, senior PLA leaders, socialized by the unique Party-army relationship that has also rewarded them with promotion to the higher ranks, are unlikely to seek greater autonomy. Thus the PLA's political culture subordinates the military to the Party leadership for decisions at the time when the use of force is considered. It is interesting to note that Chinese military thought today still regards the primary use of airpower as deterrence, deferring to the political leadership sole authority to determine whether, in fact, airpower should be used. The role the air force can play is thus more as a tool to serve national policy than as a component of national policymaking.

There have been three major occasions in the PLAAF's history during which the Chinese leadership has had to contemplate the employment of the air force and airpower beyond Chinese-controlled territory. The first was during the Korean War in February 1952. In that case, Zhou Enlai personally cancelled a PLAAF bombing mission aimed at Kimpo airfield near Seoul only minutes before takeoff. Zhou feared a Chinese raid south of the 38th parallel would upset an implicit mutual understanding that the United States would not extend its bombing campaign north beyond the Yalu River into Chinese territory.[19]

The second incident occurred during 1958 Taiwan Strait crisis when the Chinese leadership was very uncertain about the PLAAF's strike capability. Again, Zhou raised concerns about potential Nationalist bombing retaliation against the mainland should the PLAAF undertake an air bombardment of Jinmen island. He felt that the inability of the PLAAF to reciprocate by bombing Taiwan in return would signal Chinese weakness to the world. He thus strongly advised the CMC not to bomb Jinmen.[20]

The last came during China's invasion of Vietnam in 1979, when the PLAAF engaged in a brief combat action against its southern neighbor. Despite several instances where the PLA ground forces requested air support, Beijing authorities refused to grant such permission lest the use of airpower escalate the conflict; instead, the General Staff ordered the army to rely exclusively on artillery fire support.[21]

These three episodes merit careful analysis for any inquiry into what role the PLAAF could potentially play in national policymaking. Political concerns and the insufficient capability of the air force constitute the true reason for the PLAAF to have undertaken no offensive roles in military actions since its establishment. Further examination suggests that the real problem was the Chinese leadership's failure from the creation of the PRC in 1949 to appreciate the centrality of airpower in modern warfare and, hence, the critical role it could play. The PLA's subsequent war experience in Korea seemingly confirmed the leadership's position that airpower could have, and in fact had, only little impact on the victory claimed by China in that war. We should thus not be surprised that Chinese political and military leaders have long maintained the view that war will continue to be conducted in the context of dominant ground operations, with airpower used in a supporting role, to supplement the power of the army.

Furthermore, given their confidence in the human factor—that men could overcome weapons, a belief reinforced by their own guerrilla war experience—Chinese leaders were convinced that their ground forces could overwhelm any opponent and win any war. Consequently, the PLAAF had long argued that ground operations would determine the air force's contribution to final victory. The development of such thinking was supported by the objective reality confronting the PLAAF. While the PLAAF was one of the world's largest air forces, its equipment was outdated, limited in capability, and not even equal to that of some countries surrounding China. Since the creation of the PLAAF, to address technological deficiencies and maintain the air force's overall combat capabilities, China favored an air force based on quantity instead of quality.[22] When it did engage in aircraft development, the aircraft produced were outright copies or simple derivatives or extrapolations of Soviet designs such as the Ilyushin Il–28, Tupolev Tu–16, and the Mikoyan-Gurevich MiG–17, –19, and –21.[23] The sheer numerical superiority of the PLAAF compared to its potential regional opponents convinced the Chinese that the PLA had built an adequate and credible air defense force capable of deterring and, if necessary, resisting any attack into Chinese air space.

Such a view was shattered by the dominant role airpower played in *Desert Storm* and the military conflicts since the 1991 Gulf War. Even so, one political legacy remains: the latest PLA campaign theory holds that the employment of airpower is more a political matter than a military one, subordinate to the needs of China's political and diplomatic struggles. If its use is required, it will be the political, not military, leadership that will make the decision. This perhaps explains why the development of the air force still requires the personal involvement of the Chinese political leadership.[24] The question remains whether fourth- and fifth-generation Chinese political leaders, unlike their predecessors, will not hesitate to throw the air force into harmful situations.

The PLAAF's Evolving Thinking on Airpower

The early 1990s awakened the PLAAF to the realization that China had fallen far behind the West in both technology and doctrinal thinking about airpower. Time and space were no longer the allies of those who were once so confident that China's existing air defense systems could prevent any attacks deep into the nation's heartland. Serious doubts were raised about the traditional interpretation of China's defense capabilities, including the common belief that an inferior force could overcome a superior enemy. Drawing on lessons learned from Iraq's defeat in the 1991 Gulf War, the Chinese central military leadership pointed out that "a weaker force relying solely on the defensive would place itself in the position of having to receive blows," and that only by "taking active offensive operations" could the weaker force now seize the initiative.[25]

China's evolving security interests, including the longstanding prospect of a decisive confrontation with Taiwan, also favored consideration of augmenting the PLAAF's offensive capabilities. Since 1993, Beijing has adopted a new military strategy, placing an emphasis on fighting and winning a future regional war under high-technology conditions along China's periphery. The momentum of the independence movement in Taiwan was simultaneously viewed as an increasingly serious challenge to China's sovereignty and security.[26] The central military leadership made the proper readjustment to the air force's strategic missions, requiring it to maintain strong capabilities not only for defensive operations, but also for offensive ones.

The air force's new mission requirements include securing air dominance over China's own airspace, supporting the army and the navy, and directing paratrooper operations, as well as carrying out independent air campaigns. In an offensive campaign, it should be able to launch attacks against the enemy's air assets on the ground in a potential local conflict along China's coast.[27]

In early March 1999, Jiang Zemin, former secretary-general of the Chinese Communist Party (CCP) and president of China, explicated the air force's strategic objective: to transform gradually from a homeland air defense force to one that was capable of both defensive and offensive operations. He then charged the air force to "bear the brunt of, and be employed throughout the entire course" of the conflict, and "to complete certain strategic missions independently."[28] To achieve these objectives, China later that year adopted a three-step implementation strategy for air force development over the next several decades.[29]

According to its 2008 Defense White Paper, China expected to lay a solid foundation for the development of the PLA into a more high-tech and more balanced network-centric joint force by 2010, to accomplish mechanization and make major progress in informatization by 2020, and to reach the goal of modernizing national defense and the armed forces by the middle of the 21st

century.[30] This constituted a logical follow-on to a strategic vision the PLAAF introduced in 2004. That year, the PLAAF enunciated a new strategic vision calling for the development of a long-range strategic air force and the active involvement of integrated air and space (空天一体) operations with information and firepower systems (信息活力一体).[31]

Under the guidance of such a developmental strategy, the PLAAF embarked on a two-stage transformation. The first stage is laying a framework for a force capable of both offensive and defensive operations by increasing the number of high-performance offensive aircraft, combat support aircraft, and advanced surface-to-air missile systems. The second stage is wielding fighter aircraft, surface-based defense, and command, control, communication, and intelligence elements into an integrated operational system that is able to conduct both air offensive and defensive operations under "informatized" conditions.

The development of China's air force capabilities focuses on four areas:[32]

- offensive capability to protect national security and national interests from the air and space
- integrated air defensive and antimissile capability for monitoring both air and space flying objects and attacking them
- superior capability over its main opponent (presumably Taiwan) and certain counter-information capability against its strategic opponent (presumably the United States)
- strategic airlift capability to conduct both airlift and airdrop operations.

The Development of the New Air Force

China pursued a "walking on two legs" policy to modernize the air force through purchases of foreign systems and development of domestic technology. China has historically sought to be self-reliant in military production through either reverse-engineering or incorporating foreign technology. Since the early 1990s, such foreign purchases have been perceived as a stopgap measure for the PLAAF to create a sizeable fleet of fourth-generation aircraft, exemplified by acquisition of the Russian-made Sukhoi Su–27 and Su–30, and co-produced J–11 fighters. After years of effort, the development of domestic systems has borne fruit thanks to the J–10 and JH–7 that have entered service in the PLAAF since 2004. It appears that every year since 2005, one regiment of PLAAF or navy aviation has transitioned into the JH–7A, J–10, and J–11B.[33]

With its entry into the 21st century, the PLAAF has become smaller. The U.S. Department of Defense reports on Chinese military power registered

5,300 tactical fighters, bombers, and support aircraft in both the PLA Air Force's and naval aviation's inventory in 2000. That number declined to 2,300 in 2010.[34] As early as 2003, the PLAAF's operational air divisions had fallen to just 29 divisions, with some of them having only two air regiments.[35] Along with this reduction and restructuring, the PLAAF established an additional transport division and one special aircraft division, attempting to enhance its long-range airlift and airborne early warning (AEW) capabilities. Thus, although getting smaller, the Chinese air force has become much better equipped and much more technologically sophisticated.[36]

Like the United States Air Force and the Royal Air Force previously, the PLAAF's leadership seeks to create a mixed force that blends limited quantities of high-performance fighters and larger quantities of less expensive fighters. The ongoing procurement of J–7G and J–8F/H, which are upgraded versions of obsolete second-generation J–7/8s, provides the Chinese air force with less-expensive, less-capable aircraft to serve alongside J–10s and J–11s in a "high/low" combination.[37] One problem which seems to have bothered the PLAAF is that the initially purchased Su–27s and the subsequently assembled Chinese J–11s are not true multirole fighters capable of supporting the increasingly diverse mission requirements of the PLAAF, particularly the increased emphasis on offensive as well as defensive roles.[38] The real change of its offensive capabilities will only come as a significant number of J–10s and J–11Bs enter operational service over the next 5 to 10 years.

For the past 10 years, increasing focus has been placed on informatization as a leapfrog measure to close the PLAAF's cyber and electronic warfare (EW) gap with the United States and Western Europe. The development of sophisticated command, control, and communications (C3), or intelligence, surveillance, and reconnaissance (ISR) capabilities, has been the PLAAF's most urgent priority.[39] Following earlier experimental trials using an obsolete Soviet-legacy Tupolev Tu–4 modified with turboprop engines and rudimentary search radar in a saucer dome, China has developed two "high-low" versions of an indigenous AWACS (Airborne Warning and Control System): the high-end KJ–2000 based on the Russian IL–76MD airframe; and the low-end KJ–200 based on the Y–8F–200 transport platform. These platforms were handed over to the PLAAF in 2005 and 2006, respectively, to coordinate fighters and bombers via secure datalinks. Simultaneously, China developed seven other different types of EW aircraft, the High New (*Gaoxin*) series, likewise based upon the Y–8. Integration of these systems is well underway across the services to increase PLA joint operational capability.[40]

In retrospect, though the U.S. Government successfully pressured Israel to cancel the sale of the Phalcon AWACS system to the PLA in 1999, China appears to have pulled together sufficient talents and resources to build its own system despite this seeming setback. The chief engineer and designer of the Chinese AWACS project recently claimed that China's radar technology has reached the same level as that of leading foreign countries and that, in some areas, it is even better.[41] Efforts by the United States and European countries to prevent China from obtaining high-tech weapons similarly do not seem to have succeeded.

Yet, the downside of this success in improving the cutting edge of offensive and defensive forces has actually worked to delay PLAAF acquisition of transport aircraft and transport-related research and development (R&D). Russia's failure to deliver 34 IL–76MDs as scheduled in 2008 has kept the PLAAF's newly created transport division underequipped.[42] In the meantime, most of the Y–8 platforms manufactured by Shanxi Aircraft Factory have been committed to the production of the high priority High New series, and development of the Y–9, whose first prototype was begun in 2006, was delayed. (Recently, some sources suggest that the Y–9 project has resumed with first flight expected in 2011). It was not until May 2009 that the new transport division received its first Y–8C aircraft.[43] Again, this reflects how the PLAAF is restricted by numerous constraints and obstacles that confront all aspects of its development.

The PLAAF's Political and Organizational Culture as Constraints

A conventional academic consensus is that instituting change in military organizations is at best difficult. It is perhaps even more challenging to institute change in the PLA organization. In their 2007 study, Saunders and Quam look at tradeoffs in current PLAAF modernization efforts and future force structure including the allocation of roles and missions among services and branches, the balance between domestic and foreign procurement, the mix of low-technology and high-technology systems, and the relative proportions of combat aircraft and support aircraft.[44] But the PLA's political cultural tradition, systematic constraints, and the emergence of service cultures also influence the pace of modernization and the size of the air force.

Graham Allison and Phillip Zelikow note that organizational culture is a factor influencing leaders to favor maintenance of the status quo.[45] China's Party-army relationship, a relic from its founding, demands the PLA's absolute loyalty to the Party. The PLAAF is no exception to this. The current and future development of the air force is obligated to be framed within the ideological bounds of the military thinking of the Chinese leadership.

As mentioned, the PLAAF leadership has always maintained a pseudo-scientific attitude in characterizing their leadership's sporadic instructions as profound military thought on airpower, and then using those instructions as guidance. "Being prepared for offensive and defensive operations" had been long debated by air force theorists since the late 1980s. It was not until 1999 that Jiang Zemin endorsed the expression. The PLAAF felt itself officially blessed and subsequently claimed the concept to justify the strategic goal of the air force and, furthermore, to characterize it as a vital piece of Jiang's military thought on airpower.[46]

Chinese leaders are accustomed to devoting significant personal, autonomous attention to defense projects. Their involvement influences the allocation of resources as well as air force procurement decisions. The PLAAF, reportedly, has been unenthusiastic about the J–8 as its air superiority fighter, and would prefer to suspend its procurement as the J–10 becomes available. But Jiang Zemin personally took charge of this focal-point project, calling the J–8 aircraft a credit to the China's aviation industry.[47] Since then, the air force has had little choice but to continue purchasing upgraded versions of J–8 fighters, though in limited numbers.

Currying favor with the leadership is a cultural phenomenon in any political system dominated by absolute authority and arbitrary decisions by key individuals. It represents not only air force subordination to the Party (strongly entrenched in Chinese military culture), but also demonstrates the political reliability and loyalty of the air force to individual senior Party leaders. In return, the PLAAF leadership could be confident that, when they brought requests to the Party leadership's personal attention, they would receive favorable approval. Nothing should upset the continuity of this entwining Party/military bondage of mutual support.

Another well-known organizational constraint goes to the so-called "great land army" (大陆军) complex, which refers to army-centric thinking and leadership that have long dominated the Chinese military system.[48] The four general departments—the General Staff Department, General Political Department, General Logistics Department, and General Armament Department—serve concurrently as the PLA's joint staff, and as the headquarters for all services, namely the ground force, navy, air force, and Second Artillery force. These departments are still staffed primarily by army officers. Because there is no general headquarters for ground forces, the General Staff Department is assigned to perform the functions of ground force headquarters. Its overarching army bias has inevitably influenced all military aspects from force size, structure, and command and control to logistics, equipment, R&D, and procurement.[49]

Nowadays, increasing numbers of personnel from other services are assigned to "joint" positions at headquarters department levels, as well as at military region headquarters levels. This change enables the expertise and knowledge of other services to be brought into the joint and higher headquarters command environment. Though such personnel wear the uniform of their own services, they are, in fact, no longer controlled within the personnel systems of their own services. This separation keeps their representation of parochial service-specific interests in these headquarters departments at minimal level. Over the years, air force general officers have been appointed to deputy positions at the headquarters departments and to the commandership or political commissarship of the PLA Academy and National Defense University. A growing leadership role for other services within the PLA looks more symbolic than substantial as long as the existing organizational system continues.[50]

The organization of the Chinese air force along military regional lines, with an operational command in each military region, is another typical reflection of the predominant ground force institutional system of the Chinese military.[51] Military regional leadership organizations traditionally have been a command organization for ground troops and education institutions, while playing a concurrent leadership role for the personnel of other services located within their regions. Only ground force officers have commanded military regions, and the commanders of other services can only serve as their deputies.[52] Since there is no permanent joint organization at the military region level, when a joint command organization must be formed, air force officers can only assume assistant (hence subordinate) positions. Thus, even though China's most likely conflict scenarios involve possible sea and air fights over Taiwan and in the East China and South China Seas, no navy and air force general officer has been yet assigned to command either the Nanjing or Guangzhou Military Region.

In 2000, Lieutenant General Liu Yazhou, former deputy political commissar of the air force and currently political commissar of the PLA's National University, proposed Chinese military authorities consider reorganizing the PLAAF into functional air commands, separating the air force from the PLA military regional system, and thus making it a truly independent service. In order to make it a more offensively oriented air force, he further recommended the use of the U.S. Air Force's "expeditionary force" model to organize air force units into air strike groups with a mix of fighters, bombers, and EW aircraft.[53] Liu has been recognized as the "Douhet of China" because of his reputation as a daring thinker of airpower theory that goes against the PLAAF's tradition, though a better analogy might be that he is a Chinese equivalent of Lieutenant General David A. Deptula or Colonel John A. Warden III. Not surprisingly, given the ground-centric traditionalism of the Chinese military system, Liu's advocacy for eliminating the ground-centric military system has received little support from the PLA military establishment. Current evidence suggests that, in a joint operation or campaign, the air force will continue to play a support role rather than an independent or leading role.[54] Although the PLAAF currently enjoys the benefits of favorable military investment, as long as the

General Logistics Department continues to control military finances, PLAAF funding is unlikely to reach levels desired by air force officers.[55]

The rising importance of the navy, air force, and Second Artillery forces has facilitated the emergence of rival service cultures, which, in turn, have brought not only competition with the ground force tradition, but also rivalries among the other services and branches. In particular, the PLAAF's adoption of air and space integration as part of its development has instigated a struggle within the PLA over the control of space operations. China's space assets are controlled by the General Armaments Department, while the Second Artillery possesses strategic missiles. The PLAAF has been contending that it should be in control of space operations because air and space constitute a single integrated medium. But the PLAAF has been unpersuasive in making this case, and so has lost recent debates about whether these capabilities should be placed under its control.[56] It concurrently concentrates on building facilities and institutions to receive satellite services for communication, weather, navigation, and global positioning. Taking this tack, the PLAAF believes it will be able to make the transition from being a traditional air force to one enabled by space-based information (communications, positioning, navigation, timing, and intelligence, surveillance, and reconnaissance) capabilities.[57]

China's present-day security interests—preventing Taiwan from seceding and supporting the country's claims to islands in the East China Sea and South China Sea—have brought PLA naval aviation into competition with the PLAAF for the limited R&D and production capabilities of the Chinese defense industry. For example, the JH-7 fighter-bomber was initially made for PLAN aviation. The air force did not commit to this aircraft until the improved variant, the JH-7A—upgraded with two more powerful domestic-made turbofan engines and a new fire control system capable of launching precision strikes using antiradiation missiles and laser-guided bombs—became available.[58] Since 2004, its acquisition has been a priority for the PLAAF which has had to share its production with naval aviation, receiving one regiment every other year. As a result, the PLAAF's replacement program to phase out its obsolete fleet of aging Q-5 attack aircraft—a J-6 (Chinese version of the MiG-19) derivative—will stretch beyond 2015. This PLAN-PLAAF competition extends to other domestically manufactured aircraft, such as the J-10 and J-11B, produced by Chengdu and Shenyang aircraft factories, respectively.[59] With the air force increasingly training over water, the competition in terms of division of responsibility and procurement will be intensified as maritime strike missions traditionally assigned to PLAN are increasingly prosecuted by the PLAAF, echoing similar institutional struggles between the U.S. Navy and the U.S. Army Air Corps in the 1930s.[60]

PLAAF Influence within the PLA

The growing capability of the PLAAF raises the question of its influence within the PLA and what role it currently plays in national policymaking. An analysis of the PLAAF's missions versus those of other services is illuminating. In his "Essences for an Offensive and Defensive Chinese Air Force" essay, Lieutenant General Liu Yazhou argues that the air force must be capable of playing a major role in a variety of military operations against Taiwan—including air and missile attacks, a naval blockade, or even an outright invasion of the island.[61] Over the last decade, the PLAAF has striven to develop the capability for carrying out all-weather, day-night, high-intensity, simultaneous offensive and defensive operations. The 2006 *Science of Campaigns* by the PLA's National Defense University identifies the following major PLAAF missions:[62]

- military deterrence
- offensive air operations (including air-blockade, airborne forces insertion, informatized operations, and special operations)
- air defense
- assisting ground and navy forces in offensive-defensive operations
- assisting the Second Artillery force in missile attacks
- resisting a more powerful enemy's attack
- participating in United Nations operations.

In discussing air offensive campaign categories, *Science of Campaigns* pinpointed three objectives that the PLAAF is expected to achieve:[63]

- seizing air control by annihilating or crippling the enemy's offensive and defensive airpower forces
- creating favorable conditions for the army and navy to operate by destroying a large number of ground troops and the communication systems
- attacking the enemy's political, military, and economic targets to weaken his war potential or to achieve specific strategic objectives.

Two major concerns are intrinsic within PLA campaign theory: one is the presumption that the air force's offensive capability remains limited, both in terms of the quantity and quality of PLAAF forces; and the other is that the enemy—specifically Taiwan—has built up such a sophisticated air defense system (consisting of radars, EW aircraft and satellites integrated with fighters, antiaircraft missiles, and artillery) that it will be difficult for PLAAF or PLAN strike aircraft to break through it.[64]

An important discontinuity of thought is inherent within how the PLAAF and the PLA perceive the PLAAF's combat role and capabilities. While the PLAAF holds that the air force should be capable of being used throughout a conflict from the beginning to the end, PLA campaign theory argues otherwise, suggesting that the PLAAF should be employed in offensive operations at the critical time (重要时节).[65] This may reflect an intriguing fact: the officers responsible for writing PLA campaign theory come mainly from the army. Thus it is likely that this difference represents the army's influence within PLA doctrinal circles and, consequently, its own interpretation about the mission and current capability of the PLAAF. Furthermore, it explains why the PLA has attached great importance to land-based ballistic and cruise missile programs versus winged atmospheric (hence PLAAF) attack. Competition for resources between the PLAAF and Second Artillery is inevitable as the PLA pursues developing a long-range strike capability, particularly as strategic projection remains a major deficit of PLAAF capability. Perhaps not surprisingly, then, according to PLA campaign doctrine, the Second Artillery is defined as a primary player of the joint strike force to conduct preemptive attacks (先击制敌) against enemy targets from long range.[66]

In contemplating regional conflict, China's greatest concern is confronting an American intervention. Over the years after the first Gulf War, Chinese defense experts raised serious doubts whether the country could withstand air and missile attacks similar to those that had shattered Iraq's military structure and capabilities. The subsequent emphasis of the "three attacks and the three defenses" required the development of air defense systems that are capable of attacking stealth aircraft, cruise missiles, and armed helicopters (the "three attacks"), and protecting against precision strikes, electronic jamming, and electronic reconnaissance and surveillance (the "three defenses").[67] The 2008 defense white paper characterizes the PLAAF as a mixed force of aviation, ground-based air defense, airborne, signal, radar, electronic countermeasures (ECM), technical reconnaissance, and chemical defense.[68] This mixed-force structure will continue to complicate China's air and space decisions, particularly with regard to training, allocating roles and missions among the services and branches, and influencing resource allocations for Chinese air force modernization.

Division of responsibility across the services in air defense also challenges the PLAAF's effort to build an integrated air defense system. The PLAAF is primarily responsible for the air defense mission. It not only operates most of China's fighters and also most of its ground-based air defense systems, such as surface-to-air missiles (SAMs) and antiaircraft artillery (AAA). The PLA ground force and navy units also operate antiaircraft systems (short-range antiaircraft missiles and antiaircraft artillery, and navy fighters) to protect themselves. The question is to what extent the possession of air defense systems by other services represents an old service cultural preference for embracing every possible capability, particularly since many of these ground-based air defense weaponries have proven ineffective in recent warfare.[69]

The PLAAF's *Science of Modern Air Defense* describes air defense as an integrated air-space operation in all dimensions (air, sea, space, cyber, and ground), and requires joint operations of all services.[70] Yet against this confident assertion, evidence out of China is confusing. The PLAAF air defense forces operate the most sophisticated long- and middle-range SAM systems, the Russian made S-300 and China's indigenously developed HQ-9/12 series. However, the bulk of Chinese SAM batteries remain equipped with the obsolete HQ-2 systems as well as outdated Stalinist/Mao-era antiaircraft artillery.[71] Perhaps what is even more significant is that no single national air command system has ever been established equivalent to the former Soviet Union's *PVO-Strany*, or the United States' North American Aerospace Defense Command (NORAD). Lieutenant General Liu has suggested creating a Chinese "NORAD" to command China's air defense based around the Beijing Military Region Air Force. The recent Vanguard-2010 exercise suggests that the army air defense forces are attempting to assert their independent role in China's national air defense system, however it develops.[72]

Conclusion

With the existence of a ground force–dominated culture and the emergence of other cultures for the other services, the PLAAF's relationship with other services and organizations has been complicated, but not significantly changed since its earliest days. The PLAAF is a separate service (*junzhong*) along with the PLAN and Second Artillery under the CMC. The General Staff Department is responsible for operations, military affairs, training, and mobilization for the entire PLA. Allocation of missions is under the purview of the General Staff. As a result of bureaucratic politics, an analysis of missions divided between the air force and other services does not suggest that the PLAAF's role and influence are likely to change in the future, despite changes in China's security interests, technological developments, and other areas.

The growth of China's airpower in recent years has naturally raised great Western interest in comprehending the PLAAF's influence within the PLA, its relationship with other services, and the role it currently plays in national policymaking. Change is clearly underway within the ranks of the PLAAF, which has embraced a new concept of operations that emphasizes development of an air force capable of both offensive and defensive operations, fielding an increasing number of fourth-generation multirole fighters, early warning and electronic warfare aircraft, and long-range surface-to-air missiles. The force structure is being radically reshaped to become a smaller, yet more technologically capable, service. For military organizations to be able to take dramatic changes, they must also have appropriate personnel policies, organizational structure, service culture, and leader development programs. What has not changed is the PLA's political culture, service tradition, older ways of doing things, and outdated organizational system. All these form relentless constraints that will undoubtedly continue to hinder the PLAAF's modernization efforts.

In sum, then, the PLA is a titanic bureaucratic amalgamation with a leaden hand of tradition that can often block innovation. Changes in doctrine, training practices, force structure, and equipment are underway, yet many traditions and cultural characteristics of the 83-year-old PLA are rigorously maintained. On top of that, there is the Party-controlled political culture and the ground force–centric predominant organizational tradition of the PLA. Both serve as constraining mechanisms that not only restrict the PLA's drive to autonomy, but also ensure its loyalty to the Party and obedience to Party policy. No military reformation can be expected to undermine the Party's control over the military (with the CMC on the top, assisted by four headquarters departments, though not organized in Western fashion as true joint command and control apparatuses).

If new mission requirements and an emphasis on joint operations are forcing the PLAAF to rethink itself and its role, to reduce its force size, to acquire new aircraft and weapons systems, and to strengthen its command and control by informatization, none of these changes has seriously posed challenges to the existing organizational system of the PLA. The political culture and the military system of the PLA continue to ensure the Chinese air force remains as it has been—consisting of aviation, surface-to-air missiles, antiaircraft artillery, radar, and airborne troops, while space assets and strategic missiles remain separate from it. Despite the PLAAF's vision of being capable of both offensive and defensive operations, the PLA's current campaign theory defines the Second Artillery force as a preemptive strike force and projects the PLAAF to carry out offensive operations at critical, necessary moments. Thus, although the PLAAF is in the midst of a dramatic transformation with new weapons systems and growing capabilities, its role and influence remain limited within the contemporary, army-dominated, Chinese military system. As in other nations previously, differing and conflicting service cultures contribute frictions between services, though, in China, that has not brought any fundamental change of relationship among the land-air-sea forces. The continued existence of political constraints on when and how airpower should be used further limits and frustrates any role the air force can play in national policymaking.

Historically, the Chinese leadership has repeatedly demonstrated hesitation in employing its national airpower for offensive purposes. This was partly attributed to the Chinese leadership's misunderstanding of the PLAAF's actual experience in the Korean War and in homeland air defense operations during the Cold War, and to their ignorance (for various reasons) of the actual role that airpower can play in modern conflict. The other factor was because the PLAAF had been incapable, in any case, of conducting offensive operations, again for a variety of reasons such as available force structure, capabilities, and training.

The potential of a U.S. intervention is always seen as a major variable of a regional security equation, particularly in a crisis over Taiwan and the Taiwan Strait. While the PLAAF's modernization efforts may close the gap between its aircraft and avionic capabilities and those of the United States, its overall capability will continue to be inferior to that of the U.S. Air Force. The current and future Chinese leadership will continue to face and confront the same dilemmas as have its predecessors over the extent that political considerations and the PLAAF's restricted capabilities work to constrain Beijing's national security calculation and decisionmaking.

Nevertheless, it is undeniable that the PLA's warfighting potential has grown in parallel with China's economic surge. Assuming its economy continues along a steady trajectory, China will be able to commit further resources to the more challenging aspects of the three-step strategy, particularly informatization. Should these goals be realized, the United States and other powers will face a genuine challenge in preparing themselves to encounter increasingly capable Chinese aerospace power over the coming decades. This perhaps is the key rationale fueling continued interest in studying the steady evolution of the PLAAF as it progresses through the 21st century.

Notes

[1] The views expressed in this paper are those of the author and do not necessarily reflect the official policy or position of the Department of Air Force, the Department of Defense, or the U.S. Government.

2 Phillip C. Saunders and Erik Quam, "Future Force Structure of the Chinese Air Force," and Kevin M. Lanzit and Kenneth Allen, "Right-Sizing the PLA Air Force: New Operational Concepts Define A Smaller, More Capable Force," in *Right Sizing the People's Liberation Army: Exploring the Contours of China's Military*, eds. Roy Kamphausen and Andrew Scobell (Carlisle, PA: U.S. Army Strategic Studies Institute, 2007), 377–478.

[3] Kamphausen and Scobell, 12–14.

[4] Lü Liping, *Tongtian zhi lu* [The Road to the Sky] (Beijing: Jiefangjun Press, 1989), 144.

[5] From 1950 to 1956, 1 army group headquarters, 5 army headquarters, 19 divisional headquarters, and 41 regimental headquarters were transferred to air force headquarters and aviation divisions and regiments. See Liu Yalou, "The Initial Seven Years of Establishing the Air Force," in *Lantian zhi lu* [The Road to Blue Sky], eds. Gao Xinmin and Ding Wengchang, vol. 2 (Beijing: Political Department of Air Force, 1992), 4–5.

[6] For detailed discussion of the characteristics of the PLAAF in the early years, see Xiaoming Zhang, *Red Wings over the Yalu: China, the Soviet Union, and Air War in Korea, 1950–1953* (College Station, TX: Texas A&M University Press, 2002), 36–40; and "The Sixty-Year Endeavor to Increase Chinese Airpower" in *Global Air Power*, ed. John A. Olsen (Washington, DC: Potomac Books, Inc., 2011).

[7] He Tingyi, "The Establishment of Air Force Headquarters," in Gao and Ding, vol. 1, 199–205.

[8] This also results in Western misunderstanding of the PLAAF. See Kenneth W. Allen, Glenn Krumel, and Jonathan D. Pollack, *China's Air Force Enters the 21st Century*, RAND Document MR-580-AF (Santa Monica, CA: RAND, 1995), 37.

[9] Liu Pushao et al., "Biography of Zhu Guang," in *Zhongguo renmin zhiyuanjun renwu zhi* [Nanjing: Jiangsu People's Press, 1992], 309.

[10] Xiaoming Zhang, "Air Combat for the People's Republic: The People's Liberation Army Air Force in Action, 1949–1969," in *Chinese Warfighting: The PLA Experience Since 1949*, eds. Mark A. Ryan, David M. Finkelstein, and Michael A. McDevitt (Armonk, NY: M.E. Sharpe, 2003), 279–282.

[11] Lin Hu, *Baowei zuguo lingkong de zhandou* [Fight to Protect the Motherland's Airspace] (Beijing: Jiefangjun Press, 2002), 96. Xiaoming Zhang, "The Vietnam War, 1964–1969: A Chinese Perspective," *The Journal of Military History* 60, no. 4 (October 1996), 739–746.

[12] Lin, 272. For details about the establishment of the air force as the best example for other services to learn, see Wu Faxian, *Wu Faxian huiyilu* [Memoirs of Wu Faxian] (Hong Kong: Star Books, 2006), 510–511.

[13] "Sixty Years of the Chinese Air Force and the Capability of Its Equipment Grows," *Wenweipo* (Hong Kong) (November 22, 2009).

[14] According to the PLAAF encyclopedia, in addition to Mao, other Chinese political and military leaders who also made contributions to Chinese military thought on air force (*kongjun junshi sixiang*) are Premier Zhou Enlai, Chairman of CMC Deng Xiaoping, Party Secretary-General Jiang Zemin, and Marshalls Zhu De, Peng Dehuai, Xu Xiangqian, Nie Rongzhen, and Ye Jianying. Yao Wei, chief ed., *Zhongguo kongjun baike quanshu* [Encyclopedia of Chinese Air Force], vol. 1 (Beijing: Aviation Industry Press, 2005), 9–19.

[15] According to the authors of General Liu Yalou's biography, "elimination of the remnant enemy" was the PLAAF's contemporary mission, while "the consolidation of national defense" was its future one. "Mao's message to the air force, April, 1950," in *Liu Yalou jiangjun zhuan* [Biography of General Liu Yalou], Yang Wanqing and Qi Chunyuan (Beijing: CCP History Press, 1995), 284.

[16] Ibid., 18. This specific view was given by Marshall Xu Xiangqian.

[17] For example, see Deng Keyang, chief ed., *Deng Xiaoping kongjun jianshe sixiang yanjiu* [Study of Deng Xiaoping's Thought on the Construction of Air Force] (Beijing: National Defense University Press, 1997). Shang Jinshuo, chief ed., *Mao Zedong junshi sixiang yu xiandai kongjun zuozhan* [Mao Zedong's Military Thought and Modern Air Force Operations] (Beijing: Blue Sky Press, 2004).

[18] "Sixty Years of the Chinese Air Force."

[19] Zhang, *Red Wings over the Yalu*, 185.

[20] Zhang, "Air Combat for the People's Republic," 284.

[21] Zhang Zhizhi, "The Air Force Troops in the Self-Defensive Counterattacks against Vietnam," in Gao and Ding, vol. 2, 355.

[22] Wang Hai, *Wo de zhandou shengya* [My Career in Warfighting] (Beijing: Central Archival and Manuscript Press, 2000), 281.

[23] Lin Hu, "The Air Force's Armament Work during the Seventh Five-Year-Plan Period," in Gao and Ding, vol. 2, 514.

[24] Zhan Yulian, ed., *Zhanyu xue* [Operational Art] (Beijing: National Defense University Press, 2006), 543–44.

[25] Hua Renjie et al., *Kongjun xueshu sixiang shi* [The History of the Academic Thinking of the Air Force] (Beijing: Jiefangjun Press, 2008), 368.

[26] Liu Huaqing, *Liu Huaqing huiyilu* [Memoirs of Liu Huaqing] (Beijing: Jiefangjun Press, 2004), 581–582; Ye Huinan, "Four Major Changes of Our Country's National Defense Strategy since Its Founding," *Dangdai Zhongguo shi yanjiu* [Studies of Modern Chinese History], no. 3 (1999), 8.

[27] Shao Zhenting, Zhang Zhengping, and Hu Jianping, "Theoretical Thinking on Deng Xiaoping's Views on the Buildup of the Air Force and the Reform of Operational Arts," *Zhongguo junshi kexue* [China Military Science], no. 4 (1996), 47.

[28] He Weirong, "Military Thought on the Air Force," in Yao, 1, 4.

²⁹ Dong Wenxian, *Xiandai kongjun lun (xupian)* [On the Modern Air Force (continuation)] (Beijing: Lantian Press, 2005), 47.

³⁰ "China's National Defense Paper in 2008," at <www.gov.cn/english/official/200901/20/content_210227.htm>.

³¹ Dai Xu, "Goodbye, Old J–6 Fighters: A Complete Examination of the Service History of the Last Meritorious Fighter in the Chinese Air Force with Combat Victory Record," *Guoji zhanwang* [World Outlook], no. 19 (2005), 21.

³² Shang Jinsuo, chief ed., *Kongjun jianshe xue* [Science of Air Force Construction] (Beijing: Jiefangjun Press, 2009), 557–558.

³³ China does not make the PLAAF aviation order of battle publicly available. China-Defense.com forum provides some order of battle information. Currently a total of 13 Su–27/30 and J–11 regiments are operational with two more coming. See <www.china-defense.com/forum/index.php?showforum=5>.

³⁴ Office of the Secretary of Defense, *Military Power of the People's Republic of China* (Washington, DC: DOD, 2000), 21; and Office of the Secretary of Defense, *Military and Security Developments Involving the People's Republic of China* (Washington, DC: DOD, 2010), 62.

³⁵ Lanzit and Allen predict that the PLAAF operational air units would have reduced down to fewer than 30 divisions. "Right-Sizing the PLA Air Force," 446, 465.

³⁶ China News reported that the PLAAF's 1950s vintage Jian–6s had been completely phased out from the air force by June 2010. *China [Xinhua] News*, June 13, 2010, <www.news.xinhuanet.com/mil/201006/13/content_13661716.htm>.

³⁷ For China's military aircraft program, see "Procurement, China," Jane's *Sentinel Security Assessment—China and Northeast Asia*, July 8, 2010, Jane's Information Group, at <www.janes.com>.

³⁸ Cai Fengzhen and Tian Anping, *Kongtian yiti zuozhan xue* [Study of Integrated Aerospace Operations] (Beijing: Jiefangjun Press, 2006), 287–301.

³⁹ Ibid., 554–556.

⁴⁰ According to a *Jiefangjun bao* [People's Liberation Army Daily] report on March 31, 2008, for the first time, during a regular training day of an unidentified air division, a regiment commander conducted his command and control role in an Airborne Warning and Control System (AWACS) aircraft. See "The Change of Command Mode by One Air Force Division Increases Its Combat Capability: Command Post Flies from the Ground into the Sky," *Jiefangjun bao*, March 31, 2008, 2. Another *PLA Daily* report indicates that Chinese AWACS aircraft flew command and control missions for the 2008 Olympic Games. See Xu Qiliang, "The Dream Flies in Reform and Opening Up," *Jiefangjun bao*, November 4, 2008.

⁴¹ He Yi, "Special Interview of Wang Xiaomo, Member of Chinese Academy of Engineering, and Chief Designer of Our Country's Early Warning Aircraft," *Bingqi zhishi* [Ordnance Knowledge] no. 11A (2009), 12–16.

⁴² Martin Sieff, "Airlift the Key to True Superpower Capability Part One," December 12, 2008, <www.spacewar.com/report/Airlift_The_To_True_Superpower_Capability_Part_999.html>; Vladimir Isachenkov, "Russia Faces an Aging Defense Industry," July 20, 2008, at <http://article.latimes.com/2008/jul/20/world/fg-russia20plr>, accessed March 21, 2009.

⁴³ *Jiefangjun bao* [People's Liberation Army Daily], June 24, 2009.

⁴⁴ Saunders and Quam, 401.

⁴⁵ Graham Allison and Phillip Zelikow, *Essence of Decision: Explaining the Cuban Missile Crisis*, 2ᵈ ed. (New York: Addison-Wesley Educational Publishers, 1999), 175.

⁴⁶ Yao vol. 1, 15, 39.

⁴⁷ "From a Soldier to a Member of Chinese Academy of Engineering: A Story of Li Ming," on the Web site of Chinese Academy of Engineering, at <www.cae.cn/cn/yuanshifengcai/yuanshifengcai/20090615/cae474.html>.

⁴⁸ Dong Wenxian, *Xiandai kongjun lun (xubian)* [On the Modern Air Force (continuation)], 263–265.

⁴⁹ For example, the air force and navy have long experienced the technological generation gap, but it is not the case for the army, which has been close to the top level of the world except for army aviation.

⁵⁰ Lanzit and Allen, 461.

[51] For a detailed discussion, see Kenneth Allen, "PLA Air Force Organization," in *PLA as Organization: Reference*, eds. James C. Mulvenon and Andrew Yang, vol. 1.0 (Santa Monica, CA: RAND, 2002), 346–457.

[52] Dong, 268–269.

[53] Liu Yazhou, "Essences for an Offensive and Defensive Chinese Air Force," in *Liu Yazhou zhanlue wenji* [A Collection of Liu Yazhou's Papers on Strategy] (n. p.: n. p., n. d.), 394–397.

[54] During the recent joint military exercises either inside or outside China, air force officers have been always assigned to a deputy position.

[55] Ren Lijun, Wang Deshun, and Wang Yehong, "Identify the Major Strategic Direction, Strengthen Air Force Finance Development," *Junshi jinji yanjiu* [Military Economic Study], no. 7 (2008), 52–53.

[56] Dong 327–328, 373, 389.

[57] Cai Fengzhen et al., *Kongtian yiti zuozhan xue* [Study of Integrated Air and Space Operations] (Beijing: PLA Press, 2006), 287–301; Shan Jinsuo and Li Niguang, "Creative Development of the Party's Guiding Theory of Air Force Building," *Zhongguo junshi kexue* 20, no. 5 (2007), 45.

[58] "The Development of the Joint Strike Flying Leopard for the Air Force," *Hangkong shijie* [Aviation World], no. 5 (2005), 38–39.

[59] Chinese Military Aviation Web site, at <http://cnair.top81.cn/J-10_J-11_FC-1.htm>.

[60] Yan Zhen, "Training Fighting Eagles to Fly to the Ultimate Limit," *Jiefangjun bao* [People's Liberation Army Daily] (February 22, 2010).

[61] Liu Yazhou, "Essences for an Offensive and Defensive Chinese Air Force," 427–430.

[62] Zhan, *Zhanyi xue*, 99.

[63] Ibid., 527–528.

[64] Ibid., 544.

[65] Ibid., 99.

[66] Ibid., 99–100.

[67] Liu, *Liu Huaqing huiyi lu*, 606–613.

[68] State Council Information Office, *China's National Defense in 2008*, 26.

[69] After several rounds of force reduction, the PLA Navy maintains its AAA units, which still operate outdated antiaircraft artilleries. A recent news report suggests they are upgraded with a new radar system. <http://news.ifeng.com/mil/jsdg/200909/0908_6242_1339093.shtml>.

[70] Wang Fengshan, Li Xiaojun, Ma Shuanzhu, et al., *Xiandai fangkong xue* [Science of Modern Air Defense] (Beijing: Aviation Industry Press, 2008), 3, 132.

[71] According to Chinese Internet information, the PLAAF has 105 SAM battalions, of which about two-thirds remain equipped with HQ-2 SAMs.

[72] *Zhongguo Qingnian Bao Online*, August 6, 2010.

PART II
ORGANIZATION, LEADERSHIP, AND DOCTRINE

Chapter 4

The Organizational Structure of the PLAAF

Kenneth W. Allen

Any examination of the People's Liberation Army Air Force (PLAAF) (人民解放军空军) must examine its organizational structure (体制编制), answering three fundamental questions: What is the PLAAF's current organizational structure and what are the historical, theoretical, bureaucratic, and other reasons for it?[1] What are the implications of the current organizational structure for the PLAAF's future development? Finally, how might the PLAAF's organizational structure change in order to operate in a joint conflict?

Introduction

During the 1990s, the PLAAF began purchasing high-tech weapons from abroad, as well as developing and purchasing them domestically, including combat aircraft (such as the Russian Sukhoi Su–27), surface-to-air missiles (SAMs, such as the SA–10), and radar and electronic countermeasures (ECM) systems that now form the cornerstone of its table of organization and equipment (TOE). In order to support these systems, the PLAAF has also begun implementing significant organizational changes that have mirrored similar changes occurring in the rest of the PLA.

Starting in the early 2000s, PLAAF officers began to assume key joint billets, including membership on the Chinese Communist Party's (CCP's) Central Military Commission (CMC), commandant of the Academy of Military Science, commandant and political commissar of the National Defense University, and deputy director billets in the General Staff Department (GSD), General Political Department (GPD), and General Logistics Department (GLD). Although these appointments are impressive, not all of them are permanent PLAAF billets. In addition, the army still dominates the majority of the leadership and working billets in all of these organizations, along with the General Armament Department (GAD), which has yet to have a PLAAF (or PLA Navy) deputy, and all seven of the Military Region (MR) Headquarters. There are no indications this pattern of army domination will change in the next decade.

Concerning the PLAAF's branches, one of the most significant organizational changes occurred within the last decade, when the PLAAF redesignated its radar branch as a specialty force. Even though the PLAAF's ECM troops are also considered a specialty force, the PLAAF has consolidated their administrative structure into a PLAAF Electronic Countermeasures and Radar Department under the Headquarters Department and merged the research and development for the two forces into a single research institute under the Air Force Equipment Research Academy. Yet another significant change occurred in 1993, when the 15th Airborne Corps upgraded its three brigades to divisions, was designated the lead element for the PLA's rapid reaction force, and changed from being subordinate to the Guangzhou Military Region Air Force (MRAF) to being directly subordinate to PLAAF Headquarters.[2] Although the airborne corps still lacks sufficient airlift capabilities, since the early 1990s it has shifted from having primarily an internal security mission to a combined internal and external security mission.

Starting in the late 1990s, the PLAAF began to restructure its academic institution and equipment support structures. To help provide better education to its cadets and meet operational support requirements, the PLAAF consolidated several colleges into two universities—Air Force Engineering University (1999) and Air Force Aviation University (2004)—and restructured some of its other colleges—Xuzhou (Logistics) Air Force College, Guilin (Antiaircraft Artillery and Airborne) Air Force College, and flight colleges. At the same time, however, the PLAAF has increased the number of new officers who have graduated from the Defense Student (国防生) program at 18 civilian academic institutions. This program is also called the Reserve Officer (后备军官) program. The goal for 2010 was to have 60 percent of all new officers come from civilian academic institutions, of which two-thirds would come from the Defense Student Program and one-third from directly recruited civilian college graduates with science and engineering degrees; however, a November 2009 *Jiefangjun Bao* article stated that the PLA's officer corps receives about 100,000 graduates per year, of which 70 percent come from military academic institutions and 30 percent from the Defense Student program.[3] The number of pilot cadets who have been recruited from civilian college graduates and students rather than from high school graduates and enlisted personnel is also rising. These changes will continue to challenge the size and structure of the PLAAF's academic institutions and may necessitate further consolidation over the next decade.

Over the past decade, the PLAAF's logistics support structure has mirrored changes that have occurred in the GLD, which is roughly equivalent to the U.S. Joint Chiefs of Staff's J–4 (Logistics) Directorate. One of the biggest changes occurred in 1998 when the PLAAF's Logistics Department, which had been responsible for providing maintenance support for all nonaviation equipment and weapons systems (e.g., SAMs, AAA, radars), turned over support for all of this equipment, except vehicles, to the PLAAF's restructured Equipment Department. In addition, during the 2000s, the GLD and PLAAF consolidated their Quartermaster Department, Materials Department, and Petroleum, Oil, and Lubricants (POL) Department into a single Quartermaster, Materials, and POL Department. Even though these organizations have been merged at the top, they remain separated as individual branches at the regiment level.

Concerning the equipment support structure, two major changes have occurred since the late 1990s. The first occurred in 1998, when the PLA established the GAD and the PLAAF adjusted its existing equipment support structure, so that the restructured Equipment Department took responsibility for developing and supporting all combat equipment and weapons systems, except vehicles, from birth to death. In 2004, the PLAAF also created a new Air Force Equipment Research Academy that became responsible for managing the research and development for all PLAAF combat equipment and weapons systems. There are no indications the equipment support structure, which is fully integrated with the logistics support structure at the regiment and below levels, will change appreciably over the next decade.

Current Organizational Structure

The PLAAF's organizational structure is a complicated one.[4] The 2002 and 2008 editions of *China's National Defense* state:[5]

> Concerning the PLA Air Force organizational structure, the Air Force practices a leadership system that combines operational command with Air Force building and management. The organizational system consists of Air Force Headquarters, seven Military Region Air Force Headquarters, [deputy] corps- and division-level command posts (CPs), divisions, brigades, and regiments. The Air Force [has] four branches—aviation, surface-to-air missile (SAM), antiaircraft artillery (AAA), and airborne—plus five types of specialty forces—communications, radar, electronic countermeasures, chemical defense, and technical reconnaissance. The Air Force also has education, research, testing, and training institutions.

According to PLAAF writings, the air force's organizational structure or military system (空军军制) consists of 11 components, each of which has various subcomponents, some of which overlap.[6] These are the organizational system (组织体制);[7] leadership and command system (领导指挥体制);[8] establishment (e.g., table of organization and equipment / TOE) system (编制);[9] education and training system (教育训练体制);[10] scientific research system (科学研究机构组织体制);[11] political work (整治工作);[12] logistics support (后勤保障体制);[13] equipment management (装备管理体制);[14] equipment technical support (装备技术保障);[15] personnel management (人事管理);[16] and mobilization (动员体制) and reserve forces (后备力量建设).[17] Each is subsequently examined.[18]

PLAAF Grade Structures

Familiarity with the PLA's 15-grade and 10-rank structure, which applies to officers and organizations for all the services and branches, is the key to understanding the PLAAF's organizational structure. The current system became effective in 1988 and is based on ground force terminology. Although this paper refers to the grade and rank system only in passing, it is important to understand the basics of the system as it provides the basis for hierarchical and cross-organizational relationships throughout the PLA.[19]

According to *PLAAF 2010*, there are four key differences between the U.S. military and the PLA in terms of their use of grade and rank. First and most importantly, in the PLA, rank is not as important as grade. The PLA uses rank insignia primarily as a visual cue to identify an individual's approximate status; military grade is the more accurate reflection of one's status.[20] Second, the PLA assigns billets based on one's grade, not rank. Third, promotion in grade, not rank, is what determines how one moves up the career ladder. For example, moving from senior colonel to major general while remaining in the same grade is not as important as moving from one grade to the next, even if one retains the same rank. Finally, the PLA assigns every organization, not just officers and billets, a grade, as shown in table 4–1. The grade system is what defines the organizational structure and the relationship among organizations.

Organizational System

The PLAAF organizational system includes PLAAF Headquarters (空军 / 军委空军), seven MRAFs (军区空军), four branches (兵种), operational units (作战部队), and logistics support units (后勤保障部队).[22] The PLAAF further divides it into two separate systems based on missions (任务) and work characteristics (工作性质). The mission-based system is discussed below; the work characteristics system is discussed in the leadership and command section.

The role of PLAAF Headquarters is a crucial one. Unfortunately, no PLA or PLAAF definition or specific information about the overall roles and missions of the headquarters is readily available. Nevertheless, it is safe to assume the role of the headquarters is to conduct "Air Force Building" (空军建设).[23] Air Force Building includes organizing, manning, educating and training, equipping, providing logistics and maintenance support, and providing operational, political, and support policy guidance for the strategic, operational, and tactical levels of conflict to the PLAAF during peacetime and wartime.[24] While the Party Committee system limits the role of the commander during peacetime, during wartime the commander enjoys expanded responsibilities and authorities consistent with his responsibility for implementing the war plan that the Party Committee has already approved during peacetime.

Table 4–1. PLAAF Grade and Rank System*

Grade	Primary Rank	Secondary Rank
Central Military Commission (CMC) Chairman (军委主席)	None	
Vice Chairman (军委副主席)	General**	
CMC Member (军委委员)	General	
Military Region Leader (正大军区职)	General	Lieutenant General
Military Region Deputy Leader (副大军区职)	Lieutenant General	Major General
Corps Leader (正军职)	Major General	Lieutenant General
Corps Deputy Leader (副军职)	Major General	Senior Colonel
Division Leader (正师职)	Senior Colonel	Major General
Division Deputy Leader (副师长)	Colonel	Senior Colonel
Regiment Leader (正团职)	Colonel	Lieutenant Colonel
Regiment Deputy Leader (副团长)	Lieutenant Colonel	Major
Battalion Leader (正营职)	Major	Lieutenant Colonel
Battalion Deputy Leader (副营长)	Captain	Major
Company Leader (正连职)	Captain	1st Lieutenant
Company Deputy Leader (副连长)	1st Lieutenant	Captain
Platoon Leader (排职)	2d Lieutenant	1st Lieutenant

* The People's Liberation Army (PLA) uses the term *yizhi liangxian* (一职两衔) to refer to one grade with two ranks. Xu Ping, ed., *Discussion of Chinese and Foreign Ranks* (漫谈中外军衔) (Beijing: Jincheng Press, January 2002), 199. Although most PLA grades have a leader (正职) and deputy leader (副职) grade, they are often lumped together. For example, PLA writings refer to the corps level (军级) or division level (师级), which includes both the leader and deputy leader grades.

** The chairman and civilian vice chairman do not wear military rank insignia.

Although the PLAAF and the U.S. Air Force (USAF) are organized completely differently, table 4–2 provides a rough comparison between their headquarters structures.

According to the *Air Force Encyclopedia*, the PLAAF's mission-based systems consist of four components.[25] These are the department system (机关体制), which is organized into different types and levels;[26] the unit system (部队体制);[27] the academic institutions system (院校体制); and the scientific research system (科研体制).

The PLAAF Department System

The *department system* consists of what the PLAAF calls *bumen* (部门), which is the generic term for the four first-level departments—*Headquarters* (司令部), *Political* (政治部), *Logistics* (后勤部), and *Equipment* (装备部)—and their subordinate second- and third-level departments (部), bureaus (局), divisions (处), offices (科), and/or branches (股). With only a few exceptions where a battalion has a Headquarters Department, there are no *bumen* below the regiment level. The PLAAF has three general categories of *bumen*, which include administrative departments (行政部门), functional/professional departments (业务部门), and operational departments (事业部门). Unfortunately, no clear definition is available for these three categories of departments, and some of them overlap.

Table 4–2. PLAAF and USAF Headquarters Comparison

PLAAF Headquarters	USAF Headquarters
[No Civilian/State Component]	Secretary of the Air Force
--	Secretariat
Commander and Political Commissar (PC)	Chief of Staff of the Air Force
Command Staff	Air Staff
5–6 Deputy Commanders/2–3 Deputy PCs	Vice Chief of Staff
[No enlisted advisor]	Chief Master Sergeant of the Air Force
4 Departments	A1–A9
7 Military Region Air Forces	9 Major Commands

Based on a review of the terms in various dictionaries, encyclopedias, and interviews with PLA personnel, we can conclude the following: Administrative departments conduct work that affects daily life, such as support and supplies, logistics, and housing. Functional/professional departments conduct work that affects operations, such as the operations, intelligence, training, finance, and health departments. Operating departments is a general category for all functional/professional departments (other than finance) that have some degree of financial responsibility, but with limited budgetary responsibility. Examples include military schools, hospitals, warehouses, scientific research organizations, military transportation representative organizations, and military representative organizations stationed at factories.

Overall, the department system has not changed appreciably for almost 60 years, and may be compared to a deck of cards with four suits—Headquarters, Political, Logistics, and Equipment—that have occasionally shifted a few cards from one suit to the other. It is important to pay attention, however, when a new card appears or an old card shifts to another suit, because such changes do not occur randomly. Each of these is discussed in sequence.[28]

Headquarters Department. The Headquarters Department (空司) is the highest-level functional and administrative organization within PLAAF

Headquarters that is responsible for what the PLAAF calls "military work" (军事工作) or "command work" (指挥工作) on behalf of the PLAAF's Party Committee and leadership.[29] Its primary responsibilities include managing unit deployments, battlefield development, and combat command. It is also responsible for the PLAAF's organizational structure, personnel management, enlisted force personnel records, intelligence, communications, radar, air traffic control, and weather support, as well as researching air force military theory, and managing education and safety. Leadership of the PLAAF's Headquarters Department includes the chief of staff (参谋长), who is the department director, and five deputy chiefs of staff (副参谋长). Each deputy chief of staff is responsible for guiding and monitoring activities in two or more second-level departments.

The Headquarters Department has at least 15 second-level departments, each of which has subordinate third-level departments. These are the General Office (办公室), Directly Subordinate Work Department (直工部), Operations Department (作战部), Intelligence Department (情报部), Communications Department (通信部), Military Training Department (军训部), Military Professional Education Department (军事职业教育部),[30] Military Affairs Department (军务部), Ground-Based Air Defense Troops Department (地面防空兵部), Electronic Countermeasures and Radar Department (电子对抗雷达部), Air Traffic Control Department (航空管制部), Military Theory Research Department (军事理论研究部), Pilot Recruitment Bureau (招飞局), Technology Bureau (技术局), Weather Bureau (气象局), and Flight Safety Bureau (飞行安全局). The PLAAF Headquarters' command post (CP) is subordinate to the Headquarters Department, with the Chief of Staff as its director. Personnel from throughout the Headquarters Department (especially from Operations, as well as relevant personnel from the Logistics and Equipment Departments), man the CP on a rotational basis.[31]

Political Department. The Political Department (空政) is the highest-level leadership, functional, and administrative organization within PLAAF Headquarters for political work.[32] The Political Department is responsible for keeping officer personnel records, propaganda, security, education, cultural activities, civil-military relations, Party discipline, and Party organizations within the PLAAF. The leadership of the PLAAF's Political Department includes the director (主任) and three deputy directors (副主任). Each deputy director is responsible for guiding and monitoring activities in one or more second-level departments.

The seven primary second-level departments, each of which has several subordinate third-level departments, are the following: Headquarters Department (司令部), Organization Department (组织部), Cadre (Officer Personnel) Department (干部部), Propaganda Department (宣传部), Security Department (保卫部), Discipline and Inspection Department (纪检部), and Liaison Department (联络部).

Logistics Department. The Logistics Department (空后) is the highest-level leadership, functional, and administrative organization within PLAAF Headquarters for logistics work, which includes overseeing transportation, finances, materials and supplies, POL, and medical care.[33] The leadership of the PLAAF's Logistics Department includes the director (部长), political commissar (政治委员 / 政委), three deputy directors (副部长), one deputy political commissar (副政委), a chief of staff (参谋长) (e.g., director of the Headquarters Department), and director of the Political Department (政治部主任). The 12 second-level departments, each of which has several third-level departments, are the following: Headquarters Department (司令部), Political Department (政治部), Finance Department (财务部), Quartermaster, Materials, and POL Department (军需物资油料部), Health Department (卫生部), Military Transportation Department (军交运输部), Airfield and Barracks Department (机场营房部), Directly Subordinate Supply Department (直属供应部), Air Force National Defense Engineering Development Command Department (空军国防工程建设指挥部), Audit Bureau (审计局), Real Estate Management Bureau (房地产管理局), and Air Force Engineering and Design Research Bureau (空军工程设计研究局).

Equipment Department. When the PLAAF was founded in November 1949, it created an Air Force Engineering Department (空军工程部) to manage aircraft maintenance; however, in September 1969, it was abolished, leaving the PLAAF with only three first-level departments. Because of significant aircraft maintenance problems during the Cultural Revolution, the PLAAF created the Aeronautical Engineering Department (空军航空工程部) on May 1, 1976 as the fourth first-level department with the responsibility of managing aircraft maintenance and providing representatives at aviation-related factories. In 1992, the name was changed to the Air Force Equipment Technical Department (空军装备技术部), but it still had the same responsibilities.[34] In 1998, the name was changed to the Equipment Department (装备部 / 空装). At that time, the second-level Equipment Department and Scientific Research Department from the Headquarters Department, along with the second-level Armament Department from the Logistics Department, were merged into the new Equipment Department. According to *PLAAF 2010*, the Equipment Department is the highest-level leadership, functional, and administrative organization within PLAAF Headquarters for equipment work, which includes the birth-to-death life-cycle management, repair, and maintenance of all PLAAF weapons systems and equipment.

The leadership of the PLAAF's Equipment Department includes the director (部长), political commissar (PC), five deputy directors (副部长), one deputy PC, and director of the Political Department (政治部主任).

The eight second-level departments (each of which has several third-level departments) are the following: Comprehensive Planning Department (综合计划部), which also serves the function of a Headquarters Department;

Political Department (政治部); Field Maintenance Department (外场部); Scientific Research and Procurement Department (科研订货部); Air Materiel Department (航材部); Aviation Engineering Management Department (航空工程管理部); Armament Common-Use Equipment Department (军械通用装备部); and Air Force Armament General-Use Equipment Military Representative Bureau (空军军械通用装备军事代表局).[35]

PLAAF Unit System

According to *Modern Military Organizational Reform Research*, which was written by the Academy of Military Science, the PLAAF's unit system (部队体制) consists of four components.[36] These are the PLAAF's branches and specialty/specialized forces/units; the PLAAF's leadership and command tiered structure; the PLAAF's operational units; and the personnel and force reductions within the PLAAF. The leadership and command tiered structure is discussed later in this text, so the following addresses the other three.

Branches and Specialty Forces. Until the early 2000s, the PLAAF had five branches (兵种)—aviation, SAM, AAA, radar, and airborne.[37] This apparently changed in the early 2000s, whereby the PLAAF now has only four—aviation, SAM, AAA, and airborne—plus five types of specialty forces (专业部/分队)—communications, radar, ECM, chemical defense, and technical reconnaissance.[38]

Operational Units. Depending on the type of unit, the PLAAF's branches and specialty forces are organized into divisions, brigades, regiments, battalions, companies, platoons, and squads. Today, the only operational corps is the 15th Airborne Corps, discussed subsequently. Table 4–3 provides an overview of the types of operational units and their headquarters levels.[39]

Table 4–3. PLAAF Operational Units and Headquarters Levels

	Aviation	SAM	AAA	Airborne	Radar	Communications	ECM	Chemical Defense	Technical Reconnaissance
Corps				x					
Division	x	x		x					
Brigade	x	x	x		x		x		
Regiment	x	x	x	x	x	x	x	x	x
Battalion	x	x	x	x	x	x	x	x	x
Company	x	x	x	x	x	x		x	x
Platoon				x		x		x	

AAA: antiaircraft artillery   ECM: electronic countermeasures   SAM: surface-to-air missile

According to *PLAAF 2010*, the PLAAF currently has 29 operational air divisions—20 fighter, 3 ground attack, 3 bomber, and 3 transport divisions. From 1950 to 1971, the PLAAF created 50 operational air divisions that were stationed throughout China. This situation did not change until 1986, when the PLAAF began converting one air division in each of the seven military regions to a division-level transition training base (改装训练基地). Since then, the PLAAF has gradually reduced the remaining 43 operational air divisions to 29. While most of these divisions have only two subordinate regiments, some have three. The PLAAF also has several independent helicopter and transport regiments. As a general rule, a division can have more than one model of aircraft, but each regiment has the same model for training, logistics, and maintenance support purposes. The reduction in the number of divisions has taken place in order to incorporate new types of aircraft, retire older aircraft, meet new mission requirements, and reduce personnel. Although there are fewer aircraft today, their capabilities far exceed those of the F–6, A–5, and earlier versions of the F–7, F–8, and B–6.[40]

In December 2011, the PLAAF began creating air brigades (航空兵旅) in at least the Shenyang, Lanzhou, Nanjing, and Guangzhou MRAFs. Each brigade has several subordinate battalion leader-grade flight groups (飞行大队), which are most likely treated as regiments. The goal is to have each flight group equipped with a different type of aircraft, including trainers, ground attack, and fighters, so that the air brigade is multifunctional.[41] As of early 2012, it was not yet clear if these brigades are upgraded regiments, downgraded divisions, or a combination of both.

The airborne force, the 15th Airborne Corps, consists of three subordinate divisions, each of which is organized into regiments, battalions, and companies. The three divisions are composed of infantry, motorized infantry equipped with light vehicles, mechanized infantry, artillery, air defense (AAA and SAM), special operations, communications, special forces, reconnaissance, engineering, helicopter, training, and logistics support.[42] Unfortunately, no authoritative information is available about the SAM or AAA order of battle in terms of numbers and types of units or numbers of missiles and guns. However, according to the Department of Defense's 2010 report on the PLA, "The PLAAF has continued to expand its inventory of long-range, advanced SAM systems and now possesses one of the largest such forces in the world."[43] The report does not discuss the PLAAF's AAA force.

Number of Personnel. The PLAAF has not provided public information about the current number of personnel, including the number and percentage of officers and enlisted personnel by rank; however, Xu Guangyu, a retired PLA major general from the General Staff Department, published an article in July 2010 that states the PLAAF constitutes about 12 percent of the 2.3 million-man PLA, which equates to 276,000 personnel.[44] Since 1949, the PLAAF has implemented 10 force reductions (精简), all of which were part of larger PLA force reductions. While some of the reductions affected the entire force, others focused strictly on certain levels of headquarters. Although the figures available in different PLA sources are often inconsistent, it appears that, in September 1953, the PLAAF increased its personnel from the existing 210,000 to 257,000. PLAAF reporting states that, in 1972, it had its highest number of personnel, but the number was not specified. By the end of 1976, the force was somewhere between 16.4 percent and 26.9 percent less than 1972.[45] Since then, the PLAAF has averaged force reductions of 10–20 percent each time the PLA has instituted a force reduction.[46] Again according to Xu Guangyu, the PLA will reduce its force in stages over the next 20 years to about 1.5 million, which will result in a reduction in the army's percentage and an increase in the PLAAF's percentage.[47]

According to *PLAAF 2010*, all PLAAF officers serve in one of five possible career tracks: *military officer* (军事军官, also identified as the command officer [指挥军官] track), *political officer* (政治军官), *logistics officer* (后勤军官), *equipment officer* (装备军官), and *technical officer* (技术军官). These career tracks are not further broken down into Air Force Specialty Codes (AFSCs) similar to the USAF's personnel system. Depending on the career track, they are assigned to all PLAAF organizations, including headquarters, operational, support, research, and academic organizations.[48] Military officers serve as unit commanders, deputy commanders, and staff officers (参谋) in the Headquarters Department. They are responsible for operations, intelligence, training, unit organizational structure, enlisted force records, and communications. Political officers serve as unit political commissars (PCs), deputy PCs, and staff officers (干事) in the Political Department. They are responsible for conducting all political work, which includes that related to keeping officer personnel records, propaganda, security, cultural activities, civil-military relations, Party discipline, and Party organizations. Logistics officers serve as the director, deputy director, and staff officers (参谋) in the unit's Logistics Department. They are responsible for managing logistics support, which includes overseeing transportation, finances, materials and supplies, POL, housing, airfields, and medical care. Equipment officers serve as the director, deputy director, and staff officers (参谋) in the unit's Equipment Department. They are responsible for managing the development, acquisition, maintenance, and repair of all equipment and weapons systems. They also serve as representatives in civilian research institutes and factories that develop and produce aviation systems and equipment. Technical officers serve primarily as engineers, weapons system and equipment maintenance and repair officers, computer technicians, academics, and doctors. A high percentage of civilian college graduates who join the PLAAF as officers serve in this track. The grouping based on work characteristics consists of four systems, which equate to four of the five officer career tracks, and are aligned with the four departments:[49] military (command) leadership system (军事领导体制); political leadership system (政治领导体制); logistics leadership system (后勤领导体制) and equipment leadership system (装备领导体制).

PLAAF Leadership and Command System

The PLAAF's leadership and command system (领导指挥体制) consists of the Party Congress (党代表大会), Party Committees (党委), the leaders (领导首长), and the four departments (机关, Headquarters, Political, Logistics, and Equipment, discussed previously). The PLAAF's leadership and command system also refers to the following headquarters levels: PLAAF Headquarters, MRAF Headquarters, deputy corps- and division leader-level CPs, division and brigade headquarters, and regiment headquarters.[50]

Party Congresses and Party Committees: Party members elect members of the PLAAF Party Congress, and, once elected, the Party Congress members are responsible for discussing and deciding on key PLAAF issues. The Party Congress is also responsible for electing the members of the PLAAF Party Committee.[51] The Party Committee, in turn, then elects a Standing Committee (党委常委) and Discipline Inspection Commission (纪律检查委员会).[52] According to *PLAAF 2010*, in most cases, the PC serves as the Party secretary and the commander serves as the deputy secretary. In some situations, the commander is the secretary and the political officer is the deputy secretary. For example, three PLAAF commanders—Wu Faxian, Zhang Tingfa, and Qiao Qingchen—were the also the Party secretary as a result of having previously served as the PLAAF PC.[53] The PLAAF has had eleven Party Congresses since 1956—averaging one every 5 years over the past three decades. The 11th Party Congress was held in May 2009. Over the past 20 years, the number of representatives has averaged around 280–300, the number of Party Committee members has averaged around 40–45, and the number of members of the Discipline Inspection Commission has averaged around 10–11. The PLAAF's Standing Committee currently has 11 members.

While the Party Congresses meet only once every 5 years, the Party Committee meets about twice a year to review the Standing Committee's actions and to decide important PLAAF issues. Meanwhile, the Party Committee's Standing Committee is responsible for making the daily decisions concerning the PLAAF, but is responsible to the Party Committee for its decisions. Besides each regiment and above-level headquarters having its own Party Committee (部队党委), every first-, second-, and third-level department has its own Party Committee (机关党委), with the director as the Party secretary and one of the deputy directors as the deputy secretary. In the case of the Logistics Department and Equipment Department, however, the PC is the secretary and the director is the deputy secretary.

PLAAF Leaders: The commander (司令员) and PC (政治委员 / 政委) are the air force's highest leaders (最高首长).[54] Of particular note, the PC and commander are co-equals and, with only a few exceptions, serve as the secretary and deputy secretary of the PLAAF's Party committee, respectively.[55] One PLA political works book states that, together, the commander and PC are responsible under the PLAAF Party Committee's guidance for all types of work (各项工作).[56] Under the guidance of the Party Committee's unified leadership, the commander and PC together are responsible for dividing up leadership responsibilities for subordinate units.[57] Based on interviews with PLA officers over the past two decades, in general, this means that the commander is responsible for operational and support work while the PC is responsible for political work.[58] This does not mean, however, that the PC, as the Party secretary or deputy secretary, cannot provide input into operational issues.

Most importantly, the PLAAF's leaders at every level consist of the members of the Party Committee's Standing Committee, who also make up the command staff.[59] The PLAAF's Party Committee Standing Committee, not just the commander, at every level is responsible for making important decisions. During the meeting, everyone has an equal vote; however, once the decision is made, then every member is responsible for implementing it.[60] Unlike the USAF, PLAAF Headquarters averages five to six deputy commanders and two to three deputy PCs, while units down to the regiment level can have two to three deputy commanders and one to two deputy PCs. Based on a review of PLAAF sources, each deputy commander has a portfolio that covers two or more tasks that appear to match up with the second-level departments within the first-level Headquarters, Logistics, and Equipment Departments. While some deputy commanders may have responsibilities within only a single first-level department, others have responsibilities in more than one department.[61] The following is a brief overview of the PLAAF's commanders, PCs, deputy commanders, and chiefs of staff.[62]

Since 1949, the PLAAF has had 10 commanders. As a group, they average 17 years-old when first joining the service. Given the overall poor education system and political turmoil in China until the 1980s, none of them had even a high school degree when they joined. At first, aviation experience did not constitute a command requirement; only in 1973 did the PLAAF have a commander who was himself a pilot, Ma Ning.[63] His successor, Zhang Tingfa, was not a pilot, but since Zhang, all PLAAF commanders have been pilots. Beginning with Ma, they all received 1 to 2 years of basic flight training at a PLAAF flight school, which served as their undergraduate-level education. Additionally, most of them have taken intermediate- or advanced-level professional military education courses.[64] Since 1977, five of the seven commanders took office when they were 60–63 years old and, on average, remained in office until 65–67. The current commander, General Xu Qiliang, joined the PLAAF at age 16, became the commander in 2007 at age 57 and will most likely remain on active duty until at least the CCP's 19th Party Congress in 2017. As noted earlier, the commander is only one of the members of the Party Standing Committee, thus limiting his individual authority. To date, 4 of the 10 commanders have been Party secretary and 6 have been deputy secretary. In addition, 4 commanders—Liu Yalou, Zhang Tingfa, Qiao Qingchen, and Xu Qiliang—have been CMC members. As noted earlier, the commander at each level has more authority during wartime to make decisions without first receiving approval from the Party Standing Committee or the Party Committee as a whole.

The political commissar is the leader (领导者) for all daily Party work at his level and his unit's subordinate organizations under the guidance of the Party committee at his level and the next higher level.[65] The commissar holds the same grade as commander, with the exception of the PLAAF's PC, who has the grade of military region leader, while the PLAAF commander has the grade of a CMC member.[66] Since 1949, the PLAAF has had 11 PCs, 3 of whom became the commander where they also served as the Party secretary. The current PC, General Deng Changyou, assumed his position in 2002 and will have to retire at age 65 at the time of the 18th Party Congress in 2012. There was no discernible trend in selecting these leaders. For example, the first eight PCs began their careers in the army and then transferred to the PLAAF; however, the last three have spent their entire careers in the PLAAF. In addition, only four deputy PCs and one MRAF PC have become the PLAAF PC.

The PLAAF has had over 40 deputy commanders (副司令员). The first 14 were ground force officers who had served in the army until the PLAAF was formed in 1949: not until 1973 did the PLA assign a pilot (Zhang Jihui) as a deputy commander. Between 1973 and 1982, all of the other deputy commanders had their roots in the ground forces as PCs or commanders. In 1982, Wang Hai became only the second pilot to be assigned as a deputy commander, but since then, most of the deputy commanders have been pilots. In February 2009, an anomaly occurred when the PLA assigned a career army officer, Lieutenant General Chen Xiaogong, as one of the deputy commanders. This was most likely an issue of "*guanxi*" (for example, personal relationships) rather than the army's desire to inject ground force control within the PLAAF Headquarters. Not only are deputy commanders responsible for specific tasks within their portfolio, but they can also be deployed elsewhere to serve as the commander or as a backup commander. For example, the joint commander (联合指挥员) can deploy an air force deputy commander (副职指挥员) to the antiair raid command center to take responsibility for air force operations and antiair raid operations.[67] In a "real world" example, during the 2008 Sichuan earthquake, the CMC designated the Chengdu MRAF as the PLAAF Forward CP

(前指挥所) and deployed one of the PLAAF's deputy commanders, Lieutenant General Jing Wenchun, as the commander of air force relief operations.[68]

Since 1949, the PLAAF has had 12 chiefs of staff (参谋长).[69] The chief of staff, who is the director of the Headquarters Department, is one of the unit's leaders (首长之一) along with the commander, PC, and deputy commanders and PCs. The chief of staff has the same grade as the deputy commanders. As such, he is the primary officer responsible for assisting the principal leaders in military (e.g., command) building by organizing and coordinating all related activities. He is also the command staff's leader, responsible for organizing the unit's military administrative work and implementing the command staff's intentions (意图) and resolution (决心). He is directly responsible for all Headquarters Department activities and is head of the PLAAF's CP.[70]

Leadership Structure, Tier-Command, and Establishment System

According to *PLAAF 2010*, the PLAAF currently has a three-tiered vertical command structure for its operational forces: *PLAAF Headquarters*, *MRAF Headquarters*, and the *unit and subunit* tier, from air corps level down to platoon and even squad level.

PLAAF Headquarters (空军) is the highest leadership organization in the PLAAF. Under the leadership of the CMC and the four General Departments, PLAAF Headquarters' primary missions during peacetime are to manage and oversee air force reform and modernization and to execute direct operational command authority over some PLAAF units, such as the 15th Airborne Corps and the 34th Air Transport Division in Beijing. It is not clear what PLAAF Headquarters' exact roles are during wartime. Most likely, however, it will be responsible for having full situational awareness, assigning forces to the different theaters, and providing personnel to man the Air Operations Groups in the national-level and theater headquarters.

The seven MRAF headquarters (军区空军) comprise the second tier.[71] According to the PLAAF, each MRAF is organized according to its missions and battlefield environment. Thus, no two MRAFs are organized exactly the same way. However, each MRAF has subordinate air divisions, SAM brigades or regiments, and AAA regiments, as well as radar brigades and regiments, communications regiments and companies, and support units and subunits. Following the PLA's 2003–2004 force reduction (up to 200,000 personnel), all combat units in each MRAF, with the exception of the 15th Airborne Corps and 34th Air Division, are now under the direct leadership of the MRAF Headquarters.

The final tier consists of PLAAF *units* (部队) and *subunits* (分队). The PLA defines units as organizations at the corps, division, brigade, and regiment level. For example, air divisions and regiments, SAM brigades, and communications regiments are considered units. The PLA defines subunits (分队) as organizations at the *battalion, company,* and *platoon* level, with some including even squads. Subunits can be either permanent, or ad hoc organizations such as communications, radar, vehicle, maintenance, or launch/firing subunits.[72] Prior to the 2003–2004 reduction, the PLAAF had 11 corps leader–grade organizations, including the 15th Airborne Corps plus five air corps and five bases (基地), which were subordinate to their respective MRAF headquarters and were responsible for directly commanding the PLAAF combat units (aviation, air defense, radar, etc.) in their area of responsibility. The PLAAF also had two division-level CPs (指挥所) serving the same function.[73] Today, the only corps leader–grade combat organization is the 15th Airborne Corps, which is directly subordinate to PLAAF Headquarters and has three subordinate airborne divisions in the Guangzhou and Jinan MRAFs. As a result of the force restructuring, the PLAAF reduced the grade of the remaining air corps and corps-level bases to either corps deputy leader– or division leader–grade organizations, re-designating them as Command Posts, as shown in table 4–4:[74]

The air force establishment system (空军编制) refers to the regulations governing establishing the table of organization and equipment (TOE) (建制单位) for every PLAAF organization. This includes the organizational structure, number or personnel, billets, and equipment (including order of battle) for each unit throughout the PLAAF. The PLAAF bases its establishment system according to three sets of criteria: the time period (时效性), both peacetime and wartime; functions (职能) and missions (任务), both divided into departments, units, and academic institutions; and duty status (兵役性质), including either active duty units or reserve units.[75]

Although not stated, the Headquarters Department's Military Affairs Department is responsible for managing the TOE, including assigning aircraft tail numbers and military unit cover designators (MUCDs). It also serves as the personnel center for the enlisted force.

Professional Military Education, Training, and Academic Institutions within the PLAAF

The PLAAF's education and training system (教育训练体制) consists of three main components: *leadership and management* system (领导管理体制); *academic institution professional military education* (PME) system (培训体制); and *flight training* system (飞行训练体制).[76]

The *leadership and management* system has five tiers: PLAAF Headquarters, MRAF Headquarters, corps, division (academic institutions, aviation troop training bases, brigades), and regiments. The Military Training Department (军事训练部 / 军训部) in the PLAAF Headquarters' Headquarters Department is the highest organization for leading PLAAF education and training. Each of the other four tiers has an equivalent department for leading training at their level.[77] Significantly, however, the Political Department's Cadre Department

(政治部干部部), not the Military Training Department, is responsible for managing the Defense Student program.[78] Based on a review of PLAAF-related books, journals, newspapers, and Internet articles, it appears that the Headquarters Department in each MRAF Headquarters and the 15th Airborne Corps Headquarters has a Training Division (训练处); some divisions and brigades have a Training Office (训练科), while others have a combined Operations and Training Office (训练科); and all regiments have a combined Operations and Training Branch (作训股). There are no training organizations below the regiment level.

Table 4–4. PLAAF Command Posts

Military Region Air Force	Corps Deputy Leader– Command Posts	Division Leader– Command Posts
Beijing	Datong	[None]
Chengdu	Kunming	Lhasa
Guangzhou	Wuhan	Nanning
Jinan	[None]	[None]
Lanzhou	Wulumuqi, Xi'an	Hetian
Nanjing	Fuzhou	Shanghai, Zhangzhou
Shenyang	Dalian	Changchun

The PLAAF's PME system is different from the USAF system. Basically, the United States Air Force Education and Training Command (AFETC), one of the USAF's major commands, is responsible for enlisted and officer basic education, specialty training, and PME, throughout the member's career. The exception is the U.S. Air Force Academy (USAFA), which is a Direct Reporting Unit (DRU) under Headquarters Air Force. Upon graduation from USAFA, the new officers receive their specialty training under AFETC. The differences between the PLAAF and USAF education and training systems for enlisted personnel, noncommissioned officers (NCOs), and officers are both numerous and significant. For example, whereas the USAF conducts basic training for all of its enlisted members at Lackland Air Force Base, the PLAAF does not train its new recruits and conscripts (who serve for 2 years) at a single location.[79] Instead, they receive basic training at their operational unit or at a technical training unit. All PLAAF basic training occurs between early December and late January and the instructors are assigned by that unit on a temporary basis. Upon completion of basic training, the new enlisted members either receive on-the-job training (OJT) at their operational base or at the technical training unit.

To achieve promotion, USAF NCOs must satisfactorily complete correspondence courses throughout their career, and selected senior NCOs take in-residence PME at a training organization, such as the Air Force Senior NCO Academy, for a few weeks. In contrast, the PLAAF emphasizes lengthier in-residence training. It has only one NCO school (specializing in communications), which students attend for 2 years. Several other PLAAF officer academic institutions offer separate 2- or 3-year associates degree programs for NCOs, including the Air Force Engineering University, Aviation University, Radar College, 1st Aviation (Aircraft Maintenance) College, Guilin (AAA and Airborne) College, Xuzhou (Logistics) College, and the 2d Flight College.[80] Like the USAF, the PLAAF also provides correspondence courses for its NCOs, where they can receive a high school equivalency degree or an associate's degree. If necessary, NCOs can attend a short course for squad leaders and for technical training if, for some reason, they did not receive it during their first 2 years as a new recruit/conscript.

The USAF's officers come from graduates of USAFA, Reserve Officer Training Corps (ROTC) programs, and college graduates who successfully complete a postgraduate Officer Training School (OTS) course. Upon graduation, these officers then receive their specialty training. All officers must have a bachelor's degree. In contrast, the PLAAF's officer cadre comes from graduates of one of three PLAAF universities and 15 colleges, from Defense Student programs at 18 civilian universities, or from directly-recruited civilian college graduates with a science or engineering degree. The PLAAF ceased directly recruiting enlisted personnel as officers in the early 1980s. All cadets who attend a PLAAF academic institution also receive their technical training and are assigned directly to their operational unit upon graduation. Students who graduate from the Defense Student program or who are directly recruited after graduation are assigned to their operational unit, where they receive OJT.

USAF officers must complete PME correspondence courses at each level to be competitive for promotion. Some, though not all, officers also have the opportunity to attend in-residence courses sponsored by the Air University at Maxwell Air Force Base. These programs include the 6-week Air and Space Basic Course for second lieutenants, 5-week Squadron Officer School course for captains, 40-week Air Command and Staff College course for majors and major selectees, and the 44-week Air War College course for lieutenant colonels and colonels. Some officers also have the opportunity to attend joint institutions such as the National War College, or specialized training such as the School of Advanced Air and Space Studies. Students in these courses come from all specialties, as well as from other service branches and selected civilians in government service. In addition, the Air Force Institute of Technology (AFIT) at Wright-Patterson Air Force Base provides a variety of graduate programs in science and technology-related subjects. Some USAF officers are sponsored to attend nongovernmental academic institutions such as the John F. Kennedy School of Government at Harvard University or other civilian institutions, with majors ranging from military history to aerospace engineering.

Currently, the PLAAF's officer PME academic education system is divided into two levels of education: basic and specialized education (基础与专业教育) and advanced education (深造教育).[81] Whereas all cadets who attend a PLAAF college, including pilots, receive both their basic education and specialty training before they graduate, Defense Students do not receive any technical training until after they graduate. Pilot cadets who are selected from high school graduates receive 30 months of basic education at the Air Force Aviation University (空军航空大学). Upon completion, they are assigned to the university's flight training base or to one of seven flight colleges, where they complete 6 months of flight training in a basic trainer and 12 months in an advanced trainer. Depending on the type of aircraft they will eventually fly at an operational unit, they are then assigned directly to an operational base or for 1 year to one of seven transition training bases. Pilot candidates who were recruited from PLA or civilian college graduates receive 2 years of training that includes basic flight theory and flying time in a basic trainer and advanced trainer. After graduation, they are then assigned to one of the seven transition training bases for 1 year.

Nonaviation PLAAF cadets receive basic education either at the Air Force Engineering University (AFEU) or at a PLAAF specialty college. Those finishing AFEU are then assigned to one of the PLAAF's colleges to complete their specialty training and a bachelor's degree. Cadets who do not attend AFEU remain at the same college to complete their specialty training and receive either a senior technical (associate's) or bachelor's degree. Upon graduation, all new officers are assigned to their permanent unit, where the first year is considered a probationary (见习) period, during which they spend the first 6 months as a squad (enlisted troop) leader.[82] Prior to graduation, some Defense Students spend a short period of time at an operational unit observing the daily activities. Upon graduation, Defense Students have several options, including attending graduate school. If they do not attend graduate school, they are assigned either directly to an operational unit or to a training organization where they receive specialty training. With the exception of new graduates who serve in remote areas, the first year is a probationary (见习) period.[83] Almost all Defense Student graduates serve in technical, rather than command, billets.[84]

Advanced education for intermediate- and senior-level PLAAF officers (lieutenant colonels, colonels, senior colonels, and major generals) is conducted in only a few military academic institutions. Only selected officers have the opportunity to receive advanced PME or a graduate degree. For example, command track officers receive 1 year of intermediate- and senior-level PME at the Air Force Command College (空军指挥学院), which does not award a graduate degree, while some technical officers attend specialized programs for 2 to 3 years in various PLAAF colleges, such as AFEU, the Air Force Radar College (空军雷达学院), or Xuzhou Air Force (Logistics) College (徐州空军学院), to obtain graduate degrees. Certain command track officers, such as radar and SAM commanders, can attend specific graduate programs in a PLAAF college or a civilian university where they receive an advanced degree. Some officers (senior colonels and major generals) receive their senior-level PME at the National Defense University (国防大学).

The PLAAF's various academic institutions are organized into two basic categories: flight colleges and all others.[85] Each category has three main components: a command element (领导机构), administrative departments (部门), some of which also provide certain types of training, and academic departments (系).[86]

Flight training for all new high school graduates or enlisted personnel selected for pilot training begins at the Air Force Aviation University (空军航空大学), which was created in 2004 by combining the Changchun Flight College (长春飞行学院), 7th Flight College (第七飞行学院), and the 2d Aviation (Aircraft Maintenance) College (第二航空学院). All new flight cadets spend their first 30 months at the university, where they receive their basic education. They then transfer to one of the seven numbered flight colleges for 18 months to receive their flight training.[87]

The Aviation University, which is located in Changchun, Jilin Province, has a commandant (校长), PC, and at least two deputy commandants and one deputy PC. The university has a Training Department (训练部) that serves as well as the Headquarters Department. It also has a Political Department (政治部), College/School Affairs (院务部 / 校务部), and Scientific Research Department (科研部).[88] The Scientific Research Department is responsible for overseeing all of the institution's technical training curricula and systems research work.[89] The Training Department and Scientific Research Department also have subordinate classrooms and laboratories, where personnel from the departments provide training to the cadets. The College/School Affairs Department is responsible for managing facilities and logistics issues.

All seven of the PLAAF's numbered flight colleges are division leader–grade organizations and are structured similarly to an operational air division, with a command staff plus four administrative and functional departments—Headquarters Department, Political Department, Logistics Department, and Equipment Department. Rather than academic departments, each college has a subordinate basic trainer regiment and one or more advanced trainer regiments. Table 4–5 shows the flight colleges, their location, and the types of personnel they train.[90]

Upon graduation, the pilots from the 1st and 2d flight colleges are assigned directly to their operational units. Pilots graduating from the other five colleges are assigned to one of the PLAAF's seven transition training bases for about 1 year. Upon completing transition training, they are then assigned to their permanent operational unit, where they transition into that unit's aircraft. Some of the graduates from the five colleges that train fighter pilots transition into multirole or ground attack aircraft.

Table 4–5. The Seven PLAAF Flight Colleges

Academic Institution	City, Province	Education and Training Missions
1st Flight College	Harbin, Heilongjiang	Bomber and transport pilots, navigators, and communications personnel
2d Flight College	Huxian, Shaanxi	Bomber and transport pilots and navigators, ground controllers [officers], and approach radar controllers [NCOs]
3d Flight College	Jinzhou, Liaoning	Fighter pilots
4th Flight College	Shijiazhuang, Hebei	Fighter pilots and foreign pilots
5th Flight College	Wuwei, Gansu	Fighter pilots
6th Flight College	Zhuozhou, Hebei	Fighter pilots
13th Flight College	Bengbu, Anhui	Fighter pilots

The PLAAF's nonaviation colleges are organized differently from its aviation colleges. They each have a command staff, 2–5 administrative and functional departments, academic departments, and cadet teams.[91] As shown in table 4–6, all nonaviation academic institutions have at least a Training Department and Political Department (政治部). Depending on the institution's mission, location, and curriculum, other administrative departments include a College/School Affairs, Basic Department (基础部), and/or Scientific Research Department. The Basic Department is responsible for providing instruction in certain required basic education courses that all undergraduates must take regardless of their specialty.[92] The protocol order for the five departments is Headquarters, Political, College/School Affairs, Basic, and Scientific Research.

Each institution has several academic departments and associated specialties, which prepare graduates to assume their operational duties. For example, the PLAAF's Surface-to-Air Missile College (地空导弹学院) has six academic departments—Command Engineering, Computer Engineering, Electro-Mechanical Engineering, Radar Engineering, Guided Missile Engineering, and Systems Engineering—and 12 academic specialties.[93]

Depending upon the academic institution, undergraduate students/cadets (学员) and graduate students (研究生) are grouped into various organizations, which are typically subordinate to the academic department to which they are affiliated. These include the student group (学员大队), which is a battalion-level organization; student companies (学员连); student teams (学员区队 / 学员队); and student squads (学员班). Of note, within the PLA, a cadet's graduating class year is based on the year training begins, not the year of graduation. For example, the cadets who began training in summer 2010 are identified as the class of 2010. The reason for this is that not all cadets receive a 4-year degree. In addition, their total time-in-service includes their cadet time, not just their active duty time, once they become an officer.

Table 4–6. Nonaviation Academic Institution Departments and Grades

Academic Institution (grade)	Training	Political	Affairs	Basic	Scientific Research	City, Province	Missions
Command College (corps leader)	x	x	x		x	Beijing	Command officers
Engineering University (corps leader)	x	x	x	x	x	Xian, Shaanxi	Aircraft maintenance, surface-to-air missiles (SAMs), and communications
Natural Science College (division leader)	x	x				Xian, Shaanxi	Basic education
Engineering College (division leader)	x	x	x	x	x	Xian, Shaanxi	Aircraft maintenance
Surface-to-air Missile College (division leader)	x	x	x	x		Xian, Shaanxi	SAMs
Telecommunications Engineering College (division leader)	x	x	x	x		Xian, Shaanxi	Communications
Guilin Air Force College (corps deputy)	x	x		x		Guilin, Guangxi	Antiaircraft artillery and airborne
Radar College (corps deputy)	x	x	x	x	x	Wuhan, Hubei	Radar
Xuzhou Air Force College (corps deputy)	x	x	x	x	x	Xuzhou, Jiangsu	Logistics
1st Aviation College (division leader)	x	x	x	x	x	Xinyang, Henan	Aircraft maintenance
Dalian NCO Communications School (division leader)	x	x		x		Dalian, Liaoning	Communications

Scientific Research System

The PLAAF's scientific research system (科学研究机构组织体制) is incorporated into the broader Chinese research, development, and acquisition (RDA) structure.[94] According to *PLAAF 2010*, RDA of a specific weapon or system usually involves multiple phases of development and related activities by different organizations within and outside of the PLAAF. China's RDA process allows it to plan properly and to lay a solid foundation for PLAAF modernization programs. Under the overall guidance of the GAD, the PLAAF Headquarters' Equipment Department is responsible for overseeing all of the PLAAF's equipment and weapons systems development.[95] The process involves the following sequential phases: Demonstration/Development and Evaluation (论证); Proposal (方案); Engineering Development (工程研制); Design Finalization (设计定型) and Production Finalization (生产定型).[96] Before the RDA process actually begins, preparatory research takes place for the chosen area of development under the official rubric "National Defense Science and Technology Preparatory Research." Researchers examine ongoing technology efforts that could meet operational requirements and evaluate candidate technologies that could possibly mature into useful weapons.[97]

In February 2004, PLAAF Headquarters formally established the Air Force Equipment Research Academy (空军装备研究院), consolidating administration of more than 20 PLAAF scientific research organizations.[98] The academy is a corps deputy leader–grade organization.[99] Its administrative departments include the Science and Technology (S&T) Department (科技部), Political Department (政治部), and Academy Affairs Department (院务部).[100] The S&T Department serves as the Headquarters Department, and the Academy Affairs Department most likely manages the facilities. The academy has about 1,500 S&T officers and 490 senior technical billets.

A review of the academy's activities since 2004 indicates at least two reasons the PLAAF, along with the PLA Navy and Second Artillery, created their own equipment research academy. The first was consolidating management of all RDA under a single organization. The second reason was to deal with the GAD and government RDA organizations on a more equal basis.

The academy has a dozen primary functions and responsibilities for equipment and weapons systems research and development (R&D/研制), which involve tracking foreign development of new military technology, equipment, and weapons systems; serving as the PLAAF's top level organization for equipment and weapons system design, system development, regulations, and planning for new systems, modifying older systems and special-use equipment; and conducting research for the operational use, maintenance, and technical support for new and modified equipment.[101] Some of the subordinate institutes are shown below.[102] The research institutes are either division- or regiment-level organizations.[103]

- *Air Force Equipment General Demonstration (Development and Evaluation) Research Institute* (空军装备总体论证研究所), a regiment-grade organization, has an Organization and Plans Division (组织计划处), Political Division (政治处), and Management Division (管理处), and nine research labs (研究室)[104]

- *Air Force Aviation Equipment Research Institute* (空军航空装备研究所), a division-grade organization, has an S&T Division (科技处), Political Department (政治部), and Management Division, and several subordinate research institutes and labs[105]

- *Air Force Ground Air Defense Equipment Research Institute* (空军地面防空装备研究所), a regiment-grade organization, has an S&T Division, Political Division, and Management Division, six research labs, and one testing workshop (试制车间)[106]

- *Air Force Radar and Electronic Countermeasures Research Institute* (空军雷达与电子对抗研究所), a division-grade organization, has an S&T Division, Political Department, and Management Division, and several research labs[107]

- *Air Force Communications, Navigation, and Command Automation Research Institute* (空军通信导航与指挥自动化研究所), has a General Office (办公室), several research labs, and a services subunit (勤务分队)[108]

- *Air Force Reconnaissance and Intelligence Equipment Research Institute* (空军侦察情报装备研究所), with three research labs and a testing workshop[109]

- *Air Force Weather and Chemical Defense Research Institute* (空军气象防化研究所), which has an S&T Division, Political Department, and Management Division, as well as four research labs[110]

- *SAM Technical/Technology Services Research Institute* (导弹技术勤务研究所)[111]

- *Air Force Equipment Software Testing and Evaluation Center* (空军装备软件测评中心).[112]

Political Work System

The PLAAF's political work (整治工作) system mirrors the PLA's overall political work system.[113] The PLA's political work system is the means through which the Chinese Communist Party guarantees absolute control over the military. The PLAAF political work system consists of six main elements integrated into every organization within the PLAAF Party Congress system: Party Committee system; Party Congress system; political officer system; political functional and administrative department system; discipline inspection system; and judicial system.[114]

Logistics Support System

The PLAAF's logistics support system (后勤保障体制) consists of six primary components: materials (物资), finances (经费供应), medical services (卫勤保障), equipment maintenance and repair (装备维修), transportation (交通运输), and engineering (工程).[115] These are managed by the second-level departments within the PLAAF Logistics Department's system, down to the regiment level. Of particular interest are the field stations (场站) that support air regiments. According to *PLAAF 2010*, a field station is an independent logistics support unit subordinate to the air division. Depending on their location and function, some field stations can also be directly subordinate to an MRAF Headquarters. The commander (站长) serves as the airbase commander with responsibility for all facilities and operations. He also organizes the supply of materials and equipment to each tenant air regiment at the airbase and provides logistics support for flight operations and training. A field station has three components: a command staff, functional and administrative branches, and subordinate company-level organizations. Although the field station serves as the logistics support organization for an air regiment, it also incorporates certain organizations within the Equipment Department system, such as munitions and air materiel.[116]

Equipment Management System and Equipment Technical Support System

The PLAAF's Equipment Department and its second-level departments down to the regiment level are responsible for the PLAAF's equipment management system (装备管理体制).[117] Historically, the equipment management system dealt primarily with aircraft maintenance, while the logistics system dealt with nonaviation equipment. For example, the fourth PLAAF department was known as the Aeronautical Engineering Department (航空工程部) and then the Equipment Technical Department until 1998.[118] In 1998, when the PLA created the General Armament Department, the PLAAF merged support for all equipment from birth to death into the Equipment Department. The structure of the current Equipment Department was discussed earlier. The PLAAF equipment management system also includes military representative offices assigned to regions and individual nonmilitary research institutes and factories.[119]

The *Air Force Encyclopedia* states that the primary purpose of equipment technical support (装备技术保障) is to inspect, refurbish, maintain, repair, and improve the PLAAF's equipment and weapons systems for all its branches and specialty units.[120] These components are managed by the second-level departments within the PLAAF Equipment Department's system down to the regiment level. As noted above, however, some of these functions for aircraft support are incorporated under the field station's management. Officers involved in this system come from the equipment and technical support career tracks.

Personnel Management System, Mobilization, and Reserve Forces

The PLAAF's personnel management system (人事管理) consists of separate organizations for the officer (cadre) corps and the enlisted force. The Political Department's Cadre Department down to the regiment level is responsible for managing officer records, promotions, and appointments.[121] Meanwhile, the Headquarters Department's Military Affairs Department is responsible for managing the enlisted force records and appointments, while the political officer system is responsible for gathering information on the enlisted personnel, and the Party Committee system is responsible for their promotions. One key point is that the PLAAF does not have a central promotions board. Instead, the Party Committee at the corps to regiment levels is responsible for promoting all officers and enlisted personnel at the next lower level.[122] One of the reasons for this is that most personnel remain in the same unit most of their career.

The *Air Force Encyclopedia* has several entries for the PLAAF's mobilization system (动员体制) reserve forces (后备力量建设).[123] The PLAAF's mobilization system consists of an air force mobilization organization and reserve forces, which support the air force's reserve power transition from peacetime to wartime, and for its personnel, materials, and financial power to serve operations.[124] In the 1950s, the PLAAF created a Mobilization Division (动员处) within the Headquarters Department and a similar organization in each Headquarters Department down to the regiment level. In 1998, however, the PLAAF abolished all of these organizations and placed the mobilization responsibility under the Military Affairs Department within the Headquarters Department. In 2002, the Mobilization Department created an Air Force National Defense Mobilization Committee Comprehensive Office (空军国防动员委员会综合办公室) to manage mobilization issues. This office coordinated with the air force's Military Affairs Departments, as well as local governments and army units from the military district level down.[125] PLAAF mobilization includes expanding the size of units, as well as mobilizing troops and their equipment, furnishing logistics support, and providing technical service support.[126] It is not clear how much the PLAAF has been involved in mobilization work. Shortly after a new National Defense Mobilization Law became effective in July 2010, however, the PLAAF conducted its first-ever mobilization exercise involving militia using construction equipment to repair a "damaged airfield following a surprise enemy attack."[127]

The concept of PLAAF reserve forces is fairly new. The PLAAF translates the terms *houbei* (后备) and *yubeiyi* (预备役) as "reserve," causing confusion when using only the English term. *Houbei* is a generic term for reserve forces including personnel, equipment, technology, civilian aircraft, and materials. Various definitions imply that PLAAF *yubeiyi* reserve personnel are part of the *houbei* system.[128] In 2004, the PLAAF began developing reserve forces in three particular areas: field station flight support personnel, surface-to-air missile regiments, and radar battalions. In January 2010, the PLAAF issued "Air Force Reserve Unit Work Regulations" codifying the changes in its organizational structure.[129]

Implications of the PLAAF Organizational Structure upon Its Future Development

As has been explicated, the PLAAF's organizational structure has multiple components and layers, many of which overlap, generating redundancies. From an overall perspective, the structure has not changed appreciably over the past 30 years. While some organizations and departments have been abolished or merged as a result of force reductions, the remaining ones have stayed largely intact, serving the needs of the service even as the world around it has changed dramatically.

Perhaps because of this unchanging quality, it is invariably significant—and thus important to note—when a change *does* occur. For example, when the PLAAF downgraded all the corps leader–grade headquarters in 2004 to either corps deputy leader–grade or division leader–grade CPs, it altered the command structure vertically within the PLAAF and horizontally with the other services. Specifically, under the new structure, the division leader–grade CPs cannot command an air division, which is at the same level, or interact as an equal with a group army, which is a corps–level organization. Even the corps deputy leader–grade CPs are still not at the same level as the group armies. The PLAAF is still working out the mechanics of this major change.

Unsubstantiated reports out of Hong Kong have indicated the PLA may undergo a major restructuring to replace the seven MR Headquarters with four theater commands.[130] In addition, since the PLA has already had 10 major force restructurings since the early 1950s, the last of which occurred in 2004, there is a good possibility another downsizing will occur before or shortly after the 18th Party Congress in 2012. Either or both of these events will most likely alter the PLAAF's force structure, especially the MRAF Headquarters, with major implications for the PLAAF's overall command and control structure.

In terms of its air order of battle, the PLAAF has reduced the number of air divisions from a high of 50 in the late 1980s to 29 today. This reduction occurred in conjunction with a drop in the total number of aircraft, the incorporation of newer models, and establishing a transition training base in each of the seven MRAFs in 1986. While some air divisions today field more than one type of combat aircraft, most regiments have only one type so as to simplify logistics and maintenance. The new units are still in the early stages of conducting dissimilar aircraft training, but the diverse organizational structure within each air division has made it easier to do. Given the current distribution of air divisions among the seven MRAFs, the number of divisions will probably remain the same over the next decade, but the composition and number of subordinate regiments will probably change as older aircraft are taken out of the inventory and replaced by a fewer number of modern multirole aircraft.

It is not clear how many SAM units, especially long-range SAMs, the PLAAF has, but the number is apparently growing and the units are being deployed in more MRAFs.

Another important example of change is that the PLAAF has gradually incorporated its electronic countermeasures mission and organizational structure with the radar forces. Significantly, the PLAAF Headquarters merged management of the two types of specialty forces into an Electronic Countermeasures and Radar Department (电子对抗雷达部) subordinate to the Headquarters Department and combined research for them into the Air Force Radar and Electronic Countermeasures Research Institute (空军雷达与电子对抗研究所) under the Air Force Equipment Research Academy. In addition, the Air Force Radar College has an Electronic Countermeasures Academic Department (电子对抗系) that provides education and training for officers and NCOs assigned to operational unit electronic countermeasures billets. Besides merging radar and ECM administrative and research functions as noted above, the PLAAF began merging several radar regiments into brigades during the 2003–2004 force restructuring. Although it is now easier to command more company-level radar sites as a result of information technology, the PLAAF is still concerned about span of control from a geographic perspective. Restructuring of the Equipment Department in 1998 and creation of the Equipment Research Academy in 2004 have had important implications for consolidating and managing all of the PLAAF's equipment and weapons systems. No significant organizational changes are anticipated to these two organizations in the next 5 years. That said, however, the biggest change within this system will be the inclusion of new officers and enlisted personnel who received their undergraduate education at civilian academic institutions rather than PLAAF institutions.

The education and training system will most likely undergo some more restructuring over the next decade. The Air Force Engineering University was created in 1999 and the Air Force Aviation University was created in 2004 with the goal of consolidating basic education for cadets in specific fields and then providing specialty training at subordinate colleges. In addition, the Guilin Air Force College, which had always trained AAA cadets, began educating and training the PLAAF's airborne officer cadets in 1999. Given that the goal was to have 60 percent of all new PLAAF officers in 2010 graduate from civilian colleges, including from the Defense Student Program, and that the PLA most likely did not meet this goal, the PLAAF's academic institutions will most likely undergo some more restructuring as the number of cadets is reduced to meet the 60 percent goal.[131]

Finally, the PLAAF does not have an extensive reserve program, a circumstance which most likely will not change over the next few years. However, following the implementation of the new National Defense Mobilization Law in July 2010, the PLAAF most likely will become more involved in mobilizing civilian organizations to support it. At the same time, however, the PLA has implemented some personnel changes that have allowed PLAAF flag officers to assume a few key national-level leadership positions as shown in table 4–7.

Table 4–7. PLAAF Officers in Key Joint Billets During the 2000s

Billet	PLAAF Officer	PLAAF Officer
CMC Member	Qiao Qingchen [2004–2007]	Xu Qiliang [2007–Present]
DCGS	Xu Qiliang [2004–2007]	Ma Xiaotian [2007–Present]
Deputy, GPD	Liu Zhenqi [2006–Present]	
Deputy, GLD	Li Maifu [2006–2009]	
Deputy, GAD	None	
AMS Commandant	Zheng Shenxia [2003–2007]	Liu Chengjun [2007–Present]
NDU Commandant	Ma Xiaotian [2006–2007]	
NDU Political Commissar	Liu Yazhou [2010–Present]	

AMS: Academy of Military Science
GAD: General Armament Department
NDU: National Defense University
CMC: Central Military Commission
GLD: General Logistics department
DCGS: Deputy Chief of the General Staff
GPD: General Political Department

To put narrative to these data points, in 2003, the CMC appointed Lieutenant General Zheng Shenxia to become the first air force commandant of the PLA Academy of Military Science (AMS).[132] He received his third star in 2004. Upon his retirement in 2007, another PLAAF flag officer, Lieutenant General Liu Chengjun, assumed his position, receiving his own third star in 2010. Since

2004, the commander of the PLAAF (along with the commander of the PLA Navy and Second Artillery) has been a member of the CMC—the national command authority for the PRC. General Qiao Qingchen was appointed in 2004 and was replaced by Xu Qiliang in 2007. Only two PLAAF officers, Liu Yalou (1956–1965) and Zhang Tingfa (1977–1982), had previously served as CMC members. Since 2006, the CMC has assigned the first PLAAF officers as commandant and political commissar at the National Defense University. In 2006, the CMC appointed Lieutenant General Ma Xiaotian as the first PLAAF officer to serve as commandant.[133] In 2007, Ma became one of the Deputy Chiefs of the General Staff with the important portfolio of intelligence and foreign affairs for the entire PLA. He received his third star in 2010 and will most likely have to retire in 2012. In 2010, the CMC appointed Lieutenant General Liu Yazhou as the first PLAAF officer to serve as NDU political commissar. Prior to that, he was one of the PLAAF's deputy political commissars.

Since 2006 (and as shown in table 4–7), the CMC has appointed PLAAF flag officers as one of the three or four deputy directors in the GPD and one of the four or five deputies in the GLD.[134] As a result, the PLAAF is increasingly involved in developing PLA-wide policies to a greater degree than in the past; however, these do not appear to be permanent air force billets. For example, in 2006, Lieutenant General Li Maifu became the first PLAAF deputy director of the GLD. However, when he retired in late 2009 or early 2010, it does not appear that he was replaced by a PLAAF officer.[135] No PLAAF (or PLAN) officers have served as a deputy in the GAD, which implies that the GAD is less "joint" than the other three general departments. Each MR Headquarters has an average of five deputy commanders. Since 1988, each MRAF commander and fleet commander has served concurrently as an MR deputy commander; however, no PLAAF officers have served as the director of an MR first-level department and only a few PLAAF personnel apparently hold positions in any of the departments.[136]

Based on this history, if the PLA does restructure its Military Region system into strategic theaters, there is a high probability army officers will still dominate the leadership positions in the Central Military Commission, General Departments, and Theater Headquarters, while PLAAF officers will rotate in and out as the head of the Adademy of Military Science and the National Defense University. The PLAAF will make its way onward into the 21st century, aided—and encumbered—by its unique and ever-fascinating organizational structure and culture.

Notes

[1] Key information for this paper is taken from *People's Liberation Army Air Force 2010* (Dayton, OH: National Air and Space Intelligence Agency [NASIC], August 1, 2010). Henceforth, this publication is cited as *PLAAF 2010*. This document can be found at <www.au.af.mil/au/awc/awcgate/nasic/pla_af_2010.pdf>.

² Luo Bogan, "Air Force of the Guangzhou Military Area Command," in *China Air Force Encyclopedia* [中国空军百科全书], vol. 2, ed. Yao Wei (Beijing: Aviation Industry Press, November 2005), 1239 (henceforth cited as *Air Force Encyclopedia*); *Handbook of the Chinese People's Liberation Army* (Washington, DC:, Defense Intelligence Agency, DDB-2680-32-84, November 1984); "PLA Airborne Brigades Become Divisions," *Jane's Defence Weekly* 20, no. 14 (October 2, 1993), 12; Department of Defense, "The Security Situation in the Taiwan Strait." Report submitted by Secretary of Defense William Cohen to the U.S. Senate as directed by the FY99 Appropriations Bill, February 17, 1999.

³ Sun Zhi, "The Defense Student Program Nurtures the Core of the Modern Military," *Jiefangjun Bao*, November 30, 2009, 8.

⁴ Part of the problem of understanding the PLAAF's structure exists because the PLAAF has multiple two-character terms that, either alone or in different combinations, refer to its organizational structure or system. These terms include *zuzh* [组织], *tizhi* [体制], *junzhi* [军制], *bianzhi* [编制], *jiegou* [结构], *jigou* [机构], *zhidu* [制度], *tixi* [体系], and *jianzhi* [建制]. In addition, one book uses one set of characters, while another book uses another set for the same concept.

⁵ The information in this paragraph is a combination of material from the 2002 and 2008 versions of *China's National Defense* [中国的国防], Information Office of the State Council of the People's Republic of China, published in December 2002 and January 2009, respectively.

⁶ Chen Jinxue, "Air Force Military System," in *Air Force Encyclopedia*, 212. Shang Jinsuo, ed., *Science of Air Force Building* [空军建设学] (Beijing: PLA Press, September 2009), 393.

⁷ Chen Jinxue, "Air Force Organizational System," in *Air Force Encyclopedia*, 213.

⁸ Yang Zhipo, "Air Force Leadership and Command System," in *Air Force Encyclopedia*, 214.

⁹ Xiao Mingli, "Air Force Establishment," in *Air Force Encyclopedia*, 215. Meng Zhaoxu, "Establishment Form," and Wang Guoliang, "Order of Establishment," in *China Military Encyclopedia* [中国军事百科全书], vol. 2, eds. Song Shilun and Xiao Ke (Beijing: Military Science Publishing House, July 1997), 9-10.

¹⁰ Yang Zhipo, "Air Force Leadership and Command System," 214-215.

¹¹ Qian Haihao, *Science of Military Organizational Structure* [军队组织编制学] (Beijing: Academy of Military Science Press, December 2001), 249.

¹² Zhu Rongchang, ed., *Air Force Dictionary* [空军大辞典] (Shanghai: Shanghai Dictionary Press, September 1996), 193-195. Henceforth cited as *Air Force Dictionary*.

¹³ Liu Youfeng, "Air Force Logistic Support System," in *Air Force Encyclopedia*, 424.

¹⁴ Li Zhenlin, "Air Force Materiel Management System," in *Air Force Encyclopedia*, 214.

¹⁵ Li Xuezhong, "Air Force Materiel Technical Support," in *Air Force Encyclopedia*, 493-494.

¹⁶ Wang Yuanming, "Air Force Work of Appointing and Removing Cadre," in *Air Force Encyclopedia*, 369-370.

¹⁷ Ba Jianmin, "Air Force Reserve Forces," "Air Force Reserve Duty," and "Air Force Reserve-Duty Forces" in *Air Force Encyclopedia*, 266-267; and Bai Junlu, "System of Air Force Mobilization," in *Air Force Encyclopedia*, 263.

¹⁸ Kevin Lanzit's chapter examines the education and training system in more detail.

¹⁹ For more detailed information, see chapter 2 in *PLAAF 2010*.

²⁰ One of the reasons the PLA reinstituted ranks in 1988 was its growing foreign relations program. Some countries expressed confusion when planning exchanges and during meetings, because they did not know what each person's rank was.

²¹ The PLA uses the term *yizhi liangxian* [职两衔] to refer to one grade with two ranks; see Xu Ping, ed., *Discussion of Chinese and Foreign Ranks* [漫谈中外军衔] (Beijing: Jincheng Press, January 2002), 199. Although most PLA grades have a leader [正职] and deputy leader [副职] grade, they are often lumped together. For example, PLA writings refer to the corps level [军级] or division level [师级], which include both the leader and deputy leader grades.

²² Chen Jinxue, "Air Force Military System," in *Air Force Encyclopedia*, 212. The PLAAF does not have a term for "headquarters." Depending on the context, the terms *kongjun* [空军] and *junwei kongjun* [军委空军] refer to the PLAAF in general or PLAAF Headquarters, and the term *junqu kongjun* [军区空军] refers to an MRAF in general or to the MRAF Headquarters. The term *silingbu* [司令部] is often mistranslated or

misunderstood as the headquarters, but it refers specifically to the Headquarters Department. Occasionally, the PLA uses the term *zhihui bu* [指挥部] to refer to a headquarters as in a joint headquarters [联合指挥部].

²³ This concept reflects the top-down nature of PLAAF organization development under the guidance of the CCP's CMC and through the PLAAF Party Committee.

²⁴ Lu Wenzhi, "Air Force Building," in *Air Force Encyclopedia*, 83.

²⁵ Chen Jinxue, "Air Force Organizational System," in *Air Force Encyclopedia*, 213. The fifth officer career track is technical support.

²⁶ The PLA often translates *jiguan* [机关] as *organs*.

²⁷ Hu Guangzheng, ed., *Modern Military Organizational Reform Research* [当代军事体制变革研究] (Beijing: Military Science Publishing House, October 2007), 462–469. Henceforth identified as *Military Organizational Reform*.

²⁸ The information below on the organizational structure of the four departments comes from *PLAAF 2010*, chapter 2.

²⁹ According to *PLAAF 2010*.

³⁰ In June 2008, the PLAAF created the Professional Education Air Force Military Professional University [空军军事职业大学], and its first classes began in September of that year. PLAAF Commander General Xu Qiliang is the university's commandant, and PLAAF Political Commissar General Deng Changyou is the political commissar. The university has branch campuses in each of the PLAAF's four departments, each MRAF Headquarters, and the Airborne Corps headquarters. Every independent unit at the regiment level and above also has its own study center. Wei Yinhai and Zhang Jinyu, "Air Force Military Professional University Established," <english.chinamil.com.cn/site2/news-channels/2008-07/04/content_1348728.htm>, July 4, 2008; "The PLA's First Military Professional University Is Established in the Air Force" [全军第一家军事职业大学在空军挂牌成立], <www..go81.net/news/shownews_12454.html>, July 3, 2008. In early 2009, the PLAAF created the Military Professional Education Department to manage the university and to link up with the China Central Radio and TV University. The department director is Zhang Liqun [张力群], accessed at <www.infzm.com/content/29139> and <www.crtvu.edu.cn/DDSX/file.php?id=8868>, November 7, 2010.

³¹ Interviews with PLA personnel in Beijing in November 2009.

³² According to *PLAAF 2010*.

³³ Ibid.

³⁴ Kenneth Allen, *People's Republic of China People's Liberation Army Air Force*, DIC–1300–445–91 (Washington, DC: Defense Intelligence Agency, May 1991), 8–1; "Air Force Aviation Engineering Department," *Air Force Dictionary*, 146; *World Military Yearbook 1993–1994* [世界军事年鉴] (Beijing, PLA Press, June 1994), 81. Prior to 1998, the Logistics Department was responsible for maintenance for all nonaviation equipment and weapons systems. With the exception of vehicle maintenance, which remained under the Logistics Department, the Equipment Department took responsibility for maintenance for all equipment and weapons systems in 1998.

³⁵ The Military Representative Bureau is responsible for guiding all of the PLAAF's military representatives assigned to regional offices and to individual nonmilitary research institutes and factories to monitor the development and production of PLAAF systems. It is roughly equivalent to the USAF's Air Force Plant Representative Office (AFPRO) system, except that the PLAAF's military representatives spend most, if not all, of their career in the same office, while USAF representatives rotate every 2 to 3 years.

³⁶ *Military Organizational Reform*, 462–469.

³⁷ According to the *World Military Yearbook*.

³⁸ According to the PRC's *2002 Defense White Paper* and various PLA books; what is and is not a PLAAF branch is complicated. Since at least 1991, the *World Military Yearbooks* have identified the PLAAF's five branches as aviation, AAA, SAM, radar, and airborne. Although the 2002 Defense White Paper listed and identified the four branches separately from the five specialty units, the 2002–2006 White Papers did not provide a list at all, and the 2008 White Paper lumped them all together as branches. Page 466 of *Military Organizational Reform* also separates them into four branches and five specialty forces. Page 13 of the *PLA Air Force Enlisted Force Handbook* identifies only four branches and does not list the specialty units. Meanwhile, the *Air Force Encyclopedia* identifies radar troops and communications troops as branches. *PLA Air Force Enlisted Force Handbook* [中国人民解放军空军士兵手册] (Beijing: Blue Sky Press, November 2006), 13.

³⁹ The information for this figure was taken from *PLAAF 2010*, chapters 8–12.

⁴⁰ *PLAAF 2010*, chapter 8.

⁴¹ "广空航空兵某旅科学统筹从严治训 确保节后开飞," accessed at <www.china.com.cn/military/txt/2012-02/01/content_24523647.htm> and "央视曝光：中国居然用一个歼-111B飞行旅守卫朝鲜," <http://club.mil.news.sohu.com/newclub/show.php?forumid=shilin&threadid=4114990> on March 25, 2012.

⁴² Jiang Nianping and Zou Guiyuan, "Airborne Corps," in *Air Force Encyclopedia*, 231–232.

⁴³ *Annual Report to Congress, Military and Security Developments Involving the People's Republic of China, 2010*, (Washington, DC: Office of the Secretary of Defense, August 2010), 4.

⁴⁴ Major General Xu Guangyu, "Evolution of China's Military over the Next 20 Years," *Chinese Academy of Social Sciences Journal*, July 27, 2010. Accessed at <http://theory.people.com.cn/GB/12365190.html> September 10, 2010. The International Institute for Strategic Studies (IISS) *Military Balance for 2010* has a figure of 300,000 to 330,000, which equates to 13.0–14.3 percent of the total force of 2.3 million. James Hackett, ed., *The Military Balance 2010* (London: Routledge Journals for The International Institute for Strategic Studies [IISS], February 2010), 403.

⁴⁵ For 1975, one source (*Air Force Dictionary*) cited a 100,000-man reduction, which equated to a 16.4 percent reduction; a second source (*Military Organizational Reform*) cited a 190,000-man reduction; and a third source (*Air Force Encyclopedia*) reported a 26.9 percent reduction. See the Chronology of Events Appendix in the *Air Force Dictionary*, 977; *Military Organizational Reform*, 465; and Qiao Qingchen, "Air Force of the CPLA," in *Air Force Encyclopedia*, 1233–1234.

⁴⁶ See the Chronology of Events Appendix in the *Air Force Dictionary*, 973, 977, 980, and 982; *Military Organizational Reform*, 465; Jiang Yanyu, *60 Years of New China's National Defense and Military Building* [新中国国防和军队建设60年] (Beijing: Party-founded Reading Material Press, September 2009), 25, 37, 43, and 55. Qiao Qingchen, "Air Force of the CPLA," in *Air Force Encyclopedia*, 1233–1234.

⁴⁷ Xu Guangyu, "Evolution of China's Military over the Next 20 Years."

⁴⁸ *PLAAF 2010*, chapter 3.

⁴⁹ Chen Jinxue, "Air Force Organizational System," in *Air Force Encyclopedia*, 213. Depending on their specialty, technical officers can serve in any of the four departments.

⁵⁰ Yang Zhipo, "Air Force Leadership and Command System," in *Air Force Encyclopedia*, 214.

⁵¹ This discussion draws upon the *Air Force Encyclopedia*. For the Party congresses, see Liu Feng'an, "Chinese Communist Party congresses at various levels of the CPLA Air Force," *Air Force Encyclopedia*, 361.

⁵² Regulations state that, depending on the level in the chain of command, the number of Standing Committee members ranges from 7 to 15. *Science of PLA Political Work* [中国人民解放军政治工作学] (Beijing: National Defense University Press, May 2006), 170–171. The PLAAF's Standing Committee most likely consists of the commander, PC, some (if not all) of the deputy commanders and deputy PCs, and the directors of the Political, Logistics, and Equipment Departments. It is not clear if the PCs of the Logistics Department and Equipment Department are on the Standing Committee.

⁵³ The fourth commander to serve as the Party secretary was Liu Yalou. *Dictionary of China's Communist Party Central Committee Members for 1921–2003* (Beijing: Chinese Communist Party History Press, 2004), 465–466, 587–588, 824–825, and 1052–1053.

⁵⁴ See *PLA Air Force Enlisted Force Handbook*, 12. The PLAAF has several terms that are translated as commander. These include: *silingyuan* (司令员], as in the PLAAF commander [空军司令员] and MRAF commander [军区司令员]; *zhang* [长], as in regiment commander [团长]; and *zhuren*, as in training base commander [训练基地主任]. The PLAAF often uses the generic term *zhihuiyuan* [指挥员] for commanders at all levels.

⁵⁵ Unfortunately, no information was found that describes the specific responsibilities for the PLAAF commander, including his current role as a member of the CMC, or for the PC.

⁵⁶ Li Kunming, *General Theory of Military Political Work* [军队政治工作作学通论] (Beijing: PLA Press, June 2007), 103.

⁵⁷ Liu Yan and Liang Xuemei, *Military 10,000 Why's: Military Structure Revealed* [军事十万个为什么:军制揭密] (Zhengzhou: Zhongyuan Nongmin Chubanshe, July 2002), 162–163. According to this book, the Red Army began using *silingyuan* for commander for larger headquarters, but used *zhang* for operational unit commanders. This book is part of a 10-book series that explains the basics of the PLA. The preface states that it was published as a result of Jiang Zemin's signing of the "National Defense Education Law" in April 2001. Although this series is not published by the PLA, the material appears authoritative.

⁵⁸ The author escorted the PLAAF's Political Commissar, Zhu Guang, around the United States for a week in late 1988 and had a 30-minute one-on-one conversation with the commander, Wang Hai, in April 1989, where he had the opportunity to discuss their common and separate responsibilities. The author has also had discussions with PLA officers in China about this specific topic during the past decade.

⁵⁹ The PLAAF's leaders are often identified as *lingdao* [领导], *shouzhang* [首长], or *zhuguan* [主官]. Together, these terms refer to different combinations of the command staff or command element, including the commander, PC, deputy commanders and PCs, and directors of the four departments.

⁶⁰ Shi Fang, "Senior Officer Division of Labor Responsibility System Under the Unified Leadership of the Party Committee," in *China Military Encyclopedia*, [中国军事百科全书], vol. 4, Song Shilun and Xiao Ke, eds. (Beijing: Military Science Publishing House, July 1997), 28–29.

⁶¹ For example, one of the deputy commanders, Lieutenant General He Weirong, appears to be responsible for training and foreign affairs in the Headquarters Department and possibly development of combat aircraft in the Equipment Department. He was one of the key leaders during the PLAAF's 60th anniversary in November 2009. He also chairs PLAAF training meetings. "China to Mark 60th Founding Anniversary of Airforce with Warplane Show," Xinhua, October 26, 2009, at <www.bjreview.com.cn/60th/2009-10/27/content_226062.htm>. According to a November 9, 2009, Xinhua report, He Weirong gave an interview to the state-owned China Central Television (CCTV), where he announced the next-generation fighter would soon undergo its first flight. See Russell Hsiao, "China's Fifth-Generation Fighters and the Changing Strategic Balance," *China Brief* 9, no. 23 (Washington: Jamestown Foundation, November 19, 2009).

⁶² Of note, in the PLAAF, a chief of staff is the director of the Headquarters Department and is thus the approximate equivalent to a USAF director of operations (A3).

⁶³ According to *PLAAF 2010*. See also "Ma Ning," *Dictionary of China's Communist Party Central Committee Members for 1921–2003*, 523; and "Ma Ning," *Air Force Dictionary*, 842.

⁶⁴ *PLAAF 2010*, chapter 5.

⁶⁵ "Zhengzhi Weiyuan," *Air Force Dictionary*, 206.

⁶⁶ However, the current PC, General Deng Changyou, is still the PLAAF's Party secretary and the Commander, General Xu Qiliang, is the deputy secretary.

⁶⁷ See Yuan Wenxian, ed., *Science of Military Command* [军队指挥学] (Beijing: National Defense University Press, May 2008), 286. This book was published under the auspices of the All-Army Military Science Research "10th Five-Year" Plan.

⁶⁸ "Air Force Deputy Commander Jing Wenchun Tells the Story of Parachute Drops," at <http://news.sina.com.cn/c/2008-06-23/140815799683.shtml>.

⁶⁹ The Internet has biographic information for each of the chiefs of staff. For example, information for Ma Zhanmin, who was the chief of staff from 1982–1987, can be found at <www.hudong.com/wiki/%E9%A9%AC%E5%8D%A0%E6%B0%91>. Based on a review of all 12 biographies, eight chiefs of staff have already retired: two of them retired as the chief of staff, three as a PLAAF deputy commander, one of them as an MRAF commander, one as the commandant of the Academy of Military Science, and one as the PLAAF commander. Of the remaining four, one is still the chief of staff, two are still PLAAF deputy commanders, and Xu Qiliang is still the commander. It should be noted that the chief of staff is the same grade as the MRAF commanders and PLAAF deputy commanders, so moving from chief of staff to those positions is not a promotion. It just means they have different responsibilities.

⁷⁰ Jia Fengsheng, "Chief of Staff," in *China Military Encyclopedia*, vol. 2, 24–25. In the PLA, military work [军事工作] refers specifically to officers who are in the military/command track and work in the Headquarters Department. See also, Yuan Wenxian, ed., *Discussion of Headquarters Department Building* [司令部建设论] (Beijing: National Defense University Press, July 2003), 153.

⁷¹ The seven MRAFs, listed in protocol order, are Shenyang, Beijing, Lanzhou, Jinan, Nanjing, Guangzhou, and Chengdu.

⁷² Subunits are also identified as the "grassroots" [基层] level.

⁷³ Units located in the same province as the MRAF headquarters are directly subordinate to it. Liaoning Province is an exception, because it contains both the Shenyang MRAF and the Dalian Command Post. The five air corps included Datong, Nanning, Wulumuqi, Fuzhou, and Changchun. The five bases included Kunming, Wuhan, Xi'an, Shanghai, and Dalian. Lhasa and Hetian were already division leader–grade CPs. Zhangzhou, which is also one of the 13 CPs, has a long history of being an air corps and a CP, and

having been abolished a few times in between. It was apparently reestablished in 2004. Tangshan, which had been the 6th Air Corps and became the Tangshan Base around 1993, was apparently abolished sometime in the early 2000s. Bi Chunlian, Li Jinzhi, and Chen Ping, "Beijing MRAF Certain Base [Tangshan] Supports National Day Parade," in *China Air Force* vol. 1999-5, no. 82 (Beijing: Lantian Chubanshe, 1999), 27.

[74] At least the Dalian, Datong, Kunming, Wuhan, Wulumuqi, and Xi'an CPs appear to be corps deputy leader–grade organizations. *PLAAF 2010*, chapter 2.

[75] Xiao Mingli, "Air Force Establishment," in *Air Force Encyclopedia*, 215. Meng Zhaoxu, "Establishment Form," and Wang Guoliang, "Order of Establishment," in *China Military Encyclopedia*, vol. 2, 9–10.

[76] Yang Zhipo, "Air Force Leadership and Command System," in *Air Force Encyclopedia*, 214–215.

[77] Ibid. In 1949, the PLAAF Headquarters Training Department was established as a first-level department equal to the Headquarters, Political, and Operations Department. In October 1953, it split into two first-level departments: the PLAAF Military Training Department [空军军训练部], which was responsible for unit training, and the PLAAF Military Schools Management Department [空军军事学校管理部], which was responsible for education and training in the academic institutions. The latter department changed its name to the Air Force Military Schools Department [空军军校部] in 1958. Since then, the training and schools departments have merged and separated several times. See Wang Dinglie, ed., *China Today: Air Force* [当代中国空军] (Beijing: China Social Sciences Press, 1989), and Yuan Wei and Zhang Zhuo, eds., *History of the Development of Chinese Military Academies and Schools* [中国军校发展史] (Beijing: National Defense University Press, July 2001).

[78] Overall, the General Political Department's Cadre Department [中政治部干部部], not the Military Training and Service Arms Department [总参谋部军事训练与兵种部], manages the overall Defense Student Program. See the Defense Student regulations at <www.heao.com.cn/main/html/pz/201006/content_9227.html>.

[79] Air Force Education and Training Command Fact Sheet, which can been found at <www.af.mil/information/factsheets/factsheet_print.asp?fsID=138&page=1>. Information on the U.S. Air Force Academy's subordination can be found at <www.airforce-magazine.com/MagazineArchive/Magazine%20Documents/2011/May%202011/0511FOAS.pdf>.

[80] *PLA Air Force Enlisted Force Handbook*, 214–221.

[81] *PLAAF 2010*, chapter 7.

[82] *A Guide for Applicants to Military Academic Institutions and Civilian College National Defense Student Program* [军队院校及普通高校国防生班报考指南] (Beijing: PLA Press, January 2005), 19. New officers who are assigned directly to a unit along the interior border do not have to undergo any probationary period.

[83] Information accessed at <http://xpb.xidian.edu.cn/trans.aspx?id=944> on January 17, 2011.

[84] Information accessed at <www.csust.edu.cn/pub/kjxpb/notice/t20100611_126804.htm> on January 17, 2011.

[85] The grades were taken from a combination of sources, including the *Air Force Encyclopedia* and the following Internet Web sites: <http://bbs.tiexue.net/post_4402529_1.html>, <http://wenku.baidu.com/view/15ae98b91a37f111f1855bc7.html>, <http://binsys.cn/military/overview/education.php>, and <http://guof.web.sdutcm.edu.cn/shownews.asp?newsid=212>, accessed on November 7, 2010.

[86] Yuan Wei and Zhang Zhuo, ed., *History of China's Military Schools Development*, 931.

[87] *PLAAF 2010*, chapter 8. Liu Jianxin, "Air Force Aviation University," in *Air Force Encyclopedia*, 1248–1249.

[88] See <http://school.kaoyan.com/kjhkdx/2710/kjhkdx-f8ca3586694abce1b7ea81942df1fe43.html>.

[89] Information on the various departments from a review of the PLAAF's encyclopedia, journals, and Internet, as well as interviews with PLA personnel over the past decade.

[90] *People's Liberation Army Air Force Officer's Handbook* [中国人民解放军空军军官手册] (Beijing: Blue Sky Press, November 2006), 338–340.

[91] Accessed at <www.hudong.com/wiki/> [中国人民解放军空军指挥学院] on August 9, 2010.

[92] Dong Huiyu and Mou Xianming, *Modern Military School Education Dictionary* [现代军校教育辞典] (Beijing: National Defense University, July 2009), 137. The dictionary translates *jichu bu* [基础部] as *department of elementary courses*.

[93] *PLAAF 2010*, appendix B.

[94] Qian Haihao, *Science of Military Organizational Structure*, 249; *PLAAF 2010*, chapter 15.

⁹⁵ In the PLAAF, equipment [装备] refers to both individual equipment as well as complete weapons systems, even though the PLAAF sometimes uses weapons and equipment together [武器装备].

⁹⁶ *PLAAF 2010*, chapter 15.

⁹⁷ Ibid.

⁹⁸ According to the *Air Force Encyclopedia*. The Logistics Department still has its own set of research institutes, including the Fuel Research Institute [油料研究所] and the Air Force Aviation Medicine Research Institute [空军航空医学研究所 or 航医学研究所].

⁹⁹ During 2009 and 2010, the PLA had a ceremony for corps deputy leader–grade officers who received their first star. The leaders of the Air Force, Navy, and Second Artillery Equipment Research Academies were among those who received their stars. This clearly indicates that each of those organizations is a corps deputy leader–grade organization. Information accessed at <http://webcache.googleusercontent.com/search?q=cache: 402M94YcDS0J: www.ourzg.com/bbs/read.php%3Ftid%3D87791+%222009%E5%B9%B4%E5%BA%A6%E6%99%8B%E5% 8D%87%22+%22%E6%8E%88%E4%BA%88%E5%B0%91%E5%B0%86%E5%86%9B%E8%A1%94%22&cd= 6&hl=en&ct=clnk&gl=us> for the 2009 ceremony and <http://www.ourzg.com/bbs/simple/?t149938.html> for the 2010 ceremony.

¹⁰⁰ Wang Kang, "Equipment Academy of Air Force," in *Air Force Encyclopedia*, 1252. In early 2004, Second Artillery also created a Second Artillery Equipment Research Academy. In late 2003, the PLA Navy replaced the Naval Research Center (NRC) with its own Naval Equipment Research Academy.

¹⁰¹ Liu Yazhou and Yao Jun, eds., *A History of China's Aviation: Second Edition* [中国航空史 {第二版}] (Hunan: Hunan Science and Technology Press, August 2007), 608–609.

¹⁰² Wang Kang, "Equipment Academy of Air Force," in *Air Force Encyclopedia*, 1252.

¹⁰³ Although the *Air Force Encyclopedia* entries noted in the next few endnotes do not state which grade the research institutes have, regiment-level organizations in the PLA have a Political Division [政治处], while division and above had a Political Department [政治部]. The S&T Division apparently serves the same function as a Headquarters Department and works directly with the Equipment Research Academy's S&T Department. The Management Division apparently works with the Research Academy's Academy Affairs Department.

¹⁰⁴ Wang Kang, "Air Force Institute of Equipment General Development and Evaluation," in *Air Force Encyclopedia*, 1252. The Organization and Plans Division apparently serves the same functions as a Headquarters Department.

¹⁰⁵ Zhang Hongyuan, "Air Force Aeronautic Equipment Institute," in *Air Force Encyclopedia*, 1252.

¹⁰⁶ Wang Yuzhu, "Air Force Institute of Land-Based Air Defense Equipment," in *Air Force Encyclopedia*, 1252–1253.

¹⁰⁷ Zhu Heping, "Air Force Radar and ECM Institute," in *Air Force Encyclopedia*, 1253.

¹⁰⁸ Zhu Lin, "Air Force Institute of Communication, Navigation and Command Automation," in *Air Force Encyclopedia*, 1253. Other than a General Office, no other administrative organizations were identified, so it is not clear whether this is a regiment- or division-grade organization; however, it probably has an S&T Division, Political Division/Department, and a Management Division.

¹⁰⁹ Gu Zhiming, "Air Force Institute of Reconnaissance Intelligence Equipment," in *Air Force Encyclopedia*, 1253. No administrative organizations were identified, so it is not clear whether this is a regiment- or division-grade organization; however, it probably has an S&T Division, Political Division/Department, and a Management Division.

¹¹⁰ Yu Chenglang, "Air Force Institute of Aeronautic Meteorology and Chemical Defense," in *Air Force Encyclopedia*, 1253.

¹¹¹ The *Air Force Encyclopedia* did not have a separate entry for this institute.

¹¹² The *Air Force Encyclopedia* did not have a separate entry for this institute.

¹¹³ *PLAAF 2010*, chapter 6.

¹¹⁴ The first four components have already been discussed. For further information on the last two, see chapter 6 in *PLAAF 2010*.

¹¹⁵ Liu Youfeng, "Air Force Logistic Support System," in *Air Force Encyclopedia*, 424–425.

¹¹⁶ *PLAAF 2010*, chapter 8. The branches support more than 10 companies, including navigation beacon, target range, security, four stations, airfield service, vehicle, fuel transport, cave depot, and air-to-air missile companies. The field station also has several depots, including those for fuel, air materiel, and munitions. In addition, it is responsible for communications and has a subordinate weather station.

[117] Li Zhenlin, "Air Force Materiel Management System," in *Air Force Encyclopedia*, 214.

[118] Although the Aeronautical Engineering Department changed its name to the Equipment Technical Department in 1992, it was still only responsible for aircraft maintenance. The Logistics Department was still responsible for all other systems until 1998, when the Equipment Department took over responsibility for all equipment and weapons systems. See "Air Force Aviation Engineering Department" and "Air Force Equipment Technical Department," *Air Force Dictionary*, 1996, 146.

[119] These offices are subordinate to the Air Force Armament General-Use Equipment Military Representative Bureau discussed earlier.

[120] Li Xuezhong, "Air Force Materiel Technical Support," in *Air Force Encyclopedia*, 493–494.

[121] Wang Yuanming, "Air Force Work of Appointing and Removing Cadre," in *Air Force Encyclopedia*, 369–370.

[122] The regiment-level Party Committee is responsible for promotions at the battalion and company levels.

[123] Ba Jianmin, "Air Force Reserve Forces," "Air Force Reserve Duty," and "Air Force Reserve-Duty Forces," in *Air Force Encyclopedia*, 266–267; and Bai Junlu, "System of Air Force Mobilization," in *Air Force Encyclopedia*, 263. Chen Jinxue, "Air Force Military System," in *Air Force Encyclopedia*, 212.

[124] Chen Jinxue, "Air Force Military System," in *Air Force Encyclopedia*, 212.

[125] Bai Junlu, "System of Air Force Mobilization," in *Air Force Encyclopedia*, 263.

[126] Tai Zhuhua, "Air Force Mobilization Plan," in *Air Force Encyclopedia*, 263.

[127] Li Yun and Yang Lei, "National People's Congress Standing Committee Votes Through the 'National Defense Mobilization Law of the People's Republic of China,'" *Xinhua* (February 26, 2010); no author, "China's Air Force Conducts First Airfield Repair Exercise with Militia," *Xinhua* (August 5, 2010), accessed at <http://war.news.163.com/10/0805/12/6DAR21QU00011MTO.html>.

[128] PLAAF National Defense Students are called reserve officers, but use *houbei* rather than *yubeiyi*.

[129] According to the PLA Ministry of National Defense; see Xiong Huaming, "'Air Force Reserve Unit Work Regulations' Issued," MND Website (January 8, 2010), accessed at <http://news.mod.gov.cn/headlines/2010-01/08/content_4116691.htm>. See also Ba Jianmin and Xiong Hua Ming, "Air Force Reserve Troops Strengthen Their Combat Capabilities," *PLA Daily*, January 4, 2009, accessed at <www.chinamil.com.cn/site1/xwpdxw/2009-01/04/content_1606758.htm>.

[130] Russell Hsiao, "Major Restructuring of PLA Military Regions?" *China Brief* 9, no. 16 (August 5, 2009).

[131] See *PLAAF 2010*, chapter 3, for information about the 60 percent figure and National Defense Student Program.

[132] The AMS is the PLA's highest-level institution charged with the development of PLA strategy and doctrine. It serves as a "think tank" directly subordinate to the CMC and both drives and executes major initiatives of PLA-wide reform and modernization in the realms of military strategy, the operational art, and tactics.

[133] The PLA National Defense University is the highest level of joint professional military education. Its students include general officers and senior field grade officers of all services, and NDU's research institutes are involved in cutting-edge work on all aspects of military affairs.

[134] For further information see Kenneth W. Allen, "Assessing the PLA Air Force's Ten Pillars," *China Brief* 11, no. 3 (February 10, 2011), at <www.jamestown.org/uploads/media/cb_11_3_03.pdf>.

[135] Of note, no PLAN officers have held GPD or GLD deputy billets during the 2000s.

[136] Prior to implementation of the 15-grade system in 1988, the MRAF Headquarters were *bingtuan* leader–grade [正兵团] organizations, which were one grade below MR deputy leader. When the new grade system was implemented, the bingtuan leader and deputy leader [副兵团] grades were abolished. The bingtuan leader grade was merged into the MR deputy leader grade and the bingtuan deputy leader grade was merged into the corps leader grade. As a result, the PLA was then able to designate each MRAF commander as a concurrent deputy commander. Although the PLA began designating MRAF commanders as concurrent MR deputy commanders in 1988, the CMC did not officially approve the practice until January 1993. See the Chronology of Events Appendix in the *Air Force Dictionary*, 982.

Chapter 5

The Missions of the People's Liberation Army Air Force

Murray Scot Tanner

This chapter analyzes the emerging missions of the People's Liberation Army Air Force (PLAAF). It draws on the discussions and debates over these missions contained in recent analyses of airpower and spacepower by Chinese specialists, in particular over the past half-dozen years. The chapter begins with a brief overview of the concept of the "mission" in Chinese airpower and spacepower writings.[1]

This chapter focuses on one of the most important themes that unify many Chinese analyses of the air force's emerging missions—the PLAAF's transition from an air force focused on territorial defense toward an air force that increasingly emphasizes offensive missions and trying to seize and maintain the initiative in its combat missions.

The increased emphasis on offensive power and initiative in PLAAF missions by Chinese air- and spacepower analysts reflects their assessment of the increasing military and political utility of offensive airpower and conventional deterrence, which were two major lessons they have drawn from the use of airpower in the Gulf War, Kosovo, the Iraq War, and the Afghan War. The transition to offense and initiative also reflects their assessment of the military needs of China's enduring and emerging national security interests. Coercive operations against Taiwan might require the PLAAF to deter or prevent U.S. naval and air forces from intervening in support of Taiwan. PLAAF analysts also contend that in a Taiwan scenario, the air force must be prepared to resist what they regard as the certainty of major U.S. airstrikes against Chinese forces, and try to find a way of using these strikes to regain the initiative against U.S. forces. Chinese security analysts also argue the PLA must be prepared to deter or defend against potential attacks against China's increasingly populous and wealthy southeastern coast, and strengthen its ability to assert China's territorial and resource claims in its coastal waters. Some air- and spacepower analysts also see these missions contributing to China's struggle against separatists and terrorists in China's border regions.

This transition is particularly evident in Chinese security analysts' discussion of three of the PLAAF's existing or emerging missions—deterring infringement of China's critical national security interests, carrying out offensive operations, and maintaining China's air and space defenses. Following a brief overview of the PLAAF's concept of its missions, the chapter focuses on these three specific missions and the recent thinking by air- and spacepower analysts about how the PLAAF should deepen its orientation toward offense and initiative in pursuing these missions.

The Concept of the PLAAF's Missions

Prior to the 1990s, the PLAAF's official mission was largely limited to that of a localized defensive force intended to support ground (or maritime) operations on or close to the mainland.[2] In recent years, however, Chinese Communist Party (CCP) and PLA leaders have made clear that they envision a greatly expanded combat and noncombat role for the air force. In 2004, the Party's Central Military Commission (CMC) approved the air force's first-ever service-specific strategic concept. This concept clearly suggested a much broader mission than in the past, with a greater emphasis on offense: "Integrate air and space; be simultaneously prepared for offensive and defensive operations" (*kongtian yi ti, gongfang jianbei,* 空天一体, 攻防兼备).[3] Then, in 2008, China's National Defense White Paper identified the PLAAF as a "strategic service" of the PLA.[4]

Over the past 5 to 6 years in particular, PLA analysts of air- and spacepower have produced an outpouring of articles and in-depth studies analyzing and debating the future missions that the world's most powerful air forces, including China's, will have to prepare to undertake. This chapter draws heavily upon these analyses.[5]

Some recent Chinese military reference works have tried to clarify and standardize the definitions of concepts such as "mission" and "task," and related terms such as "operations" (*xingdong,* 行动). But most PLA books and articles do not draw clear distinctions among these concepts, nor have consistent definitions for these terms emerged in recent analyses of air- and spacepower. For example, the most common terms for "mission" (*shiming,* 使命) and "task" (*renwu,* 任务) are often used interchangeably or in combination.

The *Chinese Air Force Encyclopedia* and a few other analytical sources provide distinct definitions for air force "missions" (*shiming,* 使命) and air force "tasks" (*renwu,* 任务).[6] The *Chinese Air Force Encyclopedia* defines *air force missions* as:

> The important historical responsibilities entrusted to the air force by the state, which are divided into basic missions [jiben shiming, 基本使命], special missions [teshu shiming, 特殊使命], and concrete missions [juti shiming, 具体使命].[7]

Historically, statements of basic PLA missions have been worded as slogans or broad statements of political values or goals. The PLAAF's first statement of mission, for example, appears to have been Mao Zedong's April 1950 inscription for the inaugural issue of the PLAAF's journal *People's Air Force*. It read simply "Create a Strong and Great People's Air Force; Destroy the Remnant Enemy Forces; Stabilize the Nation's Defenses."[8] Today, statements of the PLAAF's basic missions tend to be worded in somewhat more concrete terms, but are still not highly detailed. An example is the 2008 National Defense White Paper's statement that the PLAAF was responsible for "safeguarding the country's territorial air space and territorial sovereignty, and maintaining a stable air defense posture nationwide."[9]

The *Air Force Encyclopedia* defines the *basic tasks* (*jiben renwu*, 基本任务) of any nation's air force as "the important responsibilities that an air force assumes in order to carry out its missions."[10] Although "tasks" are supposed to be clearly defined responsibilities intended to carry out PLAAF missions, very few PLA analysts actually make any clear distinction between "tasks" and relatively specific or concrete "missions." Some senior analysts even use the term "tasks"—*renwu*—jointly or interchangeably with "missions"—*shiming*—both when they describe some relatively abstract missions (deterrence, for example) and when they describe far more concrete and specific missions or tasks.

For example, two leading analysts have referred to the same undertaking by air force personnel—using air and space forces to deter the enemy, for example—as different categories of concepts: one labels this a "task-mission" (*renwu shiming*; 任务使命), and the other calls some of these activities "operations" (*xingdong*; 行动) in one portion of his study and "tasks" in another.[11] This lack of consistency within the PLAAF literature indicates a clear conceptual problem—the PLAAF is presently in the process of defining a new set of missions without a clear, agreed-upon concept of what a "mission" is or how it fits into the structure of PLAAF military thought.

The PLAAF has not publicly released a list of its principal missions. Nor have PLA air- and spacepower analysts over the past several years referred to air force missions using the same list of missions and similar terms for them—something Western analysts would expect to see if an agreed-upon list of missions existed. But a review of recent PLA writings on air- and spacepower suggests that a broad consensus exists among PLA analysts concerning the importance of six core PLAAF air and space missions: deterrence; offense; defense; airlift; airborne; and blockade support. The breadth of this list underscores the terrific change in the PLA's overall view of the air force's mission and utility over the past 15 years or so.

A closer examination of some of these missions demonstrates an important theme in the PLAAF's transition away from being a largely defensively-oriented air force. Several of these missions reflect the PLA's focus on developing the air force's offensive capabilities as well as its capability to retake and maintain the initiative in deterrence and combat missions. The remainder of this chapter focuses on what most analysts would probably agree are the three most important of these missions—deterrence, offense, and defense—with a special focus on this new emphasis on offense and initiative.

Conventional Air and Space Deterrence Missions

For more than a decade, PLAAF doctrinal writings, defense white papers, and analytical studies have placed increasing emphasis on "deterrence" as one of the PLAAF's most important missions. The PLAAF's capability to achieve an important strategic goal of the state such as deterrence—either acting independently or as the lead service in joint operations—is an important aspect of what PLA analysts mean when they refer to the PLAAF becoming a "strategic air force" or a "strategic air and space force."

Recent PLA studies have also argued that conventional air and space forces have become increasingly effective as deterrent forces since the end of the Cold War.[12] One part of this contention is that the speed, range, precision and "ferocity" of modern precision-guided munitions make them especially well-suited for deterring hostile behavior by a prospective enemy.[13] Chinese analysts argue that these weapons, in addition to their battlefield effectiveness, can have a powerful political effect by dissolving the willpower of the enemy's civilian population and government to support continued warfare. Some analysts, moreover, have argued that compared to nuclear weapons, conventional air and space weapons are more controllable and flexible, cause less collateral damage, and have fewer or shorter lived aftereffects, all of which make them politically less risky to employ.[14] Apparently implicit in this last point is the assumption that the most likely opponent to be targeted by such operations is, itself, a nuclear power.

Toward a ladder of deterrence intensity. Over the past 6 years, in an apparent effort to promote China's capacity for initiative and control in its conventional air- and space-deterrence operations, several major studies of air- and spacepower have tried to develop what might be called a "ladder of intensity levels" for deterrence. These studies describe increasingly serious periods or stages in a crisis, and recommend increasingly harsh corresponding actions China could take to signal its military power, preparation, and determination to its prospective adversaries. During peacetime precrisis periods, these include many routine activities associated with China's buildup of military forces.

At the highest, most intense stages of a crisis, some analysts have even suggested the use of actual first strikes as a means of warning an opponent to desist in its actions.

A powerful implicit theme in these discussions of a ladder of deterrence is that China will be able to maintain control and initiative, selecting among these options based on the nature of the threat it faces. Unpredictable or uncontrollable responses by enemy forces are not addressed.

Low-intensity deterrence operations. During peacetime or the very early stages of a crisis, PLA analysts recommend the use of an array of "low-intensity" deterrence operations and activities. These include several gradual, nonviolent, noncoercive, and even commonplace peacetime military activities whose purpose is to communicate to a potential enemy the increasing strength of the country's air- and spacepower, as well as its resolve to use it if need be. Examples include publicizing the country's air- and spacepower buildup, training and exercises, international arms sales expositions, and testing of new weapons and equipment.[15] Analyst Yuan Jingwei of China's National Defense University (NDU) cites the publicity surrounding a reported 2001 U.S. space warfare exercise as an example, claiming that the exercise was far more valuable to the United States for its deterrent effect on potential enemies than as an actual military exercise.[16]

Medium-intensity deterrence operations. During the early or "deepening" stages of crises, analysts recommend undertaking more open and assertive deterrent measures. The purpose of these measures is to signal much more forcefully to a potential enemy the strength of China's capabilities, its intentions, and its resolve. Possible deterrent activities might include carrying out realistic exercises and weapons tests, redeploying troops, establishing no-fly zones, or undertaking intrusive patrols or reconnaissance activities.[17]

High-intensity deterrence operations. Analysts recommend these operations for when "a crisis is intensifying, the enemy is clearly making moves to prepare for real combat, and is clearly plotting to carry out an attack."[18] Their purpose is primarily to communicate will and intention to use force in the event the adversary "stubbornly persists" in offensive actions.[19]

A few PLA air and space analysts have recently begun to blur any distinction between "deterrence" and "actual combat" by explicitly proposing the possibility of launching first attacks to intimidate potential opponents during the "high-intensity" phase of a crisis. Analyst Yuan Jingwei of the Chinese National Defense University's Campaign Education and Research Department contends that a sharp, initial combat blow should be seen not so much as the initiation of full-scale combat, but rather as a signal designed to get the opponent to back down. "Military deterrence," Yuan argues, "has gradually become an important form for actually carrying out combat."[20] Widely published air- and spacepower theorists Cai Fengzhen and Tian Anping likewise identify forms of high-intensity and even super-high-intensity deterrence operations in which relatively low-intensity combat operations are used to achieve the goals of strategic and campaign-level deterrence.[21] Cai and Tian, as well as PLAAF analyst Min Zengfu, argue that this form of deterrence lies somewhere between "deterrence" and "real combat."[22]

Offensive Missions and Operations

A major transformation in thinking among PLA air- and spacepower analysts since the early 1990s has been their increasing emphasis on offensive missions and operations, and their growing faith in the broad strategic, campaign, and political utility of the offensive mission. Longtime PLAAF analyst Min Zengfu traces this change in thinking, noting that during the 1970s and 1980s, the two major tasks set forth by the Central Military Commission that defined the PLAAF's mission were air defense of the national territory and providing support for military combat operations of the infantry and navy. In the early 1990s, however, as part of China's reorientation of its "primary strategic direction" away from defense against the former Soviet Union and toward preventing Taiwan independence and securing China's interests along its southeast coast, the PLAAF's missions were redefined and expanded to include more offensive operations.[23] Along with deterrence and air defense, the PLAAF's capability to carry out offensive operations is now one of the three missions that attract the greatest emphasis and focus among analysts.

This increased emphasis on the offensive mission is reflected in the 2007 edition of the National Defense University's *The Science of Campaigns*. The text notes that the PLAAF's service mission of "being simultaneously prepared for offense and defense" (gongfang jianbei, 攻防兼备) is a combined offensive and defensive mission, but the authors then proceed to urge that the air force place greater focus on the active, offensive aspects of this mission.

> The Air Force should implement the operational thinking of emphasizing offense [zhuzhong jingong, 注重进攻], while being simultaneously prepared for offense and defense. The Air Force should give full play to its powerful aerial mobility, rapid speed, and long-distance strike capabilities, as well as its advantages in conducting multiple types of aerial missions.[24]

PLAAF analysts Cai Fengzhen and Tian Anping echo these thoughts, calling upon the air force to expand the role and power of offense and labeling this an "urgent task."

China needs to readjust its attack-and-defense structure. The urgent task facing China is to increase the ratio and power of its offensive combat strength and to increase the quality of its defense, while at the same time reducing the scope of its defense. To be able to simultaneously attack and defend has become a short-term objective for China to achieve.[25]

Accomplishing and Supporting Objectives

Chinese air- and spacepower analysts demonstrate great faith in the utility of modern air and space offensive missions, and they maintain that PLAAF offensive missions can accomplish or support a wide array of strategic, campaign, operational, and also political objectives. To underscore the concept of the PLAAF as a "strategic" service, a number of analysts stress the ability of modern, informatized air and space forces to achieve the strategic objectives of the state either singlehandedly, or as the lead service in joint operations. Their contention is that in several recent limited wars and operations around the world, the speed, range, and destructiveness of offensive air and space have not only been militarily critical, but also politically decisive—constituting "the final word" that destroyed the adversary's economic and logistical capability to sustain military operations, and that undermined the political will of an adversary's population, armed forces, and government to fight onward.

Writing in 2006, analysts Cai Fengzhen and Deng Fan described the decisive importance of the air and space offensive mission this way:

> The practise of modern warfare has already verified that "victory or defeat is determined in the air and space." Air-space superiority not only can achieve maximum military advantage. It can also be used to obtain comprehensive benefits in political, spiritual and other areas. By means of operations in air-space battlefields ... fighting speedy battles and winning quick decisions has already become the principal measure used by the United States and other major air- and space-countries for seizing comprehensive political and military benefits.[26]

The Science of Campaigns has identified three clusters of "basic tasks" that define the key strategic- and campaign-level objectives of PLAAF offensive campaigns. These focus on destroying or disabling enemy forces to achieve air dominance, supporting ground and maritime campaigns, and achieving other unspecified strategic goals of the state. More specifically, they include the following: "Destroy or cripple enemy aviation forces and ground air defense forces, and thereby seize air dominance"; "Destroy or weaken large enemy troop concentrations, and destroy enemy transportation systems, to create conditions for ground or maritime campaigns"; and "Strike enemy political, military, and economic targets, weaken the enemy's combat potential to achieve specific strategic goals, and accomplish other specially assigned strategic aims."[27]

NDU analyst Yuan Jingwei's description of the objectives of offensive missions, however, places more explicit emphasis on disabling the enemy's combat systems than the list of tasks in *The Science of Campaigns*. He describes the objectives of these missions as follows:

> to achieve air and space superiority [*kongtian youshi*, 空天优势], paralyze the enemy's combat systems [*nanhuan di zuozhan tixi*, 瘫痪地作战体系], and weaken the enemy's combat potential [*xiaoruo di zhanzheng qianli*, 削弱敌战争条件], in order to create the conditions for achieving strategic and campaign goals [*wei dacheng zhanlue zhanyi mudi chuangzao tiaojian*, 为达成战略战役目的创造条件], or to achieve these goals directly.[28]

Offensive Information Warfare Systems and Operations

Yuan's definition of the offensive mission reflects a growing consensus among PLA air- and spacepower theorists (including the authors of *The Science of Campaigns* in 2007) that a primary objective of offensive missions is to destroy or undermine the capability of the enemy's command and control, surveillance, and other information systems to function together effectively. This mission is to be accomplished by sudden, carefully targeted attacks on "key-point" (*zhongdian*, 中点) or "critical" (*yaohai*, 要害) targets. A critical aim is to disable enemy air defenses and induce paralysis, blindness, or isolation in these key combat systems at least long enough for PLAAF forces to establish and exploit corridors to carry out their main attacks.

A number of PLA air- and spacepower analysts portray these enemy information systems as fragile, interdependent "systems of systems" that are potentially subject to something like cascade failure, rather than as interconnected systems with a robust level of redundancy built in. Analysts Cai Fengzhen and Tian Anping contend that, properly carried out, "an attack on one point can paralyze the entire situation" (*ji qiyidian tanhuan quanju*, 击其一点瘫痪全局).[29] This perspective that the enemy is a vulnerable "system of systems" is spelled out in a number of other analyses as well.[30]

Toward this end, PLA analysts increasingly emphasize the critical role that achieving information superiority (*xinxi youshi*, 信息优势) and undertaking successful information operations plays in the offensive mission to incapacitate enemy systems while protecting China's own systems.[31] They distinguish three aspects of information operations that play a critical role in the overall offensive mission—reconnaissance, attacks, and defense:[32]

- *Information reconnaissance* involves expanding the campaign commanders' capability for gathering intelligence materials on enemy information operations.[33]

- *Information attacks* involve seeking information superiority by disrupting the enemy's flows of key information. A major purpose of these operations is "to completely blind the enemy's air defense system" and "to open a gap in the enemy's air defense system to make it difficult for the enemy to organize effective interception actions." PLA analysts note two forms of "soft" information attacks—electronic jamming and deception and computer network attacks—and "hard" attacks involving firepower destruction of enemy information assets.[34] Key targets include enemy reconnaissance and early warning satellites, airborne early warning and control aircraft, ground-based long-range warning and fire-control radars, surface-to-air missile radars, and command guidance systems.[35] *The Science of Campaigns* specifically recommends that attack planners assign a portion of China's most capable fighters to attack enemy airborne warning and control system (AWACS) planes in order to "chop down one of the enemy's important information pillars" (*qieduan di de zhongyao xinxi zhizhang,* 切断地的重要信息支撑).[36] Some analysts contend that China's electronic jamming and deception resources are limited at present, and hence these information attacks are likely to rely more heavily on air attacks.[37] This strongly suggests that Chinese forces may be forced to place much greater emphasis on destroying enemy warning and command and control and guidance systems through use of firepower destruction.

- *Information defense* involves organizing defensive operations to prevent enemy jamming, firepower destruction, and computer network attacks.

Evading, Suppressing, and Penetrating Enemy Air Defenses[38]

Chinese analysts contend that penetrating enemy air defenses to establish corridors through which the main assault forces can reach their targets (*kongzhong tufang,* 空中突防) is one of the most difficult tasks of the offensive mission. But they also underscore the importance of this task to the successful execution of the overall mission.[39] Their assessments are heavily influenced by their very high evaluation of the air defense systems of the countries of their most likely prospective adversaries (the United States, Taiwan, and probably Japan), as well as by their concerns about the shortcomings of China's own forces. Some argue that penetration will be extremely difficult because "presently our main operational targets are the established and tightly integrated long, medium, and short range, and high, medium, and low altitude air defense systems." They also argue that the PLAAF should expect to encounter enemy air defenses with advanced intelligence warning systems, continuous 360-degree monitoring of the battlespace, and other features that create an "unprecedented" level of battlespace transparency. All of these, they contend, will make the execution of penetration very difficult.[40]

In order to penetrate advanced air defenses, Chinese analysts have advocated using a combination of "stealth penetrations" and "storm penetrations." Stealth assaults emphasize deception, concealment, flying at ultra-low levels and a variety of other radar avoidance techniques to avert detection and mislead enemy defenses. Storm assaults involve preceding and escorting the actual attack group with as many as five other groups assigned to such tasks as reconnaissance, electronic interference, air defense suppression, screening, and support.[41]

To maintain China's initiative following the initial assault, Chinese analysts urge preparations to launch quick follow-on attacks. They emphasize that this requires very rapid assessment of the damage inflicted by the first wave, which, in turn, places a heavy burden upon all surveillance and reconnaissance assets—air, space, naval, ground, and other assets—to quickly supply data for follow-on assaults.[42]

Another aspect of the assault that Chinese analysts emphasize is the early and continuous preparation to defeat enemy counterattack operations. In addition to defending the security of key war zone targets, these analysts stress that preparing to block counterattacks is critical to allowing Chinese forces to remain on the offensive and facilitate the overall "smooth progress" of the mission.[43]

The PLAAF's Increasing Interest in Space

A few air- and spacepower analysts have been increasingly frank in discussing the future role of space orbital attacks as a means of seizing the initiative and rapidly gaining air and space superiority, although the studies reviewed for this chapter also insist that China has an overall peaceful space policy. These analysts have outlined space orbital attacks as an important future means of disrupting, crippling, or destroying an adversary's satellites and other space-based assets. Some also speculate about more futuristic attacks by space-based weapons. Writing in 2006, analysts Zhang Zhiwei and Feng Chuangjiang recognized the critical connection between control of space and seizing initiative, arguing that space would ultimately become "the true first battlefield" in modern war, with countries using the first wave of attacks to induce satellite paralysis and seize space supremacy.⁴⁴ Chinese NDU Professor Yuan Jingwei has taken this analysis a step further, spotlighting three potential methods of carrying out these space orbital operations: physically destroying satellites and other enemy targets, using lasers, bursts of electromagnetic energy, directed energy weapons, armed satellites, or antisatellite/antiballistic missiles; disabling the target's ability to function, employing low-energy lasers, particle beams, or "space junk"; and even seizing (捕捉) an enemy space vehicle or other target, using one's own space vehicles.⁴⁵

Yuan has argued that this type of warfare represents the future of integrated air and space combat, and that Russia, the United States, and "every militarily powerful country" are engaged in research on weapons systems for carrying out space orbital attacks. He maintains that in the future "these attacks will be one of the principal methods of combat for seizing space supremacy."⁴⁶ Although Yuan stops short of voicing the obvious policy conclusion, his implication almost certainly seems to be that China must also develop such weapons and capabilities if it is to avoid being left behind.

Integrated Air and Space Defensive Missions

For decades, providing air defense—in particular, territorial air defense—has been one of the PLAAF's two defining missions. This chapter and many other analyses have placed considerable stress on such emerging PLAAF missions as deterrence or offensive strikes. But it is worth bearing in mind that some of the PLA's most authoritative published studies and documents still emphasize the PLAAF's air and space defense mission as one of the most important and pervasive that it will be asked to undertake in any future war. The PLAAF's ability to repulse enemy air and space strikes, mitigate their political, economic, and military damage, and launch crippling counterattacks against enemy offensive capabilities will be crucial to China's success in achieving its campaign and strategic goals, and, indeed, to China's national security as a whole. The 2006 edition of *The Science of Campaigns* contends that the stakes of success or failure in defending against enemy air raid campaigns may include "crucial issues such as our country's territorial integrity, respect for our sovereignty, or the very security of the nation."⁴⁷ Likewise, when China's 2008 National Defense White Paper describes the duties the air force must undertake as a "strategic service" of the PLA, it does so primarily in terms that emphasize its defensive mission: "[The air force] is responsible for such tasks as safeguarding the country's territorial air space and territorial sovereignty, and maintaining a stable air defense posture nationwide."⁴⁸

The PLAAF's defensive mission is comprised of three main parts or dimensions that have, for the most part, remained the same for decades. These are: protective or "defensive" (*fanghu*, 防护) activities and operations; interception or "resistance" operations (*kangji*, 抗击); and "counterattack" operations (*fanji*, 反击). *The Study of Air Force Campaigns* refers to all three of these tasks that the air force would undertake as part of its air defense mission:

> Organize air defense campaigns with varying sets of arrangements and of different scales based on the objectives and scope of the enemy's air attack; intercept the enemy's attack planes and other aerial attack forces; launching sudden attacks against enemy planes and other weapons while they are still at their airfields and launch bases; and carrying out tight defense of our own airfields, bases, etc., in order to destroy the enemies' aerial attack plans and schemes.[49]

The PLAAF's "integrated" defensive mission is also very likely its most complex mission organizationally because of the sheer breadth of tasks involved and the numerous units that must collaborate effectively with the air force—including the other PLA services and national and local government and civilian organizations. PLAAF analysts note that China's "integrated" air- and space-defense system must incorporate aerial, space-based, and ground-based (including maritime) forces to undertake protection and defense, interception, and counterattack operations. The system is also expected to protect numerous political, economic, military, media, and other targets that would be essential to sustain the Communist Party's capability to rule the country and the PLA's warmaking capability and freedom of operation (including key command, control, information, defensive, and other systems).[50]

PLA air- and spacepower analysts are often very frank about the enormous challenge they believe Chinese defenses will face from multiple, large-scale air attacks by an unnamed enemy that possesses a considerable advantage in military power and technology. NDU scholar Yuan Jingwei, for example, makes little effort to disguise that he is talking about the United States and the North Atlantic Treaty Organization when he argues that aerial surprise attacks have become the method of first-choice in modern informatized warfare, and were decisive to the outcome of the Gulf War and the wars in Kosovo, Afghanistan, and Iraq. Yuan foresees China facing "severe air and space intimidation" in a future war, and argues that "air and space defense combat will be one of the primary forms of future air and space integrated combat."[51] *The Science of Campaigns* is even more blunt: "In future anti-air raid campaigns, our principal combat adversary will be a powerful enemy who possesses superiority in high technology."[52]

Active Defense, Counterattacks, and Regaining Initiative

A number of recent PLA analyses are placing growing emphasis on finding ways for the PLAAF to use defensive operations to retake the initiative by carrying out effective counterattacks against enemy bases. Counterattacks are seen as an increasingly critical aspect of the PLA's overall "active defense" strategy and "being prepared for simultaneous offensive and defensive operations."[53] Military analysts make clear that in addition to accomplishing a variety of important protective and damage limitation tasks, China's air and space defensive operations are expected to try to transform the nature of the war by lifting the air force out of a "passive" or "defensive" posture into an "active" or "offensive" posture. This transformation will require air and space defensive forces to prevent or limit fundamental damage to military command and control systems and preserve the PLA's capacity to make war. Interception and counterattack operations would likewise be expected to inflict sufficiently high attrition rates to weaken, paralyze, or confuse enemy air and space operations, and make a major contribution to China seizing air and space superiority (*zhikongquan, zhitianquan*, 制空权,制天权).

Although officially called "*counter*attacks" (*fanji*, 反击), Chinese analysts stress that these strikes can (and should) include attacks against enemy air- and ground-based assets and facilities, and possibly even before an adversary's first strike. One analyst, writing frankly about air and space counterattacks, notes that these operations are sufficiently similar to offensive strike operations (*kongtian jingong zuozhan*, 空天进攻作战) that his study analyzes counterattack operations as part of its section on offensive operations.[54] Air- and space-defense specialists Wang Fengshan, Li Xiaojun, and Ma Shuanzhu likewise define "active counterattacks" (*jiji fanji*, 积极反击) in a way that seems as though it could include first strikes to destroy or delay an enemy's plan to carry out air attacks:

> Active counterattack refers to, in the course of air defense operations, creating and seizing advantageous opportunities to actively and assertively launch air strikes [*kongxi*, 空袭] and disruption operations [*xirao xingdong*, 袭扰行动] against the enemy, to destroy his plans for air strikes, delay his air strike operations, weaken and halt his power to commit air strikes, and use attacks to help our defense and support our regular [*zhengmian*, 正面] resistance operations. The keypoint objective of our counterattack operations is the enemy's information centers for his air strike systems, his communication nodes, and other crucial command and control facilities.[55]

Chinese analysts have tried to set out several basic principles for carrying out these counterattacks, including recommending a relatively low number of small-scale, tightly focused attacks aimed at enemy gaps and weaknesses in order to cause maximum disruption. As suggested above, they also emphasize that it is better to strike early rather than to delay. Counterattacking forces are urged, as much as possible, to focus their strikes on paralyzing one aspect of the enemy's operations at a time, rather than attempting a more wide-ranging attack. The keypoint targets for operations are crucial enemy command and control facilities, information centers for air strike systems, communication nodes, bases (including carriers), air and space assets, and support facilities.[56] The NDU's Yuan Jingwei stresses in particular the importance of precision attacks against both the physical and informational "sourceheads" (*yuantou*, 源头) of incoming enemy planes and missiles—air bases, space launch bases, command and control centers, and orbiting spacecraft.[57] With success in these "active defense" counterattacks, PLAAF analysts have voiced great hope that these operations can reverse the overall trend in a war or campaign from defensive to offensive, and "thoroughly remove [us from] the passive position of air defense, and allow us to obtain the initiative in a campaign."[58]

Conclusion

In their analyses of China's emerging air force missions over the past decade or so, Chinese air and space analysts have devoted increasing attention to promoting China's preparation for offensive missions and its efforts to seize and maintain the initiative in combat. In their discussion of deterrence operations, this has included efforts to develop a ladder of signals of increasing intensity to ward off potential adversaries. In their analysis of offensive operations, these analysts have stressed the increased importance of offense in PLAAF missions. They have also emphasized the importance of targeting what they see as the fragile "systems of systems" that constitute enemy combat information systems. Finally, even within the defensive mission, analysts have placed a growing emphasis on counterattacks as a means of seizing and holding the initiative in the face of near certain large-scale air attacks.

Notes

[1] The views in this chapter are entirely those of the author and do not necessarily represent those of the Center for Naval Analyses, its corporate officers, or its sponsors.

[2] Kevin Lanzit and Kenneth Allen, "Right-Sizing the PLA Air Force: New Operational Concepts Define a Smaller, More Capable Force" in *Right Sizing the People's Liberation Army: Exploring the Contours of China's Military*, eds. Roy Kamphausen and Andrew Scobell (Carlisle, PA: Strategic Studies Institute, U.S. Army War College, 2007).

[3] Several English translations of 空天一体, 攻防兼备 are equally plausible. The one used here draws in part on Lanzit and Allen.

[4] *China's National Defense in 2008*, 45.

[5] See for example Cai Fengzhen and Tian Anping, *The Air and Space Battlefield and China's Air Force* [*Kongtian Zhanchang yu Zhongguo Kongjun*, 空天战场与中国空军] (Beijing: Jiefangjun Chubanshe, 2004); Min Zengfu et al., *The Concept of Air Force Military Thought* [*Kongjun junshi sixiang gainian*, 空军军事思想概念] (Beijing: Jiefangjun Chubanshe, 2006); Yuan Jingwei, *Research on Integrated Aerospace Combat Operations* [*Kongtian yiti zuozhan yanjiu*, 空天一体作战研究] (Beijing: Guofang daxue chubanshe, 2006); Cai Fengzhen and Tian Anping, *The Study of Integrated Aerospace Combat* [*Kongtian yiti zuozhan xue*, 空天一体作战学] (Beijing: Jiefangjun Chubanshe, 2006); and Wang Fengshan, Li Xiaojun, and Ma Shuanzhu, *Science of Modern Air Defense* [*Xiandai fangkong xue*, 现代防空学] (Beijing: Hangkong gongye chubanshe, 2008).

[6] Yao Wei, ed., *Chinese Air Force Encyclopedia*, 5–6.

[7] See Min et al., 132.

[8] Hua Renjie, Cao Yifeng, and Chen Huixiu, *A History of Air Force Academic Thought*, 347.

[9] *China's National Defense in 2008*, 45.

[10] Yao, 5–6; and Min et al., 132.

[11] Cai Fengzhen and Tian Anping refer to deterrence as a "task-mission" [*renwu shiming*, 任务使命], whereas Yuan Jingwei analyzes air and space deterrence as one of seven major integrated air and space "operations" [*xingdong*, 行动] in one part of his study but refers to it as one of several key "tasks" [*renwu*, 任务] in another part. See Cai and Tian, *The Study of Integrated Air and Space Combat*, 289; and Yuan, 124–134 and 13–15.

[12] Yao, 43–44; also Min et al., 145–147.

[13] Min et al., 145–147; Yuan, 125; and Cai and Tian, *The Study of Integrated Air and Space Combat*, 289.

[14] On the political advantages of conventional weapons, see Min et al., 145–146; Yuan, 126; Cai and Tian, *The Air and Space Battlefield and China's Air Force*, 150.

[15] Yuan, 129.

[16] Cai and Tian, *The Study of Integrated Air and Space Combat*, 289; Yuan, 129–130.

[17] Cai and Tian, *The Study of Integrated Air and Space Combat*, 289; Yuan, 130.

[18] Cai and Tian, *The Study of Integrated Air and Space Combat*, 289.

[19] Yuan, 132; Cai and Tian, *The Study of Integrated Air and Space Combat*, 289.

[20] Yuan, 125–132, and Min et al., 145–147, make a similar argument. The possible use of limited attacks is also evident in Yuan's definition of deterrence: "Air and space military deterrence is, to use powerful air and space forces as one's backup force, and threaten to use, or make limited use of [威胁使用或有限使用] this air and space power in order to overawe one's opponent and hold him in check. The goal of carrying out air and space military deterrence/intimidation is by means of comprehensive employment of offensive-style and defensive style deterrence, dynamic, and static deterrence, soft and hard deterrence, and other sorts of tactics, to demonstrate our real power and determination for air and space combat operations to our enemies."

[21] Cai and Tian, *The Study of Integrated Air and Space Combat*, 289–290.

[22] Min et al., 147; Cai and Tian, *The Study of Integrated Air and Space Combat*, 289–290.

[23] Min et al., 32–42; Hua, Cao, and Chen, 345.

[24] Zhang Yuliang, *The Science of Campaigns* [*Zhanyi xue*; 战役学] (Beijing: National Defense University Press, 2007 edition), chapter 3.

[25] Cai and Tian, *The Air and Space Battlefield and China's Air Force*, 154–155.

[26] Cai Fengzhen and Deng Fan, "Introduction to Air-Space Battlefields and National Air-Space Security System," *China Military Science* [*Zhongguo junshi kexue*; 中国军事科学], 2006, no. 2. See also Zhang, *The Science of Campaigns*, 543–544; Min et al., 37–38; Cai and Tian, *The Air and Space Battlefield and China's Air Force*, 155, 171–172. Zhang notes that the political sensitivity and importance of these missions are one of the "special characteristics" of offensive missions.

[27] Zhang, *The Science of Campaigns*, 528.

[28] Yuan, 145.

[29] Cai and Tian, *The Study of Integrated Air and Space Combat*, 204.

[30] *The Science of Campaigns* also spells out this viewpoint in some detail: "In the future when we organize to carry out an aerial assault campaign, that which will confront us will be an organically-consti-

tuted macro-system [*youji goucheng de daxitong*; 有机构成的大系统] which is made up of a reconnaissance and surveillance system [*zhencha tance xitong*; 侦查探测系统], a firepower attack system [*huoli daji xitong*; 火力打击系统], a command and control system [*zhihui kongzhi xitong*; 指挥控制系统], and other such systems. And whether or not our enemy can reach the full potential of his combat capacity will, primarily, be decided by the coordinated exercise of these major systems. Within this macro-system there exist many critical targets in which 'pulling a single hair can move the entire body' or one incident can affect the entire situation. These include communication nodes, reconnaissance and early warning systems, air bases, command and control centers, industries which are pillars of the entire national economy and its war-making potential, energy installations, and so forth." Zhang, *The Science of Campaigns*, 528.

[31] Cai and Tian, *The Study of Integrated Air and Space Combat*, 203; also Cai and Tian, *The Air and Space Battlefield and China's Air Force*, 164–165.

[32] Yuan, 135, and Zhang, *The Science of Campaigns*, 547–549.

[33] Yuan, 135; Cai and Tian, *The Study of Integrated Air and Space Combat*, 204; Zhang, *The Science of Campaigns*, 547–549.

[34] Cai and Tian, *The Study of Integrated Air and Space Combat*, 204; Zhang, *The Science of Campaigns*, 547–549.

[35] Zhang, *The Science of Campaigns*, 548–549; Yuan, 136–137.

[36] Zhang, *The Science of Campaigns*, 2006 edition, 548.

[37] The weakness of Chinese electronic jamming and deception technology is claimed in Zhang, *The Science of Campaigns*, 547–548. See also Yuan, 137.

[38] Yuan, 148–149; see also Zhang, *The Science of Campaigns*, 549–551.

[39] Ibid., 147–148.

[40] Zhang, *The Science of Campaigns*, 549–551.

[41] Yuan, 148–149; see also Zhang, *The Science of Campaigns*, 549–551.

[42] Zhang, *The Science of Campaigns*, 552; Yuan, 159–160.

[43] Zhang, *The Science of Campaigns*, 553–554; Yuan, 159–160.

[44] Zhang Zhiwei and Feng Chuanjiang, "Analysis of Future Integrated Air and Space Operations," *China Military Science* [*Zhongguo junshi kexue*; 中国军事科学] 19, no. 2 (2006).

[45] Yuan, 154–155.

[46] Ibid., 154.

[47] Zhang, *The Science of Campaigns*, 2006 edition, 331–332.

[48] This quote is from the Information Office of the State Council of the People's Republic of China, *China's National Defense in 2008* (Beijing, January 2009), 26.

[49] Zhang, *The Science of Campaigns*, 2006 edition, 331–332.

[50] Cai and Tian, *The Study of Integrated Air and Space Combat*, 225; Cai and Tian, *The Air and Space Battlefield and China's Air Force*, 174.

[51] Yuan, 158–159.

[52] Zhang, *The Science of Campaigns*, 2006 edition, 332.

[53] Cai and Tian, *The Air and Space Battlefield and China's Air Force*, 156.

[54] See also Yuan Jingwei's wording about attacks against the "source" of the enemy attack. Yuan, 158–159.

[55] Wang, Li, and Ma, especially 100.

[56] Ibid., 101.

[57] Yuan, 158–159.

[58] Wang, Li, and Ma, especially 101.

Chapter 6

The Development of the PLAAF's Doctrine

Roger Cliff

As history has repeatedly demonstrated, doctrine is key to the effective employment of air forces. No matter how capable an air force's equipment and operators are, if they lack an appropriate doctrine, their employment will be ineffective at best and self-destructive at worst. A thorough understanding of the People's Liberation Army Air Force (PLAAF), therefore, requires the fullest possible understanding of how its doctrine has evolved since its creation over six decades ago.[1]

Evolution of PLAAF Doctrine

Like the U.S. Air Force (USAF) and, indeed, the majority of the world's air forces, the PLAAF was first founded as part of China's army, the People's Liberation Army (PLA). Unlike the USAF, however, which became an independent service in 1947 and went on to develop its own doctrine and employment concepts, for over half a century PLAAF doctrine has struggled to move out of the PLA army's shadow, even though the PLAAF became an independent service in 1949.[2] Tied to the land-centric force-employment concepts of the PLA, PLAAF doctrine mostly evolved in step with that of the PLA army. In the initial years after the establishment of the PLAAF, "no consideration was ever given to making the air force a service independent of the army . . . because the PLA leadership did not want an autonomous aviation force."[3] Accordingly, the PLAAF's first commander and political commissar were chosen directly from the army.[4] The shadow cast by the PLA army over the PLAAF is evident in the early roles and missions of the Chinese air force. For example, the PLAAF's first operational mission in 1949—defending Beijing and Shanghai against Nationalist air raids—was defensive in nature.[5] In the early 1950s, one of the PLAAF's primary missions was seizing air superiority over the battlefield.[6] Both of these missions are reflective of a ground force perspective on the utility of air forces.

The Korean War, battles over Taiwan's offshore islands, and the Vietnam conflict shaped both the evolution of PLAAF doctrine and the pace of the PLAAF's growth from the 1950s to the 1980s. During the Korean War, the PLAAF's original air plan was to support ground troops as its primary mission, again a reflection of the PLA army's influence on China's air force employment concepts.[7] The PLAAF lacked the technical capability to execute this strategy, however, and had to change its mission to that of conducting air operations against U.S. forces. This caused the PLAAF to develop a basic air defense strategy and tactics.[8]

Air operations against Nationalist forces on Taiwan's outlying islands of Yijiangshan and Jinmen (the latter also known as Quemoy or Kinmen) in the late 1950s also helped to shape PLAAF doctrine. The Yijiangshan Island campaign of 1954–1955 is the only campaign in PLA history to have combined air, ground, and naval operations.[9] The PLAAF's goals were to achieve air superiority, attack Taiwanese resupply ships, conduct decoy and reconnaissance missions, and provide direct air support for landing operations.[10] Lessons learned from the Yijiangshan Island campaign resonate in subsequent PLAAF strategy and employment concepts and include a "relentless use of an overwhelming striking force to attack enemy artillery and firepower positions as well as command and communication centers."[11] Chinese military leaders also learned that they could overcome the short ranges and limited loiter times of their fighter jets by using the numerical superiority of PLAAF fighters to maintain continuous fighter patrols.[12] A third lesson was that, while attack sorties should be flown according to plan, commanders should allow flexibility "in target selection based on the need of ground forces."[13] The Yijiangshan experience became a model for the PLA's concept of the role airpower would play in future small-scale conflicts.[14] This was summarized as "air defense first, followed by air superiority, and then offensive air support."[15]

The Jinmen campaign of 1958, the most recent Chinese military conflict to truly involve air combat, was also an important shaper of PLAAF strategy and doctrine. The conflict also provides an example of how air operational principles were governed by directives issued from the very top of the PLA—the Central Military Commission (CMC).[16] According to Zhang Xiaoming, the operational guidance of the CMC stressed using massed force to achieve protection of forces and destruction of enemy forces; subservience of military battles to political battles by a strict adherence to CMC operational policy; and study and application of PLAAF experiences and tactics drawn from the Korean War.[17]

Because the Chinese leadership was uncertain about the PLAAF's counterstrike capabilities vis-à-vis Taiwan, the PLAAF was employed defensively. Thus, it "deployed large numbers of fighters to the region but could not capitalize on its numerical superiority," since it had to reserve half of its aircraft to protect home bases.[18] Along with the political concern of not wanting to escalate the Jinmen campaign into an international crisis, the limited range of Chinese MiG–17 aircraft also inhibited the offensive role that the PLAAF could play.[19]

In addition to battle experience, China's political upheavals have also shaped the evolution of Chinese air force doctrine. Beginning with the Sino-Soviet split in the 1960s and during the 1966–1976 Cultural Revolution period, Chinese airpower, and the ability to execute its strategy and doctrine, atrophied. The Sino-Soviet split significantly slowed the PLAAF's modernization efforts, as China was highly dependent on Soviet technology transfers for equipping the PLAAF.[20] And, due to the fact that air forces are, by their very nature, more technically oriented services than armies, the PLAAF suffered disproportionately from the Cultural Revolution, which discounted anything having to do with knowledge and expertise. Furthermore, the PLAAF's association with Defense Minister Lin Biao's failed coup attempt against Mao in 1971 resulted in the air force being marginalized until after Mao's death and the rehabilitation of Deng Xiaoping in 1978.[21] Partly as a consequence, PLAAF involvement during China's war with Vietnam in 1979 was limited. As in the case of the Jinmen conflict, China's air involvement during the conflict was also constrained both by political factors—not wanting to involve the United States in the former case and the Soviet Union in the latter—and by the limited capabilities of the PLAAF.

When Deng Xiaoping took control of the CMC and later became China's undisputed leader in 1978, he ushered in a new era of economic and military reform, which set all military services on a path to modernization and reform, and his perspective on airpower was elevated to official CMC dogma.[22] This perspective viewed the pursuit of air superiority as crucial to Chinese military power and winning future wars.[23]

The actual implementation of Deng's directives on Chinese airpower modernization, however, was constrained during most of his tenure as China's paramount leader, for two major reasons. First, by attaching special political weight to the PLAAF, Deng not only wanted to alleviate the decrepit state of Chinese airpower, he also wanted to keep tight control over the PLAAF so as to prevent it from becoming the politically dangerous service it had been under Lin Biao during the Cultural Revolution.[24] Second, the army-centrism ingrained during the Mao era attenuated efforts to implement near-term improvements in the PLAAF.[25] For example, when the PLA began reorganizing ground forces into group armies in the early 1980s, the PLAAF was given guidance that its role was to support the needs of ground forces and that a victory was a ground force victory.[26]

The Gulf War of 1991 spurred renewed debate within the PLAAF and Chinese military establishment about how to modernize and develop Chinese airpower. The U.S. show of force in the Taiwan Strait crisis of 1996, in which the United States deployed two aircraft carrier battle groups near Taiwan in response to Chinese military intimidation of Taiwan, further motivated doctrinal reform and technological modernization efforts in the PLAAF. The PLAAF's hopes for a strategy of "quick reaction," "integrated coordination," and "combat in depth" had to be transformed from wishful desires to operational realities.[27] "Quick reaction" meant launching an instantaneous retaliatory strike for deterrence, or even survival.[28] "Integrated coordination" meant allowing the air force to "manage the long-range bomber air groups and oversee the initial stages of joint operations with the other services and between air combat units stationed in different military regions."[29] Finally, "combat in depth" meant conducting operations over a wide geographical area.[30] However, operationalizing these concepts was difficult because, for most of the 1990s, military reform tended to stress internal organization and structural changes, as opposed to training and equipment modernization.[31] The PLAAF lacked the equipment and training needed to implement this strategy.[32]

In the early 1990s, PLAAF employment concepts assumed that future wars would be conducted according to an active defense strategy with three phases: "strategic defense, strategic stalemate, and strategic counterattack."[33] Under the umbrella of active defense, PLAAF campaigns were divided into two categories—defensive campaigns and attack campaigns—either of which could be one of two types: independent air force campaigns or air force campaigns as part of a joint campaign.[34] PLAAF publications also specified three levels of scale for an air defense campaign, with small campaigns requiring air defense of a strategic position, large campaigns requiring air defense of a battle area, and larger campaigns requiring air defense of many battle areas.[35]

A PLAAF study published in 1990 revealed both the desire to have a more unified air strategy, and the gap between desired strategy and the ability to implement it. For example, one challenge to execution of the aforementioned rapid-reaction strategy was the lack of a unified air defense plan in China.[36] Each service possessed its own air defense forces, and coordinating the different elements within each service was challenging enough; it was virtually impossible to coordinate operations across services.[37]

Other dimensions of the PLAAF strategy included two principles: the "light front, heavy rear" [前轻后重] and "deploying in three rings" concepts.[38] The light front, heavy rear principle stemmed from the PLAAF's responsibility to protect airfields, "national political and economic centers, heavy troop concentrations, important military facilities, and transportation systems."[39] Under light front, heavy rear, the PLAAF "would organize its SAM [surface-to-air missile] and AAA [antiaircraft artillery] forces into a combined high, medium, and low altitude and a far, medium, and short distance air defense net."[40] Intercept lines and aviation forces would also be organized into a series of interception layers.[41] However, in executing this concept, the PLAAF faced two daunting challenges: the limited range of Chinese aircraft, and adversaries that had aircraft capable of conducting deep strikes into Chinese territory.[42] The limited range of PLAAF aircraft was worsened by the fact that most airfields and almost all SAMs were concentrated near China's large cities, far away from China's borders.[43] For the light front, heavy rear principle to work, moreover, the PLAAF needed to develop a better command-and-control system; otherwise, there was a risk of fratricide to friendly aircraft from SAMs and AAA.[44]

To be used in conjunction with the light front, heavy rear principle, "deploying in three rings" involved organizing a small quantity of interceptors, AAA, and SAMs "as a combined air defense force into 'three dimensional, in-depth, overlapping' firepower rings."[45] Furthermore, according to Kenneth W. Allen, Glenn Krumel, and Jonathan D. Pollack,[46]

> Each weapon system would be assigned a specific airspace to defend—high, medium or low. In-depth rings means assigning each weapon system a specific distance from the target to defend—distant, medium or close. Overlapping rings means organizing each weapon system into left, middle or right firepower rings facing the most likely avenue of approach.

The American experience with airpower in the first Gulf War transformed military thought on the use of air forces and what they could contribute to modern war, and China was no exception to this pattern of influence. In 1993, after Operation *Desert Storm*, 60 airpower specialists formed an airpower theory, strategy, and development study group to investigate independent air campaigns.[47] By 1997, the Chinese air force had "claimed precedence over the other service branches, and the People's War as a unifying dogma had given way to service-specific strategies."[48]

According to another study, as of the late 1990s, the primary PLAAF missions were air coercion, air offensives, air blockades, and support for ground force operations.[49] Coercion could come in the form of demonstrations, such as deployments and exercises, weapon tests, or overflights. It could also come in the form of limited strikes to warn or punish an adversary. Air offensives, by contrast, would entail large-scale strikes with the goal of rapidly gaining air superiority, reducing an adversary's capacity for military operations, and establishing the conditions necessary for victory. An air blockade would entail attacks on airfields and seaports as well as on air, land, and sea transportation routes with the goal of cutting off an enemy from contact with the outside world. Support for ground force operations would include attacks on logistics facilities, hardened coastal defenses (in the case of an amphibious operation), reinforcements, and key choke points, such as bridges. It would also include battlefield close air support, strategic and theater airlift, airborne operations against an enemy's command headquarters, and the deployment of ground-based air defenses to protect ground forces and key facilities.[50]

As Mark A. Stokes noted, as of the late 1990s, PLAAF operational principles included "surprise and first strikes," "concentration of best assets," "offensive action as a component of air defense," and "close coordination."[51] "Surprise and first strikes" refers to the goal of crippling an opponent and gaining the initiative early in a conflict through surprise and large-scale attacks on key targets, such as the enemy's air command-and-control structure, key air bases, and SAM sites. Concentration of best assets supports this principle and refers to using the PLAAF's best assets in the initial strikes and to dedicating the majority of them to targets that will have the most influence on a campaign. Offensive action as a component of air defense refers to using offensive counterair attacks as an integral aspect of air defense by attacking those enemy assets that pose the greatest threat. Close coordination refers to coordinating the air assets of all services (army, People's Liberation Army Navy [PLAN], PLAAF, Second Artillery), as well as unified command at the theater level. As seen later in this chapter, these principles remain key elements of PLAAF employment concepts.[52]

A major change in PLAAF doctrine occurred in 1999, when it was issued campaign guidance (战役纲要) that "provides the classified doctrinal basis and general guidance for how the PLAAF will fight future campaigns."[53] Since the guidance is classified, its exact contents are unknown. What Western analysts do know is that the guidance shows that the PLAAF had deepened its understanding of the operational level of war. The PLAAF also now identified three types of air force campaigns: air offensive, air defense, and air blockade.[54]

Until 2004, the PLAAF lacked its own service-specific strategy, and the actual ability of the PLAAF to integrate its campaign and operational principles with the Second Artillery, PLA army, and PLAN was questionable. One study states that, until that time, the Chinese air force relied "almost solely on the PLA army's 'Active Defense' operational component as its strategic-level doctrinal guidance."[55] The approval of the PLAAF's active defense strategy as a component of the National Military Strategic Guidelines for air operations in 2004, however, indicated an important shift in the PLAAF's status.[56] The PLAAF's strategic component of the National Military Strategic Guidelines is now identified as "Air and Space Integrated, Simultaneous Preparations for the Offensive and Defensive" ([空天一体，攻防兼备)."[57] While it does not appear that the PLAAF yet has a service-specific strategy that is as well defined as the PLAN's strategy of offshore defense, it does seem that the PLAAF is now seen as a truly independent service. Lanzit and Allen (2007) cite Hong Kong press reports that the PLAAF should be a strategic air force that stands "side by side" with the Chinese army and navy "to achieve command of the air, ground, and sea."[58]

Current PLAAF Doctrine

Chinese military doctrine is codified in "campaign guidance" and "combat regulation" (战斗条令) documents, equivalent to the U.S. Department of Defense's *Joint Publication (JP)* doctrinal series. China's Central Military Commission issues campaign guidance documents for each of its services, including the PLAAF, as well as a joint campaign guidance document. The PLAAF thus does not have the freedom of doctrinal development that, for example, the U.S. Air Force does with its *Air Force Doctrine Document (AFDD)* series. The PLA-rooted PLAAF campaign guidance includes "standard military guidelines for PLAAF campaign operations" and is the "fundamental basis for the Air Force campaign group to organize campaign operations and exercises."[59] Signed in 1999 by China's top military leadership, its contents are said to include the nature of air force campaigns, basic campaign types, and campaign principles; air force campaign organization for command and coordination mechanisms; the campaign guiding thought, operational tasks, and operational methods for air force offensive campaigns, defensive campaigns, air blockade campaigns, and coordination with ground, naval, and Second Artillery Force campaign operations; campaign electronic countermeasures; campaign airborne duties and demands; and requirements and basic methods of campaign operational support: logistic support, armament support, and political support.[60]

In addition to its overall campaign guidance, the PLAAF has combat regulations for "composite force combat" (合同战斗条令) and for fighter aviation, attack aviation, bomber aviation, reconnaissance aviation, transport aviation, SAM, AAA, airborne, electronic warfare (EW), radar, communications, chemical warfare defense, and technical reconnaissance force combat.[61] Like the campaign guidance, however, the combat regulation documents are classified. Any information on the PLAAF's doctrine, therefore, must be derived from reference works and textbooks that are believed to be based on and consistent with these documents, but cannot be regarded as equivalent to them.[62]

General Employment Concepts and Principles

Official Chinese military publications define *airpower* as the overall term for aviation forces belonging to air forces, navies, air defense forces (such as the Russian *Protivo Vozdushnaya Oborona* [Anti-Air Defense], or *PVO*), ground forces, and special operations forces.[63] In joint operations, airpower is said to be used for high-speed, deep strikes against key targets and to be used first and throughout campaigns to seize control of the skies in support of broader campaign objectives. Airpower also is used defensively to protect the ability of an air force to conduct air operations, especially air bases, air defense positions, and radar sites, as well as to protect ground and naval operations.[64]

PLA publications assert that the struggle for dominance of the battlefield will increasingly consist of an integrated struggle for air, space, information, electromagnetic, and network superiority. Acquiring air superiority is considered a prerequisite in a variety of operations involving all services. By obtaining air superiority, one can restrict enemy air, air defense, and ground force operational movements while ensuring that one's own ground and navy forces have effective cover from the air to carry out their operations.[65] Like the USAF, however, the PLA does not assert that achieving absolute air superiority in all stages of combat and across all battlefields or theaters is necessary. Instead, it aims to achieve enough air superiority to achieve its campaign or tactical objectives.[66]

Presumably because of reservations about its ability to defeat a qualitatively superior opponent such as the United States in the air, the PLA places primary emphasis on achieving air superiority by attacking the enemy on the ground and water: enemy forces, equipment, bases, and launch pads used for air raids. Especially at the beginning of a war, the PLA will endeavor to attack enemy air bases, ballistic missile bases, aircraft carriers, and warships equipped with land-attack cruise missiles before enemy aircraft can take off or missile strikes can be launched.[67] Another means of achieving air superiority will be to carry out air and land attacks to destroy and suppress ground-based air defense systems and air defense command systems.[68] Finally, defensive operations will be an important component of air superiority throughout a campaign.[69]

In future warfare, space superiority is expected to be crucial for controlling the ground, naval, and air battlefields. To gain space superiority, offensive and defensive weapons systems will be deployed on the ground, air, sea, and space. Space control operations are said to include space information warfare, space blockade warfare, space orbit attack warfare, space-defense warfare, and space-to-land attacks.[70]

In struggles for information superiority, the goal will be to control information on the battlefield, allowing the battlefield to be transparent to one's own side but opaque to the enemy. Methods for achieving information superiority include achieving electromagnetic superiority through electronic interference; achieving network superiority through network attacks; using firepower to destroy the enemy's information systems; and achieving "psychological control."[71]

While acquiring electromagnetic superiority is described as a subset of acquiring information superiority, it is treated as a distinct type of operation in PLA publications.[72] Methods for obtaining electromagnetic superiority are said to include electronic attack and electronic defense. In electronic attack, "soft kill" measures include electronic interference and electronic deception. "Hard kill" measures include antiradiation destruction, electronic-weapon attack, firepower destruction, and attacks against the enemy's electronic installations and systems. Electronic defense is simply defending against enemy electronic and firepower attacks.[73] The primary targets of EW are said to include command, control, communications, and intelligence systems.[74]

PLAAF publications describe three major types of air combat operation: air-to-air combat, air-to-surface combat, and surface-to-air combat.[75] Air-to-air and surface-to-air operations are areas of traditional emphasis for the PLAAF, but the PLAAF seems to be moving away from focusing on air-to-air operations and toward emphasizing operations to gain air superiority by attacking enemy airfields and controlling the enemy on the ground before resorting to fighting the enemy in the air.[76] Air-to-surface operations are considered more effective, less costly, and less reactive than air-to-air operations.[77]

Campaign-Specific Employment Concepts

Chinese military publications identify four types of air force campaigns: air offensive campaigns, air defense campaigns, air blockade campaigns, and airborne campaigns. These can be either air force–only campaigns or, more frequently, air force–led joint campaigns that incorporate other services. These air force campaigns can also be part of broader joint campaigns, such as an island-landing campaign or joint blockade campaign. In all air operations, a great deal of emphasis is placed on surprise, camouflage, use of deception, meticulous planning, and strikes against critical key points.

An air offensive campaign can have one or more of several objectives: obtaining air superiority; destroying key enemy political, military, and economic targets; destroying the enemy's transportation and logistic supply system; and destroying the enemy's forces to isolate the battlefield and facilitate PLA ground and maritime operations. Obtaining air superiority is needed in order to conduct air strikes against targets, but the principal objective of an air offensive campaign is to strike political, economic, and military targets, rather than simply to achieve air superiority.[78]

Several types of combat groups are involved in air offensive campaigns: a strike group, an air defense suppression group, a cover group, a support group, an air defense group, and an operational reserve.[79] An offensive air campaign is said to consist of four tasks: conducting information operations, breaking through enemy defenses, launching air strikes, and protecting against counterstrikes. The first three are generally conducted sequentially, beginning with information operations. The last is conducted throughout the campaign.[80]

A textbook on military operations lists three primary objectives for air defense campaigns: protecting the capital against air attack, protecting other important targets within the theater, and seizing and holding air superiority.[81] Defensive air campaigns, according to Chinese military publications, can be national in scope or can be confined to a particular theater.[82] Depending on the circumstances, the entire air effort in a given war could be defensive; a single phase could be defensive; or, in the case of a geographically wide-ranging conflict, some theaters could be defensive, while others are offensive. In a war over Taiwan, for example, the PLA might conduct an offensive air campaign in the area opposite Taiwan while preparing for defensive air campaigns to the north and south in anticipation of possible retaliation or counterattack by U.S. forces.

Air defense campaigns are described as entailing three types of operations: resistance, counterattack, and close protection. Resistance operations are actions to intercept, disrupt, and destroy attacking aircraft. Counterattack operations are attacks on enemy air bases (including aircraft carriers). Close protection operations are passive defense measures, such as fortification, concealment, camouflage, and mobility.[83] China's overall approach to air defense is to combine the early interception of enemy attacks with full-depth, layered resistance to protect targets and forces while gradually increasing the tempo of counterattacks on enemy bases.[84]

Air blockade campaigns are operations intended to prevent an adversary from conducting air operations and to cut off its economic and military links with the outside world.[85] Some Chinese sources describe them as simply a special variety of air offensive campaign,[86] but most authoritative sources regard them as a distinct type of campaign.[87] They will usually be conducted as part of a broader joint blockade campaign but can be implemented as an independent air force campaign. Air blockade campaigns are regarded as having a strong political nature, being long in duration, and requiring a high level of command and control.[88] Typically, an air blockade campaign will entail the establishment of one or more no-fly zones surrounded by aerial surveillance zones.[89] Actions conducted as part of an air blockade campaign will include information operations, flight suppression operations, interdiction of maritime and ground traffic, strikes against the enemy's counterblockade system, and air defense operations.[90]

Unlike the U.S. armed forces, the PLA's airborne assault (paratroop) forces belong to its air force. Therefore, an airborne campaign in the PLA is an air force campaign, not a joint campaign. Airborne campaigns are regarded as inherently resource-intensive and difficult to organize and prosecute.[91] For an airborne campaign to be carried out, information and air superiority must be seized (at least locally) and firepower preparation around the landing zone must be conducted. Then, air corridors to the landing zone must be opened up and kept clear, and enemy land-based air defenses near the landing zone must be suppressed while airborne forces are flown to the landing zone. Once they have landed, the airborne forces must clear and secure a base for receiving additional forces and supplies, including, if they landed on or near an airfield, seizing the airfield and bringing it to operational readiness. Meanwhile, friendly air and missile forces will suppress and interdict nearby enemy ground forces. Finally, the air-landed forces can initiate ground operations.[92]

Although any of these four types of air force campaigns can be conducted as an independent single-service campaign, they are more likely to be conducted as part of a broader joint campaign, such as an island-landing campaign or a joint blockade campaign. Even if an air force campaign is conducted as an independent, single-service campaign, other services, particularly the PLAN and the Second Artillery, are likely to be involved in supporting roles. For example, conventional missiles of the Second Artillery will play a key role in air offensive campaigns, counterattack operations of air defense campaigns, and providing firepower support for airborne campaigns.

Similarly, the PLAN has responsibility for defending certain sectors of China's airspace and would be the service with primary responsibility for conducting counterattacks against air attacks launched from aircraft carriers and, thus, would likely play an important role in an air defense campaign. The PLAN is also responsible for providing air defense for surface naval forces, including, presumably, a Taiwan-bound invasion force. Little information appears to be available in published Chinese sources, however, on how PLAAF and PLAN aviation and SAM forces would interoperate when conducting air operations—a potentially significant challenge, particularly given the huge engagement envelopes (150 kilometers or more) of the land-based and ship-based SAMs the PLAAF and PLAN have begun acquiring. Conversely, naval strike appears not to be an important mission for the PLAAF, meaning that naval strike operations are primarily the responsibility of the relatively small and less-capable PLAN aviation forces (along with, possibly in the future, the Second Artillery, if it acquires an antiship ballistic-missile capability).

Conclusion

Chinese military publications on air force operations are systematic and comprehensive. Few militaries in the world have such extensive published documentation on the employment of air forces. The concepts described, moreover, appear to be realistic and practical, drawing on the experience of other air forces in recent conflicts, particularly those of the United States (the PLAAF having had no significant combat experience since the 1950s), but remaining appropriate to the current and near-future capabilities of the PLAAF. Chinese military analysts are clearly engaged in a serious process of developing specific, practical concepts for the employment of China's air forces.

In addition, although the PLAAF has traditionally emphasized defensive operations, that is no longer the case, and the United States and Taiwan would likely find the PLAAF to be an aggressive opponent in the event of a conflict. The PLA clearly prefers to achieve air superiority by attacking its enemy on the ground or water. Especially at the beginning of a war, the PLA will endeavor to attack enemy air bases, ballistic-missile bases, aircraft carriers, and warships equipped with land-attack cruise missiles before enemy aircraft can take off or missile attacks can be launched. These attacks, moreover, will be carried out not by China's air force operating in isolation but in coordination with the Second Artillery's conventional ballistic and cruise missiles.

By 2015 or so, the weapons systems and platforms that China is acquiring will potentially enable it to effectively implement the four types of air force campaigns described in the previous section. The significant numbers of modern fighter aircraft and SAMs, as well as the long-range early warning radars and secure data and voice communication links China is likely to have by 2015, for example, coupled with the hardening and camouflage measures China has already taken, would make a Chinese air defense campaign, if conducted according to the principles described in Chinese military publications, highly challenging for U.S. air forces.[93] Similarly, these same modern fighters, along with ground-launched conventional ballistic and cruise missiles, cruise missile–carrying medium bombers, and aerial refueling aircraft, will enable China to conduct offensive operations far into the western Pacific.[94]

Whether China will actually be able to fully exploit its air force doctrine and capabilities, however, is less clear. Much will depend on the quality of the training and leadership of China's air force, and it should be pointed out that the PLAAF last engaged in major combat operations in the Jinmen campaign of 1958, more than 50 years ago.

Notes

[1] Readers wishing a more extensive examination of this subject are invited to read Roger Cliff, John Fei, Jeff Hagen, Elizabeth Hague, Eric Heginbotham, and John Stillion's *Shaking the Heavens and Splitting the Earth: Chinese Air Force Employment Concepts in the 21ˢᵗ Century*, RAND Document MG-915 (Santa Monica, CA: RAND Corporation, 2011). The author wishes to acknowledge the important contributions made to this shorter study by John Fei, Elizabeth Hague, and Eric Heginbotham.

[2] Kenneth W. Allen, "PLA Air Force Organization," in *The People's Liberation Army as Organization: Reference Volume v1.0*, RAND Document CF-182-NSRD, eds. James C. Mulvenon and Andrew N.D. Yang (Santa Monica, CA: RAND Corporation, 2002), 364.

[3] Kenneth W. Allen, Glenn Krumel, and Jonathan D. Pollack, *China's Air Force Enters the 21st Century*, RAND Document MR-580-AF (Santa Monica, CA: RAND Corporation, 1995), 37.

[4] Ibid., 35.

[5] Ibid., 101.

[6] Allen, "PLA Air Force Organization," 370.

[7] Zhang Xiaoming, "Air Combat for the People's Republic: The People's Liberation Army Air Force in Action, 1949–1969," in *Chinese Warfighting: The PLA Experience Since 1949*, eds. Mark A. Ryan, David Michael Finkelstein, and Michael McDevitt (Armonk, NY: M.E. Sharpe, 2003), 271–272.

[8] Ibid., 271–272.

[9] Ibid., 279.

[10] Ibid., 280.

[11] Ibid, 282.

[12] Ibid.

[13] Ibid.

[14] Ibid.

[15] Ibid.

[16] Ibid., 283.

[17] Ibid., 284.

[18] Ibid., 288.

[19] Ibid.

[20] Allen, Krumel, and Pollack, 71.

[21] Ibid., 73.

[22] John W. Lewis and Xue Litai, "China's Search for a Modern Air Force," *International Security* 24, no. 1 (Summer 1999), 64–94, 70.

[23] Lewis and Xue, 70.

[24] Ibid. Because of these constraints, the PLAAF remained subservient to the PLA army and other strategic priorities.

[25] Ibid., 74. The Mao-era dogma of self-reliance was relaxed to permit acquisition of foreign air-launched weapons and avionics, but the purchase of foreign aircraft remained prohibited.

[26] Kevin Lanzit and Kenneth W. Allen, "Right-Sizing the PLA Air Force: New Operational Concepts Define a Smaller, More Capable Force," in *Right Sizing the People's Liberation Army: Exploring the Contours of China's Military*, eds. Roy Kamphausen and Andrew Scobell (Carlisle, PA: Strategic Studies Institute, U.S. Army War College, September 2007), 439–440.

[27] Lewis and Xue 79.

[28] Ibid., 80.

[29] Ibid.

[30] Ibid.

[31] Allen, Krumel, and Pollack, 105.

[32] Ibid., 109.

[33] Ibid., 111. These phases are clearly based on Mao's writings and the CCP's experience in the Chinese civil war.

[34] Ibid., 111–112.

[35] Ibid., 112.

[36] Ibid., 113.

[37] Ibid.
[38] Ibid., 114–115.
[39] Ibid., 114.
[40] Ibid.
[41] Ibid.
[42] Ibid., 115.
[43] Ibid., 114.
[44] Ibid., 114, 116, 124.
[45] Ibid., 115.
[46] Ibid., 115–116.
[47] Mark A. Stokes, "The Chinese Joint Aerospace Campaign: Strategy, Doctrine, and Force Modernization," in *China's Revolution in Doctrinal Affairs: Emerging Trends in the Operational Art of the Chinese People's Liberation Army*, eds. James C. Mulvenon and David Michael Finkelstein (Alexandria, VA.: CNA Corporation, 2005), 246.
[48] Lewis and Xue, 89–90.
[49] Stokes, 247. The Chinese term for coercion [*weishe*, 威慑] is translated by many analysts, including Stokes, as "deterrence." As Stokes himself argues, however, *weishe* actually encompasses both deterrence, as it is normally understood, and *compellence*—forcing an adversary to do something it would not otherwise wish to do. The more accurate translation of *weishe*, therefore, is the term *coercion*, which, in Western strategic writings, also includes both deterrence and compellence.
[50] Ibid., 247–250.
[51] Ibid., 250–254.
[52] Ibid.
[53] Kenneth W. Allen, "The PLA Air Force: 2006–2010," paper presented at the CAPS-RAND-CEIP International Conference on PLA Affairs, Taipei, November 10–12, 2005, 3.
[54] Ibid., 4.
[55] Lanzit and Allen, 448.
[56] Ibid., 450–451.
[57] Ibid., 450.
[58] Ibid., 451.
[59] People's Liberation Army Air Force (PLAAF), *China Air Force Encyclopedia* [中国空军百科全书] (Beijing: Aviation Industry Press [航空工业出版社], 2005), 328.
[60] Ibid., 328.
[61] Ibid., 328–330.
[62] The PLAAF also has a set of training and evaluation guidelines [*dagang*, 大纲] based, presumably, on the campaign guidance and combat regulations. See PLAAF, *China Air Force Encyclopedia*, 331–332, and Office of Naval Intelligence, China's Navy 2007 (Washington, DC: Department of the Navy, 2007), 28–29.
[63] PLAAF, *China Air Force Encyclopedia*, 81.
[64] Bi Xinglin [薛兴林], ed., *Campaign Theory Study Guide* [战役理论学习指南] (Beijing: National Defense University Press [国防大学出版社], 2002), 140–141, 145–146.
[65] PLAAF, *China Air Force Encyclopedia*, 41. The USAF's top-level doctrine publication provides a very similar description of the role and importance of air (and space) superiority: "Gaining air and space superiority . . . enhances and may secure freedom of action for friendly forces in all geographical environments—land and sea as well as air and space. Air and space superiority provides freedom to attack as well as freedom from attack. Success in air, land, sea, and space operations depends upon air and space superiority." See U.S. Air Force, *Air Force Basic Doctrine*, Air Force Doctrine Document 1 (Washington, DC: HQ USAF, November 17, 2003), 76–77.
[66] Zhan Xuexi [展学习], ed., *Campaign Studies Research* [战役学研究] (Beijing: 国防大学出版社 [National Defense University Press], 1997), 307. For comparison, the USAF describes air superiority as "that degree

of dominance that permits friendly land, sea, air, and space forces to operate at a given time and place without prohibitive interference by the opposing force." Air supremacy is described as "that degree of superiority wherein opposing air and space forces are incapable of effective interference anywhere in a given theater of operations" (U.S. Air Force, 2003, 77). Thus, the Chinese concept of strategic air superiority corresponds approximately to the U.S. concept of air supremacy, and the Chinese concepts of operational and tactical air superiority correspond approximately to the U.S. concept of air superiority.

[67] PLAAF, *China Air Force Encyclopedia*, 39–40.

[68] Ibid., 40; Zhan, 310–312.

[69] PLAAF, *China Air Force Encyclopedia*, 40–41.

[70] Ibid., 48–49.

[71] Ibid., 50.

[72] Ibid.; see also Zhan, 297–305.

[73] PLAAF, *China Air Force Encyclopedia*, 50–51.

[74] Zhan, 300.

[75] Under the entry on "Air Force Tactics" [空军战术] in PLAAF, *China Air Force Encyclopedia*, 108, the three types of tactics listed and described are air-to-air combat [空中战斗], air-to-surface combat [空地战斗], and ground-to-air combat [地空战斗].

[76] Zhan, 310–312. Some forward-leaning theorists believe that air-to-air operations should be deemphasized even more than they have been. For example, Liu Yazhou [刘亚洲], Qiao Liang [乔良], and Wang Xiangsui [王湘穗], "Combat in the Air and China's Air Force" [战争空中化与中国空军] in *China's Military Transformation* [中国军事变革], ed. Shen Weiguang [沈伟光], assoc. eds. Xie Xizhang [解玺璋] and Ma Yaxi [马亚西] (Beijing: Xinhua Press [新华出版社] 2003), 87–88, argue that the PLAAF needs to break through "air combat" [空战]–centered thought and work toward the idea that the main type of combat is "air raids" [空袭].

[77] For example, in its discussion of "methods" for achieving air superiority, the *China Air Force Encyclopedia* (2005, 40) remarks that attempting to achieve air superiority in the air (using air-to-air and surface-to-air operations) requires "payment of a relatively high price to be effective" [付出较大代价才能显现效果].

[78] Bi, 372. In a discussion of the missions of air offensive campaigns, Bi notes that, while gaining air superiority is the "primary" mission [首要任务], attacking political, military, and economic targets is the "main" mission [主要任务], and attacking logistics targets is an "important mission" [重要任务]. It is unclear whether he means that air superiority is "primary" in the sense of "first" mission, or "primary" in the sense of "first in importance." Other sources, however, indicate that air superiority is an important part, but not the main objective, of air offensive campaigns. Zhang Yuliang [张玉良], ed., *Study of Campaigns* [战役学] (Beijing: National Defense University Press, 2006), has a somewhat different interpretation. While there is not a distinct section on "missions" or "objectives," the introduction to the chapter on "air offensive campaigns" (p. 575) briefly notes that air offensive campaigns' "missions and objectives" can be to (1) achieve air superiority, (2) weaken the enemy forces, or (3) achieve some kind of special objective. It therefore appears that the "objective" or "mission" of air offensive campaigns has evolved in recent years.

[79] This characterization of the types of forces used in an air offensive campaign is based on Bi, *Campaign Theory Study Guide*, 377–378, and PLAAF, *China Air Force Encyclopedia*, 100–101. Bi also mentions an electronic countermeasure group [电子对抗集群], but no reference to an electronic countermeasure group can be found in the *China Air Force Encyclopedia*. Instead, the *China Air Force Encyclopedia* refers to "electronic countermeasures forces" [电子对抗兵] as being part of the suppression group.

[80] See PLAAF, *China Air Force Encyclopedia*, 99–100; Zhang , 579–588.

[81] Bi, 471–472.

[82] PLAAF, *China Air Force Encyclopedia*, 101–102; PLAAF, *Air Force Dictionary* [空军大辞典] (Shanghai: Shanghai Dictionary Press [海辞书出版社], 1996), 18–19.

[83] Cui Changqi [崔长崎], Ji Rongren [纪荣仁], Min Zengfu [闵增富], Yuan Jingwei [袁静伟], Hu Siyuan [胡思远], Tian Tongshun [田同顺], Ruan Guangfeng [阮光峰], Hong Baocai [洪宝才], Meng Qingquan [孟庆全], Cao Xiumin [曹秀敏], Dai Jianjun [戴建军], Han Jibing [韩继兵], Wang Jicheng [王冀城], and Wang Xuejin [王学进], *Air Raids and Counter–Air Raids in the 21st Century* [21世纪初空袭与反空袭] (Beijing: Liberation Army Press [解放军出版社], 2002), 210–215. On counterattack and close protection operations, see also Bi, 481.

[84] Lu Lihua [芦利华], *Military Command Theory Study Guide* [军队指挥理论学习指南] (Beijing: National Defense University Press, 2004), 267–268.

[85] Bi, 356.

[86] Ibid.

[87] Wang Houqing [王厚卿] and Zhang Xingye [张兴业], eds., *Study of Campaigns* [战役学] (Beijing: National Defense University Press, 2000); PLAAF, *China Air Force Encyclopedia*; Zhang.

[88] Wang Houqing and Zhang Xingye, *Study of Campaigns*, 363–365; Bi, 357–358; PLAAF, *China Air Force Encyclopedia*, 102; Zhang 292–294.

[89] Bi, 361–362. This is consistent with the discussion (and schematic) found in PLAAF, *China Air Force Encyclopedia*, 102–103.

[90] Bi, 368–371.

[91] PLAAF, *China Air Force Encyclopedia*, 103.

[92] Bi, 244–250; Wang and Zhang,, 480–484; Zhang, 597–601.

[93] As of early 2010, China was estimated to have at least 120 J–10s, which are roughly comparable to the U.S. F–16 in capability; 240 Su–27, Su–30, and J–11B aircraft, which are comparable to the U.S. F–15 in capability; 20 battalions of Russian-made S–300PMU, S–300PMU1, and S–300PMU2 (SA-10 and SA-20) surface-to-air missiles (8 quadruple launchers per battalion); and at least 4 battalions of the Chinese HQ–9 system, which is roughly comparable to the S–300PMU1. See International Institute for Strategic Studies, *The Military Balance 2010* (London: Oxford University Press, 2010), 402, 404.

[94] See, for example, "Xian Aircraft Industries Group: XAC H–6," *Jane's All the World's Aircraft*, August 2, 2007; Carlo Kopp, *XAC (Xian) H–6 Badger, Air Power Australia* technical report APA-TR-2007-0705, July 2007; "DF–21 (CSS–5)," *Jane's Strategic Weapon Systems*, June 18, 2007.

Chapter 7

The PLAAF and the Integration of Air and Space Power

Kevin Pollpeter

On November 1, 2009, Chinese news outlets published an interview with People's Liberation Army Air Force (PLAAF) Commander General Xu Qiliang that was interpreted by many as an official Chinese statement endorsing the development of space weapons and the establishment of a space force based on the PLAAF. Xu proclaimed that the 21st century was "an informatized century" and "an air and space century." Xu went on to say:[1]

> The air and space era and information era have arrived at the same time and the domain of information and domain of space and air have become the new commanding height for international strategic competition. Considering the global trend of a new revolution in military affairs, competition among armed forces is moving toward the air and space domain and is extending from the aviation domain to near space and even deep space. Such a "shift" represents an irresistible trend, such an "expansion" is historically inevitable, and such development is irreversible. In a certain sense, having control of air and space means having control of the ground, oceans, and the electromagnetic space, which also means having the strategic initiative in one's hands.
>
> In ground operations, the commanding height is to be found on the hilltop; in three-dimensional operations, the commanding height is to be found in the air. Since the air force's "sphere of activity is high up in the heavens," it is heaven's favored one and boasts the combination of a science gene, an expedition gene, and a military gene. The air force is a young military service branch, yet its appearance on the scene has at once twisted the curve of the evolution of two-dimensional warfare and has quickly established a status that is on a par with the land force whose history goes back several thousand years and the naval force whose history goes back several hundred years. It has evolved from a supporting subordinate force into a decisive strategic force. Since the air force is a science- and technology-based service branch, it has always occupied the commanding height of knowledge.... On the surface of the earth, the area of land is limited and so is the area of oceans and seas, only the space and the sky have no limits.

> In facing the particular nature of the developing competition in the domains of air and space, the people's air force must establish a concept of air and space security, of air and space interests, and of air and space development. It must establish an air force that corresponds to our country's building and development needs, that is in keeping with the development needs of the air and space age and that will help maintain regional stability and world peace by properly forging a sharp sword and shield capable of winning peace.

In order to develop an air force that is capable of carrying out this agenda, Xu advocated that the PLAAF should focus on carrying out the "historic missions of our armed forces in the new century" by extending the "boundary of security" to "wherever there are national interests" and by building a service capable of winning an informatized war, integrating air and space, acquiring defensive and offensive capabilities, and developing reconnaissance, early warning, air strike, antimissile air defense, and strategic airlift and airdrop capabilities.[2]

Even though Xu did not explicitly propose that China develop antisatellite (ASAT) weapons, Xu's call for the air force to forge a "sharp sword and shield capable of winning peace" and his assessment "of the inevitability of military competition in air and space" were widely interpreted as a call for the development of space weapons and for the PLAAF to be the PLA's space force. Even the Chinese new agency Xinhua reported that Xu had advocated developing "an air force with integrated capabilities for both offensive and defensive operations in space as well as in the air."[3]

The Chinese Foreign Ministry, reacting to the interview, denied that China would ever participate in a space arms race. According to foreign ministry spokesman Ma Zhaoxu, "China has all along upheld the peaceful use of outer space. We oppose the weaponization of outer space or a space arms race. China has never and will not participate in an outer space arms race in any form. The position of China on this point remains unchanged."[4]

Speaking 10 days after his interview, Xu clarified but did not retract his remarks. He stated that China's policy toward outer space had always been consistent and that the air force would firmly carry out the policies of the country. It supported using outer space for peaceful purposes and it opposed carrying out an arms race in space and deploying weapons in outer space. China also followed the principle of peace, development, cooperation, and peaceful exploration and utilization. At the same time, Xu stated that his earlier remarks were an "objective analysis" that recognized that "some countries are developing weapons for space deployment, and some phenomena of not being secure have appeared in outer space."[5]

Xu Qiliang's remarks in his November 1, 2009, interview offer provocative insights into the PLAAF's attitudes toward the use of space, and Xu's statements regarding space are supported by a substantial body of literature written by PLAAF researchers in the years preceding the interview. This correlation between Xu's remarks and PLAAF research indicates that PLAAF doctrine is shaped by an interaction between PLAAF scholars and PLAAF leadership. This doctrine regards space-based assets as the primary source of information and the seizure of the initiative in outer space as a prerequisite for victory in the domains of the ground, air, and sea. The necessity to seize the initiative in outer space requires the PLAAF to achieve *space supremacy*—defined as the ability to use space and deny its use to others.

Moreover, the correlation of this research and Xu's remarks indicates that the PLAAF has committed itself to become both an air and space force in which the PLAAF is the main orchestrator of space-enabled operations. Under the rubric of an "integrated air and space force," the PLAAF describes itself as the service most responsible for the PLA's space enterprise. In this role, the PLAAF will be the primary entity facilitating network-centric warfare and jointness in the PLA and the main defender of China's interests in outer space. Because of this, PLAAF analysts argue that the air force is the ideal institution to lead the PLA's space efforts. Consequently, the doctrine of integrated air and space operations is not only about how the PLAAF should conduct future operations, but also about the PLAAF position within the PLA hierarchy.

The fullest analysis and comprehension of Xu Qiliang's remarks and PLAAF writings on the role of space in the PLAAF strategy of integrated air and space operations (空天一体作战) first require examining the role of space in the strategic guidance of the "New Historic Missions." This examination will provide context for the importance of space in future operations and the organizational changes proposed by PLAAF researchers to effectively carry out space missions.

The "New Historic Missions": Extending the Boundary of Security

Xu's comment that "the boundary of security should extend to wherever there are national interests"[6] is firmly rooted in the strategic guidance provided by the PLA under the banner of the "New Historic Missions." The New Historic Missions were first introduced by President Hu Jintao in 2004—the same year the PLAAF introduced its concept of integrated air and space operations—and ratified by the Communist Party in 2007. They direct the PLA to carry out four missions:

- *Guarantee Chinese Communist Party rule.* The PLA is to remain the ultimate backer of the Communist Party.

- *Safeguard the strategic opportunity for national development.* The PLA is to serve as a powerful defensive force that can deter aggression against China and protect its national sovereignty and territorial integrity so that China may develop economically.
- *Safeguard national interests.* The PLA must defend China's interests, not only within its land borders, territorial waters, and territorial air space, but also in distant waters, outer space, and in the electromagnetic sphere.
- *Play an important role in world peace.* China will maintain a defensive military strategy and will participate in United Nations peacekeeping missions and international cooperation on counterterrorism.

The New Historic Missions reflect the Chinese leadership's intention to have the PLA protect the Communist Party's and country's interests by meeting the challenges of the 21st century. While the New Historic Missions direct the PLA to continue with its legacy missions of guaranteeing Communist Party rule and maintaining territorial integrity, they expand the PLA's missions in important ways. For the first time, the PLA is directed to defend China's economic interests, not only within China's borders but also in the new areas of distant waters, outer space, and the electromagnetic sphere. In this respect, these missions are partly aspirational, serving as a guide for the development of operational concepts and capabilities.

Space plays two roles in the Historic Missions context, constituting both a domain in which China has interests, and a domain through which China defends its interests. Not surprisingly, China's interests in outer space are becoming more pronounced and varied as it becomes more vested in space. China's increasingly robust and varied space program is made up of communications satellites, remote-sensing satellites, and navigation and positioning satellites that not only provide military benefits but also commercial opportunities. Communication satellites can relay voice and television transmissions and support credit card transactions. Remote-sensing data can be used in urban planning and environmental studies. Navigation and positioning satellites have given rise to commercial and private navigation products and services. Outer space also holds vast natural resources, such as those deposited in asteroids or on the surface of the moon. One of the primary reasons for China's lunar exploration program is to search for Helium-3, touted as a potential source of clean energy.[7]

Indeed, a common theme in Chinese writings is that outer space and its associated technologies are of increasing economic value. Chinese space industry representatives cite reports, such as those by *The Space Foundation*, that revenue from the global space industry increased 7 percent to $261.61 billion in 2009.[8] According to one source, the value of a spacecraft and rocket is $150–200 million. If a satellite is lost, not only is there the monetary loss of a satellite that cannot be easily replaced, there is also the loss of the services it provides.[9]

As a result, space takes on a much more strategic character than its military applications alone would suggest.[10] PLAAF writers assert that if China does not develop space capabilities, it will neither be able to exploit the benefits of space nor will it be able to defend itself from threats from countries with strong space capabilities.[11] Furthermore, those countries that have strong space capabilities will be able to garner higher international prestige and more influence from which to promote military, economic, science and technology, and cultural interests.[12]

In fulfilling the Historic Missions, Xu states that the air force will face "numerous difficulties" in "scientifically planning" its innovative development.[13] Indeed, air force analysts state that the service is required to transform itself from being homeland defense–oriented to being offensively and defensively capable, from being mechanized to being informatized, from being air-oriented to being air- and space-integrated, and from being a tactical and campaign-oriented force to being a strategic force.[14]

The concept of the PLAAF as a strategic air force was codified at the same time as the New Historic Missions during the 17th Communist Party Congress held in November 2007. The Party Congress called on the PLAAF to strive "to build a modernized strategic air force that will be compatible with the international stature of our country and capable of carrying out the historical mission of our armed forces."[15] Being a strategic air force requires the PLAAF to participate in joint operations as well as independent strategic actions to support the military and national development strategy of the country.[16] The PLAAF intends to carry out its strategic mission through the use of "integrated air and space operations."

Toward an Integrated Air and Space Force

Xu's call for the air force to establish a concept of "air and space security" is directly related to its strategy of integrated air and space operations. Integrated air and space operations refer to the organic combining of airpower and spacepower to form an integrated air-space force. According to PLAAF analysts, the air and space battlefield is the main domain for information collection in which the space component plays an important role. Spy satellites, for example, can legally conduct reconnaissance over other countries. Navigation satellites can provide accurate positioning data. Communication satellites can provide global communications support.[17] In addition, seizing air and space superiority prevents the enemy from gaining strategic air and space superiority.[18] According to two prominent PLAAF researchers, "military activities in the air and space battlefield have already matured into the main military force of high technology local wars."[19]

Research on integrated air and space operations began in 1990 when Dong Wenxian at PLAAF Headquarters proposed "the control of high-altitude three-dimensional territorial airspace"—a euphemism for operations in outer space.[20] In 2000, a project championed by the President of the Air Force Engineering University, Major General Cai Fengzhen, was initiated with Senior Colonel Tian Anping as the project lead. This project was inspired by a book published by the PLA Navy (PLAN) entitled *Looking Toward the Pacific* (向太平洋看). These researchers realized that while the navy was extending its look *horizontally*, the air force had to extend its look *vertically*, to outer space.

This project resulted in two monographs entitled *The Air and Space Battlefield and China's Air Force* (空天战场与中国空军) published in 2004, and *Integrated Air and Space Operations* Studies (空天一体作战学) published in 2006. At the same time, in 2003, Li Rongchang (Dean of the Telecommunications Engineering School at the Air Force Engineering University) published *Integrated Air and Space Information Operations* (空天一体信息作战), as one of the projects of the air force's 10th Five-year Plan for military theory research. Since then, researchers at the Air Force Command College, including Wang Mingliang (Deputy Department Head of Research), Ji Yan (Deputy Director of the Institute's Strategic Research Office), and strategist Major General Qiao Liang, among others, have also researched integrated air and space operations.[21]

Integrated air and space operations are defined differently by various sources, but all involve the integration of battlespace, forces, and activities. A 2003 article defines *integrated air and space operations* as:[22]

> air forces, structure, and operational activities integrating aviation and space, air defense and space defense. Integrated air and space warfare refers to aviation and space offensive and defensive equipment merged into one to conduct simultaneous offensive and defensive operations. It includes aircraft, cruise missiles, and to different degrees includes ballistic missiles, satellites, orbiting space stations, and space planes. At the same time it includes aviation interceptors, all types of ground-to-air missiles, air-to-air missiles, and new concept weapons such as high power lasers, high power microwave weapons, and particle beam weapons.

The Air Force Informatized Work Office and the Air Force Informatized Expert Advisory Committee, in the book *Air Force Informatized Knowledge: Concept Volume,* define *integrated aerospace operations* as:

> integrated aviation and space forces in the atmosphere and outer space as well as related terrestrial integrated operations. Its characteristic is "three integrations" under a unified command, namely the integration of operational space, operational forces, and operational activities.
>
> 1. *Integration of operational space.* Although physical differences exist between the atmosphere and outer space, there is no definite line that distinguishes them. The air and space battlefield is a seamless whole that is an integrated battlefield in which different platforms and methods can be used to carry out identical military activities.
>
> 2. *Integration of Operational Forces.* The organization, training, and command and control of aviation and space forces are basically the same. It includes using aircraft, intercontinental ballistic missiles, satellites, space stations, space planes, interceptors, ballistic missiles, spacecraft, missiles, kinetic energy weapons, and lasers. Space forces are responsible for global reconnaissance, seizing the information initiative, launching spacecraft, and achieving space supremacy.
>
> 3. *Integration of operational activities.* The integration of aviation and space operations as well as ground forces that directly support aviation and space forces.

The authors of *Strategic Air Force* offer a similar definition in which air and space integration refers to integration of aviation and space in terms of structure, and the management of air defense, missile defense, and space defense in order to build a "new concept air force" made up of air and space forces. The integration of air and space is based on the lack of a boundary between the atmosphere and space, which leads the authors to conclude that an air and space integrated force is inevitable from the standpoint of technology, operations, environment, and experience.[23]

According to Cai Fengzhen and Tian Anping, integrated air and space operations are "operations in which aviation and space forces are the main operational components. It includes other operational forces related to integrated air and space operations and is represented by joint operations in the air and space battlefield."[24] In another venue, these authors define the air and space battlefield as an "integrated and information-oriented land (sea), air, and space battle arena, which fully connects organizationally fused and organically combined space and aerospace and related capabilities in the domains of the surface of the Earth, and the land (sea)."[25] Cai and Tian also describe the air and space battlefield as the principal battlefield.[26]

These various definitions, if differing somewhat in scope and precision, nevertheless present important common and cohesive themes regarding the integration of the air and space battlespace and the integration of air and space forces and operational activities.

Integration of Operational Battlespace and Forces

One of the most important aspects of the concept of integrated air and space operations as it relates to space is the characterization of the air and space battlespace as a "seamless whole." This characterization is based on the lack of a distinct boundary separating the atmosphere from space. This characterization, however, holds several conceptual problems based on the nature of the atmosphere and space, physics, and operational and legal considerations. First, satellites and most air-breathing engines cannot readily operate between the altitudes of 20 and 100 kilometers. Aerodynamic heating and atmospheric drag inhibit the former, while the increasingly tenuous atmosphere works against any form of air-breathing propulsion other than the high-hypersonic supersonic combustion ramjet (scramjet). This "nether region" has been largely left unexploited for military use, except as a region to transit into orbit. Second, the different operating environments of air and space vehicles force them to operate in fundamentally different manners. Aircraft are maneuverable, can group together, and can respond to operational demands relatively quickly. Spacecraft, on the other hand, are less maneuverable than aircraft and can only maneuver occasionally through the expenditure of limited quantities of fuel. Third, aircraft and spacecraft are treated differently by international law. Aircraft do not have unrestricted use of a foreign country's territorial air space whereas overflying a country in space is legal.[27]

Chinese analysts do acknowledge that there are important differences between outer space and the atmosphere. But Chinese analysts also assert that the integration of air and space operations will lead to a virtual single battlespace. This is reflected in three activities: operations that utilize the force enhancement aspects of space-enabled operations; the use of space and near-space vehicles that operate in the nether region described above; and space-based platforms that attack terrestrial targets.

The foremost activity that promotes the integration of air and space is the use of space-based force enhancement technologies that act as a force multiplier for air force and other service operations.[28] Space forces provide reconnaissance, communications, and navigation and positioning capabilities that cannot normally be achieved through other means. These capabilities provide and transmit information to increase the precision of strikes and facilitate long-range strikes. For example, reconnaissance satellites provide high-resolution, global, real time intelligence over a vast area without consideration of national borders; communication satellites provide global communications; and global navigation satellites can provide three-dimensional positioning data for navigation and for guiding long-distance precision strike weapons.[29]

The ultimate goal of the PLAAF's use of space is to build a network-centric force in which disparate forces divided by function and distance will be fused into an organic whole through the use of information technologies. Networked capabilities will allow the air force to carry out four activities: information, air, and space superiority; precision strike; rapid maneuver; and multidimensional support. These capabilities are intended to achieve information superiority across all domains. In fact, the level of network capabilities is said to define the level of modernization of air forces.[30]

The capabilities derived from a space-enabled, networked air and space force will also better integrate disparate services into a joint force, an essential prerequisite for winning informatized wars. Jointness is realized in two ways. First, space-enabled air operations allow the air force to provide better operational support to other services, for example, through precision strikes. Second, the C^{4}ISR [command, control, communications, computers, intelligence, surveillance, and reconnaissance] capabilities provided by satellites will allow all services to share a common battlefield picture and to better communicate with each other.[31] Through the use of these capabilities, practitioners of air and space integrated operations will be able to achieve synergies in which the whole is more than the sum of its parts.[32]

Technologies that transit through or operate in the nether world of near space between the altitudes of 20 and 100 kilometers, where neither conventional aircraft nor spacecraft can operate, likewise facilitate the integration of air and space. These technologies include high-flying balloons and airships, inhabited aircraft such as the venerable Lockheed U–2, and uninhabited, remotely piloted systems such as the Northrop-Grumman Global Hawk that provide persistent intelligence, surveillance, and reconnaissance (ISR) capabilities at altitudes between 20,000 and 25,000 meters (approximately 65,000 to over 80,000 feet). While the U–2 or Global Hawk may be able to stay above a target for hours or days, high flying balloons can remain aloft for months, although station-keeping of lightly loaded craft in the midst of high-altitude winds poses a significant challenge. These technologies blur the line between the atmosphere and outer space and will result in near space becoming as much of a battlespace as the lower atmosphere is today.

Another technology which blurs the distinction between the air and space mediums is transatmospheric space planes. Space planes, such as the proposed U.S. Falcon hypersonic near-space vehicle, are launched into the atmosphere and then accelerate to hypersonic speeds (speeds in excess of five times that of sound, Mach 5+) climbing to and cruising at altitudes ranging from 20 to over 100 kilometers (from over 12 to over 60 miles). Space planes include low-hypersonic Mach 5–8 remotely piloted aircraft, missile-launched hypersonic penetration systems operating at near-orbital (Mach 25) velocities, and even, well into the future, piloted global-ranging vehicles operating across this velocity range. Chinese analysts believe space planes will ultimately be important platforms for achieving air and space superiority[33] due to their ability to conduct operations in less time and at less cost than spacecraft, aircraft, or even cruise missiles.[34] Chinese writers often refer to space planes' global reach and information-sharing and precision strike capabilities[35] as both something China must possess and something which presents a great threat. According to one author, space planes will become "the most serious military blackmailing China has encountered since the invention of the atomic bomb."[36]

A third, though less discussed, aspect of integrated air and space operations will be the ability of space-based platforms to strike ground, air, and sea targets.[37] This includes the use of orbital bombs, so-called "rods from God," and directed energy (DE) weapons such as lasers and microwaves.

Securing Space Supremacy

Xu's comments that space is a "new commanding height for international strategic competition," that competition in space is an "inevitable trend," and "having control of space means having control of the ground, oceans, and electromagnetic space" are also common themes in PLAAF writings. PLAAF analysts assess that the role space plays in providing information and in linking units together into a networked force will turn the space domain into a contested battlefield. This conclusion is rooted in Chinese military doctrine that now regards the use of information as the main determiner of success on the battlefield. In fact, PLA analysts widely consider space as the dominant domain from which to collect intelligence and to facilitate network-centric warfare practices.[38]

This conclusion is partially based on the U.S. military's experience in the 1991 Gulf War and the wars in Afghanistan and Iraq. According to Chinese analysis, the United States used over 100 satellites during the 1991 Gulf War and 70 satellites during Operation *Allied Force*. The use of these satellites and the C⁴ISR systems they supported were the primary reason for U.S. victories. These capabilities allowed the U.S. military to have an asymmetric superiority over its opponents gained through battlefield transparency and long-range precision strikes.³⁹ The primacy of information gained from space has led many PLAAF analysts to conclude that space is the new commanding high ground of the battlefield.⁴⁰ Because of this, PLA analysts conclude that the primacy of information derived from space will make satellites irresistible targets. As a result, space will become a battlefield and seizing that battlefield will determine the success of air, naval, and ground operations.⁴¹ Operations to seize control of space are referred to as space warfare, called *tian zhan* (天战), *taikong zhan* (太空战), or *kongjian zhan* (空间站) in Chinese, involving military engagements that mainly take place in space between two parties trying to seize or maintain space superiority.

Space warfare is described as a new operational method in air and space integrated operations and an important method of achieving military superiority.⁴² Space warfare operations can be divided into space-based, air-based, and ground-based operations. These can include ground-based directed energy strikes and space-based kinetic energy strikes, airborne lasers, and electronic countermeasures. Chinese writers also refer to using space stations and space planes to conduct ASAT attacks.⁴³ Space stations can also serve as a command and control base, a communications node, and a logistics and maintenance hub for spacecraft and as a platform for strategic weapons.⁴⁴

Including the goal of achieving space supremacy in the definition of space warfare indicates that the PLAAF is attempting to take on the counterspace role. The same source that defined air and space integrated operations defines *space supremacy* as:⁴⁵

> During times of war, the control of a certain area of space for a certain period of time by one side. Its goal is to ensure one's freedom of action in space and its full access to space resources and to limit the other side's freedom of action in space and access to space resources.

Seizing space superiority is also described as one of the necessary conditions for achieving ground, naval, and air superiority, leading many analysts to conclude that whoever controls space will seize the initiative.⁴⁶

This definition of space supremacy is largely consistent with other Chinese definitions of space supremacy, and is, as well, consistent with the U.S Air Force (USAF) definition found in *Air Force Doctrine Document 2-2, Space Operations*:⁴⁷

> Space Superiority is that level of control in the space domain that one force enjoys over another that permits the conduct of operations at a given time and place without prohibitive interference by the opposing force. Space superiority may be localized in time and space, or it may be broad and persistent. Achieving space superiority is of primary concern since it allows control and exploitation of the space domain in order

to provide space effects in and through space. The Air Force achieves space superiority through counterspace operations, including offensive and defensive operations, both of which are based on robust space situational awareness.

One important difference between the two definitions is the Chinese reference to space superiority occurring within a certain time and area, whereas the USAF definition states that space superiority "may be localized in time and space, or it may be broad and persistent." The Chinese definition reflects doctrinal writings, which stress seizing the initiative at a certain place and period of time in order to open a window of opportunity that can be used to strike a decisive blow. This limited goal also recognizes that the PLA, as a weaker force compared to the U.S. military, will most likely not be able to maintain the initiative for long periods of time over an expansive area.

Organizing for the PLAAF Assuming the PLA's Space Mission

PLAAF writers conclude that the essential nature of the space battlefield and the central role that the PLAAF will play in conducting operations in outer space make the PLAAF the ideal service to take over the PLA's space mission.[48] PLAAF researchers argue several points in making their case. The first is that the air force is critical to any operation's success. As one researcher writes, "Seizing air dominance in the war zone relies on the entire military force. Still, it will only succeed by the integrated offense and defense operations in the air assisted by space-based information. Consequently, an integrated air and space force is a crucial force. This is a conclusion we have come to from all high-tech limited wars."[49] Xu makes a similar, if not more ostentatious, statement in promoting the superiority of the air force by stating, "Since the air force's 'sphere of activity is high up in the heavens,' it is heaven's favored one and boasts the combination of a science gene, an expeditionary gene, and a military gene."

A related argument is the characterization of the air force as the most highly technical branch of the military, which makes the air force more suitable to warfare in the information age than other services.[50] Scientific and technological achievements in aviation and space technology have led to dramatic changes in how wars are fought. These achievements have transformed warfare into a three-dimensional battlefield fought at ever increasing altitudes and eventually in space. This evolution has directly led to the concept of integrated air and space operations and network-centric warfare.[51]

Another argument used by PLAAF analysts is the requirement for a unified command of China's space forces. According to this argument, the increasing diversity and number of Chinese satellites has increased the difficulty of coordinating China's space enterprise and only by a unified command can the PLA bring together these disparate functions and organizations into an effective military force.[52]

In fact, PLA analysts and those involved in the space industry have for some time argued that China requires an organization to unify space efforts.[53] They point out that China's space enterprise is too widely spread out among a number of different organizations, including the General Armament Department (GAD), the China National Space Administration, the Ministry of Science and Technology, and the National Weather Administration. In addition, PLAAF analysts argue that the GAD, while responsible for research and development and the launch and tracking of satellites, is less suited for conducting space operations. According to a PLAAF author, this makes the GAD incapable of meeting the needs of space operations and integrated air and space operations.[54] These inefficiencies result in the waste of human, material, and financial resources and the failure to identify priorities and coordinate development. Moreover, the lack of a unified command organization has resulted in a lack of space doctrine at the campaign and tactical levels.[55] This was most recently demonstrated during the 2008 Wenchuan earthquake which revealed shortcomings in the ability of the Chinese government and military to effectively utilize space-based assets.[56]

Another compelling rationale for the PLAAF to lead the space mission is the inevitable deployment of space planes and near-space vehicles. Since the PLAAF will be the main organization operating aircraft, space planes, and near-space vehicles, it is thus best suited to control their flights. This also makes the PLAAF the logical organization to defend China from enemy space planes, near-space vehicles, and satellites.[57]

A final argument made by PLAAF analysts is that every other military in the world places the responsibility for the command of space forces with its air force. As one author writes, "as of today, no country, from the large such as the United States and Russia to the small such as Israel, puts the country's space force under a service other than the air force, let alone under the establishment of the rocket forces."[58]

PLAAF writers acknowledge that not all agree the PLAAF should command the PLA's space forces. According to one account, the PLAAF is accused of a having "too long of a reach." One analyst, however, argues that the PLAAF is the only logical choice based on military structure, development, and economic benefits. This author concludes that if the PLAAF's "reach is too long," then so is the reach of other air forces, who also happen to be supported by their military leaders; he writes:[59]

> An authoritative report concluded that it is unadvisable to have the Air Force take on the command of space forces, given its other responsibilities.

The implication is that the Air Force does not have what it takes. I have argued against that conclusion at different conferences. The question comes to: it should fall under the Air Force's responsibility based on the attributes and inherent function of the service. Foreign countries let their air force take it on. The Chinese air force must be capable of doing it as well. ... My view is as follows: our military is currently at a time of reestablishing itself as a new air force, so as to transform from a mechanized air force into an informatized air force, an air defense–oriented air force into an offense-defense capable air force, a tactical air force into a strategic air force, and an aviation-oriented air force into an integrated air and space air force. In short, to transform a "small air force" into a "big air force," and achieving "air force first" as put forward by Deng Xiaoping. "Air force first" does not mean the Air Force being the "big brother." All services and combat arms were spun from the ground force and nurtured by the glorious tradition of the ground force. As a result, the army will forever be the "big brother." "Big air force" refers to breaking away from the traditional mind-set of the Air Force and to build a new model air force called for by the new times, to play a major role in wars, as well as a strategic role in national defense.

Whether the PLAAF's space force should be an independent force or a force subordinated to a joint organization appears to be under debate, however. One author recommends that the air force should be the PLA's primary space force that will conduct independent operations as well as operations in support of other services.[60] Another researcher, however, argues that the Central Military Commission (CMC) and General Staff Department (GSD) should establish a joint organization which would command all PLA space forces, including air force space launch, tracking, situational awareness, operations, and information application units.[61]

Conclusion

Chinese writings on integrated air and space operations reflect the PLAAF desire to integrate space into military operations. This desire is based on the assertions that space-based information will become a deciding factor in future wars, that space will be a dominant battlefield, and that in order to achieve victory on Earth, one must first seize the initiative in space. This will require China to achieve space supremacy, defined as the ability to freely use space and to deny the use of space to adversaries.

PLAAF analysts acknowledge that the role of space in modern military operations is largely aspirational and is mainly limited to information support given to air and air defense operations. Nevertheless, as space operational capabilities improve, integrated air and space operations will become more effective.[62]

In making these conclusions, however, PLAAF analysts fail to question their assumptions. In addition to the conceptual problems related to the characterization of air and space as a seamless medium discussed earlier in the paper, the description of space as the dominant domain ignores the vulnerability of space-based assets and the primacy of offense over defense in space. Indeed, while space provides vital force enhancement functions, the fragility of spacecraft and the difficulties in defending relatively unmaneuverable satellites suggest that outer space will not remain the dominant domain in the face of counterspace operations. PLAAF analysts also seem inordinately interested in manned space missions on the premise that manned spacecraft are more responsive in combat—a notion discarded by the U.S. Air Force in the 1960s.

Ultimately, PLAAF analysts argue that the primacy of the outer space domain will require the PLA to establish a space force to unify China's military space program into a cohesive whole and that the air force is the best institution to take on this mission. In this regard, while PLAAF researchers may firmly believe their conclusions, it cannot be ignored that such arguments also support PLAAF equities in its efforts to expand its mission. In this respect, integrated air and space operations are as much about bureaucratic interests as they are about doctrine.

This approach is not without its risks. RAND Corporation analyst Benjamin Lambeth argues that U.S. Air Force claims to the air and space domains under the rubric of an "aerospace force" had opportunity costs. Even though the term *aerospace force* successfully claimed the two domains for the USAF, the USAF never revised its operational concepts to include space and simply replaced "air" with "aerospace." When the USAF subsequently did become more involved in space, it had a difficult time receiving budget increases to cover its increased activities since its rhetoric had led Congress to believe that it had already been conducting the space mission.[63]

The case of the PLAAF may be different, however. The PLAAF, though in existence for more than 60 years, is still relatively undeveloped in terms of technology, training, and doctrine. In fact, PLAAF writings refer to the PLAAF as a "new air force" that is just beginning to modernize its technology and doctrine. Adopting space as an inherent mission for the PLAAF would thus appear to hold less risk since it is not doctrinally wedded to acting as a pure air force. However, this would only be true if the PLAAF can properly balance the obligations of its air and space missions.

Whether the PLAAF will or should take over the PLA's space enterprise is, of course, a different question. Despite the air force's assertion that the GAD is not properly suited to take on space military operations, an argument can be made that the GAD's present role of researching, developing, launching, and operating spacecraft makes it the best organization to run the PLA's space program. Alternatively, the PLA could divide responsibility for space between the GAD and the services. Under this scenario, the GAD would maintain responsibility for launching spacecraft while the air force would operate space planes and air-launched ASAT weapons and the Second Artillery would operate direct ascent ASAT weapons.

Despite these shortcomings, the analysis of PLAAF researchers should not be disassociated from official PLAAF policy and doctrine. In fact, the conformity of the writings of PLAAF researchers with Xu Qiliang's comments in November 2009 suggests that the concept of space warfare within the context of integrated air and space operations has been officially adopted by the PLAAF. Most of the writings presented in this paper were published well before Xu's 2009 statements, indicating that PLAAF analysts play a critical role in shaping PLAAF doctrine. Doctrinal assumptions advanced by PLAAF analysts and stated by Xu include outer space as a commanding height, the inevitability of combat extending to outer space, and the seizure of the initiative in outer space leading to victory on Earth.

Moreover, there is evidence that these concepts are being disseminated throughout the PLAAF. In June 2010, the PLAAF organ *Air Force News* reported that the Air Force Command Academy held a "PLAAF aerospace strategy advanced seminar" which "was aimed at strengthening the research of the major issues concerning the Air Force's building, development, and strategy implementation in the new stage of the new century so as to lay a good human resources and theory foundation for the Air Force's capability to 'move up to space and use space.'" The seminar was designed to "help senior and intermediate-level Air Force commanders fully and clearly understand the development tendency of military space technology in the contemporary world and the situation of the international competition in the space domain."[64]

While the conformity of PLAAF writings on space with the comments of Xu Qiliang indicates official PLAAF strategy, does official PLAAF strategy reflect official PLA and Chinese government doctrine and policy? First, there is no doubt that the PLA is using space's force enhancement capabilities. China's development of space-based remote sensing and its development of a global navigation system have admitted national security applications. The more important question concerns China's counterspace efforts. In this regard, any interpretation of Xu's comments and subsequent Chinese reactions must first recognize that China has an active, if not extensive, ASAT weapons program at the same time that it appears to be opposed to them. According to the 2010 Pentagon report on the PLA, China is continuing to refine and develop its direct ascent ASAT weapon successfully tested in 2007, and is developing laser, high powered microwave, and particle beam weapons for use in the ASAT role.⁶⁵ The challenge then is reconciling the seeming contradiction among Chinese statements opposing space weaponization, China's ASAT programs, PLAAF writings, and Xu Qiliang's statements.

First, a careful exegesis of Chinese statements on ASAT weapons and space warfare must be conducted to determine their exact meaning. China's official stance on space arms control is opposition to the "deployment of weapons in outer space and the threat or use of force against objects in outer space so as to ensure that outer space is used purely for peaceful purposes."⁶⁶ Other statements express opposition to an arms race in space and the weaponization of space (反对在外空进行军备竞赛和武器化). This policy was stated by the Chinese Foreign Ministry in response to Xu's comments as well as by Xu in his November 11 *Nanfang Zhoumo* interview.

Chinese policy is widely regarded as unconditionally opposed to all types of ASAT weapons. In fact, official Chinese policy, as well as Xu's November 11, 2009, statement, only expresses opposition to weapons deployed in outer space and to arms races that occur in outer space. Chinese statements do not oppose the development of terrestrially-based ASAT weapons, such as its direct ascent kinetic kill vehicle. For example, in the draft "Treaty on Prevention of the Placement of Weapons in Outer Space and of the Threat or Use of Force Against Outer Space Objects (PPWT)" submitted with Russia to the United Nations Conference on Disarmament, China defines "weapon in outer space" as "any device placed in outer space ... to destroy, damage or disrupt the normal functioning of objects in outer space, on the Earth or in the Earth's atmosphere, or to eliminate a population or components of the biosphere which are important to human existence or inflict damage on them." "Use of force" or the "threat of force," on the other hand, means "any hostile actions against outer space objects including, inter alia, actions aimed at destroying them, damaging them, temporarily or permanently disrupting their normal functioning or deliberately changing their orbit parameters, or the threat of such actions."

Neither definition constrains or limits the research and development of any ASAT weapon. It neither prohibits the deployment of terrestrially-based ASAT weapons nor the terrestrial storage of space-based ASAT weapons. This treaty would even allow the development of space-based ASAT weapons and their storage on Earth. Moreover, the prohibition against the "use of force" or the "threat of force" is nullified during armed conflict. The draft states that nothing in the treaty "may be interpreted as impeding the exercise by the States Parties of their right of self-defence in accordance with Article 51 of the Charter of the United Nations."⁶⁷

This last condition renders the treaty useless since most countries claim the right of self-defense before going to war.

This point is especially important in the case of China. Indeed, while people tend to regard their country as peace-loving, the Chinese appear to perceive their country as more peace-loving than others. This predilection for using peaceful methods to resolve conflicts is historically based and continues to influence China's contemporary behavior.[68] According to China's 2008 national defense white paper, China pursues a national defense policy that is "purely defensive in nature" and "places the protection of national sovereignty, security, territorial integrity, safeguarding of the interests of national development, and the interests of the Chinese people above all else."

China's national defense policy is reflected in its national defense strategy of active defense. Active defense was first formulated by Mao Zedong in the 1930s and is described as "offensive defense or defense through decisive engagements" and is "for the purpose of counter-attacking and taking the offensive."[69] Active defense involves seizing the initiative through offensive strikes and gaining mastery after the enemy has struck.[70] Yet any strategic concept that emphasizes gaining mastery only "after the enemy has struck" would seem to have an inherent weakness given the speed in which modern conventional warfare is conducted, a detail not lost on Chinese military analysts.

This contradiction is best explained by the little apparent operational difference between China's active defense strategy and an offensive strategy. Within the context of protecting China's sovereignty and national interests, Chinese writers make clear that the full range of offensive actions, including preemptive strikes, are permissible.[71] As a result, active defense is best thought of as a politically defensive but operationally offensive strategy in which China will rhetorically maintain a defensive posture up until the time that war appears imminent. Thus, any U.S. military support or deployment that is deemed to be a precursor of U.S. action could be grounds for a preemptive strike.[72]

The inclusion of preemptive strikes within China's official strategy of active defense indicates that China may initiate armed conflict when it determines that its national sovereignty or interests are at stake. Characterizing this strategy as defensive becomes more complicated when China's national interests butt up against the interests of other countries. For example, China's defense of claims in the South China Sea may be viewed as aggressive by other claimants to the area as well as by countries, such as the United States, that have an interest in maintaining freedom of navigation in the region.

China's position against a space arms race also does not necessarily mean that it is opposed to developing ASAT weapons. A space arms race connotes an attempt by China to develop more weapons than an opponent, which could unnecessarily divert resources from other weapons programs, lead to China being unnecessarily provocative, or retard economic growth. It does not prohibit China from developing a sufficient number of ASAT weapons of a sufficient quality that can both act as a deterrent force and have an operational capability.

In this regard, China's development of ASAT weapons is akin to its nuclear weapons posture. China has substantially fewer nuclear weapons than the United States and Russia and is not attempting to equal their number. China's possession of nuclear weapons, however, is meant to deter opponents from threatening and conducting nuclear strikes and, in case deterrence fails, to provide a viable retaliatory strike capability. This operational deployment of nuclear weapons, however, has not prevented China from supporting "the complete prohibition and thorough destruction of nuclear weapons."[73]

Xu's comment that China should develop an air and space force that will help maintain regional stability and world peace suggests that China views its ASAT programs as defensive and partially based on the belief that the United States has at least latent capabilities and intends to use them. Chinese researchers point to the U.S. ASM–135 direct-ascent ASAT weapon test in 1985,[74] the U.S. Alpha space-based laser program,[75] and the 1997 U.S. Mid-Infrared Advanced Chemical Laser (MIRACL) test,[76] as evidence that the United States possesses ASAT capabilities. As a result, PLA researchers argue that China must develop its own indigenous ASAT capabilities, especially as China's presence in space grows. Chinese ASAT capabilities, they believe, can have a deterrent effect as well as provide warfighting options.

Indeed, Xu's comments that China is a force for peace is based on the premise that China needs to develop space technologies to thwart U.S. aggression. The U.S. military's adoption of air- and spacepower and statements that the USAF should achieve space superiority lead PLA analysts to conclude that the U.S. military is intent on seizing a preeminent position in space in order to develop an asymmetric military supremacy over other nations, which will in turn start a space arms race. As two prominent scholars write:[77]

> The American air-space strategy constitutes challenges to the rest of the world. Other developed countries, in order to protect their "air-space" strategic interests and international status, as well as to compete for the possession of larger "capital" in international affairs, also are not content to be left behind and emphatically develop their air-space strength. Russia, Western Europe, Japan, and India, all strive to catch up and overtake one another, thereby making the air-space a new military "wrestling" ground.

In conclusion, Xu's remark that China's policy on space weapons has been consistent and that the air force will carry out the country's policies is accurate. Neither Xu Qiliang's remarks, Foreign Ministry statements, nor official Chinese policy rule out the development, testing, deployment, and use of ASAT weapons. Consequently, Xu's remarks that China should develop a "sharp sword" and "shield" for maintaining peace are best taken as expressions of support for the development of space-enabled capabilities and ASAT weapons and as a proposal for the air force to assume responsibility for developing a "space force" which would be the main military organization responsible for conducting the space mission. In conducting this mission, the PLAAF will follow a strategy of "integrated air and space" that is "simultaneously prepared for offensive and defensive operations."

Notes

[1] "Flying with Force and Vigor in the Sky of the New Century—Central Military Commission Member and PLA Air Force Commander Xu Qiliang Answers Reporter's Questions in an Interview [奋飞在新世纪的天空: 中央军委委员、空军司令员许其亮答本报记者问]," *PLA Daily* [解放军报], November 1, 2009. Hereafter cited as Xu Interview.

[2] Ibid.

[3] "China's PLA Eyes Future in Space, Air: Air Force Commander," *Xinhua*, November 1, 2009.

[4] "China Disavows General's Comments on Space Militarisation," *Agence France Presse*, November 5, 2009, accessed on August 22, 2011, at <www.spacewar.com/reports/China_disavows_generals_comments_on_space_militarisation_999.html>.

[5] Chun Feng and Zhang Jiajun, "China Responds to the Guesses that the United States Has about the Anti-Satellite Facilities of the People's Liberation Army" [中国回应美关于解放军反卫星设施猜测], China Space News [中国航天报], November 9, 2009; and Yao Yijiang, "The Sky Cannot Be Turned Into a 'Dangerous Skylight' Above People's Heads—Exclusive Interview of General Xu Qiliang, Member of the Central Military Commission and Commander of the Air Force," *Nanfang Zhoumo* [南方周末], November 11, 2009.

[6] Xu Interview.

[7] Zhang Yi and Wang Zi, "An Expert Explains the Lunar Exploration Project: Why Do Chinese Want to Explore the Moon" [专家解释绕月工程：中国人为什么要探测月球], *People's Daily*, March 17, 2004. Note: Helium-3 (^{3}He) is an isotope of helium having two protons and one neutron. Rare on Earth, it can be manufactured in limited (and hence highly expensive) quantities as a byproduct of tritium (^{3}H) decay, typically from dismantled nuclear weapons. Large natural deposits are thought to be entrapped in loose lunar soil (the regolith), from eons of accretion from the solar wind. Energy enthusiasts believe a cheap source of ^{3}He could revolutionize fusion energy production.

[8] The Space Foundation, *The Space Report 2010* (Colorado Springs, CO: The Space Foundation, 2010), 30.

[9] Pan Youmu, "Exploring National Air and Space Security Strategies in View of Air and Space Integration" [着眼空天一体化探索国家空天安全战略], *China Military Science* [中国军事科学] 19, no. 2 (2006), 66.

[10] Chang Xianqi, *Military Astronautics* [军事航天学] (Beijing: National Defense Industry Press, 2002), vi.

[11] Pan, 65.

[12] Dong Wenxian, "Emergence of Modern Air War" [现代空中战争的崛起], *PLA Daily* [解放军报], May 9, 2000.

[13] Xu Interview.

[14] Shang Jinsuo, Li Zhen, Li Liguang, and Ye Haiyuan, "Expansion and Development of the People's Air Force Along With the Progress of the People's Republic of China" [人民空军伴随共和国的步伐开拓发展], *China Military Science* [中国军事科学] 22, no. 4 (2009), 30.

[15] Dong Wenxian, "Part I of the 'Strategic Air Force' Series: The Expansion of National Strategic Space Calls for a Strategic Air Force" [战略空军系列谈之一：国家战略空间扩展呼唤战略空军], *Air Force News* [空军报] February 2, 2008, 2.

[16] Ibid.

[17] Cai Fengzhen and Tian Anping, *The Air-Space Battlefield and China's Air Force* [空天战场与中国空军] (Beijing: Liberation Army Press, 2004), 27.

[18] Ibid., 33.

[19] Ibid., 27.

[20] "The Chinese Air Force's Road to Leapfrog" [中国空军的" 跨越之路], *Liaowang* [瞭望], August 5, 2010.

[21] Ibid.

[22] Zhang Wei, "Discussion on Speeding up the Development of Integrated Air and Space Warfare Equipment" [试论加快空天一体战装备发展], *Ground-based Air Defense Weapons* [地面防空武器], no. 1 (2003), 2.

[23] Zhu Hui, ed., *Strategic Air Force* [战略空军论] (Beijing: Blue Sky Press, 2009), 39.

[24] Cai Fengzhen and Tian Anping, *Integrated Air and Space Operations Studies* [空天一体作战学] (Beijing: Liberation Army Press, 2006), 2.

[25] Cai Fengzhen and Deng Fan, "Introduction to the Air and Space Battlefield and National Air and Space Security System" [空天战场与国家空天安全体系初探], *China Military Science* [中国军事科学] 19, no. 2, (2006), 44.

[26] Ibid.

[27] For the roots of air and space law and overflight policy, see Stuart Banner, *Who Owns the Sky? The Struggle to Control Airspace from the Wright Brothers On* (Cambridge: Harvard University Press, 2008); Nathan C. Goldman, *Space Policy: An Introduction* (Ames, IA: Iowa State University Press, 1992), 24–30; R. Cargill Hall, "The Evolution of U.S. National Security Space Policy and Its Legal Foundations in the 20th Century," *Journal of Space Law* 33, no. 1 (2007), 1–103; and Benjamin Lambeth, *Mastering the Ultimate High Ground: Next Steps in the Military Uses of* Space (Santa Monica, CA: RAND Corporation, 2003), 45–46.

[28] Zhu, 256.

[29] Ibid., 260–261; and Cai and Tian, *The Air-Space Battlefield,* 160.

[30] Dong Wenxian, "Integrated Development of Firepower and Information Networks: A Hallmark of the Compound Development of Mechanization and Informatization—Fifth Installment of the 'Strategic Air Force' Series," *Air Force News (*April 5, 2008), 2.

[31] Zhu, *Strategic Air Force*, 65.

[32] Cai and Deng, "Introduction to the Air and Space Battlefield," 44.

[33] Guo Rui, Qi Ming, Cheng Jian, and Tong Zhuo, "An Application of Value-Focused Thinking to Near-space Weapons Systems" [价值中心法在临近空间武器装备体系中的运用], *Journal of the Academy of Equipment Command and Technology* [装备指挥技术学院学报] (February 2010), 94.

[34] Zhu, *Strategic Air Force*, 42; and Pan, 63.

[35] Guo, Qi, Cheng, and Tong, "An Application of Value-Focused Thinking," 94.

[36] "The Chinese Air Force's Road to Leapfrog" [中国空军的" 跨越之路], *Liaowang* [瞭望] (August 5, 2010); and Cai and Tian, *The Air-Space Battlefield,* 201.

[37] Ibid., 201.

[38] Cai and Tian, *Integrated Air and Space Operations Studies*, 12.

[39] Dai Xu, "Space, A Rising Power's New Opportunity" [太空, 大国崛起的新机遇], *Huanqiu Shibao* [环球时报], December 21, 2006.

[40] Cai and Tian, *Integrated Air and Space Operations Studies*, 59.

[41] Cai and Tian, *The Air-Space Battlefield,* 178–179.

[42] Ibid.

⁴³ Zhu, *Strategic Air Force*, 247–248.

⁴⁴ Cai and Tian, *The Air-Space Battlefield*, 131.

⁴⁵ Ibid., 213.

⁴⁶ Ibid., 214.

⁴⁷ United States Air Force, *Space Operations, Air Force Doctrine Document 2-2* (Washington, DC: Headquarters Air Force, November 27, 2006), 31.

⁴⁸ See, for example, "China Should Build a Mighty Air Force," *China Military Online* (August 29, 2009), accessed at <http://english.chinamil.com.cn/> on August 21, 2011; Cai and Deng, "Introduction to the Air and Space Battlefield," 50; and Dong Wenxian, "Air Force Culture—the Distinct Characteristics of the Strategic Air Force (Part VI of the Strategic Air Force Series)," *Air Force News* [空军报], April 19, 2008, 2.

⁴⁹ Zhu, *Strategic Air Force*, 48.

⁵⁰ Chen Ling and Chen Peng, "Interview with Major General Lu Gang, Head of the PLAAF Informatization Specialists Advisory Committee and Director of the PLAAF Equipment Research Institute," *Air Force News*, April 19, 2007, 2.

⁵¹ Dong, "Air Force Culture," 2.

⁵² Zhu, *Strategic Air Force*, 30–31.

⁵³ See, for example, Li Xin, Lei Xu, and Li Jun, "Preliminary Analysis of Future Space Unit C⁴ISR System Construction" [未来航天部队C⁴ISR 系统建设初探], *Winged Missile Journal* [飞航导弹] no. 3 (2006), 41; and Yang Zhiqiang and Zhang Dongliang, "Space Power and Joint Operations System" [空间力量与联合作战体系], *Winged Missile Journal* [飞航导弹] (July 2008), 32.

⁵⁴ Zhu, *Strategic Air Force*, 145.

⁵⁵ Ibid., 32.

⁵⁶ "Scientists: China Should Integrate Space Resources to Improve Emergency Response," *People's Daily Online* (March 4, 2009).

⁵⁷ Zhu, *Strategic Air Force*, 43.

⁵⁸ Ibid., 48.

⁵⁹ Ibid., 51.

⁶⁰ Ibid., 44.

⁶¹ Ibid., 146.

⁶² Cai and Tian, *The Air-Space Battlefield*, 181.

⁶³ Lambeth, 48–49.

⁶⁴ Qiao Songbai, "Air Force's First 'Aerospace Strategy Advanced Seminar' Begins" [空军首期 空天战略 高级研修班开班], *Air Force News* [空军报], June 2, 2010, 1.

⁶⁵ Office of the Secretary of Defense, *Military and Security Developments Involving the People's Republic of China* (Washington, DC: Department of Defense, 2010), 36.

⁶⁶ Full text of white paper on arms control: State Council Information Office, "China's Endeavors for Arms Control, Disarmament and Non-Proliferation," at <www.china.org.cn/english/2005/Aug/140343.htm>.

⁶⁷ Russian Federation to the Conference on Disarmament and People's Republic of China to the Conference on Disarmament, CD/1839, available at <http://daccess-ods.un.org/TMP/2082939.74399567.html>, accessed on August 29, 2010.

⁶⁸ Andrew Scobell, *China's Use of Military Force: Beyond The Great Wall and The Long March* (New York: Cambridge, 2003), 27.

⁶⁹ Mao Zedong, *Selected Military Writings of Mao Zedong* (Beijing: Foreign Languages Press, 1967), 105.

⁷⁰ Wang Houqing and Zhang Xingye, ed., *The Science of Campaigns* [战役学] (Beijing: National Defense University Press, 2000), 90.

⁷¹ Liu Zhenwu, "National Security and the Active Defense Strategy" [论国家安全与积极防御战略], *Military Art Journal* [军事学术], no. 4 (2004), 9.

⁷² Ibid.

⁷³ State Council Information Office, "China's Endeavors for Arms Control, Disarmament and Non-Proliferation."
⁷⁴ Zhu, *Strategic Air Force*, 255.
⁷⁵ Cai and Tian, *Integrated Air and Space Operations Studies*, 169.
⁷⁶ Ibid., 221.
⁷⁷ Cai and Deng, "Introduction to the Air and Space Battlefield," 45.

PART III

EQUIPMENT, PERSONNEL, AND EDUCATION/TRAINING

Chapter 8

Equipping the PLAAF: The Long March to Modernity

David Shlapak

Since the early 1990s, and rapidly accelerating after the latter half of that decade, China has undertaken an ambitious program of military modernization, one that continues vigorously today.[1] A primary focal point of this effort has been to update and upgrade the People's Liberation Army Air Force (PLAAF), which for the first 40-plus years of its existence had been a backward force, equipped with numerous but antiquated aircraft flown by poorly trained pilots. While it has yet to completely outgrow this modest past, the PLAAF has undergone a remarkable transformation over the last 20 years, a process that seems certain to continue through the foreseeable future.

This paper addresses one aspect of the PLAAF's ongoing evolution: its aircraft and weapons. This assessment leads to a conclusion that the point of the PLAAF's spear—its fleet of modern combat aircraft along with their munitions—has mostly caught up to the standards of other advanced air forces. In terms of its physical hardware, the PLAAF will soon have the ability to credibly challenge the United States over the nearby waters of the Taiwan Strait, if it is not capable already. However, the PLAAF's ability to project airpower against a first-rate adversary in an arena farther from China's shores—over the South China Sea or beyond—remains more doubtful, although this could change in the next decade.

Equipment is of course only one piece of the airpower puzzle; without adequate doctrine, leadership, training, and ground support, the most modern aircraft and equipment are at best a static display and at worst a target array. So, this paper's judgment of China's air force must be partial; larger and more integrated assessments are needed to understand the PLAAF more thoroughly. What can be said is, should the PLAAF falter in a Taiwan contingency, its leaders will be hard put to lay the blame on their tools.

PLAAF Order of Battle, 1990–2010

Table 8–1 lists the composition of the Chinese air force at 5-year intervals from 1990 to 2010. It shows that as late as 1995, almost 80 percent of the PLAAF's combat aircraft were variants of 1950s vintage Soviet MiG–17 and MiG–19 fighters. To put this in perspective: the original MiG–19 was introduced in the Soviet air force in the mid-1950s and entered Chinese service around 1962. In 1962, the most common combat aircraft in the U.S. Air Force was the F–100 *Super Sabre*. While the F–100 was an excellent airplane in its own right, it is hard to imagine the U.S. Air Force (USAF) in 1995 being built around it, as the PLAAF was built around the MiG–19/J–6.[2]

Table 8–1. PLAAF Aircraft Inventory by Type, 1990–2010

Class / type	1990	1995	2000	2005	2010
Fighter Aircraft					
J–5 / MiG–17	400	400	—	—	—
J–6 / MiG–19	3,000	3,000	—	—	—
J–7 / MiG–21	500	500	700	756	552
J–8	50	100	250	245	312
Su–27 / J–11A	—	26	65	116	116
J–10	—	—	—	62	120
Su–30	—	—	—	73	—
Ground Attack Aircraft					
Q–5	500	400	300	408	120
J–6	—	—	1,500	722	—
JH–7	—	—	—	39	72
Su–30	—	—	—	—	73
J–11B	—	—	—	—	18
Bomber Aircraft					
H–5	350	300	—	94	—
H–6	120	120	120	128	82
Total	4,920	4,846	2,935	2,643	1,465

Source: International Institute for Strategic Studies (1990, 1995, 2000, 2005, 2010)

As notable—though perhaps less remarked upon—is the dramatic reduction in the number of combat aircraft in the PLAAF inventory. Between 1990 and 2010, almost 3,500 obsolete aircraft—*70 percent* of the force—were retired, mostly since 1995. Again by way of comparison, the USAF's fleet of fighter-bombers shrank from a Cold War level of 3,620 in 1990 to 2,650 in 2010—a little over 25 percent.[3] That the PLAAF was willing to shed so many of its aircraft indicates the scope of the PLAAF's modernization efforts equally as much as its acquisition of modern aircraft.

One way of understanding the impact of the past 20 years on the PLAAF's fighter force is to compare the number of its modern fighters with the numbers owned by the air forces of other advanced countries; table 8–2 shows that comparison. It reveals that the third-largest fleet of advanced fighters in the world may be found within the PLAAF, smaller only than those of the United States and Russia, and larger than the combined inventories of, for example, the British and French air forces.

Table 8–2. Comparative Numbers of Modern Fighters, 2010

Air Force	Number of Modern Fighters
U.S.	1,490
Russia	523
China	399
Taiwan	331
Israel	294
South Korea	201
France	191
Great Britain	183
India	182
Japan	160
Germany	150

Source: International Institute for Strategic Studies (2010).
Counts include: U.S. (Active component only): F–22, F–15, F–16, F/A–18); Russia (Su–34, MiG–29, Su–27); China (J–10, Su–27/J–11, J–11B, Su–30, JH–7); Taiwan (F–16, F–CK–1); Israel (F–15, F–16); France (Rafale, Mirage 2000); Great Britain (Typhoon, Tornado F.3, Tornado GR.4); India (MiG–29, Su–30, Mirage 2000); Japan (F–15); South Korea (F–15K, KF–16C/D); Germany (Eurofighter, Tornado IDS).

Finally, figure 8-1 presents a third way of visualizing the reshaping of the PLAAF's fighter fleet by depicting its order of battle according to fighter "generation." Today, almost a third of the PLAAF's fighter-bombers are fourth-generation jets; yet as recently as 2000, they made up only 2 percent of the force. (Chinese writings refer to fourth-generation fighters as "third-generation" aircraft; this book employs the Western terminology throughout.)[4]

PLAAF Aircraft and Weapons in Service[5]

Q–5. The last second-generation aircraft in combat service with the PLAAF is the Q–5 Fantan. The Q–5 evolved from the J–6, which itself was a Chinese-produced MiG–19; it first flew in 1965 and entered service in 1970. In keeping with what we will see is PLAAF practice, the Q–5—nearly obsolescent already by North Atlantic Treaty Organization (NATO) or Warsaw Pact standards at the start of its operational career in China—has been modified and updated several times over the years. The newest variant, the Q–5L, has been fitted with a conformal belly fuel tank and a laser designator under the nose, and Chinese Internet photos show it equipped with a targeting pod on a ventral pylon and laser-guided bombs hung on the wings. Despite its age, the Q–5L could be an effective light attack aircraft if employed in a very forgiving air defense environment.

Figure 8-1. Size and Composition of the PLAAF Fighter Fleet, 1990–2010

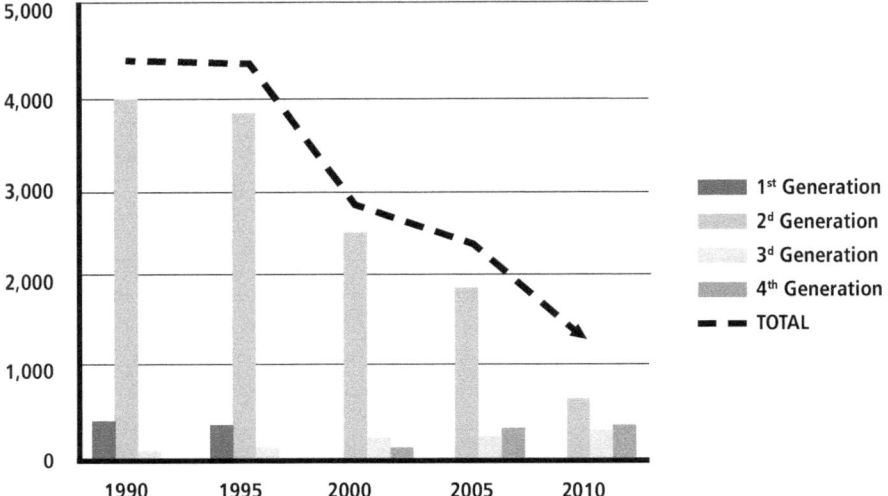

J–7. A reverse engineered MiG–21, the J–7 Fishbed was put into production in the early 1960s, entered PLAAF service in 1965, and has since been produced in a bewildering variety of subtypes.[6] It is still the most numerous type of fighter in the PLAAF's inventory; the latest (and probably last) model, the J–7G, first flew as recently as 2002. In production for nearly 4 decades—a time span that likely will never be approached, let alone surpassed, by another combat aircraft—the J–7 has been improved over time, including several upgrades to its radar, addition of a head-up display (HUD) and other updated avionics, a larger, double-delta wing, and integration of more modern air-to-to air missiles (AAMs), including the infrared (IR)-guided PL–8. Production of the J–7G reportedly continued at least into 2009.

J–8. Originally an enlarged, twin-engine development of the J–7, the J–8 Finback is yet another PLAAF aircraft that has been progressively upgraded since its introduction in 1981.[7] A major redesign was undertaken in the late 1980s, which saw the forward fuselage with its MiG–21-style nose intake give way to one featuring a solid nose—accommodating a more powerful radar—and two lateral air intakes, one on each side of the aircraft. It is this version, the J–8II or J–8B, which continues to serve and has also been the platform for several generations of progressively more capable models. The latest confirmed variant is the J–8F, which has been equipped with new cockpit avionics, more powerful engines, and a probe for in-flight refueling.[8] The most significant upgrade is the installation of a newer radar that enables employment of the PL–12 active homing radar–guided "fire and forget" medium-range AAM (MRAAM). Although not as capable as the most modern aircraft in its arsenal, these late-generation J–8s provide the PLAAF another, presumably cheaper, platform capable of using its most up-to-date air-to-air weapons.

JH–7. The JH–7 Flounder is an indigenously designed twin-engine attack fighter that entered PLAAF service by 2004.[9] The current production model is the JH–7A, equipped with improved radar, digital flight controls, and modernized cockpit instrumentation. The aircraft's empty weight has been reduced via utilization of composite materials and the number of stores hardpoints increased from 7 to 11. The JH–7A can be equipped with navigation, targeting, and data link pods mounted under the forward fuselage and is capable of carrying a wide array of land attack and maritime strike weapons of both Chinese and Russian origin. It, too, has been photographed carrying the PL–12 MRAAM. There are reports that a second update, the JH–7B—with improved engines and some radar signature reduction—is under development, although no solid evidence of this has yet appeared.

J–10. The J–10 is a single-engine multirole aircraft developed by Chengdu Aircraft Industry Corporation (CAC). First flown in March 1998, the J–10 reportedly entered PLAAF service in 2003. A tailless design with canard foreplanes, the J–10 strongly resembles the cancelled Israeli Lavi fighter though it is unclear how much design assistance, if any, CAC received from either Israel or Russia (although the latter has to date provided the J–10's engine). It has 11 weapons stations and has been photographed with what appear to be navigation and targeting pods mounted ventrally just aft of the underslung air intake, and with a removable fixed air refueling probe on the starboard side of the fuselage. Around the time that the first J–10s were being deployed by operational units, development began on an upgraded version of the aircraft. Dubbed the J–10B, the new model features a simplified engine inlet ramp that reduces weight and improves the aircraft's radar signature. The J–10B also adds an electro-optical targeting system (EOTS), visible as a bulge forward and to the starboard side of the canopy. Featuring an infrared search and track (IRST) sensor and a laser rangefinder, the EOTS allows a pilot to passively detect and target enemy aircraft without requiring telltale signals from the J–10's radar.

Su–27SK/UBK, J–11A. The first variants of the Sukhoi Flanker to join the PLAAF were the single seat Su–27SK and the two-seat operational trainer, the Su–27UBK.[10] These were also the first fourth-generation combat aircraft to enter PLAAF service when they appeared in the mid-1990s. Initially, the PLAAF purchased its Flankers from the Russian production line, but these have been supplemented over time by more than 100 aircraft built from Russian-supplied kits by Shenyang Aircraft Corporation (SAC), aircraft that are designated J–11A. Chinese assembly of these J–11A kits was ended about halfway through the planned 200 aircraft run because PLAAF requirements had reportedly evolved such that the single-role air superiority Su–27/SK/J–11A no longer suited the service's needs. As originally built, China's Su–27SK/J–11 fighters can carry neither the Chinese PL–12 nor the Russian R–77 (AA–12) active-homing MRAAMs. There are, however, reports that at least some of these aircraft have been fitted with the radar modifications needed to fire the R–77/AA–12. Like the J–10B, all Flankers feature an EOTS mounted in front of the canopy. In an intriguing development, the PLAAF apparently sent several Su–27/J–11 aircraft to Turkey in October 2010 to participate in an exercise called "Anatolian Eagle." This is the first time a NATO country has hosted an exercise that included the PLAAF.[11]

J–11B. The J–11B is SAC's response to the PLAAF's requirement for a true multirole Flanker variant. Based on the Su–27SK airframe, the J–11B features Chinese-manufactured engines and avionics, including indigenous radar, and can be armed with a wide variety of air-to-air and air-to-surface weapons, including the PL–12 MRAAM. Among other improvements, SAC claims that the radar cross-section of the J–11B has been reduced by 75–80 percent from the Su–27SK by reconfiguring the engine intakes and employing radar-absorbing paint. This degree of signature reduction may strain credulity absent more substantial changes to the airframe, but the assertion alone indicates that the PLAAF understands the advantages afforded by stealth. The J–11B appears to have entered PLAAF service in 2007. A two-seat version, the J–11BS, is under development.

Su–30MKK. The Su–30MKK is yet another derivative of the Flanker family, a two-seat multirole aircraft developed from the Su–27 for the PLAAF. China has reportedly purchased 76 of these Russian-manufactured fighters, which incorporate improved avionics, including a more advanced radar with improved air-to-ground capabilities. The Su–30 can be fitted with a wide array of "smart" and "dumb" weapons and munitions, and it also features a retractable refueling probe. Licensed production of the Su–30 in China was once expected but now appears unlikely, with the two-seat J–11BS potentially occupying what might otherwise have been the Su–30's "strike fighter" niche in the PLAAF force structure.[12]

China's Fifth-Generation Fighter (J–20).[13] The first public flight in January 2011 of a stealthy new Chinese fighter, the J–20, came as a surprise to many observers who had agreed with then-Secretary of Defense Robert Gates that China would "have no fifth-generation aircraft by 2020" and only "a handful" by 2025.[14] The flight took place while Gates was in China, an irony that may or may not have been intended by the Chinese.

The J–20 appears to be a large airplane, estimated to be about the size of an F–111 by at least two analysts. Its appearance shows that substantial care was taken in the design to shape the jet for low observable (LO) characteristics.[15] At this point, all performance specifications are wholly speculative, but the J–20 is thought to have two internal weapons bays and to be capable of "supercruising" flight. In both regards, the aircraft resembles the USAF F–22.

Some accounts report that J–20 prototypes had been flying at a PLAAF test center for several months before the fighter's official debut in January, and that a total of four airframes are being used in the test program.[16]

Late in 2009, the PLAAF's deputy commander, General He Weirong, said that a new fighter would soon "undertake its first flight" and be in service "8 to 10 years" after that.[17] This schedule would appear to bring the jet into service around 2016, earlier than previous intelligence assessments had projected.

H–6. The H–6 Badger is the PLAAF's only true bomber, a twin-engine medium-range aircraft copied from the Soviet Tupolev Tu–16 of the mid-1950s, with which it shares the same Western reporting name, Badger. The H–6 has been built in a number of versions for both air force and naval use since its first delivery in 1969.[18] The newest versions in PLAAF use are the H–6G, which is the carrier platform for China's first air-launched land attack cruise missile (LACM), the KD–63, and the H–6K, which can carry up to six smaller Tomahawk-like LACMs. The H–6K in particular appears to be a fairly radical reworking of the Badger, with modern turbofan engines apparently replacing the less powerful and less efficient turbojets that powered all previous models, composite materials being used to reduce weight, a modern "glass" cockpit installation, improved avionics, and a thermal-imaging sensor under the nose.

Special Purpose Platforms. The PLAAF has long sought to acquire an airborne early warning and control (AEW&C) platform along the lines of the U.S. E–3 Airborne Warning and Control System (AWACS). A program to buy four A–50I aircraft—a Russian Il–76 Candid airframe equipped with Israeli radar and mission equipment—collapsed in 2000 when Israel succumbed to substantial U.S. pressure and dropped out of the deal. After this disappointment, China moved forward with its own aircraft, also based on the Il–76 platform, but with an indigenously developed mission suite. At least four of these KJ–2000 AWACS aircraft are in active service with the PLAAF, providing it with its first sophisticated airborne battle management assets.[19]

Another area of interest to the PLAAF is aerial refueling, which is a necessary competence if China intends to extend the reach of its airpower beyond its immediate environs. Today, the PLAAF possesses a fairly rudimentary capability, owning about a dozen H–6U tankers equipped with a "probe and drogue" refueling pod under each wing. Relatively few of China's combat aircraft can be refueled in the air: some late-model J–8s have probes fitted, and a fixed probe can be installed on the J–10. The PLAAF's Su–30s have retractable refueling probes, but their system is allegedly not compatible with the H–6U.[20]

In 2005, China ordered 34 additional Il–76 Candid transports and four Il–78 Midas tankers from Russia, but none have been delivered to date due to a dispute between the Russian export company and the factory responsible for building the aircraft.[21] The PLAAF needs not only additional tankers but also more strategic airlifters—if not from Russia, then from its own aviation industry—to achieve any aspirations it might have for possessing a credible power projection capability. In fact, a new large transport aircraft, sometimes called the "Y–20" is reportedly under development; a first flight "around 2012" has been suggested.[22]

The PLAAF has also developed about a dozen specialized platforms based on the Y–8 four-engine turboprop transport.[23] The "Gaoxin" series includes another AEW&C aircraft, a maritime surveillance variant, an airborne command post, and a number of platforms for various electronic warfare functions, such as jamming and signals intelligence (SIGINT).

Unmanned Aerial Systems. Table 8–3 lists unmanned aircraft systems (UAS) deployed or under development in China. They range from a copy of the Vietnam-era U.S. Firebee reconnaissance drone to the Xianglong high-altitude long endurance (HALE) UAS that bears a passing resemblance to the U.S. RQ–4 Global Hawk.

Table 8–3. PLAAF Unmanned Aircraft Systems

Vehicle Designation	Vehicle Type	Payload (kilograms)	Mission radius (kilometers)	Endurance (hours)
Harpy	Armed UAS	32	400–500	2
CH–3	Armed UAS	63–90	1,200	12
Xianglong	HALE	650	7,000	unknown
Yilong	MALE	200	unknown	20
BZK–005	MALE	150	unknown	40
ASN–206	MAME	50	unknown	4-8
ASN–209	MAME	50	100	10
LT series	MAV	unknown	10–20	0.3–0.6
ASN–104	RPA	30	60	2
Chang Hong*	RPA	65	1,250	3
ASN–105B	RPA	40	150	7
AW series	Tactical	unknown	5	1–1.5
W–30	Tactical	5	10	1-2
Tianyi	Tactical	20	100	3
W–50, PW–1	Tactical	20	100	4–6
PW–2	Tactical	30	200	6–7
U8E	VTOL	40	75	4
Soar Bird	VTOL	30	150	4

Source: Data from *Jane's* (2010) and *SinoDefence* (n/d).
HALE: high altitude, long endurance   MALE: medium altitude, long endurance   MAME: medium altitude, medium endurance
MAV: micro air vehicle   RPA: remotely piloted aircraft   VTOL: vertical takeoff and landing
*The Chang Hong may also be referred to as the "WuZhen–5."

In the past decade, China has displayed a dizzying array of various UAS models at air and trade shows; many if not most seem never to have gone into production. A look at the table suggests that China is experimenting with many classes of UAS, mostly for surveillance and reconnaissance. Of particular interest is the Harpy, an Israeli-made antiradiation drone. It flies to a target area and loiters until an appropriate target begins to emit, at which point it dives into the target and detonates. Harpy is an interesting hybrid of UAS and cruise missile, somewhat akin to the cancelled American AGM–139A Tacit Rainbow program of the late 1980s.

Air-to-air missiles: Table 8–4 lists air-to-air missiles (AAMs) in service with the PLAAF. As can be seen, for many years the PLAAF was equipped with obsolete AAMs. Through to the mid-1980s, the most common missile in its inventory was the PL–2, a Chinese copy of the Soviet AA–2 Atoll AAM, itself a copy of the first-generation U.S. AIM–9B Sidewinder. But, in the early 1990s, this began to change. Along with Russian Su–27s came modern Russian missiles: the R–27/AA–10 Alamo radar-guided medium-range air-to-air missile (MRAAM) and the R–73/AA–11, short-range AAM (SRAAM), which at the time was probably the best visual range "dogfight" missile in the world. As well, China developed two indigenous infrared homing SRAAMs, the PL–8 and PL–9. The PLAAF fielded its first indigenous MRAAM, the PL–11 semiactive radar homing missile, developed from the Italian Aspide (which Beijing had purchased in small numbers) around the turn of the century. Along with its Su–30s, China procured a number of R–77/AA–12 "fire and forget" MRAAMs from Russia. Shortly thereafter the PLAAF also began fielding the PL–12, an indigenous active-homing MRAAM compatible with most of its modern fighters.[24]

Table 8-4. Current PLAAF Air-to-Air Missiles

Designation	Year introduced	Type	Range (kilometers)	Notes
PL–2	~1970	IRH	3	Copy of AIM–9B
PL–5	~1987	IRH	16	Similar to AIM–9G
PL–8	~1990	IRH	15	Based on Python 3
PL–9	early-1990s	IRH	15–22	
PL–11	~2001	SARH	25	Based on AIM-7, Aspide
R–27/AA–10	mid-1990s	SARH/IR	60–80	On Flankers
R–73/AA–11	mid-1990s	IR	30	On Flankers
R–77/AA–12	~2003	ARH	50–80	On Flankers
PL–12/SD–10	~2004	ARH	70	

Source: *Jane's* (2010)
ARH: active radar homing   IRH: infrared homing   SARH: semiactive radar homing

Both the AA–11 and the PL–9 are reportedly compatible with helmet-mounted sights, which allow the missile to be locked onto an air target when the pilot looks at it. When combined with the missile's "off boresight" capability—it can be fired at targets to one side or another of the launching aircraft up to some specified limit—the sighting system streamlines the engagement dynamics of close-in aerial combat.

Looking ahead, it has been reported that China is working on at least three new AAM designs: an extended-range ramjet powered version of the PL–12, a short-range active radar homing missile, and the PL–ASR, an IR missile employing thrust vector controls which would provide greater agility to the weapon.[25]

Air-to-surface missiles: Table 8–5 lists air-to-surface missiles (ASM) reportedly fielded by the PLAAF. They range from the Hellfire-class AR–1 to the HN–1, a Tomahawk-like long-range cruise missile (LRCM). In addition to these missiles, China is also beginning to deploy laser- and satellite-guided bombs, although it is not clear whether they are yet available in operationally significant quantities.[26]

Table 8–5. Current PLAAF Air-to-Surface Missiles

Designation	Type	Guidance	Range (kilometers)	Warhead (kilograms)
AR–1	ATGM	Semiactive laser	8	10 AP
Kh–31/AS–17/YJ–91	ARM	INS/passive radar	15–110	87kg HE
KD–88	ASM	INS/EO/RF	"100+"	(unknown)
KD–63*	LACM	INS/EO	200	512 HE
HN–1	LACM	INS/GPS/TERCOM	600	400 HE/SM

Source: *Jane's* (2010).
AP: armor-piercing
EO: electro-optical
INS: inertial navigation system
SM: submunition
ARM: antiradiation missile
GPS: global positioning system
LACM: land attack cruise missile
TERCOM: terrain comparison and matching
ATGM: antitank guided missile
HE: high explosive
RF: radio frequency
*The KD–63 is also referred to as the YJ–63.

Surface-to-air missiles. The PLAAF operates China's long-range strategic surface-to-air missiles (SAMs); as table 8–6 shows, these are a mix of indigenous and Russian designs. While the HQ–2 is obsolete, the HQ–9, HQ–12, and SA–300 variants are all very capable systems. Of particular interest is the HQ–12, which appears to have been designed expressly to attack AWACS-type aircraft and jamming platforms; it is unique in being a surface-to-air antiradiation missile (ARM). The table includes the new S–400 SAM system that has entered service in Russia. No exports of this very long-range SAM—the intended successor to the S–300 series—are as yet reported, but China, which is said to have paid for a substantial portion of the system's development, is likely to be an early customer for it.

Table 8–6. Current PLAAF Surface-to-Air Missiles

Designation	Guidance	Range (kilometers)	Notes
HQ–2	Command	35	Similar to Russian S–75/SA–2
HQ–7	Command	12	Similar to French Crotale
HQ–9	Track via missile	200	Merges S–300 / Patriot technology
HQ–12/FT–2000	Inertial navigation system / passive radar	100–120	Targets airborne warning and control, electronic warfare aircraft
S–300PMU	Radar homing	90	5V55RUD missile
S–300PMU1	Track via missile	150	48N6E missile
S–300PMU2	Track via missile	200	48N6E2 missiles
S–400	Inertial navigation system / command / radar	up to 400	9M96, 40N6 missiles

Source: *Jane's* (2010)

Measuring Up: The PLAAF's Equipment versus the United States

Consider the circumstances had U.S. and Chinese fighter pilots encountered one another in the skies near Taiwan in 1995. The American would have been flying a fourth-generation F–15, F–16, or F/A–18, armed with AIM–120 advanced medium-range air-to-air missiles (AMRAAMs) and AIM–9L/M short-range air-to-air missiles (SRAAMs). The U.S. pilot would almost certainly have been supported by a controller in an E–3 AWACS, and would have found a KC–135 tanker orbiting nearby in the event that fuel became an issue.

For his part, the PLAAF pilot would most likely have flown a MiG–21 variant without any medium-range missiles, being armed instead with only obsolescent PL–2 or PL–5 short-range IR weapons. While a ground controller back on the mainland would have helped manage and inform the PLAAF pilot's sortie, that controller's picture of the relevant airspace would have been substantially inferior to the one being monitored inside the AWACS as it cruised high above. And there would have been no tankers available to provide additional fuel should that have been necessary or desirable. In short, the Chinese airman would have been flying an obsolete aircraft carrying antiquated missiles, have modest situational awareness, and, as is discussed elsewhere, would himself have been the product of inferior training and preparation compared to the U.S. pilot. Thus, he would have been overmatched and outgunned.[27]

Now fast-forward 15 years. While the U.S. pilot would most likely be in essentially the same plane with essentially the same weapons and essentially the same support, the picture on the PLAAF side would be very different. Consider the following changes:

The PLAAF Now Has Platforms Comparable to U.S. Platforms

The PLAAF's Su–27/J–11s are often compared to the U.S. F–15, the J–10 to the F–16, and the Su–30 to the F–15E. As table 8–7 shows, these comparisons are not far-fetched; though hardly identical, the two sides' jets clearly seem to fill parallel slots in their respective force structures.

Table 8–7. USAF vs. PLAAF Fourth-Generation Fighters

Type	Initial operational capability	MTOW (kilograms)	Range (kilometers)	Armament
F–15C	1979	30,845	>2,500	Up to 8 air-to-air missiles
Su–27/J–11	~1997	33,500	4,900	Up to 10 air-to-air missiles
F–15E	1989	35,741	2,540	11,113 kilograms
Su–30	2001	34,500	3,000	8,000 kilograms
F–16C	1984	21,772	1,550	4,200 kilograms
J–10	~2006	18,500	~1,100	4,500 kilograms

Source: *Jane's* (2010)

The similarities between each side's "fourth-gen" fighters go beyond static comparisons of size and payload. Plotted in figure 8–2 are two factors for each of eight aircraft: weight-to-thrust and wing loading. The first shows the relationship between an aircraft's weight and the power of its engines, and the second the relationship between its weight and the surface area of its wings.[28] These factors help determine a fighter's maneuverability in both the horizontal (banks and turns) and vertical (climb and dive) dimensions. Lower is better for each factor, so the farther down and to the left an aircraft lies, the better.

Unsurprisingly, the USAF F–22—seen in the figure's lower left corner—is superior on both counts; in the upper right are the F–16C and the F/A–18E/F, which trail the pack in these two regards. Clustered in the middle are five aircraft, the F–15C, F–15E, F–35, J–10, and J–11, which are in more or less the same neighborhood on these two important characteristics. While weight-to-thrust ratio and wing loading vary over the course of a mission as fuel is burned and ordnance expended, these platforms themselves start out broadly similar in these important factors.

Figure 8-2. Weight-to-Thrust Ratio and Wing Loading, PLAAF vs. U.S. Fighters

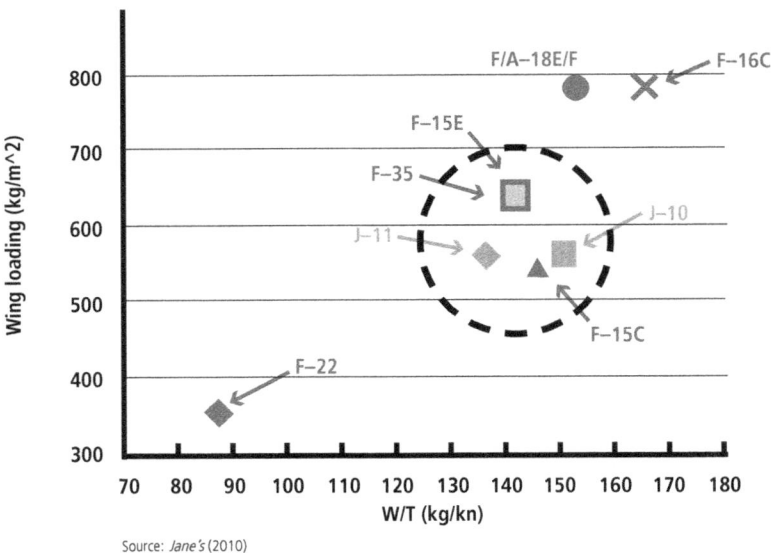

Source: *Jane's* (2010)

The J-10B and Flanker variants are equipped with passive IRSTs. These sensors can permit a pilot—without emitting a radar signal— to detect another aircraft by "seeing" the heat from its engines, the friction produced as it moves through the air, or the heat signature from the launch of a powered missile. Sukhoi claims that the OLS-35—developed for its Su-35 advanced Flanker—has a front hemisphere detection range of 50 kilometers (30+ miles), and as much as 90 kilometers (55+ miles) in the rear hemisphere, where it is "looking" at the hot exhaust of a target aircraft.[29] While the OLS-27 and OLS-30 that equip China's Su-27/J-11s and Su-30s, respectively, are less capable, it is worth noting that no current generation U.S. fighter has an IRST at all, not even the F-22.[30] The forthcoming F-35 (now in advanced flight testing) will mount an IRST, and programs are underway to retrofit both the F-15C and F/A-18E/F.[31]

The PLAAF Now Has Weapons Comparable to U.S. Weapons

The weaponry—air-to-air, air-to-surface, and surface-to-air—available to the PLAAF has obviously advanced dramatically since the mid-1990s. As discussed above, new AAMs and precision-guided munitions (PGMs) are entering the force, providing China with much improved capabilities across the board. Whereas in 1995 the PLAAF would have gone to war with outmoded AAMs and "dumb" bombs, its inventory today includes weapons—of both Russian and Chinese manufacture—that are in the same class as those carried by USAF and U.S. Navy combat aircraft, including laser- and satellite-guided bombs and guided missiles of various sorts. Tables 8–8 and 8–9 compare similar weapons from each side's arsenal.

Table 8–8. U.S. and Chinese Air-to-Air Missiles

Designation	Year Introduced	Type	Range (kilometers)
AIM–9X (U.S.)	2003	IRH	>10
PL–9	early-1990s	IRH	15–22
R–73/AA–11	mid-1990s	IR	20
AIM–120–C5 (U.S.)	1996	ARH	50
R–77/AA–12	~2003	ARH	50+
PL–12/SD–10	~2004	ARH	70

Source: *Jane's* (2010)
ARH: active radar homing   IRH: infrared homing

Table 8–9. U.S. and Chinese Air-to-Surface Missiles

Designation	Type	Guidance	Range (kilometers)	Warhead (kilograms)
AGM–114 *Hellfire* (U.S.)	ATGM	Semiactive laser	9	12
AR–1	ATGM	Semiactive laser	8	10
AGM–88 HARM (U.S.)	ARM	INS/passive radar	80	66
Kh–31/AS–17/YJ–91	ARM	INS/passive radar	15–110	87
AGM–84E SLAM (U.S.)	ASM	INS/GPS/IIR	95	222
KD–88	ASM	INS/EO/RF	"100+"	u/k
AGM–84H SLAM–ER (U.S.)	ASM	INS/GPS/IIR	280	360
KD–63	LACM	INS/EO	200	512
BGM–109 TLAM (U.S.)	LACM	INS/GPS/TERCOM	1,200	535–1,360
HN–1	LACM	INS/GPS/TERCOM	600	400

ATGM: antitank guided missile   ARM: antiradiation missile   ASM: air-to-surface missile
EO: electro-optical   GPS: global positioning system   IIR: imaging infrared
INS: inertial navigation system   LACM: land-attack cruise missile   TERCOM: terrain comparison and matching

The PLAAF Is Beginning to Field "Force Multipliers"

For decades, the United States has fielded dozens of noncombat aircraft that increase the effectiveness of its fighters and bombers. These "force multipliers"—the E-3 AWACS, the E-8 JSTARS (Joint Surveillance Target Attack Radar System), the KC-135, the RC-135, and others—help manage air combat, track moving targets on the ground, refuel aircraft to extend their range and endurance, and provide a variety of intelligence and electronic warfare (EW) capabilities. They are linchpins of not just U.S. air operations but also of the Pentagon's overall concept for joint operations.

Until recently, the PLAAF has only aspired to such capabilities, and in the realm of in-flight refueling its capabilities remain minimal. With the deployment of the KJ–2000 AEW&C platform and multiple EW aircraft based on the Y–8, however, it has begun to make progress in a number of these areas. These specialized aircraft exist in small numbers and it is not at all clear how adept the PLAAF is in operating and exploiting these emerging capabilities, nor do we know how well they are integrated into Chinese operational concepts. But the steps we have seen them taking are significant and bear very close attention going forward.

In China's Backyard, the PLAAF's SAMs Weigh Heavily

In almost any plausible near- to mid-term Sino-U.S. confrontation, China would have home-field advantage, at least relative to the United States. Whether across the Taiwan Strait, over the Senkaku/Diaoyu Islands, or in the South China Sea, Beijing would be able to bring more of its military power to bear than could the United States. This is especially true in the early hours, days, and weeks of a conflict. For the PLAAF, that means that it will at least initially likely enjoy a numerical advantage over U.S. forces, and—depending on the circumstances—perhaps even over the combined forces of the United States and its partners.[32]

Operating close to China's shores could also bring the PLAAF's modern SAMs into the picture. Figure 8–3 shows the ranges of today's S–300PMU2 (200 kilometers) and tomorrow's S–400 (400 kilometers) in the context of the Taiwan Strait and South China Sea areas.[33]

At maximum range these missiles can engage only high-flying targets, but many important U.S. aircraft—the "force multipliers" described above along with high-endurance UASs like Global Hawk—typically operate at precisely those altitudes. Especially after the S–400 enters Chinese service, those U.S. platforms will either have to operate in the face of a much-increased SAM threat or fly farther away from the action and so compromise their performance.[34] U.S. bombers carrying cruise missiles might be compelled to launch farther from the Chinese coast, which would limit the depth into the mainland that the missiles could reach. Closer in, these advanced SAMs could constrain the operation of even high-performance fighter aircraft; nonstealthy, so-called legacy jets—the F–15, F–16, and F/A–18—would be greatly at risk if called upon to fly within the S–300/400's envelope.

Figure 8–3. Range Rings for S–300PMU2 and S–400 Surface-to-Air Missiles

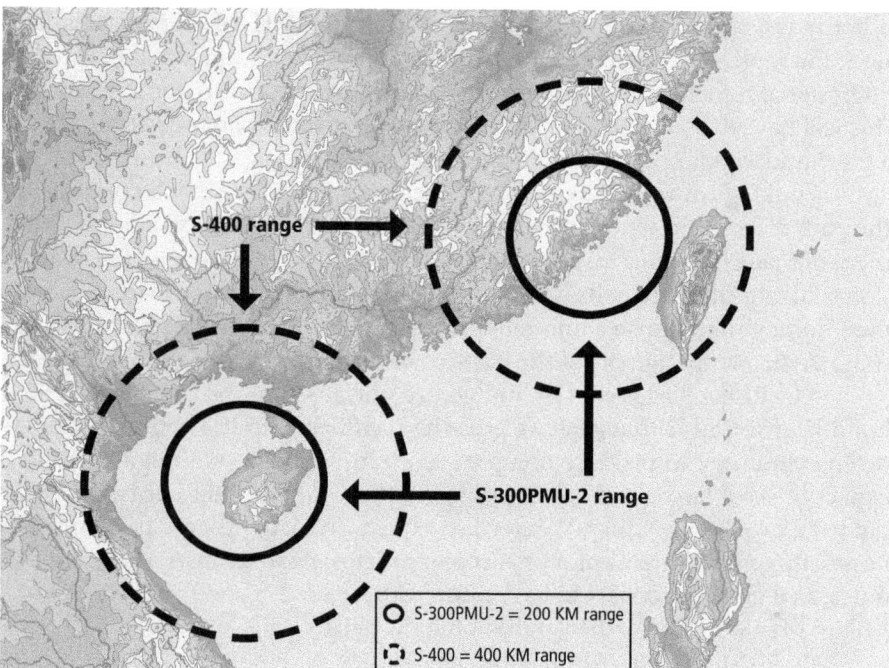

The Big Picture: The PLAAF Today and Tomorrow

If the PLAAF is not capable of challenging U.S. airpower in a nearby scenario like a Taiwan Strait contingency, its major items of equipment are no longer the main culprits. Its radical downsizing and steady modernization have, since 1995, brought the Chinese air force up to advanced world standards in many regards. Its growing fleet of fourth-generation fighters, stockpiles of advanced air-to-air and air-to-surface weaponry, emerging AEW&C and EW capabilities, and up-to-date surface-to-air defenses represent remarkable advances in technology and capacity since 1995.

In the event of a confrontation farther afield—for example, in the Malacca Strait, or closer to home, in the Spratly Islands—the PLAAF's capabilities remain limited. Conducting high-tempo combat operations is much more challenging 1,500 or 2,500 kilometers from home versus 200 or 300 kilometers. Under these conditions, the PLAAF would require a much more robust in-flight refueling capability and enough AEW&C assets to compensate for the absence of ground-based control. Recent years have seen the PLAAF begin to step up to the latter challenge; its intentions regarding tanker aircraft, on the other hand, appear modest. With only a dozen or so H–6Us operational and no known plans to acquire more than the four MIDAS tankers it ordered in 2005, aerial refueling does not appear to be a current priority for the Chinese; this will have to change if the PLAAF is to project significant power more than a few hundred kilometers from Chinese territory.

Looking toward 2020, it seems likely that the PLAAF will continue on the path it has been following since the mid-1990s. This will mean the retirement of many J–7s and early model J–8s accompanying the acquisition of additional advanced fighters. It seems unlikely that China will choose to replace its own "legacy" fighters on a one-for-one basis, so the PLAAF will probably continue to shrink, though not at the pace we have witnessed over the last 15 years.

The PLAAF's decision to "indigenize" the Su–27 as the J–11B rather than build licensed Su–30s suggests a growing confidence in the ability of China's defense industry to produce complex modern weapons. We might therefore expect to see a larger and larger proportion of Chinese-built hardware filling out the PLAAF's inventory. We can also expect China to progressively upgrade its fourth-generation inventory to accommodate new weapons, radars, and avionics, as it already appears to have done with its Su–27s—to fire R–77/AA–12 MRAAMs—and the J–10, by developing the J–10B.

By 2020, the PLAAF may be operating at least small numbers of J–20 stealth fighters; we should also expect to see the introduction or enhancement of other PLAAF platforms and weapons. These include the following: more, and more advanced, AEW&C capabilities, and improved EW capacities overall; improved air-to-air weapons, including a very long-range AAM to threaten an adversary's high-value assets like the E–3; the proliferation of "smart" weapons throughout the force; increased use of drones and UASs, likely including analogues to the U.S. Predator and Global Hawk aircraft; and continued deployment of the indigenous HQ–9 long-range SAM and acquisition of the S–400.

Although it seems less likely given available evidence, by 2020 China could also be well on the way to equipping the PLAAF with a new long-range strike aircraft to replace its antediluvian H–6s as bombers and cruise missile carriers. The PLAAF might also seek to increase its modest long-range airlift capabilities. Receiving the 34 Il–76 Candids it bought in 2005 would appreciably expand its transport fleet, but, as with tankers, the development and/or acquisition of more airlifters beyond those already booked would be needed if the PLAAF sought to support power projection over long distances.

The progress made in recent years by the PLAAF is impressive. Not too long ago, it was an unsophisticated congeries of ancient aircraft and weapons, its pilots poorly trained and poorly supported. As late as the early 1990s, it was likely too weak to have even defended China's home airspace against a serious, modern adversary. In the early- to mid-1990s, as Chinese doctrine changed from focusing exclusively on territorial defense to contemplating limited power projection campaigns, the PLAAF found itself confronting a number of daunting learning curves that led from where it was to where it needed to be to fulfill its new missions. In terms of major items of equipment, it has successfully climbed many of these curves and appears at least to understand the ones that are left, even if it is not yet poised to climb them.

The revolution in the PLAAF's order of battle is over. It has made up the four decades separating the MiG–17/MiG–19 generations from the Su–27SK /Su–30MKK generation in just 15 remarkable years. Whether or not the PLAAF can close the remaining gaps between its capabilities and those of the most advanced air forces remains to be seen. But given how it has transformed itself over the last 15 years, one would be foolish to bet heavily against it.

Notes

[1] This paper reflects the analysis and judgments of its author alone. It in no way represents or purports to represent the views of the RAND Corporation or the sponsors of RAND's research.

[2] The last F–100s retired from reserve component service in 1979 while the final J–6 reportedly left combat service with the PLAAF only in June 2010; see RIA Novosti (RIAN), "China says farewell to J–6 fighters," June 13, 2010, at <http://en.rian.ru/mlitary_news/20100613/159405610.htl>, accessed October 2, 2010. In 1995, F–15s and F–16s constituted three-quarters of the USAF's fighter-bomber inventory; see International Institute for Strategic Studies [hereafter IISS], *The Military Balance 1995* (London: Routledge, 1995), 27.

[3] IISS, *The Military Balance 1990* (London: Routledge, 1990), 29; IISS, *The Military Balance 2010* (London: Routledge, 2010), 40.

[4] We take as "first-generation" fighters the earliest, gun-armed, subsonic jets like the F–86 or, in China's case, the MiG–17/J–5. In the second generation are the aircraft fielded in the late 1950s: capable of supersonic flight, usually radar-equipped, and in at least some cases missile-armed. The aforementioned F–100 and MiG–19/J–6 are representative types. The third generation includes fighters that were introduced to service in the 1960s through the early 1970s. They featured vastly improved avionics and weapons, carried the first beyond visual range (BVR) radar-guided air-to-air missiles (AAMs), and were often intended as multirole platforms. The quintessential "third-gen" aircraft is probably the F–4; the various subtypes of J–8 fit into this class. Finally, fourth-generation fighters were introduced into service in the late 1970s and early 1980s. These jets had further improved avionics fits, such as "look-down, shoot-down" radars, sophisticated flight control systems, and designs that generally emphasized maneuverability rather than raw speed. An example on the U.S. side is the F–15; for the PLAAF, the Su–27.

[5] Except as noted, all data is taken from the following 2010 editions of Jane's Publishing publications: *Jane's Aircraft Upgrades*, at <http://jau.janes.com/public/jau/index.shtml>; *Jane's Air-Launched Weapons*, at <http://jau.janes.com/public/jalw/index.shtml>; *Jane's All the World's Aircraft*, at <http://jawa.janes.com/public/jawa/index.shtml>; *Jane's Land-based Air Defence*, at <http://jau.janes.com/public/jlad/index.shtml>; and *Unmanned Aerial Vehicles and Targets*, at <http://jau.janes.com/public/juav/index.shtml>. See also Michael J.H. Taylor, ed., *Jane's World Combat Aircraft* (Alexandria, VA: Jane's Information Group Inc., 1988); and *SinoDefence.com*, at <www.sinodefence.com>.

[6] *Jane's Air-Launched Weapons*, lists 9 domestic variants; 15 others have been offered for export.

[7] The J–8 first flew in 1969. The long gap between first flight and operational introduction can be blamed on the chaos attendant to the Cultural Revolution and its aftermath.

[8] There are reports of still another model, referred to as the J-8T or F-8T, but no definitive information appears to be available.

[9] The JH-7 had already been operational in China's naval air arm for several years.

[10] For this impressive warplane, see Yefim Gordon and Peter Davison, *Sukhoi Su-27 Flanker* (North Branch, MN: Specialty Press and Wholesalers, 2006).

[11] "Turkey invited China to join NATO air exercise after U.S. withdrew," at *WorldTribune.com* (October 4, 2010); and Burak Ege Bektil and Umit Enginsoy, "Turkey, China in Exercises," *Defense News*, October 17, 2010), at <www.defensenews.com/story.php?i=4921329>.

[12] The two-seat J-11BS version was first photographed in 2009 at a Chinese flight-test facility.

[13] Chinese sources often refer to the planned new fighter as "fourth- generation" vice fifth, which is the generation for low-observable "stealth" aircraft developed in the West.

[14] Robert M. Gates, "Remarks before the Economic Club of Chicago," July 16, 2009, at <www.defense.gov/speeches/speech.aspx?speechid=1369>, accessed August 24, 2011.

[15] Carlo Kopp and Peter Goon, "Chengdu J-XX [J-20] Stealth Fighter Prototype: A Preliminary Assessment," *Air Power Australia*, Technical Report APA-TR-2011-0101, at <www.ausairpower.net/APA-J-XX-Prototype.html>, accessed January 15, 2011; Bill Sweetman, "Chinese J-20 Stealth Fighter In Taxi Tests," *Aviationweek.com*, at <www.aviationweek.com/aw/generic/story.jsp?id=news/awst/2011/01/03/AW_01_03_2011_p18-279564.xml&channel=defense>, accessed January 3, 2011.

[16] "CAC J-20," *Jane's All the World's Aircraft* online, May 17, 2011; by subscription only.

[17] Bradley Perrett, "China Close To Testing Next-Gen Fighter," *Aviation Week & Space Technology* (November 13, 2009) at <www.aviationweek.com/aw/generic/story_generic.jsp?channel+awst&id=news/CHINA111309.xml>, accessed August 24, 2011.

[18] The original Soviet Tu-16 entered production in 1953. Like the MiG-19 and MiG-21, current versions of the H-6 testify to China's ability to squeeze the last drops of operational capability out of the most antiquated designs.

[19] The delivery of an additional two KJ-2000s was reported in 2008. Roger Cliff, in *The Development of China's Air Force Capabilities—Testimony presented before the U.S.-China Economic and Security Review Commission, May 20, 2010*, RAND Document CT-346 (Santa Monica, CA: RAND Corporation, May 20, 2010), 3, writes "China operates at least a dozen AEW&C aircraft," a number that probably includes the Y-8-based model mentioned on the next page.

[20] Gabe Collins, "Air time—increasing China's aerial range," *Jane's Intelligence Review* (June 12, 2008).

[21] RIAN, "Delivery terms for Il-76 aircraft to China may be revised," July 3, 2007, at <www.globalsecurity.org/wmd/library/news/china/2007/china-070307-rianovosti01.htm>, accessed October 4, 2010.

[22] Craig Caffrey, "Chinese military aircraft: Up and coming" in *Jane's Defence Weekly* (July 5, 2010).

[23] The Y-8 is a Chinese version of the venerable Soviet-era Antonov An-12 Cub transport.

[24] The "indigenousness" of the PL-12 can be overstated. There is evidence that the seeker, the guidance system, and some of the control systems were developed with substantial Russian help. The PL-12 is sometimes referred to by its export designation, SD-10.

[25] Robert Hewson, "Air supremacy club loses exclusive status" in *International Defence Review* (November 13, 2008).

[26] China's surface strike capabilities of course also include over a thousand short-range ballistic missiles (SRBMs) and some hundreds of ground-launch cruise missiles (GLCM). See U.S. Department of Defense, *Military and Security Developments Involving the People's Republic of China 2010* (Washington, DC: Department of Defense, 2010), 31.

[27] The MiG-21 was, in its heyday, a fine airplane: small and hard to see, light, and maneuverable. In the hands of a pilot who could exploit these strengths, it could be a capable day fighter. The tradeoffs inherent in designing any high-performance aircraft, however, meant that these qualities came at the expense of range and armament. See Bill Gunston, *Mikoyan MiG-21* (London: Osprey Publishing Ltd., 1986).

[28] I have used the maximum takeoff weight and maximum thrust with afterburner for each aircraft.

[29] Andrey Fomin, "Su-35 a Step Away from the Fifth Generation," in *Take-off* (June 2007), 51, at <www.sukhoi.org/files/su_news_29-08-07_eng.pdf>.

[30] IRST's have been installed on some export versions of U.S. F–15s and F–16s; see "U.S. 'Teen Series' Fighters to Get IRST," *Defense Industry Daily*, November 17, 2009, at <www.defenseindustrydaily.com/f-18-super-hornets-to-get-irst-03429/>.

[31] For the F–15C, see Steven Trimble, "USAF adds IRST pod for F–15s," *Flight International* (September 18, 2009), at <www.flightglobal.com/articles/2009/09/18/332380/usaf-adds-irst-pod-for-f-15s.html>; for the F/A–18E/F, see the previously cited "US 'Teen Series' Fighters to Get IRST," *Defense Industry Daily*.

[32] The author led a study that examined the possible dynamics of an air war over Taiwan in the 2010–2015 timeframe. If China can successfully suppress operations from Taiwan air bases and the U.S. base at Kadena on Okinawa—and the study concluded it most likely can—the PLAAF could have up to a 4:1 numerical advantage in the air over the USAF, U.S. Navy, and Taiwan; see David A. Shlapak, David T. Orletsky, Toy I. Reid, Murray Scot Tanner, and Barry Wilson, *A Question of Balance: Political Context and Military Aspects of the China-Taiwan Dispute*, RAND Document MG-888 (Santa Monica, CA: RAND Corporation, 2009).

[33] In both cases, analysts placed the SAM unit 50 kilometers (31 miles) back from the nearest coastline.

[34] Long-range SAMs may not be the only weapon capable of threatening AWACS, JSTARS, and the like. Russia has worked on at least at two very long range AAMs, the R–37 and R–172/K–100, and the latter program is likely ongoing. These missiles, whose ranges are reportedly in excess of 200 kilometers (125 miles), are sometimes called "AWACS-killers" and may have been designed explicitly to engage large, slow, loitering aircraft like the E–3. There is no evidence that either weapon has entered service with the Russian air force let alone the PLAAF, but to the extent that China has access to leading-edge Russian weapons and technologies, it would not be surprising to see a like missile appearing in the PLAAF's arsenal at some future date.

Chapter 9

Meeting the Challenge of the Upcoming PLAAF Leadership Reshuffle

You Ji

The transformation of the People's Liberation Army Air Force (PLAAF) has entered a fast track, as new fourth-generation fighters (third-generation, by Chinese terminology) are introduced to the force. This has placed huge pressure on the air force to groom, select, and place talented commanders at various levels. This is an enormous task, as the service has about 250 posts at or above deputy corps level (major generals or above). The foundation of this large pool of senior officers is in a constantly changing mode, especially for the majority of major generals who come and go due to the PLA age rules. This paper concentrates on officers at the corps level (正军级), totaling about three dozen commanders. For reasons of space, it does not examine purely political officers. Instead, the emphasis is on professional airmen and those responsible for combat forces.

Today the PLAAF is about to reshuffle its top and regional leadership because of the age requirement and the reshuffling of the Central Military Commission (CMC) in the 18th Party National Congress to be held in 2012. For the top leaders, all PLAAF deputy commanders would step down before the 18th Congress, as they were all born in 1949 and thus—according to regulations governing officers at the deputy military region (DMR, 大区副) level—must retire at 63. Among the regional commanders who are also at the DMR rank, two were born in 1947 and two in 1948, which means that they should step down this year or the next. The rest were all born in 1949 and will retire at about the same time with deputy commanders of the PLAAF. Thus, by 2012, over two dozen senior air force commanders at the rank of lieutenant general (including those in the political affairs system) will vacate their positions and make way for the new blood to take over. This changeover of the top PLAAF leadership is unprecedented.[1]

This paper examines the reshuffle of air force leadership in the context of CMC personnel changes in the 18th Party Congress, which will be equally profound. The impact on the PLAAF is significant, particularly if General Xu Qiliang (徐其亮) gets promoted and General Ma Xiaotian (马晓天) returns to the air force, a very logical scenario. It argues further that the future PLAAF leadership will be made up of three age echelons:

- Top leaders born at about the same time as the founding of the People's Republic of China (Xu and Ma)
- PLAAF deputy commanders and commanders at the military regions (MRs). (These leaders were born in the mid-1950s, with one or two born in the early 1960s.)
- Younger officers appointed to corps rank, e.g., deputy chief of staff of the air force and deputy commander/chief of staff at the military region air force (MRAF) rank (born in the late 1950s and early 1960s).

The Duumvirate of Xu and Ma: The Top Echelon

There is no doubt that the career path of Generals Xu and Ma presents a very useful case for the study of PLAAF leadership. Their past experience exposes broadly how the PLA top command selects top brass, trains them with various difficult tasks, and finally realizes their potential to be the highest-level leaders. More significantly, the study of Xu and Ma is integral to that of the 18th CMC. Therefore, in studying them, research of the emerging PLAAF leadership is linked to that of the future PLA leadership as a whole.

In the make-up of the current CMC, the age structure of its members may lead to retirement of all but Xu and Chang Wanquan (常万全), director of the General Armament Department (GAD), in the Party's 18th National Congress in 2012.[2] Being the youngest CMC member and with the highest seniority (Xu became divisional, corps, and service commander much earlier than Chang), it is likely Xu would be promoted further. Yet there are only two positions for him at this level of power: either deputy CMC chair, or minister of defense.[3] In this case he would vacate his current position of PLAAF commander. Ma would likely be the first in line to succeed Xu, following Xu's own path from the PLAAF Headquarters to the General Staff Department (GSD), and thence to the CMC as the PLAAF representative.

If this occurs, it would constitute a groundbreaking development within the elite politics of the PLA and its service relationships. First, since the ouster of Wu Faxian (吴法宪) in 1971, the PLAAF has not had another person in the second rank of CMC. Secondly, for the first time since the founding of the air force, it would now have two officers, Xu and Ma, at the apex of power. This is conducive to the PLA's efforts to erode the "army-first" mentality (大陆军主义) affecting its overall strategic orientation.[4] Given Ma's background—previously he was the deputy commander of Lanzhou and Guangzhou Military Regions; president of the National Defense University; currently, most senior deputy chief of staff; and most importantly, a member of the Party's Central Committee (CC) since 2002—his further promotion is a perfect fit to PLA personnel advancement patterns.⁵ Failure to promote Xu and Ma would be regarded as unfair and discriminatory according to PLA norms and standards (军中伦理). If this is indeed the case, both of them would take a veritable great leap forward in their political and military careers. As CMC deputy chair, Xu would acquire the Party rank of Standing Committee member in the Politburo; if he is made defense minister he would hold the rank of State Council counselor. Ma would hold the rank of a Politburo member as a CMC member. And as such they would both enjoy the prestige of Party and state leaders.

Certainly there are high odds against such a dual PLAAF membership in the CMC. Today, service representation in the CMC is basically functional. This is especially true of specialized, highly technical services, such as the air force, the navy, and the strategic missile force (二炮). The initial concept in 2004 of absorbing service commanders into the CMC was to turn it into the top body for commanding joint warfare, increasingly seen as the primary type of warfare for the PLA in the decades to come.⁶ It drew upon the example of the U.S. joint chiefs of staff system in integrating service functions as part the PLA's preparation for war, the central theme of China's defense policy since 1999.⁷

As the PLAAF contemplates its future, it faces a number of intriguing questions. Would the potential dual air force representation upset the functional balance among the different services? Would this dual representation be viewed as fair by other services? The perception of fairness in the PLA is an important concept in maintaining factional and service equilibrium, something that may impact force stability. The navy, for instance, would be jealous; its current CMC representative, Admiral Wu Shengli (吴胜利) will be over 65 years of age in 2012 and will likely retire.⁸ Admiral Sun Jianguo is 3 years younger than Ma Xiaotoan and would be the primary choice to replace Wu, but the naval headquarters does not have a figure comparable to Ma.⁹ The situation with the leadership of the strategic missile force (Second Artillery Corps) is similar.

Ma's future is tangled up with Xu's in that if Xu is not promoted, there is no vacancy for Ma in the CMC, unless Ma would be made chief of the general staff or a director of either GAD or the General Logistics Department (GLD), both relatively unlikely. If Ma does not advance, it is a loss not only for the air force, but the PLA as a whole. In the GSD he has been praised as the most competent deputy chief of staff, evidenced by his being given a wider range of duties than his GSD colleagues, including war preparation and training; strategic planning; foreign affairs (a euphemism for intelligence); the air force; and the PLA professional military education (PME) institutions. In particular, Ma has impressed his colleagues and others (including the present author) with his ability to grasp and analyze even casually presented information in briefings and during various conferences.¹⁰

It is possible that the CMC would regard the issue of two PLAAF CMC members not strictly from the viewpoint of service representation. This is to say that one of the two would be functional, representing the air force, but the other would be regarded simply as a competent top leader who can make great contribution to PLA transformation, regardless of whether he is a seaman, airman, or foot soldier. Both are well qualified for either position. Ma's experience at the National Defense University (NDU) and as the executive deputy chief of GSD in the lead-up to General Ge Zhenfeng's (葛振峰) retirement testified that the CMC had great expectations of him. The NDU experience was meant to broaden his strategic vision and theoretical depth in the "ivory tower" of ideas. It also familiarized Ma with key candidates (then at corps rank) for future top PLA leadership positions. His position as executive deputy chief of the GSD furnished a rare opportunity to grasp the overall military situation, from the nuclear button, foreign military exchanges and joint exercises, weapons research and development, operations and training, and the PLA's domestic missions to budgetary allocations among services and interservice coordination.

Xu and Ma: Two Remarkable Careers

Xu and Ma are believed to share similar career advancement paths. They both joined the air force and became jet pilots in the mid-1960s (Ma in 1965 and Xu in 1967) and have a very similar and impeccable track record in military service. They both enjoy sports, particularly basketball.

Xu has enjoyed good fortune while in the air force. After graduation from the 8th Aviation Academy in 1969 he became a fighter pilot in the Independent Detachment of Air Force (AF) Division 4. This detachment was a battalion unit, but had regiment rank. As a result, Xu skipped the conventional regiment step on his way up. He was made commander of the 26th Division at 33 years of age and deputy corps commander of the 4th Corps (later reorganized as the PLAAF's Shanghai Commanding Headquarters) at just age 34 in 1984, becoming the youngest army-level commander of the PLA at the time. He became commander of the new 8th Corps (deployed in Fujian for Taiwan missions) at the age of 40 in 1990, still holding the record of youngest corps commander to this day. In 1994, he became chief of staff of the air force, achieving the crucial deputy MR rank. In 1999 the PLA leadership transferred him to the Shenyang MR as deputy commander. In 2004, he was made the PLA's deputy chief of general staff, a full MR rank post. Three years later, he became air force commander, the fourth youngest PLAAF commander following Liu Yalou, Wu Faxian, and Ma Ning (马宁), and thus a member of the CMC as well.[11]

Ma was born in 1949 and quickly proved a model officer. In 1972, because of his birth date, he was selected to appear in a documentary film *As the Same Age of the Republic*, representing the PLA. Thereafter he entered the fast track of promotion. He became commander of the 72^d Regiment in 1973, at the age of 23(!), and then, a decade later, was promoted to deputy commander of the 24th Air Force Division, part of the 6th Corps, at 34. In 1995, he became commander of the 10th Corps, and then, just 2 years later, the PLA leadership promoted him to deputy chief of staff for the PLAAF. Only a year later, he was transferred to be chief of staff of Guangzhou Air Force Region.[12]

The Guangzhou transfer was unusual, in that he moved at the same rank. Seldom is a transfer from the center to the region at this level made without a promotion. But even this reflected his favored status, for the underlying reason was to broaden Ma's command experience and familiarity with operational combat units in different war zones. Two years later, in 1999, he was promoted to the position of deputy commander of Lanzhou MR, and commander of Lanzhou Air Force Region, making the crucial climb into the deputy MR rank. Within 2 years he was transferred to be deputy commander of Nanjing MR and commander of PLAAF Nanjing Region. In 2003 he became deputy PLAAF commander. In 2006 he assumed the presidency of the National Defense University, thus entering the full MR rank. The following year he was given his current position as the PLA's executive deputy chief of general staff.

It is very interesting to compare Xu and Ma's career paths, something that can shed a lot of light on PLA elite selection, advancement, and career termination. From the information mentioned above, it is clear that both Xu and Ma were identified early by the air force and the CMC as candidates for top leadership. They had excellent performance qualifications, were top-grade fighter pilots (特级飞行员), and were well respected by their peers and subordinates. Both Xu and Ma piloted J–10s, Su–27s, and Su–30s to gain first-hand experience with these aircraft.

Yet, in this invisible race, Ma was left behind, virtually from the starting point. There are some clues why. First, Xu served in one of the PLAAF's elite fighter divisions, while Ma's was a relatively less prestigious one. This gave Xu an advantage in attracting the attention of the PLA/PLAAF leadership. Later his 8th Corps was deployed in a key strategic location—Fujian, near the Taiwan Strait—where it was on constant combat readiness, while Ma's corps was based in more distant Hebei with more routine service. Second, Xu's skip of the regimental step in the upward ladder allowed him to enter the cadre reserve list of the military region earlier than Ma. Therefore, once there was an opportunity for promotion, Xu was the first to be considered. Third, Xu served in the 4th Corps (later the Air Force Shanghai Commanding Headquarters (上海空军指挥所) as its chief of staff. This corps historically produced many more key PLAAF leaders (for example, Gao Houliang [高厚良], Qao Qingchen [乔清晨], and Han

Decai [韩德彩]) than Ma's 6th and 10th Corps. These leaders naturally favored subordinates following the same career track. Fourth, Xu was younger than Ma by 1 year, a seemingly small difference, but one that could be a key cut-off factor in Chinese Communist Party (CCP)/PLA succession politics.[13]

Thus, Xu accelerated ahead of Ma as early as the late 1980s, even though Ma's own upward progression was a veritable "helicopter" compared with his peers. Xu acquired deputy corps rank about a decade earlier than Ma (1983 versus 1993). When Xu became the PLAAF chief of staff in 1994, Ma was only chief of staff of the 10th Corps. This was a crucial difference, as Xu entered the CMC cadre management list while Ma stayed in the air force list. The gap was finally closed on the eve of the 16th National Party Congress as both were at the same military rank: Ma was then Nanjing MR deputy commander and its air force chief, and Xu held the same ranks in Shenyang. At the congress, they were both elected to be CC members, and thus equal to the parallel third-most-important personages in the air force (the first two CC members being the commander and political commissar of the PLAAF).

But when the selection of the PLAAF commander came down to Xu and Ma, Xu's early seniority over Ma played a crucial role in his promotion. This difference is a huge one, because Xu as a CMC member is ranked as the leader of the PLA (军委领导), while Ma can only be dubbed the leader of a headquarters (总部首长). It is interesting to watch if Ma can again match up with Xu in the forthcoming PLA leadership reshuffle. Certainly in no aspect is Ma inferior in ability and performance to Xu. Their relative career progression is evidence, yet again, that sometimes the factor of luck is more important than anything else.

The Second Echelon of the PLAAF Headquarters Elites

The second echelon of PLAAF leadership consists of the PLAAF's deputy commanders, chief of staff, deputy chiefs of staff, and assistant chiefs of staff. Readers are advised that these elites at the headquarters belong to two clusters in CMC nomenclature. The deputy commanders and chief of staff are at the deputy MR rank and fall into the CMC "Category B" management list, requiring that (though nominated by the CMC's professional soldiers) their appointments be approved by the CMC chair personally. The deputy chief of staff and assistant chief of staff are Corps-level leaders whose appointments are basically decided by the PLAAF, approved by the CMC in regular meetings, and signed by the CMC chair. Their appointments are professional, not political. In fact the PLA is no longer subjected to impositions of blatantly political appointments, though this was a widespread phenomenon in the now-past eras of Mao Zedong and Deng Xiaoping.[14] Currently, the PLAAF has five deputy commanders, five deputy chiefs of staff, and five assistant chiefs of staff.

Deputy Commanders

All five PLAAF deputy commanders were born in 1949, meaning that they have little or no prospect of upward progression, since the deputy MR rank requires compulsory retirement age at 63. Among them are three fighter pilots of the top grade and two army officers transferred to the PLAAF, with distinctive military family backgrounds.

Lieutenant General He Weirong (何为荣) is executive deputy commander, responsible for operations and training. He commanded Fighter Division 6 and was deputy commander of the Jinan MR and the Jinan AF Region (2003). He was PLAAF chief of staff (2003) before assuming his current position (2005).

Lieutenant General Jing Wenchun (景文春) is in charge of the departments of supporting arms in the Headquarters (electronic warfare, radar and communications, education institutions, and key weapons projects).[15] He was commander of the 10th Corps (1998) and deputy commander of the Beijing MR and the Beijing AF Region (2002–2006) before assuming his current position.

Lieutenant General Zhao Zhongxin (赵忠新) is in charge of headquarters affairs and air force MR affairs. He was commander of the 19th Fighter Division and the Dalian base (2000) and chief of staff for the Nanjing (2002) and Chengdu (2004) AF Regions and deputy chief of staff (2004) and chief of staff of the PLAAF (2005) before assuming this position.

Lieutenant General Yang Dongming (杨东明) is in charge of the PLAAF Research Institutions (basic weapons design, research and development), the Engineering Department, and logistics. Although recruited into the PLA as an air force technical officer—he graduated from the Beijing Aero-Space and Aviation University in 1977 as a rocket engineer—his career advancement came mostly in the army, with postings to the Defense Technology Commission, the Hebei Military District, and the Beijing Garrison. He was transferred back to the PLAAF as deputy commander from the GLD (where he was director for the Material and Oil Department). Without the connections of his father (General Yang Chengwu [杨成武], former PLA chief of general staff), he would not have come this far in the air force, for he was not an airman and possessed no prior experience in PLAAF combat units or headquarters.

Lieutenant General Chen Xiaogong (陈小工) is in charge of intelligence, training safety, and foreign affairs. He is probably the only senior commander in the PLAAF with battlefield combat experience, having fought in the Sino-Vietnam border war as a battalion commander. He was PLA defense attaché in Washington (2001) and then the PLA's intelligence chief (director of the 2d Department of the GSD). He represented the PLA as deputy director of the Politburo's Foreign Affairs Leading Small Group (FALSG) office and was appointed assistant chief of general staff in 2007, temporarily filling the vacancy left by General Xiong Guangkai.

Chen's career progression is intriguing. It is not clear how he was transferred to the PLAAF, which had already filled its four deputy-commander quota. Chen belongs to the PLA category of "cadre to be rescued" (抢救干部), a commander with a distinctive service record who, due to lack of a compulsory experience or lack of a vacancy, is transferred elsewhere as a way of promotion. General Pei Huailiang (裴怀亮) was a good example of this category when he was promoted as president of the NDU. General Zhang Qingsheng was promoted to be deputy chief of general staff without experience as a group army (GA) and MR Commander. For Chen Xiaogong, assistant chief of general staff is still between the army and DMR ranks that he achieved long time ago (准大区级).[16]

But without experience as a commanding officer at or above divisional level (军事主官), it went against the norm to create an exception for him to become deputy chief of general staff. Overall, Chen's career progression was frustrated despite his extensive connections with top leaders while working in the Politburo's FALSG and his father's connection as China's first ambassador to Japan. He thus went to the PLAAF because the PLAAF was a place that could adopt him.

Lieutenant General Yang Guohai (杨国海) is the PLAAF chief of staff. From his resume, we can see that he has been Xu's old associate in Shanghai and is the same age as Xu. The relations between a commander and his chief of staff are always special, and this makes the post of chief of staff a key position in the PLA. According to PLA regulations, the chief of staff is in a way more important than deputy commanders. For instance, if the commander is killed in combat, the next person in line to fill the commanding job is not one of the deputy commanders, but the chief of staff because the former are in charge of specific areas while the latter is more familiar with the overall responsibilities and workings of the unit.[17] Although deputy commander and chief of staff are at the same military rank, in recent years more chiefs of staff have been promoted to lead MRs and Corps-level units than deputy commanders.

Yang was born in 1950, and became commander of the 4th Fighter Division in his late 30s and commander of the Shanghai base in 1998. He stayed in the post of chief of staff of the Lanzhou AF Region for 6 years from 2000, a bit too long for a designated candidate for a future PLAAF leader and, as a result, his future is relatively limited. But after he was appointed to deputy chief of staff of the Air Force in 2006, he held that post for hardly a year before being promoted to chief of staff. Obviously his deputy period was transitional, waiting for the incumbent chief of staff (Zhao Zhongxin) to vacate the position.

Deputy Chiefs of Staff

The PLAAF deputy chief of staff and assistant chief of staff positions are at Corps rank (young assistant chiefs of staff are usually at the deputy Corps level) and normally serve as an important stepping-stone to more senior posts.

The importance of these roles is to bring promising commanders of tactical units (divisional and forward bases) to the headquarters to familiarize them with higher command and strategic management. If the top PLAAF leadership is composed of generals of different age clusters separated by about 5 years, deputy chiefs of staff are reserved for candidates for deputy MR positions either in air force headquarters in Fuxingmen (复兴门空军大院) or in the seven air force regions. Since the mid-1990s, almost all PLAAF deputy chiefs of staff have advanced further, to the deputy MR rank or higher.

The following is the list of past deputy PLAAF chiefs of staff since that time:

- Xu Qiliang (徐其亮, 1993–1994, AF commander)
- Wang Liangwang (王良旺, 1994–1996, deputy AF commander)
- He Weirong (何为荣, 1996–2002, deputy AF commander)
- Jia Yongsheng (贾永生, 1996–2003, regional commander)
- Ma Xiaotian (马晓天, 1997–1998, deputy PLA chief of general staff)
- Liu Zuoxin (刘作新, 1998 regional commander)
- Jiang Jianzeng (江建曾, 2000–2004, regional commander)
- Zhou Liaqian (周来强, 2000–2004, regional commander)
- Zhao Zhongxin (赵忠新, 2004–2005, deputy AF commander)
- Yang Guohai (杨国海, 2005–2006, PLAAF chief of staff).

The present deputy chiefs of staff have an average age of 53 and are destined to take over more senior commanding positions, as the entire pool of incumbent deputy PLAAF commanders and regional commanders (whose average age is about 62) will be replaced in accordance with the "63 and out" regulation.

Currently, there are four deputy chiefs of staff in the PLAAF headquarters:

Major General Zhang Jianping (张建平) was born in 1956 and enlisted in the PLAAF in 1974. He now assists the chief of staff, overseeing operations and training. For instance, he was the PLAAF representative in the Sino-Russo joint military exercise Peace Mission 2009 in the Zhaonan Joint Tactical Training Base in the Jinan MR in July 2009. After the exercise, he made a widely circulated speech on how the PLAAF should learn the best air force theory and practices of the foreign counterparts, noting "Joint exercises and exchange of personnel with other militaries would be a very useful means for absorbing the good experiences of foreign air forces and this will have profound impact on PLAAF transformation."[18]

Zhang had already served in various key commanding posts before coming to the PLAAF headquarters. He was regimental commander at the age of 27 and commander of the 3ᵈ Fighter Division a few years later (the elite of all elite divisions in the PLAAF). Being the first "fist unit" equipped with the Su–27 in the mid-1990s, he led the first team from the division to Russia to receive the Su–27 and become the first of the Su–27 pilot cadre in the PLAAF. He was promoted to be commander of the 9th Corps and deputy commander of the Beijing MRAF. There is no doubt he was marked early as a candidate for the service's senior leader. As first deputy chief of staff, he is poised to replace Yang Guohai.[19]

Major General Yi Xiaoguang (乙晓光) was born in 1958 into a military family and was one of 296 PLA deputies to the 17th Party National Congress.[20] In charge of training and headquarters affairs, he is the most promising and the youngest officer at the full corps rank in Fuxingmen, and the second youngest in the entire PLAAF. His rise was swift and impressive: joining the PLAAF in 1974 at the age of 16, he studied at the Baoding Aviation School (预校) for a year, and became a commander at the battalion level 3 years later at the age of 20. He studied in the PLAAF Command Academy in 1984, laying the foundation for his own subsequent "helicopter rise." He reached the post of deputy division commander in 1989 at the age of 31 and division command in 1992, director of the Department of Training in the PLAAF Headquarters in 1996 (the youngest grade-two Department head at the time), and deputy chief of staff of Guangzhou AF region in 2002.

Before being appointed to his current post, Yi was president of the famous Air Force Command Academy (AFCA) in Haidian, Beijing. In PLA tradition, it is relatively easy to find a capable corps commander, but very difficult to locate a capable president for a top military university.[21] When he was divisional commander in 1992, Yi composed *The Chinese/English Manual for Jet Pilots*, something quite unique for a combat pilot with no formal higher education and an achievement helpful for his appointment to the presidency of the AFCA.[22] Clearly, Yi was brought back to the PLAAF headquarters to manage the routine work at the apex of power before taking on more senior positions elsewhere in the future.

Major General Wang Yisheng (王义生) was an interesting appointment in 2009, for he was clearly a "rescued cadre." He was commander of the AF Weapons Experimental Base in Jiuquan (Shuanchengzi Base, 双成子基地), Gansu Province, having spent fully 38 years in the base since joining the PLAAF in 1968.[23] He transformed it into the PLA's most sophisticated and largest electronic warfare center. Wang was transferred to Beijing following Hu Jintao's instruction that the CMC should take good care of the cadres who have served in remote and poor provinces for a lengthy period of time, such as

Tibet, Xinjiang, Gansu, and Qinghai, where living conditions are harsh. Wang is now assisting the chief of staff in managing technological affairs and weapons research and development programs.

Major General Dan Zhiping (但志平), born in 1957, assists the chief of staff in matters of training and foreign affairs in the headquarters. He was assistant chief of staff between 1994 and 1999 in his late 30s (a remarkably young age for the post). He assumed the current position after transfer from deputy chief of staff of the Chengdu AF region in 2008. Before that, he also served as deputy chief of staff of the Lanzhou AF region. In 2007 he was sent to study at "the Generals' course" (将军班) in the PLA NDU where he was cited as an excellent student. His graduation thesis on training in a combat situation using simulation facilities furnishing "Red" versus "Blue" force scenarios and practice won high praise. He was subsequently chosen to supervise further study resulting in an influential colloquium in which the main ideas expressed by participants were subsequently published in the *PLA Daily*.[24] Clearly he is a rising star in the PLAAF.

Assistant Chiefs of Staff

The post of assistant chief of staff serves as a stepping-stone for further promotion for most of the assistant chiefs. They are selected from promising young commanders at the deputy corps rank, either from combat units at campaign levels or specialized/technical departments in Fuxingmen. Oftentimes they are hand-picked by chiefs of staff personally and work closely with top commanders there. They usually enjoy good personal ties with the top AF brass and link the top command to the grass-roots forces. Currently the PLAAF has four assistant chiefs of staff, each with a unique background.

Major General Li Shaomin (李绍敏) joined the PLAAF in 1968 and now specializes in air force education. He was a top-grade jet pilot and regimental commander until 1996 when he was promoted to be deputy commandant of the 1st Flying Academy. From then on he served as commandant of the 3d Flying Academy (1999); deputy president of Air Force University of Engineering (2001); and president of PLAAF Aviation University in 2003. He has held his current position since 2008. He assists the chief of staff in overseeing university education in the air force. Given his age, his career prospects seem to be limited, particularly as his current duty is not directly related to combat operations.

Major General Wang Weining (王卫宁) was recently promoted to the position from the directorship of the second department (intelligence) of the PLAAF. He assists the chief of staff in managing intelligence-related matters, public affairs, and foreign affairs.

Major General Lin Tao (林涛) has long served in air force units in northwest provinces such as Tibet. He was recently promoted to the major general rank (2009). In Fuxingmen, he assists the chief of staff in headquarters affairs and daily running of the staff department.

Major General Zheng Yuanlin (郑元林) is also a rising star in the PLAAF, as seen from his fast upward advancement in the last 3 years. In 2008 he was commander of the 13th Division (the PLA's strategic transportation division). The next year he became commander of the PLAAF's Wuhan Base at deputy corps rank. The following year he was appointed deputy chief of staff of the PLAAF Guangzhou MR. He was in Guangzhou for barely a year before being brought back to Beijing to be an assistant chief of staff of the Air Force.

Zheng has excelled both as a transport pilot and transport commander. He was selected as one of the best air force commanders in 2007, following his command of Il-76s deployed in the Sino-Russian Peace Mission 2007 exercise in Russia. During the catastrophic snow and ice storm in South China in January 2008, he was placed in charge of the PLA's air relief missions. In a week, the 13th Division's Il-76s conducted 75 emergency sorties and carried about 800 tons of goods to 19 airports in eight provinces. In the Wenchuan earthquake rescue operations, the 13th Division made a huge contribution.[25] It was very difficult for large transports to take off and land in concentrated sorties, in tough weather conditions (e.g., visibility less than 100 meters), and on airports with only rudimentary facilities.[26] Even so, operations were conducted with complete safety. Just days after he arrived in Beijing to take his current job, the Yushu earthquake struck; again the PLA entrusted him to command relief operations by both the 13th Division and the Chengkong Division.

Given that he is both in his early 50s and in the right place at the right time—on the verge of the forthcoming massive leadership reshuffle—it might be expected that his future is a bright one. But he faces a serious obstacle: in the entire PLAAF history of pilot cadre management, an airlift pilot has never risen very far in the leadership. As in other air forces, young and accomplished fighter pilots form the traditionally favored cadre. Within the PLAAF, the fighter divisions comprise over 55 percent of the total, attack aircraft divisions 30 percent, and bomber/transport divisions just 15 percent.[27] Three transport divisions (the new division in the Chengdu AF Region, and the 13th and 34th Divisions) form a "minority" in the PLAAF structure. As a result, given the PLAAF's past tradition, it will be interesting to see how far Zheng goes.

The Commanders of PLAAF Military Regions

As this is written, the military region air force commanders are all transitioning to retired status. The youngest commanders were born in 1949 and the oldest in 1947. Jia Yongsheng of the Beijing MRAF and Liu Zhongxing are already over the retirement age.[28] The CMC has applied a level of flexibility in service age to some special cases in recent years.[29] The current MRAF commanders will all retire before the end of 2011, unless some "historical accidents" happen, such as an outbreak of conflict.

Attention should therefore be focused on the younger and rising stars in the MRAFs, who are in their early 50s, have served in operational frontline posts, and have held senior commanding positions for a number of years. Most are chiefs of staff of MRAFs who proved themselves as the top-grade fighter pilots, commanders of the "fist units," and as staff officers in headquarters assignments. They are:

Major General Ma Zhenjun (麻振军), deputy commander and chief of staff of the Beijing MRAF. Born in 1964, he is probably the only major general at the full corps rank in the air force who was born in the 1960s.[30] This indicates that Ma has distinguished himself in the race to the apex of power. He is now in a unique position to succeed either Jia Yongsheng, his current superior, or to be transferred to another MRAF as commander. It is worth noting that by March 2010 the PLA had only eight post-1960s major generals at the corps level, the youngest being Yang Hui (杨晖), director of the 2^d Department of the GSD.[31] Mao Xinyu (毛新宇) (Mao Zedong's grandson) is the only one born in the 1970s. So far, apart from Ma, no other post-1960s corps level officer is found in the PLAAF.

Ma earned his fast promotion after proving himself as a top-grade fighter pilot, an outstanding fighter division commander, and a keen proponent of training. Instead of emphasizing routine technical training, Ma emphasized tactical combat training. When he commanded the 2^d Fighter Division, it was rated as having displayed the most proficiency in training for three successive years. He also won three PLA science and technology awards.[32]

In 2007 Ma was promoted from commander of the 2^d Fighter Division to deputy chief of staff of the Guangzhou MRAF, when he was 43. Two years later, he was promoted to deputy commander of the Jinan MRAF (a full corps rank) and again within 1 year he was transferred to his current position. The frequent transfers clearly reflect the air force leadership's confidence in Ma and their crafting a succession plan for him involving gaining intimate familiarity with various MRAFs and combat units.

Major General Ding Laihong (丁来杭) was born in 1957 and is the second youngest senior officer among the seven PLAAF MRs (at the full corps rank). He became regimental commander of Regiment 71 of Fighter Division 24 while in his early 30s. From the position of division deputy commander he moved to command of a training base in the Beijing MRAF, a divisional unit.

Like Ma, he emphasized combat-realistic "Red versus Blue" training. In 2001 he was swiftly promoted to chief of staff of the 8th Corps, deployed on the Taiwan Front, reaching the deputy corps level at the age of 44. When the 8th Corps was reorganized down to the Fuzhou Forward Commanding Post in 2003, Ding remained its foundational head. In 2007 he was promoted to be president of the Air Force Command Academy. One year later he was transferred to the Chengdu MRAF as its chief of staff. Looking back, Ding has been at the corps-command level for almost a decade. In terms of seniority or in terms of the PLAAF's demand for a large pool of candidates to complete the forthcoming reshuffle, Ding is certainly at the front in the queue.

Major General Zheng Qunliang (郑群良), born in 1954, is older than Ding, but is still a valid candidate to "catch the last train" to reach deputy MR rank. Previously he was a corps commander who would have had to retire at the age of 55 if he could not advance further; but now, his active service can be extended, perhaps to age 58.[33] Zheng, as commander of the PLAAF's elite 1st Fighter Division, was selected to participate in a PLA senior officers' delegation to visit the United States in July 2000, a sign of the PLA having identified him as a future PLAAF leader.

After his trip, he wrote a widely distributed article recounting his experiences visiting various U.S. Air Force bases.[34] For instance, he noticed it took only 15 minutes for an F–15 wing to change munitions, as compared with his division's 3 hours. He was highly impressed that USAF F–15 Eagle fighter pilots took off in formation, even under heavy clouds below 200 meters (something his own pilots could only do individually under the same conditions) and landed out of steep, descending turns.

At one base in California, he was particularly surprised to find Air Force male and female personnel working together and was impressed with the orderly and systematic airfield operations. He was surprised to find non-commissioned officers supervising flight operations (a task performed only by commanders in a PLAAF fighter division). Zheng concluded that if his commanders could be freed from such duties, they could devote their attention to more important tasks. He concluded that the more the PLA understood the U.S. military, the more the PLA would know its own shortcomings and be motivated to catch up.

Zheng is a top-grade jet fighter pilot. When he reached the PLAAF's compulsory nonflight age of 47, he had accumulated 2,200 flying hours. He became commander of Regiment 3 of the 1st Division in 1992, then divisional commander in 1997. In a transregional combat drill under no pre-set flying conditions, he led the division to a deployment at another air base, breaking PLA records for the largest number of aircraft moved on a single mission, traveling the longest distance, and the longest flying time under instrument-only (blind flying) flight conditions. In 1999 he was the in-flight commander for the Air Force National Day Military Parade. The review formation was 7 kilometers (4.34 miles) long, and passed the review stand at Tiananmen Square exactly on time, to the second. This exhibition won him high praise from PLAAF leaders.[35] In 2002 he was promoted to commander of the Wuhan base and concurrently deputy commander and chief of staff of the Shenyang MRAF. Clearly, if age is not an obstacle for his advancement, he will receive a more senior post in the PLAAF's leadership reshuffle.

Major General Zhuang Kezhu (庄可柱), chief of staff of the Lanzhou MRAF. He was born in 1955 and rose quickly in his early career. He was commander of the 33^d Fighter Division, the top division in Southwest China and always the first combat unit to equip with new generation aircraft in that region. He was promoted to commander of the Kunming Forward Headquarters in 1999. In 2005 he was transferred to Beijing to serve as assistant chief of staff of the PLAAF, in charge of combat plans and training of air force units in the southwest. He has thus gained valuable access to the top AF leadership on the one hand and had rich commanding experience at the basic campaign units on the other. His future upward movement is certain.

Major General Xu Anxiang (徐案祥) is chief of staff of the Nanjing MRAF. In his early 50s, Xu has already acquired valuable experience in commanding divisional and corps-level operations and training. In 2002 he was commander of the 14th Fighter Division, a unit on constant combat duty in the Nanjing War Zone. He was in charge of the MR's air force units in the Wenchuan operation when he was deputy chief of the staff. He personally oversaw preparation of aircraft in the Special Rescue Regiment that received emergency mobilization orders at 10:30 p.m. on the night of the earthquake, departing 3 hours later with all necessary materials.[36] In 2007 Xu was front-line commander for PLAAF fighters deployed to the Sino-Russian joint military exercise Peace Mission 2007. This was the first time that PLAAF aircraft had entered a foreign country for combat drills. Xu directed 24 sorties of eight Chinese J–7s and Il–76s within a short period of time. Xu's division achieved its tactical objectives, even though in a strange location, against unfamiliar targets, and under uncertain circumstances.[37] Given the fact that the PLAAF top leadership always selects the most competent commanders to command transnational military missions, Xu's experience in the mission was a telling proof of how the PLAAF leadership regarded him. As a richly experienced commander in charge of operations and training in an important air force war zone, he held heavy responsibilities, a contributing factor likely to influence his promotion to higher command in future years.

Major General Sun Herong (孙和荣) is chief of staff of the Jinan MRAF (2009). He was deputy chief of staff of Shenyang MRAF (2003–2006) and commander of the Dalian Forward Headquarters (2007). His seniority is about the same as that of Ding, Zheng, and Xu, and he is a clear candidate for more important positions. In 2003 he coauthored with Yi Xiaoguang (乙晓光) a book entitled *The Stealth Aircraft: A Difficult Adversary* (隐形飞机及其克星). This highly acclaimed work subsequently proved popular with the PLAAF, then in the midst of examining high-tech warfare.

Clearly, there are many promising commanders among this cluster of relatively young major generals at the MRAF level. A number of other officers are also potential candidates; however, due to limited space, they can only be briefly noted:

Major General Chang Baolin (常宝林), deputy commander of the Nanjing MRAF, was chief of staff of the 1st Corps in 2000 at the age of 44 and then the Guangzhou MRAF's chief of staff and deputy commander (2005). He is a candidate for commander for one of the MRAFs.

Major General Yang Weidong (杨卫东), commander of PLAAF Wuhan Base, was commander of the 31st Fighter Division and deputy chief of staff of the Jinan MRAF. He served briefly as assistant chief of staff of the PLAAF, which gave him close access to top PLAAF leaders. His current job is meant to increase his experience in regional command and campaign level units. He is poised to become chief of staff of one of the MRAFs.

Major General Wang Tieyi (王铁翼). Born in 1959, Wang is deputy chief of staff of the Shenyang MRAF. He was commander of the 9th Fighter Division, which is one of the top divisions in the air force, in 2000. He was selected to study at National Defense University in 2005 and was a deputy leader in the 54th Base of the Strategic Missile Force under the PLA senior officer exchange program of different services. In his capacity of deputy chief of staff of the Shenyang MRAF, Wang was the first-line commander of PLAAF units in the 2009 Sino-Russian Peace Mission joint exercise.

Major General Li Xiangmin (李向明). Born in 1959, Li became commander of the PLAAF Nanning Forward Headquarters in 2004 at the age of 45, younger than Ding Laihang (Fuzhou) and Zheng Qunliang (Wuhan) who held the same rank at the same time.

Summary

This chapter's research tentatively reveals a few commonalities in PLAAF leadership politics, especially in regard to the patterns of elite selection and promotion.

First, the leadership selection process is increasingly based upon meritocracy and even "expertocracy." The candidates for top leadership are inevitably well-trained, learned, and internationally exposed. The level of professionalism is very high, both in terms of their careers as airmen and their experience as commanders. Mediocre officers simply do not make it to the top, given the extremely tough competition among peers. The officers in the CMC and PLAAF cadre reserve lists have to go through several rounds of performance tests, through various commanding posts and at different levels of command. In this regard, the PLAAF is much like professional air forces in other parts of the world.

Second, fighter pilots have dominated the PLAAF leadership from its formative years to the present day. Virtually all top service leaders and leaders at the region level are fighter pilots. Partly this is due to the PLAAF force structure that gives numerical advantages to fighter divisions and partly to a tradition dating to the earliest years of the service. Functionally, fighter jets undertake a proportionally higher responsibility for homeland air defense. It is interesting to watch how this tradition will evolve and change, as the air force increasingly emphasizes power projection missions away from home, which will require other types of aircraft to play a larger role. In terms of personal networks, it is logical and commonplace for the incumbent fighter-pilots turned AF leaders to groom their subordinates into commanding positions. This situation is unlikely to change much any time soon.

Third, the age of the PLAAF's current leadership will soon force a massive leadership reshuffle at the service and MRAF levels. The generational succession can be expected to be orderly, as an array of candidates is already in place to take over key positions as they become available. This chapter lists a number of them, although it is not an exhaustive examination. If there is no substantial intervening surprise, they will become the next generation of air force leaders. They are younger, better educated, with more flying hours, and more capable of piloting various types of third-generation (fourth-generation in Western terminology) fighter aircraft.

Fourth, the PLA as a whole and the PLAAF in particular have developed a sophisticated, institutionalized, and comprehensive personnel selection and promotion system. It is multi-layered, with a CMC reserve list, a PLAAF list, an MRAF list, a corps list, and a divisional list. Each list normally has 1.5 times the number of personnel who can be promoted to the next level to guarantee that the best make it through the selection filter.[38] Different tiers are mutually supportive, as a promising PLAAF candidate can enter the CMC list simultaneously, to be groomed with a variety of opportunities, as takes place in the other services. As far as the air force is concerned, a pattern of upward mobility is thus clearly visible for those lucky enough to be screened as future top leaders.

They are identified early compared with those in other PLA services, thanks to the service age regulations for combat pilots, whose flying career ends at age 47. In their early 30s they become regimental commanders, get to the divisional rank in their mid to late 30s, and then to corps level posts before age 50. From there they are transferred frequently to gain familiarity with central affairs and different MRAFs, normally staying in one place no more than 2 years. A top air force leader is thus tempered with as much necessary experience as possible.

To stress yet again, meritocracy and expert knowledge of one's professional career field are now the core defining qualities for the deepening professionalization of the PLAAF's top elites. This is seen by the following facts:

- They are all top-grade pilots, typically rated in several kinds of high-performance aircraft (typically fighters), or other aerospace professionals.

- By the time a commander is selected for a corps-level command, he has gone at least three times to advanced training in military academies (for a deputy MR commander, at least four times).

- PLAAF officers are given special missions to test their ability in the process of being selected and promoted, such as joint combat drills with foreign military services and large-scale military operations other than war (MOOTW) experience.

- The selection of future leaders is increasingly open and competitive, using measures such as a satisfactory graduation thesis, peer opinion survey, and examination marks on technological tests (for instance, computer knowledge and skills). All these and others heavily impact subsequent personnel selection. Thus, the scope of arbitrary nomination of favored candidates by individual leaders is markedly decreasing.

In conclusion, the PLAAF is capable of identifying potential leaders and giving them the experience and skills needed to undertake the complicated and tough transformation of turning the air force from a purely defensive force to one with reasonable long-range offensive and defensive power-projection capabilities. The next years will bring about a major reshaping of the PLAAF leadership as those born in the late 1940s and early 1950s give way to younger officers. This will take place in an orderly fashion, though some disruption is likely to occur, with gaps between the right people in the right posts being narrowed and bridged only in a gradual manner.

By December 2011 the reshuffle of the military region air force leadership had seen five new MRAF commanders: Jiang Jianzeng (江建曾), Beijing MR, transferred from the Nanjing MR; Zhang Jianping (张建平), Guangzhou MR; Zhuang Kezhu (庄可柱), Lanzhou MR; Yi Xiaoguang (乙晓光), Nanjing

MR; and Zheng Qunliang (郑群良), Jinan MR. Two other air force military region commanders Fang Dianrong (方殿荣),Chengdu MR and Zhou Laiqiang (周来强), Shenyang MR have not been changed.

Notes

[1] This paper does not examine any personnel in the air force's political affairs system. The main reason is the limited space. Yet no less significant is the fact that political affairs staff have traditionally played a subordinate role as compared with commanders (军事主官) since the Liu Yalou (刘亚楼) era. This is similar to other specialized services that are more technologically intensive. But in the air force, the commanders have always been assertive. An interesting example is that in 1984 Politburo member and air force commander Zhang Tingfa (张庭发) clashed with Yang Shangkun (杨尚昆) in a Central Military Commission meeting over the issue of PLAAF streamlining. Yang asked Gao Houliang (高厚良), political commissar, to express his view. Gao simply said "I was with Commander Zhang." Yang was enraged. He said "Your air force commissars never had any independent view against the commanders." Both Zhang and Gao were removed from office in a few years.

[2] Under PLA regulations, generals do not actually retire. They have permanent military status, but simply leave their active duties. They can still wear the PLA emblem and retain military rank. This gives them concrete privileges such as reading classified documents, utilizing a supporting staff, having official cars, and receiving full salaries as with active officers.

[3] If the current CMC dual leadership structure continues, namely with a military officer and a political officer at the apex of power, Xu would be more likely given the defense minister portfolio. He would then be the first defense minister from the air force.

[4] "One Million Reduction of PLA Soldiers Ends the Era of Big Army" [百万大裁军: 中国大陆军时代的终结], *PLA Daily*, August 19, 2009.

[5] Ma became Lanzhou deputy MR commander in 1999, arriving at the deputy MR rank 5 years earlier than Zhang Qinsheng (章沁生) and Sun Jianguo (孙建国), who reached the rank in 2004 as assistant chief of general staff and naval chief of staff, respectively, and 6 years earlier than Hou Shusen (候树森), who was promoted to chief of staff of the Shenyang MR in 2005. Ma was a Central Committee (CC) member in 2002, while Zhang in 2007, and Sun still an alternate CC member now. Hou is not a CC member yet. On the other hand, Zhang, Sun, and Hou also have their chances to enter the CMC. For instance, Sun would replace Wu Shengli (吴胜利) as naval commander and Hou Liao Xilong (廖锡龙) as director of the General Logistics Department (GLD) in the 18th Congress in 2012.

[6] When General Guo Boxiong (郭伯雄) inspected National Defense University (NDU) on September 18, 2010, he pointed out that all the war operations that would involve the PLA would be joint operations. The primary task for the NDU was to train commanders capable of commanding joint operations in the future wars. "Daily Military Report" [军事报道], *CCTV Channel 7* (September 19, 2010).

[7] Accelerating military struggle was a Politburo and CMC joint decision in 1999 in response to the U.S. bombing of the Chinese embassy in Belgrade during Operation *Allied Force*, and Lee Teng-hui's "two-state thesis" in that year.

[8] There is some possibility that Wu might not retire in 2012, as both Liang Guanglie (梁光烈) and Liao Xilong (廖锡龙) were retained in the 17th National Party Congress at the age of 67 in 2007. The likelihood is low, though, as one unwritten age rule for CMC membership selection is for the person to serve for two terms for the sake of leadership and policy stability. A younger person who can serve two terms from 2012 would be better for the PLA Navy (PLAN).

[9] Vice Admiral Ding Yiping (丁一平) was groomed earlier to be the candidate. He was 6 years younger than Admiral Wu Shengli and had comparable command experience. He was as well an alternate CC member in 2002, as Wu was in the CC only 5 years later. However, Ding was penalized following a fatal accident with the Type 035 *Ming*-class submarine 361 on April 16, 2003. Seventy officers and men were lost, though the submarine was later salvaged. In the accident's aftermath, Ding was lowered in rank by one grade, removing him from contention. Thus the promotion went to Wu.

[10] According to General Xiong Guangke (熊光楷), Ma invited him to give a speech on global strategic issues in the PLA NDU in 2006. During the talk Xiong listed eight major points that he did not tell Ma prior to the talk. He noticed that Ma did not take notes. But when Ma made the summary speech, he elaborated these

eight points with great accuracy and his insights. This greatly impressed Xiong. In the three Shangri-la Security Dialogues, except for the first one where he looked a bit nervous, Ma was calm, eloquent, and firm in presenting China's view amidst clear situational pressure and addressed the most complicated issues with confidence. I was present for the 9th Shangri-la Dialogue on May 30, 2009, when Taiwanese scholar Liu Fu-kuo (刘复国) asked Ma a question in the first preliminary session. Liu first praised the improvement in bilateral relations across the Taiwan Strait. Then he said the improved bilateral ties should lead Taiwan to contribute to multilateral security regimes in the region. Ma immediately saw that the crux of the question was not bilateral but multilateral. He did not bother with the first part and stressed Beijing's stance on Taiwan's international pursuits.

[11] Information from various official sources, such as Air Force News Paper, and PLA related Web sites, e.g., <www.ourzg> [军政在线], and <www.chinagate.com.cn> [中国发展门户网].

[12] Information from <www.k6j.cn> [空6军战友网]. This is a Web site run by active and retired officers of the former 6th Corps of the Air Force where Ma started his first years as a pilot in the 24th Division until he became the division's commander.

[13] For instance, in order to reinforce a sense of fairness or to arrive at a reluctant compromise, the 17th National Party Congress imposed an unwritten rule that those Politburo members born in the 1930s should step down and only those in the 1940s remained. Zeng Qinghong (b. 1938) thus had to go but Jia Qinglin (b. 1940) stayed on. See You Ji, "17th Party Congress and the CCP's Changing Elite Politics," in *China's Reform at 30*, ed. Dali Yang and Zhao Litao (Singapore: World Scientific, 2009), 55-92.

[14] Lieutenant General Jia Tingan (贾庭安), deputy director of the General Political Affairs Department (GPAD), is the only exception. He was Jiang Zeming's chief secretary. His appointment to the PLA was both political and functional, as he was basically a liaison officer for Jiang prior to Jiang's retirement.

[15] On August 2, 2010, Jing inspected the Yanliang Aviation R&D Complex, accompanied by Zhang Wei (张伟), deputy director of the Armament Department of the PLAAF and others. The purpose was likely to gain first-hand knowledge of new aircraft. He also personally tested the simulation cabin of a key aircraft project. *Chinese Aviation* [中国航空报], August 5, 2010.

[16] The position of assistant chief of general staff can be at a corps rank if the holder is not senior enough (appointed from a grade-one department at the GSD), but most get a DMR status. The majority of assistant chiefs of general staff receive promotion to the military region commander level when they become deputy chief of general staff, with the one exception of Li Yu (李玉) who retired with a DMR rank. Chen would be another exception, as his career would end with a DMR rank in the air force. His fatal weakness is that he did not have group army command experience.

[17] Senior Colonel Jiang Daohong (姜道洪) et al., *Theory of Improving the Quality of the Chief of Staff* [参谋长素质论] (Beijing: National Defense University Press, 2006), 19.

[18] Zhang Jianping's interview with Li Jin in *International Online* [国际在线], July 24, 2009.

[19] After the drafting of this chapter in late 2010, Zhang Jianping was promoted to be deputy commander of the Jinan MR and commander of the Jinan MRAF in an enlarged CMC conference in early 2011. He was the PLAAF representative in General Chen Bingde's (陈柄德) U.S. tour in May 2011, and accompanied Admiral Michael Mullen's visit to a PLAAF unit in Jinan in June 2011. In the same month, however, he was transferred to Guangzhou AF Military Region to be commander. Clearly his brief role in Jinan was associated with Mullen's visit, which exposed him to an important diplomatic event. He is widely tipped as the air force's next commander.

[20] After the drafting of this chapter in late 2010, Yi Xiaoguang was promoted to be deputy commander of Nanjing MR and commander of Nanjing MRAF, at the same time with Zhang Jianping. Logically, Yi and Zhang have formed a potential team to succeed Xu and Ma in due time.

[21] The AFCA was originated from the Air Force Academy, and used to be a DMR rank institution. The PLAAF leadership always tries to appoint the best person to be its president. Its incumbent president is Major General Ma Jian (马建), formerly the AF operations chief and first deputy director general of the Department No. 1 in the GSD, who is also a promising future AF leader. Ma attended the Australian Chief of Army Conference as the representative of General Liang Guanglie (then PLA chief of staff) in Canberra in August 2005. He was probably the first PLA military officer to participate in such international activities (most of the time it would be an officer from the 2[d] department). He was seated with Australian Governor General (former Australian defence force chief) in the conference banquet and chatted with him directly for the whole evening without an interpreter, as I watched from a few tables away. He also led the PLA delegation to observe the U.S. Pacific Command's 2007 annual multinational naval exercise in 2007.

[22] Shuyanghouqiu Web site [沭阳厚丘网] (May 29, 2009) accessed on August 1, 2010. Shuyang is Yi's hometown.

[23] "Li Peiwen Meets with Wang Yisheng Major General of the Air Force" [李沛文会见空军首长王义生少将], *Jiuquan Daily* [酒泉日报], February 21, 2009.

[24] "Speech Abstract of the PLANDU Student Training Transformation Symposium" [国防大学基本系学员'训练转变座谈会'发言摘要], *PLA Daily*, June 12, 2007.

[25] "The Air Force Officer Shuffle Highlights Military Transformation" [空军军官調整凸顯軍事變革], *Wenhui Daily* [文汇报], May 17, 2010.

[26] Speech on the 13th Division's Wenchun Operations by Senior Colonel Cheng Xiaojian (程晓键), now commander of the new transport division in Chengdu AF Region and the only female divisional commander in PLA combat troops at present. *Hunan TV,* June 18, 2008.

[27] Senior Colonel Tian Yueying (田越英), "Liu Yalou's Theory and Practice in Building the People's Air Force" [刘亚楼的人民空军建设的理论与实践], *Chinese Military Science* [中国军事科] 15, no. 5 (2002), 120.

[28] After the writing of this paper in late 2010, Jiang Yongsheng retired in early 2011. Oddly enough, Jiang Jianzeng (江健曾), the person who replaced him, was formerly commander of the Nanjing MRAF and is only 2 years younger (b. 1949). This is a rare case, unless the CMC has plans to further promote Jiang Jianzeng, who is likewise near retirement age.

[29] In 2005 the PLA adjusted the age rule, making it a bit flexible for non–front-line commanders. This applies to university and research staff, specialists in military technology, and unique cases.

[30] "Guangzhou Military Area Air Force Deputy Chief of Staff Inspires Armed Forces to Promote Jinan Military Region Air force Assistant Commander"[广州军区空军副参谋长麻振军少将调升济南军区空军副司令员], *Dazhong Ribao* [大众日报], January 12, 2009.

[31] After the writing of this paper in late 2010, Yang was promoted to chief of staff of the Nanjing MR in early 2011, the youngest PLA officer arriving at a DMR post. He was on General Chen Binde's [陈炳德] U.S. tour in May 2011, and is tipped to replace Ma Xiaotian in charge of PLA foreign affairs and intelligence when Ma is transferred to another post.

[32] "Divisional Commander of the Guangzhou MRAF Ma Zhenjun Tabs Potential of New Generation Aircraft and Turns it into an Ace Division" [广空某师师长麻振军挖新机潜力打造王牌], *China's Air Force* [中国空军], January 17, 2004.

[33] See Article 134 of PLA Active Duty Officers' *Regulations re service age, in Regulations of the PLA Active Duty Officer of the PRC* [中华人民共和国现役军官法规定 第十四条]. This is according to Amendment 6 of the *Regulation* approved by the 7th plenary session of the 8th Standing Committee of the National People's Congress on May 12, 1994, which allows maximum expansion of 3 years for divisional commanders and 5 years for corps commanders; see China.com [中国网], accessed on October 10, 2010.

[34] "East Asia Armed Forces Network" [亚东军事网] at <http://bbs.warchina.com/bbs1/read.php?tid=7542> (November 9, 2005), accessed on October 10, 2010.

[35] *PLA.net* [中国军网], August 15, 2010.

[36] *Air Force News* [空军报], May 14, 2008.

[37] "Chinese Air Force in Peace Mission 2007" [和平使命 – 2007军演中的中国空军], CNR.CN [Chinese Broadcasting Network, 中国广播网], Febuary 23, 2009.

[38] From the rank of wing commander upward, the PLAAF has adopted a selection criterion of 1.5 times the available positions. The age and other qualifications are very tough. For wing commanders to be in the reserve list they must be younger than 30, have college degrees, 2 years of battalion commander experience, and be pilots of fighter and attack aircraft. This is the beginning step for all senior leaders to climb. See "The PLAAF Announces the Regulation on Enhancing Promotion of Wing Commander" [空军出台关于加强飞行大队长培养工作的意见], *Air Force News* [Newspaper of the PLAAF, 空军报], July 29, 2010.

Chapter 10

Education and Training in the PLAAF

Kevin Lanzit

Strengthened military education and training programs are fundamental to Chinese People's Liberation Army Air Force (PLAAF) efforts toward "air force building" and are essential to China's efforts to construct a modern 21st century military.[1] The PLAAF recognizes that its modernization goals cannot be fully realized merely through the acquisition of advanced weapons and revision of military doctrine; it will also require the institutionalization of strong education and training programs capable of developing personnel with the requisite knowledge and skills to operate effectively in today's increasingly complex operational environment.[2] To that end, the PLAAF announced the following at the beginning of 2009:[3]

> Taking into full account preparations for combat and its own transformation and development, the Air Force is exploring training systems and methods tailored to the development of the latest generation of weaponry and equipment. It stresses technical and tactical training in complex environments, combined training of different arms and aircraft types, and joint training; conducts mission-oriented and confrontational training; and is increasing on-base, simulated and web-based training. It is working to optimize the tripartite pilot training system composed of flying colleges, training bases and combat units, and intensifying the training of aviation units in counter-air operations, air-to-ground attacks and joint operations. It is deepening reforms and innovations in institutional education by improving the system of discipline, and making innovations in teaching programs, means and methods. It is strengthening on-the-job training, and exploring a new model of personnel development, namely the triad of institutional education, training in units and professional military education. For this purpose, the Air Force Military Professional University was established in July 2008.

The principal target of air force education and training programs is the officer corps (cadre), whose members serve as the primary warfighters; secondarily, the focus is on the noncommissioned officer (NCO) corps, which is beginning to take on additional responsibilities in logistics and mission support. Education provides the officers and NCOs with the intellectual foundation needed to master the typical entry-level jobs in today's military and to advance to jobs of increasing complexity as technology evolves and they grow in rank and responsibility. Training provides technical knowledge and hands-on skills to achieve proficiency and perform consistently under the stress of uncertain and dynamic operational conditions. Together, education and training underpin the disciplined and agile combat forces that China seeks to build.

To fully harness the potential of its new arsenal—including aircraft, sensors, munitions, and space-based systems—China's air force must resolve long-term deficiencies in education and training that have stood in the path of its advancement. Over the years, PLAAF education and training programs have been influenced and molded by a variety of factors, including Marxist-Leninist thinking and the influences of Mao Zedong, continuous comprehensive air force building and operational training experience, and the selective adoption of foreign operational practices. Although education and training programs of the PLAAF remain highly influenced by their early course of development, today's training structure has undergone a number of recent reforms and adjustments which are now reaching maturity and show signs of producing solid results.

The ongoing modernization drive that encompasses the whole of the PLAAF education and training infrastructure is part of a much broader People's Liberation Army (PLA) effort to transform its legacy mechanized force into a force that will be capable of fighting and winning in modern, informatized conditions.[4] Promoted by President Hu Jintao in his capacity as Chairman of the Central Military Commission (CMC), this strategic policy direction provides the basis for the advancements and developments that are reshaping air force education and training programs. The PLAAF recognizes that this effort entails a long-term commitment and has established achievable goals for the path forward. This chapter will examine the historical development of PLAAF education and training programs, look at the features of current programs, assess the effectiveness of these programs, and consider how the programs are likely to evolve in the future. It will not attempt to assess sufficiency and quality of tactical or operational training. Rather, it will focus on the education and training structure and programs of the PLAAF.

Development and Evolution of PLAAF Training and Education

PLAAF education and training exist in a historical background that pre-dates the People's Republic of China (PRC) and the establishment of the nation's air force. In fact, China's earliest experience with aviation dates back to 1905, when Zhang Zhidong (张之洞), the governor of Guangdong-Guangxi and Hubei-Hunan Provinces, imported two Japanese reconnaissance balloons to set up China's first military aviation unit.[5] In March 1909, the Qing government sent a delegation to England and France to investigate European aircraft construction and flight technology. By August 1910 a Chinese team successfully assembled and tested an aircraft at Nanyuan, to the south of Beijing. The Qing government fell in 1911, leaving it up to its successor, the Beiyang government, to open China's first "aviation school for the development of army and naval aviation personnel and the institute for research and development of aircraft manufacturing technology," at Nanyuan Field in September 1913.[6]

The Nanyuan Aviation School (南苑航空学校) provided aviation academics as well as technical training. Academics included flight theory, mechanics, meteorology, military tactics and military history, and foreign languages. Technical instruction was primarily flight training, with supplemental training in engine installation and aircraft maintenance. The students were principally recruited from graduates of army schools. Initially, the curriculum was achieved during a year-long course that was divided into primary and advanced phases of flight training. Subsequently, the curriculum was extended to 2 years to incorporate instruction in reconnaissance, bombing, and air patrolling during the advanced training stages.

Nanyuan Aviation School operated 15 years and produced 158 aviators. These graduates became the backbone of the Nationalist Army's aviation units as well as other military forces operating in the provinces. By May 1928, the Beiyang government had fallen and the Nanyuan Aviation School was disbanded. Yet, the establishment of the Nanyuan Aviation School represented a significant step in China's endeavor toward aviation education; it ended China's complete reliance on foreign training and laid the foundation for what would eventually develop as the PLAAF's aviation and military education programs. Nanyuan not only produced a group of Chinese pilots and flight mechanics, it also provided China with a significant source of experience in the conduct of flight instruction as well as aircraft production, repair, and logistical support. The military significance of aviation was not lost on the provincial warlords during this turbulent period in Chinese history and additional flying schools and units were eventually established by the Northeast, Guangdong, Guangxi, Sichuan, and Yunnan armies. Of particular note was the early lead taken in China's Northeast and in Guangdong to establish schools to support military flight training and aircraft maintenance.

In 1920, 10 of Nanyuan Aviation School's aircraft along with support equipment and personnel were dispatched to Fengtian, Shenyang Province, to establish a military aviation training base in the Northeast. On April 1, 1921, Northeast Flight Division (东三省航空处) was established, with the standup of the Northeast Aviation School at Dongta Airfield coming a year later in September 1922.[7] The new school conducted a 2 to 2-1/2 year curriculum stressing flight technology with courses in aircraft manufacturing, aircraft engines, aviation, aeronautics, and meteorology. In order to accelerate the pace of development, Zhang Xueliang sent three groups of faculty abroad to France and Japan to pursue advanced studies in flight techniques, tactics, and aviation equipment, as well as obtaining expertise on tactical theory, air reconnaissance, air combat, and aerial bombardment. In July 1930, the Northeast Aviation Headquarters Department selected 16 cadres to form an air command training class, thus establishing the first air tactics training course in China.[8]

Early steps were also undertaken to promote military aviation in southern China. In November 1911, the Guangdong Military Government established a military flying unit under the direction of Feng Ru, an aviation pioneer who returned to China after receiving flight training in the United States.[9] Although Feng's career was cut short—he died while staging a flight demonstration over Guangzhou in 1912—his legacy lived on as flight operations continued to develop in China's south and President Sun Yat-sen ultimately turned to military aviation to help establish control over the divided nation. In 1924, President Sun established the Guangdong Military Aviation School (广东军事飞机学校) under the Aviation Bureau of the Nationalist Government.[10] The Guangdong school offered curriculum for both aviators and aircraft mechanics. The flying course included instruction in flight theory, aeronautics, aviation mechanics, meteorology, wireless communications, cartography, politics, and music, while providing foundational, intermediate, and advanced flight training. The aviation mechanics curriculum stressed engine, aircraft, and equipment maintenance.

The first class of the Guangdong Military Aviation School entered in the fall of 1924 and graduated the next fall after completing the 1-year course. The actual flight training for this class was relatively limited because the faculty and aircraft were frequently transferred to the war efforts. In order to accelerate personnel development, in August 1925 the Guangdong Military Government sent an initial group of six Chinese exchange students to the Soviet Union to study aviation and aviation technology. In June 1926 and February 1927, the government sent additional student groups to Russia for flight training and coursework in aviation engineering.[11] Altogether, the former Soviet Union trained 37 Guangdong students, including 24 pilots, 8 aviation mechanics, and 5 others in related studies.[12]

In December 1928, after the Nationalist Government had largely consolidated its power over China, it established the Aviation Bureau (航空署) under the Ministry of War (军政部) and set up the Aviation Section within the Central Army Officer School to conduct flight training and develop aviation personnel. In April 1929, the Nationalist forces established separate army, navy, and air force commands, with an air headquarters that signified its status as an independent branch.

By 1936, the Nationalist Chinese Air Force had established nine air groups, five directly subordinate squadrons, and four air transports units, with 314 fighter aircraft and over 300 air transport and trainer aircraft, operated by 620 aviators flying from 262 airfields.[13] To accelerate development of personnel, the Nationalist Air Force set up an Air Force Officer School, Air Force Mechanics School, Air Force Air Defense School, Air Force Noncommissioned Officer School, Air Force Youth School, Air Force Communications School, and Air Force Staff School, as well as several additional training courses for specialized technical personnel. Although these schools were hastily set up in a war-torn China—with rudimentary equipment, inferior facilities, evolving courseware, and frequent relocations—confronting Japanese occupation forces, these schools nevertheless produced large groups of trained personnel in a variety of specialties.

Underacknowledged in PLA renderings of their historical development is the significant boost Chinese military aviation programs received from Soviet and U.S. military aid from the 1930s through the 1940s. Although the assistance was directed primarily toward building up the Chinese Nationalist air forces of Chiang Kai-shek, arguably these efforts ultimately laid the foundation for the PLAAF's development after Nationalist forces departed mainland China in 1949. For example, between 1937 and June 1941, the Soviet Union supplied China with 900 military aircraft and 31,600 aerial bombs.[14] During that same period, 1937–1940, the United States supplied China with 279 military aircraft.[15] Although the Soviets ceased military aid in 1941, U.S. aid continued and by the end of World War II, the United States had supplied China with nearly 1,400 combat and transport aircraft and trained over 1,300 aviators and 320 aviation technicians.[16]

Although the PLAAF was not formally established until 1949, after the Chinese Communist Party fully consolidated its control over the Chinese mainland, the earliest foundations of the PLAAF's education and training programs began shortly following the termination of World War II. Upon Japan's surrender on August 15, 1945, the Central Committee of the Chinese Communist Party (CCP) sent personnel to Jilin Province in China's northeast to take possession of the Japanese aviation materials and set up an aviation school at Tonghua Field. In March 1946, the CCP's Northeast Field Army formally announced the establishment of the Aviation School of the Northeast Democratic United Army (东北民主联军航空学校) and began training aviators.[17] This was the first aviation school established under the authority of the CCP and it served as the initial foundation for the PLAAF military education system. In

March 1949, the school relocated to Changchun and the name was officially changed to the Chinese People's Liberation Army Aviation School. The Changchun school closed in December 1949, after graduating 560 personnel, including 126 pilots, 322 technicians, 26 navigators, and 88 airfield operations and communications staff.[18]

Formally established in 1949, the PLAAF was thrown immediately into battle conducting air operations in the Korean War, defending the nation's air space, and suppressing rebellions in the west. This forced the PLAAF to develop its education policies, procedures, and operational training programs while fighting. In February 1951, it was formally announced at the conclusion of an expanded meeting of the air force party committee that "Air Force construction was to be based on the Army" (在陆军基础上建设空军).[19] In addition to adopting the "structure and fine traditions of the Army," this declaration also reaffirmed the commitment to Marxist-Leninist ideals and Mao Zedong thought.

Following the formal establishment of the PLAAF in November 1949, the PLAAF successively set up seven aviation schools—numbered simply as the 1st through the 7th Aviation Schools—adopting accelerated training programs for air service (空勤) and ground support (地勤) personnel. These seven schools represented the PLAAF's initial steps at establishing an air force military education and training structure, and provided the basis for subsequent regularization of the PLAAF. Within a few years, over 20 schools were hastily set up, graduating over 31,300 aviators and ground personnel prior to China's entry into the Korean War.[20]

On September 15, 1950, following the eruption of the Korean War, the PLAAF Party Committee quickly established a Volunteer Army Air Force.[21] At the time, many of the aviation units were transitioning to new aircraft and had not yet fully completed training in basic flying skills or combat skills. In order to speed up the technical and tactical training of the forces, the PLAAF Party Committee adopted the principle of "study warfare through warfare"(从战争中学习战争), a term that continues to resonate with the PLA during national emergencies.[22] The PLAAF set upon applying this dictum to develop military education and training programs that would speed the building of aviation and maintenance skills. In other words, the PLAAF's focus was on operational expediency to the exclusion of other longer term development needs during this early stage of PLAAF growth.

After the termination of the Korean War, the PLAAF Party Committee's focus shifted to regularization and modernization of the forces. This new stress on education and training led to the establishment of specialized schools for each professional specialty. By the mid-1960s the PLAAF had set up schools and academies for the command, political, logistics, weather, communications, navigation, surface-to-air missile (SAM), and health fields. Additionally, the service established advanced air defense schools for air defense artillery and radar.

The period of the Cultural Revolution between 1966 and 1976 was particularly turbulent for PLA schools with serious disruptions in military education and training. Large numbers of PLAAF schools simply closed and disbanded classes. The PLAAF education infrastructure collapsed with losses in experienced teaching staff, collapses in academic standards, cutbacks in curricula, and an overall erosion of teaching capacity. This 10-year period was a major setback for the academic program development, nullifying the progress that had been achieved during the first 15 years of PLAAF history.[23]

In 1978, based on guidance promulgated by the CMC, the PLAAF entered a new era of educational development with the reconstitution of a large number of schools that had been disbanded during the Cultural Revolution.[24] At this juncture, in order to speed up personnel development, the PLAAF resolved to selectively develop education and training curriculum based on the particular needs of individuals and various training responsibilities and targets of the units and schools. Military units were to primarily support doctrine education in professional knowledge, operational knowledge and military psychology, military hygiene, and foreign military studies; schools were responsible for determining curriculum content based on the educational development objectives. For example, education in command academies and schools primarily covers the principles of military theory and the foundations of organizational command. Within these schools, entry-level command schools are responsible for comprehensive and systematic military foundational education, mid-level command schools engage in advanced studies education, and senior-level command schools conduct comprehensive education at high levels. Education at professional technical academies and schools is primarily basic systems theory, professional theory, and professional technical training. These reforms in educational methods and content, along with improved management, are credited with enhancing the capability of military education programs to meet the PLAAF's development needs.

In June 1986, in response to the CMC's promulgation of the "Resolution Concerning Military Educational Reform," PLAAF military education took further steps to rationalize its training structure, reform training content, and improve conditions and standards, through the adoption of multilevel, multichannel personnel development. To accomplish this goal, seven of the PLAAF academies—Air Force Engineering Academy, Surface-to-Air Missile (SAM) Academy, Weather Academy, Command Academy, Political Academy, Radar Academy, and Communications Academy—began offering master's studies, moving these schools beyond run-of-the-mill to more modernized educational institutions offering advanced technical degrees. The development of PLAAF advanced studies programs represents a significant milestone in the development of the education and training system, providing the PLAAF with the capability to develop personnel with higher competencies in professional and technical areas.

During the 1980s, in order to improve the caliber and capability of its aviation personnel, the PLAAF raised aviation training standards, requiring aviators to attain higher education (高等教育). Subsequently, in the 1990s, the PLAAF education and training programs entered a stage of "planned overall development," whereupon academies and schools established new personnel development goals, restructured curricula, and specialized training programs. Regarding officer personnel, emphasis was placed on recruiting college graduates with baccalaureate degrees, strengthening graduate-level research programs, and developing high-caliber military commanders and technical staff.[25] The 1990s also represented a period in which the PLAAF invested considerable resources toward the rethinking of its strategic vision and air doctrine, while simultaneously introducing new, advanced weapons into the force.

Today's In-service Education and Technical Training

> PLAAF military education emphasizes integration of systematic and specialized, stressing the promotion of personnel development based on PLAAF development needs. Basic level command schools emphasize the complete development of student technical skills and knowledge, promoting military specialty education with particular stress on foundational theory, knowledge, and skills for the specialty. Mid-level command schools promote occupational education, stressing essential education and innovative abilities to develop suitable command talents.[26]

Historically, PLAAF education and training programs have focused on providing military job skills training and this remains true today, although there is evidence that PLAAF is committed to broadening the educational experiences of its officers and NCOs. The quote above, from the 2007 publication *The Science of Air Force Military Education and Training*, stresses that the emphasis is on "development based on PLAAF development needs" and "development of student technical skills and knowledge, promoting military specialty education." This principle reflects the operational and developmental considerations of a service that was born during the Korean War, when the urgent task was to recruit young men with enough education to rapidly assimilate the training before launching off to war. PLAAF military schools continue in this tradition today—although new programs encouraging broader and deeper levels of academic education are beginning to emerge.

Officer Education and Training

Air forces are unique among the military services in that it is the officers who do the fighting and therefore the bulk of the education and training focus is aimed at their development and proficiency. This axiom holds especially true in the PLAAF because technical officers continue to play a critical hands-on role in the maintenance and repair of aircraft and other weapons systems. Consequently, PLAAF education and training programs are principally focused on officer development across all branches and specialties and secondarily aimed at raising the skill levels of NCOs.[27] Airmen, on the other hand, may only receive rudimentary training while serving in their first 2-year enlistment, as they are essentially on probationary status awaiting determination of their suitability for potential development into NCOs or officers.[28]

As with other air forces, the PLAAF has established a comprehensive military education structure which focuses on four common objectives: schools and institutes must strive to achieve compatibility between force development requirements, force composition and career specialties, and the categories of schools, training allocations, and levels of education and training; officer development capacity of air force schools and institutes must be balanced against and consistent with the requirements of peacetime replacement rates; division levels within the air force training structure must be consistent with officer development regulations; and, the structure must combine officer academic education with military specialty training and integrate pre-assignment coursework with post-assignment advanced studies.[29]

Estimates by Western PLA military experts suggest that the PLAAF commissions approximately 4,000–6,000 new officers each year, of whom approximately 1,000 are aviators.[30] Until recently, the PLAAF has relied on its own colleges and academies to educate and develop new officers (cadres), but that paradigm changed in May 2000 under a new policy document issued jointly by the State Council and the CMC entitled "Decision on Establishing a Military Cadre Training System that Relies on Civilian Higher Education [关于建立依托普通高等教育培养军队干部制度的决定]."[31] The "decision" was announced following an initial trial program conducted at 22 of China's top universities—including Beijing, Qinghua, and Fudan—beginning in 1999.[32] The new policy opened up three new commissioning channels to a civilian university inclined toward a national defense direction (国防定向). First, the new program permits the direct recruitment of university students for direct entry into one of the PLAAF military colleges. Second, it provides a path of direct accession to college graduates, although they may be required to complete a full year of military training prior to commissioning. And third, it established the National Defense Student (国防生) program which operates similarly to the Reserve Officers Training Corps (ROTC) in the United States.[33] The PLAAF has established National Defense Student programs on multiple campuses throughout China and detailed air force officers to the faculty to instruct military courses as part of the academic load. Additionally, National Defense Students participate in drills at assigned units during summer academic breaks. Following graduation, National Defense Students receive an additional 3 months of military skills training and political education prior to commissioning. Operating on the campuses of leading universities throughout China, this program has become a common gateway for many of today's new PLAAF officers.[34]

While the induction of civilian college graduates into the PLAAF represents a monumental adjustment to the military education and training structure, the PLAAF continues to rely on its own command academies and technical schools to recruit and develop over half of its new officers. These academies accept graduates of public high schools and qualified airmen from the ranks with high school equivalency–level education. Officer accession schools provide either a 3-year vocational education (任职教育) leading to a technical degree (专科) or 4-year academic education (学历教育) leading to an undergraduate degree (本科). Specialty programs have been established at the flight academies, the Guilin Air Force College, and the First Aviation Academy, developing officers for various air force branch specialties (aviation, communications, radar, SAM, etc.). The PLAAF Engineering University, the PLAAF Aviation University, and the Xuzhou Air Force Academy are 4-year institutions which confer undergraduate degrees. PLAAF Aviation University cadets receive an abbreviated academic curriculum that includes 30 months of academics, 6 months of aviation theory, and 12 months of basic flight training. Depending on the school and specialty, the PLAAF appoints graduates of 3-year and 4-year schools as either a commanding officer or technical officer, with some technical officers holding civilian rank (文职).[35] With the exception of aviators who receive their undergraduate education through the PLAAF Aviation University or civilian university before reporting to one of the flying academies, the foundational education for PLAAF officers in other career fields is normally completed through attendance at a single college or school.[36]

PLAAF command academies are organized into a three-level structure providing pre-accession education and training at the foundational level, and professional military education (PME) at the intermediate and senior levels.[37] Mid-level command colleges, such as the PLAAF Command College, are targeted at active duty officers who have attended a foundational command college and possess a senior technical degree or higher. The mid-level school curriculum varies from 6 months to 1 year and prepares graduates to perform work in operational, political, logistical, or equipment sections at the regimental and division levels. PME for senior air force officers is conducted through the National Defense University (NDU) for those who have completed a mid-level command course and possess a senior technical degree or higher. Graduates are prepared to assume responsibilities at Group Army– or Military Region–level command positions. In recent years, the PLAAF has gradually improved its PME courses through efforts to increase the contact and coordination between its faculty and operations. Air force officers—whether in operational, political, logistical, or equipment branches—are offered various opportunities for attendance at PME and graduate degree programs during their careers.[38]

The PLAAF graduate education program consists of master's candidates, Ph.D. candidates, and military specialty master's candidates, with programs lasting 2-1/2 years, 3 years, and 2 years, respectively. The graduate studies program is implemented to address the full spectrum of knowledge required within the service, and now includes programs in military professional studies.

In addition to the in-residence formal education programs offered to officers and NCOs, in 2008 the PLAAF established the Air Force Military Professional University, offering service personnel opportunities for study through correspondence courses, mini-courses, seminars, and study at civilian colleges. This new program appears to operate as a virtual university to promote the individual development of officers and NCOs in various career fields.

NCO Technical Training

With the emergence of the of NCO corps in 1998, the air force determined that the primary development focus for NCO schools was to be "professional theory knowledge and training in procedures and rules for the proper operation, employment and care of weapons and equipment."[39] In other words, NCO schools are focused on providing technical or occupational specialty training.

NCO education is conducted at special NCO schools and through special NCO programs conducted at the PLAAF officer academies. Qualified personnel with a high school or middle school equivalency education are enrolled in 2-year and 3-year academic programs that confer secondary or senior technical degrees as well as occupational specialty training. NCO education is characterized as occupational (specialty) training, aimed at developing entry-level technicians. NCO schools of all categories are founded on the principle of "promote suitability while furthering development" (突出 适应性, 兼顾 发展), indicating that there is a strong element of political education along with the development of technical skills.

The PLAAF has approximately 300,000 active duty personnel with as many as two-thirds of these serving in enlisted ranks. Of those, perhaps as many as one-quarter (50–60,000) are first-term recruits who are serving an initial 2-year term of service.[40] The PLAAF draws its recruits from both rural and urban residents, with varying entry requirements for each locale. China's military service law stipulates that rural recruits must have graduated from middle school (初中) while urban recruits must have graduated from high school (中学), a vocational high school (中专), or a 3-year technical college (大专), or be enrolled in a 4-year college (大学) to be eligible for enlistment.

Following a PLA-wide strategy to increase the quality of its recruits, the PLAAF is making efforts to increase its enlistment of college students by offering preferential treatment and other incentives. For example, the maximum age for female recruits with 4-year college education or higher has been lifted from 22 to 24, while the limit for female graduates with a 3-year education was raised from 21 to 23. In addition, the students-turned-soldiers are entitled to receive "a one-off refund of up to 24,000 yuan ($3,500) as compensation for college tuition fees or student loans."[41] In addition, candidates may be promised preference while seeking jobs at police and other law-enforcement departments. According to the *Global Times*, the PLA recruiting effort on Chinese college campuses may be producing desired effects in view of an oversaturated labor market that leaves as many as one-third of each year's 6 million graduates unable to find suitable jobs.[42]

Assessing the Effectiveness of Education and Training

> The key to strengthened national defense and military modernization is to foster and raise a large batch of high quality, new-model, talented military personnel, while vigorously increasing the ability to make innovations in science and technology. We must grasp these two requirements as the primary responsibility of the military academies, properly grasping the developing trends of modern technology and the developing patterns of military education, diligently pressing for military academies to successfully become the cradles for development of high quality, talented military personnel—the foundations of new high technology and military theory innovation.[43]

While the PLAAF aspires to set up educational infrastructures that "become the cradles for development of high-quality, talented military personnel," it remains to be seen whether the programs that are now being put into place will deliver the desired results. Accurately assessing the competency of PLAAF personnel has been and remains a difficult endeavor. The PLAAF has not been operationally tested since the Korean War, and it has been absent from

Chinese military interventions since the 1950s. The air force was never committed into battle during ground force skirmishes on Vietnam's border in the late 1970s. Since then, PLA operations have been limited to humanitarian relief efforts in response to flooding or earthquakes. In these instances, the PLAAF's limited airlift capacity has left it sidelined during the army-led operations. Nor has the PLAAF participated widely in United Nations peacekeeping missions, although the PLA is expanding its support of logistics and medical teams in Africa and Asia. And, the PLAAF has not established the type of bilateral training exercises with other regional air forces that would provide insights into the level and sophistication of its tactical forces. Although the PLAAF Command College has cracked opened its doors to foreign military students, these officers are segregated into a separate international seminar which limits their interaction with and exposure to Chinese field grade officers. Thus it is necessary to look for other proxies that can yield insights into the progress, professionalism, and operational capacity of the officers and airmen of the PLAAF.

Despite recent progress and increased accessions of graduates of civilian universities, the PLAAF may be a long way from reaching its education goals. The PLAAF has announced that improved officer education is a top priority and an enduring long-term goal. In fact, the PLAAF has set as a near-term goal to ensure all new officers attain a 4-year undergraduate degree prior to accession. In the mid-to-long term, the PLAAF hopes to build an officer corps in which 100 percent have undergraduate degrees and over 30 percent have advanced degrees. Additionally, the PLAAF intends to see that over 95 percent of commanding officers at the division, brigade, and regimental levels are equipped with basic degrees, with 80 percent or more having advanced degrees.[44] Yet, as late as 2009, fewer than 40 percent of officers leading the air force's front line units (空军应急机动作战部队) possessed an undergraduate degree and less than 1 percent of those commanders held a postgraduate degree.[45] This lack of credentials among PLAAF commanding officers may be explained by PLAAF restrictions placed on their course attendance. Senior command track officers—at the colonel and senior colonel level—are only authorized to attend a 1-year, nondegree PME program, while support and technical officers are afforded opportunities to pursue graduate degrees in multiyear programs at either PLAAF or civilian colleges.

Another measure of the professional development of the PLAAF is the volume and quality of military professional publications that are being developed by its officer corps. The PLA's airmen have published extensively during the past 10 years, oftentimes in the performance of directed research on key topics—strategy, doctrine, tactics, air force building, education and training, logistics, etc.— assigned by the PLAAF Headquarters. Officially developed publications are generally produced by a research team under the guidance of a senior officer and vetted through a formal review prior to publication. Top-level writings are endorsed by the PLAAF Commander or the Political Commissar, or both. In recent years, the PLAAF has written extensively on military education and training, and a listing of relevant recent publications can be found in the appendix.

Although the volume of PLAAF military writings is an important indication of the transformation that is taking place in PLAAF education and training, significant variations and gaps remain in both the substance and the operational concepts articulated by various authors and institutions. For example, *Science of Air Force Training* (空军军事训练学), published in 2006 under the guidance of Lieutenant General He Weirong, was the air force's contribution to a PLA series that includes separate volumes on army, navy, and joint training.[46] The book provides a comprehensive overview of the PLAAF training structure, laying out the hierarchy of training organizations, classifications of training, specific training responsibilities at various levels of command, and categorization of training methods. But, one must ask: what is the purpose and motivation behind this publication? And, who is the target audience? The publication lacks the authority of a service regulation or manual, and it does not include sufficient detail to either develop or execute training programs. In effect, the *Science of Military Training* series serves only as a primer on PLAAF service training programs and infrastructure, and therefore may be an indication that the PLAAF (and the PLA) are still at a very early stage of revamping military training programs.

Yet another indicator of professional development within the PLA—and by extension within the PLAAF—is the well-defined process for compilation, review, and validation of training standards. The PLA has demonstrated a consistent pattern of managing operational training as it has twice revised and promulgated new *Outlines for Military Training and Evaluation* (OMTE) within the past 10 years. The most recent effort was undertaken beginning in 2006 to correct recognized training deficiencies in the 2002 version of the OMTE. From initial review in December 2006 through promulgation in July 2008 and implementation in 2009, the OMTE development and review process took slightly over 2 years to complete. As the event sequence and timelines in table 10-1 demonstrate, the procedures and deadlines for the development of the 2009 OMTE followed a pattern of development similar to the previous OMTE revision cycle that ran from January 2000 and October 2001.

Field units played a substantially greater role in the initial development of the 2008 OMTE. Standards development and field testing were carried out during the 2007 and 2008 annual training cycles with 163 division- and brigade-level units participating in the trial training and validation of the 2008

OMTE.⁴⁷ The 2-year process of revision, experimental training, and validation was a PLA-wide effort that included participants from each of the seven military regions, the PLA Navy, the PLA Air Force, Second Artillery, People's Armed Police, and 21 departments within the four General Headquarters.⁴⁸

The new OMTE was designed to address the training shortfalls that have repeatedly been cited in *Kongjun Bao* and other PLA newspapers, including expanded training for noncombat military operations; increased proportion of informatized knowledge skills and simulated training with high-technology weapons and equipment, including aircraft; standardized methods, procedures, and criteria for network-centric and "opposing force" training; clarified conditions, styles, methods, and requirements for training in complex electromagnetic environments, training at night, and training under adverse weather conditions; established capabilities-based training standards and assessment system; raised standards for basic training; expanded scope of training appraisals; revised evaluation program; and defined training management scheme, specified duties, and functions of training.

Table 10–1. Outlines for Military Training and Evaluation (OMTE) Revision Process and Timelines

Event	2001 OMTE	2008 OMTE
New Operational Tiaoling	September 1999	March 2008
OMTE Drafting Guidance Complete	January 2000	December 2006
Revision, Experimental Training, and Validation OMTE	February 2000–July 2001	January 2007–June 2008
Promulgation	October 2001	July 2008
Transition Phase	October–December 2001	August–December 2008
Implementation	January 1, 2002	January 1, 2009
Key Objectives	Scientific, combat realism, efficiency, effectiveness, realism, new standards for new high-tech weapons	Informatized conditions joint and complex electromagnetic environments, noncombat actions

Sources:
— "Jiang Zemin Signs 13 Operational Rules for Military," *Xinhua* in English January 24, 1999
— "CMC Promulgates New Operation Regulation," *Ming Pao* in Chinese September 10, 1999, A19.
— Military People Destined for Victory: Our Army's Fifth Generation Operations Regulation Just Promulgated" [军人生来为战胜: 我军第五代作战条令正在报批], Peoplenet March 23, 2008, accessed April 29, 2009, available at <http://military.people.com.cn/GB/7032628.html>.
— "Trial Training by 'Military Training and Checkout Outline,'" April 17, 2008.
— "Training Class on New MTEPs Held Recently at Location of an Unidentified Group Army," *Qianwei Bao*, October 21, 2001.
— "Details on the New PLA OMTE: Establishes New System of Informatized Military Operations" [解读解放军新大纲: 构建信息化军事作战新体系] *Chinanews Online* in Chinese, August 1, 2008, available at <www.chinanews.com.cn/gn/news/2008/08-01/1332272.shtml>, accessed July 1, 2009.
— "PRC Officers Discuss Training Outline Reform," *Jiefangjun Bao* (Internet Version) in Chinese August 15, 2000, 6.

Summarizing Developments in PLAAF Training

Education and training are clearly at the forefront of the PLA drive toward comprehensive force modernization that has been underway for nearly 30 years. Since the early 1980s, Chinese leaders have recognized a need to build "regularized" (正规化) military forces better able to respond in China's evolving security environment.[49] To that end, the leaders of China's air force have undertaken a series of steps to build a more professional, competent, and capable air force.

The PLAAF regards officer professional development a cornerstone of its force modernization program, a viewpoint consistent with the goals of three generations of CMC chairmen. Beginning with Deng Xiaoping in the 1980s, the chairmen of the CMC have stressed the strategic requirement to build "a young and knowledgeable, revolutionized and professionalized officer contingent."[50] In the 1990s, then-CMC Chairman Jiang Zemin expressly pointed out that unless the PLA emphasized professional development as a strategic mission, it would be "impossible to build a modernized army and defeat enemies having high-tech advantages."[51] Under Hu Jintao, the PLA is continuing to pursue professional development "centered on enhancing competence and integrating training and employment" through a pattern of "connected academic education and military training, parallel development of military education and national education, and the combination of domestic cultivation and overseas training, so as to effectively develop and make a full use of the human resources of the military."[52]

The PLAAF's transition toward improved education and training is being driven by overarching guidance from the CMC and shaped by a recognized need for a new generation of operators and support personnel with vastly greater knowledge and skills to employ and manage weapons systems of increasing technical complexity. Although the PLAAF has made substantial progress in recent years, it has not yet achieved the development goals it seeks for officers and NCOs. In particular, increased academic education for air force officers remains a priority, and it appears that PLAAF academies will move from military specialty training programs to course work focus on formal academics. As the air force continues on this development path, it can be expected that future officers will be universally educated at the university level, adept in the employment of modern technologies, and competent in multiservice joint operations.

As the PLAAF evolves to address the demands of integrated joint operations, greater demands will be placed on the officer corps, further raising the requirements for professional military education and training. These changes are also certain to create pressure to expand the authorities and responsibilities of air force NCOs, who will be required to take on greater responsibilities in the more demanding joint environment. Going forward, it can be expected that along with the reform and development of PLAAF colleges and schools, the development of mid- and senior-level NCO curriculum and training programs will be a primary focus, with education and training for junior ranks remaining a goal for the future.

Appendix: Recent PLAAF Publications

These titles are offered as evidence of the surge in air-relevant publications within the past several years. Many of these titles may be for internal distribution only and thus unavailable to the general public.[53]

Reference Books (参考书)

Air Force Development Strategy to 2020 (2020年前空军发展战略)
Chinese Air Force Encyclopedia (中国空军百科全书)
Deng Xiaoping's Thoughts on Air Force Building [邓小平空军建设思想研究]
The History of Air Force Academic Thought (空军学术思想史)
In Depth Research on Air Force Transformation (空军转型建设深化研究)
An Introduction to PLAAF Military Thought (空军军事思想概论)
Jiang Zemin's Thoughts on National Defense and Army Building and the PLAAF (江泽民国防和军队建设思想与人民空军)
Mao's Military Thought and Contemporary Air Operations (毛泽东军事思想与现在空军作战)
Military Terminology of the PLAAF (中国解放军空军军语)
Philosophical Underpinnings of Scientific Development Concepts (科学发展观的哲学底蕴)
The PLAAF at the Beginning of the 21st Century (21世纪初期人民空军)
Science of Air Force Political Works (空军政治工作学)
Science of Air Force Strategy (空军战略学)
The Science of Flight Analysis (飞行诊治工作学)
Scientific Development Concepts and the Political Development of Military Thought (科学发展观与军队思想政治建设)
Theory Treatises (理论专著)
World Air Force History (世界空军史)

Teaching Materials (教材)

Air Force Aviation Equipment Management (空军航空兵装备管理)
Air Force Political Works for Flight Training (空军飞行训练政治工作)
Air Strategy Curriculum (空军战略教程)
Introduction to Jiang Zemin's Thoughts on National Defense and Army Building (江泽民国防和军队建设思想概论)
Lectures on Our Nation's Air Strategy (我国空军战略讲义)
Methods of Leadership and Leadership Thought (思想方法与领导方法)
The Party and Innovation Theory: Special Study (党的创新理论与实践专题研究)
Political Works for a New Era Air Force (新时期空军政治工作研究)
Science of Air Campaign Logistics (空军战役后勤学)
Science of Air Force Logistics (空军后勤学)
The Science of Air Force Operational Logistics (空军作战运筹学)
Science of Air Force Training (空军军事训练学)
The Science of Air Tactics (空军战术学)
The Science of Commanding Air Operations (空军作战指挥学)

Selected Research by Air Force Personnel—Volumes 1 through 4 (空军人才研究成果选编 (第一至四辑))
Space Operations (空天作战概要)

Research Reports and Major Topics (研究报告和主要题目)

Building Foundational Training for a New Era Air Force (关于空军新时期打基础训练问题的研究)
Cultural Development for a Modernized Strategic Air Force (现代化战略空军文化建设研究)
Preliminary Concepts for Right-sizing the Air Force Training Structure (理顺 空军训练体制的初步设想)
Steps to Hasten the Cultivation of Women Cosmonauts (加快培养女航天员步伐)
Strategic Concepts for the Major Issues for Transforming our National Air Defense (我国防空 转型建设若干 重大问题的战略构想)
Suggestions on Establishing a Pilot Reserve System (建立飞行员预备役制度的建议)
Suggestions to Rapidly Elevate the PLAAF's Ability to Win a Limited Air and Space Integrated Battle (加速提高空军打赢有限空天一体战能力的建议)
Suggestions on Reforming the PLAAF AAA Reserve Division Leadership Structure (改革空军高炮预备役师领导体制的建议)
Thoughts on Five Breakthroughs in Air Force Military Training (对空军军事训练 五个突破 的思想)

Notes

[1] The views and opinions expressed in this paper are solely those of the author and do not necessarily reflect the views of Alion Science & Technology, Inc., the Department of Defense, or the U.S. Government.

[2] "Air force building" [空军建设] is defined as "the organization of forces and those measures adopted and actions taken to increase the combat power, including active duty and reserve forces."

[3] *China's National Defense in 2008, Section VI The Air Force* (Beijing: Information Office of the State Council of the People's Republic of China, January 2009).

[4] Zhong Xun, "The Strategic Policy Decision for Invigorating Military Training and Strengthening the Army in the New Period of the New Century—On the Scientific Connotations and Epoch-Making Significance of Transforming Military Training," *PLA Daily*, November 28, 2006, at <http://news.xinhuanet.com/mil/2006-11/28/content_5399475.htm>, accessed September 27, 2010.

[5] Zhang Yanbing [张彦冰], *The Science of Air Force Military Education and Training* [空军军事教育训练学] (Beijing: Blue Sky Publishing [蓝天出版社], 2007), 15.

[6] Ibid.

[7] Ibid., 17. Northeast Aviation School is also known as Dongta Aviation School.

[8] Ibid.

[9] Ibid. While Feng Ru is unknown in the United States, in China his fame is equivalent to the Wright brothers. Middle and high schools are named in his honor, and his childhood home is a museum. China even considers its space program to be based upon the foundations of Feng's work.

[10] Ibid. Sun Yat-sen's government adopted the slogan 航空救国 [*Hangkong jiuguo*] during this period of war with Japan. Although the school's official name was 广东军事飞机学校 [Guangdong Military Aircraft School], the school was commonly referred to as the Guangdong Military Aviation School [广东军事航空学校].

[11] Ibid., 18.

[12] Ibid.

[13] Shang Jinsuo [尚金锁], *Science of Air Force Construction* [空军建设学] (Beijing: PLAAF Command College Press, 2009), 81.

[14] Yu Maochun, *The Dragon's War: Allied Operations and the Fate of China 1937–1947* (Annapolis, MD: Naval Institute Press, 2008), 194.

[15] Xu Guangqiu, "The Issue of US Air Support for China during the Second World War, 1942–1945," *Journal of Contemporary History* 36, no. 3 (July 2001), 464–465.

[16] Ibid., 465.

[17] Liu Zhejun [刘哲君], 东北民主联军航空学校, posted November 28, 2008, accessed September 18, 2010, at <http://military.people.com.cn/GB/8221/71065/137783/139906/139912/8430886.html>. The school was colloquially known as the Northeast Aviation School [东北老航空校, Dongbei Lao Hangxiao].

[18] Ibid.

[19] Shang, *Science of Air Force Construction*, 82.

[20] Zhang Gang [张刚], "PLAAF Preliminarily Achievement of Five Major System Crossovers" [人民空军初步实现五大体系跨越], November 4, 2009, accessed September 18, 2010, at <http://mil.nen.com.cn/military/314/3379814.shtml>.

[21] Fierce Sino-US Battles in Skies over Korea: Volunteer Army Air Force Creates Air Combat Miracle [朝鲜上空的中美激战：志愿军空军创造空战奇迹], March 12, 2009, accessed September 18, 2010, at <http://military.china.com/zh_cn/dljl/kmyc/01/11043607/20090312/15369499.html>.

[22] "Study Warfare through Warfare—The 35 Lessons Learned from the Mass Response to Earthquake Recovery" [从"战争"中学习战争—关于抗震救灾部队群众性总结经验活动的35条笔记], a reprint from the *PLA Daily*, August 26, 2008, accessed September 16, 2010, at <http://military.people.com.cn/GB/1076/52984/7731007.html>.

[23] Lonnie D. Henley, "Officer Education in the Chinese PLA," *Problems of Communism* 36, no. 3 (May-June 1987), 70–71.

[24] In 1978, the CMC promulgated "Resolution Concerning the Strengthening Military Education and Training" [关于加强部队教育训练的决定] providing new guidelines on education and training programs. See <http://news.xinhuanet.com/mil/2008-12/25/content_10556112.htm>, accessed September 17, 2010.

[25] Zhang, *Science of Air Force Military Education*, 25.

[26] Ibid., 66 (translated by author).

[27] Ibid., 58–60.

[28] Dennis J. Blasko, "PLA Conscript and Noncommissioned Officer Individual Training," in Roy Kamphausen, Andrew Scobell, and Travis Tanner, *The "People" in the PLA: Recruitment, Education, and Training in China's Military* (Carlisle Barracks, PA: U.S. Army War College Strategic Studies Institute, 2008), 104. Estimate based on numbers provided by this article and estimated strength and composition of PLAAF force structure which has not been officially published by the PRC.

[29] Zhang, *Science of Air Force Military Education*, 64–65.

[30] John Corbett, Edward O'Dowd, and David Chen, "Building the Fighting Strength: PLA Officer Accession, Education, Training, and Utilization," in Kamphausen, Scobell, and Tanner, eds., *The "People" in the PLA*, 141–144. Corbett et al., estimated that the PLA commissions 29,000 new officers annually to sustain an officer corps for a total end-strength military force of 2.3 million. With an estimated total force size of 300,000, the PLAAF's proportional share of new officer accessions would be 4,000–5,000 per year.

[31] "PRC Military Official on Cadre Recruitment," *Xinhua Domestic News Service*, June 23, 2000, in *Foreign Broadcast Information Service* (FBIS)-CPP20000623000046.

[32] Zhang, *Science of Air Force Military Education*, 70.

[33] Corbett et al., "Building Fighting Strength," 141–144.

[34] Ibid.

[35] Ibid., 141–142, 147–153.

[36] Zhang, *Science of Air Force Military Education*, 58.

[37] The PLAAF also provides other avenues of entry into the officer ranks. Some recruits are offered the option of a participating in a "2+2" program in which they complete 2 years at a civilian followed by 2 years at an academy. See Corbett et al., "Building Fighting Strength," 151–153.

[38] PLAAF professional technical colleges and schools support a two-level—mid- and high-level—education structure that offers five levels of degrees, including middle technical degrees (中专), senior technical degrees (大专), baccalaureate degrees (本科), master's degree (硕士), and doctoral (博士).

[39] Zhang, *Science of Air Force Military Education*, 26.

[40] Dennis J. Blasko, "PLA Conscript and Noncommissioned Officer Individual Training," in Kamphausen et al., *The "People" in the PLA*, 104. Estimate based on numbers provided by this article and estimated strength and composition of PLAAF force structure which has not been officially published by the PRC.

⁴¹ Guo Qiang, "PLA Lures Talent with Incentives," *Global Times* [Huanqiu Shibao], November 2, 2009.

⁴² Ibid.

⁴³ Jiang Zemin, speaking September. 1, 2003, at the National University of Defense Technology, upon the 50th anniversary of its founding.

⁴⁴ Shang, *Science of Air Force Construction*, 442–443.

⁴⁵ *Strategic Air Force* [战略空军论] (Beijing: Blue Sky Publishing [蓝天出版社], 2009), 98.

⁴⁶ He Weirong, ed., *Science of Air Force Training* [空军军事训练学] (Beijing: Academy of Military Science Press, 2006). The senior editor for this publication was a strong advocate for training reforms during his tenure as both a deputy chief of staff and a deputy commander of the air force. The book was actually prepared by a research team led by the Training Instruction and Research Office of the PLA Air Force Command College.

⁴⁷ Liu Fengan and Wu Tianmin, "New Generation Outline of Military Training and Evaluation Promulgated" [新一代《军事训练与考核大纲》颁发], *Jiefangjun Bao* [Internet Version-WWW], July 24, 2008, available at <www.chinamil.com.cn/site1/2008b/2008-07/25/content_1378924.htm>.

⁴⁸ Ibid.

⁴⁹ Deng Xiaoping, "Build Powerful, Modern, and Regularized Revolutionary Armed Forces" in *The Selected Works of Deng Xiaoping* (Beijing: Foreign Languages Press, 1984), 372–373. "Regularization" is a distinctively Chinese term that is understood to embody the creation of a rational set of capacities, institutions, and directions that will create an armed force which will be based on and emphasize standardization, systemization, and the scientific process.

⁵⁰ Hong Hengwu, Gu Zhenjun, and Zhang Gugu, "Roundup of Officer Contingent and Military Talent Building of PLA (I)," *Jiefangjun Bao* (Internet Version) in English, January 6, 2009.

⁵¹ Ibid.

⁵² Ibid.

⁵³ Zhang, *Science of Air Force Military Education*, 6–7. Publication details were not provided for this list of reference materials. While some of the tiles can be found through Internet search, many cannot be found, indicating that these references may be internal military publications and not publicly available.

PART IV
INDUSTRIES AND MILITARY IMPLICATIONS

Chapter 11

China's Aviation Industry: Past, Present, and Future

Shen Pin-Luen

China's aviation industry has been plagued by problems of inefficiency, redundant leadership, and overlapping organizational and bureaucratic structures. In a closed system that had a planned economy and prioritized military development, such problems would not create much of an impact. But along with the inception of reform and opening-up and People's Liberation Army (PLA) modernization, problems in China's outdated aviation industry began to surface, prompting the People's Republic of China (PRC) leadership to initiate a series of reforms. In January 2006, the PRC State Council released the *National Guideline on Medium and Long-term Program for Science and Technology Development (2006–2020),* which listed the development of large aircraft as a key national science and technology project.[1] In May 2008, China established the Commercial Aircraft Corporation of China, Ltd. (COMAC), and in November 2008, China merged China Aviation Industry Corporation I (AVIC I) and China Aviation Industry Corporation II (AVIC II) to found China Aviation Industry Corporation (AVIC). This overhaul of the aviation sector is an indication that the pace of development and reform in China's aviation industry is picking up. Therefore, China's determination and injection of resources into the industry should not be underestimated by the outside world.

Due to the complexity of the development of China's aviation industry and China's tight control, most of the public information about the sector is general in nature and gives only an overview and the objectives of the industry. Truly useful analysis and documentation are rare. Therefore, this article seeks to provide a relatively objective and comprehensive analysis of the issue based on available information and personal observations.

The System of China's Aviation Industry: Evolution and Revolution

The origin of China's aviation industry can be traced back to April 18, 1951, when China established the Bureau of Aviation Industry under the Ministry of Heavy Industry for the purpose of maintaining military aircraft. In other words, China's aviation industry started from military applications. At the end of December 1953, the former Soviet Union transferred manufacturing technology for the Yak–18 trainer (including engine) to China, along with complete technical information and prototypes. In July 1954, the Yak–18 trainer was assembled successfully at China Nanchang Aircraft Manufacturing Corporation (CNAMC) under the designation CJ–5. In October of the same year, the former Soviet Union transferred manufacturing technology for the production of MiG–17 fighters to China. In September 1956, Shenyang Aircraft Corporation assembled the MiG–17 fighter successfully, which the PRC named the J–5. These two types of aircraft are milestones in the development of China's aviation industry. On June 4, 1965, the Q–5 attack aircraft, a variant of the later J–6 that CNAMC produced from copying the MiG–19, made its maiden flight. Mass production of the Q–5 began in 1969. The Q–5 can be regarded as the first military jet developed and manufactured by China.

China's Bureau of Aviation Industry was reorganized successively into the Third Ministry of Mechanical Industry (1960–1982), the Aviation Ministry of Industry (1982–1988), and the Aviation and Astronautic Ministry of Industry (1988–1993). Starting in 1993, China ushered in three waves of organizational transformation in its aviation industry.

The first wave began in 1993, when the PRC restructured the defense industries under its direct administration into large, state-owned enterprise groups including China National Nuclear Corporation, China Aerospace Corporation (CASC), China Aviation Industry Corporation (CAIC), China Shipbuilding Corporation, and China Ordnance Industry Corporation. CASC and CAIC were incorporated by splitting the Ministry of Aerospace Industry. It was hoped that through an enterprise-oriented structure, the industry's manufacture, research and development (R&D), maintenance, and sales could be integrated and better managed so as to enhance its operation and productivity, and the industry could be run and developed from the perspective of enterprise management.

The second wave began in 1998 when China abolished the Commission of Science, Technology, and Industry for National Defense (COSTIND), which was set up by the PLA in 1982, and created in its place an institution of the same name directly under the State Council. The new COSTIND's main duties were to supervise production of military products and development of defense industry; study and formulate policies, regulations, and laws on the conversion of military technologies and products to civilian use; and administer biddings from defense firms. In the same year, the PLA formed the General Armament Department (GAD) to assume the procurement function of the former COSTIND, and integrate equipment-related offices within the General Staff and General Logistics systems and some procurement units under the General Logistics Department. The GAD is responsible for defense procurement, life-cycle management of weapons, and maintenance of the weapons research and testing base of the PLA.

In 1999, China divided each of the big five military conglomerates into two independent companies, forming 10 major defense science and technology groups. In 2002, China created China Electronics Technology Group Corporation (CETC) as the 11th large military enterprise group.[2] One of the reconstruction efforts is to split CASC into AVIC I and AVIC II.

It was out of this climate that China embarked on its third wave of defense industrial organizational reform. China's 2006 defense white paper outlines the development direction of its defense industry and the focuses on "consolidating its foundation, making independent innovation, and speeding up the implementation of the strategy of transition and upgrading, so as to ensure the production and supply of military equipment and promote the development of national economy."[3] In September 2007, COSTIND, the State Development and Reform Commission (NDRC), and State-owned Assets Supervision and Administration Commission (SASAC) jointly issued the "Guiding Opinions on Promoting the Transformation of Defense Industries into Joint-Stock Enterprises."

This document encourages military enterprises to implement shareholding system reform and structural transformation, while making full use of civilian strengths in national defense building.[4] In October of the same year, Hu Jintao revealed in his report to the 17th National Congress of the Communist Party of China (CPC) that the country should "adjust and reform the systems of defense-related science, technology and industry and of weapons and equipment procurement," and "establish a sound system of weapons and equipment research and manufacture that integrate[s] military with civilian purposes and combine[s] military efforts with civilian support."[5] These developments indicated that to facilitate military modernization, China was paving the way for the third wave of reform of the defense industry.

On April 1, 2008, China established a new state agency, the Ministry of Industry and Information Technology (MIIT), and reorganized COSTIND into the State Administration of Science, Technology, and Industry for National Defense (SASTIND), which is subordinate to the MIIT. The MIIT assumed authority to oversee the 11 major military-industrial enterprise groups originally under COSTIND, basically achieving unified management over the military and civilian industries.

With regard to the aviation industry, AVIC I and AVIC II were set up with the goal of fostering internal competition and undertaking international outsourcing business as original equipment manufacturers (OEMs). The two conglomerates produce different lines of products to reduce overlapping businesses. Nonetheless, the split caused resource diversion, redundancy, and low efficiency, and went against the growth-through-merger trend of the leading aviation giants in the world.

Once China decided to undertake the development of large aircraft, COMAC was founded in 2008, and AVIC I and AVIC II were merged to form AVIC. On the surface, the newly established groups look similar to their predecessors. However, they have completely new structures and market positioning. The primary duties of COMAC include the design, assembly, sale, maintenance, and after-sale service of large passenger aircraft. AVIC is mainly responsible for the development and production of military aircraft, small to medium civil aircraft, helicopters, and engines, and for carrying out aviation research and flight testing. For its secondary tasks, AVIC also functions as a supplier to COMAC, manufactures airframes, engines, and airborne equipment for large passenger aircraft, and undertakes outsourcing business for foreign civil aircraft companies. In addition, AVIC Commercial Aircraft Engine Co., Ltd. (ACAE) was set up in 2009 to be the main contractor producing the engine to be used in the large aircraft project.

Aviation Industry Corporation of China. AVIC has a registered capital of RMB 64 billion, nearly 200 subsidiaries, and about 400,000 employees. The company has total assets reaching RMB 290 billion. The reorganization of AVIC was an endeavor to regroup and adjust each subsidiary according to its specialties, and realign and optimize company resources. After the reorganization, AVIC headquarters has 14 divisions directly under it in charge of 10 key business segments.[6] At present, the restructuring of AVIC headquarters and subsidiaries has been completed, and consolidation of the 10 business segments is in full swing. After its birth in the wake of the reorganization, AVIC launched a development strategy of "market-oriented reform, center-of-excellence-based integration, capital operation, globalization-based development, and industrial-scale-based growth," and "integration into the world aviation industry chain, integration into the regional economic development circles." According to AVIC, the company is aiming to grow more than 20 percent annually and achieve 1 trillion yuan in sales by 2007.

Commercial Aircraft Corporation of China (COMAC) and AVIC Commercial Aircraft Engine Corporation (ACAE). COMAC has a registered capital of RMB 19 billion and six primary shareholders—SASAC, AVIC, the Shanghai Guosheng Group (representing the Shanghai Municipal People's Government), Aluminum Corporation of China (CHINALCO), Shanghai Baosteel Group Corporation, and China Sinochem Group Corporation (Sinochem). COMAC can be regarded as a fully state-owned company of the PRC.[7] COMAC leadership came from senior government officials; COMAC Chairman Zhang Qingwei and General Manager Jin Zhuanglong are the former COSTIND Minister and Vice-Minister, respectively. COMAC is the executive body of China's special science and technology project for the R&D of large passenger aircraft. It has three centers—the R&D Center, the Final Assembly Center, and the Customer Service Center, and a consortium of subsidiaries such as AVIC I Commercial Aircraft Co., Ltd. (ACAC), Shanghai Aircraft Design and Research Institute, and Shanghai Aircraft Manufacturing Co., Ltd. COMAC is responsible for the overall design, system integration, marketing, airworthiness certification, and service of large passenger aircraft.

Short-term goals proposed by COMAC include the following: through the introduction and absorption of foreign technology and independent innovation, making breakthroughs in key technologies concerning the C919, and obtaining airworthiness certification; completing research and development of the ARJ21 regional aircraft, obtaining airworthiness certification, making delivery to customers, establishing mass-production capacities, and expanding market shares; and setting up a system of R&D, production, marketing, and customer service for civil aircraft. Long-term goals include achieving the industrialization and series production of civil aircraft; carrying out maintenance and repair of civil aircraft, developing financial leasing and other related businesses, and expanding the industry chain of the civil aviation sector; and becoming a civil aircraft manufacturer that owns independent intellectual property rights and enjoys international competitiveness.

With a registered capital of RMB 6 billion, ACAE is invested by its controlling shareholder AVIC and shareholders such as Shanghai Electric Group and Shanghai Guosheng Co., Ltd.[8] The remaining 30 percent of ACAE shares is planned to be bought by private enterprises. The main function of ACAE is to carry out R&D, production, sales, and maintenance of civil aircraft engines, and to provide technical consultation. Its key tasks include constructing an engine R&D center and a basic technology center, recruiting engine experts at home and from abroad, establishing technical cooperation with foreign engine manufacturers, seeking to build up an international R&D team and hiring professional organizations for technical advice and marketing consultation.

Recent Achievements by China's Aviation Industry

Through its long-term effort on the introduction of foreign technology and independent R&D, China has built a complete aviation research, testing, and manufacturing system. Its aeronautical manufacturing technology is sufficient to support the production of airframes and airborne equipment for fourth-generation fighter aircraft. Airborne missiles made by China are close to international standards. China has the capability to research, develop, and produce air-to-air and air-to-surface missiles. China has accumulated a certain degree of skill and experience in avionics technology, and is capable of supporting the R&D and manufacture of avionics system for fourth-generation fighters. China has also built up the capability to develop and produce the turbojet engine, the turbofan engine, and the turboshaft engine, and has successfully developed and produced medium-thrust engines. Now China is making an all-out effort to develop high-performance, high-thrust engines.[9] The achievements of China's aviation industry in recent years involve both civil and military aviation. Civil aviation programs include the C919 and the ARJ21; military ones include a variety of fighter-bombers and larger aircraft, including the JH–7, J–10, J–11, H–6, airborne early warning and transport projects, and military engines. Each is detailed below.

C919. The C919 is the first large passenger aircraft built by China indigenously. "C" is the first letter of China as well as COMAC, the acronym for Commercial Aircraft Corporation of China. It implies China's intention to form an A-B-C tripartite competition with Airbus and Boeing in the world's large passenger aircraft market. The number "19" means that the aircraft is designed to accommodate 190 seats. The designation shows that COMAC intends to build a series of larger aircraft. Preliminary design for the 168-seater C919 has been completed. The aircraft is due to make its maiden flight in 2014 and will be available for delivery in 2016. COMAC plans to produce 150 C919s a year and, ultimately, 3,000 aircraft in total.[10]

ARJ21. The ARJ21 is the first short-to-medium-range regional passenger aircraft developed and produced indigenously by China, and the first passenger aircraft that is developed and produced in strict accordance with international airworthiness standards. The ARJ21 made its first flight in November 2008. The base model of the aircraft has a maximum range of 3,700 kilometers, and 2,225 kilometers when fully loaded. With a maximum take-off weigh of 40 tons, the ARJ21 has a designed capacity for 78 or 90 seats, and is expected to be sold for U.S. $28 million per aircraft, lower than the price of similar foreign aircraft. COMAC claims that it has received 210 orders for the ARJ21, including 30 from foreign customers. The first ARJ21 was scheduled to be delivered to its first customer at the end of 2010, but problems in late stages of flight testing delayed delivery, which is now expected in late 2012. According to unofficial estimates, the ARJ21 will generate more than U.S. $1 billion for COMAC. Before the C919 can bring in any economic benefits, the ARJ21 will be the only source of revenue for COMAC.[11]

JH–7. The JH–7 resulted from an indigenous R&D program that China initiated in the 1980s for a new fighter-bomber. Its performance and role are roughly equivalent to those of the early models of the European Tornado fighter-bomber. The JH–7 is outfitted with twin WS–9 turbofan engines, and first entered service in the PLA Navy Air Force (PLANAF) to carry out anti-ship missions. The upgraded JH–7A has also entered service in the PLA Air

Force (PLAAF), and is capable of firing precision-guided weapons such as the KD–88 and YJ–91. The JH–7A is gradually replacing the old Q–5 strike aircraft, to furnish the ground-attack backbone of the PLAAF.

J–10. China started contact with Israel secretly in the 1980s, and introduced the technology that was used in the terminated Israeli Lavi fighter for the development of its own new fighter aircraft. The J–10 fighter made its maiden flight in 1998, and was delivered to the military in 2006. The performance of the J–10 is roughly comparable to that of the F–16C/D Block 30/40. Observations on the aircraft in service in the PLAAF suggest that China utilized a phased approach toward the development of the plane. In the early stage, the J–10 had only air superiority capabilities. The J–10B, under development at the moment, will be fitted with the WS–10A turbofan engine, new radars, fire-control systems, and a modified intake. New multipurpose combat capabilities will be added to the aircraft including the capability to employ precision-guided weapons.[12]

J–11. China acquired the Su–27SK fighter in 1992, and secured an agreement for licensed production of 200 Su–27SK aircraft under the name of J–11. The assembly of the aircraft in China proceeded very slowly due to the lack of experience and because China intended to make partial improvement to the aircraft to enhance its performance by using its own technology. The J–11B, which China claims to be completely self-made, is outfitted with the indigenously produced WS–10A engines, new radars, avionics systems, and air-to-air missiles. The J–11B already outperforms the early models of Su–27s.[13]

J–15. In addition, to pursue the development of an aircraft carrier fleet, China acquired the prototype (the T–10K) of the Su–33 carrier-based fighter from Ukraine earlier in the 21st century, for reverse engineering. In 2009, China produced the J–15 ship-borne fighter prototype based on the J–11B. The prototype is now undergoing testing at Shenyang Aircraft Corporation (SAC).[14] At least five J–15 prototypes have been built and are undergoing testing. It is expected that early production examples will be introduced into service in 2012 or 2013.

J–20. China's new-generation J–20 jet fighter first appeared in December 2010. Estimated J–20 weight is 20 tons, with a maximum takeoff weight of 36 to 38 tons, and an operational radius of more than 2,000 kilometers (over 1,240 miles). The J–20 has frontal stealth with careful fuselage design, but not rearward stealth, as its all-moving fins and vertical tailfins, front canards, and nozzles are not currently compatible with an all-aspect low observable design such as the American F–22. This could change in time with, for example, introduction of 2–D exhausts, and careful attention to incorporating radar absorbent structure, coatings, and edge treatments. The two prototypes are respectively fitted with AL–31 and WS–10 engines. They do not have vectored thrust and supersonic cruise ability, such as that possessed by the F–22. The J–20 fighter is thus still very much an experimental aircraft. Any combat-worthy production derivative can be expected to attain its initial operational combat capability no earlier than 2018 to 2020.

H–6M/K. Until very recently, China did not have the technology necessary for the development of new bombers and could not introduce them from abroad. Inspired by the U.S. experience of continuously upgrading the B–52 bomber, China upgraded the H–6 medium-range bomber as an air-launched cruise missile (ALCM) carrier. Fitted with four under-wing pylons, a few of the upgraded H–6Ms are believed to have entered service. China is researching on how to increase the number of H–6 pylons to six, and put in a new digital cockpit, avionics systems, the D–30 engine (used in the Il–76), and ventral tanks. The new H–6 variant is designated H–6K. Given the H–6K's combat radius and China's cruise missile range, for the first time China will have the combat capability, in theory at least, to strike Guam from the air with H–6K-launched subsonic cruise missiles and, given current PRC research interests, perhaps with hypersonic air-launched missiles in the more distant future.[15]

Airborne Early Warning and Control (AEW&C). In the 1990s, a proposed PLAAF AEW&C deal with Israel was canceled because of U.S. pressure. However, it is possible that through Israeli and Russian technical assistance, China nevertheless developed an airborne active phased-array radar system, subsequently modifying four of its active Il–76 transports into the KJ–2000 AEW&C aircraft, and thus giving the PLAAF its first long-range airborne early-warning capabilities. Earlier, China had modified the Y–8 turboprop transport (a derivative of the Antonov An–12) to incorporate search radar, generating the KJ–200 AEW&C aircraft. Together, these two types provide an early-warning capability covering both low and high altitudes.

Large transport aircraft. Xi'an Aircraft Industry Group (XAC) is responsible for the R&D and manufacture of the transport aircraft, which is projected to enter service in 2016 and will have a maximum take-off weight of 200 tons. According to Ukrainian media reports, China's development of large military transport aircraft is backed by Ukrainian technical assistance. The Antonov Design Bureau has offered two proposals for modifying either the An–70 or the Il–76. Ukraine's FED Corporation has proposed to upgrade the Il–76, and hoped to set up a joint venture in China to carry out research, development, and assembly of the new transport aircraft.[16]

Aircraft engine programs. Though China does not possess the ability to design, develop, and manufacture large civil aircraft engines, it is increasingly active in manufacturing military engines. The WS–9, WS–10 and WS–13 are the best representatives of such engines made by China. The WS–9, a copy of the 1960s-vintage Rolls-Royce Spey afterburning turbofan engine, is one of a few aircraft engines made in China that originated from Western technologies. The engine is used in the JH–7. The WS–10 is a copy of the Russian AL–31, and has been installed in the J–10 and the J–11B since 2009. During test flights, PLAAF test pilots reported abnormal engine vibrations, and thus, for a while, the PLAAF refused to accept new deliveries of the aircraft. The JF–17 fighter aircraft, developed jointly by China and Pakistan, uses Russian RD–93 engines. China has long drawn upon Russian engine technology, but now, to lessen its dependency, it is pursuing a Chinese derivative of the RD–93 under the designation of WS–13. Though China has a certain degree of military engine manufacturing capability, Chinese-made engines in general, compared with similar types of engines made by Western countries, have short overhaul intervals and are slow in acceleration to maximum power following rapid throttle application. This indicates that there is still a significant technical lag in China's engine development capabilities.

Observations on the Development of China's Aviation Industry

Airpower strategy and the aviation industry have advanced together. Observations on the evolution of the PLAAF's strategic objectives and the reform of the aviation industry since the 1980s suggest that China has managed to keep them up to speed. After Den Xiaoping put forward the guideline of "building an armed forces with quantity and quality" in 1985, the PLAAF started to study its strategic role. After the Gulf War in 1991, the PLA realized that a modernized air force is the key to victory in battle, and thus established CAIC. In 1999, China restructured AVIC I and AVIC II. In November of the same year, the PLAAF's commander outlined on the 50th anniversary of the PLA the idea of shifting the air force from "territorial air defense" to "both offense and defense."[17] In 2004 and 2007, the PLAAF Party Congress passed resolutions on building a "strategic air force" and "an air force that matches the status of a great power."[18] In 2008, China once again restructured AVIC. It is believed that these developments are not coincidental. Instead, they are calculated measures adopted after comprehensive considerations on the two major objectives of strengthening airpower and developing the aviation industry.

The aviation industry has been selected as a key development project. The *Outline of the National Program for the Medium- and Long-Term Development of Defense-Related Science, Technology and Industry (2006–2020),* released by COSTIND in 2006, stipulates clearly that by 2020, defense-related science and technology must be able to meet basically the needs of the independent R&D, as well as the manufacture and information-based development of modern weapons and equipment.[19] According to the *Outline,* China will step up research on basic aviation science, and develop advanced aviation technology. Moreover, the development of the aviation industry should be unaffected by the government's macroeconomic control measures. On the whole, the PLA's effort to develop new-type fighter-bombers, AEW&C aircraft, air-launched missiles, aircraft engines, and large passenger aircraft, to which the government has committed significant resources, are all concrete manifestations of the *Outline*.

However, the biggest problem of China's aviation industry is that its ability of independent innovation and invention needs to be enhanced, since Chinese-made fighter aircraft, guided missiles, engines, and other systems are more or less the results of suspected piracy and some are even exact reproductions of foreign inventions. If China is unable to acquire advanced products from foreign countries, the development of its aviation industry will be limited. Furthermore, internal R&D expenditure by China's aircraft manufacturing industry in 2007 amounted to merely RMB 3,722.68 million,[20] far behind that of its European and American counterparts. Inadequate investment in R&D is another factor constraining the development of China's aviation industry.

Foreign assistance is needed if China is to develop advanced technology. Though it has built up some measure of strength, China's aviation industry still lags behind advanced countries to a great extent. According to the Stockholm International Peace Research Institute (SIPRI) and the U.S. Department of State, China belongs to the "third-tier" states in terms of military-industrial strength. The strength of the military industry in Russia, which ranks no. 1 in the second-tier states, is about one-sixth of the military-industrial strength of the United States.[21] For a long time, China has used procurement to boost its own technological capabilities. Nonetheless, in the face of U.S. high-tech export controls, the European Union arms embargo, and Russia's growing wariness of Chinese piracy, China's attempt to acquire high-end technologies from foreign countries has run into a severe challenge.

Recent measures adopted by China's aviation industry are worthy of attention. In December 2009, AVIC XAC acquired a 90 percent stake in Austria's Future Advanced Composite Component (FACC).[22] FACC is a company specializing in the development and production of aviation composite materials.[23] The acquisition was the first of its kind that China had made in a foreign aviation industry. AVIC will use FACC as an R&D and test center for aviation composite materials. Relevant technologies will be transferred to China for production, assisting considerably the R&D and manufacture of advanced composite materials in China. AVIC and ACAE have devoted about 4,000 people to research and develop the C919 and its engine. To drive forward follow-up works in each stage, both companies have launched a global talent recruitment program. The management personnel AVIC hired initially in August 2009 have been appointed senior managers at five subsidiaries. AVIC's goal is to recruit 3,000 people of various talents in 5 to 8 years. This indicates that lack of talent has constrained China's ability to make breakthroughs in key technologies. Therefore, China wishes to acquire foreign technology through the recruitment of international specialists.[24]

Blazing a path of development with military and civilian integration. PRC research suggests that the United States has created a matchless military by harnessing the infinite power of the civilian sector and that the separated civil-military research systems in China are one of the factors causing China to trail behind. Hu Jintao stressed at the 17th Party Congress that China would "establish sound systems of weapons and equipment research and manufacture that integrate military with civilian purposes and combine military efforts with civilian support, and blaze a path of development with Chinese characteristics featuring military and civilian integration."[25] Take the development of China's aviation industry, for instance. The strategy adopted to develop large civil passenger aircraft and large military transport aircraft is based on the principle of "1 project, 2 models, civil-military coordination, and series development." Technologies acquired from international cooperation—such as structural designs for airframes, composite materials, aircraft engines, and automatic control systems—can be used in the R&D and manufacture of military aircraft in China, making it difficult for foreign countries to implement effective controls. In Western countries, most AEW&C, electronic warfare, and command and control aircraft use civil passenger aircraft as the basic platform to build upon. The C919 also has the same potential. China will be able to produce a synergistic effect for the development of its military power if it can promote the "civil-military integration" strategy effectively.

Export and domestic demand: the prospects for China's aviation industry. There is no doubt that the primary mission of China's aviation industry is to support the development of the PLA. With regard to the export market, China has found a niche in the arms markets of some Asian and African countries through the sales of the J–7, Q–5 and K–8. If the production agreement between China and Pakistan on 150 JF–17s is taken into account, China will become the world's third-largest exporter of military aircraft, behind only the United States and Russia.[26] Two Pakistan JF–17 aircraft were displayed for the first time at the 2010 Farnborough International Air Show in London. During the air show, China and Pakistan discussed matters relating to possibly exporting JF–17 fighters to eight countries: Congo, Egypt, Nigeria, the Philippines, Sri Lanka, Sudan, Turkey, and Venezuela. In addition, Pakistan, Iran, North Korea, and others have expressed high levels of interest in the Chinese-made

J-10. If China can avoid Russian control over engine production, the global export of Chinese-made military aircraft would seem to have a bright future.

Airbus predicted in 2006 that China would need to add more than 2,800 passenger aircraft and freighters in the next 20 years. Moreover, an AVIC market forecast for the period up to 2028, released at the Beijing Air Show in 2009, predicts that China will need 2,922 large and 874 short-to-medium-range aircraft.[27] From these data, it seems that China's domestic market will be able to shore up the sales of the C919 and its follow-up models. However, to form a complete civil aviation industry, China will have to face up to the competition from Boeing and Airbus, and the key is whether China can obtain Federal Aviation Administration and European Aviation Safety Agency airworthiness certifications. If China fails to get the certifications, then large civil aircraft made by China could only fly in the sky in China and in a few other countries.

Conclusion

Since its founding in 1949, the People's Republic of China has weathered many troubles at home and from abroad. Driven by the goal of a modern military, China has listed the development of its aviation industry as a key project from the beginning. After 60 years of development and reform, the aviation industry in China, though growing slowly with limited transformation, has achieved some results. For a long time, China has sought to enhance the standards of its aviation industry by copying finished products that are acquired from abroad or through OEM production. Initial results generated from this approach include the key technologies that China lacked but has now learned, and the improvement of foreign products with some innovations. In general, China already has a considerable capacity for indigenous production. Once reaching a certain level, China's indigenous production capacity will begin to transform quantitatively and qualitatively, ultimately allowing China to achieve its aspiration toward independent innovation and invention. China's aviation industry still faces many unsolved problems and lags far behind advanced countries. Despite that, in time, the standards of China's aviation industry may progress to an extent unimaginable to the outside world.

Notes

[1] "The National Guideline on Medium and Long-term Program for Science and Technology Development (2006–2020)," *Xinhua*, February 9, 2006, at <www.gov.cn/jrzg/2006-02/09/content_183787.htm>.

[2] The 11 major military-industrial groups include: China National Nuclear Corporation (CNNC), China Nuclear Engineering and Construction Corporation (CNEC), China Aerospace Science and Technology Corporation(CASC), China Aerospace Science and Industry Corporation (CASIC), China Aviation Industry Corporation I (AVIC I), China Aviation Industry Corporation II (AVIC II), China State Shipbuilding Corporation (CSSC), China Shipbuilding Industry Corporation (CSIC), China North Industries Group

Corporation (CNGC), China South Industries Group Corporation (CSG), and China Electronic Science and Technology Corporation (CETC).

[3] State Council Information Office of the People's Republic of China, "China's National Defense in 2006," December 2006, 19.

[4] COSTIND, NDRC, and SASAC jointly released the "Guiding Opinions on Promoting the Transformation of Defense Industries into Joint-Stock Enterprises," June 23, 2007, PRC Central Government's Official Web Portal at <www.gov.cn/gzdt/2007-06/23/content_658955.htm>.

[5] Hu Jintao, "Hold High the Great Banner of Socialism with Chinese Characteristics and Strive for New Victories in Building a Moderately Prosperous Society in All Respects," Report, 17th National Congress, CPC, *Xinhua*, October 15, 2007, at <http://news.xinhuanet.com/newscenter/2007-10/24/content_6938568_8.htm>.

[6] The 15 divisions directly under AVIC headquarters include administration, strategic planning, management, human resources, financial management, science and information, capital operation, corporate culture, major project management, international affairs, policy and legal affairs, quality and safety, discipline, inspection, and audit. The 10 business segments include AVIC Defense, AVIC Asset Management, AVIC Aircraft, AVIC Engine, AVIC Helicopter, AVIC System, AVIC General Aircraft, Chinese Aeronautical Establishment, AVIC Flight Test Establishment, and AVIC International.

[7] The share proportions of the six main shareholders are as follows: SASAC, 31.58; percent; AVIC, 26.32 percent; SGG, 26.32 percent; CHINALCO, 5.26 percent; Boasteel, 5.26 percent; and Sinochem, 5.26 percent.

[8] The share proportions of the three original shareholders are AVIC, 30 percent; Shanghai Electric Group, 30 percent; and Shanghai Guosheng Co., 30 percent.

[9] Wu Weiren, ed., *An Overview of the World Defense Technology and Industry* (Beijing: Aviation Industry Press, 2004), 208.

[10] "C919 Chinese-made large aircraft first flight in 2014," *China Review News*, September 16, 2010, at <www.chinareviewnews.com/doc/1013/9/1/2/101391250.html?coluid=0&kindid=0&docid=101391250&mdate=0724093004>.

[11] "About the ARJ21 aircraft," AVIC I Commercial Aircraft Company," ACAC Consortium, at <www.acac.com.cn/product02.asp>.

[12] "The UK media explains the advanced air intake of J-10B, and claims its electronic capabilities enhanced," *Global Times Online*, March 24, 2009, at <http://mil.huanqui.com/Exclusive/2009-03/412695.html>.

[13] "Jane's Defence Weekly: J-11B has been modified by China to a multipurpose aircraft with partial stealth capabilities," *China Review News*, June 23, 2010, at <http://3g.cnrn.tw/doc/1013/6/1/6/101361683.html?coluid=4&kindid=101361683>.

[14] "Kanwa Defence Review: test flights for the J-15 ship-borne aircraft, a Chinese copy of the Su-33, will take place soon," *Xinhua*, April 26, 2010, at <http://big5.xinhuanet.com/gate/big5/news.xinhuanet.com/mil/2010-04/26/content_13425387.htm>.

[15] "The PLA's H-6K bomber fitted with large cruise missiles," *Wen Wei Po*, August 19, 2009, at <http://paper.wenweipo.com/2009/08/19/YO0908190008.htm>.

[16] "Russian media reports Ukrainian participation in China's large aircraft project," *China Review News*, March 20, 2010, at <www.chinareviewnews.com/doc/1012/7/4/4/101274492.html?coluid=4&kindid=18&docid=101274492>.

[17] Zhang Nongke, "The PLAAF is transforming from a defensive force to an offensive and defensive force, an Interview with Air Force Commander Liu Shunyao and Political Commissar Qiao Qingchen," *Bauhinia Magazine*, no. 109 (November 5, 1999), 5–9.

[18] "Jian Zemin and Hu Jintao met with representatives attending the 10th PLAAF Party Congress," *Xinhua*, May 20, 2004, at <www.wutnews.com/news/news.aspx?id=3556>.

[19] "The Outline of the National Program for the Medium- and Long-Term Development of Defense-related Science, Technology and Industry," *Xinhua* Online, May 25, 2006, at <http://big5.xinhuanet.com/gate/big5/news.xinhuanet.com/newscenter/2006-05/25/content_4597459.htm>.

[20] *China Statistical Yearbook on High Technology Industry* (Beijing: China Statistics Press, 2008).

[21] Ma Jie and Guo Chaolei, "The revolution in military affairs and the important task of national defense, technological and industrial development," in *Defence Industry Conversion in China*, no. 59 (January 2005), 21.

[22] "XAC bought FACC, the aviation industry's first overseas acquisition," *People's Daily* Online, December 14, 2009, at <http://caac.people.com.cn/GB/114104/10515071.html>.

[23] Established in 1989, FACC's main business is the R&D and manufacture of composite materials. It currently has four production facilities, two engineering centers, one service company (in Canada), and one customer service center (in the United States) with a total staff of 1,500-plus persons.

[24] AVIC Website at <www.avic.com.cn/index_jtfc.asp>.

[25] See note 2.

[26] "U.S. World News Network: Chinese military exports distinguished, Ranks No. 3 worldwide," *Global Times* Online, July 23, 2010, at <http://war.news.163.com/10/0724/11/6CBT36RC00011MTO.html>.

[27] "China's aviation market immense; 3,796 aircraft need to be added by 2028," PRC Central Government's Official Web Portal, September 24, 2009, at <http://big5.gov.cn/gate/big5/www.gov.cn/jrzg/2009-09/24/content_1424846.htm>.

Chapter 12

China's Quest for Advanced Aviation Technologies

Phillip C. Saunders and Joshua K. Wiseman

Although China continues to lag approximately two decades behind the world's most sophisticated air forces in terms of its ability to develop and produce fighter aircraft and other complex aerospace systems, it has moved over time from absolute reliance on other countries for military aviation technology procurement to a position where a more diverse array of strategies can be pursued. Steps taken in the late 1990s to reform China's military aviation sector demonstrated an understanding of the problems inherent in high-technology acquisition, and an effort to move forward.[1] However, a decade later it remains unclear how effective these reforms have been. Where are the People's Liberation Army Air Force (PLAAF) and China's military aviation industry headed? What obstacles must be overcome for China to join the exclusive ranks of those nations possessing sophisticated air forces and aviation industries capable of producing world-class aircraft? Answering these and related questions is at the heart of this study. Because advanced fighter aircraft exemplify the most sophisticated level of aerospace technology, are important for air force combat capabilities, and present unique design and fabrication challenges for a military aviation industry, the authors' analysis focuses primarily on China's efforts to acquire, produce, and develop fighter aircraft and related technology. It also includes some discussion of bombers, transports, and airborne early warning aircraft where relevant to Chinese technology development and acquisition efforts.

Approaches to Technology Development and Procurement

Few things differentiate the lethality of an air force more than the level of technology in its most advanced aircraft. Historically, advantages in aviation technology have often translated into significant advantages in combat environments, especially for fighter aircraft. In the current environment, the world's most advanced air forces have access to fifth-generation fighter aircraft technology.[2] Fifth-generation fighters are characterized by the incorporation of advanced technologies such as stealth, integrated avionics systems, thrust vectoring, and helmet-mounted sights.[3] The technological demands of designing and producing advanced fighters present considerable challenges for developing countries. They may want an air force that is on par qualitatively with the world's most advanced, but usually lack an aviation industry capable of producing cutting-edge fighter aircraft technology. A developing country may be able to produce some highly sophisticated components, but lack the knowledge or industrial capacity to design and build all necessary components or to integrate them into a finished product. Industrial capacity refers to the ability to fabricate each component part that goes into the final product and assemble it using indigenous labor. Knowledge encompasses the know-how to design and manufacture component parts, together with requisite competence in areas such as systems engineering, which is critical to integrating various complex systems into a working unit.[4]

Developing countries incapable of producing cutting-edge fighters on their own must seek to acquire complete aircraft or technologies from countries willing to sell them advanced aircraft or to export or codevelop the relevant technologies. However a number of factors might dissuade countries with an advanced aviation technology base from exporting aircraft or advanced aviation technologies to a particular developing country. The exporter country might view such transfers as potentially harmful to its security interests if it is unsure about the developing country's long-term intentions. It might seek to avoid entering into a technology transfer relationship out of deference to its relationship with allies or other customers. Allies might use leverage to dissuade potential exporters from making arms sales or technology transfers to developing countries about which they have security concerns. Nevertheless, access to foreign advanced fighters and aviation technology is critical for developing countries seeking to build a modern air force.

Buy, Build, or Steal

Countries whose overall level of economic development and relatively backward aviation industry limit their aircraft production capability have the three basic options of purchase (buy), indigenous development (build), or espionage (steal) in their efforts to develop a modern air force. For countries in this situation, all three options have significant limitations.

Buy

Buying imported aircraft allows a developing country to obtain more advanced fighters than its indigenous aviation industry can produce. Buying complete aircraft offers a developing country a relatively fast way to build its air force's combat capability (although in practice it may take 4 to 5 years from the time a deal is signed until a unit equipped with a new fighter reaches initial operational capability). Often a deal to purchase advanced fighters includes flight training, assistance with maintenance, and the acquisition of spare parts necessary to maintain operational readiness. This can not only speed the introduction of the aircraft into service, but also improve the acquiring air force's human capital and overall capabilities. Because purchasers usually have the opportunity to "fly before they buy," there is a clearer sense of what the capabilities of the aircraft will be and less risk of technological failure or inadequate performance.

The disadvantages of building a modern air force using imported aircraft include the relatively high cost, limited transfer of technology to the aviation sector, and continuing dependence on foreign suppliers. Buyers are also limited to the aircraft that supplying companies are willing to sell; advanced countries often restrict the type of aircraft or the sophistication of avionics and weapons systems that can be exported due to strategic concerns or to maintain a technological advantage for their own air force. A common approach is to export last generation systems or watered-down versions of the most advanced fighters. This enables the United States, Russia, and European powers to maintain a long-term competitive advantage in military aviation technology and a measure of airpower dominance over their customers.

Purchases of complete aircraft do not produce jobs or technological spin-offs for the acquiring countries (though this may be partly overcome by the use of offsets in the contract that require the seller to accept payment in the form of goods produced by the buyer). Finally, the acquiring country will usually have a limited capacity to produce spare parts for an imported aircraft or to modernize its systems, resulting in long-term dependence on the seller in order to keep the aircraft flying or to update an older aircraft's systems. This can be problematic if the seller's economy goes through a major transition (note, for example, India's difficulty in acquiring spare parts for its Soviet aircraft following the breakup of the Soviet Union) or if changes in political relations make the supplier unwilling to continue to provide spare parts and maintenance (compare Iran's U.S.-built McDonnell-Douglas F–4, Northrop F–5, and Grumman F–14 aircraft following the Iranian revolution in 1979). Variations on the "buy" option such as coproduction are discussed later in this study.

Build

The pure "build" option requires planning, designing, and producing the desired fighter system utilizing only indigenous knowledge and production facilities. A developing country may invest significant resources in research and development (R&D) to build its domestic aviation technology production base. However, this requires a significant investment of both capital and human knowledge and presents large opportunity costs on both fronts. If a developing country seeks to push its aviation sector well beyond the technological development of its broader economy, this entails costly efforts with limited broader payoffs as scarce engineering talent and resources are focused on narrow military applications. If a developing country tries to push the overall technological capacity of the broader economy, this entails a much longer time period before improvements spill over and raise the technological level of the aviation industry.

The chief advantages of indigenous development are that a developing country can master the technologies required to design and build a fighter, limit its reliance on imported parts and technologies (and thus its potential vulnerability to a cutoff that might limit combat readiness), and diffuse some benefits of aircraft R&D and production into the broader economy (in the form of jobs and technology spin-offs). Over time, indigenous production can lay the foundation for a domestic aviation industry capable of designing, producing, and potentially exporting complete fighter aircraft.

The disadvantages are that a developing country's aviation industry may only be able to produce low-quality aircraft with limited combat capability, that large technological hurdles and a high learning curve must be overcome to establish an advanced aviation industry, and that the long period required to learn to develop and produce a modern fighter may yield aircraft that are obsolete before they are fielded. There is also no guarantee that investments in aviation R&D and production capacity will pay off. Few defense projects historically have been more costly, slower, or more prone to unforeseen difficulties than those undertaken to produce new fighter aircraft.[5] It is possible for a developing country pursuing the economic and technological spinoffs from indigenous design and production to spend much more than it would have cost to buy an advanced fighter from a foreign supplier, only to wind up with an inferior aircraft. Japan's F–2 fighter provides a good illustration.

Steal

A developing country can use surreptitious means to steal design and technology information on aircraft and aircraft components that it lacks the knowledge to design and produce domestically. This can be accomplished using covert procurement (often through third countries), traditional espionage methods, or computer network intrusion methods to exfiltrate the desired information. Individuals with access to information on classified weapons systems are prime targets of foreign intelligence organizations. Cyber espionage attacks against U.S. targets including military/government organizations and defense contractors have reportedly been successful in obtaining sensitive, though not classified, data.[6] The "steal" option can be used to gain blueprints or examples of weapons to use in reverse engineering a subsystem or to develop countermeasures that make a threat aircraft less effective in combat.

The principal advantage of the "steal" option is the potential to acquire advanced systems or technologies that other countries are unwilling to sell. In some cases, espionage can allow a country to acquire advanced technology without spending funds on its own research and development. The disadvantages include a developing country's limited ability to absorb or replicate stolen systems and technologies without technological support from the manufacturer, the haphazard and potentially incomplete access to systems and technologies through clandestine or surreptitious means, and the potential for espionage to send a country's aviation industry down a blind alley. In discussing the degree to which China has employed the "steal" option, we should differentiate its comprehensive efforts to collect and assimilate open source defense information (for example, through the China Defense Science and Technology Information Center) from its efforts to obtain restricted technologies covertly, by way of either traditional or cyber espionage. Exploiting the volumes of technical open source information produced in developed countries is an effective, legitimate, and predictable way to acquire knowledge.[7]

Of these three main avenues to technology procurement, the "build" option is the only one with the potential to stimulate innovation and create a broad-based domestic aviation industry from a low initial starting point. The United States and Russia produce the world's most complex fighter aircraft and, although they gained the ability in the midst of different economic and political circumstances, both were only able to reach this status through the ability to develop new technologies. Simply buying fighter aircraft from another country, with no plans to reverse engineer or coproduce, does not help a developing country move toward self-reliance. The steal option can have benefits if a developing country is able to obtain the information it needs without having to expend the necessary resources on R&D. However, simply possessing a blueprint does not guarantee success in reproducing the design, especially for a developing country with a limited aerospace production capacity.

Hybrid Approaches: Reverse Engineering, Coproduction, and Codevelopment

Hybrid approaches blend elements of buy, build, and steal in different combinations. This section considers reverse engineering, coproduction, and codevelopment as means of developing and acquiring aviation technology and building an advanced military aviation industry.

Reverse Engineering

Reverse engineering is the process of acquiring an aircraft, weapons system, or component and then taking it apart to understand how it works and potentially how to replicate or defeat it. The initial acquisition may be done through legitimate purchase (buy) or covert procurement (steal). Successful reverse engineering requires a certain level of technological sophistication in a country's aviation industry (for example, some degree of "build" experience and capacity).

Reverse engineering can serve several functions. Disassembling a mechanical or electronic device reveals its inner workings, yielding understanding of how it functions, the specific technologies and components involved, and identifying successful design paths that can be emulated. It may be possible to replicate the system or component by producing an exact clone of an aircraft component or weapons system. The knowledge gathered from reverse engineering may be incorporated into a newly designed subsystem that bears some resemblance to the original but is not an exact copy. As in the case of the "steal" option, a developing country might use reverse engineering to gain understanding of an aircraft's weapons systems or radars so that it can develop effective countermeasures.

Developing countries often assume that reverse engineering can help accelerate development in certain sectors of the economy.[8] Examples of weapons reverse engineering do not validate this assumption in each case but rather suggest that success depends on a number of country-specific factors. Developing countries sometimes attempt to purchase a small number of sophisticated fighters or advanced components from another country for the sole purpose of trying to reverse-engineer them in order to produce copies or gain knowledge about the component parts. (China was notorious for its efforts in the 1980s and early 1990s to purchase small quantities of advanced fighters and aviation components.) If a country is able to purchase small quantities and successfully reverse engineer them, the savings in development time (compared to completely independent development) and money (compared to a purchase of large quantities of aircraft or components) may be significant. However, this runs counter to the seller's best interests. Advanced arms suppliers such as the United States or Russia have no motivation to sell a small number of fighter aircraft to a country with the industrial capacity to copy them. A more usual variant can occur when a developing country procures a large quantity of an aircraft and then attempts to reverse engineer parts and components to reduce its dependence on the original seller for spare parts. (Both India and China have often pursued this approach.) This option is often explicitly banned by the sales contract, but the buyer may have a limited capacity to enforce these provisions once the sale is complete.

A developing country may also use covert procurement through a third party in order to acquire access to small quantities of an aircraft or component. An ally with legitimate access to advanced fighters or aviation technology may act as a "cut out" and either sell or turn over a working example of the aircraft for reverse engineering purposes. One widely cited example is the assumption that Pakistan, which purchased F–16 fighters from the United States, may have provided China with access to F–16 fighters and components. It is impossible to definitively determine the extent of access China may have had to Pakistani F–16s in the 1980s, but sources claim that Chinese technical personnel visiting Pakistan in the early 1980s were allowed to examine the U.S.-made fighter.[9] China may also have obtained some access to F–16 technology through its defense cooperation with Israel.[10]

In some cases, a country may be able to acquire an adversary's military hardware as a result of serendipitous circumstances, such as cases where a pilot loses his way in bad weather or defects with his aircraft.[11] For example, during the second Taiwan Strait crisis in fall 1958, the United States equipped Taiwan's F–86F Sabres with the AIM–9 Sidewinder infrared (IR)-guided air-to-air missile (AAM). On September 28, 1958, an F–86F fired and hit a PLAAF MiG–17 with a Sidewinder that lodged in the MiG's fuselage without exploding. The Soviet Union convinced China to turn over the unexploded missile and successfully reverse engineered it as the K–13. Soviet engineer Gennady Sokolovskiy described acquisition of the Sidewinder as, "a university offering a course in missile construction technology which has upgraded our engineering education and updated our approach to production of future missiles."[12]

The biggest benefit of reverse engineering is that a developing country can sidestep some of the R&D investment required to develop advanced weapons technologies. Unlike the pure "buy" option where a developing country merely operates the system it purchases, reverse engineering can lead to significant technical discoveries that propel a nation's defense industry forward. (The Soviet effort to reverse engineer the AIM–9 Sidewinder AAM is one such instance.) This is not always the case, however. Reverse engineering might allow for better understanding of a complex piece of military hardware, but there is no guarantee that a country can produce an exact clone or functional equivalent. Individual components may incorporate materials or be produced using advanced production processes that cannot be easily replicated by a developing country's aviation industry. (This was initially the case with composite materials and stealth aircraft designed using advanced computer systems, and remains the case for some materials used in high-performance jet engines.) Fighter aircraft present a particular reverse-engineering challenge because of the vast number of complex subsystems (for example, radars, avionics, and engines) that must be integrated into a functional whole. A developing country may obtain access to an advanced fighter, but lack the production capacity to reproduce it. A developing country may be able to reverse engineer and replicate key components, but lack the design skills to integrate them into an existing aircraft.

Coproduction and Codevelopment

The terms *coproduction* and *codevelopment* are sometimes used interchangeably. For the purposes of this paper, *coproduction* refers to a contract where the supplying country sells the purchaser the right to produce copies of a complete aircraft or key components. Coproduction deals can range from assembly of imported complete knock-down (CKD) kits with all necessary components to transfer of blueprints, machines, technical assistance, and relevant production technologies that give the purchaser an independent capability to build complete aircraft from scratch. *Codevelopment* refers to cooperation in the design stage of aircraft development where two or more countries work as partners.

Technology transfer and how expensive research and development costs are allocated are the principal issues in coproduction or codevelopment projects. The country with the more advanced industry has the motivation to withhold technical details from partners to protect its competitive advantage; the country with the less developed aviation industry typically has to agree to pay a premium price in order to gain access to relevant production (in the case of coproduction) or design/systems integration expertise (in the case of codevelopment).

Developing countries often seek coproduction arrangements as a means of starting an aviation industry or improving the technological capacity of their existing industry. The developing country typically seeks the maximum possible transfer of design information and production technology to allow fully independent production. Unless suppliers have a strategic reason for wanting to build up the recipient country's defense industry, they typically seek to retain control over key design information and production technology and prefer to supply components for assembly rather than give the purchasing country an independent production capability. The exact nature of the deal is often a function of the relative bargaining power of the parties involved. Coproduction usually involves a licensing agreement stipulating the number of systems the producer country can build at an agreed upon cost.

As a technology procurement strategy, coproduction is basically a combination of "buy" and "build." The developing country typically assembles aircraft from imported parts (often in the form of a complete knockdown kit) rather than producing them from scratch, at least initially. Contracts sometimes allow replacing imported components with indigenously produced components as the purchasing country's aviation industry gains the ability to successfully produce them.

Developing countries sometimes evade contractual restrictions by using knowledge gained in the production process to design compatible subsystems or components that can either be integrated into an existing aircraft or that can be part of an improved variant of an existing aircraft. Because the supplier often provides knowledge about how to assemble the aircraft rather than complete design information, the buyer country still has a fair amount of work to do if the goal is to reverse engineer an exact clone or to develop an improved variant incorporating indigenous subsystems.

The nature of defense cooperation between countries is a good indicator of the overall political relationship. Coproduction agreements imply a basic level of political trust between partner countries. A supplier country will not enter into an agreement to sell a developing country the rights to build a fighter aircraft if there is a fundamental divergence of strategic interests or if the purchasing country poses a significant security threat. Coproduction is less of a risk than codevelopment to the supplier country from a technology procurement perspective because it does not usually grant the purchaser access to state-of-the-art aircraft or subsystems. As the next section will detail, China relied on coproduction with the Soviet Union in the 1950s to launch its military aviation industry and on coproduction deals with Russia in the 1990s to improve its capability to build advanced fighter aircraft.

Codevelopment in aircraft design implies that both partners possess a relatively well developed aviation industry. The partners typically share the costs of R&D efforts; partners with less advanced aviation industries typically pay a premium price or commit to purchase significant quantities of the finished aircraft in order to gain access to advanced technologies, design processes, and systems integration expertise. In some cases, codevelopment will produce new technologies and intellectual property that will be shared by the partners.

A good recent example of codevelopment involves the joint venture between Russia's United Aircraft Corporation (UAC) and India's Hindustan Aeronautics Limited (HAL) to develop a fifth-generation fighter.[13] The work is split on a 75–25 percent basis, with Russia contributing the larger share.[14] "Codevelopment" is also sometimes used to describe projects where parties contribute to development costs without participating in the actual work. From a technology procurement standpoint, this is much closer to the "buy" avenue than to coproduction or codevelopment.

The F–35 Joint Strike Fighter program is an example of an unequal codevelopment partnership where a number of countries contributed financial support and committed to purchasing the aircraft without any involvement in development work.[15] The United States and Britain have carried out the vast majority of technical development work, with Italy making minor contributions.[16] The other six partners (Netherlands, Turkey, Australia, Canada, Denmark, and Norway) have bought into the project by contributing development funds and agreeing to purchase a specific number of F–35s. True codevelopment implies not just cost-sharing, but shared ownership of the intellectual property generated by the project.

The decision to codevelop a fighter aircraft can be motivated by different circumstances, but the logic in forming joint partnerships is the same: both countries benefit more through codevelopment than they would by working alone. Defense industries can share the substantial burden of R&D costs while bringing their technological comparative advantages to the fore. Perceived economic, political, and strategic benefits drive the decisionmaking process, with the relative importance of each depending on the relationship, political situation, and threat perceptions of the partner countries.

The UAC/HAL joint venture between Russia and India illustrates the complex economic and geopolitical pressures that drive defense technology decisionmaking. India was an end user and coproducer of Soviet military aircraft since a cooperative defense relationship was established in the early 1960s.[17] The relationship persisted throughout the Cold War, and after the Soviet Union dissolved, India helped Russia's defense industry stay afloat in the 1990s.[18] The plan to codevelop a fifth-generation fighter was hatched at a time (2000) when the dire Russian economic situation gave India a significant degree of bargaining power.[19] If not for economic necessity, Russia might never have proposed a codevelopment deal given the major step forward it provides the Indian aerospace industry.[20] Some Russian defense industry experts have been skeptical about the value India will bring to the project, citing Russia's half century of experience designing award-winning fighter aircraft.[21] Indian media reports have highlighted HAL's potential contributions in aircraft body design through its work on composites gained during the design of its indigenous Tejas Light Combat Aircraft (LCA).[22] Russia has designed mostly metal aircraft and thus lacks experience with composites. HAL will also design the mission computer, navigation, and countermeasure dispensing systems, and critical software.

PLAAF Technology Procurement Strategies: Past, Present, and Future

How have the pros and cons of the potential methods of building or acquiring military aircraft and aviation technology described above affected Chinese decisions about whether to "Buy, Build, or Steal"? This section briefly develops a concise model of a developing country's decision calculus, and then applies that model to explain Chinese choices over the period from 1949 to the present. We organize the analysis into five distinct periods defined by Chinese economic and technological capacity and the sources of foreign aircraft and aviation technology available to China at a given time.

The model we develop involves four factors. (See table 12-1.) The first is the level of development of the overall Chinese economy, which defines China's general technological capability. The level of overall development constrains the indigenous technological capacity of China's aviation industry and defines the potential for China to "spin on" technologies from the civilian sector to the military sector. The second factor is the technological capacity of the aviation sector. The level of development of the overall economy constrains the indigenous capacity of the aviation sector, but it is possible to use foreign assistance and imported technology to build advanced capabilities in the aviation sector that surpass those in the broader civilian economy. To the extent that advanced fighter aircraft require technologies that do not have civilian applications ("single-use technologies"), the military aviation sector must be ahead of the overall economy in some specific areas if indigenous production is to be an option.

Table 12–1. Four Factors in Chinese Military Aviation Technology Procurement Calculus

Development level of overall Chinese economy	Technological capacity of Chinese aviation sector	Willingness of foreign suppliers to transfer technologies	Chinese relative bargaining power vis-à-vis foreign suppliers

The third factor is the willingness of foreign countries to sell advanced military aircraft, key components and armaments, and related production technology. Who is willing to sell to China and what aircraft and aviation technologies they are willing to sell define the available options in terms of purchasing ("buy"), coproduction, and codevelopment. The fourth and final factor is China's bargaining power vis-à-vis potential sellers of aircraft and aviation technology. This can be influenced by ideological and security factors (including the seller's calculus about whether China represents a potential ally or a potential threat), the health of the potential seller's overall economy and defense sector, and supply and demand within the broader military aviation market (for example, whether it is a "buyer's market" or a "seller's market"). Bargaining power influences whether potential sellers are willing to sell their most sophisticated fighters and whether they are willing to transfer production technology or consider coproduction or codevelopment deals. Sellers generally prefer to sell complete aircraft and spare parts (to maximize profits, maintain control of the supply chain, and limit potential competition) while buyers often want technology transfer and coproduction arrangements which provide employment opportunities and reduce their dependence on the seller.

We divide the time under examination into five periods. (See table 12-2.) The first, from 1950 to 1960, is the period of Sino-Soviet defense cooperation. The Soviet Union's willingness to sell aircraft, designs, and production technology provided the foundation for China's modern defense aviation industry. At the same time, the United States and Western countries used a trade embargo and export controls to ban the sale of military aircraft and military technology. The second period is marked by the Sino-Soviet split and the withdrawal of Soviet advisors and technicians from China. With the Western embargo continuing, China was essentially cut off from legitimate access to military aircraft and related technology from 1960 to 1977. The third period, from 1977 to 1989, was marked by increasing Chinese access to Western commercial technology, including selected military systems, components, and technologies. Access to Eastern bloc technologies, which lagged behind Western systems but were more compatible with China's existing industrial base, remained very limited. China's cooperation with Israel on fighter aircraft began during this time.[23] The fourth period, from 1989 to 2004, is characterized by the U.S. and European ban on military sales to China following the Tiananmen incident in June 1989 and the gradual opening of the window for arms sales and technology transfers from the Soviet Union and its successor states. Western countries sought to limit the transfer of military and dual-use technologies to the Chinese defense industry, but the Chinese commercial sector gradually gained access to increasingly sophisticated civilian and dual-use technologies for commercial applications. Despite efforts to use end-use certificates and inspections to monitor where dual-use technologies were employed, many of these technologies could eventually be "spun on" to defense production.

Table 12–2. Five Periods of Chinese Technological Development

1950–1960	1960–1977	1977–1989	1989–2004	2004–Present
Sino-Soviet defense cooperation	Chinese isolation	Window of access to Western technologies	West cuts access, Russia reopens; diversification of strategies	Russian reluctance; increased indigenous capacity

The fifth period, from roughly 2004 to the present, is marked by Russia's growing reluctance to provide China access to its most advanced military fighters and production technology as Russian economic recovery increased Moscow's bargaining power and control over the Russian defense industry. Despite China's efforts to persuade the European Union to lift its arms embargo, access to Western military aircraft remained denied. However, some European countries did sell China components and technologies that could be employed in military aircraft.[24] At this time, Israel, under heavy U.S. pressure, cancelled a deal to upgrade unmanned aerial vehicles (UAVs) it had previously sold to China (having cancelled an earlier project to upgrade Chinese airborne early warning aircraft in 2000).[25] Although Chinese access to state-of- the-art military technology remains limited, the Chinese aviation industry made significant strides in absorbing foreign technology and demonstrated the ability to reverse engineer the Su–27 Flanker (as the J–11B) and to serially produce its own fourth-generation fighter (the J–10). It was also recently discovered that China is farther ahead in the development of its fifth-generation stealth fighter (the J–20) than many foreign sources anticipated.[26] Overall, China's level of economic development has advanced significantly, and its civilian industry has enjoyed significant access to state-of-the-art commercial (and sometimes dual-use) technology.

The Era of Sino-Soviet Defense Cooperation (1950–1960)

Table 12–3. The Era of Sino-Soviet Defense Cooperation (1950–1960)

Buy	MiG–15bis (1951)	MiG–17 Fresco-As (early 1950s)	Il–28 bomber (early 1950s)	
Coproduce	4 Core Aviation Enterprises established with Soviet assistance (1952–1954)		Shenyang J–5: Chinese MiG–17F (1956)	J–6 rejected by PLAAF due to poor quality workmanship (1959–1960)
Build			JJ-1 trainer: first indigenously developed military aircraft (1958)	CJ–6 fighter trainer (1960)

In the aftermath of the Communist takeover and the establishment of the People's Republic of China (PRC) in 1949, the Chinese economy's level of development was relatively backward. Some pockets of industry employed modern technologies, but China was still predominantly a rural economy with limited industrial capacity. Given its limited technological base, China essentially had no ability to indigenously produce military aircraft. The first armed air contingent (and precursor to the PLAAF), the Nanyuan Flying Group, operated an assorted collection of around forty aircraft captured from the Nationalist air force.²⁷ There is no sourced record of the fighters operated by the short-lived Nanyuan Group, but they likely included U.S.-built Curtiss-Wright aircraft like the Hawk 75M, 75A-5, and CW-21, as well as the Soviet Polikarpov I-15bis and I-16, all operated by the Nationalist air force in the war against Japan. It is estimated that at the time the PLAAF was officially founded in late 1949, it had approximately 115 ex-Nationalist aircraft, though some sources place its strength approximately 40 percent higher.²⁸ Several dozen of these were not obtained until near the end of the Chinese civil war, when the Nationalist air force began to experience frequent uprisings and pilots defected to the Communist side along with their aircraft.²⁹ The Soviet Union soon augmented China's air force with an additional 434 aircraft and sent 878 experts to seven flight schools that had recently been approved by the Central Military Commission (CMC) of the People's Liberation Army.³⁰ Chinese involvement in the Korean War led to the rapid expansion of the PLAAF in terms of both equipment and capable personnel. By 1953, the last year of the war, there were 13 air force schools which had trained nearly 6,000 flight crew members and 24,000 maintenance personnel to service 28 PLAAF air divisions (around 3,000 aircraft).³¹

From the outset of Sino-Soviet defense cooperation, Moscow had considerable bargaining power vis-à-vis China, which had no alternative source for advanced military technology. Trade agreements that allowed for the transfer of technology boiled down to what Chinese Premier Zhou Enlai described as "selling agricultural products to buy machines."³² In a conversation with Indonesian President Sukarno, Mao Zedong gave a candid assessment of the Chinese economy circa 1953 saying, "Frankly speaking, we haven't got a lot of things to export apart from some apples, peanuts, pig bristles, soy beans."³³ Despite this imbalance, the Soviet perception of China as a fellow Communist state and natural ally led Moscow to view a Chinese capacity to produce military aircraft as an asset in the Cold War against the West. As a result, the Soviet Union did not fully employ its potential leverage and provided the PLA Air Force with its first jet fighters and the Chinese aviation industry with its first capacity to produce modern jet fighters. So keen, in fact, were the Soviets to bring China online that some Chinese armament producing plants were turning out sophisticated weaponry before the Soviet defense industry itself could.³⁴ The decision to allow China to coproduce sophisticated fighter aircraft was part of the larger effort to transform it quickly into a capable, self-sufficient defense partner.

Archives maintained by the Communist Party of the Soviet Union Central Committee (CPSU CC) assert that ten thousand "specialists" were sent to China in the 1950s, but there is no corresponding record of who these specialists were, where they went, or how long they stayed.³⁵ It is clear that from the early 1950s the Soviet Union committed a massive amount of resources to build up Chinese industrial enterprises, with special attention given to the defense industry. The initial agreement pertaining to military aviation, signed by Stalin and Chinese Premier Zhou Enlai in October 1951, laid out the terms under which the Union of Soviet Socialist Republics (USSR) would render technical and repair assistance as well as construct new factories for the manufacture of aircraft.[36] This agreement was reached against the backdrop of the Korean War. In 1954, Moscow issued another memorandum to the People's Republic of China outlining cooperation on 15 new defense enterprises.[37] The Soviets agreed to perform design work, deliver equipment, and provide technical support for the fledgling enterprises. It is no exaggeration to say the Soviets helped China build a military aviation industry essentially from the ground up.

After a protracted civil war, which resumed after 7 years of Japanese occupation, China was left with almost no means to produce military aircraft indigenously. Several years after the founding of the PRC, China's nascent defense industry lacked the capability to produce advanced Western designs, or even to absorb Western technology into its Soviet-designed fighters, making the steal option impractical even if China could gain access to controlled Western designs and technologies. Initial purchases of Soviet fighters and aggressive pursuit of coproduction arrangements were logical responses to this set of constraints and opportunities, despite the implicit dependence on continuing access to Soviet designs, spare parts, and technical assistance. The massive infusion of Soviet personnel and equipment enabled China to design and produce several prototypes of its own fighter trainer (based largely on Soviet designs) by 1960, and to coproduce Soviet fighters, bombers, and transport aircraft throughout the 1950s.

China's leadership assessed the technical challenges implicit in licensed coproduction of Soviet aircraft and incorporated conclusions in the first five-year plan for the development of the aviation industry. The plan anticipated China's heavy reliance on the USSR to get the core enterprises that would form the backbone of military aviation up and running, but the end goal was for China to independently manufacture advanced Soviet aircraft within 3 to 5 years of facilities coming online. Four main production plants were established in the early to mid 1950s: the Nanchang Aircraft Factory, Shenyang Aircraft Factory, Zhuzhou Aero Engine Factory, and the Shenyang Aero Engine Factory.[38] Once these core enterprises were established, the emphasis shifted to manufacturing components. Construction of the Xian Aircraft Accessory Factory, Xinping Aviation Electronic and Wheel Brake Factory, and the Baoji Aviation Instrument Factory began in 1956. During the era of Sino-Soviet cooperation, these seven enterprises formed the core of China's military aviation industry. Though the degree of direct Soviet assistance varied by factory, the USSR was instrumental in the development of each.

Metallurgy in China prior to the 1950s was not suitably advanced for the production of advanced aero engine materials, which rely on the mastery of high temperature alloys including steel-titanium and aluminum-magnesium alloys. The PRC government made the development of high temperature alloys a priority for the Ministry of Metallurgical Industry.[39] Joint efforts of the aviation and metallurgical industries led to development of China's first high temperature alloy in 1956. A great deal of labor resources was devoted to this task, enabling the PRC to produce its first turbojet engine, the WP5.[40] Conversion from the WP5 to the next generation WP6 turbojet proved difficult, first due to technical differences—the WP6 had 2,521 parts, 46 percent more than its predecessor[41]—making it impossible to use the same production lines, and second, due to the chaotic work conditions resulting from the Great Leap Forward. Performance standards were not met when the WP6 underwent initial testing in 1958. It was not until 1963 that the engine was finally approved and paired with the J6.

China's first indigenously produced military aircraft, the CJ–5 trainer manufactured at the Nanchang Aircraft Factory, made its first successful test flight on July 11, 1954. The CJ–5, which was built around the M–11 powerplant produced by the Zhuzhou Aero Engine Factory, was a nearly exact copy of the Soviet Yakovlev Yak–18 fighter trainer. Based on ambitions laid out by China's military leadership to transition from repairing aircraft to manufacturing complete designs in 3 to 5 years, domestic production of the CJ–5 was ahead of schedule. The Shenyang Aircraft Factory was also able to produce its copy of the MiG–17 ahead of schedule. Originally slated for completion at the end of 1957, the J–5 fighter, powered by the domestically produced WP5 engine, made a successful test flight on July 19, 1956.[42] Coproduction of the J–5 went relatively smoothly, with the Soviet Union providing two MiG–17 pattern aircraft, manufacturing documentation, and 15 complete knock-down kits to the Shenyang Aircraft Factory. Over its 14-year production run from 1955 to 1969, the Chinese military aviation industry produced 767 J–5/J–5A fighters, first at the Shenyang Aircraft Factory (SAF) and later at Chengdu State Aircraft Factory No.132 (later Chengdu Aircraft Industry Group), which was established with the help of Soviet technicians in 1958. Around the time China successfully tested the J–5, preparations were underway for the first Chinese-designed and -produced fighter aircraft. This project culminated in the JJ–1 jet fighter trainer, which was test-flown in the summer of 1958. Although the JJ–1 met PLAAF inspection standards, it was not serially produced. Military planners opted for an alternate Chinese-designed fighter trainer, the CJ–6, which was tested successfully in 1960 and serially produced up until the mid 1980s.[43] Indigenous modifications made to the CJ-6 were meant to improve upon its predecessor, the CJ-5, itself a copy of the Yakovlev Yak-18 fighter trainer.

The J-6, based on the more sophisticated MiG-19P,[44] was the first Chinese-produced supersonic fighter.[45] Manufacturing rights for the MiG-19P were transferred in 1957, and in 1959 Moscow agreed to license coproduction of the MiG-19PM and S. As the Great Leap Forward began to affect China's industrial enterprises, the production quality of the J-6 rapidly declined. Rules and regulations adapted from the Soviet model were cast aside and "an unhealthy tendency of neglecting quality while pursuing quantity" appeared.[46] Soviet assistance was still available during initial production of the J-6 but China chose to manufacture the necessary tooling and assemble the aircraft without outside help. The end result was a large number of J-6 fighters produced in the period 1958–61 that were of such poor quality that they were not delivered to the PLAAF and PLA Navy Air Force. Performance appraisals of the J-6 that appear in the Chinese literature for this time period are unduly optimistic given SAF's inconsistent production record.[47] Although it had yet to master independent MiG-19 (J-6) production, China nevertheless sought access to more advanced Soviet fighters. In the last deal before the Sino-Soviet split ended all defense cooperation, Moscow licensed production of the MiG-21F-13 to China in 1961.[48] China received three pattern aircraft, as well as 20 kits, but did not take possession of all relevant technical information before defense cooperation ended in 1962. The MiG-21 served as the template for China's long running J-7 fighter program which began in the early 1960s.

Moscow also provided the PLAAF with a fleet of modern bomber aircraft. China took delivery of the Ilyushin Il-28 tactical bomber beginning in the early 1950s. A repair shop to service the Il-28 was set up in Harbin, but China did not receive licensing rights to coproduce the bomber before Soviet advisors were withdrawn in July 1960. China later reverse engineered the Il-28 and produced it as the It-5.[49] The Soviet Union licensed production of its state-of-the-art Tupolev Tu-16 Badger bomber in 1957, supplying China with two production aircraft, a semi knock-down kit, and a complete knock-down kit.[50] Soviet technicians and engineers were on hand to set up serial production of the aircraft the Chinese designated H-6 (or B-6) at factories in Harbin and Xian. The Xian factory was built specifically for production of the H-6 and was facilitated with help from over 1,500 skilled industry workers transferred from the Shenyang Aircraft Factory. H-5 repairs were already being made at the Harbin location, but serial production of the H-6 required a doubling of floor space and an expansion of the work force with experienced Shenyang workers.[51] Although Moscow granted China access to the latest fighter and bomber technologies—even allowing Beijing to produce copies of the MiG–17's Klimov VK–1F and Tumansky R–9BF–811 turbojet engines—the Soviets withheld the transfer of key technologies that would have allowed China to build a long- range strategic missile force.

While it had access to Soviet assistance, China's military aviation industry made steady, quantifiable progress on almost every front. In addition to mastering production of several fighters and bombers, the PRC also began to form a research and development infrastructure meant to advance the end goal of self-reliance. In 1956, Mao Zedong called for a "march towards modern science," which was embodied in a 12-year development plan directed by Zhou Enlai, Chen Yi, Li Fuchun, and Nie Rongzhen.[52] Advancing military aviation technology, particularly fighter technology, was one of five objectives in the plan. To this end, Chinese technicians constructed a transonic wind tunnel for testing jet body designs based on the Soviet AT–1. The Shenyang Aircraft Factory began construction in September of 1958 and completed the tunnel in March 1960.[53] Design and research institutes were established to build China's knowledge base in aerodynamics, thermodynamics, and avionics development, with a total of 19 research and design departments employing approximately ten thousand employees operating at the end of 1960.[54] Overall, military aviation in the 1950s was technologically advanced compared to most of the Chinese economy. Of the handful of countries able to produce modern fighters and bombers, China was the poorest and most backward in terms of other scientific development. This situation was indicative of the importance Mao placed on strengthening China's defensive capabilities (at great cost to other areas of development) as well as Soviet willingness to transfer the necessary set of technologies and know-how.

Sino-Soviet Split to the Reform Era (1960–1977)

Table 12–4. Sino-Soviet Split to the Reform Era (1960–1977)

Buy		50 Spey fan-jet engines from Britain (1975)	SA–321 Super Frelon helicopter from France (1977)
Coproduce	Chengdu J–5A: Chinese MiG–17PF (1964)	Spey fan-jet engine coproduction (1975)	Harbin H–6: Chinese Tu–16 bomber (1968)
Reverse Engineer	Harbin H–5: Chinese IL–28 bomber (1966)	Shenyang J–7: from incomplete MiG–21 production documents (1966)	Shenyang J–8: based on MiG–21 airframe (1969)
Build			Shenyang/Tianjin JJ–6 (1970)

At the time of the Sino-Soviet split, China possessed a military aviation industry with fully operational production facilities, almost a decade of experience manufacturing advanced fighter and bomber systems, and a reasonably well-equipped air force modeled along Soviet lines. However the withdrawal of Soviet advisors and technical assistance in July 1960 and the intensification of the Sino-Soviet split in the early 1960s had major consequences for the PLAAF and the Chinese aviation industry.[55] As relations between China and the Soviet Union deteriorated, the PLAAF lost the option of buying new and updated Soviet fighters and the Chinese aviation industry lost access to technical support from Soviet advisors to help improve aircraft production and master key technologies. The Chinese defense industry would spend much of this period struggling to absorb and extend the technology it had acquired from its coproduction deals with the Soviet Union or reverse engineered from its Soviet aircraft.

In the wake of the Sino-Soviet split, China lacked a relationship with another advanced country to acquire cutting-edge military hardware. Western export controls focused on preventing exports of militarily relevant technologies to the Eastern bloc foreclosed the "buy" option. Even after China's rapprochement with the United States in 1971, it took a number of years before the United States and European countries were prepared to ease export controls on military technology, pursue arms sales, or engage in defense industrial cooperation. The one noteworthy exception was a 1975 agreement (negotiations began in 1972) whereby Britain supplied China with 50 Spey fan-jet engines, the powerplant used in British versions of the multirole F–4 Phantom (the RN F–4K and RAF F–4M), as well as the Vought A–7 Corsair light attack aircraft.[56] China was given full production rights and began trial manufacturing the Spey RB–168–25R as the WS9 at its plant in Xi'an. Under the terms of the agreement, Rolls Royce provided both manufacturing facilities and technical expertise involved with testing the Chinese-produced Speys. To date, the Xian JH–7 fighter bomber is the only PLAAF aircraft powered by a variant of the original Rolls Royce Spey or the Chinese-manufactured WS9.[57] While the Spey arrangement was not a direct transfer of weaponry per se, it involved a single-use technology applicable only to combat aircraft and should thus be considered a transfer of military equipment.

Political restrictions on importing military hardware from the West were further aggravated by the fact that very few Chinese citizens were permitted to go abroad (even Chinese diplomatic missions were withdrawn from most countries during the Cultural Revolution), making it difficult to access the sorts of restricted technologies worth stealing. Obtaining access to information about improvements in Soviet weapons systems from other members of the Eastern bloc and developing country customers would have been a logical approach, but little information is available about the extent to which China pursued this direction and what success it might have had.

These challenges were compounded by the massive social upheavals and the cumulative impact of the Great Leap Forward and the Cultural Revolution, which stymied development of the Chinese economy for a decade, limiting the ability of the Chinese civilian economy to produce technologies that the military could incorporate into weapons systems. Industrial output not related to the defense sector was severely affected by the Cultural Revolution as capable individuals with managerial and planning roles in key enterprises were branded bourgeoisie reactionaries and removed from their positions. The damage done in this respect had long-term consequences for many sectors of the Chinese economy. Despite efforts to protect scientists and engineers working on high-priority defense projects, chaos in the wider economy inevitably had a negative impact on China's aviation industry.[58]

Although the Central Military Commission ordered the aviation ministry to commence R&D programs on some 27 new types of aircraft in 1971,[59] in reality China's aviation industry had its hands full mastering production and extending the designs of Soviet fighters and bombers designed in the late 1950s. For example, the design of the J–7 (China's MiG–21 variant) was not finalized until more than a decade after its initial flight test in 1966 and it was not approved for serial production until 1979.[60] China's aviation industry eventually proved capable of absorbing 1950s Soviet aviation technology and by the end of this period had developed some limited design innovations (for example on the J–7/F–7) via reverse engineering efforts that went a step beyond copying. However, by the time the Chinese industry reached this point, both Western and Soviet air forces had moved on to more advanced fourth-generation aircraft that made China's most advanced aircraft effectively obsolete as soon as they rolled off the production line.

Coproduction

As previously mentioned, the Shenyang Aircraft Factory refused Soviet assistance on the J–6A and set out to manufacture the required tooling domestically.[61] These efforts were not particularly successful; production was halted at various times as the result of poor quality manufacturing and the PLAAF refused to fly the J–6A until improvements were made.[62] Under the guidance of SAF vice general secretary Wang Qigong and vice chief technician Luo Shida, a document was drafted outlining 10 standards to follow in the second series of J–6 prototype production.[63] With better quality control procedures in place, SAF was able to finally produce a J–6 prototype which met state standards for mass production in 1963. Once mass production was approved, the Nanchang

Aircraft Factory (NAF) began manufacturing the J–6. This required NAF to convert from a propeller aircraft factory to one that produced jet fighters.[64]

Improvements to J–6 production quickly eroded with the onset of the Cultural Revolution. Aircraft designers and engineers were among the group of "intellectuals" targeted in the mass movement, and their marginalization along with a number of other technical issues plagued China's defense industries.[65] By the early 1970s, hundreds of substandard J–6s had to be dismantled and rebuilt (to the tune of millions of yuan).[66] Though the J–6 and J–7 represent the height of Chinese advancement in terms of the serial production of military aircraft during this time period, efforts continued to improve upon previous J–5, J–5A, and JJ–5 designs. These improvements were for the most part cosmetic (the lengthening of a fuselage, relocation of components, etc.) and though Chinese writings are sanguine about the progress made, there was very little in the way of actual innovation.

Bomber production made some modest advances during this period, with a domestically manufactured Xian H–6 medium bomber taking to the air on December 24, 1968, and serial production beginning shortly thereafter.[67] Efforts to produce the H–6 were delayed significantly by the withdrawal of Soviet advisors, but Chinese engineers were eventually able to use the plans and tooling to successfully produce the bomber. Chinese serial production of the H–6 was a notable achievement for the military aviation industry, but the aircraft was based on the Tupolev Tu–16 Badger, which had been in service with the Soviet air force since 1954.[68] The H–6 has remained China's mainstay bomber over the decades with modified versions of the aircraft comprising the bulk of the PLAAF bomber fleet even today.

Reverse Engineering and Independent Production

China received licensing rights for the MiG–21F–13 and its Tumansky turbojet engine, but transfer of other MiG–21 technical information ended with the Sino-Soviet split.[69] Despite incomplete information, China managed to produce various models of the J–7/F–7, as well as the Tumansky engine, in the 1960s and 1970s. Some variants featured limited upgrades and improvements. SAF had taken possession of several completed models of the MiG–21, along with a number of assembly kits, before the USSR withdrew assistance. This provided a decent base to start from, though SAF only succeeded in producing upgraded J–7/F–7 fighters through intense efforts at reverse engineering.[70] The original J–7 experienced numerous teething problems before making its maiden flight in 1966, but was reworked and ultimately entered service with the PLAAF, and was exported as the F–7A. Both the Tanzanian and Albanian air forces operated this aircraft.

SAF later came out with the upgraded J–7I that featured a variable air intake with translating shock cone, an indigenous add-on developed due to missing information in the Soviet manufacturing documents.[71] The PLAAF operated the J–7I interceptor along its southern borders during the Vietnam War, where it shot down six U.S. combat aircraft that entered Chinese airspace.[72] The J–7 program demonstrates that although China was unable to design and produce its own fighters, it had mastered coproduction and reverse engineering well enough to produce reasonably capable (though by no means state-of-the-art) fighters without Soviet assistance. This production capability allowed China to produce F–6 (MiG–19) and F–7 (MiG–21) variants to customers seeking low-cost fighters. The J–6 export variant (F–6C) was produced from complete Soviet blueprints and with initial Soviet assistance.

Although China had not received a license to coproduce the Il–28 bomber, it ultimately decided to try to reverse engineer and independently produce the bomber as the H–5 (or B–5). As a result, China did not possess the same level of design information and Soviet technical support as with its fighter aircraft or the H–6 bomber. When the project finally began in 1963, there were some significant design alterations in the Chinese version.[73] Chinese-produced H–5 bombers did not enter service with the PLAAF until 1967.[74]

The result of forced reliance on indigenous production and reverse engineering was a PLA Air Force equipped throughout the 1960s, 1970s, and 1980s with large quantities of obsolete aircraft based on 1950s vintage Soviet designs that were all the Chinese aviation industry could produce. Although PLAAF leaders (and to some extent Chinese civilian leaders including Deng Xiaoping) were aware of the extent to which China was falling behind advances in Western and Soviet military aviation technology, they had few options available to rectify the situation. In addition to limited access to international aircraft and aviation technology potential, the loss of Soviet support highlighted the importance of self-reliance in military technology for Chinese political leaders and reinforced the interest of key civilian and military leaders in building a defense industry capable of independently designing and producing advanced systems. The result has been an enduring tension between PLA leaders focused on equipping the military with technologically advanced systems (acquired from abroad if necessary) and civilian and defense industry leaders focused on the Maoist goal of building an independent, indigenous defense industry (even if the weapons it produced fell well short of state-of-the-art Western systems).

New Windows of Opportunity (1977–1989)

Table 12-5. New Windows of Opportunity (1977–1989)

Buy	British firm GEC Marconi sells China advanced avionics for J–7II/F–7 fighters (1979)	French Dauphin 2 attack helicopter (1980)	U.S "Peace Pearl" transfer of advanced avionics for J–8 fighters (1984)
Coproduce		France gives China production rights for Dauphin 2 attack helicopter (1980)	
Reverse Engineer	Chengdu J–7II: Based on MiG–21; indigenous add-ons (1978)	Chengdu J–7C: Reverse engineered from Egyptian MiG–21MF (1984)	Shenyang J–8A: Based on MiG–21 airframe (mid 1980s)
Build		China develops first indigenous fire control radar—Type 204 (1984)	

Deng Xiaoping's emergence as China's top leader and the initiation of economic reforms and opening in 1978 offered new opportunities for the Chinese economy generally, and for the defense industry in particular. An initial focus of the reforms was the Four Modernizations campaign (Agriculture, Industry, Science and Technology, and National Defense). Although defense was the last of the Four Modernizations and given lower priority than the first three, the strategies used to modernize China's national defense were consistent with the broader economic development strategy's emphasis on opening and reform. Creating a self-sufficient Chinese national defense infrastructure based on a modern technology base had been a goal since the first five-year plan.[75] The pursuit of air superiority and the role the Chinese military aviation industry played in this pursuit took on a new level of importance once Deng became Chairman of the CMC in 1977.[76] After consolidating all top positions within the Chinese Communist Party (CCP) and becoming "paramount leader," Deng continued to develop his case for airpower, stating to the CMC in January 1979: "Without the air force and air domination, winning a future war is out of the question. . . . Stress investment in the development of the aviation industry and the air force to ensure air domination."[77]

China's ten-year plan for developing both the national economy and the science and technology base was published on February 26, 1978.[78] The plan outlined many of the key elements necessary to produce modern military equipment: more raw materials, better understanding of modern scientific techniques, and access to foreign technology and production practices. China would increase trade by opening its economy, allowing foreign direct investment, and purchasing capital goods and technology from the developed world. Investment from abroad would be obtained by expanding China's export-oriented light industries (i.e., textiles, clothing, and handicrafts), which required low amounts of capital, could be rapidly established, and had "high foreign exchange earnings potential."[79] Earnings originating from light industries could then be recapitalized to continue expanding that sector, applied to the import of advanced foreign technology, or both. China was also in a position to leverage its ample energy resources to finance technology acquisition from abroad. This was the basis of an 8-year, 20 billion dollar agreement signed with Japan in 1978.[80] Casting military modernization in a subordinate role to the other three modernizations inverted Mao's "superpower" strategy, which stressed building national defense as the first imperative in elevating China to great power status. The more pragmatic reform-era leadership understood that national defense capability improved as a function of overall economic progress. Moreover, it realized that to achieve self-reliance in the long term, China would have to pursue the transfer of advanced foreign military and dual-use technologies in the near term.

China continued to refine its industrial policy throughout the 1980s, with the goal of developing a modern, science and technology–driven economy in the first half of the 21st century. Evan Feigenbaum notes the contributions of scientists involved with China's nuclear program in the 1950s and 1960s in crafting and pushing forward the set of policies establishing a new national development trajectory.[81] Prominent nuclear scientists like Zhang Jingfu and Song Jian were among a small group of Chinese technical personnel involved in Mao era programs requiring "'scientific' decision analysis."[82] This gave them valuable experience organizing research and development to meet specific scientific objectives, and applying lessons learned in the process to other related areas. Observing the state of global technological innovation in the late 1970s and early 1980s led the group of scientists advocating China's new industrial policies to the conclusion that novel state-of-the-art technologies (semiconductors, integrated circuits) would be increasingly dual-use in nature and thus result in a "spin-on" paradigm.[83] Because commercial and military technologies would be inextricably linked in the future, China would have to reengineer its entire state R&D system and not focus solely on developing military technologies. The Chinese government's efforts to bridge the technology gap with Western military powers rely on spurring innovation, stressing market competition, and emphasizing civil-military integration (*Junmin Yitihua*) to create greater efficiencies. These policies seek to construct an effective dual-use technology base that can support both the civilian economy and the needs of the military.[84]

China's opening and reform efforts built upon its rapprochement with the United States and the West in the early 1970s. The primary impetus for rapprochement was strategic, but improved relations also created a favorable climate for China's economic reforms and, eventually, for defense industrial cooperation with Western countries. Mirroring the Soviet logic of the 1950s, the United States and other Western military powers sought to improve China's defense capability as a means of tying down the vast Soviet military. There was obviously not the same strong ideological affinity between China and the West that there had been during the Sino-Soviet partnership. There was, however, a mutual understanding that certain common objectives—namely, undermining Soviet power and influence—could be advanced by assistance to China's defense industry. China did not view the West as an ally per se, nor did the West expect a close defense relationship to emerge from new circumstances.

The strategic rationale for cooperation was paired with the realization by Western defense industries that significant profits might be available by selling arms to China and assisting in the modernization of China's backward defense industries. Continuing export controls and legal restrictions on the export of arms and advanced technologies to China also meant that cooperation expanded at a gradual, modest pace with considerable oversight by Western governments. On China's side, the opportunity to take advantage of new access to Western military aviation technologies clashed with the desire to build an independent aviation industry and Maoist concerns about self-reliance. As Lewis and Xue write, "The ensuing compromise restricted the definition of self-reliance to the outright purchase of aircraft, while extending the meaning of Deng Xiaoping's Open Door policy to permit the acquisition of foreign air-launched weapons and avionics."[85]

Buying, Coproduction, and Integration

China chose to pursue acquisition of armaments and avionics rather than outright purchases of Western combat aircraft (which Western governments would have been reluctant to allow). Helicopters were an exception to this general rule. In 1977, the French delivered the SA–321 Super Frelon helicopter to China, and allowed China to coproduce it as the Z–8 beginning in 1981.[86] France also agreed to let China coproduce its Dauphin 2 attack helicopter as the Z–9 beginning in 1980.[87] The earliest fighter technology transfers came in 1979, in the form of a license agreement between China and the British defense firm GEC-Marconi (now BAE avionics) to supply the J–7II tactical fighter, as well as F–7 export variants, with a complete avionics suite. This upgrade, which included the Type 226 Skyranger radar, weapons-aiming computer, and state-of-the-art display systems, represented a huge boost for China's military aviation industry. Chinese-produced F–7s with Western avionics sold well on the export market with the air forces of Sri Lanka, Iran, Myanmar, Bangladesh, and Pakistan all signing purchase agreements in the 1980s. The F–7s were not actually delivered until the late 1980s and early 1990s and many remain in service today. J–7/F–7 aircraft produced in the 1970s and 1980s with advanced avionics were an improvement over the J–6/F–6 series, but still lagged far behind Western and Soviet fourth-generation fighters that were entering service in the same time period.[88]

The Shenyang J–8A (a twin-engine MiG–21 derivative) was the most sophisticated fighter China operated in the late 1980s. Shenyang Aircraft Corporation (SAC)[89] proved that it could go beyond simply reproducing Soviet designs by modifying the MiG–21 airframe to accommodate the J–8A's two Wopen–7A turbojet engines. However, the derivative body design limited top speed to a "modest" Mach 2.2, making the J–8A slower than third-generation Soviet fighters like the MiG–23.[90] China sought to use its newfound access to Western avionics to improve the J–8A's combat capability. By the mid-1980s, China had developed its first indigenous fire control radar (Type 204), but this system lacked some state-of-the-art features embedded in Western and Soviet radar systems, most notably beyond-visual-range capacity. One of the four programs under the U.S./China "Peace Pearl" initiative launched in the mid 1980s involved the U.S. firm Westinghouse equipping 50 J–8 fighters with advanced, beyond-visual-range capable radar systems. Sanctions banning sale of U.S. arms to China were imposed in the wake of the 1989 Tiananmen massacre, but in 1992 President George H.W. Bush issued a waiver stating that it was "in the national interest" to fulfill the terms of four suspended weapons sales programs on the grounds that none of them "significantly" boosted Chinese military capabilities.[91] The waiver also stated that fulfilling these programs would "improve the prospects for gaining further cooperation from China on nonproliferation issues."[92] The PLAAF ultimately received two modified J–8 fuselages and four avionics kits to close out the "Peace Pearl" effort.

China also reportedly developed a variant of the J–8, the ACT control variant, which featured analogue fly-by-wire (FBW) controls. A working test bed was flown in 1988. The ability to produce an aircraft incorporating this technology is noteworthy given the fact that China had no legal access to it through Western or Soviet channels (FBW controls had been incorporated into new Western and Soviet fighters by the mid-1970s). Chinese military aviation had not mastered less challenging aspects of avionics development at the time the J–8ACT program was underway, and it is unlikely that the knowledge to produce FBW controls came about via indigenous R&D. There is no way to draw definitive conclusions about where China acquired the knowledge to produce this technology, but its defense relationship with Israel provides one possible answer. Development work on the FBW-capable Israeli Lavi fighter began in 1982 and by the time Sino-Israeli defense cooperation was established in 1984, the Lavi project was in full swing. A range of open source information suggests that Israel transferred advanced military aviation technologies to China long before formal diplomatic relations were established in 1992.[93]

Advances in Chinese military aviation from the late 1970s to the late 1980s came primarily as a result of exposure to more sophisticated Western aviation technologies and their integration into PLAAF aircraft. Access to the GEC Marconi radar and to FBW technology required Chinese technical personnel to perform design modifications necessary to accommodate these new systems. It also provided a starting point for reverse engineering efforts, though due to China's inexperience with Western production practices there was no guarantee of success. Despite newfound access to some state-of-the-art military hardware and innovations in airframe design, China's defense sector remained incapable of producing modern weapons systems.[94] Numerous deficiencies prevented China from turning out cutting-edge equipment. The issues it faced were specific to its system of economic and political organization, not merely the byproducts of central planning. (The Soviet case proves that an economy based on central planning can produce some of the world's most advanced military hardware.)

During the 1980s and 1990s, state-owned Chinese defense enterprises received cost plus 5 percent for all equipment produced, providing no incentive to cut costs or maximize production efficiency.[95] There was no competition to determine which enterprise would build which system. Enterprises were (and still are to some degree) assigned projects based on ministerial bargaining, nullifying a great deal of the incentive to turn out a better end product.[96] The story of this time period for the aviation industry is mixed: from an organizational perspective, the objectives articulated in the Four Modernizations campaign and attention to airpower at the highest levels of leadership set a course for progress. On the other hand, the industry made almost no tangible progress in closing the technology gap with Soviet or Western air forces in the 1980s.

Three significant developments would come to shape the trajectory of Chinese military aviation in the next time period we analyze. First, there was the decision to emphasize the development and diversification of the overall Chinese economy via deeper market reforms. The initial impact on the defense industry was negative, as funding for the military was reduced and the defense industry was encouraged to convert to civilian production. Over the longer run, however, development of the broader economy produced both financial resources and access to technologies that would support a more advanced defense technology base. The second important event was the Sino-Soviet rapprochement. Soviet Premier Mikhail Gorbachev's visit to Beijing in May 1989 marked the official return of normal relations between the two sides and was eventually followed in the early 1990s by new arms sales agreements, including the sale of the Sukhoi Su–27 Flanker.[97] These deals were largely negotiated on Chinese terms, offering China the opportunity to pursue new procurement strategies. Finally, the Tiananmen massacre in June 1989 led to an immediate end of Chinese legitimate access to most Western arms and military aviation technologies.

New Partners, New Strategies (1989–2004)

The immediate Chinese leadership response to Tiananmen was a political clampdown and economic retrenchment, but by early 1991 economic growth had resumed and the stage was set for further economic reforms that would lay the foundation for sustained Chinese growth. Openness to trade and foreign investment helped the Chinese economy grow rapidly and develop a deeper civilian technology base. Although the United States and Western European countries sought to limit Chinese access to Western arms and military technology through export controls and sanctions, the lure of access to China's market ultimately gave China's defense industries access to considerable dual-use technology that could be "spun on" to military applications. Moreover, the rapid advancement of computer, communications, and material technologies in a globalized economy meant that technologies once used primarily in military industries became ubiquitous (and free from export controls).

Table 12-6. New Partners, New Strategies (1989–2004)

Buy	12x Su–27 Flanker (1992)	24x Su–27 Flanker (1995–1996)	80x Su–30MKK (2000–2001)	Ukraine sells China single Su–33 (2000)
Coproduce		Sino-Russian agreement for SAC to manufacture 200 Su–27s as J–11 (1996)	SAC masters coproduction of J–11 (2002)	
Reverse Engineer	Shenyang J–8D (1990)	Shenyang J–8F (2000)		
Steal		China begins reverse engineering Su-27 subsystems for use in indigenized J–11B (2002–2003)	Chinese cyber espionage efforts target information on foreign military aviation technologies (mid 2000s)	
Codevelop	Espionage emerges as technology acquisition strategy with increased Chinese presence abroad (mid 1990s)			
Build	China begins to develop indigenous fourth-generation fighter (J–10); significant technical assistance from Israel (mid 1990s)	China develops JH–7 fighter/bomber with assistance of imported U.S. supercomputers (mid 1990s)		China violates terms of Su–27 contract with Russia; develops indigenized J–11B (2003–2004)

The Chinese defense industry's access to advanced computers in the mid-1990s supported efforts to develop more sophisticated design capabilities. Supercomputers obtained from the United States after export laws were loosened in 1996 and 1998 were later used to simulate the detonation of nuclear warheads without actual underground testing.[98] China's shipbuilding industry also made new advances enabled by computer-assisted design (CAD) technology to improve both the quantity and quality of maritime vessels.[99] The Xian FBC-1 fighter-bomber (also known as the JH–7) presents the most compelling example of U.S. supercomputer technology being used to expand Chinese military aviation capabilities. Designed to replace outdated light bombers like the Nanchang Q–5 and Harbin H–5, the development program for the JH–7 began in the 1980s. Six prototypes were developed in the early 1990s and delivered to the PLAAF and PLANAF for evaluation. An upgraded variant, the JH–7A, came out around 2000 and was the first Chinese aircraft based solely on CAD design. Chinese engineers reportedly bragged that the fighter-bomber was designed using supercomputers imported from the United States. The fact that Xian Jiaotong University houses a supercomputer and has ties to the Xian Aircraft Industry Corporation (XAC) and the 603[d] Aircraft Design Institute, the principal contractors on the JH–7A, may explain why CAD technologies were applied to the JH–7A rather than the more advanced J–10 fighter. In the wake of discoveries during the 1990s that China had diverted some supercomputers acquired from the United States for military purposes, Congress passed a law in 1998 tightening restrictions on the technology. China's indigenous efforts to develop its own supercomputers since the late 1990s have made the law (at least as it applies to China) somewhat irrelevant.[100] A 2003 report cites the twin seat J–10BS variant as the first Chinese fighter produced with CAD, noting that the software decreased the time it took to render design drawings from 10 to 6 months.[101] The fact this achievement was reported publicly does not contradict the conclusion that the JH–7 was China's first CAD assisted fighter, but instead hints at the fact that the J–10BS was the first example of a military aircraft designed using domestically produced CAD technology. All subsequent Chinese military aviation development projects almost certainly utilize CAD.

Although China lost legitimate access to most Western defense technologies after Tiananmen, it continued existing defense technology ties with Israel and reestablished them with Russia. Ukraine also emerged as an important source of air-to-air (AAM) and air-to-surface missiles (ASM) for the PLAAF.[102] Unlike the previous Sino-Soviet defense arrangement where Beijing was dependent on Moscow and negotiated from a weaker bargaining position, the economically tumultuous post-Soviet Russian state was much more dependent on China as a buyer. This allowed China to gain access to both advanced fighters and aviation technologies that a more solvent Russian government likely would have preferred not to sell.

In response to these new opportunities, China pursued multiple options to advance military modernization. The PLA purchased limited quantities of advanced Russian aircraft, ships, and submarines in order to gain experience operating modern weapons systems. For the PLAAF, this included acquisition of the Su–27 fighter and the S–300 surface-to-air missile. The deal eventually evolved into a coproduction arrangement intended to produce 200 aircraft and then into efforts to reverse engineer key components to create an independent production capability. Chinese defense industries continued efforts to develop their own new systems, seeking to integrate advanced imported technologies and components into the design where Chinese equivalents were not available. The J–10 fighter, which uses Russian engines, is one such example. Chinese defense industries also sought to adapt imported and indigenous avionics and armaments to improve the capabilities of older platforms.

At the strategic level, in keeping with Deng's earlier pronouncements regarding the centrality of airpower in winning modern wars, the Chinese began investing more time in related research. Academics and military strategists examined U.S. and Soviet theories on how to achieve maximum effect through the use of airpower.[103] Beijing was realistic about the relative weakness of the PLAAF when measured against its U.S. and Soviet counterparts. While it assimilated airpower strategy as conceived by the superpowers, China was equally interested in understanding how countries with qualitatively less advanced air forces could employ airpower against more powerful opponents. Several works cite surprise attacks by the Argentine air force against British naval forces during the Falklands War as an illustrative example.[104] It was also during this time period that Chinese defense analysts and military planners began to translate the emphasis on expanded airpower into concrete technology acquisition and procurement goals. In the early 1990s, the PLA was still operating under significant budget constraints; since the outset of opening and reform, resources had been shifted to nondefense areas of the economy. Despite this situation, PLAAF planners mapped out a development trajectory for the air force which has been more or less followed: (1) phase out equipment based on antiquated technology; (2) place emphasis on aircraft quality over quantity; (3) graft, when possible, new technology (radar, avionics, missiles) onto older airframes to increase combat effectiveness and extend service life; and (4) focus on long-term self-reliance, while filling existing technology gaps in military aviation via procurement of foreign equipment/knowledge.[105]

In 1998, China undertook a massive restructuring of its defense industry with the aim of ensuring that the PLA was adequately involved in procurement decisions. Prior to creation of the General Armaments Department (GAD), the intermediary between the end user of weaponry (PLA) and the supplier (the defense industry) was the Commission of Science, Technology, and Industry for National Defense (COSTIND). This system resulted in a fundamental misalignment of interests as COSTIND failed to properly represent the needs of the Chinese military, instead allowing the weapons producers to advance their own institutional interests at the expense of the PLA.[106] The defense reforms of the late 1990s allowed the PLA, through the GAD, to take the lead in dictating procurement requirements based on actual need.[107] While the reforms did not specifically address resource competition among the service branches, they did provide a mechanism for the PLAAF to align procurement with its strategic development objectives. Leadership support for increased airpower capability also helped the PLAAF advance its procurement agenda.

Buying, Coproduction, and Reverse Engineering

After Gorbachev's 1989 visit to Beijing, Sino-Soviet rapprochement was solidified by various arms sales agreements including the 1991 deal for China to purchase a dozen Sukhoi Su-27 fighters.[108] At the time, the Soviet Union had just collapsed and the new Russian economy was in a shambles. Strapped for cash, Moscow was ready to leverage the defense industry—one of the few performing sectors of the economy—in order to profit. China was quick to take advantage of the deteriorating situation in the early 1990s, getting Moscow to accept poor quality "barter goods" in exchange for weaponry.[109] Russia had little choice but to put longer-term strategic security concerns on the back burner and do what it could to keep its arms industry operational. To provide some idea of how important Chinese arms sales became to the Russian defense industry, a U.S. Department of Defense report estimated the value of weaponry delivered to China (not simply agreed upon) from 1990 to 2002 at between $7 and $10 billion.[110]

China took delivery of its initial order of 12 Su-27s in 1992, and an additional batch of 18 Su-27SKs and 6 Su-27UBKs in 1995–1996. Altogether China purchased 48 Su-27 Flankers before deciding to build the aircraft domestically as the Shenyang J-11.

The J-11 story began in 1996, when Russian arms export organization Rosoboronexport signed a $2.7 billion licensing agreement with Shenyang Aircraft Corporation allowing coproduction of 200 Su-27s.[111] The agreement came with two provisos: that China would not export the J-11 and that the fighters would be fitted with Russian engines, radar, and avionics which would not be licensed for coproduction.[112] This important agreement, which moved China's military aviation industry from third-generation to fourth-generation production capacity, came about through the actions of the General Director of the Sukhoi Design Bureau, Michael Simonov, who negotiated the deal without Moscow's approval and later presented it to the Yeltsin government as a *fait accompli*.[113] Simonov (acting more in the interests of Sukhoi than the new Russian state) knew that forming a strategic partnership with China was the cornerstone of Yeltsin's Asia policy and that a reversal of the Flanker deal on Moscow's part might sabotage these efforts. The terms of the arrangement were finalized and SAC received manufacturing documents for the Su-27 in 1997 along with complete knock-down kits from which it assembled its first two J-11s. Although both fighters were test flown, they proved to be of such poor workmanship that Russian technicians were called in to rebuild them.[114]

During the first 3 years of production, SAC assembled just five J–11s. Over the next 3 years it quadrupled this number, turning out 20 aircraft by 2003. As SAC began to successfully produce its own replacement parts, the Russian supplier (KnAPPO) began to reduce the contents of the knock-down kits it provided. By 2002 China was not just coproducing the J–11, but doing it at a high level of quality—a remarkable development given that just 4 years earlier SAC could not even put the fighter together correctly without Russian technical assistance.[115] By late 2004, SAC had taken possession of all 105 CKD kits delivered from Russia and had managed to assemble and deliver 95 of those to the PLAAF. After mastering coproduction China quickly moved on to developing its own version of the J–11. Russia cancelled plans to fulfill the remainder of the order after discovering that China had an indigenous J–11 in the pipeline.[116] The 1996 agreement stipulated that China would equip its J–11s solely with Russian-made engines, radar, and avionics, which left China dependent on KnAPPO. Russia had no objection to China producing replacement parts not related to engine, radar, or avionics; the violation occurred when it began to develop these three systems indigenously. By doing so, China ensured that it would not be reliant on Moscow for any component part of its J–11s. This presented the Russian aviation industry with a loss of future revenue and also presented the possibility that China would attempt to sell its J–11 on the international arms market. To date China has made no effort to export any J–11 variant, nor has it expressed any interest in doing so. Chinese officials justified the decision to violate the contract by claiming that the 95 Su–27s on order were no longer adequate to serve the needs of the PLAAF—an interesting claim given the large number of third-generation J–8s still in service. China's decision to abrogate the terms of the Su–27/J–11 contract has had lasting consequences. Since 2006, Russia has refused to enter into any substantive military aviation transfer agreement. We discuss some of the repercussions for China in the next section.

It took 4 years to produce three prototypes of the J–11B multirole fighter, and another 2 years to build the twin-seat J–11BS variant. Sources in the Chinese defense industry report that the J–11B is based on roughly 90 percent Chinese-designed parts and subsystems, including the Type 1474 serial radar system, 3-axis data system, power supply system, emergency power unit, brake system, hydraulic system, fuel system, environment control system, and molecular sieve oxygen generation systems.[117] The J–11B/BS is also fitted with indigenous PL–12 air-to-air missiles. There have been several cases since 2008 of Russian authorities in the Transbaikal region arresting Chinese citizens for attempting to smuggle spare Su–27 parts into China.[118] This might suggest that China is not able to design 90 percent of the original fighter's parts and subsystems (the 10 percent gap in design capability alluded to presumably refers to engines, avionics, and radar which were not among the smuggled items). The engine is the only major subsystem China has openly acknowledged it has yet to master, relying on the imported Russian AL- 31F turbofan for both the J–11 and J–10 fighters.[119] Shenyang Liming Motor Corporation has produced a turbofan engine in the WS–10A Taihang (likely the product of substantial reverse engineering) that approaches the performance of the AL–31F, but takes twice as long to "spool up," or obtain the same thrust output, as its Russian counterpart.[120] This lag time could have life or death consequences for a pilot needing to restart his engine.

Chinese military aviation worked hard to incorporate indigenous systems into the J–11B. The upgraded systems were developed as improvements to the original Su–27SK, which was dated technology by the mid 1990s (the Soviet Air force began operating the Flanker in 1985). China's subsequent decision to lobby Sukhoi to sell it an upgraded version of the Flanker was precipitated by a handful of factors. China was looking for a faster way to obtain increased fighter capability than was presented by developing indigenous upgrades. The 1995–1996 Taiwan Strait crisis highlighted the real possibility of an armed conflict, which in turn reinforced previous conclusions about the centrality of Chinese airpower in prevailing in a Taiwan scenario. Displays of overwhelming U.S. airpower in the 1991 Gulf War were undoubtedly still fresh in the minds of Chinese military planners during the Strait crisis. In addition, the Russian government's inability to regulate military transfers and the tenuous state of the national economy ensured that China could gain access to fighter technology that was closer to state of the art than Russia might have been willing to sell in better circumstances.[121]

The Su–30MK (*modernizeerovannyy kommercheskiy*—upgraded export variant) was already available on the international arms market at the time China was seeking an upgraded Flanker. Russia agreed to sell China a version of this aircraft, appending "K" to the name to denote the customer (*kitayskiy*—Chinese), in 1998. While the two-seat Su–30MKK was not the best fighter Russia was able to produce, it represented a significant jump forward for the PLAAF, particularly in terms of subsystems. The avionics suite incorporated cutting-edge digital processors that linked the primary avionics subsystems together via multiplex databuses.[122] This made it possible for China to integrate new avionics components, either indigenously produced or purchased from a third party, as they became available. The first batch of 10 Su–30MKK aircraft entered service at Wuhu airbase in December 2000.[123] Another 70 were delivered to China in 2001. China and Russia signed a contract in 2003 for the sale of a Su–30 variant with maritime strike capability (MK2), with the PLANAF taking possession of 24 of the aircraft in early 2004. The Su–30MKK is the most sophisticated fighter the PLAAF operates to this day—a mantle it is likely to wear until China's fifth-generation fighter comes into service.

Buying, Building, and Stealing

In addition to acquisition and coproduction of the Su–27, China also continued to pursue indigenous development efforts in parallel through the J–10 fighter program, which drew significantly on Israeli-rooted technology and design assistance.[124] Defense collaboration between the two countries was in full swing as early as 1984 with arms sales reaching an estimated $3.5 billion in that year alone.[125] A great deal of speculation remains regarding the amount and type of technical assistance Israel provided in the development of the J–10, but open source materials clearly indicate that Israel used some expertise gained from developing the U.S.-financed Lavi fourth-generation fighter to assist in the development of the J–10.[126] It is difficult to determine whether the design assistance provided by the Israelis on the J–10 rises to the level of codevelopment as articulated in the model. It is likewise difficult to determine from open source materials what, aside from money, China offered Israel in exchange for design assistance on the J–10. One logical possibility is that Beijing shared technical information on the missiles it sold to countries hostile to Israel—Iran being a prime example. Arguments have also circulated that China had access to a Pakistani F–16, parts of which it may have reverse engineered and integrated into the J–10. The J–10 is clearly not a Lavi clone, however. It has significant design differences from the Lavi including its larger size, canard positioning, wing platform, and two-dimensional air intake.[127] It was originally designed to use the Israeli Elta EL/M–2035 radar, which can simultaneously track six air targets and lock onto the four most-threatening, but is also able to incorporate Russian and Chinese avionics. Both the original J–10 and the J–10B/AS/AB upgrade variants that came into PLAAF service in 2006 sport specially designed Russian Lyul'ka Saturn AL–31N turbofan engines.[128]

Israel was China's second largest source of military aviation technology transfer in the 1990s.[129] While this data point is undeniable, some clarification should be added. Russian arms sales to China during the 1990s topped those of all other countries combined; Israel's stake in the market was trivial by comparison. Nevertheless, it assisted Chinese military aviation in several other areas. In the mid-1990s Israel agreed to sell China its Phalcon Airborne Early Warning and Control (AEW&C) platform and the Harpy unmanned aerial vehicle. At the time, some defense experts rated the Phalcon as the most advanced AEW&C system in the world. This might explain why China approached Israel rather than Russia for access to the technology. With Western arms embargoes still in full force, there was a very short list of states willing and able to sell China advanced military aviation hardware. Israeli Aircraft Industries (IAI) received an initial $319 million deposit from China to secure the Phalcon. News of the deal provoked a strong reaction in Washington, where there was growing concern over Chinese military modernization, particularly as it applied to a potential Taiwan scenario. Chinese military planners understood that in order to prevail in a Taiwan scenario (with U.S. military intervention likely), it was essential to control the airspace over the strait. The first Gulf War confirmed to Beijing the extent of the gap between the PLAAF and its potential U.S. rival. AEW&C was one of a set of capabilities that China needed to develop in order to stand a chance of contesting the U.S. Air Force over the Taiwan Strait. From Israel's perspective, a supplier-client relationship with a rising power like China was a golden opportunity for its small yet capable indigenous defense industries.

Israel ultimately decided that its relationship with the United States was too important to jeopardize, and in July 2000 it canceled the Phalcon sale and refunded China's deposit. Beijing was furious when Israel announced it was backing out of the deal. Prime Minister Ehud Barak had promised that China would receive Phalcon technology, leading President Jiang Zemin to make public statements to that effect.[130] Jiang lost face over what turned out to be empty promises and a substantial diplomatic rift between the two sides ensued.[131]

Since the Phalcon deal fell through in 2000, China has pursued its own domestic AEW&C development program, encountering numerous difficulties along the way. In 2006 a prototype aircraft undergoing flight testing crashed in Anhui province, killing 40 people, among them 35 technicians who were intimately involved with the project.[132] China has since succeeded in producing several types of AEW&C aircraft: the KJ–200, based on the Soviet Yak–8 transport, and the KJ–2000, based on the Russian A–50 MAINSTAY airframe.[133] The PLAAF has taken possession of, and is presumably operating, at least four KJ–2000s.[134] Little is known about the exact capabilities of these aircraft, though there is speculation that they are similar in design, though technically inferior, to the Phalcon.[135] The degree to which China's AEW&C aircraft were developed domestically remains an open question. Despite the fact that Israel cancelled its sale of the Phalcon, it is not implausible that it might have provided China design and technical assistance after the fact.

Israel's reversal on the Phalcon damaged its military aviation technology transfer relationship with China (and also affected overall bilateral relations), but the Harpy fiasco in 2004 was the knock-out punch. Designed to "detect, attack, and destroy radar emitters with a very high hit accuracy," the Harpy is an unmanned aerial vehicle (UAV) with all-weather capability.[136] Its range, the fact that it is launched from a ground vehicle outside the immediate battlespace, and its ability to neutralize SAM and radar sites for long periods of time made the Harpy a sought-after item for Chinese military planners looking out over the Taiwan Strait. The Harpy deal was negotiated in the mid-1990s, with China having taken possession of around one hundred of the UAVs by 1999.[137] The deal was reported to the United States at the time it was negotiated and although there were objections, Washington did not pressure Israel to cancel it. Because the Harpy was a system wholly designed and produced by Israel there was no basis to block the sale on the grounds of illicit technology transfer. It was only when China sent its Harpy inventory back to Israel for service and repair in 2004 that the United States objected. The Bush administration claimed that the true purpose was to upgrade the systems with new sensors that could detect radar emitters even when they are not actively transmitting a signal.[138] Taiwan was reportedly already in possession of the new, upgraded Harpy.[139]

Concerned about the threat the Harpy posed in the case of a Taiwan scenario, the United States demanded that Israel not return the drones that China had already purchased and thus legally owned. What finally happened to China's Harpy aircraft remains unclear (at least in open source material).[140] Israel did refund China a considerable sum of money related to the UAV upgrade indicating that some part of the work was not completed, though whether this included technical upgrades (as Washington claimed) or routine maintenance is still unknown.[141] There is also the possibility that Israel confiscated Harpy components and paid China off in order to mitigate political fall-out over the incident. Whatever the case, the Harpy episode marked the last significant military aviation transfer between Beijing and Jerusalem. It also had negative repercussions for U.S.-Israeli relations: Amos Yaron, Director General of Israel's Ministry of Defense, resigned after the incident.

Ukraine also emerged as a source of advanced military aviation technology during this period. It has not played as prominent a role in equipping the PLAAF as has Russia, but Ukraine has served as an important conduit for Russian military hardware that China has been unable to procure directly. In 2000–2001, the Ukrainian firm Progress reportedly supplied both Iran and China with Soviet Kh–55 cruise missiles, which have an active range of 3,000 kilometers and can be armed with both nuclear and conventional warheads.[142] The highly accurate guidance system used in the Kh–55 was more advanced than anything China was producing indigenously at the time, and expanded the capability of its aged bomber fleet (the Kh–55 is an air-to-surface missile fired solely from bomber platforms). Around this time China also gained access to a single Su–33 (air frame T–10K–7) prototype from Ukraine.[143] China has used this aircraft as a template for its J–15 naval fighter, which is reported to have made a successful test flight in August 2009.[144]

From 1989 to 2004, China actively pursued acquisition of advanced aircraft and aviation technology from Russia, Ukraine, and Israel; used a combination of coproduction and reverse engineering to make advances in subsystem design and manufacturing; and came up with innovations in its own capacity to build fighter aircraft at least partially based on indigenous design. China also appears to have greatly expanded its efforts to steal restricted technologies by way of industrial espionage using both traditional and computer network intrusion techniques. While there are few documented examples citing fighter aircraft technology, there are a number of cases where China obtained, or attempted to obtain, restricted dual-use technologies from the United States using surreptitious means. By 1993 approximately 50 percent of the 900 technology transfer cases handled by U.S. federal law enforcement agencies involved the Chinese.[145] Cases of cyber espionage that track back to China provide more detail about the types of military aviation–related technical data attackers are after. It should be noted that the relative anonymity afforded cyber attackers often leads to problems of attribution. Forensic investigators can trace the origin of a certain exploit back to a computer server in China, for example, but the attacker might be using Chinese commercial networks, which are notoriously porous, as an intermediary point. We therefore only cite examples where evidence exists linking the source of espionage attempts to China, and suggests the involvement of the military or intelligence organizations.

Although the intrusions did not target fighter technology, the 2004 attacks on a number of computer networks belonging to the U.S. military and defense contractors that came to be known as Titan Rain were definitively traced back to a location in Guangdong Province by a computer specialist working at Sandia National Laboratories in New Mexico. The specialist, a former U.S. military intelligence officer, surreptitiously monitored the activities of the attackers after the Sandia networks he was responsible for safeguarding were attacked. He discovered an operation that involved 20 or more individuals connecting through three separate end nodes in Guangdong. While this is not hard proof of a Chinese military or intelligence operation, the sort of data being targeted suggests a military end user. The attackers reportedly breached the systems of the Redstone Arsenal, home of Army Aviation and Missile command, and stole technical data for the mission planning system used by U.S. Army helicopters, as well the Falconview 3.2 flight planning software used by both the U.S. Army and Air Force.[146]

Chinese cyber espionage operations aimed at extracting sensitive technical data began in the period under consideration (1989–2004), and expanded rapidly in terms of both volume and sophistication since. In a 2009 case, computer networks belonging to at least one defense contractor working on the F–35 Joint Strike Fighter program were reportedly compromised, giving intruders access to Pentagon computer systems that contained sensitive, though not classified, data on the J–35's design, performance, and electronics systems. There is not as much evidence linking this exploit to Chinese attackers, but U.S. officials interviewed about the breach reported that it had been traced to China and bore the hallmark of a state-sponsored operation.[147] In this particular case, the stolen information could not be used to reverse engineer F–35 systems, but could have been helpful in learning how to better defend against them.

This chapter has examined the evolution of China's military aviation industry over the decades and discussed the various procurement strategies it has used at different points in time. The approach has been based on four main variables: (1) the state of China's domestic economy, in particular the state of its technological and industrial base; (2) the technological capacity of China's military aviation sector; (3) the willingness of foreign countries to sell China advanced military aircraft, key components, armaments, and related production technology; and (4) China's bargaining power vis-à-vis potential sellers of military aircraft and aviation technology. Between 1989 and 2004 China was able to diversify avenues of aviation technology procurement. Expansion occurred as a result of favorable developments across each of the four main variables. China's civilian technology base grew as a result of trade and foreign investment, generating access to dual-use technologies which the military aviation sector leveraged to improve design and production capacity. Rapprochement with Russia once again gave China access to advanced military hardware that was blocked by Western embargoes post-Tiananmen. Moreover, China's newfound economic clout afforded it a much stronger negotiating position with a Russian state that faced myriad economic difficulties after the Soviet collapse. Defense cooperation with Israel, though ultimately problematic, provided China a window of access to technical knowledge and design expertise which moved its aviation industry forward. Engagement with the outside world resulted in an increased Chinese presence abroad, providing avenues to restricted military technologies via espionage. Finally, cyber espionage emerged in the later part of this time period as a new vector for the extraction of data related to restricted military aviation technologies.

Looking Forward: Chinese Military Aviation Technology Procurement (2004–Present)

Table 12–7. Looking Forward: Chinese Military Aviation Technology Procurement (2004–Present)

Reverse Engineer		J–15: Chinese Su–33 (2009)	
Steal		China successfully exfiltrates terabytes of data on U.S. Joint Strike fighter electronics systems (2007–2008)	
Build	J–10 enters PLAAF service (2006)	J–11B enters PLAAF service (2008)	J–20 flight test (2011)

Building

China's overall economic development continues to progress rapidly, both in terms of growth and technological sophistication. Investment by developed countries, imports of sophisticated production technology, and indigenous production have created an advanced-Chinese economy that approaches world-class standards in many areas. Chinese companies do not necessarily have full knowledge of all the advanced technologies embodied in equipment operated on Chinese territory, but the situation has changed fundamentally. The government's focus on developing indigenous innovation with Chinese characteristics (*zizhu chuangxin*, 自主创新) emphasizes the importance of foreign technology and knowledge in moving China's overall level of industrial and scientific development forward. The most recent iteration of the Medium- and Long-Term Science and Technology Development Plan (MLP), released in 2006, outlines a path to "promote original innovations by reassembling existing technologies in different ways to produce new breakthroughs and absorb and upgrade foreign technologies."[148] The idea at the core of this approach is to assimilate and absorb preexisting foreign technologies and in the process of merging them with domestic technologies, realize new breakthroughs and improvements.[149] The decision of many advanced Western companies to locate technology R&D labs in China has led to an improvement of China's technology knowledge base which has in turn enabled overall economic progress.

This economic progress has benefited the Chinese defense industry in general and the military aviation industry in particular. Globalization has increased China's access to technologies originally developed by the West for military applications, and then applied widely for civilian purposes. This allows China to benefit from a "spin-off, spin-on" dynamic to apply these technologies to its defense industries. Advances in information technology (IT) and communications technology are providing new design tools and the basis for improved avionics systems that can be applied to Chinese fighters. Key companies in this sector such as Huawei and Julong were founded by ex-PLA officers and are closely tied to the Chinese defense industry.[150] China has been involved in commercial joint ventures with Western aviation companies since the 1980s, producing subassemblies and parts for civilian aircraft and has continued to expand its role in the global aviation supply and production chain. However, unlike the IT sector, there have been relatively few opportunities for Chinese civil/military aviation integration and technology sharing.[151] This is partly due to the limited applicability of civilian aviation technologies for military use. Compartmentalization also prevents useful transfers of personnel, knowledge of production practices, and materials. Commercial and military aviation projects are conducted by different enterprises on different production lines with apparently little or no interaction on areas that might be of common interest.[152] There are a few isolated cases where technologies and process improvements derived from civilian production may spill over to the military side, but this is not an institutional feature of the Chinese aviation industry.[153] Despite these inefficiencies and continuing problems, the Chinese military aviation industry's ability to "build" a more sophisticated PLAAF has advanced significantly.

China's potential to continue to "build" its way to a more sophisticated air force in the future depends on the degree to which it will be able to meet its indigenous innovation objectives, which continue to depend on access to advanced foreign technologies. Examples of true indigenous innovation are still few and far between. Even with the benefit of "follower's advantage," Chinese military aviation is still unable to copy some subsystems at a level equivalent to those of the original. Continuing limitations are most apparent in the industry's inability to design a turbofan engine that meets the requirements of its fleet of indigenously produced advanced fighters. In April 2009, the head of Aviation Industries of China (AVIC), Mr. Lin Zuoming, admitted that the WS-10A (China's most advanced turbofan at the time) was still "unsatisfactory in its quality" and that engine production for military aircraft has been a "chronic illness" in China's defense industry.[154] AVIC is investing $1.5 billion into jet engine research and development to try to overcome persistent problems with quality control and reliability.[155]

Flight tests of the new J-20 stealth fighter may reveal whether China has overcome this hurdle. Chinese news sources reported after the initial test flight that two J-20 prototypes had been produced, one with a Russian engine and the other with an indigenously produced engine. It is not clear which engine is coupled with which prototype. Photographic analysis reveals that the exhaust nozzles of one prototype are "jointed in a way that implies thrust vectoring capability."[156] China has been using the thrust-vectored Russian AL-31FN-M1 in its two-seat J-10 AS/BS fighters since 2006.[157] This is most likely the engine in one of the J-20 prototypes, although there is speculation that the production model will be powered by thrust-vectored WS-10G turbofans, manufactured by the Shenyang Liming Aircraft Engine Company.[158] If Chinese media reports are accurate and one prototype sports a non-thrust vector capable indigenous engine (probably, based on past instances where Russian and Chinese engines were simultaneously tested in the same model aircraft), this engine is likely some version of the WS-10.[159]

The unveiling of the J-20 is the most significant recent event for Chinese military aviation. The J-20 prototype's maiden flight coincided with U.S. Defense Secretary Robert Gates' January 2011 visit to China. Learning of the successful test flight, Gates commented, "They may be somewhat further ahead in the development of that aircraft than our intelligence had earlier predicted." The J–20 reportedly made a second round of successful test flights on April 17, 2011, to commemorate the sixtieth anniversary of the PLAAF.[160] Most recently, Chinese military bloggers posted photos of the J–20 making what appears to be a third and fourth set of test flights.[161] The fighter is expected to enter into service with the PLAAF between 2018 and 2020. While the development of J–20 prototypes is a significant achievement for Chinese military aviation, the flight tests provide no insight into whether the industry is any closer to overcoming its engine impediment or whether it has mastered critical challenges in avionics and radar. J–20 test pilot Xu Yongling made statements to the Chinese media touting technological breakthroughs embodied in the fighter, including supersonic cruise capability.[162] Publicly available data on the test flights does not provide enough evidence to support Xu's assertion. About the only thing that can be determined from them is that China can produce a few prototypes of an aircraft that appears to incorporate some stealth technology and that one of these prototypes can be flown for a short period of time without crashing. Interpreting the appearance of the J–20 as proof that China is right on the heels of U.S. military aviation capability is a misinterpretation of the known facts. Russian and Western military aviation experts maintain that the PLAAF is still 15 to 20 years behind the most advanced air forces in terms of equipment.[163]

Buying

Given continuing limitations in China's domestic military aviation industry, the PLAAF's ability to compete on an equal footing with the most advanced air forces will rest on China's ability to purchase, acquire, or codevelop advanced military aviation technology from foreign sources or partners. This access may be problematic. The United States is likely to continue to ban arms exports to China and to restrict the transfer of advanced military technologies. U.S. pressure on the European Union to maintain its ban on arms sales and on European countries and Israel to restrict the transfer of advanced military technologies will likely continue to restrict Chinese access from these countries. Ukraine has served as an important secondary point of access for Russian military aviation technology in the past, but its military aviation design and production capability lie primarily in the area of transport aircraft, limiting its ability to provide state-of-the-art fighter technologies. Ukrainian aerospace cooperation with China in recent years has focused primarily on civilian projects and military transports. The Ukrainian aviation firm Antonov signed an agreement with AVIC II in 1997 to help China develop a large transport aircraft and to assist in the design of light- and medium-sized transport platforms. Antonov has also agreed to improve the PLAAF's existing fleet of Y–8 turboprop aircraft.[164]

This leaves Russia as the only plausible source of advanced fighter aircraft and aviation technologies. Military aviation technology transfer is a key component of Sino-Russian relations. As this study has documented, the relative bargaining power of the two countries has shifted over time as a function of economic status, threat perceptions, and shifts in the broader geostrategic landscape. The terms of transfer have been based on a calculus of dependence and risk.

China's decision to violate the Su–27/J–11 coproduction contract in 2004 was an important factor influencing Russian decisionmaking on military aviation transfers to China. The official Chinese explanation, proffered only after Russia discovered that China was developing an indigenized J–11, was that the Su–27 no longer met the needs of the PLAAF. China was clearly aware that its decision to violate the contract with Russia would create strains in the relationship and might threaten Russia's willingness to sell additional fighter aircraft or components, yet it went ahead anyway. This decision may have reflected China's confidence that its domestic aviation industry could meet current and future aircraft needs of the PLAAF through indigenous development without Russian assistance. Alternatively, it may have reflected the belief based on experience that the Russian reaction would be minimal and would not impede future technology cooperation.

China may have miscalculated the scope of Moscow's reaction to the aborted Flanker deal, possibly due to the belief that Russia was more reliant on China as a buyer than China was on Russia as a seller. There is obviously a much larger dimension to Sino-Russian relations than one failed weapons system deal, but the Russian side has cited repeatedly China's 2004 contract breach as a reason it is reluctant to enter into another aircraft coproduction agreement with Beijing. It was likely a contributing factor in the stalled deal for China to purchase additional Il–76/ CANDID heavy transports and Il–78/MIDAS tankers to extend the range of its Russian fighters. China's primary indigenous in-flight refueling platform, the H–6U tanker, has significant limitations in that it holds only 37,000 pounds of transferable fuel (PLAAF analysis calls for a platform capable of holding 80,000–100,000 pounds), and cannot be used to refuel China's Su–30 fighters.[165] On the other hand, Russia has continued to sell China S–300 surface-to-air missile systems and large quantities of advanced turbojet engines. Moscow also announced in November 2010 its willingness to sell China the Su–35 fighter, which it bills as "fourth generation plus": a fourth-generation fighter that incorporates some fifth-generation technologies.[166] According to Sukhoi, the Su–35 will see a 10-year production run (through 2020) and be available for foreign purchase in 2011. Russia has not expressed interest in a coproduction agreement with China on the aircraft, nor is it likely to. In order to maintain control of its most advanced aviation technologies, Russia will likely offer a watered-down export version of the Su–35, possibly choosing to sell clients like India a more capable variant than China.[167]

A relationship of mutual advantage still exists, at least for now; each side's perception of its interests and relative bargaining power will influence how much cooperation occurs and on what terms. A stronger Russian state under Putin has managed to rein in much of the economic chaos that plagued Russia during the Yeltsin years and re-exert centralized control over many issues, including arms sales and technology transfers. The ability of Russian leaders to maintain economic growth and political stability in the face of fluctuating energy prices, systemic corruption, and limited economic reforms will affect Russia's long-term bargaining power vis-à-vis China.[168]

Conclusion

The Chinese military aviation industry is now capable of producing two fourth-generation fighters roughly equal to those operated by the most advanced air forces: the J–10 (indigenously developed with Israeli assistance) and the J–11B (based on coproduction and reverse engineering of the Su–27). The J–15 naval fighter (based on reverse engineering of the Su–33), which was successfully test flown in 2009 and is likely to enter serial production in the next 3 to 5 years, will give China a capable fourth-generation fighter that can be operated from aboard aircraft carriers. China also now operates functional AEW&C systems in the KJ–200 and KJ–2000, though the technical sophistication of these systems falls well short of systems fielded by the world's most advanced air forces. Test flights of the new J–20 stealth fighter prototype demonstrate Chinese ambitions to build fifth-generation fighters, though the extent to which the J–20 will match the performance of state-of-the-art Russian and Western fighters is unclear. Significant hurdles in engine design, avionics, and systems integration are likely to delay operational deployment of the J–20 until around 2020. This would be 15 years after the F–22 entered service with the U.S. Air Force, supporting the overall assessment that the Chinese military aviation industry remains 15–20 years behind.

Over the last 20 years, China has benefited significantly from "follower's advantage." Its military aviation industry has accessed the innovations of others via coproduction, espionage, and reverse engineering while making limited developments in genuinely new technology. In order to bridge the technology gap, China's military aviation industry will have to develop the capacity to master dual-use and especially militarily unique technologies that go into state-of- the-art fighter aircraft components. It will also have to develop the competence in systems integration to make the complex components work together. Developed countries with more advanced techno-industrial bases than China, like Japan and Taiwan, have struggled to achieve the systems integration know-how necessary to produce cutting-edge fighter aircraft. The ability to reach the technology frontier across a range of related civilian and dual-use modalities (for example, Japan's space program) is not necessarily transferable to the military aviation realm. Even if the technical knowledge and industrial capacity exist, opportunity costs involved with developing single-use military technologies might prove too great. Further Chinese integration into the global economy will increase its capacity to develop and apply dual-use technologies, but legitimate access to "single-use" military specific technologies will remain problematic.

Restrictions on advanced Western military technologies are likely to remain in place, leaving Russia as the only viable source. China remains dependent in the near term on access to Russian engines to power its indigenous fourth-generation fighters,[169] Russian spare parts for its inventory of Su–27 and Su–30 fighters, and Russian advanced surface-to-air missiles. The overall state of the Sino-Russian relationship will shape what systems and technologies Russia is willing to transfer to China, and the bargaining power between Russia and China will influence whether transfers take place in the form of sales of aircraft and complete components, coproduction of aircraft and components, or codevelopment of new aircraft and technologies. Russia's significant concerns about China as a potential strategic competitor and rival in the fighter export market suggest that Russia will seek to maintain a degree of control and leverage by supplying complete aircraft and components rather than transferring advanced technologies, which is China's preference. Paradoxically, the development of China's aviation industry to the point where it can participate in aviation technology and fighter aircraft codevelopment efforts on a more equal footing will likely make Russia less willing to engage in such cooperation. Russia's improved bargaining position as the sole source potentially willing to provide China with advanced aviation technology will likely allow Russia to exert more control over the aircraft and technologies it decides to sell.

Advanced technology is a key factor in the performance of state-of-the-art military fighters. Many relevant technologies have equivalent applications in the civilian sector and can be acquired legitimately in the global technology marketplace. But advanced fighters (especially fifth-generation aircraft) also incorporate a number of unique single-use technologies developed solely for their military applications that are not readily available on the commercial market. The likelihood that China will have no foreign source of advanced military aviation technology supports two important conclusions. First, the Chinese military aviation industry will have to rely primarily on indigenous development of advanced "single-use" military aviation technologies in the future.

The Chinese government is pursuing a range of "indigenous innovation" and technology development programs, but mastering advanced technologies becomes more difficult and expensive as a country moves closer to the technology frontier. This leads to a second, related conclusion: China will likely rely more heavily on espionage to acquire those critical military aviation technologies it cannot acquire legitimately from foreign suppliers or develop on its own.

Notes

Note: The authors would like to thank Ken Allen, Roger Cliff, Andrew Erickson, Richard Hallion, Michael Hughes, and Christopher Yung for their helpful comments and contributions in improving this paper. They also thank Jenny Lin for her diligent translation efforts, and Scott Devary for his assistance gathering research material. Richard Hallion did initial editing and provided an improved introduction. At NDU Press, we would like to thank George Maerz and Tara Parekh.

[1] Evan S. Medeiros et al., *A New Direction for China's Defense Industry*, RAND Document MG-334 (Santa Monica: RAND Corporation, 2005), 27–48.

[2] "Fifth generation" reflects the Western generational classification for American aircraft such as the F–22 and F–35, Russia's Sukhoi T–50, and China's own Chengdu J–20. The Chinese use a different classification scheme that refers to F–16s and Su–27s as "third-generation" fighters, and the F–22 and F–35 as "fourth-generation" fighters. Because this paper draws on international examples, we employ the Western terminology, which classifies the F–15/F–16 (and MiG–29 and Su–27) as fourth generation, and their stealthy successors as fifth generation.

[3] Joe Yoon, "Fighter Generations," June 27, 2004, at the Web site <aerospaceweb.org>. Accessed August 1, 2011, at <www.aerospaceweb.org/question/history/q0182.shtml>.

[4] "The systems engineering method recognizes each system is an integrated whole even though composed of diverse, specialized structures and subfunctions. It further recognizes that any system has a number of objectives and that the balance between them may differ widely from system to system. The methods seek to optimize the overall system functions according to the weighted objectives and to achieve maximum compatibility of its parts." From Harold Chesnut, *Systems Engineering Tools* (Somerset, NJ: J.W. Wiley and Sons, 1965).

[5] The U.S. F–22 Raptor, arguably the world's most sophisticated aircraft, took 20 years to develop. See "Chronology of the F–22 Program," accessed October 15, 2010, at <www.f22-raptor.com/about/chronology.html>.

[6] Brian Grow, Keith Epstein, and Chi-Chu Tschang, "The New E-spionage Threat," *Business Weekly* Web edition. (April 10, 2008). Accessed August 4, 2010, at <www.businessweek.com/magazine/content/08_16/b4080032218430.htm>.

[7] For the purposes of this chapter, we assume that China's military aviation industry is always trying to fully exploit available open source information (although its ability to do so varies depending on its technological capacity).

[8] Carol Evans, "Re-appraising Third World Arms Production," *Survival* 28, no. 2 (March 1986), 98–117.

[9] Wei Chen Lee, "The Birth of a Salesman: China as an Arms Supplier," *East Asia International Quarterly* 6, no. 4 (Summer 1987), 32–46.

[10] David Isenberg, "Israel's role in China's new warplane," *Asia Times Online* (December 4, 2002), at <www.atimes.com/atimes/China/DL04Ad01.html>.

[11] Legally speaking, an aircraft is sovereign property of the state and should be returned, although this does not always happen in practice.

[12] Federation of American Scientists Military Analysis Network, "AA 2 Atoll," accessed September 3, 2010, at <www.fas.org/man/dod-101/sys/missile/row/aa-2.htm>.

[13] The aircraft, based on the Sukhoi T-50 prototype, is referred to by Russia as "*Perspektivny aviatsionny kompleks frontovoy aviatsii*" (PAK FA, or "Future Airborne Complex—Frontline Aviation"), and by India as "Fifth Generation Fighter Aircraft" (FGFA). The variants operated by the Russian and Indian air forces will differ in many respects, though both parties will share in funding costs and will benefit equally in terms of engineering and intellectual property generated from the project. The Indian air force plans to purchase 200 two-seat models of the FGFA and only 50 single-seat models. Russian procurement plans call for the opposite balance, with the air force buying 200 single-seat PAK FA models and 50 two-seat models.

[14] Ajai Shukla, "India to Develop 25% of Fifth Generation Fighter," *Business Standard* (January 6, 2010), accessed September 7, 2010, at <www.business-standard.com/india/news/india-todevelop-25fifth-generation-fighter/381786/>.

[15] Katherine V. Schnasi, "Joint Strike Fighter Acquisition: Observations on the Supplier Base," GAO-04-554, accessed September 3, 2010, at <www.gao.gov/new.items/d04554.pdf>.

[16] "F-35 Joint Strike Fighter (JSF) Lightning II: International Partners," *Global Security*, accessed September 5, 2010, at <www.globalsecurity.org/military/systems/aircraft/f-35-int.htm>.

[17] The Soviets sided with India in the Sino-Indian border war of 1962, which represented essentially the last straw in deteriorating Sino-Soviet relations.

[18] Sudha Ramachandran, "India, Russia Still Brothers in Arms," *Asia Times* (October 27, 2007), accessed September 9, 2010, at <www.atimes.com/atimes/South_Asia/IJ27Df01.html>.

[19] Ajai Shukla, "India, Russia Close to Pact on Fifth Generation Fighter," *Business Standard* (January 5, 2010).

[20] Shukla, "India to Develop 25% of Fifth Generation Fighter."

[21] Ramachandran.

[22] Shukla, "India to Develop 25% of Fifth Generation Fighter."

[23] David Isenberg, "Israel's role in China's new Warplane," *Asia Times Online* (December 4, 2002), accessed July 31, 2011, at <www.atimes.com/atimes/China/DL04Ad01.html>.

[24] Kristin Archick, Robert Grimmett, and Shirley Kan, *European Union's Arms Embargo on China: Implications and Options for U.S. Policy*, CRS Report for Congress RL32870 (Washington, DC: Library of Congress Congressional Research Service, May 27, 2005), accessed July 31, 2011, at <www.fas.org/sgp/crs/row/RL32870.pdf>; and Government Accountability Office (GAO), *China: Military Imports from the United States and the European Union Since the 1989 Embargoes*, Report NSIAD-98-176 (Washington, DC: GAO, June 1998), accessed August 20, 2010, at <www.gao.gov/archive/1998/ns98176.pdf>.

[25] Luke G.S. Colton, "A Chinese AEW&C Threat? The Phalcon Case Reconsidered," *Chinese Military Update* 1, no. 7 (January 2004), 9–12.

[26] Austin Ramzy, "China Flexes Its Muscles with Stealth Fighter Test," *Time* (January 11, 2011), accessed August 5, 2011, at <www.time.com/time/world/article/0,8599,2041755,00.html>.

[27] Yefim Gordon and Dmitriy Komissarov, *Chinese Air Power: Current Organisation and Aircraft of All Chinese Air Forces* (Surrey: Ian Allan Publishing Ltd., 2010), 3.

[28] National Air and Space Intelligence Center (NASIC), *People's Liberation Air Force 2010* (Wright-Patterson Air Force Base, OH: NASIC, August 1, 2010), 11–12, accessed April 19, 2011, at <www.au.af.mil/au/awc/awcgate/nasic/pla_af_2010.pdf>; Chinese aviation historians Liang-yen Wen and Lennart Andersson conclude that at the beginning of December 1949, the PLAAF's strength was 159 aircraft of 21 different types, ranging from three B-24s to P-47s, P-51s, and even two British-built Mosquitoes; see Lennart Andersson, *A History of Chinese Aviation: Encyclopedia of Aircraft and Aviation in China until 1949* (Taipei: Ko-lo Color Printing Company—Chu-men Company, 2008), 176–177.

[29] Wu Chun Guang, *Zhongguo Kongjun Shi Lu* [Record of the Chinese Air Force] (Beijing: Chun Feng Wenyi Chubanshe, 1997).

[30] Ibid., 39.

[31] Zhang Xiaoming, *Red Wings over the Yalu: China, the Soviet Union, and the Air War in Korea* (College Station: Texas A&M Consortium Press, 2002), 45–51.

[32] Jung Chang and Jon Halliday, *Mao: The Unknown Story* (New York: Anchor Books, 2005), 374.

[33] Ibid., 375.

[34] Sergei Goncharenko, "Sino-Soviet Military Cooperation," in *Brothers in Arms: The Rise and Fall of the Sino-Soviet Alliance*, ed. Arne Westad (Washington DC: Woodrow Wilson Center Press, 1998), chapter 4.

[35] Deborah A. Kaple, "Soviet Advisors in China in the 1950s," in *Brothers in Arms*, Westad, chapter 3, 120.

[36] Duan Zijun, ed., *China Today: Aviation Industry* (Beijing: China Aviation Press, 1989), 18.

[37] Sergei Goncharenko, "Sino-Soviet Military Cooperation," in *Brothers in Arms*, Westad, chapter 4, 147.

[38] Duan, ed., *China Today: Aviation Industry*.

[39] Ibid., 352.

[40] Duan, ed., *China Today: Aviation Industry*: In addition to challenges posed by creating high temperature alloys, production of the WP5 was also compounded by the "high precision of nozzles, the complexity of blade profiles, and many thin wall welding parts in the combustion afterburner systems. Therefore, apart from precision machining and advanced heat and surface treatment technologies, it was also necessary to set up precision casting and forging production lines which can make parts with little or no machine allowances, as well as various welding production lines such as seam welding, butter welding, DC electrode welding, hydrogen atom welding, high frequency brazing, manual and automatic argon arc welding, etc."

[41] Duan, ed., *China Today: Aviation Industry*, 203.

[42] The Chinese military aircraft naming convention is to designate models for domestic use as 'J' and those for export as 'F.' The F–5 is, for example, the export version of the J–5. As the Chinese military aviation industry improved its productive capacity, it was able to turn out export models designed to suit the particular needs of purchasing countries.

[43] Ibid.

[44] In a PBS NOVA interview, former U.S. Air Force Historian Richard Hallion argues that the Soviets were likely able to close the fighter gap with the United States as a result of technology transfer gained via espionage. The MiG–19 and the U.S. F–100 were the first two supersonic fighters produced. When both came out in 1953, the MiG–19 outperformed its American counterpart. Hallion traces the technology transfer that enabled the Soviet breakthrough to an individual who was part of the infamous atomic espionage ring established by Julius Rosenberg. While the Rosenberg spy ring is known primarily for its role in atomic espionage which enabled the USSR to develop its first nuclear weapon, it also actively targeted the U.S. aeronautical and electronics industries. William Perl, a government aeronautical scientist who held posts at the National Advisory Committee for Aeronautics' (NACA, the predecessor to NASA) Langley and Lewis research centers, was a key player in the Rosenberg spy ring, providing the USSR with the results of highly secret tests and design experiments for American military aviation technology; see <www.pbs.org/wgbh/nova/barrier/history.html>. Perl was unmasked by the Venona intelligence collection program, arrested, and, after interrogation, was charged, tried, and convicted of perjury (after denying he knew the Rosenbergs). More serious charges were not placed for fear of compromising the ongoing Venona effort. For a further discussion of Perl's espionage activities, see Richard Hallion, "Sweep and Swing: Reshaping the Wing for the Jet and Rocket Age," in *NASA Contributions to Aeronautics*, 1, NASA SP-2010-570-Vol-1, ed. Richard P. Hallion (Washington, DC: NASA, 2010), 17, n. 30; Katherine A.S. Sibley, *Red Spies in America: Stolen Secrets and the Dawn of the Cold War* (Lawrence, KS: University Press of Kansas, 2004), 10, 115, 196–198, 315, n. 126; John Earl Haynes and Harvey Klehr, *Early Cold War Spies: The Espionage Trials that Shaped American Politics* (Cambridge: Cambridge University Press, 2006), 161–163, 167, 172, 175, 188, 236; and Robert L. Benson, *The Venona Story* (Fort Meade, MD: Center for Cryptologic History of the National Security Agency, 2001), 8, 24–25.

[45] Gordon and Komissarov, *Chinese Air Power*, chapter 2.

[46] Duan, ed., *China Today: Aviation Industry*, 115.

[47] See Wu Chun Guang, *Zhongguo Kongjun Shi Lu* [Record of the Chinese Air Force], 128.

[48] Gordon and Komissarov, *Chinese Air Power*.

[49] Ibid., chapter 3.

[50] Ibid.

[51] Ibid.

⁵² Duan, ed., *China Today: Aviation Industry*, 35.

⁵³ Ibid.

⁵⁴ Ibid., 36.

⁵⁵ For early accounts, see Donald S. Zagoria, *The Sino-Soviet Conflict, 1956–1961* (Princeton, NJ: Princeton University Press, 1962); and Roderick MacFarquhar, *The Origins of the Cultural Revolution*, 2: *The Great Leap Forward 1958–1960* (New York: Columbia University Press, 1983), 255–292. For a later account that incorporates Russian and Chinese archival materials, see Lorenz M. Luthi, *The Sino-Soviet Split: Cold War in the Communist World* (Princeton, NJ: Princeton University Press, 2008).

⁵⁶ Jonathan Pollack, "The Modernization of National Defense," in *China's Four Modernizations: The New Technological Revolution*, ed. Richard Baum (Boulder, CO: Westview Press, 1980), 249.

⁵⁷ The JH–7 was not delivered to the PLANAF for evaluation until the mid-1990s, giving some sense of the time it took for Chinese military aviation to absorb the Spey. Coproduction of the WS–9 succeeded in bringing the engine industry to a higher technical level due to the precision tooling required and introduction of new equipment to meet these requirements, yet its integration into just one combat aircraft (only operational 20 years after the original import agreement) must have been disappointing. The Spey case is a prime example of an aviation industry ill-prepared to absorb more advanced technologies in a timely and meaningful way.

⁵⁸ For an illustration, see Marc J. Blecher and Gordon White, *Micropolitics in Contemporary China: A Technical Unit during and after the Cultural Revolution* (White Plains, NY: M.E. Sharpe, 1979).

⁵⁹ Duan, ed., *China Today: Aviation Industry*.

⁶⁰ Gordon and Komissarov, *Chinese Air Power*, chapter 3.

⁶¹ Ibid.

⁶² Ibid.

⁶³ Duan, ed., *China Today: Aviation Industry*, 115.

⁶⁴ Ibid.

⁶⁵ John Wilson Lewis and Xue Litai, "China's Search for a Modern Air Force, *International Security* 24, no. 1 (Summer 1999), 64–94.

⁶⁶ Ibid.

⁶⁷ Ibid.

⁶⁸ Hans Heymann, Jr., *China's Approach to Technology Acquisition: Part I—The Aircraft Industry*, RAND Document R-1573-ARPA (Santa Monica, CA: RAND Corporation, February 1975), 18, 23–24.

⁶⁹ For Jian–7 Interceptor Fighter, see *Sinodefence.com*, accessed September 19, 2010, at <www.sinodefence.com/airforce/fighter/j7.asp>.

⁷⁰ Chinese writings seldom mention reverse engineering and instead use either *fangzhi* "manufactured imitation"—or *zixing yanzhi* "self-researched and manufactured."

⁷¹ Ibid.

⁷² Walter J. Boyne, *Air Warfare: An International Encyclopedia* (Santa Barbara, CA: ABC-Clio, 2002).

⁷³ Gordon and Komissarov, *Chinese Air Power*, chapter 3.

⁷⁴ See <www.sinodefence.com/airforce/groundattack/h5.asp>.

⁷⁵ "Imbued with revolutionary fervor, but confronting backwardness on nearly every front, China's Communist leaders committed themselves from the earliest days of the People's Republic to a broad-based modernization of their country. Inevitably, the military's powerful claim on a limited pool of resources, and its policy and technological priorities, became a subject of intense political controversy. To sustain these priorities, key leaders of the PLA argued for more than simply new and better weapons; they fashioned a powerful set of ideas about the relationship between state, technology, and national power in China." From Evan Feigenbaum, *China's Techno-Warriors: National Security and Strategic Competition from the Nuclear Age to the Information Age* (Stanford: Stanford University Press, 2003), 2

⁷⁶ Lewis and Xue, "China's Search for a Modern Air Force," 70.

[77] Shao Zhenting, Zhang Zhengping, and Hu Jianping, "Theoretical Thinking on Deng Xiaoping's Views on the Buildup of the Air Force and the Reform of Operational Arts," *Zhongguo Junshi Kexue* [China Military Science], no. 4 (1996), quoted in Lewis and Xue, "China's Search for a Modern Air Force."

[78] Hua Guofeng, "Report on the Work of Government to the 1st Session, 5th National People's Congress," Peking Review (February 26, 1978).

[79] Baum, ed., *China's Four Modernizations*, 5.

[80] Ibid.

[81] Evan Feigenbaum, "Who's Behind China's High-Technology 'Revolution?'" *International Security* 24, no. 1 (Summer 1999), 95–126.

[82] Ibid.

[83] Ibid., 100.

[84] Tai Ming Cheung, *Fortifying China: The Struggle to Build a Modern Defense Economy* (Ithaca, NY: Cornell University Press, 2009), 246.

[85] Lewis and Xue, "China's Search for a Modern Air Force," 74.

[86] Government Accountability Office, *China: Military Imports from the United States and the European Union*, 8.

[87] Ibid.

[88] Phillip C. Saunders and Eric Quam, "Future Force Structure of the Chinese Air Force," in *Right Sizing the People's Liberation Army: Exploring the Contours of China's Military*, eds. Roy Kamphausen and Andrew Scobell (Carlisle Barracks, PA: U.S. Army War College, Strategic Studies Institute, 2007), chapter 8.

[89] Shenyang Aircraft Corporation (SAC) began as a single enterprise, the Shenyang Aircraft Factory (SAF), which was established with Soviet assistance during the Korean War to coproduce MiG fighter aircraft. SAC went on to encompass a number of enterprises and in 1994 became the "core enterprise of the newly formed Shenyang Aircraft Industries Group." See Yefim Gordon and Dmitriy Komissarov, *Chinese Aircraft: China's Aviation Industry since 1951* (Manchester: Hikoki Publications, 2008), 15–16.

[90] Duan, ed., *China Today: Aviation Industry*, 192.

[91] Government Accountability Office, *China: Military Imports from the United States and the European Union*, 6.

[92] Ibid.

[93] See for example, Yitzhak Shichor, "Israel's Military Transfers to China and Taiwan," *Survival* 40, no. 1 (Spring 1998), 68–91.

[94] Medeiros, et al., *A New Direction for China's Defense Industry*, 51–52.

[95] Keith Crane, Roger Cliff, Evan Medeiros, James Mulvenon, and William Overholt, *Modernizing China's Military: Opportunities and Constraints*, RAND Document MG-260 (Santa Monica, CA: RAND Corporation, 2005), 144.

[96] Ibid.

[97] Jennifer Anderson, *The Limits of Sino-Soviet Strategic Partnership*, Adelphi Paper 315 of the International Institute for Strategic Studies (Oxford: Oxford University Press, 1997).

[98] Bill Gertz, "China Uses Supercomputers Illegally; Nuclear Facility Simulates Blasts," *The Washington Times*, June 27, 2000.

[99] Richard Bitzinger, "Civil-Military Integration and Chinese Military Modernization," *Asia Pacific Center for Security Studies* 3, no. 9 (December 2004).

[100] As of November 2010, China was home to the world's second most powerful supercomputer, the Tianhe-1A, which has a peak computing rate of 2.507 petaFLOPS per second, that is 2.5 quadrillion calculations per second. (FLOP = Floating Point Operations per Second; a petaFLOP is 1015 FLOPS.) The fastest computer as of this editing is the K Computer in Kobe, Japan, which computes at the rate of 8.162 petaFLOPS (8.2 quadrillion calculations per second).

[101] Huang Tung, "'Xiaolong,' New Model of Chinese-Built Foreign Trade-Oriented Fighter Plane," *Kuang Chiao Ching* [Wide Angle], October 23, 2003, 72–73, in Foreign Broadcast Information Service CPP20031023000106.

[102] Richard D. Fisher, Jr., "The Impact of Foreign Weapons and Technology on the Modernization of China's People's Liberation Army," *Report for the U.S.-China Economic and Security Review Commission* (Washington, DC: U.S.-China Economic and Security Review Commission, January 2004).

[103] Teng Lianfu and Meifu Sheng, *Kongjun Zuozhan Yanjiu* [Air Force Operational Research] (Beijing: Guofang Daxue Chubanshe, 1990), 78–94.

[104] Ibid., 278–279.

[105] Wu Chun Guang, *Zhongguo Kongjun Shi Lu* [Record of the Chinese Air Force] (Beijing: Chun Feng Wenyi Chubanshe, 1997).

[106] Tai Ming Cheung, "The Chinese Defense Economy's Long March from Imitation to Innovation," *Journal of Strategic Studies* 34, no.3 (June 2011), 325–354.

[107] Ibid.

[108] Robert Benjamin, "As Pace of Rapprochement Quickens, China Offers Soviets 'Commodity Loans,'" *The Baltimore Sun*, March 1, 1991.

[109] Fisher, "The Impact of Foreign Weapons and Technology."

[110] U. S. Department of Defense, *Report to Congress Pursuant to the FY2000 National Defense Authorization Act: Annual Report on the Military Power of the People's Republic of China* (Washington, D.C.: DOD, July 28, 2003).

[111] "Jian 11 Multi-role Fighter Aircraft," at Web site <Sinodefence.com> (February 20, 2009).

[112] Rick Kamer, "Flankers of the People's Liberation Army," *Chinese Military Update* 1, no. 7 (January 2004), 5–8.

[113] Stephen J. Blank, "The Dynamics of Russian Weapon Sales to China," *Army War College Strategic Studies Monograph* (Carlisle Barracks, PA: U.S. Army War College, March 4, 1997), 5.

[114] Gordon and Komissarov, *Chinese Air Power*, 105.

[115] Fisher, "The Impact of Foreign Weapons and Technology."

[116] Wendell Minnick, "Russia Admits China Illegally Copied Its Fighter," *Defense News* (February 13, 2010), accessed May 2, 2011, at <www.defensenews.com/story.php?i=3947599andc=ASIands=AIR>.

[117] Andrei Chang, "China Imitates Russian Su-27SK Fighter," UPI Asia (February 25, 2008), accessed September 28, 2010, at <www.upiasia.com/Security/2008/02/25/china_imitates_russian_su-27sk_fighter/1740/>.

[118] "Russia charges man with smuggling military equipment," *RIA Novosti* (July 8, 2011), accessed July 14, 2011, at <http://en.rian.ru/russia/20110708/165082151.html>.

[119] Saunders and Quam, "Future Force Structure of the Chinese Air Force," in *Right Sizing the People's Liberation Army*, Kamphausen and Scobell, eds., 19.

[120] Jane McCartney, "Chinese J-10 fighter in televised drama," *The Sunday Times Online* (March 24, 2009).

[121] Russia sold India a more sophisticated version, the Su-30MKI, which features the thrust-vectoring version of the Al-31F turbofan engine.

[122] Gordon and Komissarov, *Chinese Air Power*, 80.

[123] Ibid.

[124] Richard D. Fisher, "How America's Friends are Building China's Military Power," *Heritage Foundation Backgrounder* (November 5, 1997).

[125] Ken Allen and Eric A. McVadon, *China's Foreign Military Relations*, Report no. 32 (Washington, DC: Henry L. Stimson Center, October 1999), 25.

[126] Aron Shai, *Sino-Israeli Relations: Current Reality and Future Prospects*, Memorandum 100 (Tel Aviv: The Institute for National Security Studies, September 2009).

[127] Gordon and Komissarov, *Chinese Air Power*, 96.

[128] Ibid.

[129] Shai, *Sino-Israeli Relations*, 26.

[130] Ibid., 27.

131 Ibid.

132 Joseph Kahn, "Crash of Chinese Surveillance Plane Hurts Efforts on Warning System," *The New York Times*, June 7, 2006.

133 NASIC, *People's Liberation Air Force* 2010.

134 Photos of these four KJ–2000s can be seen at <www.china-defense-mashup.com/?p=3266>.

135 Michael Sheridan, "China's Hi-Tech Military Disaster: Bid to Copy Israeli Electronics Kills Experts," *London Sunday Times*, June 11, 2006.

136 Yitzhak Schichor, "The U.S. Factor in Israel's Military Relations with China," *China Brief* 5, no. 12 (June 2005).

137 Ibid.

138 Shai, *Sino-Israeli Relations*.

139 Schichor, "The U.S. Factor in Israel's Military Relations with China."

140 Shai, *Sino-Israeli Relations*, 28.

141 Ibid.

142 "Russia says Ukraine sold banned missiles to Iran, China," *RIA Novosti* (June 30, 2006), accessed July 6, 2011, at <http://en.rian.ru/russia/20060630/50710729.html>.

143 Guillaume Steuer, "Chinese J–15 Soon in Air," *Air and Cosmos* [Paris], May 6, 2011, 16–17.

144 Ibid.

145 Nick Eftimiades, *Chinese Intelligence Operations* (Annapolis, MD: Naval Institute Press, 1994).

146 Nathan Thornburgh, "The Invasion of the Chinese Cyber Spies," *Time* (August 29, 2005).

147 Siobhan Gorman, August Cole, and Yochi Dreazen, "Computer Spies Breach Jet Fighter Program," *The Wall Street Journal*, April 21, 2009.

148 Cheung, "The Chinese Defense Economy's Long March," 325–354.

149 Ibid.

150 Bitzinger, "Civil-Military Integration."

151 The push to develop an indigenous engine for China's C919 commercial airliner has "spin-on" potential for a future large military transport aircraft, but official Chinese sources have not confirmed whether this is the intent. See Samm Tyroler-Cooper and Alison Peet, "The Chinese Aviation Industry: Techno-Hybrid Patterns of Development in the C919 Program," *Journal of Strategic Studies* 34, no. 3 (June 2011), 325–354.

152 Roger Cliff, Chad J.R. Ohlandt, and David Yang, *Ready for Takeoff: China's Advancing Aerospace Industry*, RAND Document MG-1100 (Santa Monica, CA: RAND Corporation, 2011).

153 One author claims that Chengdu Aircraft Corporation (CAC) subcontracting facilities have reported gains in production efficiency as a result of military and commercial production lines being located close together. See Fisher, "The Impact of Foreign Weapons and Technology."

154 Jonathan Weng, "China AVIC Top Head Admits Poor Quality of Jet Engine," *China Defense Mashup* (April 2, 2009), accessed August 1, 2011, at <www.china-defense-mashup.com/?p=3179>.

155 Gabe Collins and Andrew Erickson, "Jet Engine Development in China: Indigenous High-performance Turbofans Are a Final Step toward Fully Independent Fighter Production," *China SignPost*, no. 39 (June 26, 2011), accessed August 1, 2011, at <www.chinasignpost.com/wp-content/uploads/ 2011/06/China-SignPost_39_-China-Tactical-Aircraft-Jet-Engine-Deep-Dive_20110626.pdf>.

156 Gabe Collins and Andrew Erickson, "China's New Project 718/J-20 Fighter: Development Outlook and Strategic Implications," *China SignPost*, no. 18 (January 17, 2011).

157 Gordon and Komissarov, *Chinese Air Power*, 101.

158 "Chengdu J–20 Multirole Stealth Fighter Aircraft," accessed June 8, 2011, at <www.airforce-technology.com/projects/chengdu-j20/>.

159 "China's stealth fighter takes to air," *People's Daily Online* (January 12, 2011), accessed June 1, 2011, at <http://english.peopledaily.com.cn/90001/90776/7257512.html>.

[160] "Global Times: J20 'appears' to have made second flight," *People's Daily Online* (April 19, 2011), accessed April 21, 2011, at <http://english.peopledaily.com.cn/90001/90776/90786/7354617.html>.

[161] See, for example, <http://bbs.tiexue.net/default.htm?ListUrl=http://bbs.tiexue.net/index.htm>; and <http://bbs.huanqiu.com/thread-697950-1-3.html>.

[162] Song Shengxia, "J–20 Stealth Fighter Jet; Innovative, Not Stolen from U.S.," *Global Times*, January 25, 2011.

[163] See, for example, Ilya Kramnik, "The Future of China's Fifth-generation Stealth Fighter," *RIA Novosti* (December 29, 2010), accessed July 1, 2011, at <http://en.rian.ru/analysis/20101229/161986565.html>; Nathan Hodge, "China's J–20 Fighter: Stealthy or Just Stealthy Looking?" *The Wall Street Journal Online* (January 19, 2011), accessed July 1, 2011, at <http://blogs.wsj.com/washwire/2011/01/19/chinasj-20-fighter-stealthy-or-just-stealthy-looking/>.

[164] "AVIC II, Antonov to design aircraft," *China Economic Net* (September 20, 2007), accessed August 1, 2011, at <http://en.ce.cn/Industries/Aerospare/200709/20/t20070920_12975829.shtml>.

[165] Gabriel Collins, Michael McGauvran, and Timothy White, "Trends in Chinese Aerial Refueling Capacity for Maritime Purposes," in *Chinese Aerospace Power: Evolving Maritime Roles*, eds. Andrew Erickson and Lyle Goldstein (Annapolis: Naval Institute Press, 2011), 198–200.

[166] "Russia ready to sell Su–35 fighter jets to China," *RIA Novosti* (November 16, 2010), 11; accessed June 22, 2011, at <http://en.rian.ru/mlitary_news/20101116/1 61359301.html>.

[167] The Su–30MKI sold to India featured upgrades not included in the Su–30MKK sold to China.

[168] John W. Parker, *Russia's Revival: Ambitions, Limitations, and Opportunities for the United States*, Institute for National Strategic Studies (INSS) Strategic Perspectives, no. 3 (Washington, DC: INSS, January 2011).

[169] Reports indicate that the WS–10 Taihang is being used in some J–11Bs, and that it might possibly replace the Russian Al–31 series engines in the J–10 and be used in the J–15; see Collins and Erickson, "Jet Engine Development in China."

Chapter 13

The Employment of Airpower in the Taiwan Strait

Hsi-hua Cheng

Since May 20, 2008, when the new Taiwan administration of President Ma Ying-jeou came into office, the cross-strait policies of both the People's Republic of China (PRC) and Taiwan have become more peaceful and friendly.[1] Yet, although military tension has decreased, it must be noted that the two sides are still in contention and facing an uncertain future. Unfortunately, there is evidence indicating that the PRC still considers military force to be an important tool for potentially solving the Taiwan issue.

First, the PRC has never renounced the use of military force against Taiwan, and, indeed, as it has steadily modernized its forces, the PRC has continued to maintain an aggressive posture toward Taiwan. For example, a recent report of the United States Office of the Secretary of Defense (OSD) noted: "By December 2009, the PLA had deployed between 1,050 and 1,150 CSS–6 and CSS–7 short-range ballistic missiles (SRBMs) to units opposite Taiwan. *It is upgrading the lethality of this force, including by introducing variants of these missiles with improved ranges, accuracies, and payloads* [emphasis added]."[2] Taiwan sources indicate that, since 2005, the People's Liberation Army Air Force (PLAAF) has annually flown 1,300 to 1,700 fighter sorties that have crossed the center line of the Taiwan Strait.[3] In April 2010, the People's Liberation Army Navy (PLAN) carried out its annual exercise far from coastal waters, intentionally conducting those activities without informing Japan, a key neighboring country. Indeed, the PRC held an amphibious exercise along its coastal area during which, pointedly, it practiced a simulated invasion against Taiwan.

Since World War II, airpower has played an ever more important role in almost all military operations. Powerful air strikes have changed the nature of war, exemplified by the first Gulf War, which constituted a revolution in military history. Precision air attack has made airpower a decisive element in war. Allied air forces have operated together in a perfect harmony, and their speed and precision have produced decisive effects much faster. High technology enables building "stealth" fighters to fly invisibly to radar without losing speed or maneuverability. Precision-guided munitions enable a small number of weapons to produce a vast effect. All of these achievements have demonstrated to the world that a new way of waging war has been created.[4]

The PLA learned the importance of military technology and the new concept of contemporary warfighting from the Gulf War. The whole world was shocked that Iraq, a nation with the world's fourth-largest army, became so vulnerable after it had been stripped of its air defenses under air strikes by the U.S-led coalition.

Since then, PLAAF modernization has become the PLA's paramount undertaking. However, due to the restrictions imposed by limited defense expenditures and insufficient technology of military industry, there had been no significant improvement until the import of the Russian-built Su–27 in 1992.[5] By purchasing advanced fighters from Russia, the PRC received access to advanced aviation technology through licensed joint-production with Russian help. Acquisition of the Su–27 pushed PRC aviation industry technology to a new level, accelerated further when the PRC imported the Su–30 multirole fighter, which can perform long-distance air strikes and can reach out from the coast line as far as 1,500 kilometers (930 miles). With these advanced fighters, the airpower of the PLAAF has transformed the PRC's strategic capabilities. Since then, the cross-strait airpower balance has tended toward the PLAAF's advantage for the first time since 1949.

Unifying Taiwan with the mainland is the ultimate goal of the PRC, and the use of force is always an option. As with the German air attacks in the Battle of Britain in 1940, the only way to effect the subjugation of Taiwan is to win the battle for air supremacy. Indeed, airpower would be the only way to cross the Taiwan Strait and attack Taiwan immediately. All PLA military action against Taiwan will surely be led by airpower. Thus this paper examines air campaign invasion scenarios, to furnish some useful suggestions for better defending Taiwan.

Key Factors Concerning Airpower over the Taiwan Strait

"Airpower," Sir Winston Churchill once stated, "is the most difficult of all forms of military force to measure or even to express in precise terms"; definitions abound, one of the most succinct being: "The ability to project power from the air and space to influence the behavior of people or the course of events."[6] In this regard, the key factors affecting airpower in the Taiwan Strait would include weapons technology such as aircraft, surface-to-air missiles, ballistic missiles, cruise missiles, airfields and runway availability, and unmanned aerial systems; crisis circumstances such as military intimidation, blockade, and employment of limited force or coercive options; and full-scale military action such as air and missile strikes, the dispatch of an amphibious invasion force, and landing assault. All of the latter can be expected to be accompanied by a fierce battle to control the airspace over the Taiwan Strait. Each of these is subsequently discussed in detail.

Aircraft

According to a January 2010 U.S. Defense Intelligence Agency (DIA) report,[7]

> Although Taiwan has nearly 400 combat aircraft in service, far fewer of these are operationally capable. Taiwan's F–5 fighters have reached the end of their operational service life, and while the indigenously produced F–CK–1 A/B Indigenous Defense Fighter (IDF) is a large component of Taiwan's active fighter force, it lacks the capability for sustained sorties. Taiwan's Mirage 2000–5 aircraft are technologically advanced, but they require frequent, expensive maintenance that adversely affects their operational readiness rate.

This U.S. DIA report may exaggerate the facts, but undoubtedly it reveals some of challenges that Taiwan's airmen face. A U.S.-Taiwan Business Council study concluded that same year as follows:[8]

> In qualitative terms, Taiwan's F–16A/Bs and Mirage 2000–5s are roughly comparable to Chinese Su–30s, Su–27/J–11s, and J–10s in performance and combat capability. The F–CK–1A/Bs are generally considered superior to J–8s, but lack the aerodynamic performance of some of the newer PLA aircraft types, while the F–5E/Fs should be a match for the J–7s.

Table 13–1. Principal Taiwan Combat Aircraft

Aircraft	Type	Quantity
F–16A/B	Multirole fighter	145
Mirage 2000–5	Air defense fighter	56
F–CK–1A/b	Multirole fighter	126
F–5E/F	Multirole fighter	60

Source: U.S-Taiwan Business Council, *The Balance of Air Power in the Taiwan Strait*, 17, available at: <www.us-taiwan.org/reports/2010_may11_balance_of_air_power_taiwan_strait.pdf>.

That same year, the U.S. Department of Defense concluded the following:[9]

> The PLAAF and the PLA Navy have approximately 2,300 operational combat aircraft. These consist of air defense and multi-role fighters, ground attack aircraft, fighter-bombers, and bombers. An additional 1,450 older fighters, bombers and trainers are employed for training

and R&D. The two air arms also possess approximately 450 transports and over 100 surveillance and reconnaissance aircraft with intelligence, surface search, and airborne early warning capabilities. The majority of PLAAF and PLA Navy aircraft are based in the eastern half of the country. Currently, 490 aircraft could conduct combat operations against Taiwan without refueling. However, this number could be significantly increased through any combination of aircraft forward deployment, decreased ordnance loads, or altered mission profiles.

Table 13–2. Principal PLA Combat Aircraft

Aircraft	Type	Quantity
Su–30MKK/MK2	Multirole fighter	100+
Su–27SK/J–11B	Multirole fighter	190
J–10A	Multirole fighter	150+
J–8	Air defense fighter	390
J–7	Air defense fighter	580
Q–5	Ground attack fighter	235
JH–7A	Ground attack fighter	130+
H–6	Bomber	160+

Surface-to-Air Missiles (SAMs)

The PRC's first surface-to-air missile, like that of other Communist Bloc countries, was the Soviet-developed S–75 Dvina, known to the West as the SA–2 Guideline, five batteries of which were delivered from the USSR in 1959. Then, the growing Sino-Soviet political crisis flared into open disagreement, bringing further deliveries to an end. On October 7, 1959, one of these Chinese SA–2 batteries shot down a Taiwan twin-engine two-crew Martin RB–57D reconnaissance aircraft while it was flying at 60,000 feet near Beijing. This loss came almost 7 months before the Soviets shot down Francis Gary Powers' Lockheed U–2 with an SA–2 on May 1, 1960.[10]

After the Sino-Soviet split, the PRC reverse-engineered the SA–2 and its SNR–75 Fan Song radar, and placed it into service as the HQ–2A, subsequently developing the more sophisticated HQ–2B. China's air defenses remained heavily dependent upon this system until the end of the Sino-Soviet split furnished China the opportunity to upgrade its surface-to-air missile defenses. In particular, it acquired advanced "double digit" SAM systems from Russia, notably the S–300 (SA–10/20) which has, like the SA–2 before it, undergone reverse engineering to further China's own indigenous SAM development programs. The PLA also acquired and manufactured derivatives of such Western SAM systems as the Crotale, Aspide, and Stinger.[11]

Though the HQ–2B remains an important element of PLA air defense, the nature of PLA missile defenses is increasingly built around the S–300 and equivalent high-technology systems. As one source suggests:[12]

> The PLA Air Force (PLAAF)'s Surface-to-Air Missile Corps has been operating the S–300 (NATO reporting name: SA–10 Grumble) family of surface-to-air missile system since the mid-1990s. The S–300 missile system was regarded as one of the world's most effective all-altitude regional air defense systems, comparable in performance to the U.S. MIM–104 Patriot system. The PRC remains the largest export customer of the S–300, mainly due to its incapability to produce a similar system domestically or acquire it from another country. A Chinese indigenous system analogous with the Russian S–300 series, the HQ–9, has had a long gestation but is now being deployed in some numbers.

A typical S–300 regiment has four to six batteries. One regiment in the PLAAF would thus have 16 to 24 transporter-erector-launchers (TELs) that could fire a total of 64 to 96 missiles (before reloading) to protect one area. The high performance (and high lethality) of the S–300 makes this a formidable system for any nation to "crack," even the United States, particularly if flying "legacy" third- and fourth-generation aircraft such as the F–CK–1, F–16, and Mirage.[13]

Table 13–3. PLA Surface-to-Air Missiles

System	Quantity (batteries)	Range (kilometers)	Altitude (kilometers)	Maximum Speed (Mach)
HQ–2	50	34	27	3.6
S–300 PMU (SA–10B)	8	90	27	5.1
S–300 PMU–1 (SA–20)	16	150	27	6
HQ–9	10	90	27	??
HQ–12	10	50	25	3.6
S–300 PMU–2 (SA–20B)	16	195	27	6

Source: *Bluffer's Guide Fortress China*, "Air Defense," accessed September 11, 2010, at:<www.sinodefence.com/special/airdefence/fortress-china2.asp>.

Taiwan currently deploys a plethora of SAM systems. As reported by the U.S. Defense Intelligence Agency, "Taiwan uses layered SAM coverage to protect its major population centers, key national leadership installations, military facilities, and national infrastructure. The air defense network consists of 22 SAM sites utilizing a mix of long- and medium-range systems, augmented by short-range tactical SAMs to provide overlapping coverage."[14] Table 13–4 offers a survey of the types, numbers of batteries, and numbers (where known) of the various missiles.

Table 13–4. Taiwan Surface-to-Air Missiles

Missile System	Batteries	Missile Type (Quantity)
Tien Kung I/II	6	(500)
PAC–2	3	Patriot (200)
I–Hawk	4	375
M–48 Chaparral	37	MIM–72C (727)
Antelope	6*	Tien Chien I (unknown) Made in Taiwan
Avenger	74	FIM–92 Stinger (1,299)
Man-portable Stingers	N/A	FIM–92 Stinger (728
RBS–70	20	

Source: Defense Intelligence Agency, *Taiwan Air Defense Assessment*, accessed September 20, 2010, at: <www.globalsecurity.org/military/library/report/2010/taiwan-air-defense_dia_100121.htm>.

* Partially fielded (6 batteries planned)

Ballistic and Cruise Missile Systems

In 2009, the Taiwan Ministry of National Defense reported that:[15]

> The PLA has currently deployed more than 1,300 short-range ballistic missiles and cruise missiles in areas opposite Taiwan . . . various kinds of improved missiles continue to be mass-produced and gradually assigned to the PLA. In the future, the PLA will continue to research and manufacture high precision and interception-resistant ballistic missiles, and deploy supersonic cruise missiles, which will enable rapid multi-wave missile assaults against Taiwan, and it can conduct precision strikes against Taiwan's critical political and military infrastructures, airports, sea ports, and military bases.

In May 2010, the Pentagon noted that the "PRC's Second Artillery maintains at least five operational SRBM brigades; an additional two brigades are subordinate to PLA ground forces—one garrisoned in the Nanjing

MR [Military Region] and the other in the Guangzhou MR. All SRBM units are deployed to locations near Taiwan."[16] Table 13-5 lists the PLA's ballistic missiles.

Table 13–5. PLA Ballistic Missiles

Designation (CN/NATO)	Quantity/Launchers	Class	Payload (kilograms)	Range (kilometers)
DF–3/CSS–2	15–20/5–10	IRBM	2,150	2,800
DF–4/CSS–3	15–20/10–15	IRBM	2,200	4,750
DF–5/CSS–4	20/20	ICBM	3,000	13,000
DF–21/CSS–5	85–95/75–85	MRBM	600	1,770
DF–15 (M–9)/CSS–6	350–400/90–110	SRBM	500	600
DF–11 (M–11)/CSS–7	700–750/120–140	SRBM	500	500
DF–31/CSS–9	<10/<10	ICBM	700	8,000
DF–31A/CSS–9 Mod–2	10–15/10–15	ICBM	700	10,700
JuLang–1/CSS–N–3		SLBM	600	2,500

ICBM: intercontinental ballistic missile   IRBM: intermediate-range ballistic missile   MRBM: medium-range ballistic missile
SLBM: submarine-launched ballistic missile   SRBM: short-range ballistic missile

Source: Office of the Secretary of Defense, *Military and Security Developments Involving the People's Republic of China 2010*; "Strategic Missile Systems," at SinoDefence.com, accessed September 28, 2010, at: <www.sinodefence.com/strategic/weapon.asp>. The more conservative estimate was used.

Land attack cruise missile (LACM) systems are proliferating in the global defense community, and the PLA had been quick to pick up on their significance. As with its earlier aircraft and missile programs, it has moved to acquire foreign cruise missile technology from abroad, going to Russia and the Ukraine, but seeking to exploit relevant technologies from other countries as well. Reportedly, between 1999 and 2001, Ukraine delivered Kh–55 (NATO AS–15) cruise missiles to the PRC, which also reportedly received detailed design information of another variant of the Kh–55 from Russia.[17] According to one analyst:[18]

> Current development projects reportedly include Chang Feng (CF), Hong Niao (HN), and Dong Hai (DH), with possible range between 400~1,800km. It is likely that even if the U.S. tried to deny GPS [global positioning system] signals to China, the PLA's cruise missiles could still function via the Russian GLONASS, or in the future the European GALILEO navigation signals. China is also developing its own "Compass Satellite Navigation System,"

which would eventually comprise 5 geostationary Earth orbit (GEO) satellites and 30 medium Earth orbit satellites to provide a global cover.

The Second Artillery, which established a conventional missile force in the 1990s, complementing its strategic nuclear force established earlier, is credited with possessing up to 300 DH-10 LACMs.[19] The PLAN possesses numerous YJ-62 (C-602) and YJ-82/YJ-83 (C-802/803) antiship cruise missiles (ASCMs), giving it a robust capability to interdict and offset Taiwan's naval forces, and perhaps those of other parties, such as the United States, that might intervene on its behalf.[20]

Regarding the Second Artillery's long-range cruise missile (LRCM) capabilities, Martin Andrew has noted that:

> The Chang Jian (Long Sword) CJ-10 (DH-10) long-range cruise missile system reportedly started trials with the Second Artillery Force in 2004 and between 50 and 250 missiles had been deployed along with between 20 and 30 launch vehicles as of September 2009. The Chinese media initially revealed their existence during the 60th Anniversary Parade. The CJ-10 is identified by three long launch canisters, square in circumference, mounted on the rear of the Chinese WS 2400 8 x 8 tractor-elevator-launcher (TEL), and the missile has a reported range of over 1,500km and up to 2,000 km.[21]

Airfields and Runway Availability

Both the PRC and Taiwan possess numerous airfields and operating locations in the Taiwan Strait region, and the PRC also has extensive basing facilities farther inland that give it a measure of security that Taiwan, because of its island status, cannot possess. In the Nanjing Military Region alone, there are more than 40 airfields, all of whose runways are longer than 7,000 feet, easily capable of supporting fighter and strike aircraft operations. On Taiwan, there are 12 air bases, with more than 23 runways longer than 7,000 feet. There are five highway strips longer than 8,000 feet that can be used as emergency runways.[22]

Unmanned Aerial Systems

In recent years, the PRC has been actively scouting, purchasing, and developing technologies to support its indigenous unmanned aerial systems (UAS) programs. The PRC's unmanned aerial vehicles (e.g., W-50 pilotless aircraft) have already entered into active service with PLA units and have reportedly attained "combat effectiveness."[23]

In 2007, Hsu Sho-hsuan of the *Taipei Times* reported that:

> A large number of recently decommissioned fighter aircraft have been turned into pilotless drone planes to be used together with Harpy anti-radar unmanned aerial vehicles purchased from Israel. These could help PRC punch holes in Taiwan's air defense systems and destroy key targets.[24]

As for Taiwan, its UAS aircraft are assigned to army aviation forces and to the Special Forces Command, and are used for intelligence, surveillance, and reconnaissance (ISR) purposes.

Possible PRC Military Actions against Taiwan

According to Taiwan and U.S. Government documents, the possible PRC military actions against Taiwan can be categorized into five phases: military intimidation, blockade, surgical strikes, asymmetric warfare, and amphibious invasion.[25] Air operations clearly figure prominently in all of these, consistent with Deng Xiaoping's pronouncement that "No matter what, the Air Force is most important in all operations: Army, Navy and Air Force, the first is a strong Air Force."[26] A 2008 White Paper on national defense issued by the PRC stated that:[27]

> The Air Force is a strategic service of the PLA, and the main force for carrying out air operations. It is responsible for such tasks as safeguarding the country's territorial air space and territorial sovereignty, and maintaining a stable air defense posture nationwide. It is mainly composed of aviation, ground air defense, airborne, signal, radar, ECM [electronic countermeasures], technical reconnaissance and chemical defense sections.

Certainly, the PLAAF can be expected to join all the possible military actions against Taiwan. In this regard, the following discussion examines possible PRC military actions against Taiwan, focusing on the role that airpower forces and air warfare would play in them.

Military Intimidation

In its 2009 Quadrennial Defense Review, the Taiwan government noted that:[28]

> The PLA may wage psychological warfare against Taiwan by means of escalation [of] the intensity of its military activities, adjusting force deployments, including forward deployments, field training exercises, firepower demonstration, and use or combine media influences to exaggerate the seriousness of military situation over the Taiwan Strait, so as to stoke internal panic in Taiwan and undermine their will and morale.

From the PLA's perspective, air intimidation offers the prospect of flexible, wide-ranging action having strong political and military effect yet with low political and military risk.[29] Airpower has the inherent ability to project power at high speed and over long distance without being hindered by the obstacles and difficulties afflicting surface power projection. The combination of airplane and missile make air intimidation a very real prospect. With regard to Taiwan, the PLA's joint-service missiles and aircraft, with their newer fighters like the Su–27, J–11, and Su–30, can project power across the entire Taiwan area. Indeed, already, Taiwan is "under" a missile-threat envelope of considerable depth and density. The coupling of this with precision navigation and sensing systems—like the various space-based navigation and cuing systems now on line (such as GPS and GLONASS)—make air intimidation more effective and more likely by largely removing the threat of counterproductive collateral damage.

Missile intimidation is a core Second Artillery mission, and works to restrain the enemy's strategic attempts or important risky military actions. The SRBMs of the Second Artillery offer long range, high accuracy, hypersonic speed, high-explosive effects, deep target penetration, and low risk of both interception and collateral damage, thus constituting a very important means of military intimidation. Air intimidation can be performed by means of airpower exercises, which not only demonstrate the threat and potentiality of airpower, but the national determination of the PRC as well. Further, routine air demonstration and intimidation can swiftly and readily transform into higher intensity military action against Taiwan, and, if done gradually and carefully, without necessarily alerting Taiwan's air defenders.

Blockade

Though traditionally thought of in naval terms, military blockade can take many forms. During World War II, for example, the U.S. Fifth Air Force effectively established an air blockade on New Guinea, routinely denying Japanese relief and supply forces from reaching the island. Taiwan's Ministry of National Defense recognized this when it issued its Quadrennial Defense Review in 2009, noting:[30]

> The PLA may use its Second Artillery, navy, and air force to conduct blockades against Taiwan's ports, offshore islands, and routes connecting to outside world, and blockade or seize Taiwan's offshore or remote islands, in order to shatter the will and morale of the populace, cripple the economic lifeline, depress the internal and external environment and force a peace negotiation on their terms.

In the event of a PRC blockade of Taiwan, it could be expected that the PLA's airpower forces will be employed to: establish and enforce a "no-fly zone" (NFZ); seize and maintain air dominance over the battlespace; establish defensive air caps and protect PLA forces from Taiwan air and missile strikes; prosecute electronic warfare and cyber warfare against Taiwan's forces; support the PLAN's sea blockade of Taiwan; support PLA littoral actions such as seizing the islands of Kinmen and Matsu; and, finally, conduct antiaccess operations against Taiwan's forces and their potential allies or coalition partners.[31] PLA airpower forces would prosecute these missions by attacking Taiwan's airfields, air bases, and important installations; seizing air dominance via air-to-air combat; conducting aerial mining operations; providing routine combat air patrols and air reconnaissance over the battlespace; and conducting air defense operations in coastal areas.[32]

Limited Force or Coercive Operations

The PRC might use various disruptive, punitive, or lethal military actions in a limited campaign against Taiwan, and the means could include computer network, special operations force, and kinetic attacks against Taiwan's political, military, and economic infrastructure to induce fear and degrade the populace's confidence in the leadership.[33]

One possible form of coercion would involve amphibious operations short of the full-scale occupation of Taiwan itself. Looking at the possibility of such coercive amphibious operations, the U.S. Department of Defense noted that:[34]

> The PLA is capable of accomplishing various amphibious operations short of a full-scale invasion of Taiwan. With few overt military preparations beyond routine training, China could launch an invasion of small Taiwan-held islands such as the Pratas or Itu Aba. A PLA invasion of a medium-sized, defended offshore island such as Mazu or Jinmen is within China's capabilities. Such an invasion would demonstrate military capability and political resolve while achieving tangible territorial gain and simultaneously showing some measure of restraint. However, this kind of operation includes significant, if not prohibitive, political risk because it could galvanize the Taiwan populace and generate international opposition.

For the limited force and coercive options, airpower can provide precision bombing, air strike, or support special operations force transportation by airdrop. The airpower employed in a punitive or lethal strike mission would be similar to an air strike as described below.

Aerospace Coercion

Aerospace coercion is a possible form of PRC action against Taiwan. As noted by the U.S. Department of Defense, the PLA may use ballistic missiles, cruise missiles, and precision-guided weapons to strike Taiwan's air defense systems, including air bases, radar sites, missiles, space assets, and communications facilities, so as to degrade Taiwan's defenses, neutralize Taiwan's leadership, and break the Taiwan people's will to fight. As well, the PLA could employ airpower and some of its ground forces, to target Taiwan's surface, underground, sea-going, and underwater military targets and infrastructure.[35] Modern airpower has the ability to seize the initiative and decide a war's outcome swiftly and irrevocably. In the case of a PLA move against Taiwan, only by massive air and missile operations can the PLA ensure its ability to land forces and secure a lodgment area. Air strikes, which in the precision era can result in swift degradation of an opponent's military strength and potential, could include attacks targeting Taiwan's air assets, to prevent them from attacking PLA forces; Taiwan's command and control facilities; naval and army forces that could counter a PLA amphibious assault; and Taiwan's overall warfighting potential and the morale of the populace.[36]

Invasion: The Ultimate Threat

A full-scale amphibious invasion is obviously the most serious form of military action the PRC could undertake against Taiwan, and would constitute a military "culminating point" in the relationship between the two entities. For the PLA, full-scale invasion constitutes an ultimate solution if the PRC perceives its unification goal and territory threatened, or the ongoing dispute is deemed impossible to be solved in any other way. From a military perspective, it will involve neighboring countries, a sensitive interregional area, and will necessarily greatly change the international political climate and global political affairs. From a financial standpoint, an invasion would obviously affect the global economy. From a military perspective, the PRC would have to expect that Taiwan would likely be assisted by a coalition of strong enemies acting to prohibit the PRC from unifying Taiwan by force, with a high probability that PRC forces would have to fight multiple enemies, not just the forces of Taiwan.[37] Under these circumstances, the PLA may employ the Second Artillery to undertake sustained missile bombardment, with the objective of forcing Taiwan to plead for peace before possible foreign powers can intervene, and thus creating an irreversible *fait accompli* before international intervention can work to thwart the PRC's aggressive plans.[38]

Former Taiwan Deputy Minister of National Defense Lin Chong-pin, in an interview during a visit to London in 2009, told a Central News Agency journalist that using military force to attack Taiwan is the PRC's final choice. To fight quickly and win quickly, he believed, the PLA will not resort to blockade, since blockades take time and provoke international outrage and intervention. Rather, he said, since 1990, the PLA has stressed quick and decisive military action, embodied in the slogan "First battle decides the war"; the PLA, he believed, would seek to launch and win an amphibious action "probably within one week."[39]

Since ancient times, amphibious operations have historically been extremely difficult to prosecute. Even for highly trained forces possessing asymmetric advantages in power projection, landing in the face of opposition has proven costly, even if ultimate victory has been secured. Such landings are recognized by military experts from the PRC, Taiwan, and the United States as among the most demanding and risky of all military operations.[40] The U.S. Department of Defense has noted the following:[41]

> Large-scale amphibious invasion is one of the most complicated and difficult military maneuvers. Success depends upon air and sea superiority, rapid buildup and sustainment of supplies on shore, and uninterrupted support. An attempt to invade Taiwan would strain China's untested armed forces and invite international intervention. These stresses, combined with China's combat force attrition and the complexity of urban warfare and counterinsurgency (assuming a successful landing and breakout), make amphibious invasion of Taiwan a significant political and military risk. Taiwan's investments to harden infrastructure and strengthen defensive capabilities could also decrease Beijing's ability to achieve its objectives.

An island landing invasion would involve joint operations by the PLA Ground Force, PLAN, PLAAF, and Second Artillery, supported by the People's Armed Police (PAP), PLA Reserve Force, and Militia, all acting in accordance with a unified joint campaign plan and command structure.[42] It would involve most, and potentially all, aspects of land, sea, air, and electronic warfare, including use of space-based assets and cyber attack. The crucial PLA challenge, obviously, would be circumventing or breaching Taiwan's shore defenses, establishing and building a beachhead, transporting personnel and materiel to designated landing sites along Taiwan's western coastline, and launching attacks to seize and occupy key targets or the entire island.[43]

PLA amphibious doctrine logically sets forth the progression of an amphibious operation in three phases: *preliminary operations, embarkation and movement*, and *assaulting and establishing the beach-head*. Each of these is addressed below, based upon Zhang Yuliang's *Science of Campaigns*.[44]

Preliminary Operations are undertaken to paralyze an enemy's operational system, to seize the initiative in the battle, and to set the conditions for amphibious landing operations. The missions in this phase include seizing information dominance via electronic combat and cyber warfare, and air and sea dominance via a comprehensive opening air and missile strike. Information dominance of the landing battle is the critical element of seizing air and sea dominance and the initiative of battle. The purpose is to greatly reduce the opponent's capability of electronic equipment and secure the PRC's own electronic warfare efficiency. Generally, it will start before the comprehensive fire assault, or at the same time, and will be proceeding throughout the whole battle process. Besides using airborne electronic countermeasures against Taiwan's air defense equipment, the PLA is likely to use precisely targeted special operations forces against Taiwan's electronic infrastructures, since use of broader-effect attacks, such as electromagnetic pulse weapons (EMP) or broad-area cyber attacks, might affect the PRC as much as Taiwan.

A preliminary comprehensive raid would employ missiles and other airborne fires to strike essential targets like command structures, air and naval bases, missile sites, and air defense systems in a sudden, massive, overwhelming manner. The purpose would be to paralyze Taiwan's military operations, incapacitate its warfighting abilities, and thereby set up favorable conditions for seizing information, air, and sea dominance. In general, this action would consist of a primary raid, and follow-up raids.[45] The first raid is the most critical, involving joint force attack by missiles and the service air components, particularly Second Artillery and the PLAAF.

Considering likely risk, efficiency, penetration, and costs, the PLA would probably choose SRBMs to execute the first raid. The high-priority targets of the raid might be SAMs, air defense radars, and fighter bases, because these targets, if untouched, could inflict heavy losses on PRC follow-on air and surface forces. The follow-on raids would be based on the result of the first raid. If the first raid degraded Taiwan's air defenses sufficiently so that PLAAF attack aircraft could operate with relative safety, then following raids would likely use aircraft primarily. Otherwise, follow-on attacks might continue to employ SRBMs until conditions favorable for PRC air dominance over Taiwan were achieved. Once Taiwan's integrated air defense system (IADS) had been destroyed or seriously degraded by SRBMs, the PRC's aircraft would become more active, furnishing a more precise, flexible, functional, and efficient means to apply military force in support of PRC campaign objectives.

Thus, the type, frequency, and interval of follow-on raids depend on the assessed battle damage and recovery time of Taiwan's air defense ability. This is, it might be noted, a very different form of air attack from that employed by coalition forces during the opening hours of Operation *Desert Storm* in 1991. In that case, there was essentially no pause for assessment between the first and follow-on strikes. Rather, following the first paralyzing strike by stealth aircraft and cruise missiles, a follow-on "gorilla package" strike was immediately undertaken.

This strike, enhanced by UAS systems mimicking manned aircraft, intimidated the surviving elements of Iraq's air defense network into revealing themselves so that they could be jammed by EW and destroyed by coalition SEAD (suppression of enemy air defenses) strikes. After this second strike, Iraq had essentially lost any hope of maintaining any semblance of air control over its own territory. Nonstealthy coalition aircraft could then fly with relative impunity across Iraq for the next 6 weeks of war.[46] In contrast, the PLA's writings imply a longer assessment period between the initial opening strike and follow-on attacks.

According to a RAND study, about 60–200 submunition-equipped SRBMs could temporarily neutralize most of Taiwan's fighter bases. They could effectively suppress Taiwan air defense operations, allowing follow-on PLAAF strike aircraft to attack air bases and other targets with modern precision weapons.[47]

Seizing air dominance by conducting surprising, fierce, continuing, and precision strikes is thus a crucial prerequisite for any landing force's grouping, embarkation, navigation, assault, and landing. Operations would be mainly conducted by the PLAAF, and joined by the Ground Force, PLAN, and Second Artillery, suppressing the enemy on the ground or jointly destroying the enemy in the air.[48] Unless Taiwan's air defense assets are mobile, bombproof, invisible, quickly recoverable, redundant, and numerous, the result can only get worse when the PLAAF is able to strike freely across the island. Seizing sea dominance would primarily involve the PLAN, joined by the PLAAF, ground forces, and Second Artillery, working together to control the area of the anticipated naval campaign, securing the landing force's abilities to undertake embarkation, seaborne transportation (coupled with defensive mine sweeping), and the assault landing.[49] The naval campaign poses challenges for both sides. Given the profusion and range of the antiship weapons available to both sides, it is difficult for both the PLAN and Taiwan naval forces to hide and survive in the Taiwan Strait because of its limited and constrained operational space.

Preparatory attacks against Taiwan's coastal defenses prior to an amphibious landing invasion would be mainly conducted by the PLAAF, joined by ground forces, PLAN, and Second Artillery forces. Depending upon the results of the previous missile and air attacks, PRC forces would seek to destroy enemy coastal defense facilities, artillery positions, missiles, radar sites, command structures, communication nodes, and other key targets. Through these, the PRC would seek to reduce enemy defense capability, stop enemy movements, isolate the landing area, and create favorable conditions for landing PLA ground forces.[50]

Embarkation and movement would proceed upon the basis of successful preliminary operations. The mission of embarkation is organizing landing forces, with their attendant logistical requirements, and loading them for transportation. Movement means all formation of landing forces en route to the respective staging area from the rendezvous area. According to a Jamestown Foundation study by Dennis Blasko, the PLAN lacks strategic sealift capacity, and thus cannot meet the requirements of a full-scale amphibious landing invasion against Taiwan, at least in the short term.[51] If this is the case, the PLA should employ more than one wave of amphibious fleets in a secured environment when it intends to invade Taiwan directly. The embarkation point must be a short distance from landing beaches to reduce time spent at sea. This is quite risky, for PLAN forces would be under near-constant Taiwan countersea attacks. Since, as Blasko notes, "Naval units from the South Sea Fleet would have to travel at least 500 nautical miles and those from the North Sea Fleet would have to travel at least 700 nautical miles to reach Taiwan," the employment of fires against PLAN forces would be near-constant, and grow ever more deadly as forces came within reach of increasingly numerous shorter-range weapons, such as aircraft, sea- or-land-based antiship missiles, coastal gun fire, and battlefield rocket artillery such as the multiple-launch rocket system (MLRS).[52]

Assaulting and establishing the beach-head is primarily conducted by landing groups and assisted by other services to fight and assure the joint operation's success. In the view of PLA analysts, it is the most critical of any of the invasion's operational phases, the time of greatest stress, intensity, difficulty, and decisiveness. It is incumbent upon the invasion commander to assure the landing operations are successful by all means. The landing beach must be as swiftly established as possible after the first echelon of landing forces have assaulted and secured the beach front, and then developed rapidly in depth so that follow-on landing forces can exploit it. All these operations must be assisted by on-call, persistent, close air support, which would be provided primarily by the PLAAF.[53]

Employing the Air Force in the Taiwan Strait: Some Thoughts

As the PLA's descriptions of amphibious landing invasion phases and scenarios are more deeply examined, considerations of employing airpower in the Taiwan Strait emerge more clearly. Reviewing all the phases of amphibious landing operations in the Taiwan Strait, we may conclude several points:

Taiwan's purpose for employing airpower is for self-defense only, not for offense. Taiwan's airpower forces must be employed in accordance with the agreed Taiwan defense strategy, and for the purpose of self-defense. Indeed, it may not be necessary to kill the enemy or to destroy enemy air bases, missile sites, naval ports, etc. To speak more clearly and practically, *Taiwan's purpose in employing airpower is to keep enemy forces out of its territory and lifeline. As long as the enemy does not step on Taiwan's territory and impede its lifelines, they don't win and Taiwan doesn't lose, and its national security is secured.* Any operations out of this scope would be a waste of resources, attrite limited assets, and could prove disastrously counterproductive. After all, national defense strategy is not about a matter of face, but about economy of force.

Taiwan must employ its airpower after the PLA initiates the first strike. To be consistent with the first point, it is impossible to apply airpower to attack the enemy prior to its first move. The reason is simple: *Taiwan can't afford the international liability of initiating the war.* During the period of any preliminary operations and the embarkation phase, all targets are shielded under the PLA's layered and integrated air defense umbrella. Taiwan would need to penetrate these defenses prior to prosecuting any attacks on those radars, missile sites, and air force bases—facilities that are typically hardened or well-protected by intensive air defense firepower. It is most unwise to conduct such a mission, which would simply consume Taiwan's airpower assets for nothing in return. Even in the name of a preemptive defense attack (such as Israel conducted in June 1967 against Egypt, Syria, and Jordan), it is unnecessary. Indeed, any Taiwan offensive operations prior to the PLA's first raid would furnish an excuse for the PRC to invade Taiwan and thus work to legitimize the invasion.

Retaining substantial airpower is dependent upon Taiwan's critical air assets surviving the PLA's first strike. Although it may seem counterintuitive, Taiwan's force-structure airpower and air defense inventory prior to the PLA's first raid may not count. Instead, we need to take the PLA's preliminary operations into account, considering what assets would likely remain following the opening SRBM attack. We need to deduct those which are not mobile, bombproof, invisible, loss-tolerable, or quickly recoverable. Frankly, sooner or later all fixed facilities will be destroyed. This means most of Taiwan's major airpower assets will be eliminated in the opening strike, leaving its defenders with only a few sheltered aircraft, mobile radars, mobile air defense missiles, and (hopefully) some recovered runways (if the PLA's raid frequency or lack of accuracy allows this). Therefore, a mobile defense is needed to ensure Taiwan's forces survive the PLA's missile and air strikes.

Taiwan's limited airpower should be concentrated to a critical time and place. Avoiding attrition of Taiwan's limited resources of airpower little by little is important. We should join the navy and army's resources and apply airpower only at a decisive time such as during the PLA's crossing of the Strait, selecting amphibious ships as the core targets. They are the "center of gravity," and must be struck before personnel debarkation by joint-service antiship weapons employed by the joint land, sea, and air forces. There is a historical precedent: the Battle of the Bismarck Sea in February 1943, in which American and Australian land-based attack forces destroyed a vital Japanese convoy carrying troops and supplies to New Guinea, effectively dooming Japanese plans to retain control of New Guinea.

Taiwan's should broaden its air defense by connecting all mobile radar and antiair weapons of all services. Taiwan must construct a mobile, diffuse, and widespread air defense umbrella covering point, area, and then theater air defense. It is technically workable and economically affordable. One example of this approach would be data-linking truck-mounted and sea-based radars and air-to-air missile launchers to provide air defense against follow-on PLA raids.

Taiwan should develop a multifunctional air force using advanced aircraft, helicopters, and UAS vehicles. Taiwan requires advanced aircraft for air superiority especially since the PLA now has more and more new, advanced aircraft of its own. But Taiwan also needs aircraft that can take part in countersea operations. In this regard, Taiwan should have some attack helicopters which can deliver antiship weapons, making a vertical take-off from a hidden point and flying at tree-top height. And it should have some small or unmanned aircraft taking off in a short distance to cruise and observe along Taiwan's coastline to search for important targets and collect information for use in antiship operations by land- and sea-based forces.

Taiwan should develop a decentralized, network-centric command and communication structure. Understandably, Taiwan's command, control, communications, computers, intelligence, surveillance, and reconnaissance (C4ISR) system constitutes a high-priority target for initial strikes by the PLAAF, Second Artillery, and special operations forces. Since Taiwan's current command and communication system is fixed in place (although there are some back-up systems), there is a high probability it will be quickly destroyed, thus not lasting long enough to be a significant element in Taiwan's defensive operations. To ensure the command and communication function will survive the opening missile and air strike, Taiwan should duplicate it by decentralizing and duplicating the command and communication center downward through the defense infrastructure, and possibly combining the military and civilian communication systems.

Taiwan's current airpower assets should be enhanced. Airpower is inherently powerful, speedy, and flexible. While this is its strength for an attacker, it is also its vulnerability for a defender. In cross-strait conflict, due to the vulnerability of runways, shelters, radars, and missile sites, there is very high risk to Taiwan's current facilities. Taiwan should improve current facilities to withstand future air and missile attack. This can be done in several ways: increasing the strength of runways, shelters, and other facilities likely to be raided; undertaking structural strengthening, increasing material preparedness, and practicing repair and recovery operations to quicken post-raid recovery and reconstitution;[54] and researching and developing new facilities or equipment to reduce runway dependence, such as RATO (rocket-assisted take-off), catapult launch, VTOL (vertical take-off and landing), STOL (short take-off and landing), and naval-style arrested landing systems.

Taiwan should adopt a "Starfish" strategy to enhance its survivability. Starfish usually have five or even more arms. Their multi-arms not only can tolerate more damage, but also can regenerate automatically. Once its arm is cut, the body will regenerate another arm to become a normal starfish again. Also, the separated part of the arm will regenerate to become another small starfish.[55] Applying this to Taiwan's defense system means that when some part of its force is hit by the enemy, it will not be paralyzed but will survive and fight independently if it cannot recover to its original body (unit). Taiwan should try to apply this strategy to decentralize the commanding activity to the very basic units of its organizations, equipment, facilities, or personnel, to ensure that sustainability and survivability will expand.

In conclusion, many articles study the balance of airpower across the Taiwan Strait, with a consensus that Taiwan has lost both its quality and quantity advantages of airpower. There is no evidence to show that the balance of airpower across the Taiwan Strait will get better in the near future. Accordingly, when facing a continually modernizing airpower projector like the PLAAF, Taiwan should become more creative and think beyond the traditional scope of airpower options. Taiwan shouldn't limit its imagination just to airpower. It needs to prevent cross-strait conflict by any means, even those other than airpower, like political or cultural power. For example, Taiwan can create a peaceful atmosphere by cultural power and economic power; it can construct a firm government by psychological power, and employ soft power so that the PRC has no excuses to justify an invasion. It will take joint efforts to fight this war: joint air force, navy, and army partnership will strengthen defensive airpower. Joint airpower, sea power, and land power will strengthen Taiwan's overall defensive power. Then, joint efforts linking hard power with soft power will form smart power, ensuring everlasting peace in the Taiwan Strait.

Notes

[1] See Ma Ying-jeou, "Taiwan's Renaissance," in *Taiwan's Renaissance: President Ma Ying-jeou's Selected Addresses and Messages, 2008–2009* (Taipei: Government Information Office, 2010), 1–9; this was Ma's inaugural address presented on May 20, 2008.

[2] Office of the Secretary of Defense, *Annual Report to Congress: Military and Security Developments Involving the People's Republic of China 2010* [hereafter cited as OSD, *2010 Military and Security Developments Involving the PRC*] (Washington, DC: U.S. Department of Defense, May 2010), 2, at <www.defense.gov/pubs/pdfs/2010_CMPR_Final.pdf>, accessed August 20, 2010.

[3] Taiwan Ministry of National Defense, *2008 National Defense Report* (Taipei: Ministry of National Defense, 2008).

[4] For a PRC perspective, see Cui Guoping and Zhang Zhanbing, *Air Warfare Is as Powerful as a Thunderbolt* [雷霆萬鈞空中戰] (Shijiazhuang: Hebei Science and Technology Publishing House, November 2000).

[5] Shirley Kan, Christopher Bolkcom, and Ronald O'Rourke, *China's Foreign Conventional Arms Acquisitions: Background and Analysis*, Report RS22079 (Washington, DC: Congressional Research Service of the U.S. Library of Congress, October 10, 2000), 11, at <www.fas.org/man/crs/RL30700.pdf>, accessed July 23, 2011.

[6] United Kingdom Air Staff, *AP 3000: British Air and Space Power Doctrine, Fourth Edition* (London: HMSO, 2009), 7, at <www.airpowerstudies.co.uk/New-CAS-AP300.pdf>, accessed July 23, 2011.

[7] U.S. Defense Intelligence Agency, *Taiwan Air Defense Assessment*, Report DIA-02-1001-028 (January 21, 2010), at <www.globalsecurity.org/military/library/report/2010/taiwan-air-defense_dia_100121.htm>, accessed July 23, 2011.

[8] Lotta Danielsson-Murphy, ed., *The Balance of Airpower in the Taiwan Strait* (Arlington, VA: U.S.-Taiwan Business Council, 2010), 17, at <www.us-taiwan.org/reports/2010_may11_balance_of_air_power_taiwan_strait.pdf>.

[9] OSD, *2010 Military and Security Developments Involving the PRC*, 62.

[10] Chris Pocock with Clarence Fu, *The Black Bats: CIA Spy Flights over China from Taiwan* (Atglen, PA: Schiffer Military History, 2010), 54 and 135, note 118.

[11] See "Surface to Air Missile Systems and Integrated Air Defense Systems," *Air Power Australia*, at <www.ausairpower.net/sams-iads.html>, accessed 24 Jul. 2011.

[12] *Bluffer's Guide: Fortress China* "Air Defense," at <www.militaryphotos.net/forums/showthread.php?152230-Bluffer%92s-Guide-Fortress-China>, accessed September 11, 2010.

[13] Kan, Bolkcom, and O'Rourke.

[14] U.S. Defense Intelligence Agency, *Taiwan Air Defense Assessment*.

[15] Taiwan Ministry of National Defense (MND), *Quadrennial Defense Review 2009* (Taipei: MND, 2009), 37, at <www.mnd.gov.tw/QDR/file/ec1.pdf>.

[16] OSD, *2010 Military and Security Developments Involving the PRC*, 66.

[17] "Land-Attack Cruise Missile (LACM)," *SinoDefence.com*, at <www.sinodefence.com/strategic/missile/cruisemissile.asp>, accessed September 20, 2010.

[18] Ibid.

[19] The PRC's view of Second Artillery's role is in State Council of the People's Republic of China, *China's National Defense in 2008* (Beijing: PRC State Council, 2008), a PRC White Paper, accessed July 25, 2011, at <www.china.org.cn/government/central_government/2009-01/20/content_17155577_8.htm>.

[20] Joseph Carrigan, "Aging Tigers, Mighty Dragons: China's Bifurcated Surface Fleet," *China Brief* 10, no. 19 (September 24, 2010), 5; Richard Fisher, "The Air Balance on the Taiwan Strait," *International Assessment and Strategy Center*, at <http://strategycenter.net/research/pubID.224/pub_detail.asp>, accessed September 20, 2010.

[21] Martin Andrew, "China's Conventional Cruise and Ballistic Missile Force Modernization and Deployment," *China Brief* 10, no. 1 (January 7, 2010), 5, at <www.jamestown.org/uploads/media/cb_010_01.pdf>.

[22] PLAAF-PLAN basing data from *Air Power Australia*, at <www.ausairpower.net/APA-PLA-AFBs.html>, accessed September 27, 2010.

[23] L.C. Russell Hsiao, "Advances in China's UCAV Program," *China Brief* 10, no. 19 (September 24, 2010), 1–2.

[24] Hsu Sho-hsuan, "PRC's Preparations to Attack Taiwan Accelerate: Report," *Taipei Times*, July 19, 2010, at <www.taipeitimes.com/News/front/archives/2010/07/19/2003478290/2>, accessed July 24, 2011.

[25] MND, *Quadrennial Defense Review 2009*, 41–42, and OSD, *2010 Military and Security Developments Involving the People's Republic of China 2010*, 51–52.

[26] Editing Group of Yearbook on Chinese Communist Studies, *2009 Yearbook on Chinese Communist Studies* (Taipei: Institute of Chinese Communist Studies, 2010), 3–47.

²⁷ State Council of the PRC, *China's National Defense in 2008*.

²⁸ MND, *Quadrennial Defense Review 2009*, 41.

²⁹ See Cui Changchi, *21ˢᵗ Century Air Raids and Air Countermeasures* [21世紀空襲與反空襲] (Beijing: PLA *Publishing* House, 2002) 28–29.

³⁰ MND, *Quadrennial Defense Review 2009*, 41–42.

³¹ Zhu Aihua, *Coastal Island Blockade Operations* [近岸島嶼封鎖作戰] (Beijing: Military Science Publishing House, July 2002), 64.

³² Ibid., 9.

³³ OSD, *2010 Military and Security Developments Involving the PRC*, 51.

³⁴ Ibid., 52

³⁵ Ibid., 51.

³⁶ Chen Xinmin, Xu Guochen, and Luo Feng, *Insular Operations Study* [島嶼作戰研究] (Beijing: Military Science Publishing House, May 2005), 155–157; see also Sun Jianbo, *Island War* [島嶼戰爭] (Beijing: Weapons Industry Publishing House, March 2003).

³⁷ Chen, Xu, and Luo, 20–21; see also Yu Guohua, *A Study on Modern Offensive Campaigns* [現代進攻戰役主要問題研究] (Beijing: National Defense University Press, June 1998).

³⁸ MND, *Quadrennial Defense Review 2009*, 42.

³⁹ "Lin Chong-pin: Military Attack on Taiwan is Beijing Final Option" [林中斌：軍事攻擊台灣是北京最後選項] Central News Agency News [中央社], March 27, 2009, at <http://n.yam.com/cna/international/200903/20090327419164.html>, accessed September 30, 2009.

⁴⁰ Chen, Xu, and Luo, 183.

⁴¹ OSD, *2010 Military and Security Developments Involving the PRC*, 52.

⁴² Zhang Yuliang [張玉良], ed., *Science of Campaigns* [戰役學] (Beijing: National Defense University Press, February 2006), 310.

⁴³ OSD, *2010 Military and Security Developments Involving the PRC*, 51–52.

⁴⁴ Zhang, 316–330.

⁴⁵ Ibid., 318.

⁴⁶ For the Gulf air campaign, see Thomas A. Keaney and Eliot A. Cohen, *Gulf War Air Power Survey: Summary Report* (Washington, DC: Government Printing Office, 1993), 11–13, 56–64.

⁴⁷ David A. Shlapak, David T. Orletsky, Toy I. Reid, Murray Scot Tanner, and Barry Wilson, *A Question of Balance: Political Context and Military Aspects of the China-Taiwan Dispute*, RAND document MG-888 (Santa Monica, CA: RAND Corporation, 2009), 51, available at <www.rand.org/pubs/monographs/2009/RAND_MG888.pdf>.

⁴⁸ Zhang, 319.

⁴⁹ Ibid., 319–321.

⁵⁰ Ibid., 322.

⁵¹ Dennis J. Blasko, "PLA Amphibious Capabilities Structured for Deterrence," *China Brief* 10, no. 17 (August 19, 2010), 5–9.

⁵² Ibid., 8.

⁵³ Zhang, 326–329.

⁵⁴ Practice builds both skills and confidence, and, as well, publicized demonstrations can increase the credibility of deterrence, so as to persuade the enemy to give up the option of using force.

⁵⁵ Not all species can regenerate and become a new small one, but some of them do.

Chapter 14

The U.S.-China Military Balance Seen in a Three-Game Framework

David Frelinger and Jessica Hart

This chapter presents an alternative framework for approaching the discussion and assessment of the "military balance" between the United States and China, with an emphasis on the effect of People's Liberation Army Air Force (PLAAF) modernization. This approach provides for a more comprehensive means of thinking about the military balance and illuminates some deficiencies in current assessments. The framework assesses PLAAF modernization through the lenses of three "games"—the Game of Influence, the Battle over a Third Party, and the Great Power Game—that represent the range of relationships the United States and China could forge, with a focus on the military aspects of those games. As this analysis will demonstrate, the effect of PLAAF modernization is most fully understood not as an input in one overall U.S.-China military balance, but as a series of moves occurring in the context of the game or games the United States and China are playing.

Why a New Framework?

The U.S.-China military balance is most often spoken of in Cold War terms of force-on-force counts, defense expenditure comparisons, and other metrics that are relatively straightforward to calculate. These calculations are then used to define the balance within future "worlds" that could exist between the two nations.[1] These analyses assume that the United States and China are playing the same game in these worlds, that both recognize the other side is playing that game, and that the game remains dominant and consistent for an extended period of time. Assessing the balance through this narrow aperture misses important nuances in what is in fact a fluid military context—one in which PLAAF modernization plays many roles. This type of assessment also does not account for the facts that powers may play more than one game simultaneously, that both sides are not necessarily playing the same game, and that both may fail to recognize what game the other has chosen.

An alternative framework is necessary to address these analytical deficiencies. By acknowledging the range of games and the fluidity of their context, the framework allows for a fuller assessment of the effects of PLAAF modernization on the military balance within the games. This avoids viewing PLAAF modernization through the lens of only one game while also highlighting the fact that there is not one military balance, but several. By adopting a more comprehensive framework, this assessment also avoids utilizing familiar—and inappropriate—analytical narratives. Many attempt to frame at least a portion of the U.S.-Chinese interactions in Cold War terms—what we call here the Great Power Game. In the Cold War, the positions of the United States and the Soviet Union as the only two remaining great powers were relatively ossified from the outset, and the overarching ideological narrative provided a grounding framework for understanding the game that both sides were playing. This is not the case for the United States and China. The relationship is not yet mature, and there are multiple, competing narratives about interests and goals on both sides. Those narratives as well as U.S. and Chinese actions provide no convincing indications that either side has made a deliberate decision as to which game it wishes to be playing—much less what game the other is playing or will choose to play in the future. Instead there are elements of multiple games that must be assessed.

Finally, assessing the potential U.S.-China relationship in these three games provides some first-order conclusions. Ultimately, the game framework points to the need for the United States to hedge—to show caution when making decisions about what course to take because multiple outcomes are possible and are difficult to predict. As a result, no course of action should be seen as immutable, and the United States should consider multiple paths. Furthermore, this framework leads to the conclusion that it is quite likely that neither side understands what game the other party may be playing, a misunderstanding that could result in unnecessarily strong reactions from both powers to fairly minor military moves—including PLAAF modernization.

Because this framework seeks to assess the military balances, the games are best understood through the different roles military power plays in each. The *Game of Influence* is one where military power is utilized in an essential supporting role to advance national interests, but military victory in a conflict is not the ultimate goal. The Game of Influence is not necessarily a zero-sum game. In the *Battle over a Third Party*, military power in the context of a conflict over a third party plays the central role, but asymmetric stakes tend to prevent a zero-sum character. In the *Great Power Game*, military power is the central aspect, and it is the most comprehensive game in scope as it ranges across all military and political spheres. It is also the only true zero-sum game discussed.

The Game of Influence

The Game of Influence is largely political in nature, with the major powers vying for greater influence in a variety of arenas. As a result, the game's scope may be confined to a region or along a much broader scale. For instance, a major power may seek to wield influence on a global scale, as the United States does, or the goal may be more limited in nature, such as China attempting to assert dominance in the South China Sea. The major powers seek to dictate the "rules of the road" and to be accepted as the legitimate authority in their desired spheres. And while the game's scope ranges across political and military arenas, the Game of Influence will not necessarily be played in every, or even the majority, of possible spheres. Instead, each power will only engage the other major power in the areas most relevant to its national interests.

Military power is often utilized in an important supporting role, but the focus of the two sides is not military victory or conquest. The major powers will largely seek to advance their goals through political posturing, economic power, and diplomatic dealings, but "soft" power is not sufficient when engaging another major military power. The political narrative of a state must be backed up by military power, by the credible threat of force. Force is one of the keys to deter violent actions by others and also serves as a tool for compellence. Military power is thus necessary to "enforce" and make credible political moves.

Despite this essential military aspect, the game remains largely non–zero-sum. Both powers will attempt to achieve their own interests, but one side's "gain" is not necessarily the other side's "loss" because both powers do not value all aspects of the game equally. The stakes in the game vary from incident to incident; one power may view an aspect of the game as more important than the other power does or both sides may hold similar views of the stakes. Nevertheless, the overall stakes are relatively symmetric in that both sides see the totality of maintaining and gaining influence in the game as important to their national interests. Responses to moves by the other side are determined by the nations' levels of interest. Because the stakes vary, a response to an opposing move may not always be seen as necessary, and each side can escalate or deescalate within the same game as interests dictate. Finally, the Battle over a Third Party may be played at the same time as the Game of Influence. But if a Game of Influence is played after a Great Power Game begins, the Game of Influence will take on a significantly different character due to the Great Power Game's encompassing nature.

Rationale/explanation for the game. Military power in the Game of Influence is utilized much differently than in the models of war familiar to Western militaries before the Cold War. Force is not used directly to prepare for or to engage in large-scale battle, but is utilized as a means of influencing the actions of the adversary.[2] Now one of the primary goals of utilizing military power is shaping the national populations' opinions of the ongoing competition, and both powers must be aware that there are internal and external audiences to be addressed. The primary objective for using force is not destroying an adversary's military, though that may play a role in limited situations. The central objective for military power is to serve as a tool in convincing a power to accept the other side's objectives.

What would it look like if the United States and China were engaged in this game? The ongoing South China Sea dispute over maritime boundaries and acceptable behavior in international waters is illustrative of this type of game. This is not primarily a military conflict, although military power is a necessary tool for both sides. China's goal is apparently to have its interpretation of maritime laws and conduct accepted as the international norm. The United States, on the other hand, seeks to maintain the current norm. For both parties, this involves crafting different political narratives for regional and international audiences. But it is also likely that both the United States and China may seek to gain influence and/or demonstrate influence by shows of military presence. This is not necessarily a demonstration of force, but, in the case of the United States, it is demonstrating that its navy maintains its right to operate in international waters. In this game, it is possible that a military incident will occur, but military conquest or victory in a conflict is not the end game. The end game is the ability to define and, if necessary, legitimately enforce the norms in the region.

The Game of Influence is also taking place in the broader maritime arena. China is seeking greater control of exclusive economic zones (EEZs) as well as waters it defines as core interests outside EEZs or territorial waters. For China, regional and international acceptance of its control in the region and of its right as a naval power to engage in limited policing is crucial to its interests. China maintains intermittent patrols and limited interdiction in these relevant sea areas with the goal of limiting resource extraction or transit by other nations. And even if not acknowledged fully in the international arena, a limited acceptance of Chinese control by fishermen or resource extraction companies in the region would be a win in this game for the Chinese because it would show that Chinese norms were accepted over those promulgated by the United States. Military power thus serves to bolster political control, but the use of military force is not the focus of this competition.

Battle over a Third Party

The Battle over a Third Party focuses on the role of military power in a possible conflict over a third party, and this game's scope is the most limited of the three described because it is confined to a third party territory or region. In this game, there is a threat of one major power using force either in an active defense of a third party or in an attack against the other major power to maintain the third party's independence. Military forces have a direct impact here, and both powers have a fairly well defined role in the ongoing military competitions. There are many possible stratagems available to both sides, but the most severe threat is seizing physical control of the third party. Lesser threats include large-scale strategic attacks, blockades, and other higher-end compellence mechanisms.

The stakes are the most interesting aspect of this competition. The game can have highly asymmetric stakes, with one power viewing control of the third party as much more central to its national interests than does the other power. This asymmetry creates interesting conflict dynamics but, fortunately, little chance of escalation because the degree of importance both sides place on the conflict is below the threshold required for either to escalate into a much more costly general war.[3] By choosing this game, both sides implicitly declare they have limited interests that do not extend to general war. And while military power in the confines of the third party game is the main focus, the third party situation is not the driving force for both sides' overall military strategy and choices—though it may be the central focus for the side with the higher stakes.

Because of its non–zero-sum nature, military improvements or political posturing by either side may not require a countermove, though changes that improve the capabilities of one side in the third party battle may cause the other side to respond directly if interest levels are high enough. In other words, each power will escalate or deescalate within the game as interests demand. Additionally, this game may be played alone or as part of the Game of Influence. Importantly, if a Battle over a Third Party is played within the Great Power Game, the nature of the game is fundamentally altered as the third party competition now plays a role in a broader, higher-stakes game.

Rationale/explanation for the game. Military power is used here in a more traditional sense than in the Game of Influence, though the use of that power is limited in scope. Both sides, for any number of reasons, have decided that they have interests in a third party nation that are important enough to engage military force to achieve. Neither side views the Battle over a Third Party as part of a larger, more comprehensive game. Military capabilities are generally highly tailored to the contours of a particular conflict, and the evaluation of forces is viewed through this conflict's lens. Other interactions and games between the two powers will undoubtedly occur, but those interactions are largely divorced from this military context and are reflective of interests that exist outside this limited contest.

This asymmetry is particularly important to the game's outcome as the military capabilities of the two parties begin to approach parity in the area of interest. The differences in stakes will alter the relative attractiveness of various defense strategies.[4] Essentially, the gains associated with some strategies will no longer be worth the risks for the side with lesser stakes in the game. And, of course, the changes in the two sides' relative military capabilities impact the potential game outcome by altering how well either side can accomplish particular missions or thwart the other power's ability to accomplish its own missions.

What would it look like if the United States and China engaged in this game? The Battle over a Third Party has been the main competition between the United States and China during the last 60 years. This competition has manifested itself both in Taiwan and Korea, where control was seen as by both parties as important but was not seen as a means of defining regional influence or a greater direct competition between the United States and China. Instead, for the United States, these were elements of the broader Cold War competition with the Soviet Union and were seen as part of a perceived Communist threat that existed throughout the world. Both of these conflicts seem to have been about narrow interests and not about serving as a stepping-stone to a larger competition.[5]

In this game, the biggest unknown when the forces begin to approach local parity in capabilities is how each side defines operational success or failure. Taiwan is an illuminating example because of the asymmetric levels of interests and the very different potential standards for success or failure on each side. China regards Taiwan as one of its core interests, but the United States does not elevate its interests in Taiwan to a comparable level.[6] In the military dimension, these differing levels of interests might manifest themselves through planners on the two sides defining success or failure in different ways. For instance, a Chinese planner might want to possess a military option to land a significant ground force on Taiwan that could be used in extreme cases and that would use Chinese air and missile forces as tools for accomplishing the mission. On the other side, an American planner might be satisfied with preventing the Chinese from effectively exploiting a landing and would therefore be more willing to accept higher levels of damage from Chinese air and missile forces. Because the bars of success or failure are different for both sides, improvements in one dimension such as airpower might not increase military capabilities enough to deny a fairly modest military objective and therefore might not be enough to alter the "balance."

The forces necessary for each side to succeed in these competitions may be far from symmetrical, and the ways in which the forces are trained could likewise be very different. For instance, a U.S. force optimized for conflicts near China might look very different from typical U.S. force configurations, unless the infrastructure (bases, country access, level of competence of military partners) for U.S. forces proved to be far more robust and extensive than in any other part of the world. Much of the U.S. force structure was inherited from the Cold

War, and even the modest changes from Cold War threat assumptions have tended to adapt the force to operate under more benign instead of more hostile conditions.[7] These changes included reliance on unfettered access to large bases and entry areas for effective employment of air and ground forces, judging that the threat to those bases that existed during the Cold War was gone.[8]

Great Power Game

The Great Power Game is the most comprehensive in scope and ranges across the majority of or all military and political spheres. It is therefore the game with the greatest focus on military power. The game's central focus is on the opposing military, extending across the full spectrum of military actions and not confined to a single issue. Indeed, while conflicts over third parties may occur within this game, they are differentiated from those occurring at the same time as the Game of Influence because they are now primarily viewed as part of the larger competition between the two powers. For this reason, a Battle over a Third Party would have very different implications within the context of this game. In this game, the area of competition is no longer confined but spreads across the global arena.

The stakes in this overall game are largely symmetric, and both powers view all interactions in light of the overall game. As a result, this is a zero-sum game, and some type of response to every move is dictated simply because of the nature of the game. In other words, because all spheres are in play, not to respond to an action within any sphere is to assure some type of loss in the game. As a result, one of the game's defining features is that it is extremely difficult for a power to disengage from participation once the game begins. This makes the Great Power Game the most dangerous and costly of the games. Just as war termination methods are more crucial in this game because of the stakes, so are game termination strategies. Short of withdrawing and "losing" or of engaging in a decisive conflict, there is no viable way for a power to end the competition. This game is a road with few exit ramps. While there are plausible de-escalation routes in the Game of Influence, particularly for the power with the lesser stakes, once the situation escalates to a Great Power Game, a power must be concerned about every conflict or risk a loss in the overall game. This means that the Great Power Game is a superset of the Game of Influence and the Battle over a Third Party. As such, aspects of the two other games will likely occur in the Great Power Game, but they have a different character and a greater significance when played within the Great Power Game.

Despite its largely military focus, there are important political implications to this game as well. One of the most notable is that alliances take on increased importance within the game's context. Both powers will focus increasingly on building alliances, many of which will be military in nature. It becomes a question of each power attempting to convince nations to side with it over the adversary. The more expansive the coalition, the more influence and power one side will wield. In many ways, the sizes of alliances are viewed as one of the metrics of success.

Rationale/explanation for the game. Major military powers seek to ensure that their military capabilities will be sufficient to counter a wide range of threats from a variety of possible adversaries across the operational spectrum. Even in an environment where there are no clear military adversaries, a major power will build capabilities as part of a hedging strategy against other powers.[9] While a major power would thus develop capabilities to counter other powers, without the impetus of a Great Power Game, it would not predicate the majority of its military strategy and acquisition on the actions of only one potential adversary. But when the choice to engage in a Great Power Game is made, the strategy shifts to one dominated by forces and capabilities to counter the one specific adversary.

Engagement in this game would begin if the United States decided that a power had become an "an adversary capable of challenging U.S. power in all dimensions of modern warfare."[10] Both the "adversary" and "capability" are necessary for this decision. The power must be viewed as an adversary, as a threat to at least some substantial national interests, and as having the capability and not just the probable intentions to harm U.S. interests. This Great Power Game drives all other games the powers may play. Every military move by the other side would now require a U.S. reaction because the United States has declared, explicitly or otherwise, that any movement on the other side is detrimental in what is now a zero-sum game. Prior to engaging in this game, the United States could dismiss a wide range of military actions by the other side as unimportant to its overall strategic interests. But choosing to play the Great Power Game requires the United States to respond to any military improvement by its adversary as a potential threat. Challenges need to be directly countered in some fashion, lest there be a perception of waning strength that would undermine the nation's position in the larger competition. This may mean building a new weapons system, acquiring more of a particular weapons system or platform, or a force posture move.

During this game, operations on the periphery of the opponent might occur, but they will have a different character because they are occurring within the Great Power Game context. Because of the high stakes of the Great Power Game, a defeat or strategic reversal for either party in a peripheral operation makes it far more plausible that the losing power will escalate in an attempt to reverse its perceived loss. This escalation could include attacks throughout the full strategic depth of the opponent both in terms of area targeted and of the relevant target set. This type of game therefore carries explicit risks of escalation for both parties as one side might transition from playing one of the lesser games and suddenly reframe the game in this much broader context. Such an escalation is extremely dangerous for both sides, and it appears to be a distinct possibility, particularly if internal politics drive one side to adopt a stronger stance against its adversary.

What would it look like if the United States and China were engaged in this game? The United States and China have never engaged in this sort of competition. The most antagonistic period between the two powers occurred during the Korean War, and even then China was a secondary concern for the United States relative to the Great Power Game with the Soviet Union. U.S. forces were focused very heavily on the Soviets, and Soviet improvements throughout the spectrum of conflict were met and countered. This has not been the case with China, but a movement by either party to frame its own military improvements within the perspective of this type of competition would begin to drive the relationship toward a Great Power Game even in the absence of a clear decision to do so. These types of military moves may have unintended and serious consequences.

Despite the dangers, a Great Power Game remains an approach one or both sides may deliberately pursue. If so, the understanding of changes in the military balance would be dependent on how the participants perceived that competition. Just as the Cold War spurred many technological improvements in forces, a move to play a Great Power Game by the United States and China would likely result in the same type of technological competition. For instance, an improvement in a key intermediate metric, such as exchange ratio of fighters, may be sufficient for the other party to embark on a major improvement in its own forces to maintain performance in that area. This response would likely occur even if the opposing force improvement was not particularly relevant to the most likely or serious potential conflicts with the opponent.[11] The rationale for the other party would likely be the perceived necessity to improve the performance of its forces in relation to the intermediate metric, either in terms of operating in a neutral space or in terms of a particular conflict where war outcomes would be the focus. An alternative response might involve choosing a strategy that emphasizes deep attack and punishment as key elements of operations, which in turn might lead to the selection of new deep attack systems.[12] Ultimately, the key is not to focus on specifics, but to understand that if this game is being played, it fundamentally colors perceptions of both parties so that any line of operation has a very different level of importance from other games.

While this game is not being played by the United States, there is evidence that other nations in the Pacific region fear that this type of game could arise between the powers. In particular, recent defense white papers from Pacific region governments have expressed concern. Australia has been the most explicit. An Australian 2009 Defense White Paper states, "As other powers rise, and the primacy of the United States is increasingly tested, power relations will inevitably change. When this happens there will be the possibility of miscalculation. There is a small but still concerning possibility of growing confrontation between some of these powers."[13] Other nations, such as Vietnam, express concerns about potential military competitions between "major powers"[14] and speak of a shifting balance of power toward "multipolarity."[15] That this concern has made a significant enough impression for these governments to address it in their official documents demonstrates that the possibility of such a game occurring resonates with other nations.

When viewed through the lens of these three games, more than one military balance must be assessed, as each game will present its own "balance."[16] A move by either side may have one impact in one game and an entirely different impact in another, meaning that PLAAF modernization may achieve a variety of results.

The Impact of PLAAF Modernization

The highlights of PLAAF modernization are:

- Aircraft have improved in terms of overall performance, particularly in regard to longer-range fighter-bombers, but the total force has shrunk in size.

- Munitions for air-to-air and air-to-surface operations are greatly improved as less capable air-to-air weapons and ground attack weapons such as dumb bombs and cluster bombs are supplanted by modern guided weapons.

- Electronic attack capabilities have improved.

- Training and tactics have improved.

- Supporting systems such as early warning, C4I (command, control, communications, computers, and intelligence), and battle management systems have been improved.

Specific examples of PLAAF improvement include:

- fourth-generation fighters (the Su–27, J–10, Su–30, and J–11, called third generation in PLAAF doctrine) that are equipped with modern avionics for targeting and electronic countermeasures and that enable employing precision air-to air and air-to ground munitions[17]
- longer-range upgraded variants of the B–6 medium bomber employing long-range cruise missiles
- new air-to-surface weapons such as long-range land-attack cruise missiles for medium bombers and fighter-bombers, and shorter-range near-precision and precision weapons
- Modern early warning, surveillance, and battle management systems to facilitate control of forces.

To fully understand the effects of PLAAF modernization, the role of the Second Artillery must also be assessed.[18] The Second Artillery's ability to threaten base operations has continued to grow substantially, meaning that the U.S. ability to reliably generate fighter sorties from close-in bases will be challenged during the period of time that the Second Artillery's force persists in substantial numbers. This would occur in cases where the conflict is of sufficient importance to China to substantially draw down the Second Artillery's missile forces by firing the missiles and potentially engaging in attacks in several countries.[19] The mere existence of these capabilities in Chinese hands creates a number of challenges, alters the way that all informed parties view operations in the region, and provides a means of challenging the U.S. style of air operations as conducted in the early phases of a serious conflict since the end of the Cold War.

Given these improvements, the potential impact of PLAAF modernization on the three games can be considered, along with possible actions these improvements cause the United States to take in response to those problems if it is playing that particular game. The ranges of actions are representative of possible U.S. actions within these games and are not exhaustive or reflective of official U.S. policy. The PLAAF's impact on the Game of Influence is outlined briefly below. Table 14–1 highlights a few of the major impacts of the current PLAAF modernization and the significance within the game, plausible strategies the United States might adopt, and concrete steps the United States could take to implement the strategies. This is intended to be illustrative and to provide an overview of the actions the United States could take and of the implications of those actions.

Table 14–1. The Game of Influence

Impact of People's Liberation Army Air Force Modernization	Significance of Action within the Game	Plausible U.S. Strategic Approach for Counter	Plausible Future U.S. Actions within the Game
Provides extended operational area for fighter aircraft	Introduces People's Liberation Army (PLA) airpower into new regions	Increase the operational area of deployed U.S. forces	Increase area of responsibility forces to counter threat [ubiquity of presence]
Provides improved air-to-air and air-to-surface capabilities and effectiveness	Changes perceived PLA effectiveness by key observers in military domain	Improve U.S. tactical engagement effectiveness to influence opinion	Improve air combat capability; counter munitions' effectiveness
Serves as a symbolic statement of military competency	Creates a perception of military/technical parity to broader audiences	Be perceived as better than opponent within a military context relevant to key audiences	Create/leverage capabilities relevant to key populations

For the purposes of this discussion, we will focus on the three aspects of the PLAAF modernization that have the most significant consequences for the United States: extended areas of operations and influence, an increase in perceived effectiveness of operations, and a statement of military competence by operating the PLAAF as a modern air force.

The PLAAF's extension of its area of potentially effective operations is significant because of the resulting increase in the PLAAF's relevance to situations of importance to other nations in the region. PLAAF fighter-bombers can now extend their capabilities to not only Taiwan, but to significant regions in other countries. Fighter-bombers have also begun to extend their reach to sea areas that hold interest for countries including Japan and South Korea, as well as to countries in the South China Sea.[20] Observers in Australia, where there are keen concerns over the Northern Territory and approaching sea areas, have noted Chinese air assets' increased range of influence. Other nations, notably Singapore, also view increased range of Chinese forces with concern. To address other nations' concerns, the United States may be required to simultaneously exert influence in more regional areas. When this requirement is combined with qualitative changes in the Chinese force, both a larger and more capable U.S. force will be necessary to maintain situational relevance. A force that would operate quite successfully in an array of combat situations is simply not relevant if it is not present when and where the adversary is operating. The presence requirement drives a buy-in force posture for the United States to maintain presence in areas where it retains interests.

The increased effectiveness of the Chinese force also influences how military technical experts who assess operational implications of Chinese capabilities in a narrow military sense perceive the Chinese air force. The effectiveness of the PLAAF in one-versus-one and small "M-v-N" combat engagements forces the United States to allocate more of its own forces and potentially to operate them in a manner acknowledging its opponent's capabilities.[21] This might translate into different numbers of fighters allocated to certain situations, a need to allocate the most capable fighters to the theater (even if basing them forward might expose them to damage or destruction from the Second Artillery), or, in the longer run, improving key U.S. capabilities to operate under conditions where U.S. assumptions of large-scale conflicts are no longer obtainable.[22]

Aside from their direct operational impact, these combinations of capabilities are also important because they are viewed by outside observers as symbolic of China's rise to the level of a great military power. Possible U.S. approaches to address these capabilities focus on strategies to maintain the desired equilibrium in theater by stepping up the presence of U.S. forces. This increased presence is intended to be visible to allies and to clearly demonstrate relevant defensive capabilities to both the general populations and to the national decisionmakers. These U.S. capabilities are generally associated with protecting key partners from attack, as the PLAAF represents a force of significant utility in a variety of coercion campaigns against neighboring states. The U.S. counters to these Chinese capabilities need to be relevant to the observers to have a significant impact. For instance, threats of escalation must not only be viewed by the Chinese as credible and potentially successful, but they also need to be seen as credible and sufficient for protection by the nations seeking protection. Defensive postures are probably easier to demonstrate and to have accepted by other nations, provided they are compatible with potential sensitivities about U.S. military presence in the region. In practice, this is a difficult line to walk, and building a useful narrative about when, where, and how U.S. forces would be used requires a careful alignment of strategies, capabilities, and operational concepts that can prove difficult and time-consuming to enact. Table 14–2 offers a perspective of impacts and likely fall-outs from the Battle over a Third Party game.[23] Because this game is a military problem where the array of forces and strategies is associated with protection of a key party, standard military metrics are relevant.

Table 14–2. The Battle over a Third Party Game

Impact of People's Liberation Army Air Force Modernization	Significance of Action within the Game	Plausible U.S. Strategic Approach for Counter	Plausible Future U.S. Actions within the Game
Makes U.S. assured air superiority more challenging in key periods of operations	Creates potential for greater damage to third party from air attack	Disrupt sortie generation; engage forces absent general air superiority	Emphasize longer-range forces and munitions, raids, and disruption operations early in the conflict
Makes routine air operations (coercive air operations and intelligence, surveillance, and reconnaissance) within China's airspace much more difficult	Creates potential for greater damage from China's air operations as U.S. counterforce and disruption capabilities are eroded	Shift to operations in area where U.S. advantages persist; emphasize easier targets not requiring persistence; emphasize focused deep operations	Engage forces outside most heavily protected areas; configure forces to have a total capacity and rate of target servicing to meet defense objectives
Renders effective operations by the third party military much more difficult	Creates greater demand for U.S. contribution	Have U.S. forces take over the missions from the third party	Deploy more forces or deliver capabilities that compensate for loss of friendly sorties

The key PLAAF improvements focus on three elements: significant air-to-air capability improvements that make air superiority operations significantly more difficult (especially in cases where force ratios might be unfavorable because of airfield suppression by the PLAAF); increased overall effectiveness resulting in a decrease in the U.S. ability to operate in contested airspace which makes deep attacks and intelligence, surveillance, and reconnaissance (ISR) operations more difficult and costly; and greater PLAAF offensive impact that is largely directed at the third party military which prevents it from effectively waging a defense. Although the area where the PLAAF can operate extends the battlespace, the focus of the Battle over a Third Party operation is still most likely to be within areas where other Chinese forces can play a substantial role. The cases where the PLAAF is the only military arm playing are degenerate cases where the Chinese would be forgoing much of their advantage.[24]

Improving PLAAF capabilities manifest themselves as an erosion of U.S. capabilities to prevent PLAAF operations from inflicting damage both on the third party military and on U.S. forces. The detrimental impact of PLAAF operations on the third party air forces and air defense assets also increases the demands on U.S. forces. The PLAAF's ability to challenge opponents in the air-to-air arena and the addition of better munitions and improved tactics for air-to-surface operations mean that the force is much more capable in operations where relatively simple tactics and operational concepts can be employed to facilitate actions by other forces. The PLAAF thus becomes an enabler for other operations, rather than strictly a supporting force. The PLAAF defensive improvements mean that its opponents' offensively focused air operations reliant on relatively free access to airspace over some or all of the key battle areas become problematic. The great difficulty of maintaining loitering ISR in a modern air defense environment, as well as the difficulty in engaging mobile forces such as mobile rocket and missile forces that are themselves enablers of air operations, creates a problem for U.S. planners.

The potential paths that the United States might take to counter these improvements are quite distinct, and the underlying logic is predicated on very different strategies. For instance, the United States might shift attention from a comprehensive protection strategy to operations that seek to defeat a certain class of attack such as a land or sea invasion, deeming acceptable a somewhat higher degree of damage from early air attacks. The United States might likewise emphasize operations against fixed targets supporting a set of combat operations. It might also consider strategies that punish the adversary for attack by engaging in either vertical or horizontal escalation, employing force in a manner to its relative advantage.[25]

Each of these notional approaches requires a different emphasis on force types. Some approaches may focus on destroying certain classes of targets (such as land forces), while others may focus on fixed targets supporting combat operations.[26] Improving this capability with strictly shorter-range forces requires an extremely robust (i.e., hard and redundant) basing posture with forces close to the defended areas to minimize logistical vulnerabilities. Absent that type of posture, forces capable of longer-range combat operations (air-to-air and air-to-surface) are required since they might minimize the threat from Second Artillery units and still retain some combat capability in both domains during the period of greatest Second Artillery threat.[27]

The Great Power Game is particularly interesting because of the competition's comprehensive nature and the scope of the competition that locks the participants into a fundamentally antagonistic relationship across all aspects of the competition. When viewed from this game perspective, PLAAF changes in the quality/quantity mix of forces, area of influence, and rate of development become the central issues of its modernization. The Great Power Game is also the least desirable of the games because, as table 14–3 reveals, it tends to lock parties into adversarial relationships and is more prone to drive arms race dynamics because of the pervasive nature of the competition and the strong and broad military character of many interactions.[28]

Table 14–3. The Great Power Game

Impact of People's Liberation Army Air Force Modernization	Significance of Action within the Game	Plausible U.S. Strategic Approach for Counter	Plausible Future U.S. Actions within the Game
Produces challenges to the U.S. within the region because of quality/quantity mix of forces	In 1-v-1 and M-v-N engagements, U.S. dominance is not assured	Increase number and quality of forces; focus on robust operations near enemy homeland; redefine the game	Shift U.S. forces from other regions; secure more bases and harden posture in region; invest in new long-range forces that operate without tactical air dominance
Results in increased area of influence because of expansion of effective air operations	Increase of adversary's influence results in a decrease of U.S. influence	Increase presence	Create more robust force postures; focus on long-range projection missions into area; emphasize increased naval operations
Results in a rate of change in improvements and a slope greater than the U.S. response	Potential allies make projections based on visible trends	Increase visible U.S. actions to have trendlines shift in U.S. favor; have allies committed to operations to decrease aggregate change; lock-in allies to prevent sudden shifts in relations	Engage in tit-for-tat programs and operations; focus on combined allied and U.S. operations; forge formal security relationships

The quantity/quality improvement of the PLAAF (along with improvements in munitions) means that it has evolved into a modern force that is capable of challenging in many dimensions the ability of the United States to conduct the sort of dominating combat operations it desires. The challenge to the balance may not be per se about engaging in combat in a specific area, but about the perceptions of dominance and perceived changes in capabilities across the broad spectrum. For instance, the assessment of the changes in the few vs. few and one-on-one combat outcomes become significant because these outcomes, whether favorable or unfavorable, are widely viewed as surrogates for engagements between the powers at a variety of levels. But simple superiority may not be adequate given either the plausible employment scenarios or the narrative used to describe the situation. In order to address this, the United States might alter the deployment of its forces, alter the quality/quantity mix of its forces, or even redefine the game as to render moot the specific discussion of force performance. This could be accomplished by concentrating on Chinese homeland targets or forces outside of China without emphasizing the U.S. forces that are being matched. Such an approach might mean that the United States would accept a decrease in tactical air dominance by utilizing different strike options, focusing on secure strike against targets at all depths, building more robust basing, and allocating more forces. This approach also might build new combat systems to reestablish superiority in the air-to-air arena and build the basing infrastructure for those cases. The United States also might go in a completely new direction by trying to redefine the game it is playing.

Another challenge to the United States is the number of potential states that feel they may be forced to deal with the PLA threat as the effective range of PLAAF operations increases. To allay these concerns, the United States might need to aid in the defense of a wider geographic area. The purpose for the United States is not only to defend that area in wartime; it is to provide reassurance in peacetime to prevent erosion of confidence in U.S. abilities. Defense of the relevant areas needs to be plausible to the interested parties and must cope with the problem of third parties wanting to be supported by the United States while simultaneously not wanting to be antagonistic to China. Increasing U.S. presence in several ways would be a reasonable top-level description of U.S. actions here. This increased presence might be manifested in a host of operations that demonstrate the U.S. ability and willingness to commit forces to the area. To more demanding allies, the ability of the United States to commit forces in the face of the substantial Chinese challenge as well as the U.S. ability to defend the assets that the supported country deems important might be required. The specifics would need to be tailored based on the nature of the perceived challenge, but could include long-range operations, maritime operations, and demonstrated robustness of the regional force posture in the face of attack.

The rate of change and acceleration of the change in relative capabilities define another aspect of the Great Power Game. These measures are an assessment of the projected capabilities of the two forces some number of years down the road. In a Great Power Game, this assessment defines the research and development (R&D), force development, and force planning futures of each side. In turn, potential allies look at the projected paths of the major powers in order to make their own investments and strategic decisions well in advance of the possible outcomes. These projections are arguably the most interesting and contentious aspect of the game, since it is about what *might* be and is not bound to current reality.

High rates of change and significant accelerations of that rate of change that are adverse to the United States are potentially alarming for allies, who will seek to make their way through a future based on extrapolations from near-term actions. Australia, which frames its own strategic arguments about future plans in terms of how situations might change in response to U.S. actions, is an example of a nation that is forward looking in its defense policy.[29] An absence of a U.S. response to alter the changes in apparent airpower capabilities might necessitate changes in Australia's own defense policies years before the immediate balance has been affected. The United States cares about these actions by allies because the overall assessment of the balance in this game is heavily influenced by allies whose association with the United States has not been effectively locked in by factors such as shared existential threats, and/or standing alliance arrangements like the relationships typified by the North Atlantic Treaty Organization's (NATO's) arrangements for mutual defense.[30]

For the United States, the implications of this sensitivity to projections are quite striking because it has significant incentives to take actions across several levels to address the revealed changes. One possible U.S. action is an essentially symmetric response of improving U.S. capabilities such that the apparent improvements in basic combat effectiveness of the opposing forces are largely reversed. However, this might initiate an ongoing arms competition that can degenerate into a type of arms race if left unconstrained by other forces. Another action might be to pursue and then exercise military operations with allies to demonstrate commitments in the wake of PLAAF improvements. Exercising forces that might be effective in combat operations tends to undercut perceived gains of the opposite side and also improves the prospect of basing and cooperation of allies in situations where the United States might need support for defense of other nations. Finally, the United States might seek to negate any Chinese gain by pursuing stronger formal arrangements to bind allies together. This binding would buffer to a certain extent the need to respond to deficiencies created by increased PLAAF capabilities by giving the United States more basing options, adding the contributions of partner military and logistical capabilities to those of the United States, and making it less likely allies will question U.S. commitments to a region.

Concluding Thoughts on the Games

Given these three possible games, it is clear the implications of PLAAF modernization for the United States vary between the games. In both the Game of Influence and within the Battle over a Third Party, the types of adaptations are essentially incremental, with force additions tailored to fairly specific problems. In the Great Power Game, the types of U.S. responses encompass much bolder moves to bolster regional positions and improve symmetric combat capabilities to maintain relative superiority. These differences affect how the balance is perceived and also frame the type of actions that might be taken within the game.

In both the Game of Influence and the Battle over a Third Party, the shifting of existing forces, as well as tailored responses focused on localized problems, appears adequate. In these cases, the focus is on crafting a strategy to solve specific problems created by the PLAAF and on ascertaining the steps necessary for solving them. The changes in the PLAAF make some operational concepts more difficult than in the past and undercut current assumptions as to how the United States could operate at will with airpower in almost any region of the world. However, the moves to counter these elements can be fairly well tailored and manageable in terms of what might be required for new operational concepts, munitions, and, perhaps most importantly, the level of engagement with other countries in the region. Dispersal and remote basing of forces, selective hardening and defense, a greater use of longer-range systems, and changing the threshold for success (defeating certain types of military attacks and accepting damage from others) can all help address the immediate problem of creating the broader perception of an effective U.S. response as well as help address specific issues in regard to problems associated with defense of third parties. Therefore, to the extent PLAAF modernization drives game changes, they will be relatively focused and bounded.

The balance in the Great Power Game is more sensitive than those in the other games in terms of the U.S. need to maintain relative position through such actions as addressing perceived rates of change and rate of acceleration of change for a variety of reasons that are not directly related to the security situation in the particular geographic region. Even if marginal improvements such as a force shift might address the immediate security problem, they would not address the broader aspect of the military competition that is integral to the game itself. It is not only the qualitative improvements of the PLAAF that are significant; after all, they are essentially only matching earlier generations of U.S. force capabilities. Instead, the dynamic of the broader region is driven by the twin problems of U.S. forces operating at a distance (the United States is acting as a global power and is expected by many to be anywhere a threat occurs) and the fear of what China's rapid rise in capability might presage. The balance in the Great Power Game incorporates elements of predictions and wagers about the future that are not dominant in the other games. This is partially due to the fact that in some narratives the immediate influence of the United States in the game is discounted and thereby diminished if the United States is not seen as actively addressing a possible negative future.

Implications for the United States

This paper provides the framework for how the United States should view and assess the impact of PLAAF modernization. This framework also yields important insights for U.S. decisionmaking within the overarching game structure. Most significantly, the United States must make a deliberate choice as to what game or combination of games it wants to play and how it will respond (force structure, political stances, etc.) within the games it chooses. This will allow the United States to best utilize its military and political tools to achieve its national interests and to avoid being forced into a nonoptimal decision.

When the United States is choosing which game to play, it will of course be influenced by Chinese military choices (one being continued PLAAF modernization) and political moves. There will also be other factors influencing the United States, and the choice between games will be predicated on the strategic importance assigned to the situation, relevant political considerations, fiscal constraints, and other factors. But whatever game it chooses to play, the United States must always be aware of the range of possible Chinese countermoves and be careful not to lock itself into a course of action that may prove detrimental if and when the game being played changes. And, of course, it is necessary for the United States to both recognize that China is not obligated to play the same game the United States chooses and to understand that such a situation would lead to potential disconnects that would need to addressed. Furthermore, once a game is chosen and is being played, the United States will continue to face choices about its specific set of actions. These choices will require the United States to prioritize different aspects of its power. Given these uncertainties, it will be prudent for the United States to hedge.

The United States and China have largely confined themselves to Game 2—The Battle over a Third Party—and the impact of PLAAF modernization has been widely evaluated through this lens. PLAAF modernization does have a direct impact on this game—and a negative impact for the United States if it does not take steps to counteract it—but the only way that modernization shifts the overall military balance across the spectrum of possible games is if the United States holds all other factors in its relationship with China constant. There is no reason for the United States to do so. The United States can define which game it is going to play by what it chooses to address as important. And in that context, the United States has a wide range of options that do not necessarily require a new force structure or more defense expenditures, but instead may call for an altered military and political emphasis.

The bottom line for the Chinese is that PLAAF modernization is contributing to conditions that compel a reaction from the United States. If the United States chooses to continue to play the same game in the same way it has since the end of the Cold War, the results may be to China's advantage. But if the United States chooses to play another game where its significant military and political assets can be more fully utilized, PLAAF modernization may lead to a Pyrrhic victory for the Chinese.[31]

The U.S. bottom line is the recognition that there is no compelling reason for it to maintain its current game. Instead, it is extremely prudent for the Nation's policy and military planners to assess the current situation and determine if another course should be pursued. This is because once the current equilibrium with China is interrupted, as it inevitably will be, the situation will shift and it is difficult to predict the course that events will take from that point.

If the United States does not then already have a plan in place or if the issue has not already been extensively discussed, the Nation's leaders could be pushed by the domestic political climate, fiscal constraints, or a variety of other factors to make a choice they would not have otherwise made. This type of situation would be metastable, and because of that lack of stability, it is a situation that could be significantly impacted by small military changes on the Chinese side. The United States must be aware that it will be necessary to make a decision before it reaches any such tipping point. Otherwise, the United States could be forced into making not only a nonoptimal decision as to which game it is going to play and how it is going to play it, but a nonsatisfactory one as well.

Notes

[1] An example is Malcolm Cook, Raoul Heinriches, Rory Medcalf, and Andrew Shearer, *Power and Choice: Asian Security Futures* (Sydney: Lowy Institute for International Policy, 2010).

[2] This viewpoint and the reasoning behind it are discussed extensively in General Sir Rupert Smith's *The Utility of Force: The Art of War in the Modern World* (New York: Alfred A. Knopf, 2007).

[3] It is possible that the stakes could be relatively symmetric for both sides. But even if the stakes were equal and the game was zero-sum, it would only be zero-sum in that confined sphere.

[4] Example strategies might include those emphasizing horizontal or vertical escalation options.

[5] Stephen Kaplan's discussion of why the United States was deterred from attacking China during the Korean War (by fear of possible Soviet reprisal) provides evidence that, though China played a role in the conflict, the United States did not view expanding the conflict to attacks on China as worthwhile given the larger battle with the Soviet Union. See Stephen Kaplan, *Diplomacy of Power: Soviet Armed Forces as a Political Instrument* (Washington, DC: The Brookings Institution, 1981), 332–333.

[6] However, past actions in regard to Taiwan during the Quemoy-Matsu Crisis of 1954–1955, the missile crisis of 1996, and the Taiwan Relations Act would suggest to a prudent Chinese planner that the United States might use force even if it maintained a lesser level of interest.

[7] The United States has used these forces from earlier periods against less capable conventional opponents during the 20 years since the first Gulf War.

[8] Alan Vick's unpublished work on the "American Way of War" provides more information.

[9] An example of U.S. thinking on the matter is the 2006 Quadrennial Defense Review's statement that "the choices that major and emerging powers make will affect the future strategic position and freedom of action of the United States, its allies and partners. The United States will attempt to shape these choices in ways that foster cooperation and mutual security interests. At the same time, the United States, its allies and partners must also hedge against the possibility that a major or emerging power could choose a hostile path in the future." Secretary of Defense Donald Rumsfeld, *Quadrennial Defense Review Report* (Washington, DC: Department of Defense, February 2006), 26–27, available at <www.defense.gov/qdr/report/Report20060203.pdf>.

¹⁰ David Shlapak provided this definition of great power war as part of his unpublished research on possible great power conflicts.

¹¹ Such improvements in forces might generate an undesired cycle of action-reaction that will produce at least a qualitative arms race even if a numerical arms race is avoided.

¹² These sorts of pure motives are intended as examples for explanatory purposes. The actual decision to build any costly weapons system is usually predicated on a mix of rationales, one of which might be the top-level appreciation of the competition.

¹³ Australian Department of Defence, *Defending Australia in the Asia Pacific Century: Force 2030* (Canberra: DoD, 2009), 33.

¹⁴ Socialist Republic of *Vietnam, Vietnam National Defence* (Hanoi: Ministry of National Defence, December 2009), 14.

¹⁵ Ibid., 13.

¹⁶ Because this assessment is focused on the role of PLAAF modernization, it does not explicitly address other aspects of Chinese military modernization such as improvement in maritime assets. But this framework can certainly be used to assess the effect of any aspect of Chinese military modernization on the military balances.

¹⁷ Office of the Secretary of Defense, *Annual Report on the Military and Security Developments Involving the People's Republic of China* [hereafter OSD, *2010 Military and Security Developments Involving the PRC*] (Washington, DC: Department of Defense, May 2010), 31–32, at <http://www.defense.gov/pubs/pdfs/2010_CMPR_Final.pdf>.

¹⁸ Roger Cliff's work provides an overview of the antiaccess threat to U.S. bases and Second Artillery. See Roger Cliff, Mark Burles, Michael S. Chase, Derek Eaton, and Kevin L. Pollpeter, *Entering the Dragon's Lair: Chinese Antiaccess Strategies and Their Implications for the United States*, RAND Document MG-524-AF (Santa Monica, CA: RAND Corporation, 2007), available at <www.rand.org/pubs/monographs/MG524/>.

¹⁹ OSD, *2010 Military and Security Developments Involving the PRC*, 29–34.

²⁰ The addition of longer-range standoff weapons to the medium bomber force increases the potential range of influence ever farther.

²¹ "M v N" refers to engagements involving varying numbers of forces in a two-sided engagement. This might be a few-on-few tactical engagement that could be replicated across larger battles or campaigns.

²² These assumptions, including allowed proximity of forces, beyond-visual-range (BVR) effectiveness, nominal superiority, and freedom to mass forces might all be challenged.

²³ The United States may also attempt to forge alliances in this game, but because there are no clearly drawn "sides" there is little incentive for other nations to cooperate solely with the United States. Thus formal alliances with the United States against the other major power do not seem likely.

²⁴ These cases would devolve rapidly to a series of airpower duels where the situation would work to the advantage of a qualitatively superior force that could choose to maximize exchange ratio rather than be compelled to defend a target where its advantage would erode as the aircraft stayed in less desirable tactical situations (such as close-in combat) for longer periods of time.

²⁵ "Escalation that involves an increase in the intensity of armed conflict or confrontation, such as employing types of weapons not previously used in the conflict or attacking new categories of targets, is often collectively described as vertical escalation, in contrast to horizontal escalation, which refers to expanding the geographic scope of a conflict (for example, by conducting operations into or through territory previously treated as neutral by the combatants)." From Forrest E. Morgan, Karl P. Mueller, Evan S. Medeiros, Kevin L. Pollpeter, and Roger Cliff, *Dangerous Thresholds: Managing Escalation in the 21ˢᵗ Century*, RAND Document MG-614-AF (Santa Monica, CA: The RAND Corporation, 2008), 18, available at <www.rand.org/pubs/monographs/MG614/>.

²⁶ It would seem that there is a clear benefit to improving strike assets that work well against both mobile and fixed surface targets (at sea and on land). Since the country that will be defended might not be well defined, a flexible attack system such as a modular missile, low-cost missile, or aircraft with suitable weapons would be prudent.

²⁷ Again, these strategies do not incorporate strong alliance-building because there is little incentive for other nations to side with one major power over the other given the parameters of this game. Alliances

here tend to be more dependent on the specific situation and would be focused on addressing specific issues rather than on an enduring alliance.

[28] For further explanatory detail, see Chapter Four of Michael Mandelbaum, *The Nuclear Revolution: International Politics Before and After Hiroshima* (New York: Cambridge University Press, 1981), particularly pages 114–115, on the German-British naval arms race before World War I.

[29] Australia's Department of Defence said in 2009 that "Australia's strategic outlook over the coming decades will continue to be shaped by the changing global distribution of economic, political and military power, and by the future role and weight of the United States;" and "Any future that might see a potential contraction of US strategic presence in the Asia-Pacific region, with a requirement for allies and friends to do more in their own regions, would adversely affect Australian interests, regional stability and global security." See the previously cited *Defending Australia in the Asia Pacific Century*, 30, 32.

[30] NATO represents one of the strongest such relationships, and typifies a high-water mark in terms of the degree of political and military commitments to the defense relationships among the key partners of the alliance.

[31] For instance, the United States could choose to play a Great Power Game where it would turn its considerable military power more fully against a range of possible Chinese threats. Or the United States could ramp up its participation in the Game of Influence and significantly modify its force posture or buy new weapons systems that would play more fully to U.S. advantages against China.

About the Contributors

Kenneth W. Allen is a Senior China Analyst at the Defense Group, Inc. (DGI), where he focuses on Chinese military issues. Prior to this, he worked in various nonprofit research organizations dealing with China and Taiwan relations. From 1971 to 1992, he served in the U.S. Air Force, including assignments in Taiwan, Berlin, Japan, Headquarters Pacific Air Forces, and Washington, DC. He also served as the Assistant Air Force Attaché in China from 1987 to 1989. He has written several books and articles on China's military. He received a B.A from the University of California at Davis, a B.A from the University of Maryland in Asian Studies, and an M.A. from Boston University in International Relations.

Hsi-hua Cheng retired from the Taiwan Air Force as a colonel in November 2011. His military assignments include a tour as acting deputy commandant of the Air Command and Staff College at Taiwan's National Defense University. Cheng was a visiting fellow at the Atlantic Council of the United States from July 2006 to June 2007 and graduated from the U.S. Air Force Air Command and Staff College in 1994.

Roger Cliff is a Non-resident Senior Fellow at the Center for Strategic and Budgetary Assessments. His areas of research include China's military doctrine, defense industries, and future military capabilities and their implications for U.S. strategy and policy. He has authored, coauthored, or edited more than a dozen research monographs and more than a dozen journal articles, book chapters, and op-eds on these topics. He is currently writing a book on China's future military capabilities. Dr. Cliff has previously worked for the Project 2049 Institute, the RAND Corporation, the Office of the Secretary of Defense, and VERAC, Inc. He received his Ph.D. in International Relations from Princeton University, and holds an M.A. in Chinese Studies from the University of California, San Diego, and a B.S. in Physics from Harvey Mudd College. He is fluent in written and spoken Chinese.

David R. Frelinger is a Senior Policy Analyst at the RAND Corporation with experience in leading technical and policy analytic studies for senior government consumers. His research interests include intelligence operations, information technologies, and the interaction of commercial and governmental activities, as well as an ongoing interest in assessing advanced weapons systems concepts. Mr. Frelinger holds an M.A. in Political Science from the University of California, Los Angeles, and a B.A in Political Science from the University of California, San Diego.

Richard P. Hallion is an aerospace analyst and historian who has written widely on defense, aerospace, military affairs, and technology. He received his B.A and Ph.D. from the University of Maryland, and is a graduate of the Federal Executive Institute and the National Security Studies Program for Senior Executives at the John F. Kennedy School of Government, Harvard University. He has served as a founding curator, Lindbergh Professor, and Verville Fellow at the National Air and Space Museum; as a National Aeronautics and Space Administration and Air Force historian; as the Johnson Chair at the U.S. Army Military History Institute; as a senior issues and policy analyst and senior advisor for air and space issues to the Secretary of the Air Force; and as a special advisor on aerospace technology to the Air Force Chief Scientist. Currently, he is a senior advisor to Commonwealth Research Institute/Concurrent Technologies Corporation; Vice President of the Earthshine Institute; and a research associate in aeronautics for the National Air and Space Museum. He has taught and lectured widely, is active in professional associations, and is a Fellow of the American Institute of Aeronautics and Astronautics, a Fellow of the Royal Aeronautical Society, and a Fellow of the Royal Historical Society.

Jessica Hart is an Analyst at a defense contractor. From 2008 to 2011, she worked as a research assistant for the RAND Corporation where she focused on defense policy and nuclear deterrence issues. Ms. Hart holds an M.P.I.A. in Intelligence and Defense Studies from Texas A&M University, and a B.A. in Political Science from Clemson.

You Ji is Reader/Professor in the School of Social Science, University of New South Wales. He has published widely on China's political, military, and foreign affairs. He is the author of three books, including *China's Enterprise Reform: Changing State/Society Relations after Mao* (1998) and *The Armed Forces of China* (1999). He has authored numerous articles and book chapters, including: "China's Response to the Deadly Triangle: Arms Race, Territorial Dispute and Energy Security," *CLAWS Journal*, Summer 2010; "Managing the Cross-Taiwan Strait Military Conflicts in a New Era of Political Reconciliation," in *30 Years of Sino-US Relations*, Sujian Guo, ed. (Lexicon Books, 2010); "Changing Civil-Military Relations in China," in *The PLA at Home and Abroad*, David Lai, Roy Kamphamsen, and Andrew Scobell, eds. (National Bureau of Asian Research and Strategic Studies Institute of the U.S. Army War College, 2010).

Kevin Lanzit is a Senior Analyst at Alion Science & Technology, Inc. with over thirty years in national security affairs. During his Air Force career he served in a variety of operational and national security planning positions, including multiple fighter assignments in the United States, Western Europe, and the Southwest Pacific. As a foreign area officer specializing on China and East Asia, he completed two assignments with the United States Embassy in Beijing, China (1989–1991 and 2000–2003), where his language skills and operational acumen facilitated the successful execution of both diplomatic and operational missions. Following military service, Mr. Lanzit has worked in both private and government positions. From 2005 to 2006, he served as a senior analyst with the U.S.-China Economic and Security Review Commission where he shaped the research, analysis, and written reports related to China's growing military power and its effect on U.S. national security interests in the region. Since leaving the Commission he has continued to lend his regional knowledge and operational experience to national security analysis. Mr. Lanzit received a B.S. in Economics from the USAF Academy in 1975, an M.S. in Systems Management from the University of Southern California, and studied National Security Affairs at the U.S. Air War College and Mandarin Chinese at the Defense Language Institute.

Forrest E. Morgan is a defense policy researcher working in the RAND Corporation's Pittsburgh Office. Prior to joining RAND in January 2003, Dr. Morgan served a 27-year career in the U.S. Air Force. His military assignments included duty as a signals intelligence analyst and as a space operations officer in various operations and staff positions. Later he served on the strategy and policy staff at Headquarters, U.S. Air Force, Pentagon, and did a tour of duty as a professor of comparative military studies at the School of Advanced Air and Space Studies. Since coming to RAND, Dr. Morgan has done strategy and doctrine research examining such issues as preemptive and preventive attack, escalation management, deterrence, information operations, and assessing performance of the Air Force and Army in Operation *Iraqi Freedom*.

Kevin Pollpeter has been the China Program Manager at Defense Group, Inc. since 2005. He manages a group of 11 analysts focused on primary source research on Chinese security issues. Mr. Pollpeter writes on a range of issues, but is a specialist on the Chinese space program. He previous worked at the RAND Corporation from 2000 to 2005 as a Research Assistant and a Project Associate. His other work experience includes time at the Monterey Institute's East Asia Nonproliferation Project, the Office of Naval Intelligence, and the Marine Corps Reserves. Mr. Pollpeter has an M.A. in International Policy Studies and a Certificate in Nonproliferation Studies from the Monterey Institute of International Studies and a B.A. in Chinese Studies from Grinnell College.

Phillip C. Saunders is Director of the Center for the Study of Chinese Military Affairs and a Distinguished Research Fellow at the Center for Strategic Research, part of National Defense University's Institute for National Strategic Studies. Dr. Saunders previously worked at the Monterey Institute of International Studies, where he was Director of the East Asia Nonproliferation Program from 1999 to 2003, and served as an officer in the U.S. Air Force from 1989 to 1994. Dr. Saunders is coauthor with David Gompert of *The Paradox of Power: Sino-American Strategic Restraint in an Era of Vulnerability* (NDU Press, 2011) and co-editor of *Cross-Strait Relations: New Opportunities and Challenges for Taiwan's Security* (RAND, 2011) and *The Chinese Navy: Expanding Capabilities, Evolving Roles* (NDU Press, 2011). He has published numerous articles and book chapters on China and Asian security issues in journals such as *International Security, International Studies Quarterly, China Quarterly, The China Journal, Survival, Asian Survey, Pacific Review, Orbis, Asia Policy,* and *Joint Force Quarterly*. Dr. Saunders attended Harvard College and received his M.P.A. and Ph.D. in International Relations from the Woodrow Wilson School at Princeton University.

Shen Pin-Luen is an assistant research fellow at the Cross-Strait Interflow Prospect Foundation in Taiwan. His research focuses on People's Republic of China national policy and the development of People's Liberation Army modernization. He has an M.A. in mainland China studies from Taiwan's National Chengchi University, Taiwan.

David Shlapak is a Senior International Policy Analyst working in the RAND Corporation's Pittsburgh Office. His areas of research include U.S. defense strategy and policy, Asian security, Chinese military modernization, and airpower operations. During his time at RAND, Mr. Shlapak has completed projects on reshaping the U.S. joint force for future challenges, countering nuclear-armed adversaries, and U.S-China security relations. He holds a B.A. in Political Science from Northwestern University.

Mark A. Stokes is Executive Director of the Project 2049 Institute. During 20 years of service in the U.S. Air Force, Lt Col (Ret.) Stokes was assigned to a variety of electronic warfare, intelligence, planning, and policy positions. From 1984 to 1986, he was assigned to the 6922nd Electronic Security Squadron, Clark Air Base, Philippines. From 1986 to 1989, he served as a signals intelligence and electronic warfare officer in the 6912th Electronic Security Wing, Berlin, West Germany. In July 1989, Mr. Stokes entered the Air Force's foreign area officer training program as a China specialist. From 1992 to 1995, he served as the assistant air attaché at the United States Defense Attaché Office in Beijing, People's Republic of China (PRC). He subsequently was assigned to Headquarters, Air Force's Plans and Operations Directorate, where he was responsible for operational and strategic planning for the Asia-Pacific region. Between 1997 and 2004, Mark served as Team Chief and Senior Country Director for the PRC, Taiwan, and Mongolia in the Office of the Assistant Secretary of Defense for International Security Affairs (OASD/ISA). For 7 years, he was responsible for developing, coordinating, and managing U.S. defense policy with respect to China. He holds a B.A in History from Texas A&M University, and M.A.s in International Relations and East Asian Studies from Boston University and the Naval Postgraduate School.

Murray Scot Tanner has published widely on Chinese and East Asian politics and security issues, and is recognized as one of the country's top specialists on internal security, social unrest, policing, and intelligence in China. Among his many books and articles are *Chinese Economic Coercion against Taiwan: A Tricky Weapon to Use* (RAND, 2007), *The Politics of Lawmaking in China* (Oxford, 1998), and "China Rethinks Unrest," *Washington Quarterly*, 2004. Dr. Tanner has previously served as Professor of Political Science at Western Michigan University, Senior Political Scientist at the RAND Corporation, as a senior staff member for the U.S. Congress, and as a China analyst for the U.S. Government. Raised in Syracuse, New York, Dr. Tanner received his B.A. and Ph.D. from the University of Michigan.

Joshua K. Wiseman is a Research Analyst at National Defense University's Institute for National Strategic Studies. Prior to joining the Institute as a Contract Researcher in 2010, he worked as a Chinese language translator for the Department of Commerce. His research focuses on Chinese security issues, specifically the Chinese defense industrial sector, Sino-Russian strategic relations, and China's expanding aerospace power. Mr. Wiseman attended The George Washington University, where he completed an M.A. in Security Policy Studies with a China regional focus. He has extensive experience working, traveling, and studying in China.

Xiaoming Zhang is Associate Professor in the Department of Leadership and Strategy at the Air War College. Dr. Zhang holds a Ph.D. in history from the University of Iowa and has authored a number of articles on Chinese military involvement in the Korean and Vietnam Wars and Sino-Soviet relations during these conflicts, as well as *Red Wings over the Yalu: China, the Soviet Union and the Air War in Korea* (Texas A&M University Press, 2002).

Index

Page numbers in italics refer to tables and figures.

068 Base Near-space Flight Vehicle R&D Center, 55

1st Aviation (Aircraft Maintenance) College, 112
1st Corps, 228
1st Division, 226
1st Fighter Division, 226
1st Flying Academy, 223
10th Corps, 217–19
13th Division, 224
14th Fighter Division, 227
15th Airborne Corps, 96, 103–4, 109–11
17th Party Congress, 267
18th Party Congress, xxiv, 108, 121
19th Fighter Division, 219

2d Aviation (Aircraft Maintenance) College, 114
2d Fighter Division, 225
2d Flight College, 112
24th Air Force Division, 217
26th Division, 216

3d Fighter Division, 222
3d Flying Academy, 223
31st Fighter Division, 228

4th Fighter Division, 220
4th Corps, 216–17

54th Base of the Strategic Missile Force, 228

6th Corps, 217

7th Flight College, 114
72d Regiment, 217
75A–5, 284

8th Corps, 216–17 226

9th Corps, 222
9th Fighter Division, 228

A–10 Thunderbolt II (Warthog), 15–16
A–5, 104
A–50 MAINSTAY, 197 306
AA–2 Atoll AAM, 199
AAA. See antiaircraft artillery (AAA)
Absolute Weapon: Atomic Power and World Order, 12
Academy of Military Science (AMS), 123, 131n132
ACAE. See Commercial Aircraft Engine Co., Ltd. (ACAE)
Active Defense doctrine, 17
active electronically scanned array (AESA) radar, 50
ACTS. See U.S. Army's Air Corps Tactical School (ACTS)
advanced medium-range air-to-air missiles (AMRAAMs), 202
aerospace campaign
 coercive, 44, 58
 conceptual theory, 49
aerospace force, 179
Aerospace power, 33, 37

AESA. See active electronically scanned array (AESA) radar
AEW. See airborne early warning (AEW) capabilities
AF Weapons Experimental Base, 222
AFCA. See Air Force Command Academy (AFCA)
AFETC. See Air Force Education and Training Command (AFETC)
AFEU. See Air Force Engineering University
Afghan War, 133
AFIT. See Air Force Institute of Technology (AFIT)
AGM–139A Tacit Rainbow program, 199
AIDC F-CK-1 Ching-Kuo, xix
AIM–120, 202
AIM–9 Sidewinder, 200, 202, 277
Air and Space Battlefield and China's Air Force, 170
air blockade, 153
   campaign, 158
   coercive, 45
   historical PLAAF missions, 153
   in Chinese military doctrine, 155
   New Guinea, 334
   PLAAF campaign, 154, 157
Air Campaign: Planning for Combat, 18
Air Corps doctrine
   pre-WWII, 9
   WWII, 11
aircraft factories, 84, 102, 105, 285, 287
Air Force Aviation University, 96, 113–14, 123
Air Force Building, 98
Air Force Command Academy, 180, 226
Air Force Command Academy (AFCA), 222
Air Force Command College, 114, 170, 244, 247
Air Force Doctrine Document (AFDD), 155
Air Force Doctrine Document 2-2, Space Operations, 175
Air Force Education and Training Command (AFETC), 111
Air Force Encyclopedia, 99, 120, 135
Air Force Engineering University, 96, 112–14, 122, 170
Air Force Equipment Research Academy, 96, 117, 122

Air Force Informatized Knowledge: Concept Volume, 171
Air Force Institute of Technology (AFIT), 113
Air Force National Defense Mobilization Committee Comprehensive Office, 120
Air Force News, 180
Air Force Reserve Unit Work Regulations, 121
Air Force University of Engineering, 223
air strike campaign, 43
air superiority
   "Three Superiorities", 40
   achieving, 160
   air defense campaigns, 158
   air offensive campaign, 157
   air offensives, 153
   airborne campaign, 159
   as a prerequisite to success, 4
   at the operational level, 37
   capabilities for winning, 13, 15
   and China's traditional concept of airpower, 46
   Chinese military pursuit of, 293
   Chinese military theory, 73
   deep-strike operations, 45
   difficulty of, 360
   essential to ground operations, 10–11
   facilitating, 38
   facilitating air and landing operations, 45
   gaining strategic leverage, 38
   limited, 34, 37, 50, 60n8
   obtaining, 156–57
   of the U.S. during the Korean War, 73
   over battlefields, 149
   PLA's inability to gain, 33
   PLA's shortcomings, 34
   space superiority, 175
   success in future wars, 44
   theater, 37
   winning future wars, 151
   Yijiangshan experience, 150
Air University, 112
Air War Planning Document 1 (AWPD-1), 9
airborne early warning (AEW) capabilities, 207, 208, 264, 305, 314
   acquisition of, 305, 306
   development, 266–67, 306

of the KJ-2000, 206
of the PLAAF, 80
production, 306
technological innovation, 264
airborne warning and control system (AWACS), 141
   acquisition, 197
   development, 80–81, 198
   Phalcon, 80
Airbus, 262, 268
AirLand Battle Doctrine, 18, 20, 24
Air-Land Force Application (ALFA), 17–18
air-to-to air missiles (AAMs), 194, 199, 204
air-turbo rocket (ATR) propulsion system, 54
AL– 31F turbofan engine, 264–65, 304, 311
al Jazeera, 25
al Qaeda, 23
ALFA. See Air-Land Force Application (ALFA)
Allen, Kenneth W., xxi
Allison, Graham, 81
Aluminum Corporation of China (CHINALCO), 260
AMRAAMs. See advanced medium-range air-to-air missiles (AMRAAMs)
AMS. See Academy of Military Science (AMS)
Anatolian Eagle, 196
antiaircraft artillery (AAA), 97, 103
   as a branch of the PLAAF, 103
   combat regulations, 155
   deploying in three rings, 153
   equipment support, 96
   organizational support, 97
   regiments under MRAF, 109
   the 15th Airborne Corps, 104
   training, 123
anti-satellite (ASAT) weapons, 53, 180–82
   ASM-135, 183
   Chinese policy, 181
   development, 166, 181, 183
   guidance technology, 53
   space warfare, 175, 180
   testing, 57
   weapons program in China, 180
antiship ballistic missile (ASBM), 39, 51
   defense against sea-based assets, 39
   guidance technology, 53

Antonov An–12, 264
AP 1300, *Royal Air Force War Manual*, 4
AR–1, 201
ARJ21, 261–62
Army of the Republic of Vietnam (ARVN), 16
Army Tactical Missile Systems (ATACMS), 18
army-first, 214
ARVN. See Army of the Republic of Vietnam (ARVN)
As the Same Age of the Republic, 217
ASAT. See antisatellite (ASAT) weapons
ASBM. See antiship ballistic missile (ASBM)
AT–1, 288
ATACMS. See Army Tactical Missile Systems (ATACMS)
ATR. See air-turbo rocket (ATR) propulsion system
Aviation Bureau of the Nationalist Government, 238
Aviation Industry, viii, xi, xxv, xxvi, xxvii, 44, 50, 58, 82, 198, 326, Chapter 11, Chapter 12
Aviation Industry Corporation of China (AVIC), 260
   acquisition of FACC, 266
   aerospace systems, 50
   agreement with Antonov, 312
   development strategy, 260
   market forecast, 268
   merger, xxv, 257, 260, 269n6
   reconstruction efforts, 259
   research and development, 311
   restructuring, 265
Aviation School of the Northeast Democratic United Army, 239
Aviation University, 112, 114, 223, 244
AVIC. See Aviation Industry Corporation of China (AVIC)
AWACS. See airborne warning and control system (AWACS)
AWPD-1. See Air War Planning Document 1 (AWPD-1)

B–29, 11
B–5, 292
B–52, 16, 35, 264
B–6, 51, 54, 104, 287, 357

Baoding Aviation School, 222
Battle of France, 8
Battle of the Bismarck Sea, 342
Beijing Aero-Space and Aviation University, 219
Beijing AF, 219
Beijing Air Show, 268
Beijing Garrison, 219
Beijing MR, 219, 230
Beijing MRAF, 222, 225
Beiyang government, 237
bin Laden, Osama, 23
Blasko, Dennis, 340
Blitzkrieg (Lightning War), 6–7, 9
Boeing, 262, 268
Bohai Gulf, 51
bombers, xxiii, xxv, 73, 75, 80, 83, 160, 205, 206, 208, 264, 271, 285, 288, 290, 299, 327, 357, Chapter 1
Bosnian civil war, 21
Brodie, Bernard, 12
Bureau of Aviation Industry, 257–58
Bush administration, 23
Bush, George H.W., 20, 296
Bush, George W., 24–25

C4ISR (command, control, communications, computers, intelligence, surveillance, and reconnaissance)
 applications for HPM, 54
 capabilities, 42, 173
 of Taiwan, 342
 Operation *Allied Force*, 174
C919, 262, 268
 as a platform for military development, 267
 civil aviation program, 262
 COMAC short-term goals, 261
 development, 266
CAC. See Chengdu Aircraft Industry Corporation (CAC)
campaign guidance, 154, 155
Cai Fengzhen, 138–40, 147, 170, 171
Caproni, Gianni, 4
CAS. See close-air support (CAS)
CASC. See China Aerospace Corporation (CASC)
CASIC. See China Aerospace Science and Industry Corporation (CASIC)
Cathay Pacific DC–4, 74
CBO. See Combined Bomber Offensive (CBO)
CCP. See Chinese Communist Party (CCP)
centers of gravity (COGs), 19, 24
 aerospace campaign, 44
 during an attack against Taiwan, 341
Central Army Officer School, 238
CETC. See China Electronics Technology Group Corporation (CETC)
Chang Baolin, 228
Chang Wanquan, 214
Chang Jian (Long Sword), 332
Changchun Flight College, 114
Changchun, Jilin Province, 114, 240
Charter of the United Nations
 Article 51, 181
Checkmate (Headquarters Air Force strategy analysis center), 18–19
Chen Xiaogong, 108, 219–20
Chen Yi, 288
Chengdu Aircraft Industry Corporation (CAC), 195
Chengdu MR, 231
Chengdu MRAF, 108, 223–24, 226
Chengkong Division, 224
Chiang Kai-shek, 239
China Aerospace Corporation (CASC), 50, 53, 258–59
 aerospace systems development, 50
 defense industry restructuring, 258
 feasibility studies, 53
 research institute, 53
China Aerospace Science and Industry Corporation (CASIC), 47, 50, 56
 aerospace systems development, 50
 feasibility studies, 53
 First Academy, 56
 research institute, 55
China Electronics Technology Group Corporation (CETC), 259
China Nanchang Aircraft Manufacturing Corporation (CNAMC), 258
China National Nuclear Corporation, 258

China Sinochem Group Corporation (Sinochem), 260
China's National Defense (White Paper), 97, 134
CHINALCO. See Aluminum Corporation of China (CHINALCO)
Chinese Air Force Encyclopedia, 134
Chinese Communist Party (CCP), 218
    expanding combat and noncombat roles for the air force, 134
    first aviation school, 239
    and PLA shift toward joint operations, xxi
    succession politics, 218
Chinese/English Manual for Jet Pilots, 222
Ching Chuan Kang (CCK) Air Base, xix
Churchill, Sir Winston, 326
CJ-10, 332
CJ-5, 258, 286–87
CJ-6, 286–87
close-air support (CAS), 6
    AirLand Battle Doctrine, 18
    during Blitzkrieg, 8
    German airpower thought, 6
CNAMC. See China Nanchang Aircraft Manufacturing Corporation (CNAMC)
codevelopment, 278–81, 305, 315
    as an approach to advance aviation technology, 275
    F-35 Joint Strike Fighter program, 279
COGs. See centers of gravity (COGs)
Cold War, 12
    Chinese capacity, 284
    Chinese defense operations, 89
    joint venture between Russia and India, 280
    U.S.-China military balance, 347
COMAC. See Commercial Aircraft Corporation of China, Ltd. (COMAC)
combat regulation, 155
Combined Bomber Offensive (CBO), 9, 11, 14
Command of the Air, 3, 44
Commercial Aircraft Corporation of China, Ltd. (COMAC), 257, 260–62
    establishment of, xxv, 257
    passenger aircraft, 260
    production plans, 262
    short-term goals, 261

Commercial Aircraft Engine Co., Ltd. (ACAE), 260–61, 266
Commission of Science, Technology, and Industry for National Defense (COSTIND), 258–60, 265, 301
    restructuring of the defense industry, 258
    restructuring, 301
composite force combat, 155
coproduction, 273, 278–79, 281–82, 285, 288, 292, 303, 305, 307, 313–15
    as an approach to advance aviation technology, 275
    with Russia, 300, 302
    with the USSR, 279, 285, 289
COSTIND. See Commission of Science, Technology, and Industry for National Defense (COSTIND)
counterair operations, 235
counterair strike campaign, 39
counterair strike operations theory, 39
counterattack, 142, 144–46, 158–59
    active defense, 146, 152
    air defense campaign, 158
    blocking, 142
    China's integrated defensive mission, 144
    defensive operations, 145
    during large-scale air attacks, xxii
    in achieving China's campaign and strategic goals, 143
    Second Artillery's role, 159
counterintervention, 38
counterspace, 179
    China's efforts, 180
    leveraging military technologies, 34, 36
    PLAAF management issues, 47
    space superiority, 176
Counterstealth, 41
counterstrikes, 59, 158
CSS-5, 331
CSS-6, 325, 331
CSS-7, 325, 331
cult of personality, 74
Cultural Revolution, 151
    aircraft maintenance, 102
    aircraft production, 291
    effect of, 151

effect on educational development, 241
industrial output, 290
PLA schools, 241
political restrictions, 289
societal disruptions, xxiv
Curtiss-Wright aircraft, 284
CW–21, 284
cyber espionage, 275, 308–09

D Block 30/40, 263
D–30 engine, 264
Dalian base, 219
Dalian Forward Headquarters, 228
Dan Zhiping, 223
DARPA. See Defense Advanced Research Projects Agency (DARPA)
Dauphin 2 helicopter, 293, 295
Defense Advanced Research Projects Agency (DARPA), 35
Defense Student program, 244, See also Reserve Officer program
  management, 111
  officer recruitment, 112
  PLA officer corps recruitment, 96
  PLAAF restructuring, 96
Defense Technology Commission, 219
Defense White Paper
  Air Force as a strategic service of the PLA, 143
  informatization, 78
  national defense policy, 39
  role of the Second Artillery, 42
  strategic attacks, 43
defensive counterair missions, 44
Deng Changyou, 108
Deng Xiaoping, xxii, xxv, 44, 151, 178, 218, 250–51, 265, 292–93, 295, 333
department system, 99–100, 119
Deptula, David, 19–20, 83
DF–21, 48, 51
DF–3/CSS–2, 331
DF–31/CSS–9, 331
DF–31A/ CSS–9, 331
DF–4/CSS–3, 331
DF–5/CSS–4, 331
DH–10, 51, 332

DIA. See U.S. Defense Intelligence Agency (DIA)
Ding Laihang, 228
Ding Laihong, 225
Discipline Inspection Commission, 106
dive-bombers, 6
Dong Wenxian, 170
Dongta Airfield, 237
Dora Farm, 24
Douhet, Giulio, xix, 3–7, 27n12, 44, 83

E–3, 197, 202, 205, 208
E–8, 205
East China Sea, 84
Eastern bloc, 282, 289
ECCM. See electronic counter-countermeasures (ECCM)
ECM. See electronic countermeasures (ECM) systems
effects-based operations, 19
Eisenhower administration, 12
electromagnetic pulse (EMP), 54, 338
electronic counter-countermeasures (ECCM), 51
electronic countermeasures (ECM), 95, 103
  PLAAF restructuring, 122
  PLAAF troops, 95
  specialty forces of the PLAAF, 103
electronic intelligence (ELINT) satellites, 56
electronic warfare, 267, 335
  as a leapfrog measure, 80
  as a force multiplier, 206
  in the attainment of political objectives, 41
  integrated information firepower, 41
  PLA development, 41
electro-optical (EO) satellite, 56
electro-optical targeting system (EOTS), 195–96
ELINT. See electronic intelligence (ELINT) satellites
EMP. See electromagnetic pulse (EMP)
EO. See electro-optical (EO) satellite
EOTS. See electro-optical targeting system (EOTS)
Equipment Research Academy, 49, 122
equipment technical support, 97, 120

Escadrille Américaine. See Lafayette Escadrille
"Essences for an Offensive and Defensive Chinese Air Force", 85

F/A–18, 202, 203–04, 206
F–100 Super Sabre, 192
F–105, 13–14
F–117, 24
F–15, 15, 18, 202, 203, 204, 206, 226
F–15E, 203
F–16, xviii, 15, 202–03, 206, 263, 277, 305, 327, 329
F–2, 274
F–22, 197, 203–04, 263, 264, 314
F2T2EA theory, 40
F–35 Joint Strike Fighter, 203–04, 279, 308
F–4 Phantom, 289
F–5E/F, 327
F–6, 104, 292, 296
F–7, 104, 290–92, 296
F–8, 104
F–86F, 277
FALCON. See Force Application and Launch from the Continental U.S. (FALCON)
Fang Dianrong, 231
fanghu, 144
fanji, 144, 145
Farnborough International Air Show, 267
FBC–1, 299
F–CK–1, xviii, 327, 329
F–CK–1A/b, 327
Feigenbaum, Evan, 294
Feng Chuangjiang, 142
Feng Ru, 238
fighters, xi, xvii, xxiii, xxv, 5, 6, 13, 14, 15, 37, 71, 72, 73, 74, 75, 79, 80, 83, 85, 86, 87, 88, 104, 141, 150, 160, 191, 192, 193, 196, 200, 203, 204, 205, 207, 208, 213, 227, 230, 261, 325–327, 334, 355, 359, Chapter 12
  fifth-generation, xi, 271, 279–80, 304
  fourth-generation, xi, xxiii, 71, 79, 88, 193, 196, 202, 203, 207, 208, 213, 229, 261, 283, 290, 296, 299, 302, 305, 313–315, 329, 357,

fighters, PLAAF, 150, 227, Chapter 8, Chapter 12, Chapter 13
F–5E/F, 327
F–6, 104, 292, 296
F–7, 104, 290–92, 296
F–8, 104
FBC–1, 299
J–10, xi, xviii, xx, xxiv, xxv, xxvi, 79, 82, 84, 195–96, 198, 203, 208, 217, 262–63, 265, 268, 283, 300–01, 304–05, 311, 314, 328, 357
J–11, xi, xviii, xxiv, xxv, 79, 203, 262–63, 302–04, 313, 334, 357
J–11A, 196
J–11B, 79–80, 84, 196, 208, 263, 265, 283, 303–04, 314, 328
J–15, xi, 263, 307, 314
J–20, xi, xxv, 197, 208, 263-64, 283, 311–12, 314
J–5, xx, xxiv, 258, 286, 291
J–5A, 286, 291
J–6, xx, xxiv, 84, 192, 193, 258, 286–87, 290–92, 296
J–6A, 290
J–7, xx, 80, 194, 208, 267, 287, 290–92, 296, 328
J–7G, 80, 194
J–7II, 296
J–8, xxv, 82, 194, 208, 296–97, 328
J–8A, 296
J–8B, 195
J–8F, 195
J–8F/H, 80
J–8II, 195
fighter-bomber, xxiii, 13, 192, 193, 262, 266, 300, 327, 356–58
Fighter Command, 8
Fighter Division 6, 24, 219, 225
fire and forget, 195, 200
Firebee, 74, 198
firepower campaign, 41
Force Application and Launch from the Continental U.S. (FALCON), 35, 53
Foreign Affairs Leading Small Group (FALSG), 219
Four Modernizations campaign, 293, 298
Franks, Tommy, 23–24

Frelinger, David, ix, xxvii, 347, 371–72
Li Fuchun, 288
Fujian, 74, 216–17
Fuxingmen, 221-24

Gabriel, Charles A., 18
GAD. See General Armaments Department (GAD)
Gao Houliang, 217
Gansu Province, 222
Gaoxin, 80, 198
Gates, Robert, 197, 311
GCI. See ground control intercept (GCI)
Ge Zhenfeng, 216
General Armaments Department (GAD), 47–48
  equipment and weapons systems development, 117
  equipment support structure, 97
  future leadership, 215
  peacetime operations, 47
  PLAAF leadership, 95
  procurement functions, 258
  Science and Technology Committee, 48
  space operations, 177, 179, 180
  stealth technology development, 50
  technology working groups, 49
geopolitical dominance, 12
GLCMs. See ground-launched cruise missiles (GLCMs)
Global Hawk, 173, 206, 208
global positioning system (GPS), 22, 331, 334
Global Reach–Global Power, 19
Glosson, Buster, 20
Goring, Hermann, 6
Gotha and Giant bomber, 2
GPS. See global positioning system (GPS)
great land army, 82
Great Leap Forward, 287, 290
ground control intercept (GCI), 74
ground-launched cruise missiles (GLCMs), 43, 58
Grumman F-14, 273
Guangdong Military Aviation School, 238
Guangdong Military Government, 238
Guangdong Province, 308
Guangzhou, 238

Guangzhou MR, 83, 214, 224, 230, 331
Guangzhou MRAF, 96, 104, 110, 217, 222, 225, 228
guanxi, 108
Guilin Air Force College, 96, 112, 123, 244
Gulf War
  airpower, 21, 153, 304, 325
  COGs and effects-based operations, 19
  importance of military technology, 326
  informatized warfare, 144
  lessons learned, 78, 133

H–5, 287, 292, 299
H–6, 197, 208, 262, 264, 287, 291–92, 328
H–6U, 198, 313
Haidian, Beijing, 222
Hail Mary maneuver, 20
HAL. See Hindustan Aeronautics Limited (HAL)
Hallion, Richard P., 20, 318n44, 372
Han Decai, 218
Hard kill, 157
Harpy, 199, 305–07, 333
Hart, Jessica, ix, xxvii, 347, 372
Harvard University, 113, 372
Hawk 75M, 284
He Weirong, 50, 128n61, 197, 219, 221, 248
Hebei, 115, 217, 219
helicopter rise, 222
High New (Gaoxin) series, 80, 81
high-power microwave (HPM) projection, 50, 54
Hindustan Aeronautics Limited (HAL), 279–80
Hiroshima
  atomic bombing of, 11
  impact of bombing, 12
Hitler, Adolf, 8–9
HN–1, 201
Horner, Charles, 19
Houbei, 121
HPM. See high-power microwave (HPM) projection
HQ–12, 201, 329
HQ–2, 87, 201, 328, 329
HQ–9, 87, 201, 208, 329
HQ–9/12, 87

HTV-2. See Hypersonic Technology Vehicle-2 (HTV-2)
Hu Jintao, xxv, 167, 222, 236, 250, 259, 267
Hubei city, 57
Hypersonic Technology Vehicle-2 (HTV-2), 35

I-15bis, 284
I-16, 284
IADS. See integrated air defense system (IADS)
Il-28, 77, 287, 292
Il-76 Candid, 80-81, 197-98, 208, 224, 264, 313
Il-78 Midas, 198, 313
Ilyushin Il-28, 77, 287, 292
independent air campaign, xx, 44, 58
Independent Detachment of Air Force (AF) Division 4, 216
industrial targets, 6, 10
industrial web
   German industry during WWII, 10
   Pacific theater, 11
   theory, 5
   USAAF bombing campaign, 9
information operations
   air blockade, 158
   ballistic missile forces, 38
   command system focus, 41
   during offensive missions, 141
   effects on air strikes, 41
   offensive air campaign, 157-58
   reconnaissance, 141
   strategic and theater objectives, 40
   success in aerospace and firepower campaigns, 41
information warfare, 58
   aerospace power, 38
   space superiority, 156
information-firepower
   China's aerospace power theories, 34
   integration, 40, 42
   warfare, 41
informatization, 40, 78, 88
   of weapons systems, 53
informatized, xxiv, 79, 165-66, 169, 178, 249
   aerial surprise attacks, 144

integrating and networking aerospace systems, xi
offensive air operations, 85
prerequisite for winning, 173
strategic objectives, 139
Instant Thunder, 19-20, 30n65
integrated air and space operations, 33-34, 46-48, 55-58, 84, 143-44, 148n11, Chapter 7
integrated air defense system (IADS), 16, 338
intelligence, surveillance, and reconnaissance (ISR), 22, 173, 333, 360
   airpower, 26
   Global Hawk, 173
   in modern air defense, 361
   PLAAF development of, 80
   situational awareness, 22
   Taiwan aircraft, 333
Iraq War, 133
ISR. See intelligence, surveillance, and reconnaissance (ISR)
It-5, 287
Italian Aspide, 200
Itu Aba, 335

J-10, xi, xviii, xx, xxiv, xxv, xxvi, 79, 82, 84, 195-96, 198, 203, 208, 217, 262-63, 265, 268, 283, 300-01, 304-05, 311, 314, 328, 357
J-11, xi, xviii, xxiv, xxv, 79, 203, 262-63, 302-04, 313, 334, 357
J-11A, 196
J-11B, 79-80, 84, 196, 208, 263, 265, 283, 303-04, 314, 328
J-15, xi, 263, 307, 314
J-20, xi, xxv, 197, 208, 263-64, 283, 311-12, 314
J-5, xx, xxiv, 258, 286, 291
J-5A, 286, 291
J-6, xx, xxiv, 84, 192, 193, 258, 286-87, 290-92, 296
J-6A, 290
J-7, xx, 80, 194, 208, 267, 287, 290-92, 296, 328
J-7G, 80, 194
J-7II, 296
J-8, xxv, 82, 194, 208, 296-97, 328

J–8A, 296
J–8B, 195
J–8F, 195
J–8F/H, 80
J–8II, 195
Jamestown Foundation, 340
Jeschonnek, Hans, 6
JF–17, 265, 267
JH–7, xxv, 79, 84, 195, 210, 262, 265, 289, 299, 300
JH–7A, 79, 84, 195, 262–63, 300, 328
JH–7B, 195
jiben renwu/basic tasks, 135
jiben shiming, 134
Jiefangjun Bao, 96
Ji Yan, 170
Jia Yongsheng, 221, 225
Jiang Jianzeng, 221, 230
Jiang Zemin, xxv, 78, 82, 250–51, 306
jiji fanji, 145
Jilin Province, 114, 239
Jin Zhuanglong, 260
Jinan MR, 219, 221, 231
Jinan MRAF, 110, 219, 225, 228
Jing Wenchun, 109, 219
Jinmen, xvii, 76, 150–51, 335
Jinmen campaign, 150, 160
JJ–1, 286i
JJ–5, 291
JK–12, 55
JK–5, 55
JKZ–20, 55
joint campaign, 18, 152, 155, 157, 158, 159, 337
joint firepower, 40
joint firepower operations theory, 40
joint operations, xxi, 6, 44, 87, 88, 136, 139, 152, 155, 169, 171, 206, 235, 250, 337
Joint Publication (JP), 155
Joint Theater Command, 42, 58
JSTARS (Joint Surveillance Target Attack Radar System), 205
JuLang–1/CSS–N–3, 331
Junkers Ju–87 *Stuka* bomber, 6
junzhong, 87
juti shiming, 134

K–13, 277
K–8, 267
kangji, 144
Kármán Line, 47–48
Kasserine Pass, 10
KC–135, 202, 205
KD–63, 197
KD–88, 263
Zhuang Kezhu, 230
Kh–55, 307, 331
Kimpo airfield, 76
Kinmen and Matsu, 335
KJ–200, 80, 264, 306, 314
KJ–2000, 80, 198, 206, 264, 306, 314
Klimov VK–1F, 288
KnAPPO, 303
Knauss, Dr. Robert, 5–6
kongjian zhan, 175
Kongjun Bao, 249
kongtian jingong zuozhan, 145
kongtian yiti, gongfang jianbei, 134
kongtian youshi, 140
kongxi, 145
Korean Peninsula, 73
Korean War, xx, 13, 74, 76, 240, 242, 246, 285, 355
  expansion of PLAAF, 284
  expansion of the Air Force, 73
  historical development of PLAAF, 72
  impact on PLAAF doctrine, 149
  PLAAF air defense, 73
  PLAAF experience, 89, 150
  Volunteer Army Air Force, 240
Krumel, Glenn, 153

Lackland Air Force Base, 111
LACM. See land attack cruise missile (LACM)
ladder of intensity, 136
Lafayette Escadrille, 2
Lambeth, Benjamin, xiii, 179
land attack cruise missile (LACM), 197, 331
Langley Air Force Base, Virginia, 17
Lanzhou MR, 214, 217, 230
Lanzhou MRAF, 104, 217, 220, 223, 227
Lapchinsky, A.N., 6–7

Lavi fighter, 195, 263, 297
Lewis, John, 44, 295
Li Rongchang, 170
Li Shaomin, 223
Li Xiangmin, 228
Li Xiaojun, 145, 147
light front, heavy rear, 152–53
Lightning War. See Blitzkrieg (Lightning War)
Lin Biao, xxii, 151
Lin Chongpin, 336
Lin Tao, 224
Lin Zuoming, 311
Liu Chengjun, 123
Liu Yalou, 108, 124, 216
Liu Yazhou, 83, 85, 124
Liu Zhongxing, 225
Liu Zuoxin, 221
Lockheed P2V-5, 74
Lockheed RF-104G, 74
Lockheed RF-80C, 74
Lockheed U-2, 328
Loh, John M., 19
long-range bombers, 6–7, 12
Looking Toward the Pacific, 170
Lufthansa, 5
Luftwaffe, 5–9
Luo Shida, 290

M-11, 286, 331
Ma Ning, 107
Ma Shuanzhun, 145, 147
Ma Xiaotian, 124, 145, 147–48, 166, 213–18, 221
Ma Ying-jeou, xix, xxvi, 325
Ma Zhaoxu, 166
Ma Zhenjun, 225
Malacca Strait, 207
Mao Xinyu, 225
Mao Zedong, xvii, 75, 135, 182, 218, 225, 236, 240, 284, 288
Marianna Islands, 11
Martin P4M, 74
Martin RB-57A/D, 74, 328
Marxist-Leninist, 7, 236, 240
Matsu, xvii, 355
Maxwell Air Force Base, 112

Maxwell Field, Alabama, 4
Mazu, xvii, 335
McDonnell F2H-2P, 74
McDonnell RF-101A, 74
McDonnell-Douglas F-4, 273
Mecozzi, Amedeo, 7
medium-range ballistic missile (MRBM), 48, 51, 331
Meilinger, Phillip, 4
MEMS. See micro-electromechanical systems (MEMS)
micro-electromechanical systems (MEMS), 49, 54, 63n60
MIDAS tankers, 198, 208, 313
MiG-17, xxiii, xxiv, 74, 77, 150, 191, 209, 258, 277, 286, 288
MiG-19, xx, xxiii, xxiv, 77, 84, 191, 193, 209, 258, 287, 292
MiG-19/J-6, 192
MiG-19P, 287
MiG-19PM, 287
MiG-21, xx, 77, 194, 202, 210n27, 287, 290–91, 296
MiG-21F-13, 287, 291
MiG-23, 296
MIIT. See Ministry of Industry and Information Technology (MIIT)
Military Affairs Department, 101, 110, 120
military balance, xxvii, 347–48, 355, 366
Milosevic, Slobodan, 21
Min Zengfu, 138, 147
Ministry of Industry and Information Technology (MIIT), 259
Minotaur, 35
Mirage 2000, xviii, 327
Mirage 2000-5, 327
Mitchell, William «Billy», xix, 4
MLRS. See Multiple Launch Rocket Systems (MLRS)
mobilization system, 120
Modern Military Organizational Reform Research, 103
MRBM. See medium-range ballistic missile (MRBM)
Mueller, Karl, 14
Multiple Launch Rocket Systems (MLRS), 18, 340

Nagasaki
   atomic bombing of, 11
   impact of bombing, 12
Nanchang Aircraft Factory, 285–86
Nanfang Zhoumo, 181
nanhuan di zuozhan tixi, 140
Nanjing MR, 217–18, 230
Nanjing MRAF, 104, 227–28
Nanjing War Zone, 227
Nanning Forward Headquarters, 228
Nanyuan Aviation School, 237
Nanyuan Field, 237
Nanyuan Flying Group, 283
national aerospace security system, 35, 46
National Defense Mobilization Law, 120, 123
National Guideline on Medium and Long-term Program for Science and Technology Development, 257
National Military Strategic Guidelines, 154
National War College, xiv, 112
Nationalist cause
   Spanish Civil War, 7
Nationalist Chinese Air Force, 239
NATO. See North Atlantic Treaty Organization (NATO)
NCW. See network-centric warfare (NCW)
NDRC. See State Development and Reform Commission (NDRC)
near-space, 35, 47, 52
   aerospace flight vehicles, 52
   flight vehicle program, 53
   integrated aerospace operations, 46
   PLA investment in, 55
   PLAAF space mission, 177
   Qian Xuesen trajectory, 52
   research, 53
   surveillance, 55
   U.S. Falcon, 174
network-centric warfare (NCW), 22, 42, 167, 176
New Guinea, 334, 342
New Historic Missions, 167–69
New Look policy, 12
NFZ. See no-fly zone (NFZ)
Nie Rongzhen, 288
Nixon, Richard, 16
no-fly zone (NFZ), 335

Nonaviation Academic Institution Departments and Grades, 116
NORAD. See North American Aerospace Defense Command (NORAD)
Norden bombsight, 5
Normandy invasion, 10
North Africa campaign, 10
North American Aerospace Defense Command (NORAD), 87
North American RF–100A, 74
North American RF–86A/F, 74
North Atlantic Treaty Organization (NATO), 17, 21, 193, 196, 329, 331, 364
North Sea Fleet, 340
Northeast Aviation School, 237
Northeast Flight Division, 237
Northern Alliance, 23
Northrop F–5, 273

offensive counterair attacks, 154
offensive counterair operations, 39
offensive counterair strikes, 39
Office of Technical Development, 6
OLS–27, 204
OLS–30, 204
OLS–35, 204
OMTE. See Outlines for Military Training and Evaluation (OMTE)
Operation *Allied Force*, 21, 174
Operation *Deliberate Force*, 21
Operation *Desert Storm*, xxi, 20, 77, 153, 338
Operation *Enduring Force*, 23
Operation *Iraqi Freedom*, 24, 25, 373
Operation *Linebacker*, 16, 17
Operation *Linebacker II*, 16
Operation Plan (OPLAN) 1003–98, 24
Operation *Rolling Thunder*, 15
Operation *Sea Lion*, 8–9
OTH. See over-the-horizon (OTH)
Outline of the National Program for the Medium- and Long-Term Development of *Defense-Related Science, Technology and Industry*, 265
Outlines for Military Training and Evaluation (OMTE), 248, 249
Outlines for Military Training and Evaluation (OMTE) Revision, 249

over-the-horizon (OTH), 55, 57, 69n120

Panzer tanks, 7–8
parallel attacks, xix, 19, 24–25, 27
paralysis warfare, 44
passive defense, 39, 158
PCS. See process control systems (PCS)
Peace Mission exercises, 221, 224, 228
Peace Pearl, 296
Pei Huailiang, 220
People's Air Force, 135
People's Armed Police, 249
People's War, 153
personnel management system, 120
PGMs. See precision-guided munitions (PGMs)
Phalcon, 80, 305–06
Pin-Luen, Shen, viii, xxv, 374
PL–11, 200
PL–12, 195–96, 200–01, 303
PL–2, 199–200, 202
PL–5, 200, 202
PL–8, 194, 200
PL–9, 200
PLA Air Force (PLAAF)
  air-to-air missiles, *200*
  air-to-surface missiles, *201*
  aircraft inventory by type, *192*
  ballistic missiles, *331*
  campaigns, 43, 58, 78, 139, 143, 144, 152, Chapter 6
  command posts, *111*
  comparison with USAF headquarters, *100*
  doctrine, 44, Chapter 6, 167, 180, 357
  fighter fleet, 1990-2010, *194*
  flight colleges, *115*
  grade and rank System, 99
  leadership, xxiv, 72, 73, 81, 82, 106, 167, Chapter 9
  military education, xxiv, 107, 110, 215, Chapter 10
  missions, 85, 138
  officers in key joint billets during the 2000s, *123*
  operational units and headquarters levels, *103*
  organization, xix, 98, 105, 110, 121

  personnel, xii, xix, xxiv, xxvii, 71, 73, 82, 83, 88, 124, 135, 214, 221, 229, 230, 284, Chapter 4, Chapter 10
  principal combat aircraft, *328*
  recruitment, 101, 243, 266, 267
  surface-to-air missiles, *202*, *329*
  unmanned aircraft systems, *199*
PLA Daily, 223
PLAAF. See PLA Air Force (PLAAF)
PL–ASR, 201
PLA Surface-to-Air Missiles, *329*
Pleiku
  Viet Cong attack, 15
Pollack, Jonathan D., 153
population bombing, 7
  Chongqing, 7
  Guangzhou, 7
  Japanese in the war against China, 7
  Nanjing, 7
  Shanghai, 7
Powell, Colin, 19
Pratas, 335
precision-guided munitions (PGMs), 204
Principal PLA Combat Aircraft, *328*
Principal Taiwan Combat Aircraft, *327*
process control systems (PCS), 41
Prompt Global Strike, 53
Protivo Vozdushnaya Oborona (PVO), 87, 155
PVO-Strany, 87

Q–5, xxiv, xxv, 84, 193, 258, 263, 267, 299, 328
Q–5L, 193, 194
Qian Xuesen trajectory, 52
qieduan di de zhongyao xinxi zhizhang, 141
Qiao Liang, 170
Qiao Qingchen, 106, 108, 124, 217
Qing government, 237
Quemoy, xvii, 150

R–27/AA–10, 200
R–73/AA–11, 200
R–77/AA–12, 196, 200, 208
Radar College, 112, 114, 122
RAF. See Royal Air Force (RAF)
RAF F–4M, 289

RAND, xii, xiii, xviii, xix, xxiii, xxvii, 12, 14, 26, 179, 339, 371-74, 376
RC-135, 205
RD-93 engines, 265
RDA. See research, development, and acquisition (RDA)
Red Army, 9
Redstone Arsenal, 308
renwu shiming, 135
renwu, 134-135
Republic RF-84F, 74
research, development, and acquisition (RDA), 117
reserve forces, 97, 120-21
Reserve Officer program, 96
Reserve Officer Training Corps (ROTC), 112, 244
reverse engineering, 275, 292, 297, 304, 307, 314, 329
   F-16, 277
   fighter production, 292
   J-7/F-7, 290
   newly designed subsystems, 276
   Su-27, 314
   Su-33 prototype, 263
   to accelerate development, 276
   to avoid R&D investments, 277
RF-100A, 74
RF-84F, 74
RF-86A/F, 74
Rice, Donald, 19
Right Sizing the People's Liberation Army: Exploring the Contours of China's Military, 71
RN F-4K, 289
Rolls Royce Spey, 289
Rosoboronexport, 302
ROTC. See Reserve Officer Training Corps (ROTC)
route packages, 14
Royal Air Force (RAF), 4, 8-10
Royal Flying Corps, 3
RQ-4 Global Hawk, 198
Rumsfeld, Donald, 23-24
Ryan Firebee drone, 74

S-300, xviii, 87, 201, 206, 300, 313, 328-29
S-300PMU2, 206
S-400, xviii, 201, 206, 208
S-75 Dvina, 328
SA-10/20, xviii, 328
SA-2, xviii, 328
SA-300, 201
SA-321, 295
SAC. See Strategic Air Command (SAC)
SAM. See surface-to-air missile (SAM)
SAR. See synthetic aperture radar (SAR)
SASAC. See State-owned Assets Supervision and Administration Commission (SASAC)
SASTIND. See State Administration of Science, Technology, and Industry for National Defense (SASTIND)
SCADA. See supervisory control and data acquisition (SCADA) systems
School of Advanced Air and Space Studies, 112, 373
Schwarzkopf, Norman, 19
Science of Air Force Military Education and Training, 242
Science of Air Force Training, 248, 251
Science of Campaigns, 140, 148
   amphibious operation, 337
   anti-air raid campaigns, 144
   attacking information pillars, 141
   defense against enemy air raids, 143
   PLAAF air offensive objectives, 85
   PLAAF missions, 85, 138
   PLAAF offensive campaigns, 139
Science of Military Training, 248
Science of Modern Air Defense, 87, 147
scramjet, 35-36, 52, 54
sea-based assets, 39
SEAD. See suppression of enemy air defense (SEAD)
Senkaku/Diaoyu Islands, 206
Shanghai Aircraft Design and Research Institute, 261
Shanghai Aircraft Manufacturing Co., Ltd., 261
Shanghai Baosteel Group Corporation, 260
Shanghai Electric Group, 261
Shanghai Guosheng Co., Ltd, 261

Shanghai Guosheng Group, 260
Shenyang Aero Engine Factory, 285
Shenyang Aircraft Corporation, 196, 258, 263, 296, 302
Shenyang Aircraft Factory, 285–88, 290
Shenyang Liming Aircraft Engine Company, 311
Shenyang Liming Motor Corporation, 304
Shenyang MR, 216, 231
Shenyang MRAF, 104, 227–28
Shenyang Province, 237
shiming, 134–35
short-range air-to-air missiles (SRAAM), 200, 202
Simonov, Michael, 302
Sinochem. See China Sinochem Group Corporation (Sinochem)
Sino-Soviet cooperation, 285
Sino-Soviet defense cooperation, 282, 284
Sino-Soviet Split to the Reform Era (1960–1977), 288
Size and Composition of the PLAAF Fighter Fleet, 1990–2010, 194
skywave brigade, 57
SNR–75 Fan Song radar, 328
soft kill, 157
Sokolovskiy, Gennady, 277
Song Jian, 294
South China Sea, 35, 84, 206
    air operation suppression, 39
    China's claims, 182
    China's dominance, 349
    China's increased range of influence, 358
    dispute over maritime boundaries, 350
    PLA missile capabilities, 51
    PLA targets, 38
    PLAAF airpower capabilities, 191
    PLAAF military power, 206
surveillance, 55
South Sea Fleet, 340
space, xi, xx, xxi, xxii, xxiii, 79, 84, 87, 88, 112, 154, 156, 236, 240, 252, 315, 326, 372, 373, Chapter 2, Chapter 5, Chapter 7
Space Foundation, 168
space superiority, 170, 173, 176
    achieving ground, naval, and air superiority, 175

    achieving strategic and campaign goals, 140
    Air Force Doctrine Document 2-2, Space Operations, 175
    China's ultimate goal, xxiii
    counterspace operations, 176
    future warfare, 156
    modern warfare, 139
    space orbital attacks, 142
    space planes, 174
    space warfare, 175
    U.S. military, 183
space-based theater electronic information system, 56
SpaceshipOne, 47
Spanish Civil War, 7
Special Rescue Regiment, 227
Special Security Organization (SSO), 24
Spey RB–168–25R, 289
Spratly Islands, 207
SRAAM. See short-range air-to-air missiles (SRAAM)
SSO. See Special Security Organization (SSO)
Stalin, Joseph, 9, 285
Starfish strategy, xxvii, 343
State Administration of Science, Technology, and Industry for National Defense (SASTIND), 259
State Development and Reform Commission (NDRC), 259
State-owned Assets Supervision and Administration Commission (SASAC), 259, 260
Stealth Aircraft: A Difficult Adversary, 228
stealth penetrations, 142
Stokes, Mark A., vii, xx, 33, 154, 374
storm penetrations, 142
Strategic Air Command (SAC), 13–14, 17, 196, 302–03
Strategic Air Force, 171, 252
strategic deterrence, 40, 43
strategic intelligence, 43
strategic paralysis, 19, 24
strategic strike, 42–43
    aerospace campaign, 44
    China's aerospace power theories, 34
    OTH radar systems, 57
    PLA capabilities, 42

PLA shortcomings, 34
PLAAF as an independent service, 44–45, 58
program phases, 50
R&D, 36
strategy intellectuals, 14
Study of Air Force Campaigns, 144
Stuka dive-bomber, 7, 8
Sturzkampfflugzeug. See Junkers Ju–87 Stuka bomber
Su–27 Flanker, xi, xviii, xx, xxiv, xxvi, 79–80, 95, 196, 200, 203, 204, 208, 217, 222, 263, 283, 298, 300, 302–03, 305, 313–15, 326–27, 334, 357
Su–27SK, xxiii, 196, 209, 263, 302, 304, 328
Su–30, xviii, 79, 196, 203–04, 208, 217, 304, 313, 315, 326, 334, 357
Su–30MK, 304
Su–30MKK, xxiv, 196, 209, 304, 328
Su–33, 263, 307, 314
Su–35, 204, 313–14
Sukhoi Flanker. See Su–27.
supervisory control and data acquisition (SCADA) systems, 41
suppression of enemy air defense (SEAD), 16, 339
surface-to-air missile (SAM), 14, 16, 87, 103–04, 122, 152, 201, 206, 208, 241, 244, 300,
306, 328–30, 338
  as a branch of the PLAAF, 103
  combat regulations, 155
  deploying in three rings, 153
  light front, heavy rear, 152
  limited-range, xviii
  loss of F-105s over North Vietnam, 14
  PLAAF air defense mission, 86
  PLAAF developmental strategy, 79
  PLAAF inventory, 104
  PLAAF organizational structure, 97
  regiments under MRAF, 109
  reserve forces, 121
  Surprise and first strikes, 154
  the 15th Airborne Corps, 104
Su–UBK, 302
Sun Herong, 228
Sun Jianguo, 215

Sun Yatsen, 238
synthetic aperture radar (SAR), 53, 56
system of systems, 36, 140

T–10K, 263, 307
table of organization and equipment (TOE), 95, 97, 110
TAC. See Tactical Air Command (TAC)
Tactical Air Command (TAC), 13, 17
taikong zhan, 175
Taiwan scenario, 133, 304, 306
Taiwan Strait, 35, 206–07, 217, 306, 325–27, 332–33, 339–40, 343
  PLAAF military power, 206
  surface-to-air missile threats, xviii
  U.S. intervention, 89
Taiwan Strait crisis, xvii, 72, 76, 151, 277
Taiwan Surface-to-Air Missiles, *330*
Taliban, 23
tankers (refueling), 13, 71, 198, 202, 208, 313
TBCC. See turbine-based combined cycle (TBCC)
terror bombing, 6, 9
teshu shiming, 134
Tet, 15
three attacks and the three defenses, 86
three defenses, 86
Three Superiorities, 40
Tian Anping, 138, 140, 147, 170–71
tian zhan, 175
Tiananmen massacre, 296, 298
Tiananmen Square, xvii, xxvi, 227
Titan Rain, 308
TOE. See table of organization and equipment (TOE)
Tomahawk cruise missiles, 24, 39
Tonghua Field, 239
TRADOC. See Training and Doctrine Command (TRADOC)
Training and Doctrine Command (TRADOC), 17
transatmosphere, 46
transformational theories, 26
Trenchard, Sir Hugh, xix, 3–5
trump card weapons systems, 36, 50
Tukhachevskii, Mikhail, 6
Tumansky R–9BF–811, 288

Tupolev Tu–16, 77, 197, 287, 291
Tupolev Tu–4, 80
turbine-based combined cycle (TBCC), 54
Type 1474 serial radar, 303
Type 204 radar, 296
Type 226 Skyranger radar, 296

U.S. Air Force Academy (USAFA), 111–12
U.S. Alpha space-based laser program, 183
U.S. Army Air Corps, 9, 84
U.S. Army Air Corps Tactical School (ACTS), 4–5, 9–11
U.S. ASM–135 direct-ascent ASAT, 183
U.S. Central Command (USCENTCOM), 19, 20, 23
U.S. Defense Intelligence Agency (DIA), 327
U.S. Mid-Infrared Advanced Chemical Laser (MIRACL) test, 183
U–2, 173
UAC. See United Aircraft Corporation (UAC)
UAS. See unmanned aircraft systems (UAS)
UAVs. See unmanned aerial vehicles (UAVs)
Udet, Ernst, 6
United Aircraft Corporation (UAC), 279–80
United States Strategic Bombing Survey (USSBS), 10, 12
unmanned aircraft systems (UAS), 198–99, 332–33, 339, 342
unmanned aerial vehicles (UAVs), 55, 283, 306
Ural Bomber, 5–6
USAAF. See U.S. Army Air Forces (USAAF)
USAF. See U.S. Air Force (USAF)
USAFA. See U.S. Air Force Academy (USAFA)
USCENTAF. See U.S. Central Air Force (USCENTAF)
USCENTCOM. See U.S. Central Command (USCENTCOM)
USSBS. See United States Strategic Bombing Survey (USSBS)

Viet Cong attack, 15
Vietnamization, 16
Volunteer Army Air Force, 240
Vought A–7 Corsair, 289

W–50, 332
Wang Fengshan, 145, 147
Wang Mingliang, 170
Wang Qigong, 290
Wang Tieyi, 228
Wang Weining, 223
Wang Yisheng, 222
War in the Air, 1
Warden, John, 18–20, 24, 37, 83
Warsaw Pact, xvii, 193
Warthog. See A–10 Thunderbolt II (Warthog)
Wehrmacht, 9
wei dacheng zhanlue zhanyi mudi chuangzao tiao-jian, 140
Weight-to-Thrust Ratio and Wing Loading, PLAAF vs. U.S. Fighters, 204
weishe, 162n49
Wells, H.G., 1
Wen Wei Po, 54
Wenchuan earthquake, 177
  Wenchuan disaster response, 227
Western Desert, 10
Wever, Walther, 5–6
Woodward, Bob, 24
World War I, 3–5, 10
World War II, 4
  Air Force strategic thought, 13
  airpower as a strategic weapon, 11
  Anglo-American airpower, 9
  Blitzkrieg, 7
  lessons learned, 17
  New Guinea air blockade, 334
  North Africa campaign, 10
  PLAAF training, 239
  post WWII airpower, 325
  U.S. military aid to China, 239
WP5, 286
WP6, 286
Wright, Orville and Wilbur, 2
Wright-Patterson Air Force Base, 113
WS–10, 264, 265, 311
WS–10A, 263, 304, 311
WS–10G, 311
WS–13, 264, 265
WS–9, 262, 264–65, 289
Wu Faxian, 106, 214, 216
Wu Shengli, 215

Wuhan Base, 224, 227–28
Wuhu airbase, 304

X–15, 47
X–37B, 35
X–51A, 35–36
Xiangfan, 57
Xianglong, 198
xiaoruo di zhanzheng qianli, 140
xingdong, 134–35
Xinhua, 54, 166
Xiong Guangkai, 219
xirao xingdong, 145
Xu Anxiang, 227
Xu Guangyu, 104, 105
Xu Qiliang, 108, 124, 165–67, 169, 174, 176, 180–81, 183–84, 214–18, 220–21
    air and space security, xxiii, 169
    as current commander of the PLAAF, 107
    career path, 216
    developing integrated capabilities, 166
    development of space weapons, 165
    future PLAAF leadership, 213–14
    integrated approach to aerospace operations, 46
    space warfare, 180
Xu Yongling, 312
Xue Litai, 44
Xuzhou Air Force (Logistics) College, 96, 112, 114
Xuzhou Air Force Academy, 244
XXI Bomber Command, 11

Y–20, 198
Y–8, 80-81, 198, 206, 264, 312
Y–8C, 81
Y–8F–200, 80
Y–9, 81
Yak–18 trainer, 257–58
Yak–8, 306
Yalu River, 76
Yang Baokui, 51
Yang Chengwu, 219
Yang Dongming, 219
Yang Guohai, 220–22
Yang Hui, 225

Yang Liangwang, 221
Yang Weidong, 228
yaohai, 140
Yaron, Amos, 307
Yi Xiaoguang, 222, 228, 230
Yijiangshan Island campaign, xvii, 150
YJ–100, 51
YJ–62 (C–602), 332
YJ–82/YJ–83 (C–802/803), 332
YJ–91, 263
Yuan Jingwei, 137, 140, 143–44, 146
yubeiyi, 121, 131
Yushu earthquake, 224

Z–8, 295
Z–9, 296
Zelikow, Phillip, 81
Zeppelins, 2
Zhang Jianping, 221, 230
Zhang Jingfu, 294
Zhang Qingsheng, 220
Zhang Qingwei, 260
Zhang Tingfa, 106–08, 124
Zhang Xiaoming, vii, xiii, xv, xx, xxi, 71, 150, 376
Zhang Xueliang, 238
Zhang Zhidong, 236
Zhang Zhiwei, 142, 148
Zhao Zhongxin, 219–21
Zhaonan Joint Tactical Training Base, 221
Zheng Qunliang, 226, 228, 231
Zheng Shenxia, 123
Zheng Yuanlin, 224
zhengmian, 145
zhikongquan, zhitianquan, 145
zhongdian, 140
Zhou Enlai, 74, 76, 284–85, 288
Zhou Laiqiang, 231
Zhou Liaqian, 221
Zhuang Feng'gan, 54
Zhuzhou Aero Engine Factory, 285–86

Center for the Study of Chinese Military Affairs Staff

Dr. Phillip C. Saunders, Director

Dr. Christopher D. Yung, Senior Research Fellow

Mr. Joshua Wiseman, Research Analyst

Dr. Bernard Cole, Adjunct Research Fellow

Dr. Cynthia Watson, Adjunct Research Fellow

Dr. Ellen Frost, Adjunct Research Fellow

Mr. Michael A. Glosny, Adjunct Research Fellow

Mr. Isaac Kardon, Adjunct Research Fellow

www.ingramcontent.com/pod-product-compliance
Lightning Source LLC
Chambersburg PA
CBHW080723230426
43665CB00020B/2587